Civil Liability
in Criminal Justice

Civil Liability in Criminal Justice

Sixth Edition

Darrell L. Ross

ELSEVIER

Amsterdam • Boston • Heidelberg • London
New York • Oxford • Paris • San Diego
San Francisco • Singapore • Sydney • Tokyo
Anderson Publishing is an imprint of Elsevier

Acquiring Editor: Pam Chester
Development Editor: Gregory Chalson
Project Manager: Jessica Vaughan
Designer: Joanne Blank

Anderson Publishing is an imprint of Elsevier
225 Wyman Street, Waltham, MA 02451, USA

Library of Congress Cataloging-in-Publication Data
Application submitted

British Library Cataloguing-in-Publication Data
A catalogue record for this book is available from the British Library.

ISBN: 978-1-4557-3013-1

Printed in the United States of America
13 14 15 16 17   10 9 8 7 6 5 4 3 2 1

For information on all Anderson publications visit
our website at www.andersonpublishing.com

Working together to grow
libraries in developing countries

www.elsevier.com | www.bookaid.org | www.sabre.org

ELSEVIER   BOOK AID International   Sabre Foundation

Contents

Preface

Civil litigation filed against criminal justice agencies is an increasing phenomenon. Due to the proliferation of civil litigation against criminal justice agencies, professors and trainers can no longer just concentrate on the criminal law. As a response, college courses and training have been developed to expose students and practitioners to the civil liability process at the university, community college, and agency levels. This book has been written in an attempt to provide information that will aid in better understanding the civil process.

Due to the nature of civil litigation today, students and practitioners must not only have a working knowledge of the criminal law, but also possess a firm grasp of the civil law process. The two systems have distinct differences and implications. In contemporary society, a criminal justice practitioner must know how to function in both systems. Students must be aware that their actions as a practitioner will more than likely be probed by a citizen or a prisoner plaintiff claiming that their actions or inactions deprived them of their constitutional rights. Likewise, practitioners must be continually updated on judicial decisions that affect their job performance. This edition of *Civil Liability in Criminal Justice* has been updated with 79 new cases, including 12 new United States Supreme Court decisions. The text is written with the needs of college students, academy recruits, veteran practitioners, administrators, and agency trainers in mind. Acquiring a complete understanding of the distinctions of both systems will greatly benefit the reader.

The book can be a stand-alone text for a legal course or a supplement to an administrative course. The text has not been written as legal advice, because only attorneys may provide such advice. Rather, the text provides general information relative to the civil liability process that affects police and correctional situations. Therefore, the text has been structured to integrate United States Supreme Court decisions and to provide lower court decisions in order to illustrate how different cases have been applied to police and correctional situations. The text also integrates research on civil liability that underscores pertinent legal issues, liability trends and patterns, policy and procedure issues, training issues, and individual officer and administrative responsibilities. In this edition, 55 new research studies that address varying aspects of civil liability and criminal justice agencies have been added. Combining these features not only provides useful information in understanding the court's decisionmaking process, but also provides the reader with realistic examples and research on how cases are applied at the criminal justice agency level.

Online Instructor and Student Resources

Thank you for selecting Anderson Publishing's *Civil Liability in Criminal Justic*. To complement the learning experience, we have provided a number of online tools to accompany this edition. Two distinct packages of interactive resources are available: one for instructors and one for students.

Please consult your local sales representative with any additional questions. You may also email the Academic Sales Team at textbook@elsevier.com.

For the Instructor

Qualified Adopters and Instructors Can Access Valuable Material for Free by Registering at http://textbooks.elsevier.com/web/manuals.aspx?isbn=9781455730131

- **Test Bank** Compose, customize, and deliver exams using an online assessment package in a free Windows-based authoring tool that makes it easy to build tests using the unique multiple choice and true or false questions created for *Civil Liability in Criminal Justice*. What's more, this authoring tool allows you to export customized exams directly to Blackboard, WebCT, eCollege, Angel, and other leading systems. All test bank files are also conveniently offered in Word format.
- **PowerPoint Lecture Slides** Reinforce key topics with focused PowerPoints, which provide a perfect visual outline with which to augment your lecture. Each individual book chapter has its own dedicated slideshow.
- **Lesson Plans** Design your course around customized lesson plans. Each individual lesson plan acts as separate syllabi containing content synopses, key terms, content synopses, directions to supplementary Web sites, and more open-ended critical thinking questions designed to spur class discussion. These lesson plans also delineate and connect chapter-based learning objectives to specific teaching resources, making it easy to catalogue the resources at your disposal.

For the Student

Students Can Access all the Resources Below by Simply Following this Link: http://www.elsevierdirect.com/v2/companion.jsp?ISBN=9781455730131

- **Self-Assessment Question Bank** Enhance review and study sessions with the help of this online self-quizzing asset. Each question is presented in an interactive format that allows for immediate feedback.
- **Case Studies** Apply what is on the page to the world beyond with the help of topic-specific case studies, each designed to turn theory into practice and followed by three interactive scenario-based questions that allow for immediate feedback.

Acknowledgments

While a book may be the work and dream of the author, many individuals assist in the final product. First I would like to thank Michael (Mickey) Braswell, Ph.D., of LexisNexis/Anderson Publishing for giving me the opportunity to revise this edition of the text. His friendship, insights, patience, and suggestions greatly assisted me throughout the course of updating the book.

The substance of the text would not have been fully completed without the influence of three individuals. Thanks to Robert L. Parsons, Ph.D., who encouraged me to pursue a Ph.D. years ago, and his continued guidance, advice, and strategies for working on civil cases have been immeasurable. A debt of gratitude is owed him for sharing his knowledge in policing, use of force, and civil litigation.

Many thanks to Joe Seward and Chris Johnson, civil litigators, who successfully defend criminal justice officers and agencies in civil litigation matters. Working with them on civil cases has greatly increased my knowledge of the civil process. Their legal skills and talents illustrated during discovery, motion preparation, and in the courtroom are unmatched and have enhanced my ability to write about defenses.

Much appreciation goes to three civil liability scholars who may not be aware that their work and research in civil liability has greatly influenced my interest in the subject for several years. Thanks to professors Rolando del Carmen, Victor Kappeler, and Michael Vaughn for their pioneering and continued research and publication efforts in this area. These three individuals are without question leaders in criminal justice regarding civil liability issues. Their work has been an inspiration to me to further research, write, and publish on civil liability topics. Thanks for your work.

Many thanks go to the professors, students, and practitioners who have used the text in order to increase their knowledge in this continually changing area of the law.

And last, but certainly not least, I would also like to thank my wife Judy and my daughter Gretchen for understanding my commitment for endeavoring to continue this research.

About the Author

Darrell L. Ross is a professor and the Department Head for Department of Sociology, Anthropology, and Criminal Justice at Valdosta State University. He is the Director of the Center for Applied Social Sciences.

Overview of Civil Liability

OVERVIEW

The intrusive nature of the duties that criminal justice personnel perform exposes them to higher degrees of liability than other occupations. This is not to suggest that physicians, psychologists, social workers, therapists, teachers, or administrators are unlikely to be the subject of a civil lawsuit. It is because criminal justice practitioners restrict citizens' and prisoners' liberties and rights, and therefore are more likely to become involved in litigation than members of other professions.

Among the many job functions that criminal justice personnel perform, responding appropriately to street- and institution-level situations is paramount. Criminal justice personnel must also exercise a high degree of skill in using their authority and discretion when implementing department policy and enforcing the law. Legal actions against law enforcement officers frequently arise out of situations in which they have restricted the rights of citizens or prisoners. Other litigation may result from allegations of failing to perform legally assigned duties, performing duties in a negligent manner, misusing authority, using excessive force, or intentionally depriving a prisoner or other person of his or her constitutional rights.

Filing a civil lawsuit in the United States has become all too common since the 1970s. American society has become highly litigious, resorting to filing civil lawsuits without hesitation. Litras and DeFrances (1999) conducted a study for the Department of Justice on the overall trends of 500,000 tort cases filed in the United States during fiscal years 1996–1997. Civil cases arising out of the 75 largest counties were studied. Types of claims ranged from personal injury actions, such as airplane accidents, assaults, libel and slander, and medical malpractice, to motor vehicle accidents and product liability. Motor vehicle accident claims accounted for 20 percent of the cases, while product liability cases accounted for 15 percent and medical malpractice cases accounted for eight percent. Plaintiffs won 45 percent of all cases filed. Plaintiffs were awarded damages in 86 percent of these cases, and punitive damages in 18 percent. The median award was $141,000. In 10 percent of the cases, the plaintiff was awarded more than $1 million, and in eight percent of the cases, awards exceeded $10 million. Approximately $2.7 billion was awarded in combined compensatory and punitive damages.

Cohen (2005) studied the trends in punitive damage awards in civil trials in the 75 largest counties in the United States during 2001. He reported that slander (58%), intentional tort (36%), and false arrest/imprisonment (26%) represent three of the most common categories in which punitive damages are awarded. Of the 6,504 cases studied, the plaintiff was awarded punitive damages in six percent of the cases. This percentage has remained stable since 1992. Juries are more likely to grant punitive damages than judges. In one-half of the verdicts, the plaintiff was awarded $50,000 or more, in 12 percent $1 million was awarded, and in one percent, $10 million was awarded. Punitive damages exceeded compensatory damages in 43 percent of the cases. Medium and maximum ranges of punitive damages were reported on the three common categories: intentional torts ranged from $16,000 to $4.5 million; slander ranged from $77,000 to $700,000; and false arrest/imprisonment ranged from $8,000 to $100,000.

Kyckelhahn and Cohen (2008) performed an assessment of the trends in civil litigation in federal district courts and the outcomes of civil rights disputes from 1990 to 2006. They reported that a significant reason for the variance of trends in civil litigation is due to the expansion of civil rights law with the passage of the Americans with Disabilities Act of 1990 and the Civil Rights Act of 1991. The Civil Rights Act of 1991 amended several federal employment discrimination laws. The Act also provided for compensatory and punitive damages to be awarded, and expanded the use of jury trials.

In the 17-year assessment, Kyckelhahn and Cohen reported that overall civil rights cases filed in federal district courts more than doubled during the 1990s, then began to decline in the early 2000s, and from 2003 to 2006, filings in federal district courts decreased by approximately 20 percent. From 1990 to 2006, the percent of civil rights claims concluded by trial declined from eight to three percent. From 1990 to 2006, about nine out of 10 civil rights filings involved disputes between private parties. The trend in filing private-party disputes emerged with 16,310 cases filed in 1990, increased to a peak of 40.4 in 1997, and declined to 30.4 cases in 2006.

In 1990 jury and bench trials each accounted for 50 percent of all civil rights trials, but by 2006 jury trials accounted for 87 percent of civil rights trials held in federal district courts. During the reporting period, employment discrimination accounted for about one-half of all civil rights filings in federal district courts, but filings began to decline in 2004. The percentage of plaintiffs who won at trial amounted to about 30 percent. From 2000 to 2006, the median damage award for prevailing plaintiffs ranged from $114,000 to $154,500. The combined 2000 to 2006 median jury award was $146,125, while the median bench award was $71,500. The period from filing a civil rights suit to resolution in federal district courts took, on average, about 10 months.

Further, Lanton and Cohen (2008) examined the dispositions of civil bench and jury trials in state courts in 2005. They assessed 26,950 disposed cases, which account for a small percentage of the 7.4 million civil claims filed in state courts around the country. They reported on nine litigated categories and found that the plaintiff prevailed in 56 percent of the filings that plaintiffs were awarded punitive damages in 5 percent, and the median damage award amounted to $28,000.

Plaintiffs were more likely to prevail in claims involving motor vehicles, animal attacks, and employment discrimination, and less likely to prevail in claims of false arrest/imprisonment and product liability, to mention only a few. High combined compensatory and punitive awards of near or more than $100,000 included: premises liability, employment discrimination, medical malpractice, and asbestos. More than 60 percent of the plaintiff winners were granted final monetary awards of $50,000 or less. A jury decided 90 percent of the personal tort claims, while judges decided about 70 percent of business-related civil trials (contracts and real property) in 2005.

Moreover, Cohen and Harbacek (2011) examined punitive damage awards in state courts during 2005. As discussed in Chapter 2, tort claims like assault and battery are litigated in state courts.

Compensatory and punitive damages may be awarded to the prevailing plaintiff. Cohen and Harbacek found that in 25,000 tort claims, 12 percent of the plaintiffs sought punitive damages and they were awarded in 5 percent. Of these awards, 30 percent were awarded about $64,000 and 13 percent were awarded punitive damages of $1 million or more. The researchers also reported that punitive damages are more likely to be awarded in assault and battery, slander, or libel cases, which have elements of willful or intentional behavior that would support a punitive damage request.

Criminal justice agencies and personnel are also vulnerable and easy targets for litigation. During the 1980s and 1990s, there were unfortunately a number of high-profile civil liability cases that brought to the forefront the problem of police and correctional officer misconduct nationally. The City of Philadelphia, Pennsylvania, paid out approximately $3.2 million in 1996 in two separate lawsuits related to a bombing incident that occurred in 1985. Police officers dropped C-4 explosives from a helicopter on a residence in order to drive out members of an antigovernment group. The bomb ignited and fire spread through numerous residences, destroying 61 structures and killing 11 people.

Other incidents have created controversy about police conduct and have resulted in civil litigation. The beating of Rodney King in 1991 led to three Los Angeles police officers being criminally indicted, convicted, and sent to federal prison. Later, the City of Los Angeles, California, paid out $3.8 million in a civil judgment to King. In 1993, two Detroit, Michigan, police officers were prosecuted, convicted, and sentenced to prison for the beating death of Malice Green. In 2000, several New York City police officers were convicted and sentenced to prison for beating Abner Louima and forcing a toilet plunger handle into his rectum.

Moreover, there have been successful outcomes in high-profile cases alleging officer misconduct. In the spring of 2000, four New York City police officers were acquitted of criminal charges in the shooting death of Amadou Diallo. In that case, the officers fired their weapons 41 times. Officers approached Diallo and he made a sudden reaching movement for his wallet. Because of poor lighting in the doorway of the apartment complex, visibility was poor and officers mistakenly took his movements as threatening and the appearance of the wallet for a weapon.

In the summer of 2000, the Federal Bureau of Investigation prevailed in a civil lawsuit brought by survivors and families of the Branch Davidian group in Waco, Texas (Garcia, 2000). Agents of the Bureau of Alcohol, Tobacco, and Firearms (ATF) were executing a warrant for the arrest of David Koresh for firearms violations, when they encountered lethal resistance from him and members of his cult in February 1993. Several agents were injured and six were killed. For more than 50 days, Koresh and his followers refused to exit their compound and submit to arrest. The siege ended with the main housing structure being burned as FBI agents attempted to enter the building.

Four million dollars in damages was paid out for a deadly force incident in 1995. The Ruby Ridge standoff incident in Montana left one U.S. Marshal and the wife and two children of

Randall Weaver dead. An FBI sniper shot and killed Vicki Weaver and her infant child, and a U.S. Marshal shot and killed the Weavers' 14-year-old son, Samuel. Federal agents were attempting to arrest Weaver on charges of possessing and selling illegal firearms.

While individual civil lawsuits filed against police officers have gained momentum since the 1980s, the federal government, through the Department of Justice, has brought civil lawsuits against several police departments. These lawsuits have been brought under § 210401 of the Violent Crime Control and Law Enforcement Act of 1994 (Title 42 U.S.C. § 14141). The Pittsburgh, Pennsylvania, and Steubenville, Ohio, police departments were the first police agencies to complete federal oversight through a consent decree for five years through this law (DOJ, 1997a,b; 2005). Since this law began to be used by the Department of Justice in 1997, 22 police agencies have been investigated and are in various stages of a five-year consent decree or a Memorandum of Agreement (MOA) (DOJ, 2005).

Jails and prison systems in the United States are also subject to prisoner civil litigation and many have sustained consent decrees. Koren (1994) reported that the number of correctional systems under court order/consent decree increased from 11 in 1988 to 39 in 1994, largely due to prisoner litigation. Correctional entities have also been targets of prisoner litigation. In 2000, the Michigan Department of Corrections settled several civil lawsuits involving sexual abuse of female prisoners by male officers. In Texas, a privately operated jail incurred litigation stemming from a shakedown in which officers were alleged to have used excessive force and physically abused prisoners, violating their constitutional rights. The actions of the "shakedown" were videotaped and later broadcast on *Dateline NBC* in 1997. The videotape showed officers and command personnel requiring prisoners to crawl across the floor nude, while officers kicked, pepper-sprayed, and prodded them with stun guns, then used a dog to move them out of their cells. On several occasions, the video showed the dog biting various compliant prisoners. This incident resulted in a civil litigation claim against the sheriff, the chief deputy, and a county official in charge of the detention center's emergency response team (*Kesler v. King*, 1998). The claim alleged the use of excessive force, failure to train, failure to supervise, and a failure to screen prospective officer candidates prior to employment. The court ruled against the county, holding that it was not objectively reasonable to use force or the canine in such a situation, in which prisoners were compliant.

The purpose of this chapter is to examine the prevalence of civil liability in police and correctional work. Since the 1960s, citizens and prisoners in the United States have, with increasing frequency, filed civil lawsuits against police and correctional officers. Trends and the subject matter of these lawsuits are still emerging, and accurate data that fully tracks this area of the law is sparse. Recognizing this, emerging trends and patterns of citizen and prisoner litigation are presented.

Trends in Police Civil Lawsuits

Much of the previous scholarly research on police civil liability has focused on precedent-setting cases decided by the United States Supreme Court (Barrineau, 1987, 1994; del Carmen, 1993; del Carmen & Smith, 1997; Franklin, 1993; Kappeler, 1997; Klotter, 1999; Smith, 1995;

Wardell, 1983). Specific police civil liability research has addressed issues of police actions "under color of law" (Vaughn & Coomes, 1995; Zargans, 1985); deaths in detention due to suicide (Kappeler et al., 1991); police misconduct (Littlejohn, 1981; Meadows & Trostle, 1988; Schmidt, 1976; Silver, 2008); negligent operation of police vehicles and failure to arrest drunk drivers (Kappeler & del Carmen, 1990a,b); officers' attitudes toward police liability (Garrison, 1995; McCoy, 1987); liability for abandonment in high-crime areas and moonlighting (Vaughn, 1994; Vaughn & Coomes, 1995); trends in settling civil cases (Bureau of Justice Statistics, 1995, 1999, 2005); liability in sudden, wrongful custodial deaths (Ross, 1998, 2005, 2007); liability trends in the police use of force (Ross, 2002); liability trends in custodial suicides and sudden in-custody deaths (Ross, 2007, 2008a,b); and liability issues affecting police pursuits (Ross, 2008a,b).

While a great deal of research exists relative to civil suit analysis, a dearth of accurate statistical information exists regarding the trends and types of lawsuits filed against police. It is difficult to precisely assess the true nature of lawsuits filed against the police, partly because the courts publish only a portion of the cases they decide, and judges are selective in documenting those cases. There is no systematic method for collecting information specific to police civil litigation. The Administrative Office of the U.S. Courts (AOC) tracks federal civil actions annually, but does not specifically report cases filed against the police. Current literature reveals that civil lawsuits against police are widespread (Worrall, 1998), frequent (Kappeler, 1997), increasing (Kappeler et al., 1993), and a major concern to law enforcement officers (Garrison, 1995; Scogin & Brodsky, 1991), police chiefs (Vaughn et al., 2001), and government leaders (MacManus, 1997).

In the absence of this information, researchers are forced to speculate about the trends and patterns of police civil litigation. A limited number of researchers in the past have used surveys or content analysis methods to examine trends in police civil litigation and they suggest that the number of cases filed against police officers is growing (Americans for Effective Law Enforcement, 1974, 1980, 1982; Barrineau & Dillingham, 1983; International Association of Chiefs of Police, 1976; Kappeler, Kappeler & del Carmen, 1993). Surveys administered by Americans for Effective Law Enforcement (AELE) report civil lawsuits filed against the police rose from 1,741 cases in 1967 to 3,894 in 1971, a 124 percent increase. They also report that by 1976 more than 13,400 cases were filed against the police (1982), making a 500 percent increase from 1967. More than 40 percent of all suits during this period alleged false arrest, false imprisonment, or malicious prosecution. Claims of excessive force by officers amounted to 27 percent of the allegations, and six percent of the claims alleged the misuse of firearms. The International Association of Chiefs of Police (IACP, 1976) indicated during this same period that one in 34 police officers was sued. In the early 1980s, AELE estimated that more than 26,000 cases were filed annually (1982), and one legal scholar has estimated that since the 1990s, police have faced approximately 30,000 lawsuits annually (Silver, 2010).

Prior studies have revealed a variety of monetary awards for plaintiffs. A survey conducted by the National Institute of Municipal Law Enforcement Officers revealed that the 215 municipalities surveyed faced costs of more than $4.3 billion in pending liability lawsuits (Barrineau, 1987). The average cost of a jury award against a municipality is reported to be about

$2 million (del Carmen, 1987). In the mid-1980s, there were more than 250 cases in which juries awarded at least $1 million (National League of Cities, 1985). A study of § 1983 police lawsuits from 1983 to 1997 in two federal district courts in New York revealed that monetary damages were awarded in 30 percent of the cases (Chiabi, 1996). Damage awards ranged from $400 to $950,000, averaging $50,408. During this 14-year period, the total monetary awards amounted to $4,536,702. Damages were more likely when a case was settled (47%) as opposed to when a jury or court awarded monetary relief (22%).

In studying liability trends of § 1983 litigation in U.S. District Courts between 1978 and 1995, Kappeler (1997) found that the average award (and attorneys' fees) against police departments was $118,698, ranging from $1 to $1.6 million. Scarborough and Hemmens (1999) examined U.S. Courts of Appeals decisions from 1989 to 1993. They reported monetary damages in only 27 cases, ranging from $1 to $7,559,000. Attorneys' fees ranged from $12,500 to $325,000, with a mean of $65,898.

These figures obviously do not reflect cases that are settled out of court, which represent a majority of police litigation. Moreover, these awards do not reflect the personnel time, resources, and legal and expert witness fees spent in defending the case. Chiabi (1996) reported that 32 percent of all police litigation in two federal district courts in New York were resolved through settlement. Worrall and Gutierrez's (1999) survey of 50 attorneys representing cities with police departments with more than 100 officers found that 41 percent of cases were settled.

From 1994 to 2001, the West Virginia State Police paid out $7.8 million due to wrongful arrests; $700,000 in 2001 for the same charge; and $88,000 in 2002 and $44,000 in 2003 for claims of failing to train and supervise officers (U.S. Commission on Civil Rights, 2004). From 2001 to 2004, the City of Los Angeles, California, paid out more than $4 million in police civil lawsuits ranging from sexual discrimination against gay police officers to two cases involving the use of lethal force (Los Angeles Times, 2004).

A study of the New York Police Department conducted between 1987 and 1991 showed that the city paid out $44 million in claims to settle police misconduct litigation. During this five-year period, the average settlement or judgment awarded to the plaintiff more than doubled, from $23,000 to $52,000. In 1996, the New York Police Department settled 503 police misconduct cases for $27.3 million and complaints made to the civilian review board increased sharply (Sontag & Barry, 1997). In 1991, the Los Angeles Police Department paid $13 million in damage awards for police misconduct (Christopher Commission, 1991). A Justice Department study of Los Angeles County found that county officials settled 61 police misconduct cases, paying plaintiffs between $20,000 and $1.7 million per case. In 1999, the LAPD paid $2 million in monetary awards and settlements (McGreevy, 2000). In 1991, the City of Detroit paid $20 million in damage awards (del Carmen, 1991). One officer cost the City of Detroit $2.4 million over several years as he incurred 13 lawsuits, primarily due to excessive force claims (Ashenfelter & Ball, 1990). All of the civil lawsuits were settled.

Other studies have documented trends in police civil litigation. Swickard (2005) reported that the City of Detroit has paid out more in police civil litigation than any other large city in the country. Swickard reported that a city council study showed that Detroit paid out more than $118 million from 1987 to 2005 and nearly $45 million from 2001 to 2004 to settle police misconduct lawsuits. This rate accounts for about $4,000 per officer, or about $17.00 per person living in Detroit. Of the 4,100 officers, 261 were named in more than one suit, and 107 of these officers were sued in three or more cases. Suits naming these officers cost more than $32 million from 1997 to 1999. By comparison, the City of Los Angeles, California, paid about $3,000 per officer to settle police civil lawsuits, while New York paid about $1,300 and Chicago paid just under $1,000 per officer to settle such lawsuits.

While comparisons of the trends of civil litigation among cities are problematic, general patterns are worth noting. The City of Chicago paid slightly more than $17 million in settlements for police lawsuits from 1997 to 1999 (Swickard & Hackney, 2001). In Cicero, Illinois, the city paid out $1.1 million to settle two sexual harassment lawsuits and one excessive force lawsuit from 2000 to 2003 (McNeil, 2005). From 1991 to 2001, the City of Cincinnati, Ohio, paid about $2.4 million to settle 56 cases (McLaughlin, 2001). The settlements are but a portion of the $685 million that it takes to operate the city annually. In the largest payout in the history of the department, the City of Oakland, California, settled a class action lawsuit claiming that a few "rogue" officers victimized more than 100 citizens, amounting to $11 million (DeFao, 2003). A court awarded $1 million against the City of San Jose, California, in the wrongful death of a mentally impaired man (Associated Press, 2005).

A further review of police litigation settlement trends in reported select cities is shown in Table 1.1. The trends of these 12 cities show multimillion settlements, with the exception of Newark, New Jersey (NJACLU, 2010). While caution must be used in reviewing these figures, because city populations vary, demographics of the city vary, which in turn impact city economic variables, the number of sworn police officers employed in each city, and a host of other variables that may impact civil litigation and settlements, these figures do show the enormity of the litigation problem during the decade of 2000. It appears settlement payout amounts are increasing over previous decades as attorney wages/fees have increased, some cases involve numerous plaintiffs, and many cases get grouped into the same year the case actually settled.

Table 1.1   Trends of Police Litigation in Selected Cities: 2004 to 2010

City	Payout
New York, NY	$964 million
Los Angeles, CA	$190 million
Oakland, CA	$57 million
Chicago, IL	$44 million
Detroit, MI	$39.1 million
Philadelphia, PA	$36.8 million
San Francisco, CA	$28 million
Denver, CO	$10 million
Minneapolis, MN	$10 million
San Jose, CA	$8.6 million
Portland, OR	$3.8 million
Newark, NJ	$1.7 million

A prime example of the city population variance and the amount of settlement payouts is Oakland, CA. The population of Oakland is about 400,000 residents and is less populated than any other city represented in Table 1.1, other than Newark, NJ. Yet it is third behind New York and Los Angeles for the largest amount settled case payouts during the decade. Settled case payouts for Oakland doubled the amount of payout for San Francisco, which has twice the number of the residential population (KTVU Channel 2, 2011).

These settlement figures represent numerous litigated cases over the period per city and also show large awards that may represent "outlier payout amounts" for one incident. For example, the Rampart precinct scandal amounted to a settlement of about $90 million for involved officers' misconduct (Muhammad, 2009). The scandal involved police corruption by numerous officers, in several incidents, who violated the constitutional rights of 100 victims. Without these associated incidents, settlements within the city perhaps would have been substantially less.

The New York City payouts also involved a number of incidents with high payouts (Long & Peltz, 2010). For example, over $7 million was paid out in one officer-involved shooting and $10 million paid in another. Plaintiffs were awarded $33 million in a class action suit against New York City on behalf of thousands of New Yorkers who were arrested and illegally strip-searched. Between July 1999 and October 2007, it is estimated that about 100,000 pretrial detainees were illegally searched when they first arrived and/or when they were coming back from court appearances. Some detainees were strip-searched multiple times. Two female plaintiffs were also forced to undergo gynecological exams. The victims faced misdemeanor charges, many no more serious than jumping turnstiles, failing to pay child support, shoplifting, and trespassing. Other cases involved multimillion dollar payouts for administrative liability and over $30 million was paid out for car accidents driven by officers. The City of Detroit, MI paid out $19.1 million in several cases including (News, 2010):

- $6.7 million was paid on 50 suits for violations of constitutional rights.
- $2.4 million was paid on two suits for wrongful deaths other than shootings.
- $1.9 million was paid on 49 suits for assault and battery, false arrest, and imprisonment.

The City of Chicago settled a lawsuit for $19.8 million involving four arrestees alleging that former police commander Jon Burge supervised their torture in order to gain confessions of a murder. The torture alleged by the lawsuit included beatings and electric shocks (Huffington Post, 2010).

Several incidents in Denver, Detroit, Minneapolis, Philadelphia, and Portland represent large settlements for an officer-involved shooting (McKinney & Mitchell, 2011; Warner, 2011; News, 2010; Bernstein, 2010; Washington, 2011). For example, the City of Portland, Oregon, paid out over $1.3 million for three officer-involved shootings. The city of Detroit paid $2.2 million and the City of Denver paid $1.34 million for two officer-involved shootings. The City of Philadelphia paid out over $2 million to settle three police shooting cases.

A former Minneapolis, Minnesota, officer settled a lawsuit for $4.5 million against the city for being shot by a fellow police officer while working undercover. Officer Duy Ngo was performing undercover gang surveillance when he was shot in his car. He radioed for help and dragged himself into the street, waving his arms at the officers who responded. Instead of helping him, the two officers mistook him for a suspect and shot him with a semiautomatic machine gun. Ngo received six bullet wounds from the shooting. It was the largest settlement ever involving a Minneapolis police officer.

These trends provide limited insights into the continuing troubling patterns of settling cases out of court in select cities as reported in various media outlets. Reported settlement types ranged from false arrest, excessive force, unreasonable/illegal searches and seizures, sexual misconduct, sexual harassment, police brutality, accidents, and other actions of police misconduct.

These examples show the importance of the subject matter, show some indication of the sheer volume of the claims filed, the staggering settlement amounts, and the ongoing attention that officers and administrators need to pay to the issue. Concern about being sued has been examined by several researchers. Del Carmen (1991) commented that the fear of being sued is an occupational hazard. Breslin, Taylor, and Brodsky (1986) suggest that job performance may be hindered by a preoccupation with litigation. Scogin and Brodsky (1991) surveyed police cadets in an Alabama training academy and reported that 84 percent believed their fear of being sued was rational and nonexcessive. Only nine percent reported that their fear of litigation was irrational and excessive. A study of Kentucky police cadets (Kappeler, 1997) found that 50 percent were worried about civil liability and 31 percent thought they worried to excess. The settlement payouts shown in Table 1.1 continue to underscore these concerns.

Perhaps the most comprehensive research regarding longitudinal trends in police civil liability was reported in a content analysis by Kappeler, Kappeler, and del Carmen (1993). They reported on 1,359 § 1983 cases filed against the police that were published from 1978 to 1994 and found that police prevailed in 52 percent of the cases (706). The analysis examined 20 major topics of civil liability. Major findings revealed that plaintiffs are more likely to prevail in claims of illegal strip searches (76.4%), inadequate policy (68%), coercion (63.6%), excessive force (59.6%), infliction of emotional distress (56.7%), inadequate training (53.5%), inadequate supervision (55.4%), assault and battery (55.4%), and failure to protect (51.2%). Three of the major topics of frequent litigation pertain to managerial functions: policy, training, and supervision. The average award and attorney's fees assessed against police departments were determined to be $118,698. Vehicle pursuits and excessive force claims averaged the highest awards granted to plaintiffs, $1.2 million and $178,878, respectively.

Ross and Bodapoti (2006) completed a longitudinal analysis of the claims, litigation, and losses of law enforcement agencies insured by the Michigan Municipal Risk Management Authority (MMRMA). The trends and patterns of these claims were examined from official MMRMA records from 1985 to 1999. The total number of claims studied was 11,273 and represented incidents from municipalities (n = 94) and sheriff's departments (n = 57), including claims from detention facilities. Municipalities accounted for 89 percent of the total claims filed. These agencies were dispersed throughout the state and included metropolitan, suburban, and rural departments.

The average annual total costs paid for all claims amounted to $10 million, but from 1996 to 1999 the total amount paid out declined by three percent. Approximately 20 percent of the claims closed without a loss (a payout). A claim may include a lawsuit filed by an arrestee, detainee, or employee. A claim may also include property damage, personal injury due to a worker's compensation claim, a loss from an accident, or an act of God. Overall, county agencies were more likely to incur a claim, a loss, as well as incurring the most costs of all claims filed. The larger-sized agencies (100 + sworn officers) incurred almost twice as much in losses paid than smaller agencies. From 1985 to 1992, the average time to close a case from date of filing took 40 months. From 1993 to 1999, the average time from filing a claim to closure was 18 months.

The analysis revealed 25 common categories in which claims were filed. Of these, 15 claims specifically emerged from law enforcement agencies and the remaining emerged from detention facility incidents (see the section below for a discussion on detention claims). The most frequent claim filed was an auto accident with an injury (40%) and it was classified as moderate in monies paid out. Other common claims included: administrative liability (14%), excessive force (11%), police pursuits with or without injury (10%), false arrest/imprisonment (8%), denial of medical care (4%), property claims (4%), and wrongful deaths (3%). Common claims filed against agency administrators included failure to train, supervise, and direct. An emerging trend of claims filed against administrators were submitted by agency personnel for allegations of sexual harassment and discrimination.

On average, the agencies closed a claim without a loss in 78 percent of the cases filed. On average, claims were resolved without paying a loss in 81 percent of the cases. The highest average payout for claims lost and percentage of claims lost by an agency occurred in the following categories: wrongful deaths ($295,000/35%), denial of medical care ($151,000/38%), auto accident with injury ($50,000/80%), police pursuits ($48,000/59%), administrative liability ($40,000/20%), excessive force ($33,000/37%), and false arrest/imprisonment ($15,000/32%). The average costs to defend a lawsuit with an attorney amounted to $40,000. When an attorney was used to defend a claim in court, the defendant agency prevailed in 75 percent of the cases.

This study represents the first to longitudinally examine multiple agencies from one state, using official records to perform the analysis. The total number of claims is not alarming for the study period, nor is the average amount of payout for claims lost. Specific claim categories are similar to those of the Kappeler et al. study (1993), but the average amount of losses paid and losing percentages were less than those in their study. These seven categories represent incidents that officers confront with regularity and that pose risk-management strategies for agency administrators. Further, administrators need to work toward reducing the number of claims filed by their own personnel for allegations of sexual harassment and discrimination.

In a comprehensive study conducted by Vaughn, Cooper, and del Carmen (2001), 849 Texas police chiefs were surveyed about their experience with civil litigation. The chiefs reported that the fear of lawsuits made it more difficult for them or their officers to do their job (53%). During the three years prior to the survey, 36 percent of the chiefs revealed that they had been sued by a citizen and 78 percent indicated they had prevailed in the lawsuit. The most prevalent liability issues filed against the departments were for excessive force (22%), false arrest/imprisonment (19%), and unlawful searches and seizures (10%). The chiefs revealed that they had lost 22 percent of the cases filed by individual citizens and 41 percent of the cases brought by their own employees. Of the cases in which monetary damages were awarded against the department, 82 percent involved settlements and 18 percent resulted from a jury or court verdict. In all, the cases settled for $8,810,400 (159 cases), averaging $55,411 per settlement. Court or jury verdicts resulting in monetary awards totaled $3,335,409, and averaged $98,100.

Additional scholarly research has examined several emerging trends in police civil liability. Using LexisNexis and Westlaw searches of equal protection § 1983 claims, Blackwell and Vaughn (2003) reported on civil litigation by plaintiffs claiming that the police violated their Fourteenth Amendment rights when they improperly responded to a domestic violence call. Case analysis revealed that when the police treat a domestic violence call or arrest less seriously than other violent assaults, delay in their response to such a call, or discriminate in arrests based on gender issues, the likelihood of liability increases. Courts are seemingly more inclined to find in favor of a plaintiff when they can illustrate that the police failed to provide adequate response in domestic violence calls. They advise that the police need further training and education on family abuse in order to become more responsive to victims of domestic violence.

Cuing on the concern that civil liability poses for police officers, several studies have been designed to survey police officers' perceptions regarding civil liability. Hughes (2001) randomly selected community and beat officers from the Cincinnati, Ohio, Police Department in order to compare their perceptions regarding the potential of incurring a civil lawsuit. A total of 147 officers (29 community officers and 118 beat officers) responded to the self-administered Likert-type survey, which included 11 items. Overall, respondents held negative attitudes regarding the use of effectiveness of civil sanctions against the police. While a majority of the respondent officers had never been sued in their capacity as a law enforcement officer, the officers reported that, as seniority increases, the more likely it is that they will be named in a lawsuit. Hughes reported that most officers believed that they should be exposed to civil accountability, and that as length of service increases, the perception that civil suits are a barrier to effective law enforcement decreases. A majority of officers believed that the threat of civil litigation does not prevent an officer from violating a citizen's constitutional rights during an arrest, that civil liability is an unfortunate inevitability of the job, and that it is not a significant method for controlling officer behavior. Differences were not, however, based on gender, ethnicity, or educational background. Female and African-American officers tend to view civil liability as less of a barrier in performing their duties. Further, the more highly educated (college degree or more) and more experienced the officer, the more favorable the perception was toward civil litigation. A majority (68%) of officers agreed that good recruitment, selection practices, and training are viable methods for protecting the department from a lawsuit. Only a slight majority (50%) believed that a strong disciplinary system reduced the department's liability.

A second study focused on a comparison of police and correctional officer attitudes toward civil liability. Hall et al. (2003) distributed a 22-item survey to deputies and detention officers of a county in a southern state and all but one municipality within the same county. Of 975 distributed, 607 surveys were completed. Police officers accounted for 500 of the surveys and 107 were completed by detention officers.

Using logistic regression analyses, the researchers' findings were similar to that of previous studies (Hughes, 2001; Garrison, 1995; Scogin & Brodsky, 1991). Police respondents were more inclined to know a peer who had been sued. Police responded more frequently than detention officers that a supervisor's order placed them at risk of incurring a civil lawsuit. Both police and detention officers were more likely to agree (62%) that they should be subject to civil liability for violating the civil rights of a citizen or detainee. A majority of both groups (60%) reported that they had received adequate training pertaining to civil liability and 48 percent agreed that the threat of civil liability deters officer misconduct. The researchers found that the higher the level of education the officer had completed, and the longer he or she had been employed, significantly influenced their favorable response to survey items. The researchers concluded that only a minority of officers believed that civil litigation hindered their ability to perform their duties and that future research should be directed toward identifying the varying influences that affect their perception regarding civil liability.

Novak et al. (2003) examined whether police officers' perceptions, years of experience, and aggressive policing styles were associated with civil liability. An 88-item survey was administered to officers from the Cincinnati, Ohio, Police Department. Officers were also observed in the field as they responded to various calls for service over a 13-month period. The researchers measured three primary propositions: (1) officer beliefs about civil liability in deterring unlawful police behaviors; (2) officer beliefs about liability and a willingness to engage in lawful behaviors; and (3) liability concerns have no effect on officer behavior. As in previous studies, officers agreed that they should be subject to civil actions but that knowing that they may be sued would not, or has not, deterred their aggressive behaviors in making a lawful arrest. A majority of the officers also agreed that being sued is "just part of the job" and that it would not influence their behavior significantly. The researchers suggest that more research be conducted to compare attitudes of officers before and after a civil liability incident to measure what factors may influence officer behaviors.

Using a content analysis of 634 newspaper articles from the *New York Times*, *Chicago Sun-Times*, and the *Los Angeles Times* from 1993 to 2003, Archbold et al. (2006) studied various police liability trends. The purpose of the study was undertaken to assist in filling some of the void in the civil liability literature. The researchers found that racial and gender discrimination comprised 30 percent of all lawsuits filed against police agencies and accounted for the top two reasons lawsuits were filed in all three cities. More than 50 percent of the lawsuits were filed by police personnel compared to 47 percent filed by citizens. A majority of the lawsuits (69%) were settled out of court and eight percent of the cases were dismissed by the courts. Only gender discrimination lawsuits filed by police personnel resulted in a jury verdict. Of these verdicts, the plaintiff prevailed in 63 percent of the gender discrimination lawsuits and the defendants prevailed in 37 percent. There were several multimillion dollar settlements awarded in the racial discrimination lawsuits. In addition, the costs associated with lawsuits based on racial discrimination ranged from $250,000 to $512,000. The costs associated with gender discrimination lawsuits ranged from $4,000 to $1,500,000.

The researchers further found that 27 percent of the lawsuits were filed by police personnel while the remaining were filed by citizens. Lawsuits filed by police personnel were comprised of the following discrimination topics: gender discrimination, age discrimination, religion, disability, sexual orientation, and sexual harassment. Police personnel also filed lawsuits claiming unfair administrative practices, which included claims of: unwarranted discipline and demotion, wrongful termination, unfair hiring, promotion, and retirement practices. These claims accounted for 23 percent of allegations asserted by police personnel. In total, citizens were more likely to prevail in the lawsuit (71%) compared to 29 percent prevailing trend for police personnel plaintiffs. Note, however, that police agencies were slightly more likely to settle a lawsuit with police personnel (54%) versus 46 percent with citizens. The findings of the study revealed that police personnel did not routinely face disciplinary actions by administrators in citizen lawsuits and affirmed that their findings concur with the Vaughn, Cooper, and del Carmen study (2001). They also noted that only a few agencies attempted to make changes in policies, procedures, and police training in an attempt to reduce litigation.

In a follow-up article, Archbold et al. (2007) reported the analysis of six common categories of litigation claims made against police officers, which included: physical abuse/excessive force/assault; false arrest; negligent actions/failure to act; wrongful death; denial of civil rights; and illegal search and seizure. Just fewer than 40 percent of these categories resulted in settlements, with 51 percent of the false arrest actions settling out of court and 38 percent of the excessive force claims settling out of court. Payout information was only available for assessment in 23 percent of the total claims. Physical abuse and excessive force settlement claims averaged $2.5 million in payouts per lawsuit and about 43 percent of these claims resulted in a $1 million payout or more. More than 78 percent of the negligent actions of officers or failure to respond by officers claims accounted for payouts of $1 million or more.

Because national detailed data is nonexistent, it is difficult to identify definitively the trends in police civil litigation. The Ross and Bodapoti study, however, provides a more detailed analysis of the trends in common types of civil liability claims, costs paid out, and prevailing trends in one state than that provided in previous studies. Other studies discussed here illustrate the concern of police officers about civil litigation while performing their sworn duties. These studies are helpful in providing data regarding what shapes officer behavior in light of potential civil litigation. What appears to be clear and continues to be shown, as illustrated in Table 1.1, is that police have been and continue to be targets of litigation. Based on the nature of police work, it is also evident that the trend will continue.

Trends in Correctional Litigation

The United States Supreme Court established in *Cooper v. Pate* (1964) that state prisoners could bring lawsuits against correctional officials under Title 42 United States Code § 1983. Since 1964, prisoner litigation has flooded state and federal courts. A limited number of studies have examined the prisoner litigation trends. Turner (1979) examined 664 cases litigated between 1960 and 1977 in the federal districts of Virginia, Vermont, and the Northern and Eastern Districts of California. He found that a high proportion of these cases were filed *in forma pauperis*, and that a significant percentage (68%) of prisoner cases were disposed of at the pleading stage. The most prevalent issues raised were those of medical care, property loss or damage, and access to the courts.

McCoy (1981) analyzed 527 court records of the U.S. District Court for the Southern District of Ohio from 1975 to 1980. She found that the change in the court's philosophy regarding the acceptance of prisoner lawsuits resulted in an increase in § 1983 suits filed by prisoners from 11 in 1975 to 87 in 1979. The data, however, also revealed a marked decrease in both § 1983 suits and habeas corpus petitions filed during 1979 and 1980. A high proportion of cases sought monetary damages and a significant number were dismissed. Thomas et al. (1985) compared the filings between habeas corpus petitions and § 1983 lawsuits in the Northern District of Illinois from 1977 to 1984. They reported that prisoners filing civil rights complaints were more likely to be "repeat filers," while habeas corpus suits tended to be filed by "one-shotters." In a second study, Thomas et al. (1986) compared state and federal prisoner civil lawsuits to the general population's filing of civil rights complaints. They showed a slow but steady increase in prisoner filings from 1960 to 1984. This finding, however, failed to show strong evidence to suggest that prisoners are more likely than civilians to take complaints to court. They reported that as the national prison population increased, prisoners actually filed proportionately fewer lawsuits. In 1964 one of every 100 prisoners filed two lawsuits. The ratio reached its peak in 1981, when seven suits per 100 prisoners were filed. By 1984 approximately one prisoner in 20 filed a lawsuit, the lowest ratio since 1969.

Champion (1988) performed a content analysis of state and federal prisoner litigation trends for six southern states to determine the number and nature of civil filings by prisoners. State records were reviewed for five periods: 1975, 1978, 1981, 1984, and 1987. The study revealed a decline in the filing of habeas corpus petitions and a decrease in the number of filings under the Federal Tort Claims Act, but an increase in § 1983 lawsuits filed by state prisoners. His findings were consistent with other studies on the topic (Thomas et al., 1986; Singer, 1980; Turner, 1979).

Hansen and Daley (1995) researched 2,700 § 1983 lawsuits that were filed in nine states during 1992. They found that the aggregate profile of § 1983 prisoner litigation most frequently involved issues of physical security, medical treatment, and due process violations. The largest number of § 1983 lawsuits named correctional officers (26%), followed by administrators (22%), medical personnel (9%), elected officials (7%), and arresting officers (6%) as defendants. The overwhelming majority (94%) of the prevailing prisoners won little or nothing in terms of actual dollars. Virtually all prisoners acted as their own attorney (96%).

Using a content analysis, Ross (1997a) conducted a 25-year assessment of 3,205 published local jail and state prison § 1983 lawsuits. In 1970 the national prisoner population was 176,391 and 2,030 lawsuits were filed (1.2% of the population filing). By 1994 the prisoner population was 992,000 and 36,318 lawsuits were filed (3.7% of the population filing). For the 25-year period, 3.6 percent of the prisoner population filed § 1983 lawsuits. During the study period, state correctional officials won 57 percent of the cases.

The Ross study also revealed several common types of cases filed by prisoners. The more prevalent issues included medical care, access to the courts, discipline, administrative liability, conditions of confinement, failure to protect, use of force, and classification. In 92 percent of the cases, the prisoner filed *in forma pauperis*, without legal counsel. When a prisoner prevailed (43%), equitable relief was awarded in 87 percent of the cases. Equitable relief is a nonmonetary judgment whereby the court, through declaratory relief, declares to the defendant that a regulation is unconstitutional. A court, through injunctive relief, may also prohibit practices of the defendant by requiring certain measures to be taken or practices to be instituted to avoid further violations of the Constitution. Monetary damages were awarded in 13 percent of the cases and averaged $43,488 per case, while punitive damages averaged $30,667 per case. The total compensatory award per litigated topic ranged from $4,500 to $5.2 million during the study period. Punitive damages ranged from $12,345 to $414,000 per litigated subject matter. Nominal damages of $1.00 were awarded to prisoners on an infrequent basis. Cases involving failure to protect, medical care, administrative liability, prisoner searches, conditions of confinement, and use of force all amounted to significant compensatory and punitive damages as well as attorney's fees when a prisoner prevailed.

Ross (1997b) also reported that prisoners in jails/detention facilities were less likely to prevail in a civil lawsuit than their prison counterparts. Jail officials lost 56 percent of the detainee litigation. Study results indicated that jail inmates were more likely to prevail in cases involving administrative liability (63%), such as hiring and training of personnel, supervision of officers, deficient or nonexistent policies and procedures, conditions of confinement (62%), deficient facility (60%, i.e., overcrowding and defective buildings), medical care (60%), mental health (58%), use of force (55%), and access to the courts (52%).

As part of the MMRMA study discussed previously, Ross and Page (2003) examined claims stemming specifically from jail detainee cases in 57 jails/sheriff's departments in Michigan. These claims represented 11 percent of the total claims studied and covered 1992 to 1999. The claims filed named detention officers in 26 percent, administrators in 22 percent, medical personnel in nine percent, and elected officials in seven percent of the cases examined. The overall costs for the study period amounted to slightly more than $7 million and averaged about 36 claims per year.

While the frequency of claims reported is small in number, there are several categories worth noting in which large payouts were common. The following claims were more frequent in occurrence than other claims and show the average payout when a loss was incurred, and the percentage of cases in which the plaintiff prevailed: attempted suicide ($271,000/65%); suicide ($175,000/60%); delay/denial of medical care ($158,000/44%); wrongful death ($125,000/88%); excessive force ($120,000/18%); conditions of the facility ($45,000/45%); administrative liability for claims of sexual assault, sexual harassment/discrimination ($24,000/25%); and failure to protect claims ($15,000/33%).

Like the findings in the police study, larger jails (number of detention officers more than 100) accounted more for claims, losses, and payouts. When an attorney was used to litigate the case in court, the agency was more likely to prevail—about 60 percent of the time overall.

Table 1.2 illustrates 32 years' worth of prisoner litigation filing trends as reported by the Administrative Office of the Courts (AOC, 2007), Filing trends are also compared to prisoner population trends (West & Couture, 2008). As shown in Table 1.2, the prisoner population has significantly increased since 1975 and, until 1995, § 1983 lawsuits filed by prisoner plaintiffs increased by almost 200 percent. Since 1980, § 1983 civil actions have become the method most often used by state prisoners and jail detainees filing legal actions against correctional officials. In 1995 these figures reveal that § 1983 claims filed by prisoners were three times as high as the number of habeas corpus petitions filed by prisoners. After 1995 and continuing into 2007, however, the number of § 1983 actions filed began to decline, with only negligible increases in 2006. Concomitantly, habeas corpus petitions have steadily increased during this period and since 2000 they closely match the number of § 1983 filings. After 1995, § 1983 prisoner filings have decreased by approximately 51 percent, while habeas corpus filings have increased by about 60 percent. Since 2000, the prisoners filing a § 1983 lawsuit and/or a habeas corpus petition average about 47,000 annually, which has collectively declined from more than 53,000 in 1995, a decrease of about 13 percent. Further, the figures show that about three percent of the prisoner population commonly files a lawsuit.

These trends appear to be influenced by the Prison Litigation Reform Act (PLRA) passed by Congress in 1996 and several United States Supreme Court decisions (Schlanger, 2006). In part, the Act was legislated by Congress to curb frivolous lawsuits filed by prisoners. The Act established mandatory filing fees, restrictions on filing successive petitions, and requirements for exhausting administrative remedies before filing their legal action. It also increased the ability of the courts to immediately dismiss any lawsuit that is frivolous, malicious, fails to state a claim upon which relief can be granted, or seeks monetary relief from a defendant who is immune from such relief.

Another trend in Table 1.2 shows that as the prisoner population declined, so too has the number of filed lawsuits and the number of habeas corpus petitions, since 2005. From 2000 to 2010 the average number of lawsuits filed was 24,078, which is about 45 percent fewer filed than in 1995. Moreover, fewer habeas corpus petitions have been filed since 2005. Since that time, habeas corpus petitions have declined by about 29 percent. It appears that the PLRA is significantly impacting the decline in prisoner litigation overall.

While Table 1.2 shows a declining filing rate trend by prisoners, this does not imply that correctional litigation is dead. The trend in prisoner litigation has stabilized and shifted in focus (Schlanger, 2006). Schlanger reports that the "kitchen sink model" litigation (lawsuits

Table 1.2   Trends in Correction Litigation

Year	*Prisoner Population	**Lawsuit Filed	% Change	**Habeas Corpus Petition Filed	% Change
1975	216,462	6,128		7,943	
1980	295,363	12,397	+102	7,091	−11
1985	447,873	18,491	+49	8.534	+20
1990	689,577	24,843	+34	10,823	+27
1995	989,004	40,211	+62	13,275	+27
2000	1,381,892	25,505	−37	25,219	+90
2005	1,527,929	24,095	−6	25,456	+1
2006	1,570,115	24,801	+3	23,553	−7
2007	1,595,034	23,236	−6	22,750	−3
2008	1,408,499	23,681	+2	17,788	−22
2009	1,406,237	23,329	−1	18,310	+3
2010	1,408,499	23,880	+2	18,358	0

*Guerino, Harrison, and Sable (2010, December).
**Administrative Office of the Courts, Table C-4 (2011, December, p. 40).

attacking a broad base of topics) that was likely in the 1980s and early 1990s has been replaced with lawsuits with more narrow focus. Some of the more common litigated correctional topics that provide examples over the last 10 years include: medical care, administrative segregation, overcrowding, staffing levels, fire safety, prisoner classification, and discipline practices (Schlanger, 2006). Other researchers have found that common prisoner litigated trends include the topics of: excessive use of force, administrative liability, officer sexual misconduct, sexual harassment, custodial deaths, and prisoner-on-prisoner assaults (Cohen, 2006; Miller & Walter, 2008; Robertson, 2004; Silver, 2010). These shifts in litigation trends should be noted by correctional personnel through potential changes in policy and practices.

Summary

As the above discussion indicates, criminal justice personnel and agencies continue to be targets of civil liability. While the number of citizen and prisoner filings is high, officials often prevail in these actions. Research also reveals that a majority of lawsuits are settled out of court, and it appears that this trend is increasing. Civil litigation is costly, but many of the judgments have been instrumental in providing more resources with which to perform daily duties, increasing personnel training, and assisting in developing more efficient policies and procedures with which to guide officer decision-making.

Research on liability issues shows the trends and impact that lawsuits have on criminal justice agencies in terms of money paid out and operational and policy changes. In response, scholarly research has documented the changes in the nature of civil litigation and the differing perceptions of civil liability between officers and supervisors. While education affects an officer's perception regarding civil liability, most officers report that such litigation is a barrier to effective law enforcement. Research on civil liability helps to pinpoint areas in which lawsuits are more likely to be filed. Officers and administrators should endeavor to work toward proactive measures to minimize lawsuits in these subject areas. Research suggests that quality efforts made in recruitment, training, workplace policies, implementing an early warning and strong disciplinary system, and maintaining a liability risk management program can assist in reducing departmental liability.

Civil lawsuits can be bothersome and stressful, and the outcome can be unpredictable. Administrators must remain committed to providing personnel with training, guidance, and legal updates to better understand how to perform their sworn duties. Officers must remain committed to performing their duties within the framework of the law. Maintaining this commitment can assist in defending the next legal action the officer or department faces.

References

Administrative Office of the United States Courts (2011). Table C-4 annual report to the director (statistics division): *Civil and trial statistics: twelve-month periods*. Washington, DC: Administrative Office of the U.S. Courts. p. 40.

American Civil Liberties Union of New Jersey (July 7, 2010). *Newark police misconduct costs taxpayers.* ACLU-nj.org.

Americans for Effective Law Enforcement (1980). *Lawsuits against police skyrocket*. San Francisco, CA: Americans for Effective Law Enforcement.

Americans for Effective Law Enforcement (1982). *Impact*. San Francisco, CA: Americans for Effective Law Enforcement.

Archbold, C. A., Lytle, D., Weatherall, C., Romero, A., & Baumann, C. (2006). Lawsuits involving the police: a content analysis of newspaper accounts. *Policing: An International Journal of Police Strategies and Management, 29*, 625–642.

Archbold, C. A., Lytle, D. J., Mannis, J., & Bergeron, L. (2007). Police liability incidents that result in litigation: an examination of the causes and costs. *Law Enforcement Executive Forum, 7*, 61–74.

Ashenfelter, D., & Ball, Z. (1990, July 16). City, not cops, pays for brutality. *Detroit Free Press, 16*(1A), 8A–9A.

Associated Press (2005, June 11). $1 Million Awarded Against San Jose PD. 2D.

Barrineau, H. E. (1987). *Civil liability in criminal justice*. Cincinnati, OH: Pilgrimage Press.

Barrineau, H. E. (1994). *Civil liability in criminal justice* (2nd ed.). Cincinnati, OH: Anderson Publishing Co.

Barrineau, H. E., & Dillingham, S. D. (1983). Section 1983 litigation: an effective remedy to police misconduct or an insidious federalism? *Southern Journal of Criminal Justice, 8*, 126–145.

Bernstein, M. (2009, December 10). Claims against Portland police officers cost city millions. *The Oregonian*, Oregonlive.com.

Blackwell, B. S., & Vaughn, M. S. (2003). Police civil liability for inappropriate response to domestic assault victims. *Journal of Criminal Justice, 31*, 129–146.

Breslin, F. A., Taylor, K. R., & Brodsky, S. L. (1986). Development of litigaphobia scale: Measurement of excessive fear of litigation. *Psychological Reports, 58*, 547–550.

Bureau of Justice Statistics (1995). *Sourcebook of criminal justice statistics—1995*. Washington, DC: U.S. Department of Justice.

Bureau of Justice Statistics (1999). *Federal tort trials and verdicts: 1996–97*. Washington, DC: U.S. Department of Justice.

del Carmen, R. V. (1987). *Criminal Procedure for Law Enforcement*. Monterey, CA: Brooks/Cole.

del Carmen, R. V. (1991). *Civil liabilities in American policing: A text for law enforcement personnel*. Monterey, CA: Brady.

del Carmen, R. V. (1993). Civil liabilities in law enforcement: Where do we go from here? *American Journal of Police, 12*, 87–99.

del Carmen, R. V., & Smith, M. R. (1997). Police civil liability and the Law. In R. G. Dunham & G. P. Alpert (Eds.), *Critical issues in policing: Contemporary readings* (3rd ed.). Prospect Heights, IL: Waveland Press, Inc.

Champion, D. J. (1988). Some recent trends in civil liability by federal and state prison inmates. *Federal Probation, 2*, 43–47.

Chiabi, D. K. (1996). Police Civil Liability: an analysis of Section 1983 Actions in the Eastern and Southern Districts of New York. *American Journal of Criminal Justice, 21*, 83–104.

Cohen, F. (2006). Custodial suicide: yet another look. *Jail Suicide/Mental Health Update, 15*, 1–11.

Cohen, T. H. (2005). Punitive damage awards in large counties: 2001. *Bureau of Justice Statistics Bulletin*. Washington, DC: U.S. Department of Justice.

Cohen, T. H., & Harbacek, K. (2011, March). Punitive damages awards in state courts: 2005. *Bureau of Justice Statistics*. Washington, DC: U.S. Department of Justice.

The Columbus Dispatch (1999, October 22). The Lawsuit. 3A.

Cooper, T. W., & del Carmen, R. V. (2001). Assessing legal liabilities in law enforcement: Police chief's views. *Crime and Delinquency, 47*, 3–27.

Department of Justice (1997a, April 16). Consent Decree with the Pittsburgh, PA, Police Department. Available at: <www.usdoj.gov/crt/split/documents/pittssa.htm>.

Department of Justice (1997b, September 3). Consent Decree with the Steubenville, OH, Police Department. Available at: <www.usdoj.gov/crt/split/documents/steubensa.htm>.

DeFao, J. (2003, February 19). City of Oakland Settles Civil Rights Case. *San Francisco Chronicle*,1D.

Franklin, C. J. (1993). *The police officer's guide to civil liability*. Springfield, IL: Charles C. Thomas.

Garcia, G. X. (2000, July 17). Davidian decision is not the end. *USA Today*, 1A.

Garrison, A. H. (1995). Law Enforcement Civil Liability Under Federal Law and Attitudes on Civil Liability: A Survey of University, Municipal and State Police Officers. *Police Studies*, *18*, 19-37.

Guerino, P., Harrison, P. M., & Sable, W. J. (2010, December). *Prisoners in 2010*. Washington, DC: Bureau of Justice Statistics. 1-37.

Hall, D. E., Ventura, L. A., Lee, Y. H., & Lambert, E. (2003). Suing cops and corrections officers: Officers' attitudes and experiences about civil liability. *Policing: An International Journal of Police Strategies & Management*, *26*, 529-547.

Hansen, R. A., & Daley, H. K. (1995). *Challenging the conditions of prisons and jails: A report on Section 1983 litigation*. Washington, DC: Bureau of Justice Statistics.

Independent Commission on the Los Angeles Police Department (1991). *Christopher Commission report*. Los Angeles, CA: Independent Commission on the Los Angeles Police Department.

International Association of Chiefs of Police (1976). *Survey of police misconduct litigation: 1967-1976*. Washington, DC: IACP.

Hughes, T. (2001). Police officers and civil liability: the ties that bind? *Policing: An International Journal of Police Strategies & Management*, *24*, 240-262.

Josar, D. (1998, March 9). Cops cost Detroit millions in lawsuits. *Detroit News*, 1A.

Kappeler, V. E. (1997). *Critical issues in police civil liability* (2nd ed.). Prospect Heights, IL: Waveland Press, Inc.

Kappeler, V. E., & del Carmen, R. V. (1990a). Police civil liability for failure to arrest intoxicated drivers. *Journal of Criminal Justice*, *18*, 117-131.

Kappeler, V. E., & del Carmen, R. V. (1990b). Legal issues in police negligent operation of emergency vehicles. *Journal of Police Science and Administration*, *17*, 163-175.

Kappeler, V. E., Vaughn, M. S., & del Carmen, R. V. (1991). Death in detention: an analysis of police liability for negligent failure to prevent suicide. *Journal of Criminal Justice*, *19*, 381-393.

Kappeler, V. E., Kappeler, S. F., & del Carmen, R. V. (1993). A content analysis of police civil liability cases: Decisions of the Federal District Courts, 1978-1990. *Journal of Criminal Justice*, *21*, 325-337.

Klotter, J. C., Walker, J. T., & Hemmens, C. (2005). *Legal guide for police: Constitutional issues* (7th ed.). Cincinnati, OH: Anderson Publishing Co.

Koren, E. I. (1994). Status report: State prisons and the courts—January 1, 1994. *The National Prison Project Journal*, *9*, 9-12.

KTVU Channel 2 (2011, November 4). Oakland paying out extraordinary police abuse settlements: A review of California Public Records Act, KTVU.com.

Kyckelhahn, T., & Cohen, T. H. (2008). *Civil rights in U.S. District Courts, 1990-2006*. Washington, DC: U.S. Department of Justice, Bureau of Justice Statistics.

Lanton, L., & Cohen, T. H. (2008). *Civil bench trials in state courts, 2005*. Washington, DC: U.S. Department of Justice, Bureau of Justice Statistics.

Los Angeles Times (2004, December 26). LA to pay $650,000 to settle two lawsuits. 1D.

Litras, M. F., & DeFrances, C. J. (1999). *Three out of four tort cases settled out of court*. Washington, DC: Bureau of Justice Statistics.

Littlejohn, E. J. (1981). Civil liability and the police officer: The need for new deterrents to police misconduct. *University of Detroit Journal of Law, 58*, 365–370.

Long, C., & Peltz, J. (2010, October 10). AP Investigation: Nearly $1B in NYC police payouts. Huffington Post, Huffington Post.com.

MacManus, S. A. (1997). Litigation: A real budget buster for many U.S. municipalities. *Government Finance Review, 10*, 27–31.

McCoy, C. (1981). The impact of section 1983 litigation on policymaking in corrections. *Federal Probation, 45*, 17–23.

McCoy, C. (1987). Police legal liability is not a crisis, 99 chiefs say. *Crime Control Digest, 21*, 1.

McGreevy, P. (2000, January 11). Lawsuit settlements by City of LA increased 28% in '99. *Los Angeles Times*, 2B.

McKinney, M., & Mitchell, C. (July 31, 2011). Costs of Minneapolis-police payouts could hit record this year. *StarTribune*, StarTribune.com

McLaughlin, S. (2001, December 16). City pays for police lawsuits. *The Cincinnati Enquirer*, 1C.

McNeil, B. (2005, November 9). $1.1. Million to settle 3 Lawsuits. *Chicago Tribune*, 2C.

Meadows, R. J., & Trostle, L. C. (1988). A study of police misconduct and litigation: Findings and implications. *Journal of Contemporary Criminal Justice, 4*, 77–92.

Miller, R., & Walter, D. J. (2008). *Detention and corrections caselaw catalog* (Editions 12–19). Poolesville, MD: CRS, Inc.

National League of Cities (1985, November). Seeking solutions on liability insurance. *Nation's Cities Weekly, 25*, 3–5.

Muhammad, C. (2009, February 27). *The high cost of police brutality*. New America Media.org.

News, T. (May 27, 2011). Cop misdeeds lead to big payouts. *Detroit News*, Detroit News.com.

Novak, K. J., Smith, B. W., & Frank, J. (2003). Strange bedfellows: Civil liability and aggressive policing. *Policing: An International Journal of Police Strategies & Management, 26*, 352–368.

Robertson, J. E. (2004). The impact of *Farmer v. Brennan* on jailers' personal liability for custodial suicides: Ten years later. *Jail Suicide/Mental Health Update, 13*, 1–6.

Ross, D. L. (1997a). Emerging trends in correctional civil liability cases: A content analysis of Federal Court Decisions of Title 42 United States Code Section 1983: 1970–1994. *Journal of Criminal Justice, 25*, 501–515.

Ross, D. L. (1997b). Section 1983 Jail Litigation: A twenty-five year content analysis. *Corrections Compendium, 22*, 1–8.

Ross, D. L. (1998). Examining the liability factors of sudden wrongful deaths in police custody. *Police Quarterly, 4*, 65–91.

Ross, D. L. (2002). An Assessment of *Graham v. Connor*, ten years later. *Policing: An International Journal of Strategies & Management, 2*, 294–318.

Ross, D. L. (2005). Civil liability for custodial deaths following restraint incidents. *Criminal Law Bulletin, 41*, 625–640.

Ross, D. L. (2007). An analysis of sudden custody deaths. *Law Enforcement Executive Forum, 7*, 7–30.

Ross, D. L. (2008a). Examining the liability trends of custodial suicides in jails, lock-ups and prisons. Paper presented at the annual meeting of the Academy of Criminal Justice Sciences, Cincinnati, OH.

Ross, D. L. (2008b). *Scott v. Harris*: Seeing is believing. *Criminal Justice Review, 33*, 431–446.

Ross, D. L., & Bodapoti, M. (2006). An analysis of the claims, losses, and litigation of Law Enforcement Agencies in Michigan. *Policing: An International Journal of Police Strategies and Management, 29*(1), 38–57.

Ross, D. L., & Page, B. (2003, January/February). Jail liability: Reducing the risk by studying the numbers. *American Jail Magazine, 2*(1), 9–15.

Scarborough, K. E., & Hemmens, C. (1999). Section 1983 suits against law enforcement officers in the circuit courts of appeals. *Thomas Jefferson Law Review, 21*, 1–21.

Schlanger, M. (2006). Civil rights injunctions over time: A case study of jail and prison court orders. *New York University Law Review, 2*, 550–630.

Schmidt, W. (1974). *Survey of police misconduct litigation: 1971.* San Francisco, CA: Americans for Effective Law Enforcement.

Schmidt, W. (1976). Recent developments in police civil liability. *Journal of Police Science and Administration, 4*, 197–202.

Scogin, F., & Brodsky, S. L. (1991). Fear of litigation among law enforcement officers. *American Journal of Police, 1*, 41–45.

Silver, I. (2010). *Police civil liability.* New York, NY: Matthew Bender & Co.

Singer, R. G. (1980). Prisoner's rights litigation: A look at the past decade and a look at the coming decade. *Federal Probation, 44*, 3–11.

Smith, M. R. (1995). Law enforcement liability under Section 1983. *Criminal Law Bulletin, 13*, 128–150.

Sontag, D., & Barry, D. (1997, September 17). Using settlements to measure police abuse. *New York Times*, 1A.

Swickard, J. (2005, July 15). Police Lawsuits Drain Detroit's Pocketbook. *Detroit Free Press*, 1B.

Swickard, J., & Hackney, S. (2001, August 3). Detroit Police Lawsuits Costly. *Detroit Free Press*, 3A.

Thomas, J. D., Aylward, A., Casey, M. L., Moton, D., Oldham, M., & Wheeler, G. (1985). Rethinking prisoner litigation: Some preliminary distinctions between Habeas Corpus and Civil Rights. *Prison Journal, 65*, 83–106.

Thomas, J. D., Keeler, D., & Harris, K. (1986). Issues and misconceptions in prisoner litigation: A critical view. *Criminology, 24*, 775–796.

United States Commission on Civil Rights (2004, January). *Police Practices in Civil Rights in America.* Washington, DC: U.S. Commission on Civil Rights.

Turner, W. (1979). When prisoners sue: A study of prisoner section 1983 suits in the Federal Courts. *Harvard Law Review, 92*, 610–663.

Vaughn, M. S. (1994). Police civil liability for abandonment in high-crime areas and other high risk situations. *Journal of Criminal Justice, 22*, 407–424.

Vaughn, M. S., & Coomes, L. F. (1995). The liability of moonlighting: Are Police Officers Employed as Security Guards Acting Under Color of Law? *Police Liability Review, 6*, 6–9.

Wardell, M. J. (1983). Section 1983: A change in the meaning of Under Color of Law: *Polk County v. Dodson. Arizona Law Review, 25*, 151–175.

Warner, J. (2011, May 18). Denver police brutality scandal: A multimedia timeline, Westworld.com.

Washington, L. (2011, February 9). Cities like Philly Waste millions defending crooked, racist cops: alley car ethics & other antics, thiscan'tbehappening.net.

Weinstein, H. (2000, August 29). Judge OKs use of racketeering law in rampart suits. *Los Angeles Times*, 1A.

West, H. C., & Saboul, W. J. (2008). *Prison Inmates at Mid-Year 2008.* Washington, DC: Bureau of Justice Statistics.

Worrall, J. L. (1998). Administrative determinants of civil liability lawsuits against municipal police departments: an exploratory analysis. *Crime and Delinquency, 44*, 295–313.

Worrall, J. L., & Gutierrez, R. S. (1999). Professional notes—Potential consequences of community-oriented policing for civil liability: Is there a dark side to employee empowerment? *Review of Public Personnel Administration, 19*, 61–70.

Zargans, E. H. (1985). Under color of what law? A reconstructed model of Section 1983 liability. *Virginia Law Review, 71*, 499–598.

2 ▪▪▪
▪▪▪
▪▪▪

Foundations for Liability

OVERVIEW

Criminal justice personnel have increasingly become targets of civil lawsuits. Historically, it has been common to read about a police or correctional officer being charged with brutality. In contemporary times, issues of liability have expanded beyond limited allegations of police or correctional officer brutality to include virtually every task performed by criminal justice personnel. Liability principles apply to all public officers, not just police officers. Detention and correctional personnel, probation and parole officers, including supervisors and administrative personnel, are subject to civil liability today. It is important for all criminal justice personnel to have a fundamental working knowledge of the critical components of civil liability, regardless of their level of responsibility.

Liability Under Tort Law

The most common area of liability in criminal justice today arises out of tort law. Torts allow recovery for personal injury. Personal injury claims include battery, negligence, and emotional distress. Most states have voluntarily passed laws known as tort claims acts in order to remove sovereign immunity obstacles. These laws have allowed numerous plaintiffs to file lawsuits seeking redress for violations of their rights.

From a broad perspective, all law is tort law, because the United States is a common law country (Silver, 2010). It is important to recognize that there is no clear definition of tort. While contract or property law is more clearly defined, tort law is loosely structured and often less clearly defined. A tort is a civil wrong. The term originates from the Latin word *tortus*, meaning *bent* or *twisted*. Initially, crimes and torts were treated the same, and an individual or a group would respond to the wrongdoing by personally taking action against the accused. Over time, as private vengeance gave way to criminal laws codified and prosecuted by the state in the name of the victim, torts and crimes evolved into separate legal concepts. Tort actions are civil legal actions arising out of situations between private parties. The injured party files a lawsuit seeking legal relief in the form of damages rather than criminal sanctions. Tort actions do not include breaches of contract.

Many criminal justice personnel are more familiar with criminal law than they are with aspects of civil law, because they enforce and apply criminal law on a daily basis. Because the liability of criminal justice personnel falls into the civil law arena, a brief comparison between criminal law and civil law is necessary (see Table 2.1).

Table 2.1   Criminal Law versus Tort Law

Components of Criminal Law	Components of Tort Law
A Public Offense	Private or Civil Wrong
State vs. Individual	Individual vs. Individual
Fines, Probation, Incarceration, Death	Monetary Sanctions
Guilt Beyond a Reasonable Doubt	Preponderance of the Evidence
Acquittal Normally Not Appealable by the State	Both Parties May Appeal
The State Receives Fines and Restitution Goes to Victim	Plaintiff Receives Monetary Damages as Compensation
Both criminal law and tort law seek to control behavior and impose sanctions.	

Criminal Law

Crimes are defined in terms of conduct that is forbidden or required and the mental state of the individual at the time of the prohibited act or omission (Gardner & Anderson, 2011). Crimes can also be defined in terms of harm done to a particular victim and against the state. Crimes are viewed as offenses punishable by the state in the name of the victim, through assessing fines, probation, community service, imprisonment, or death. In the American criminal justice system, the state—through the prosecutor—brings criminal charges against the accused. The state has the burden of proving its case "beyond a reasonable doubt," which is a high standard of proof. Should a jury or judge find the accused guilty, the judge will determine an appropriate sanction for the defendant, to be administered by the state. In a criminal case, the accused has numerous constitutionally protected rights and has the right to appeal a conviction. The state generally does not have the right to appeal an acquittal.

Torts

Torts are private injuries or wrongful acts that result in an injury or harm between individuals or their property. An individual who suffers a private injury may seek redress (damages) in a civil action, rather than through the criminal law process. The injured party (the plaintiff) seeks compensation from the injuring party (the defendant). The standard of proof needed to prevail in a civil action is that of "a preponderance of the evidence," which is a lower standard than "beyond a reasonable doubt." This means that a jury reviewing the case and evidence only needs to be convinced by a 50.1 percent margin to find in favor of either party. In a civil action, the state does not represent either party; rather, both parties may be represented by retained legal counsel, or an individual may bring the case to court without assistance of counsel (known as *pro se*). In civil cases the losing party may appeal the decision to the next higher court, including the United States Supreme Court. Should the plaintiff prevail in a civil suit, the defendant may have to pay monetary damages, including compensatory damages, punitive damages, court costs, and attorney's fees. The purpose of tort law is to compensate the plaintiff, provide justice, and deter others from similar behavior.

Some torts may also be crimes. Consider a police officer engaged in the high-speed pursuit of an alleged criminal. Should the officer operate the patrol car recklessly and hit and kill an innocent party, the officer could be prosecuted for manslaughter or murder, depending on the circumstances. If the officer is convicted of a crime, the state could impose a sanction such as a fine, probation, or incarceration. The victim's family could also file a civil lawsuit against the officer, claiming that the officer violated the constitutional rights of the deceased. Should the officer lose, the plaintiff could be awarded monetary damages.

Types of Torts

Dividing torts into categories can be problematic, because the dividing lines can be unclear. There are three general categories of torts: intentional, negligent, and strict liability. Criminal justice practitioners are most often sued for intentional and negligent torts. Strict liability torts are generally associated with activities that are so dangerous or hazardous that a person who engages in such activities can be substantially certain that the conduct will result in injury or damages (Silver, 2010); for example, workers performing duties that expose them to dangerous levels of hazardous chemicals and the potential for those chemicals to seep into the public water system. The company may be held liable for such conduct. Criminal justice functions normally do not fall under strict liability torts and will not be discussed here.

Intentional Torts

More than any other occupation, the work of criminal justice practitioners requires them to intrude into the affairs of many people. Stopping, arresting, detaining, frisking, searching, and performing other tasks have provided a steady flow of intentional tort litigation against criminal justice personnel (specific types of intentional torts will be discussed in Chapter 3).

Intentional torts may be committed against a person or property (del Carmen, 1991). This discussion will focus on torts against people, because it is more likely that an intentional tort claim would be assessed against an officer in criminal justice rather than against property. In order to prevail, the plaintiff must prove that an officer's behavior was intentional. Intentional torts are behaviors that are highly likely to cause injury to another. Intent is not easily defined, but in the context of tort it means to bring about some physical or mental harm, either through omission or commission by the actor. Further, because the intent is in the mind of the officer, the plaintiff may have difficulty proving an officer's intent in court. An example of an intentional tort is a classification officer at a prison reception center intentionally placing a prisoner in a housing unit next to known enemies, and a day later that prisoner is sexually assaulted by two other prisoners. Liability most certainly would attach, because the classification officer knew of the likelihood of harm to the prisoner and intentionally housed him in the unit knowing that harm could result.

Negligent Torts

Members of society owe a duty of reasonable care to one another (Silver, 2010). While intentional torts emerge from the purposeful conduct of an officer, negligent torts frequently arise from failing to perform a particular duty. Negligence is the breach of a common law or statutory duty to act reasonably toward those who may foreseeably be harmed. The distinction between intent and negligence is a matter of degree. The line has been drawn by the courts at the point where the known danger stops being only a foreseeable risk that a reasonable person would avoid, and becomes in the mind of the actor a substantial certainty (Prosser & Keeton, 1984). Negligence is the absence of care according to the circumstances, and requires a lesser degree of foreseeability than intentional torts.

The officer's state of mind is not in question when evaluating his or her conduct, because even inadvertent behavior that causes an injury may lead to liability. An important question to ask when assessing negligent conduct is: "Did the officer's conduct create an unreasonable risk for another?" For example, it is standard practice in policing to secure handcuffs on an individual by double-locking the single bars to prevent them from rotating so that they do not tighten around the wrist and cause injury. Liability may attach if an arresting officer fails to check the tightness of the handcuffs and double-lock them, and the arrestee sustains a wrist injury during arrest and transport. The criminal justice field is replete with situations in which negligence liability may arise. Some examples include use of equipment and vehicles, failure to protect, operating defective jails or prisons, and negligence in responding to calls for service.

Negligent torts are separated into two categories: Simple negligence means that an officer failed to exercise reasonable care in the performance of his or her duties, which led to an injury. Gross negligence means that the officer performed his or her duties with reckless disregard of the consequences of the actions that caused harm to another person or property. The distinction between these two categories is important because liability depends on which type is alleged. Normally, gross negligence is required in order for a plaintiff to prevail.

Other Types of Liabilities

Tort law provides the foundation for potential liability of criminal justice personnel. There are, however, other areas of liability that affect public officers. State tort liability exists for every public officer. This area of liability will be discussed in Chapter 3. While each state has tort laws, they also have different areas of liability. State tort liability typically includes such torts as wrongful death, false arrest, failure to protect, assault and battery, and invasion of privacy.

State Civil Rights Laws

Some states have civil rights laws that are similar to various federal civil rights laws. These laws provide sanctions for violations and are implemented as federal rights laws at the state level. This provides for more effective enforcement of the law by state authorities. Normally, federal officials allow the states to implement federal law with minimal interference.

Criminal Liability

Public officers may incur criminal liability under state law. The penal codes of most states provide for criminal prosecution of public officials who commit acts that violate the civil rights of an individual. Criminal justice personnel acting within the scope of their employment may be charged with a crime if they intentionally commit unlawful acts against an arrestee or prisoner in confinement, mistreat an arrestee, intentionally subject a person in custody to bodily injury or death, or knowingly engage in sexual activities with arrestees or prisoners.

Criminal justice officers may also face criminal liability under federal law—Title 18 U.S. Code § 242 (Criminal Liability for Deprivation of Civil Rights) and § 241 (Conspiracy to Deprive a Person of Rights) which was enacted in 1886. Under § 242, the defendant officer must have acted under color of law, acted intentionally to deprive the person of a protected right, and the person must actually have been deprived of that right. The law provides for a criminal sanction and under § 241 punishes the violation for conspiracy to commit the act, which requires at least two participants. Title 18 § 242 states:

> *Whoever, under color of any law, statute, ordinance, regulation, or custom willfully subjects any person in any State, Territory, Commonwealth, Possession, or District, to the deprivation of any rights, privileges, or immunities secured or protected by the Constitution or laws of the United States, or to different punishments, pains, or penalties, on account of such person being alien, or by citizens, shall be fined under this title or imprisoned not more than one year, or both; and if bodily injury results from the acts committed in violation of this section or if such acts include the use, attempted use, or threatened use of a dangerous weapon, explosives, or fire, shall be fined under this title or imprisoned not more than ten years, or both; and if death results from the acts committed in violation of the section or if such acts include kidnapping or an attempt to kidnap, aggravated sexual abuse, or an attempt to commit aggravated sexual abuse, or an attempt to kill shall be fined under this title, or imprisoned for any term of years or for life, or both, or may be sentenced to death.*

A former Detroit, Michigan, police officer was sentenced to 27 months in federal prison on one count of felony deprivation of rights under color of law under § 242 (*Detroit Free Press*, 1999). The officer stopped a motorist for driving with an expired license plate. The officer used a racial slur and the driver objected. The officer sprayed the driver with pepper spray and hit him in the head three times with a police radio. Two Detroit officers and one state police trooper witnessed the incident and testified against the officer. In addition to the prison time, the officer's sentence included two years of supervised release.

The Criminal Section of the Department of Justice Civil Rights Division is charged with enforcement of this title and investigating complaints made by citizens and prisoners.

The trend of prosecutions in accordance with § 242 from 1999 through 2011 are shown in Table 2.2 (DOJ, 2011).

As shown in Table 2.2, criminal prosecutions are being actively pursued by the DOJ and have increased over the reporting period. Overall, prosecutions increased by 38 percent, and from 2005 to 2011, prosecutions increased by 34 percent. The number of defendants prosecuted has increased slightly over the reporting period and a majority of cases involve multiple personnel. There is a high conviction rate, averaging 87 percent of the prosecutions.

Table 2.2   § 242 Prosecutions: 1998–2011

Year	Number of Cases Filed	Number of Defendants	Convicted (%)	Sentenced to Prison (%)
1998	80	135	90	83
1999	81	121	87	85
2000	80	135	86	78
2001	83	123	85	85
2002	79	121	88	81
2003	85	126	86	83
2004	96	138	88	90
2005	84	139	85	84
2006	90	141	91	81
2007	93	150	93	83
2008	105	146	89	84
2009	108	148	90	85
2010	112	145	93	86
2011	115	150	90	84
Averages	92	137	87	84

The figures indicate that there is an 80 percent likelihood of being sentenced to prison after conviction.

The majority of prosecutions involved law enforcement officers (69%; municipality, county, state police, and federal), followed by correctional personnel (28%; jail and prison), and court personnel account for 2 percent. Of these personnel, 30 percent included federal officers and 18 percent included administrators (chiefs, sheriffs, wardens, and middle management). Prosecuted personnel pled guilty in about 72 percent of the cases and acquittals account for about 9 percent of the prosecutions. The low number of acquittals is more representative of the DOJ's decision to prosecute only highly winnable cases. This finding corresponds with Johnson and Bridgmon's (2009) research on § 242 prosecutions.

The top five charges in which § 242 actions are prosecuted include sexual assault of an arrestee or prisoner (21%), robbery/theft (20%), excessive force (19%), assault on an arrestee/prisoner (15%), and conspiracy to violate rights/deprive rights and objection of justice (13%). Sentences for § 242 prosecutions range from financial penalties including fines and restitution, and other sentences include probation, confinement in jail, and/or prison. Financial penalties averaged $10,000 in fines and $25,000 in restitution. Other sentence options included probation, jail, prison, and community supervision. Of the prison sentences, 88 percent were less than 10 years in length, and life sentences accounted for about 3 percent. In 55 percent of the cases the sentence comprised multiple components including jail and prison confinement, supervised release, and financial costs. In all convictions, law enforcement personnel forfeited their certification. Examples of this enforcement (DOJ, 2012) are:

- For their participation in beating a handcuffed detainee, two county sheriff deputies pleaded guilty of willfully depriving the detainee of his constitutional right to be free from the use of excessive force. While acting in their capacity as law enforcement officers, the deputies punched, kicked, and slapped the detainee, who was lying on the ground in handcuffs and offering no resistance. The first deputy was sentenced to serve 3 to 4 years in prison and the second deputy was sentenced to 34 months in prison (January, 2012).

- Former officers of the New Orleans Police Department were convicted by a jury for beating to death an arrestee. During the trial evidence showed that the officers stopped a man on the street and during the arrest, one officer restrained the man while the other officer kicked him in the side and struck him repeatedly with a metal baton. The arrestee offered no resistance and suffered fractured ribs, a ruptured spleen, and injuries that triggered massive internal bleeding. The officers transported the arrestee to the hospital, where they falsely informed medical personnel that he was suffering from a drug overdose. The arrestee died shortly after admission into the hospital. During an investigation of the death the officers attempted to cover up their actions and falsely stated to the FBI that they never used force on the arrestee and that he had collapsed on the street, necessitating their transport to the hospital.
  The first officer was sentenced 22 years in prison for violating the civil rights of the arrestee and for obstructing justice in the wake of the beating. The partner of the first officer was sentenced to 5 years and 10 months in prison for obstructing justice and for making false statements to the FBI. He was also ordered to pay $11,576 in restitution (September, 2011).

- While serving as a correction officer in a detention facility, the officer pled guilty to groping female prisoners in the medical isolation rooms of the infirmary. The officer admitted that he would approach female prisoners in the unit, instructed them to disrobe, assured them that he was to perform an examination of them prior to the physician's exam, and touched intimate areas of their bodies in a sexual manner. The officer was sentenced on three counts of abusive sexual contact and three counts of deprivation of rights under color of law (October, 2010).

- A former Atlanta, Georgia, police officer pleaded guilty in federal district court to conspiracy to violate civil rights in connection with a fatal shooting during the execution of an illegal search warrant. He was sentenced to 121 months in federal prison. The officer secured a search warrant based on false information and responded to the residence. At the door the victim shot at the officers and they returned fire, killing her. The officers entered the residence and planted a bag of marijuana and cocaine in the basement, and later falsified reports and lied during the homicide investigation (October 2008).

- A police officer pleaded guilty to forcing a female arrestee to engage in sexual relations with him on a traffic stop or risk being incarcerated in jail. She complied and the officer released her. After a federal investigation the officer lied to the FBI. The officer later pleaded guilty and received a federal prison sentence (October 2008).

- The former police chief of Gary, Indiana, was convicted of a felony civil rights violation for using excessive force. The jury found that the chief used excessive force during an arrest resulting in a federal civil rights investigation. The chief entered a residence and assaulted the occupants. Testimony in court by on-scene officers confirmed that the chief kicked handcuffed individuals while they were on the ground. The chief claimed he kicked only one person after he himself had been kicked (September 2008).

- The warden of a Hawaii prison was sentenced to 24 months in federal prison and a correctional officer was also sentenced to 39 months in prison in separate incidents. The warden admitted he ordered a prisoner to be brought to the central area of the prison where he handcuffed the prisoner to a pole. The warden repeatedly struck the prisoner with a board until it broke. The officer struck another prisoner in the head repeatedly without provocation and the prisoner sustained ear drum damage. The officer admitted to the beating and making false statements to the FBI (April 2008).

- A Tennessee jail supervisor was sentenced to 33 months in federal prison for subjecting a prisoner to cruel and unusual punishment. The supervisor confined a prisoner in a small holding cell amid human waste and required that the prisoner be restrained in a straitjacket while in the cell 12 hours a day for three straight weeks. A correctional officer was also convicted for beating the prisoner and throwing a chemical agent into the cell as retribution for an earlier misconduct incident (June 2007).

- Officer Justin Volpe was sentenced to 30 years in prison under § 242 for brutally sodomizing Abner Louima in New York, while acting under color of law (December 1999).

- A Mississippi police chief was convicted of striking an arrestee several times in the head with a baton while the arrestee was handcuffed in the back of a patrol car. The chief was sentenced to 13 months in prison under § 242 for a willful unreasonable seizure under color of law (February 2000).

- Six correctional officers of the Arkansas Department of Corrections beat and repeatedly shocked two naked and handcuffed prisoners with a Taser and a cattle prod. During a separate incident, three of the six defendants shocked and beat another handcuffed prisoner. Ultimately, five officers entered guilty pleas while the sixth was convicted at trial. The officers were sentenced to prison terms ranging from 24 to 78 months under § 242 for imposing unusual punishment under color of law (February 2001).

- A North Carolina police officer pleaded guilty to a felony civil rights charge for coercing women, whom he stopped or arrested, into having sex with him. He was sentenced to 10 years in prison for willful deprivation of liberty without due process under color of law (September 2003).

- An Oklahoma police officer was convicted and sentenced to prison for assault for fracturing the hip of a 67-year-old arrestee he stopped for a traffic violation. The officer was prosecuted under § 242 for the willful deprivation of the victim's liberty without due process under color of law (July 2004).

- A Texas police officer was convicted on federal civil rights charges under § 242 for repeatedly assaulting a handcuffed man while the officer was acting under color of law. The officer first kicked and choked the man, then proceeded to stick the barrel of his gun into the victim's mouth, threatening to kill him. The officer attempted to cover up his actions by submitting a false report (September 2004).

Federal Civil Rights Laws

Criminal justice personnel may also incur liability for violating the civil rights of another under federal law. Title 42 United States Code § 1983 provides remedies such as monetary damages or injunctive relief for violations of constitutional rights. The § 1983 lawsuit is filed in federal court, and claims that the officer or official, acting under color of law, deprived the plaintiff of a constitutionally protected right, either prior to or during arrest or detention, during incarceration, or after release (parole).

Title 42 United States Code § 1985 (Conspiracy to Interfere with Civil Rights) provides a civil remedy to plaintiffs who can show that two or more officers conspired to deprive them of their civil rights. Under § 1985, the burden is on the plaintiff to prove that the officers actually agreed to participate in the action. The plaintiff must also prove intent to deprive him or her of equal protection under the law. For example, two detention officers and the sheriff meet and agree to house a detainee in a cell with a known violent offender who would purposely beat the detainee on the sheriff's order. The three could be held civilly liable for violating the detainee's rights under § 1983, and under § 1985 for conspiracy.

Violent Crime Control and Law Enforcement Act

Police departments have a higher probability of incurring liability since the passage of § 210401 of the Violent Crime Control and Law Enforcement Act of 1994 (Title 42 U.S. Code §§ 14141 and 14142). Passed partly as a result of the Rodney King incident, it grants the Department of Justice (DOJ) extremely broad investigative powers and prosecutorial authority in cases of alleged use of excessive force. Sections 14141 and 14142 permit the Department of Justice to investigate patterns or practices of misconduct in local police departments and requires the collection of statistics on "police abuse." The Department of Justice has the authority to look beyond the acts of an individual officer and into the affairs of the entire police department. The statute also gives the Department of Justice authority to file civil actions on behalf of citizens to obtain declaratory or equitable relief. The Pittsburgh, Pennsylvania, and Steubenville, Ohio, police departments were the first two police departments in which the Department of Justice utilized the statute. Both departments were under five-year consent decrees with the federal government from 1997 until successful completion in 2002. Since October 1996, the DOJ has conducted 47 investigations of law enforcement agencies and there are 17 ongoing investigations. As abuses come to the attention of the DOJ, other agencies are investigated (see Chapter 8 for a detailed discussion on the trends of these consent decrees).

As an example of the application of a § 14141 investigation, the Seattle, Washington, Police Department was investigated by the Department of Justice Special Litigation section in 2011 for engaging in a pattern and practice of excessive force violating the Constitution and federal law (DOJ, 2012). Investigators and attorneys from the DOJ conducted numerous interviews with SPD officers and administrators, city officials, and community members and local advocates. Investigators also examined SPD policies, procedures, training materials, internal records and data, video footage of arrests, and investigative files of arrests. The DOJ determined from the investigation that long-standing deficiencies emerged from excessive use of force incidents, excessive force used against a high number of persons with mental illness, lack of oversight in enforcing policies, deficiencies in training officers in using appropriate use of force, deficiencies in reporting force incidents, an ineffective system of complaint investigation and adjudication, an ineffective system of early identification and intervention with problem officers, and a failure to collect adequate data to assess biased policing allegations. Resolution of these findings required a written agreement, which sets forth remedial measures to be taken within a fixed period of time, enforceable by the court.

The DOJ (2010) filed a Statement of Interest in a class action lawsuit challenging the Franklin County Sheriff's Office's use of conducted electric devices (CEDs, commonly known as "Tasers") against detainees in its jails. The DOJ filed a motion asking the Court to allow them to intervene as a party in this lawsuit. The complaint alleged that the Franklin County Sheriff's Office violated 42 U.S.C. § 14141 by engaging in an unconstitutional pattern and practice of using CEDs in an abusive manner, failing to adequately investigate use of CEDs, and failing to adequately train corrections deputies in the use of CEDs. In February 2011, the claims were resolved by entering into a court-enforceable settlement agreement with Franklin County. The Settlement Agreement requires the Franklin County Sheriff's Office to reform its policies, procedures, and training on use of CEDs, and its internal investigations of all uses of CEDs. The DOJ will monitor compliance with the Settlement Agreement.

The Civil Rights of Institutionalized Persons Act (CRIPA)

Passed by Congress in 1980, the Act ensures that the rights of institutionalized persons are protected from unconstitutional conditions. Title 42 U.S.C. § 1997 *et seq.* permits the Attorney General to bring civil lawsuits against state institutions regarding the civil rights of those housed in the facility, including the conditions of their confinement and the use of excessive force. State institutions may include jails, prisons, and other correctional facilities (juvenile or adult), nursing homes, and other institutions that house the mentally impaired or chronically ill. CRIPA allows the DOJ to bring legal actions (similar to § 14141, discussed earlier) for declaratory or equitable relief for a pattern or practice of unconstitutional conditions of confinement.

From 1980 to 2011, the DOJ initiated CRIPA actions against 646 facilities, resulting in 401 consent decrees, lawsuits, agreements, and settlements governing conditions of confinement. Since 1997 the DOJ has conducted 82 investigations performed involving jails, prisons, and juvenile facilities, and there are 11 investigations that are ongoing. Examples of these actions include (DOJ, 2012):

- In December 2011, a court enforceable Settlement Agreement was made between the DOJ and the Lake County Jail (Indiana) to remedy the unconstitutional conditions found in their investigation of the jail under the Civil Rights of Institutionalized Persons Act. The Settlement Agreement addresses problems that included suicide prevention, use of force, medical care, mental health care, fire and life safety, sanitation, and training. The DOJ will monitor compliance with the settlement agreement every six months and file a report with the Court.
- The DOJ conducted an investigation of the Miami-Dade County Jail (MDCJ) under the Civil Rights of Institutionalized Persons Act. The investigation was performed to determine whether allegations of conditions of confinement violated the rights of detainees. The DOJ found deficiencies in MDCJ's mental health care, suicide prevention, failure to protect prisoners from physical harm, and failure to provide sanitary and safe conditions (August, 2011).

- An investigation of the Mobile County Metro Jail (MCMJ) was conducted by the DOJ investigators regarding conditions of confinement under the Civil Rights of Institutionalized Persons Act. The County initially cooperated in this investigation, but ceased communicating about the investigation. The DOJ continued the investigation and found unconstitutional conditions at MCMJ, including problems with inadequate mental health care, excessive restraint, failure to protect prisoners from physical harm, and unsafe and unsanitary conditions. Based on the findings of the investigation, officials of MCMJ agreed to make changes in policies and conditions, as stipulated in the agreement (January, 2009).
- The DOJ reached an out-of-court agreement with the Wicomico County Detention Center in Salisbury, Maryland, regarding systematic violations of prisoners' federally protected rights. The investigation showed that the Detention Center failed to provide required medical and mental health care, failed to provide adequate prisoner safety, and failed to provide sufficiently sanitary living conditions. Under the terms of the agreement the Detention Center will address and correct the deficiencies identified by the DOJ (July 2004).
- The Civil Rights Division of the DOJ filed a lawsuit challenging the conditions of confinement at the Terrell County Jail in Dawson, Georgia. The complaint alleged that the jail routinely violated federally protected rights, including failing to protect prisoner safely, and failing to provide required medical and mental health care (June 2004). A more detailed assessment of the trends of CRIPA is discussed in Chapter 8.

Americans with Disabilities Act (ADA)

The Department of Justice may file a lawsuit in federal court against a criminal justice agency to enforce the ADA in accordance with 42 U.S.C. § 12131, Titles I, II, and III. The ADA prohibits discrimination on the basis of a disability in public places, including criminal justice agencies. The DOJ may obtain civil penalties of up to $55,000 for the first violation and $110,000 for a subsequent violation. The DOJ is authorized to perform investigations of ADA claims and may resolve the matter with a written formal settlement agreement. In 2007 two such settlements with county jails were resolved stemming from prisoner disabilities (DOJ, 2008). ADA claims generally focus on allegations of discrimination regarding medical care and mental health treatment issues.

Further, a plaintiff may cite an ADA violation in conjunction with a § 1983 legal action. In *O'Guinn v. Lovelock Correctional Center* (2007) a prisoner filed a § 1983 action alleging that he was denied accommodation and treatment for a mental illness under the ADA. The district court dismissed the lawsuit in accordance with the Prison Litigation Reform Act and an appellate court affirmed. The prisoner requested a lower bunk due to poor balance resulting from a brain injury and asserted that such denial by prison personnel violated his right to mental health treatment. The court ruled that the prisoner failed to exhaust internal remedies to his complaint as required in the PLRA. Prior to the lawsuit the prisoner submitted a complaint to the Department of Justice (DOJ) and the court determined that the DOJ's investigation of the complaint did not satisfy the exhaustion requirement of the PLRA as the investigation did not terminate the prisoner's rights to pursue an ADA claim.

Moreover, in *Herman v. County of York* (2007) the estate of a prisoner who committed suicide while confined in jail filed a § 1983 claim asserting that officers and health care staff violated the ADA by failing to protect the prisoner from taking his own life. Under the Eighth Amendment, the estate alleged that the officers failed to check on the prisoner and that health care staff were deliberately indifferent to his medical care needs and failed to place him on a suicide watch. The court granted summary judgment for the defendants, holding that they were not deliberately indifferent to the needs of the prisoner. Further, the court determined that neither the medical staff nor the officers discriminated against the prisoner as they did not deny him access to jail services, programs, or activities of a public entity in violation of the ADA. The court determined that the prisoner denied suicidal thoughts, informed a nurse that he did not wish to take his prescribed antidepressant medications, and that a nurse advised him to return to the medical unit as necessary.

An ADA claim was brought by the estate of a mentally ill decedent in *Waller v. City of Danville* (2007). The suspect had entered a building in an effort to elude officers and held several occupants hostage. The suspect threatened the occupants' lives and threatened the responding officers with a knife and a large metal pipe. Officers gave several verbal commands to the individual to drop the weapons as he advanced toward them and an officer fired his weapon, killing the suspect. The estate filed a legal action alleging excessive force against the officer, an ADA claim against the city for failing to train officers in properly responding to the mentally ill and for failing to make accommodations in their response based on their son's mental condition. The court granted summary judgment on behalf of the officers ruling that the officers confronted a dangerous situation and that under the exigent circumstances, the officers had no duty to reasonably accommodate the suspect's mental illness. The court opined that it was irrelevant whether the police department had effectively trained their officers in providing such accommodations to mentally ill hostage takers.

In *Seremeth v. Board of County Commissioners Frederick County* (2012) a deaf man arrested in a domestic violence situation involving him and one of his deaf children stated a viable disability discrimination claim in accordance with the Americans with Disabilities Act. He claimed that handcuffing him in the back prevented him from writing notes in order to communicate with the deputies. The injury was the failure to make communication as effective as it would have been among deputies and persons without disabilities. The deputies were entitled to qualified immunity from liability, however, based on the exigent circumstances involved in a domestic violence situation. With the deputies concerned about their own safety and the safety of the man's family, it was reasonable to try to accommodate his disability by calling an American Sign Language trainee to assist in communication, and by attempting to use his father as an interpreter.

Discipline or Termination Under Administrative Liability

Criminal justice personnel in both state and federal agencies are bound by and subject to sanctions in their respective departments in accordance with agency rules, regulations, and policy and procedure manuals. These administrative rules and guidelines govern the conduct of employees. Violating them may expose the employee to liability and subject that employee to various forms of discipline up to and including termination. These rules are binding and may be enforced as long as they comport with constitutional requirements and do not violate the employee's rights.

Summary

In order to more fully understand civil liability, the foundations of liability have been presented. The differences between criminal law and civil law have been provided. It is important to understand that in civil law the injured party, not the state, brings an action before the court and seeks to be compensated through monetary awards. Intentional and negligent torts are two types of tort actions that are commonly brought against criminal justice personnel and often form the foundation of civil liability. Other categories of torts have been presented to further expose the reader to possible liability actions against criminal justice personnel and agencies. The primary method for filing civil lawsuits against public officers is through § 1983 for alleged violations of constitutional rights. The plaintiff seeks monetary damages against the officer or governmental entity for the alleged deprivation.

It is important to underscore that the standard of proof relied upon in civil litigation is much different from that in criminal proceedings. In civil cases, a preponderance of the evidence is all that is required for a plaintiff to prevail. This is a lower standard than "beyond a reasonable doubt." This means that a jury need only believe that there is sufficient evidence to tip the scale in favor of the plaintiff or defendant. The losing party may appeal a verdict in civil litigation, while in a criminal matter only the defendant may appeal a conviction.

Criminal justice personnel may be criminally and civilly responsible for their actions or failure to act when performing their duties. They may also be investigated by their own department and, as warranted, may be disciplined or terminated from employment.

An ongoing trend that bears noting is the investigations performed by the DOJ under § 14141 into allegations of a pattern or practice of misconduct in police departments. The DOJ has implemented this section more frequently since 1999, resulting in greater use of five-year consent decrees. Under § 242, criminal prosecutions have increased since 2005 and a high percentage of convictions result in a prison sentence. A similar trend is also ongoing with investigations by the DOJ into institutional issues surrounding conditions of confinement under the CRIPA provision. These provisions are another subset of laws enforcing the civil rights of citizens and prisoners, enlarging the framework of accountability and responsibility of criminal justice practitioners. They have significant implications for police administrators and officers alike, and a more detailed discussion is provided in Chapter 8.

In the chapters that follow, each type of tort action will be thoroughly discussed. As each tort action is presented, the reader is encouraged to determine how each action may affect his or her own job responsibilities.

References

del Carmen, R. V. (1991). *Civil liabilities in American policing: a textbook for law enforcement personnel.* Monterey, CA: Brady.

Detroit Free Press (1999, August 27). *Cop who hit suspect jailed for 27 months. Detroit Free Press.* 1A, 3A.

Gardner, T. J., & Anderson, T. M. (2011). *Criminal law* (11th ed.). Belmont, CA: Wadsworth Publishing Co.

Johnson, B. R., & Bridgman, P. B. (2009). Depriving civil rights: an exploration of 18 U.S.C. 242 criminal prosecutions, 2001–2006. *Criminal Justice Review, 34,* 196–209.

Prosser, W. L., & Keeton, R. E. (1984). *On torts* (5th ed.). Minneapolis, MN: West Publishing.

Silver, I. (2010). *Police civil liability.* New York, NY: Matthew Bender & Co.

United States Department of Justice (2011). *The Attorney General's Annual Report to Congress describing the department's enforcement efforts under the Civil Rights of Institutionalized Persons Act: 1980 to 2011.* Washington, DC: Civil Rights Division, Special Litigation.

United States Department of Justice (2012). *Reports of civil rights investigations: 1998–2011.* Washington, DC: Civil Rights Division, Special Litigation.

Forum: Discuss issue of whether or not police officers have a duty to protect citizens. Justify your position.

Paper: Identify & discuss the remedies that are available to a successful claimant in a tort action
Legal means of enforcing a right
Redressing a wrong

Civil Liability Under State and Federal Tort Law

OVERVIEW

Allegations arising from public officials' misuse of authority may be filed in federal or state court. As was noted in Chapter 1, negligence and intentional torts form the foundation of civil liability. This chapter will examine liability actions brought against criminal justice personnel under both state and federal tort theories.

Negligence claims against criminal justice personnel are based on state tort law. Negligence definitions differ from state to state, but generally mean the absence of care according to the circumstances (Silver, 2010). Liability will generally attach if the person acted in disregard of the right of one to whom he owed a duty. Differences in definitions may be due to specific categories and definitions allowed under state law or court decisions. A citizen's right to sue a public entity is limited by the doctrine of sovereign immunity. Although in decline, this doctrine shields the government from being sued by citizens. Most states have constitutional or statutory provisions that delineate the extent of sovereign immunity. These acts are normally referred to as tort claims acts. These statutes should be consulted in order to determine whether a particular entity may be sued, and whether immunity exists. The type of negligence required to hold an officer civilly liable varies from state to state. Simple negligence may be the applicable standard in one state, while gross negligence may be required to establish liability in another state.

The standard applied in negligent torts is whether the officer's act or failure to act created an unreasonable risk of harm to another. Negligence occurs when a person acting unreasonably does not intend to harm another, but fails to exercise due care to prevent such harm (*Harris v. City of Compton*, 1985). More precisely, negligence can be defined as subjecting a person to an unreasonable risk of injury. When a police or correctional officer exercises control over an arrestee or prisoner, he or she has a duty to exercise reasonable care (*Wagar v. Hasenkrug*, 1980; *Abraham v. Maes*, 1983). A person is in custody when he or she is arrested and later transported by the police or confined by detention officers. This means that the police have a legal duty to take reasonable precautions to protect the health and safety of prisoners in their custody, render medical assistance as needed, and treat arrestees humanely. This, however, does not imply that law enforcement or correctional officers are the absolute guarantors of the welfare of those in their custody.

Establishing negligence is difficult. In some negligence cases, an agency's own policies and procedures have been used to determine the level of care expected of criminal justice personnel when performing their duties. For example, in *Miller v. Smith* (1995), the wrongful death by suicide of an arrestee rose to a level of negligent conduct on the part of the chief. Failing to provide directives and guidelines in handcuffing or otherwise restraining an arrestee at the scene of a drunk driving arrest prior to the suicide caused liability to attach to the city. In *Clark v. District of Columbia* (1997), the violation of a suicide prevention policy was not negligence per se. The standard of care provided to prisoners in the facility exceeded a national standard, and liability did not attach.

To prove a state tort negligence claim, four elements must be established: (1) a legal duty, (2) the breach of that duty, (3) proximate causation, and (4) an actual injury. All of these elements must be proved by the plaintiff in order to prevail in a state tort claim of negligence. If any of the four elements is absent, there is no liability.

Duty

Negligence derives generally from common law concepts, and most courts have held that the defendant must violate a duty to the person injured (Silver, 2010). It may arise from laws, customs, judicial decisions, or agency regulations (Kappeler, Vaughn, & del Carmen, 1991).

Negligence is based on two concepts: (1) the existence of a duty, and (2) fault, or the breach of that duty (Prosser and Keeton, 1986). Duty, as a matter of law, is to be determined by the court, while a jury examines fault from the perspective of a reasonable person.

Criminal justice personnel perform a variety of duties. The authority to perform these duties does not automatically create a legal duty to perform these functions or a duty to perform them with reasonable care. In *State v. Hughes* (1989), however, the court concluded that police officers have a duty to exercise reasonable care in their official dealings with citizens who may be injured by their actions. This concept also applies to correctional personnel. In *Davis v. City of Detroit* (1986), the court held that absence of a detoxification cell required by a jail rule was a defective condition in a public building. Further, in *Layton v. Quinn* (1982), the court held that prior court orders directing improvements within the jail were relevant to the issue of failing to comply and contributed to the suicide of a prisoner known to have mental problems.

In order to require an officer to act in accordance with certain standards or levels of care to avoid a risk of harm to another, there must be a legal duty. Determining whether a duty exists at all is essential. Where no duty exists, there is no liability. *Hurely v. Eddingfield* (1901) illustrates that our society continues to be reluctant to impose liability for inaction or to create too many duties to act. A classic example is the case of a drowning person. While there may be a moral duty to attempt a rescue, there is no legal duty to do so. The law of negligence is preoccupied with the notion that there is no legal duty to act in many situations where a moral duty exists (Silver, 2005). Although the outcome in *Nelson v. Trayer* (1966) might be different today under § 1983 cases, a deputy was held not negligent in arresting only a man for hitchhiking and not his wife, who was later struck and killed by a passing vehicle.

Statutes will frequently stipulate certain actions of a law enforcement or correctional officer when performing their duties. Legislatures have passed many laws that form the basis of negligence liability. A plaintiff may assert that the defendant officer violated a statute and that the violation caused his or her injury. For example, if a police officer fails to arrest a drunk driver, and that driver later causes an accident in which another person is injured or killed, that officer could be liable for failing to arrest the driver. In this example, the statute would require a sobriety test. If the driver fails the test, arrest would be required. The court could possibly conclude that the officer failed to follow a duty of adhering to departmental regulations and state law. Such failure could be construed as creating or causing the later accident, and liability would probably attach.

Breach of Duty

Identifying a legal duty owed to the plaintiff is insufficient on its own. The plaintiff must also prove that the officer failed to perform or breached the legal duty owed. Failing to perform a duty will be based on the factual situation of the incident. Police may have a duty to arrest drunk drivers, but this does not imply that if the police fail to arrest every drunk driver and an accident occurs that causes an injury or death, liability will attach (Kappeler, 1997).

Courts have recognized that criminal justice personnel are liable only to specific individuals and not the general public (*Harris v. District of Columbia*, 1991). For example, a police officer restrained a violent arrestee who was under the influence of PCP and locked him in a police van. Medical care was delayed because the emergency room physician required the officer to fill out certain forms that initially had been completed incorrectly. The arrestee subsequently died. The court determined that the officer did not breach a duty of care, because there was no clearly established obligation to provide general medical services nor to provide such services to those not formally committed.

In order to prevail, the plaintiff must show some special knowledge or circumstances that set him or her apart from the general public and show that a relationship exists between the officer and the plaintiff. For example, in *Azure v. City of Billings* (1979), officers were held liable for violating a statute requiring the police to transport intoxicated arrestees to a treatment facility. The arrestee had sustained injuries prior to arrest and was noticeably intoxicated. There were some signs that he had been assaulted, he was unsteady in his balance, and his speech was slurred. Rather than transport the arrestee to the medical facility, where his condition could have been treated, officers transported him to the local jail.

Proximate Cause

If the plaintiff is successful in establishing that there was a legal duty and that the officer breached that duty, he or she must show that the breach was the proximate cause of the injury. Proximate cause is the direct factual link between the act of negligence and the plaintiff's injury. Proximate cause is defined differently by many courts. For example, the Michigan Supreme Court in *Robinson v. City of Detroit* (2000) defined "proximate cause" as meaning the "one most immediate, efficient, and direct cause preceding an injury." It may be enough in one court to show that the officer's act or omission rose to a level that caused the plaintiff's injury, while other courts may rely on a higher standard of recklessness, wanton conduct, or gross negligence, rather than simple negligence.

A close causal link between the officer's negligent conduct and the harm to the plaintiff must be proven. This may be determined by asking, "But for the officer's conduct, would the plaintiff have sustained the injury, harm, or death?" An additional relevant question may be: "Was the officer acting recklessly?" The court in *Carlin v. Blanchard* (1988) held that a sheriff's deputy was negligent in the shooting of a fellow officer and was the proximate cause of the officer's injuries, despite the fact that the officer's own conduct contributed to his injuries.

In *Wilson v. Taylor* (2009) the estate of a detainee who hung himself in the jail filed suit against the correctional officials on state and federal constitutional claims. The court agreed with the estate, holding that there were questions as to whether the detainee's confinement was valid, that officials maintained policies and practices that failed to provide follow-up on the detainee's repeated inquiries about his release, and whether an officer acted with gross or wanton negligence when he threw the detainee against a bench in the cell by holding his throat and threatening him. The court held that these actions in their collective totality and detention officers ignoring the detainee's repeated release inquiries supported a claim of proximate cause of his ultimate death.

Occurrence of Actual Injury

The final element required in state tort actions is that of actual injury or damage to the plaintiff. The plaintiff must prove that actual damage occurred as a result of the officer's negligent conduct. Absent a showing of an actual injury, a plaintiff will not prevail. The injury or damage does not have to be physical. Emotional distress is sufficient for recovery in a tort action. Because the police are part of a public agency and are accountable to the public, they have a duty to report their activities in a reasonable manner. A false message that a prisoner died in custody was actionable on a theory of intentional infliction of emotional distress (*Texas Dept. of Corrections v. Winters*, 1989).

In *Carroll v. City of Quincy* (2006), a detainee lodged in a holding cell at a police station was injured when he fell with his hands handcuffed behind his back. The detainee filed suit under state law, alleging that the officer was negligent in performing his duties. The detainee had a blood-alcohol content of 0.37 and later at the hospital it was determined that he sustained a subdural hematoma, traumatic brain injury, and seizure disorder. The court held that the officer had subjective knowledge of the detainee's highly intoxicated state and liability attached. The court ruled that the officer's conduct of leaving the intoxicated detainee handcuffed in a cell alone was associated with the injuries sustained by the detainee and was not undertaken pursuant to any city policy or custom, as required for the imposition of municipal liability.

Special Duty and Foreseeability

Courts have established that police and correctional personnel may owe a special duty when they have reason to believe that an arrestee presents a danger to him or herself (*Thomas v.*

Williams, 1962). A special duty of care may arise when a particular arrestee is recognized to have a diminished ability to prevent self-injury or cannot exercise judgment with the same level of caution as an ordinary arrestee. Two types of individuals fall into these two categories: (1) the mentally disabled, who have diminished capacity for self-protection, and (2) those who are impaired by drugs or alcohol. When it is evident that a particular arrestee has a diminished capacity or cannot exercise the same level of care as an ordinary person because of mental illness or intoxication, police officers must ensure that reasonable measures are taken to care for that individual while he or she is in their custody.

The concept of special duty lacks precise definition but can be based on two factors: (1) the officer's knowledge of the arrestee's mental state, and (2) the extent to which the arrestee's condition renders him or her unable to exercise ordinary care. If it is foreseeable that an arrestee's condition creates a hazard in the given circumstances (if there is a reasonable anticipation that injury or damage is likely to occur as a result of an act or omission), a general duty of care can be required of the police. A combination of several factors must exist in order to indicate foreseeability, such as: (1) a level of knowledge of the arrestee's condition by the officer, (2) condition and history of the arrestee, (3) known propensities of the arrestee, etc. As these factors increase in severity, a court may be more likely to hold that a special duty existed. This may lead to liability if the duty is breached.

A special duty stems from a specific mandate (i.e., such as a statute) rather than from situational relationships (del Carmen, 1991). If an officer possesses sufficient knowledge of an arrestee's mental or intoxicated condition and the prisoner is rendered helpless, a special duty to render care may exist. A special duty of care creates a higher level of responsibility for officers. Other examples of a special duty include securing accident scenes, protecting witnesses and informants, suicidal prisoners in detention facilities, prisoner-on-prisoner assaults, failing to follow departmental rules, and operating equipment negligently.

In *Govea v. City of Norcross* (2004), the elements of negligence and foreseeability are illustrated. Officer Heiberger was specially trained to work with youths in the city and used his relationships to gather information for criminal investigations. While performing his duties for the Norcross Police Department, Heiberger was reprimanded for several safety infractions, including leaving his duty weapon unattended on the front seat of his patrol car, damaging a police radio by spilling a beverage on it, backing his patrol vehicle into a tree, and failing to submit investigative reports. His supervisor cited him for these infractions and Heiberger also received citations for excessive use of sick leave, failure to complete time sheets, failing to complete accident reports, and tardiness. The chief of police allowed him to resign rather than terminate his employment so that he could retain his police certification in Georgia. The chief also agreed not to disclose his poor performance to any hiring agency.

Heiberger was hired by the City of Chamblee and during his field training, he was cited for failing to discover a knife in the back seat of his patrol car, operating his patrol car erratically, and improperly applying handcuffs on a an arrestee. Officer Heiberger resigned from the force but requested to be re-hired within two weeks. The City of Chamblee rehired him but did not provide additional training for him. He again began working with youths in the community and a boy fatally shot himself with Heiberger's duty weapon when he allowed him to handle it. The boy's parents filed a lawsuit against the cities of Chamblee and Norcross claiming that Heiberger's position as a police officer and employment created a relationship with the boy, and that the relationship caused the circumstances that created the fatality. The lower court decided against the parents, stating that the state did allow such a lawsuit. The parents appealed. The appellate court agreed with the parents and allowed them to pursue their negligence claims.

The appellate court stated that it was wrong for the lower court to decide that negligence did not cause the boy's death. The court noted that the City of Norcross should have "foreseen" that Heiberger would obtain future employment as a police officer. Further, given Heiberger's history of carelessness and inattentiveness, Norcross should have known he would commit some safety infraction that could lead to serious injury or death. Norcross negligently breached its duty to fully and accurately report Heiberger's employment history. Additionally, the court held that the City of Chamblee could not foresee that officer Heiberger's tendencies would cause the boy's death; however, they had access to the Norcross Police Department's personnel file and knew that supervisors in Chamblee observed him in the performance of his duties where he continued a pattern of inactiveness and carelessness.

This case illustrates what a plaintiff needs in order to prevail in a claim of negligence. Both employing agencies had a duty to ensure that Heiberger performed his duties properly. The chief of police of Norcross failed to inform Chamblee's police chief about Heiberger's tendencies and breached his duty, which ultimately became the proximate cause of harm in the boy's death. In this case the link of what was known by Norcross became the proximate cause of the harm sustained by the youth. The concept of foreseeability is evidenced by the fact that Heiberger's poor performance was known, he continued his negligent performance, and it became highly predictable that his actions would injure another. The cities of Norcross and Chamblee possessed such knowledge and their failure to act on that knowledge was the proximate cause of the boy's death.

Areas of Potential Negligence in Criminal Justice

Police and correctional personnel come into contact with a variety of individuals—from the violent, the intoxicated, and the mentally impaired, to the sober and sane. They provide a myriad of functions by virtue of their 24-hour operational availability. Statutes may mandate a certain police or correctional response to such individuals. A selection of examples of potential negligence are discussed below.

Negligent Operation of Emergency Vehicles

A majority of police work involves vehicle patrol. Patrol officers regularly respond to emergency calls. State statutes authorize the use of police vehicles in emergency situations and limit how police officers may use their vehicles. Police must follow the same traffic laws as ordinary citizens. Police are obligated to operate their vehicles in a safe and reasonable manner in accordance with the law.

Even if police violate the emergency statute by pursuing an individual and the pursuit ends in an accident, the officer may not necessarily have been negligent. For example, police officers were not liable for damages in a collision that occurred after they chased an intoxicated motorist through a red light (*Reenders v. City of Ontario*, 1977). The court determined that there was no reason to believe that the motorist would not have run the red light absent the pursuit, because he was intoxicated and unaware that the police were pursuing him. In *State v. McGeorge* (1996), the court held that an officer was not negligent for engaging in a high-speed pursuit of a fleeing vehicle that collided with an oncoming car. The court held that reasonable minds could differ as to whether a continued high-speed pursuit was justifiable.

Many courts require a higher standard than mere negligence in pursuit cases. The court in a Maryland case held that gross negligence was the standard required when reviewing police conduct (*Boyer v. State*, 1991). The court determined that although the trooper may have driven at high speeds on a road with heavy traffic in an effort to apprehend an intoxicated person, he did not act with wanton and reckless disregard for the safety of others. In North Carolina, the standard for liability in police pursuits is gross or wanton negligence in cases in which the fleeing vehicle injures another (*Parish v. Hill*, 1999). An officer engaged in a high-speed pursuit that lasted for 10 miles in the early morning during light traffic. The officer did not force the car off the road, nor did he attempt to overtake it, therefore he was not grossly negligent. In *Morris v. Leaf* (1995), the Iowa Supreme Court ruled that liability for injuries to motorists caused by a collision with a pursued vehicle can only be based on reckless conduct by police in pursuits, not mere negligence. Neither the officer nor the city was liable when the pursued vehicle had already been in a hit-and-run accident and when pursuit of the already speeding car was designed to prevent further harm.

Consider, however, *City of San Antonio v. Schneider* (1990), in which the court ruled that "reckless disregard" meant something between ordinary and gross negligence. The court held that the officer acted with reckless disregard when he was speeding on a seemingly non-emergency call, knowing that a street was dangerous when wet, filled with stranded cars, and that he would have insufficient time to stop.

The Michigan Supreme Court, in *Robinson v. City of Detroit* (2000), ruled on the issue of whether police officers in vehicle pursuits face civil liability for injuries sustained by passengers in vehicles fleeing from the police when the fleeing car causes an accident. A 15-year-old boy was being brought home from work by a friend when his friend (the driver) began weaving from one lane to another. Police officers who saw this activated their overhead lights, and the driver sped off with the police officers in pursuit. The pursuit ended when the driver struck another vehicle. The 15-year-old passenger was killed in the collision. His estate sued the City of Detroit and the officers. The court held that the police first owe a duty to innocent passengers and pedestrians, but owe no duty to passengers who themselves are law violators, whether they help bring about the pursuit or encourage flight. The City of Detroit was entitled to judgment without trial, because it was not reasonable to conclude that the officers' pursuit caused the youth's death. The police vehicle did not hit the fleeing car, did not physically cause another car or object to hit the fleeing car, nor did it physically force the fleeing car off the road or into another vehicle or object. The individual officers were entitled to immunity, because their actions were not the proximate cause of the victim's injuries. The court concluded that "innocent persons who are injured as the result of police chases may sue an individual police officer only if the officer is 'the proximate cause' of the accident." The plaintiff did not have a cause of action against the others.

Operating a police vehicle in a reckless manner during a pursuit may not always be immunized. In *Mumm v. Mornson* (2006), an officer engaged in a high-speed pursuit of a female motorist (Mornson) who later was determined to be mentally disturbed. Mornson had been driving erratically and the officer's supervisor had instructed him to monitor the vehicle and later to discontinue the chase, which was in accordance to the department's policy. The court held that while Mornson's driving was potentially dangerous, she hit no vehicles or pedestrians, nor overtly threatened the officers or others, and did not commit any crime. She had actually avoided other vehicles and was not driving erratically at the time the officer rammed her vehicle. The court ruled that the officer recklessly used his vehicle when instructed to monitor and discontinue the chase, in violation of policy, and such conduct was not immunized. There was both a common law and statutory duty of care to a passenger and negligence was actionable.

Moreover, the court ruled against an officer engaged in pursuit in *Hudson v. City of Chicago* (2007). The officer assisted in a pursuit in which backup had not been requested but was merely providing his services should the need arise to enforce or execute the law. According to the court, liability attached against the officer as violation of the agency's pursuit policy was evidence of willful and wanton conduct.

In *Plaster v. City of St. Paul* (2011), officers were involved in a high speed pursuit of an individual suspected of selling drugs. Several minutes into the pursuit, the drug suspect struck a vehicle and a woman standing behind it was hit and seriously injured. The woman lost her leg as a result of the crash. She filed a lawsuit for negligence to recover damages. An appellate court in Minnesota ruled that the defendant officers were entitled to qualified immunity under state law for the exercise of discretion in deciding whether or not to initiate and continue the pursuit of a suspect attempting to flee arrest for a serious drug felony. The court found that there was no evidence that the officers acted willfully or maliciously, which would have defeated their official immunity defense.

Wrongful Death

Wrongful death torts are acknowledged in every state and usually are the result of allegations of unjustified actions by an officer. Generally, when a death occurs during police intervention, transport, or custody, a wrongful death case is likely to result. The lawsuit is filed on behalf of the deceased by the estate, surviving family members, or a guardian. This type of liability action alleges that the government entity was intentionally or grossly negligent to the needs of the deceased. In wrongful death actions against police officers, the plaintiff generally asserts that the officers' actions or the department's customs and policies (or lack thereof) were the proximate cause of the death. These lawsuits attempt to recover damages for conscious pain and suffering; loss of financial support; loss of comfort, society, and companionship; and funeral expenses. The lawsuit may also claim that the criminal justice agency conspired to cause the death of the deceased and/or covered up the death with an inadequate internal investigation. Each case will obviously be comprised of numerous variables for the plaintiff to attack.

The claim must be based on an established tort theory. Examples include deaths from lethal force incidents, fatal vehicle pursuits, in-custody suicides, restraint deaths after a use-of-force altercation, and claims arising from delay or denial of medical care for an arrestee or prisoner. In *Fruge v. City of New Orleans* (1993), the estate of a diabetic arrestee who died while in police custody brought a wrongful death claim against the city. When arrested, the prisoner appeared intoxicated and was placed in an isolation cell, where he later was observed foaming at the mouth. He was transported to the hospital and died several hours later. The attending physician stated that he had a moderately enlarged liver, which can cause sudden death. The court found the officers to be negligent in their decision to incarcerate, because they owed a duty to the prisoner to protect him from harm and preserve his safety. The court concluded that the city had failed in its responsibility (breached its duty) by not ascertaining the arrestee's medical condition and transporting him to a hospital. The arrestee's intoxication triggered the need for a higher level of care by the police.

An emerging area of liability that is occasionally addressed in state court are unexpected deaths in police custody after restraints and varying levels of force have been used to control the violent person. In *McCrumb v. Kent County et al.* (2002), the estate of a mentally impaired man filed state tort claims for gross negligence and assault and battery after he was restrained by eight officers and died. McCrumb was being admitted into a private mental health facility for treatment for bipolar disorder and began hallucinating. He assaulted two security personnel and began destroying offices and threatening nurses, physicians, and other staff of the facility. Two Kent County deputies responded to a 911 call and initially attempted to control McCrumb in the hallway of the facility by talking to him. He charged the deputies and one sprayed two bursts of pepper spray at him, which were ineffective. McCrumb fled back into the facility and more deputies and two other agencies dispatched officers. In total, the county sent two more deputies and a lieutenant, while three other officers responded from the two other agencies.

After planning a response, five of the officers and the lieutenant entered the facility as McCrumb began advancing toward an office where staff of the facility had barricaded themselves. The officers engaged McCrumb and two other officers applied three short bursts of pepper spray to McCrumb. The spray was ineffective and he charged the officers, striking two of them in the chest and head. The officers used control holds and their weight to subdue him. The officers placed McCrumb on the ground, two officers held his legs, two other officers controlled his arms, while another officer controlled his head, as he attempted to bite the officers. Only one officer had partial weight on his back and the officers were able to restrain his hands with two sets of handcuffs. McCrumb struggled and a belt was secured around his ankles. He began to calm down and a nurse left to retrieve an injection for him. Within a few seconds, the officers noticed that McCrumb had become unresponsive, radioed for emergency medical care, removed the restraints and belt, and initiated life-saving procedures.

Emergency medical personnel responded, rendered medical care, and transported him to the hospital where he died 15 minutes later.

The family filed a lawsuit and the court, seven years later, issued summary judgment for all of the officers. The court ruled that the officers had a duty to take McCrumb into custody for mental health treatment and had the right to use reasonable force to accomplish the task. The court stated that the officers also had the right to protect themselves and that the force they used was not excessive and was consistent with the degree of resistance they encountered. There was a need to control McCrumb and a need to protect the staff of the facility from McCrumb. The court further opined that officers did not act recklessly as to demonstrate a substantial lack of concern for the welfare of McCrumb. In fact, the officers had done the "exact opposite," the court noted, and held that the officers' conduct did not amount to gross negligence.

A more common wrongful death action brought against police officers involves police shootings. In *Mathieu v. Imperial Toy Corp.* (1994), the Louisiana Supreme Court overturned a $4 million award against the city for officers' shooting of a mentally impaired individual. The individual had pointed a realistic toy gun at officers and they responded by shooting him. The estate brought a wrongful death and excessive force action against the officers, claiming that the officers should have known the gun was a toy. In another case, the jury awarded $3.6 million in damages to the estate of a man who was shot and killed by a police officer during a traffic stop (*Bodan v. DeMartin*, 1994). The family argued that the deceased had placed his hands on the steering wheel when the officer stopped him, while the officer stated that the driver had reached under the front seat, causing the officer to believe that the driver was reaching for a weapon and causing him to fear for his life. A more detailed discussion on excessive force claims arising out of lethal and less-than-lethal force incidents will be provided in Chapter 10.

In *Lopez v. City of Los Angeles* (2011), the estate of a young child who was accidently shot and killed by an Emergency Response Team (ERT) sought damages for a wrongful death. The father of the child, who was using and selling cocaine, used his 19-month-old daughter as a hostage and held up in his auto body shop with firearms. He threatened to kill her, himself, and anyone else who entered the premises. Officers of the ERT responded and after attempts to negotiate the release of the baby failed, they entered the shop to rescue the baby, and accidentally shot and killed her. The father had shot at the officers first and they were returning fire. The Appellate Court of California determined that the officers acted reasonably under the circumstances.

A recurring theme of wrongful death claims emerges from police pursuits. These claims not only allege negligence of the police officers performing the pursuit, but allege that such performance by the police created the proximate cause of death of the person in the fleeing vehicle or an innocent bystander. Some allegations claim that if the police had not initiated the pursuit the person would have never eluded the police and that the pursuit was recklessly performed, which led to the death of that person or third party.

In *City of Jackson v. Perry* (2003), a bank employee summoned Jackson, Mississippi, police to report that a woman attempted to pass a forged check. Although the bank employee attempted to stall her, the woman ran outside to her car. Police arrived and observed the woman run to the only car in the parking lot and quickly drive away. A rookie and his field training officer followed the woman and a second patrol car joined in the pursuit. The woman sped through highly populated neighborhoods at speeds in excess of 80 miles per hour and on one occasion ran a red light. The patrol cars followed at 55 miles per hour. The officers in the first patrol car stated that they had stopped chasing her but continued to follow only to obtain her license plate number. Within one minute of the pursuit, the woman crashed into another person's car, killing them. While trying to flee on foot, the officers subdued the woman and arrested her.

Perry's estate filed a wrongful death lawsuit against the city and the woman. The family alleged that the officers acted in reckless disregard of public safety and violated departmental policy, which authorized a pursuit only when an officer knew a felony had been committed. At trial the judge ruled in favor of the estate, finding that the officers acted with reckless disregard for public safety and awarded $1 million in compensation to the family. The judge allocated 50 percent fault for the accident to the city and the remaining 50 percent to the woman, who ultimately settled with the estate. The judge later reduced the award against the city to $250,000, the limits of the city's insurance.

The city appealed the decision. The state appellate court affirmed the lower court's verdict, holding that the city was not immune under state law that protected police activities "unless the employee acted in reckless disregard of the safety and well-being of any person not engaged in criminal activity at the time of the injury." The court determined that the officers could have parked their patrol car behind the woman's car when they first entered the parking lot, thereby blocking her exit. The court also determined that the officers could have obtained her license plate number but instead engaged in a high-speed chase without knowing the amount of the check and not knowing whether she had committed a felony, thereby violating the department's policy. The court held that the officers performed the chase in a reckless manner by speeding through highly populated residential areas.

Suicides in lockups, jails, and prisons have spawned numerous wrongful death actions under negligence theories. In *Title v. Mahan* (1991), the estates of two deceased pretrial detainees brought a wrongful death claim under state law. The two had committed suicide in the jail, and the claim asserted that jail personnel failed to prevent the suicides. The court determined that jail personnel were liable for failing to provide adequate supervision for the detainees. In *Moore v. City of Troy* (1992), a jail detainee hanged himself with his own T-shirt shortly after being jailed. His belt, shoelaces, outer shirt, and pants were removed. Jail personnel had documented security checks and had made such a check 11 minutes prior to the suicide. The court determined that jail personnel had complied with all procedures and did not impose liability. In *De Sanchez v. Michigan Department of Mental Health* (1997), a defense of proper supervision did not defeat the "public building" exception to immunity when a suicide was facilitated by the dangerous design of a public restroom. The main liability issues of the case centered on negligent supervision and design of the building. The plaintiff argued that the bathroom was poorly designed because it contained "open" structures in which people could hang themselves. The court did not rule on the issue of whether a true defect existed.

After a suicide in a detention facility, the estate of the deceased filed a lawsuit against the county and jail officers in *Gray v. Tunica County, Mississippi* (2003). The detainee committed suicide in a holding cell by tearing a portion of his jumpsuit into several strips. The estate alleged that that the detention officers failed to perform their security checks as required by policy when the detainee was placed on a suicide watch, and that such inaction was the proximate cause of the detainee's death. The court granted summary judgment to the county, holding that the policy was not related to the suicide of the detainee, who was placed in a new cell designed for medical and suicide watch purposes. The court ruled that the policy involving intermittent checks were reasonably related to the legitimate purpose of protecting detainees from harm. The detention officer had checked on the detainee about an hour after he was placed in the new holding cell and the officer returned 30 minutes later to discover the detainee unconscious in the cell. The court reasoned that the suicide was unforeseeable and that it was doubtful that the detainee could have been helped, even if the officer had entered the cell immediately upon noticing that the detainee had altered his jumpsuit and was lying on the floor.

In *Rentz v. Spokane County* (2006), the estate of a detainee who was murdered by two other detainees in a county jail sought to recover damages from the county under Washington's wrongful death and survival statutes. The court denied the estate's claim under Washington law, holding that the estate failed to establish standing. The court, however, allowed the estate to amend the complaint under § 1988 for violations of the detainee's constitutional rights under the Fourteenth Amendment. The court determined that the jail officers and nurses were not immunized because they were involved in the placement of the detainee in the dormitory with the other detainees. As such, the estate was allowed compensation for loss of companionship with their adult son and it was held that the detainee's substantive due process rights were violated.

Failure to Protect

There is no general civil duty to prevent a crime, even in high-crime areas (*Calogrides v. City of Mobile*, 1985). This means that police are not liable for failing to protect the victim of a crime. This is in accord with the public duty doctrine. The doctrine was established by the United States Supreme Court in *South v. Maryland* (1896). An individual who was victimized by a mob requested protection from the sheriff's office. The sheriff refused, and the individual was seriously injured and filed a lawsuit against the sheriff. The Court held that the sheriff committed no misfeasance or nonfeasance to the person injured and liability failed to attach. Most states recognize this doctrine, and there is no liability for harm or injury when the police fail to protect the general public. The public duty doctrine insulates police from liability when members of the general public are harmed or injured and desire to file a lawsuit against the police for failure to protect. This helps to enhance discretionary decisionmaking on the part of the police and helps in reducing the risk of lawsuits for these types of actions.

Generally, police and correctional personnel have a duty to protect those under their control and custody. Numerous lawsuits have emerged from this "special relationship" doctrine. States define a "special relationship" in varying ways, but the concept basically means that criminal justice personnel owe a duty to the particular individual in their custody, rather than to the general public. Factors that create a special relationship include actual knowledge of a dangerous condition or situation (foreseeability); and any statute, rule, or policy that requires officers to perform and that can be reasonably said to be for the protection of the members of society. Common examples include failing to respond to a call, failing to arrest in domestic violence situations, failing to protect a witness or informant, failure to obtain medical assistance for an arrestee or prisoner, failure to arrest a drunk driver, delayed response to a call, failing to summon assistance, and failing to protect prisoners from themselves and other prisoners.

Liability did not attach against the city in *Hamseed v. Brown* (1995) for the stabbing of a woman by her boyfriend. The boyfriend had escaped from an officer who was attempting to arrest him for violating a no-contact domestic violence order. The officer allowed him to go upstairs to get some clothes, and he fled out a window. The boyfriend later found his girlfriend and stabbed her several times. The boyfriend was not under the officer's control at the time of the stabbing. In *State v. Powell* (1991), merely receiving a subpoena to testify in court did not create an affirmative duty to provide protection. A woman was subpoenaed to testify against her ex-husband in a child abuse case. He poured gasoline on her and set her on fire. She sued the state, claiming that it had a duty to protect her from him and failed in that duty. The court concluded that there was no special relationship. Conversely, in *Doe v. Calumet* (1994), the court ruled that a police officer's failure to rescue a minor girl from being raped resulted in failure to protect liability. The mother of the child ran into the street yelling for help while her daughter was being raped. The officer's refusal to intervene constituted a willful and wanton disregard for the safety of the child.

In *Mills v. City of Overland Park, Kansas* (1992), officers did not have a duty to take an intoxicated person without a jacket into protective custody in winter weather. He came into contact with the police after he was escorted out of a bar where there had been a disturbance. He walked away from the bar and was found frozen to death the next morning in a field near the bar. A state statute that allowed (but did not require) emergency detention of intoxicated persons was also not a basis for liability. In *Kerr v. Alaska* (1996), the state of Alaska was found liable for negligent failure to prevent two prisoners from planning and carrying out, with the help of others, the mail bombing of a house where an informant who helped to convict them was living. The court awarded $11.85 million to the individual who lost his father in the explosion, which also severely injured his mother.

Occasionally a plaintiff will file a claim that the officer's failure to protect an arrestee in his or her custody was the direct cause of the harm sustained and that such failure amounted to gross negligence. This is a high standard to prove and many courts give deference to police officers when warranted. In *Kruger v. White Lake Twp.* (2002), police took a woman into custody pursuant to her mother's request, fearing that she posed a danger to herself and others due to her level of intoxication. Responding to the call, the police learned that the woman had an outstanding warrant issued for her arrest by a neighboring township. The police arrested her and transported her to the White Lake Police Department to wait for her transfer to the adjacent township. Lacking a vacant holding cell, the woman was left unattended in the booking room, where she was able to free herself from the handcuffs and escaped. As she fled from the station, she ran into traffic and was struck and killed by an unidentified vehicle. The decedent's family filed a lawsuit alleging gross negligence on the part of White Lake Township's officers.

The lower court dismissed the claim and the estate appealed. The appellate court affirmed the lower court's decision, noting that the officers' actions were not grossly negligent and that the more direct cause of the woman's death was her escaping from the police station, running into traffic, and being struck by the car.

In *Pappas v. Union Township* (2010), an officer who served as a crash investigator was dispatched to the scene of an accident that took place between a female motorist and a male motorcycle rider. The officer, who observed the motorcycle rider lying face down after having been thrown and landing head first on the street, believed that he was dead. The officer later claimed that the female motorist, though "a little shaken up," had told him that she was not injured. He handed back her driver's license, registration, and insurance card, and suggested that she could leave her disabled car at the parking lot of a nearby gas station, which she did. The officer returned to his vehicle to complete paperwork, and did not inquire as to how the motorist was getting home or offer to assist her in doing so. The elderly female motorist declined an offer from the gas station attendant to drive her home if she would wait there until closing time, and she stated that she could walk home. As she began walking across the street, she was struck by a hit-and-run driver, suffering serious injuries, and was hospitalized for various surgeries and treatments until she died. A lawsuit against the township and officer contended that they were responsible for her injuries at the hands of the hit-and-run driver by "abandoning" and failing to protect her at the scene of the first accident.

The trial court and intermediate appeals court entered summary judgment for the defendants, finding them immune from liability for the officer's performance of discretionary acts at the scene of the first accident. The court rejected an argument that the officer negligently performed ministerial duties in connection with the accident, for which state law does not provide immunity, since the female motorist had not asked him to provide aid. This was also not a case in which the motorist was plainly incapacitated, so that even if the officer was not exercising discretion, there was no evidence that he negligently performed a ministerial task.

False Arrest and Imprisonment

False arrest is the imposition of unlawful restraint upon another's freedom of movement and requires willful detention. It is an intentional tort and the intent lies in the act of arrest, not in the knowledge of falsity. An officer who fails to ascertain with due diligence that the plaintiff is in fact the person named in an arrest warrant is liable, regardless of the fact that the warrant sanctions the arrest of some person (Silver, 2010). The elements of an action for false imprisonment are the detention of a person and the detention is unlawful. The detention may be accomplished by actual or apparent barriers, physical force, a threat of physical force, or the assertion of legal authority. Plaintiffs prevailing in false imprisonment cases have shown an intent to confine, acts resulting in confinement, and knowledge of the confinement or harm (*Brown v. Bryan County, Oklahoma*, 1995). False arrest can occur when an officer arrests a person other than the one named in a warrant and, if the warrant is illegal, providing false information to a magistrate. Liability is created when the officer obtains a warrant with malice, knowing there is no probable cause (*Malley v. Briggs*, 1986).

Numerous lawsuits have been filed under state tort law for false arrest and false imprisonment. In *Byrd v. New York Transit Authority* (1991), an award of $250,000 in compensatory and
$125,000 in punitive damages was granted to the plaintiff. He had sustained injuries as a result
of false arrest, malicious prosecution, and assault by transit officers during arrest. In *Marshall v.
District Court* (1992), police officers assisted medical personnel in restraining the plaintiff while
an emergency mental health evaluation was performed. The officers had advised her that she
would be forcibly detained if she did not cooperate. She sued, claiming that the officers had
falsely imprisoned her. The officers were immune from liability, because under state law they
were responding to a call for assistance and acted in the belief that she was mentally ill and in
need of confinement. In *Diogaurdi v. City of New Rochelle* (1992), the existence of a domestic
protective order as well as the wife's complaint that her husband was harassing her gave the
police a defense in a false arrest claim filed by her husband after he was arrested for violating
the order. Liability did not attach for the arrest.

Courts routinely examine claims of unlawful detention. The court's decision in *Lopez v. City
of Chicago* (2006) provides an instructive example of police detaining a prisoner without afford-
ing him a hearing within a reasonable period of time. An arrestee who was held shackled in an
interrogation room for four days brought a claim in accordance with the Fourth and Fourteenth
Amendments for unlawful detention and emotional distress against the City of Chicago. The
arrestee presented evidence that detectives kept him shackled for four days in a small window-
less room and deprived him of food, drink, water, sleep, and the use of a bathroom until he repeatedly screamed for assistance. The arrestee claimed that there was no sink in the room, he was fed
only one bologna sandwich, was made to undergo two lineups, and was forced to make a false
confession, which did not match the details of the crime. The detectives denied the allegations. The
district court ruled in favor of the detectives, but the appellate court held that the officers violated
the arrestee's Fourteenth Amendment right to a prompt judicial probable cause hearing, amounting to an unlawful detention. The arrestee was arrested for a murder that he did not commit.

Under state and federal law, the primary action for false arrest and imprisonment is the
illegal detention of an individual without lawful process or by an unlawful execution of such
process. The United States Supreme Court held in *Wallace v. Kato* (2007) that an unlawful detention (detention without legal process) of an individual equates with the tort of false
imprisonment and is remediable. The Court also clarified that the essential elements of
false imprisonment include: the detention or restraint of one against his or her will, and the
unlawfulness of the detention or restraint.

Officers failing to thoroughly investigate a correct residence to respond to a call or to effect
an arrest may be held liable for false arrest and imprisonment. In *Marlowe v. Pinal County*
(2008) an officer's arrest was not immunized when the court held that he responded to an
incorrect residence and arrested and lodged the wrong person. A deputy was dispatched
to a residence to investigate an emergency call about a family fight in progress. The deputy
responded to the Marlowe residence instead of responding to the Schwartz residence, which
was 11 houses away. Dispatch gave the deputy a description of the suspect and the deputy
learned that he would be looking for a 73-year-old man who was severely intoxicated and
belligerent. The wife, who called 911, had locked herself in the bathroom.

At the house, the deputy noted that it was dark and quiet, and that the Marlowes were in bed sleeping. The deputy knocked on the front door and did not receive a response. He then opened the back gate, moved to the back porch and knocked on the sliding glass door. Hearing the knocking, Mr. Marlowe got out of bed and went to the back door and told the deputy to get off of his property. The deputy instructed him to step outside immediately to avoid being in more trouble than he was presently. Mr. Marlowe put on pair of pants, looked out the window and observed that the person was indeed a deputy. Mr. Marlowe exited the house, complied with the deputy's commands, and handcuffs were secured on him without incident. Mr. Marlowe was placed in the patrol car and other deputies responded. They informed the deputy, as did dispatch, that he was at the wrong address but the deputy maintained that he was at the correct address and could smell alcohol on Mr. Marlowe. The deputy's supervisor arrived and determined that the deputy had arrested and detained the wrong person and released Mr. Marlowe. The Marlowes filed a lawsuit for false arrest and detainment and the court ruled in their favor. The court held that the deputy should have performed a more thorough investigation before subjecting Mr. Marlowe to a forceful arrest and detention.

With a high degree of certainty, the courts will not protect officers or prosecutors when they deliberately file false charges. In *McGhee v. Pottawattamie County* (2008) investigators were involved in an investigation of several suspects on charges of distributing illegal substances. Unable to secure actual evidence, prosecutors and police investigators knowingly made false charges and fabricated false evidence, culminating in false arrests. Under Iowa Code § 669.2, the prosecutor and investigators were not protected by state sovereign immunity because these acts were outside the scope of employment and occurred during the investigative phase. Qualified immunity was absent because procurement of tainted evidence for use at trial violated clearly established law.

In *Virginia v. Moore* (2008), the United States Supreme Court examined the status of state law when a law enforcement officer makes an arrest based on probable cause when such state law prohibits the arrest, and examined whether evidence seized should be suppressed. The question before the court was: Does such action by a police officer violate the Fourth Amendment? Believing a motorist (Moore) was driving with a suspended license, two police officers performed a vehicle stop. Upon determining that Moore's license was indeed suspended, the officers arrested him for the misdemeanor offense. Moore was arrested and searched, and the officers found 16 grams of cocaine. Moore was later convicted of possession with intent to distribute. He appealed the conviction, arguing that, under Virginia law, he should have received a summons as opposed to being arrested and searched, and such the arrest was unlawful and the evidence discovered should be suppressed. The Virginia State Court agreed, concluding that the search violated the Fourth Amendment. The United States Supreme Court agreed to hear the case.

In a unanimous decision the Court overturned the Virginia Supreme Court's ruling that the officers had probable cause to arrest Moore and that the search incident to arrest was also lawful. The Court held that an arrest for even a minor crime committed in an officer's presence is always reasonable under the Fourth Amendment and additional state law protections prohibiting custodial arrests under certain circumstances was irrelevant. The Court reiterated that they "ruled over 50 years ago that officers having probable cause to believe that crime has been committed in their presence may make an arrest and perform a search in order to safeguard evidence and for officer safety." Virginia's decision to exclude the offense within the criminal code did not render the officers' actions unreasonable under the Fourth Amendment. The Court also stated "it is not the province of the Fourth Amendment to enforce the state law." The Court's decision in *Knowles v. Iowa* (1998) was distinguished because an actual arrest, not merely issuance of a citation, had occurred.

In *Thomas v. City of Galveston* (2011), Thomas and his wife decided to remain in their home during a hurricane, because in a former hurricane his house had been vandalized. Several days after the hurricane had ended, Thomas purchased a generator and placed it on a flatbed truck and parked it on the street in the front of his home so that it could provide power to his house and to a few neighbors' houses. One night Thomas heard his dog barking and looked out the front window, observed several flashlights moving around the generator, and yelled out for the persons to show themselves several times. The individuals did not respond and Thomas retrieved his rifle, opened the front door, yelled at the persons to identify themselves, while pointing the barrel down at the ground. Suddenly, the individuals shined their flashlights in Thomas' eyes, they identified themselves as Galveston police officers, and directed Thomas to put the weapon down. He complied, and placed his hands above his head.

The three officers rushed the porch and threw Thomas down the five stairs to the sidewalk. Thomas screamed in pain and was immediately placed in handcuffs, which were placed tightly around his wrist. Thomas did not resist arrest. While on the ground the officers kicked Thomas in the back, shoulders, and in the head several times, and he lost consciousness. An officer picked Thomas up by the chains of the handcuffs which caused severe damage to the joint. The officers transported Thomas to jail, where he regained consciousness, and was in severe pain. Due to the hurricane there were no hot water or toilet facilities or phones operational, and he was not offered any medical attention. After two days, a nurse examined Thomas but was unable to treat him. Bail was set at $40,000 and Thomas was released. A bond hearing was held two weeks later and the bond was increased to $100,000. Two days later the prosecutor dropped the charges and the judge agreed.

Thomas filed a lawsuit claiming false arrest, excessive force, and denial of adequate medical treatment. The court rejected the city's motion to dismiss the case. The court agreed with Thomas that he had a legitimate right to protect his property and that the officer's lacked probable cause to arrest him. The court concluded that Thomas's actions were provoked by the officers' conduct and such, an officer would have known that Thomas was only attempting to rightfully protect his property, and found that on this basis the officers lacked probable cause to arrest him. The court noted that since the officers made a false arrest, the force used against Thomas, who did not offer any resistance, was excessive. The claim of denial of medical care was also supported as the court noted the officers intentionally ignored Thomas's request for medical care and knew that he had lost consciousness. The behavior of the officers amounted to a wanton disregard to the serious medical needs of Thomas and the beating delivered by the officers could also not escape the officers' attention.

Malicious Prosecution

Malicious prosecution claims are made by a plaintiff who alleges that he or she was illegally prosecuted in a criminal or civil proceeding that was instituted for an improper purpose and without probable cause. The plaintiff must show: (1) the institution or continuation of original judicial proceedings, either criminal, civil, or administrative; (2) by or at the request of the defendant, (3) the termination of such proceedings in the plaintiff's favor; and (4) the suffering of injury or damage as a result of the prosecution (Plitt, 1997). Proximate cause is also critical in malicious prosecution cases if the initiator of a criminal proceeding loses control of it due to the actions of a prosecutor or judge—actions that may be deemed to supersede the original complaint.

Malice is a core element of malicious prosecution and involves an intentional wrongful act done without legal justification. Malice may consist of any improper and wrongful motive for bringing a criminal proceeding and does not require hatred of, or ill will toward, the plaintiff (*Davis v. Muse*, 1992). Further, a lack of probable cause for the institution of the original proceeding must be shown. The court in *Stitle v. City of New York* (1991) ruled that a claim of malicious prosecution can arise only after an arraignment, indictment, or some other evaluation by a neutral body that the charges were warranted. The claim cannot arise from an arrest only.

In *Carver v. Hartville Police Department* (1992), police officers and the police department were held not liable for malicious prosecution of a woman for aiding and abetting her son in a drug distribution organization. There was no evidence of malice and there was probable cause for the arrest. The officers had made observations as well as controlled buys. *Strong v. Nicholson* (1991) allowed circumstantial evidence to show that a prosecution was brought with reckless disregard and to obtain property allegedly in dispute, especially when the defendants had been legally advised to bring a civil lawsuit. Thus, malice was proven.

Malicious prosecution actions are generally not subject to qualified immunity found in many states, particularly where "bad faith" or acting outside the scope of employment is involved (*Kapper v. Connick*, 1996). In *McDaniel v. City of Seattle* (1992), prosecutorial immunity was not applicable to immunize a city against malicious prosecution by police officers, especially where false representations may have been made to the prosecutor.

Frequently a plaintiff may combine claims of false arrest and malicious prosecution in one lawsuit. In *Wilder v. Village of Amityville* (2003), the plaintiff Wilder and others protested the removal of a tree in the village. Citing pro-tree environmental and religious concerns, she allegedly attempted to block municipal workers from cutting the tree down by standing in the way. A police sergeant ordered her to move on three occasions and she refused to move. The sergeant arrested her for obstructing a governmental function in the second degree. Wilder filed a lawsuit and claimed that the sergeant used excessive force when he tightly applied handcuffs on her wrists, resulting in inflammation and soreness to her wrists. She claimed the sergeant denied her medical attention. She also filed claims of false arrest, malicious prosecution, and interference with her free speech rights.

The court granted judgment to the village and the sergeant, noting that the plaintiff's claim of excessive force failed because her allegation of sore, yet uninjured, wrists was not enough to be considered unlawful conduct in the lawful arrest situation. Further, the court noted that the sergeant made the arrest based on probable cause and that her false arrest and malicious prosecution claims failed as well. The court ruled that the law prohibited a person from intentionally preventing public servants from performing an official function. Finally, the court held that the plaintiff failed to prove that the village or the sergeant prevented her from expressing her pro-environmental or religious views through police brutality or abuse of the legal process.

In *Allen v. City of New York* (2007), a detainee filed suit against a city and officers, claiming a violation of his constitutional rights for false arrest and malicious prosecution arising from a beating administered by officers during escort to a cell. The court ruled that the arrest, confinement, and prosecution were lawful under New York law. The court, however, ruled that other officers should have intervened to keep an officer from banging the head of the detainee against a wall and denied a motion for qualified immunity. Further, the court denied a criminal complaint for assault filed by the officer, who claimed that the detainee assaulted him, holding the officer committed malicious prosecution when he filed the false charge against the detainee.

Assault and Battery

Many civil actions arise from claims of assault and battery, because the use of force is inherent in police and correctional work. Such claims may arise from an arrest, because physical force is always necessary to take custody of the arrestee. In correctional facilities, some physical force is used to move prisoners, search prisoners, or prevent prisoners from harming themselves or others.

Assault is an intentional attempt to physically injure another, coupled with the present ability to complete the intention. There must be an intent to cause harmful contact, or the fear thereof, with the person of another. Acting recklessly or wantonly is generally not sufficient for an assault. Generally, words alone are insufficient to constitute an assault.

Battery is a voluntary act that results in harmful or offensive contact with another. It is not necessary that the offensive or unpermitted touching actually cause physical harm; it is sufficient if the contact is offensive. Under this definition, every time an officer uses force to control an arrestee or prisoner, there is the potential for this claim to be made when the force used is unjustified. The distinction between assault and battery is that assault is conduct that results in an individual fearing an imminent battery, while battery pertains to unlawful, offensive, unwarranted touching, even if slight (del Carmen, 1991). The two terms are normally applied together, because as in many jurisdictions assault is an attempted battery (*Johnson v. Suffolk County*, 1997).

In *Jackson v. North Carolina Dept. of Crime Control* (1991), liability attached when an officer used a blackjack (a short, leather-covered piece of lead) on an intoxicated, handcuffed arrestee. The arrestee was restrained and cooperative, and using force in this manner was regarded as negligent. Using a weapon in an unreasonable manner may give rise to liability. In *Moody v. Ferguson* (1989), a state trooper was found to be liable for assault under South Carolina law. The plaintiff was stopped by a state trooper, and when asked for his driver's license, he placed the car in reverse and fled from the trooper. The trooper unholstered his weapon and ran after the driver. The driver moved the car toward the trooper, and the trooper fired his weapon, hitting the rim of the tire. The court concluded that the trooper used his weapon in a negligent, unreasonable manner, and was liable for assault. In *Baker v. Chaplin* (1994), the court concluded that hitting a political demonstrator with an impact weapon while he was complying with police instructions and not resisting was not only excessive, but was deadly force. The impact weapon was thrust into the chest of the demonstrator, and the court determined that this constituted deadly force and violated state law and § 1983.

The estate of a detainee confined in a county jail filed a lawsuit under the state tort claims act and § 1983, claiming that the detainee was beaten to death by detention officers, in *Pizzuto v. County of Nassau* (2003). The family sued the officers, the supervisors, and the county. The detainee had been sentenced to 90 days for driving under the influence of methadone, a misdemeanor. While in a holding cell, the detainee boisterously complained that he needed treatment for his narcotic addiction and a heated argument ensued between the officers and the detainee. The supervisor directed the officers to enter the cell to control the detainee. The officers entered the cell and punched and kicked the detainee in his face, legs, and torso for several minutes. An extensive cover-up followed and two days later the detainee collapsed in his cell. He was transported to the hospital where he died from his injuries several days later.

The officers pleaded guilty to assault and conspiracy and were convicted. The court ruled in favor of the estate's claims and liability attached against the officers and the other officers who stood by and watched and failed to intervene. The court held that the supervisor was also liable for his personal involvement and for the acts of the officers.

In *Slusher v. Carson* (2007), a civil action was brought against an arresting deputy for an alleged assault. In order to assist in enforcing a divorce judgment two deputies were dispatched to a barn were farm equipment was to be retrieved by the husband. The former wife challenged the reason why her former husband and deputies were on her property. One of the deputies showed the court order to the former wife (Ms. Slusher) and she began to review it while the husband entered the barn. Ms. Slusher began to protest the entrance into the barn and the deputy asked for the order back and she withdrew her hand away from the deputy. The deputy asked for it again and she refused to comply. The deputy reached for her arm and according to Ms. Slusher, the deputy pressed his thumb into her hand and palm, and squeezed her wrist, twisting her fingers backwards. She screamed, saying "that was her bad hand." Ms. Slusher filed suit in accordance with Michigan law, claiming the deputy assaulted her.

The deputy argued that he was immune from lawsuit under Michigan's Governmental Tort Liability Act and that his behavior failed to amount to gross negligence. The act defined gross negligence as conduct so reckless as to demonstrate a substantial lack of concern for whether an injury results. The court held that the deputy's actions were reasonable under the circumstances. By Ms. Slusher's own admission she failed to comply with the deputy's instructions. The court held that it was objectively reasonable for the deputy to grab Ms. Slusher's hand after she failed to comply with the instructions and that the deputy would not know Ms. Slusher had a bad hand and that, therefore, his actions would cause her harm. The court awarded summary judgment on behalf of the deputy.

In *Becker v. Porter County* (2009), deputies were executing an active warrant for Becker's arrest for violating a domestic violence order. The warrant had been rescinded but not entered into the computer prior to the deputies serving it. Becker demanded that there was a mistake and entered his house to retain paperwork to show the deputies. The deputies followed him into the house without permission. A dispute of the facts varied between Becker's account and the deputies. Becker claimed that officers assaulted him—one deputy hit him in the face and he fell into a wall, another officer tackled him, and a third officer used a Taser on him eight times for no reason.

The deputies claimed that Becker ran into the kitchen against their instructions, they wrestled with him, Becker continued to fight them, and a deputy activated the Taser one time on his thigh. The deputies also claimed that Becker fell to the floor, continued to resist, kicked the Taser from the hand of the deputy, and after the struggle, they were able to control and restrain him. Becker was transported to the hospital, treated, and then transported to the jail. Later Becker was found not guilty for violating the domestic violence order but found guilty of battery of a law enforcement officer and resisting arrest. Becker filed claims of assault against the deputies from injuries sustained during the service of the warrant, which was found to be rescinded at the time of arrest.

Becker argued that the deputies violated his rights by unreasonably using the Taser and other force measures. As a result of his injuries, he argued, the deputies did not know how and when to properly apply the Taser and the county failed to adequately train them in the proper use of the Taser. The court granted the defendant's motion to dismiss the claims of assault, finding that it was reasonable to apply the Taser when Becker actively resisted in the kitchen where numerous potential weapons were present. Claims of failure to train were also dismissed.

In the course of performing their duties, correctional officers have also been sued for claims of assault. In *Reid v. Wakefield* (2007), a prisoner claimed that while confined in a state correctional facility and while he was being escorted to the shower, several officers assaulted him. The prisoner claimed that as he approached the shower his hand slipped from the handcuffs and the officers threw him against a gate and slammed him to the floor. He claimed that another officer choked him from behind and others kicked and punched him. The prisoner claimed that he sustained injuries and was left untreated in an adjustment cell. The prisoner filed an assault claim and the officers filed a motion to dismiss. He also filed a claim against the officers' supervisors for failing to prevent the assault. The court granted the motion to dismiss against the supervisor, noting that he was not at the shower at the time of the alleged incident and personal involvement was required for liability to attach. The court also dismissed the assault claim filed against the officers as there was no credible evidence to support the assault charge against the officers. A more complete discussion of liability issues surrounding claims of excessive force will be presented in Chapter 7.

Federal Tort Claims Act

As discussed above, tort actions asserting misconduct on the part of police officers or correctional personnel are brought under state tort law. An individual bringing an action against a federal agent, however, cannot file an action under state tort law theories, but must file a claim in accordance with the Federal Tort Claims Act (28 U.S.C. § 1346 [b] and §§ 2671–2680). The FTCA waives the immunity of the federal government but not its employees. Federal employees are responsible for ensuring that the rights of individuals are protected just as their state and local counterparts are; however, they may not be sued under state tort law or § 1983. A plaintiff suing a federal officer must base his or her action on a complaint arising out of the scope of the federal officer's employment (*Simmons v. United States*, 1986) and must file his or her complaint in accordance with the FTCA. The FTCA authorizes the partial waiver of sovereign immunity from the federal government. A lawsuit filed under the FTCA cannot be based on a constitutional violation, but must be based on tort claims (del Carmen, 1991).

Plaintiffs filing claims against federal employees do so under provisions set forth in the United States Supreme Court's decision in *Bivens v. Six Unknown Federal Narcotics Agents* (1971). Bivens was restrained with handcuffs, searched, and arrested on drug charges while federal agents searched his apartment for evidence of drug violations. The search was conducted without a warrant or probable cause, thereby violating his Fourth Amendment rights. Bivens sued the agents, claiming mental suffering and damages from the invasion of his privacy. The Supreme Court agreed with Bivens and concluded that the agents were acting within the scope of their employment, giving rise to a cause of action.

A *Bivens* action may only be brought against federal employees—not the federal government (*Federal Deposit Insurance Corp. v. Meyer*, 1994). Plaintiffs filing an FTCA claim must do so within two years after the violation (28 U.S.C. § 2675 [a]). The Supreme Court has specifically upheld the bringing of *Bivens* actions for violations of the Fifth Amendment's due process clause (*Davis v. Passman*, 1979), and for federal prisoners claiming Eighth Amendment violations (*Carlson v. Green*, 1980; *Farmer v. Brennan*, 1994).

In *Papa v. United States* (2002), the widow and children of an alien who been killed by another detainee while being held by the Immigration and Naturalization Services (INS) brought *Bivens* and Federal Tort Claims Act claims against the INS. The district court granted the defendant's motion to dismiss and the plaintiffs appealed. The appeals court reversed the lower court's decision, holding that the officers knowingly placed the alien in danger in disregard of, or with deliberate indifference to, his due process rights, which supported a valid *Bivens* claim. The appeals court further noted that a limited right under the due process clause extends to detained aliens.

The estate of a federal prisoner who was killed by his cellmate brought a claim under the Federal Tort Claims Act (FTCA) and also brought a *Bivens* action against the correctional officials, in *Alfrey v. United States* (2002). The district court dismissed the *Bivens* claim and granted summary judgment for the defendants based on the discretionary function exception to the FTCA. The estate appealed and the appeals court held that plaintiff failed to state a *Bivens* claim and that the discretionary function exception barred an FTCA claim based on the officers' response to the report of the cellmate's threat. The appeals court, however, ruled that the federal officers had a nondiscretionary duty to perform a prisoner monitoring assessment of the prisoner, who was to be held at a federal facility pending trial on a federal charge, before assigning the prisoner to share a cell with a federal prisoner, precluding summary judgment on the FTCA claim.

Questions have surfaced regarding whether a private corporation could be successfully sued under *Bivens*. Like many correctional entities, federal correctional entities have turned to private corporations to provide operational and medical responsibilities for confined detainees. This question was addressed in *Sarro v. Cornell Corrections, Inc.* (2003). A federal pretrial detainee brought a *Bivens* action against the private operator of a prison facility, officers employed by the operator, and others. A federal magistrate recommended that summary judgment be entered for the defendants and the prisoner objected. The district court held that the prisoner could maintain a *Bivens* claim against the officers employed by the private operator, but the private corporation that operated the facility could not be sued under *Bivens*. The court held that officers and operators were not subject to *Bivens* actions because they did act under color of law, because only federal prisoners were housed in the facility.

In *Watson v. United States* (2007), a guardian brought a legal action under the Federal Tort Claims Act (FTCA) alleging that the government responded negligently to the prisoner's medical condition, which resulted in a brain hemorrhage that left him permanently disabled. The district court ruled in favor of the defendant and the appellate court affirmed. The court noted that there was sufficient evidence that the government lacked notice of the need to closely observe the prisoner for post-surgical complications upon his return to the correctional facility after surgery. Evidence indicated that the prisoner did not require observation upon his return to the facility. The court upheld the lower court's finding that the government did not breach any applicable standard of care by failing to summon an air ambulance after the prisoner was found unconscious in his cell, where expert physicians testified that the use of an air ambulance was dependent upon distance, necessity, and the patient's best interest, but did not suggest that such factors applied to the prisoner's case.

The United States Supreme Court granted certiorari to examine whether a private person may use the Federal Tort Claims Act (FTCA) to redress allegations of malicious prosecution, extortion (under RICO), and retaliation against federal agents attempting to obtain property for the federal government. In *Wilkie v. Robbins* (2007), Robbins owned a ranch in Wyoming that intermingled with federal lands. A previous owner allowed the Bureau of Land Management (BLM) right of way access across the property but when Robbins purchased the property he refused to re-grant such access. Robbins brought legal action, alleging that the BLM threatened and harassed him with meritless criminal charges in violation of his constitutional rights. He brought a lawsuit under the Federal Torts Claims Act seeking damages and declaratory and injunctive relief against the federal agents for extortion, malicious prosecution, and retaliation. The District Court dismissed the claims, but the Tenth Circuit Court of Appeals reversed. The government argued before the Supreme Court that BLM officials should be granted qualified immunity and therefore could not be sued for extortion. The government also argued that an FTCA suit could not be brought because review of the official's actions was available under the Administrative Procedures Act.

The Court, in a 7-to-2 decision, agreed with the federal government, holding that neither the FTCA or RICO provided Robbins a cause of action. The Court ruled that Congress did not design the FTCA to align with the types of claims made by Robbins and determined that his argument did not fit into the framework of the FTCA. The Court reasoned that "the FTCA is not a remedy available for a claim against a law enforcement official to address malicious prosecution." The Court was not prepared to allow the FTCA to become a remedy within a landowner's toolkit. According to the Court, Robbins had other administrative and judicial remedies available as provided in the Administrative Procedures Act to vindicate his complaints and he failed to fully access them. The Court also reasoned that the FTCA did not provide an intuitively meritorious measure for recognizing a new constitutional cause of action.

In *Padilla v. Yoo* (2009), a detainee, a U.S. citizen designated as an "enemy combatant" and detained in a military brig in South Carolina, brought numerous claims under *Bivens* against a governmental official. Padillia alleged denial of access to counsel, denial of access to court, denial of freedom of religion, unconstitutional conditions of confinement, cruel and unusual confinement, and other violations of his constitutional rights. Defendants moved to dismiss the lawsuit. The court noted that the detainee, who had been detained for two years incommunicado with no access to counsel and very tight restrictions and monitoring, stated a claim and was hindered from bringing his claims before the court. The prisoner claimed that he suffered prolonged periods of shackling in painful positions and prolonged periods of illumination and intentional interference with sleep by means of loud noises at all hours, and that he was subjected to extreme psychological stress and impermissibly denied medical care without support of legitimate penological interests. The court held that national security issues were not a factor to deny a U.S. citizen the rights afforded through the Constitution and denied qualified immunity to the senior governmental official.

Defenses to Negligent Tort Actions

There are a number of defenses to tort actions. For purposes of this chapter, only three types will be discussed: contributory negligence, comparative negligence, and assumption of the risk. Defenses and immunity strategies will be presented in more detail in Chapter 11.

Contributory Negligence

Contributory negligence doctrine has a lengthy history. The first case to apply this legal concept was the English case of *Butterfield v. Forrester* (1809). It was later used in the United States in *Smith v. Smith* (1824). The concept has been used in both state and federal courts.

Contributory negligence is conduct on the part of the plaintiff that contributed, as a legal cause, to the injury sustained by the plaintiff (Prosser & Keeton, 1984). The argument is that the plaintiff was partially at fault for his or her injuries (Silver, 2005). It may operate as a complete or partial defense for the defendant, thereby relieving the defendant of liability. If the defendant can show that the plaintiff's action caused his or her own injury, the defendant will not be liable.

The defendant must show that the unreasonable actions of the plaintiff, by a preponderance of evidence, contributed to his or her own injuries. This may be accomplished through discovery, outside evidence, or testimony from an expert witness (Franklin, 1993). If the defendant is successful in showing that the plaintiff contributed to his or her own injuries, the plaintiff will be unable to recover any damages.

In *Fruge v. City of New Orleans* (1993), a diabetic arrestee, wearing a medical notification bracelet, foamed at the mouth while confined for public intoxication. The court concluded that the officers were negligent in failing to provide timely medical care to the prisoner. The court also found that the prisoner contributed to his own injuries, because he had consumed a considerable amount of alcohol, which exacerbated his condition.

Most courts have not applied contributory negligence and assumption of the risk concepts to suicides in custody (*Saunders v. County of Steuben*, 1998). It appears that the duty of providing care outweighs contributory negligence on the part of the detainee. The court in *Miga v. City of Holyoke* (1986) found liability when the decedent was known to the police agency, prior to being stopped, for drunk driving from previous stops. Despite a desire to place her in protective custody and a regulation forbidding the placement of unconscious detainees in jail cells, the defendants made no effort to obtain background information on her or to call a detoxification center. The exception to this may be cases in which a suicide in custody was unforeseeable. In *Murdock v. City of Keene* (1993), the court concluded that liability will not attach unless a jailer has actual knowledge of facts indicating that the prisoner is likely to commit suicide. The prisoner's intentional act will preclude a finding that the jailer's breach of duty was the proximate cause of the prisoner's harm. This holding was also affirmed in *Thomas v. City of Parma* (1993).

Comparative Negligence

Most states have instituted the doctrine of comparative negligence (Silver, 2008). A jury must determine the portion of the injuries sustained by a plaintiff that they think is attributable to his or her negligence and the portion that is attributable to his or her adversary's negligent conduct. There are four categories in which a state's comparative negligence law may be classified:

1. pure comparative negligence, in which the plaintiff's recovery is never barred, unless his or her negligence caused 100 percent of the injuries;
2. fifty percent modified rule, which bars recovery when the plaintiff's negligence is greater than the defendant's negligence;
3. forty-nine percent modified rule, which bars recovery unless the plaintiff's negligence is less than the defendant's negligence; and
4. slight-gross rule, which bars recovery unless the plaintiff's negligence was slight in comparison to the defendant's negligence (Minzer et al., 2002).

Comparative negligence compares the plaintiff's and the defendant's levels of negligence. It acknowledges that both parties may have contributed to the injury. Even though the plaintiff bears a percentage of the responsibility for causing his or her own injuries, he or she can still recover damages. It does not eliminate liability for the defendant, but rather mitigates the amount of the award. For example, an officer may be 25 percent at fault in causing harm to the plaintiff, while the plaintiff is 75 percent at fault. If the jury were to award $1,000, the plaintiff would recover $250. The comparative negligence doctrine allows the court to determine the degree of fault of both parties in a particular incident.

In *Del Tufo v. Township of Old Bridge* (1996), the estate of an arrestee who died from a cocaine overdose while in police custody brought a wrongful death action for negligence. The arrestee had not informed officers that he ingested cocaine prior to his arrest, when he had the ability to do so. Medical care was provided for him when he began to show signs of seizures. The individual died an hour later in the hospital from cardiac failure due to the cocaine. The New Jersey Supreme Court found that comparative negligence was a defense to an action for negligent failure to summon medical care for an arrestee. The court rejected the idea that drug abusers fall into the same category as the elderly and mentally impaired; they have a responsibility to advise the police that they have consumed drugs. Self-inflicted harm equals self-care responsibility. Although seemingly absurd, in *McRoy v. New Orleans Police Department* (1990), the court held that, even though the arresting officer used excessive force while handcuffing an arrestee, fracturing his wrist, the arrestee resisted the arrest. A reduction of 50 percent for comparative negligence resulted.

In *Ayers v. O'Brien* (2009), a sheriff making a U-turn to pursue a speeding car was struck by another motorist's vehicle. In a lawsuit by the sheriff against the motorist for his resulting injuries, the court ruled that the sheriff, as a plaintiff, could not use a statute providing a legal standard of "reckless disregard" for the liability of an emergency vehicle operator as a "shield" against a comparative negligence defense by the motorist. The reckless disregard standard only applies when the driver of an emergency vehicle is sued or countersued.

Assumption of the Risk

While in many jurisdictions the doctrines of contributory and comparative negligence prevail, assumption of the risk is still used by some courts in determining degree of responsibility. Assumption of the risk applies when a plaintiff knew or should have known of the existence of certain risks. Thus, the plaintiff knowingly engaged in certain activities and was harmed. If the defendant can prove the elements of assumption of the risk, the plaintiff is precluded from recovering damages.

There are three elements the defendant must prove in asserting the defense of assumption of the risk. First, the defendant must show that the plaintiff knew or should have known of the risk involved, or had actual knowledge. Evidence such as the plaintiff's behavior prior to the injury may support this element. Second, the defendant must show that the plaintiff had the ability to recognize the risk associated with the activities (behavior and knowledge). Finally, the defendant must show that the plaintiff had the opportunity to disengage from the harmful activity, but failed. There would be no risk had there been an opportunity for the plaintiff to remove himself from it. The general principle is that the plaintiff knowingly placed himself in a dangerous situation and should therefore be liable for his actions. For example, a police officer responds to a silent alarm of a robbery at a local bank. As the officer exits his vehicle, the bank robber exits the bank, notices the officer, flees on foot, and runs into the street, where a truck strikes and severely injures him. The bank robber cannot anticipate recovering damages when he knowingly chose to commit the robbery and also chose to flee from the officer by running into a busy street. The robber assumed the risk of the activity and the officer would not be liable.

In *City of Jackson v. Perry* (2003), previously discussed in the wrongful death section, the court applied the three elements of assumption of risk theory to the woman who eluded the officers after attempting to pass a forged check. The court ruled that the woman shared in the liability of causing harm to the innocent victim through her risky behavior of operating her car at speeds in excess of 80 miles per hour in a highly populated residential area. The court further noted that the woman had knowledge that such behavior would and could cause harm to another in the residential area and failed to disengage from such harmful activity. The judge determined that the woman assumed the risk when she operated her vehicle in a reckless fashion and assessed an undisclosed amount against her. The woman settled her claim with the family.

Remedies in Tort Actions

As noted in Chapter 2, a plaintiff in a civil action files a claim to recover monetary damages for an injury. There are three primary types of monetary damage awards available to a prevailing plaintiff in tort actions: compensatory, punitive, and nominal.

Compensatory Damages

The cardinal principle of compensatory damages in Anglo-American law is that of compensation for the plaintiff's injury caused by the defendant's breach of duty (Harper & James, 1956). The plaintiff receives a monetary award for actual damages. This can include physical injury and pain and suffering. For example, a plaintiff prevailing in an excessive force case may assert that he sustained a fracture as a result of a blow to the head with the butt of a shotgun. He would be awarded money for the injury. He may also claim that he has endured mental anguish, pain and suffering, humiliation, loss of income, and incurred enormous debt in medical bills as a result of the officer's actions. Compensation could also be granted for these claims. The Pennsylvania Supreme Court in *Catalano v. Bujak* (1994) upheld compensatory damages of $1,543,440 for medical expenses on a claim that a police officer used excessive force in making an arrest. Catalano was stopped for speeding and arrested for disorderly conduct. He claimed the arresting officer forced him over the hood of his car in order to handcuff him, and in the process Catalano injured his wrists when he extended his arms to break the fall against the hood. Catalano later underwent surgery on his wrists, lost work due to the surgery, was no longer able to perform his job as a manager at a supermarket, experienced pain and suffering, and his future earnings were reduced. The jury returned a verdict in favor of the plaintiff, concluding that the officer had engaged in willful misconduct.

Also recall that in the *City of Jackson* pursuit case that the court awarded the estate $250,000 in compensation. The court noted that the officers' actions were reckless, proximately causing the death, and such actions violated the department's pursuit policy.

Punitive Damages

Punitive damages are assessed primarily to punish the errant officer and to send a message to others that the court will not tolerate such misconduct. They are awarded for particularly egregious misconduct, far outside the scope of the officer's authority. Punitive damages are normally awarded for reckless or intentional misconduct on the part of the officer. Generally, the award is proportional to the severity of the wrong committed by the officer, although it is difficult to predict the amount of the award when there has been blatant misconduct. Further, if punitive damages are assessed, it is the individual officer's responsibility to pay the plaintiff. In *Smith v. Wade* (1983), the Supreme Court ruled that punitive damages may be awarded against an officer for displaying reckless and callous indifference, as well as evil motive and intent toward the rights of the plaintiff. In this case, a prison classification officer was held liable for $5,000 in punitive damages for recklessly assigning a prisoner to a housing unit with the knowledge that he probably would be assaulted. Several days later, the prisoner was sexually assaulted by other prisoners.

In *Moore v. City of Philadelphia* (1990), a robbery suspect was punched, kicked, and racially insulted by officers who forced him to strip to the waist and placed him in a cold room in an attempt to elicit a confession. He was awarded $581,977 in compensatory damages and $100,000 in punitive damages.

Punitive damages were awarded by the court in *Siggers-El v. Barlow* (2006). A prisoner filed a lawsuit against a prison official of the Michigan Department of Corrections after the official transferred him to another facility in retaliation for exercising his First Amendment rights. The prisoner complained about the official's misconduct in administering the facility. The court held that the prisoner experienced emotional distress, found that the official's transfer of the prisoner was sufficiently reprehensible to warrant denial of immunity, and that such behavior was worthy of a punitive damage award. The court awarded $200,000 in punitive damages to the prisoner and awarded $90,875 in attorney fees to the law students who assisted the prisoner in the lawsuit.

In *Ferguson v. City of New York* (2010), the estate of a man shot in the head and killed by an officer sued the city for wrongful death, and a jury awarded damages. An intermediate appeals court found that the trial judge had properly set aside $3 million in damages awarded for conscious pain and suffering, because the man's death was almost instantaneous and there was no evidence of his consciousness for any period of time following the shooting. The appeals court, however, upheld jury awards of $55,020 for loss of past economic support, $261,091 for past and future loss of services, and punitive damages of $2.7 million, finding them amply supported by the evidence. The appeals court stated that the trial judge had improperly concluded that the jury awarded punitive damages in part on a finding that the officer had negligently handled his weapon. The appeals court found that the jury award of punitive damages was based on a finding of excessive force, and conduct that was wanton, reckless, or malicious.

Nominal Damages

Nominal damages are awarded as a symbolic gesture. The court may award nominal damages as a token, recognizing that the plaintiff prevailed in the civil action, but did not sustain an actual injury. Generally, nominal damages are quite small and frequently only $1.00 is awarded.

Table 3.1 State Tort Negligence Components

Four Elements of Negligence	Definition
Legal duty	Existence of a duty
Breach of duty	Commission/omission
Proximate cause	Causal link
Injury	Actual injury sustained
Special Duty	Sufficient knowledge
Foreseeability	Reasonable anticipation
Defenses	
Contributory negligence	Plaintiff caused his/her own injury
Comparative negligence	Plaintiff and defendant share liability
Assumption of the risk	Plaintiff willingly engaged in activity
Damages	Monetary awards
Compensatory	Actual/consequential damages
Punitive	To punish blameworthy conduct
Nominal	Symbolic

Summary

The primary thrust of this chapter has been a discussion of state tort claims and defenses. The distinction was made between state and federal tort claims. Tort actions arising out of the conduct of federal employees are filed as *Bivens* actions, although they are similar to state tort actions.

This chapter has highlighted the more common types of torts—intentional and negligent—with case examples, and was designed to present general principles of tort theories. Tort law varies from state to state and can be complex, because intentional torts and negligence may be defined by statute in varying ways. As illustrated in Table 3.1, to prevail in a state tort claim, a plaintiff must prove four components: (1) a legal duty, (2) breach of that duty, (3) proximate causation, and (4) injury. An injury sustained by the plaintiff does not have to be a physical injury. A discussion of damages was presented with defenses to illustrate how the law is applied in varying circumstances.

The differences between state torts and federal court claims were addressed, with case examples. Defenses to these claims show that criminal justice personnel can defend against a state tort claim, but they must show that their actions did not breach duty to perform a certain action in regard to the plaintiff. Criminal justice personnel should become familiar with state tort actions, as the potential to be sued in state and federal court simultaneously is a possibility. Criminal justice personnel should also closely examine the various types of defenses that exist as this will assist in averting a civil action.

References

del Carmen, R. V. (1991). *Civil liabilities in American policing*. Englewood Cliffs, NJ: Prentice-Hall.

Franklin, C. J. (1993). *The police officer's guide to civil liability*. Springfield, IL: Charles C Thomas.

Harper, F., & James, F. (1956). *Law of torts*. New York, NY: Matthew Bender.

Kappeler, V. E. (1997). *Critical issues in police civil liability* (2nd ed.). Prospect Heights, IL: Waveland Press, Inc.

Minzer, M., Nates, J., Kimball, C., Axelrod, D., & Goldstein, R. (2002). *Negligence*. New York, NY: Matthew Bender & Co.

Plitt, E. A. (1997). *Police civil liability and the defense of citizen misconduct complaints manual*. Chicago, IL: Americans for Effective Law Enforcement.

Prosser, W. L., & Keeton, R. E. (1986). *Tort law* (5th ed.). St. Paul, MN: West Publishing Co.

Silver, I. (2010). *Police civil liability*. New York, NY: Matthew Bender & Co.

Vaughn, M. S., & del Carmen, R. V. (1991). Death in detention: an analysis of police liability for negligent failure to prevent suicide. *Journal of Criminal Justice, 19*, 381–393.

4

Civil Liability and Federal Law: Section 1983 Litigation

OVERVIEW

Federal civil lawsuits arising out of allegations of deprivations of constitutional rights by local officials are filed in accordance with § 1983. It provides remedies for violations of federal rights. Section 1983 lawsuits may include claims of abuse of authority by police and correctional personnel with arrestees and prisoners, issues of school desegregation, and other institutional reform litigation. For 40 years, § 1983 litigation has made up the majority of civil litigation in the United States. This chapter will provide an overview of the historical and contemporary use of § 1983 and the methods that are used to bring a constitutional claim against criminal justice personnel.

History of § 1983

At the conclusion of the Civil War, Congress enacted the Civil Rights Act (Title 18 U.S. Code § 242 [1866]) to put an end to the lawless activities of the Ku Klux Klan. The Act provides federal criminal penalties for state and local officials who violate guaranteed rights of citizens (Eisenberg & Schwab, 1987; Gressman, 1992). In April 1871, Title 42 United States Code § 1983 was passed by Congress, and it provides a vehicle for citizens to sue for violations of constitutional rights. Section 1983 added civil remedies to the criminal penalties that were enacted in 1866.

Prior to the Reconstruction period, there were only a handful of constitutional provisions that gave protection against actions by state and federal governments. State courts and the common law were virtually the only protections for citizens' lives, liberty, and property. The conclusion of the Civil War changed this. Between 1866 and 1870, Congress enacted three constitutional amendments: the Thirteenth Amendment (abolishing slavery), the Fourteenth Amendment (due process and equal protection clauses), and the Fifteenth Amendment (right to be free from discrimination in voting). In 1866, Congress enforced the Thirteenth Amendment by passing a civil rights statute guaranteeing rights to African-American citizens. In 1867, Congress enacted a habeas corpus statute that gave those held in state facilities the right to challenge the constitutionality of their incarceration in federal court. Section 1983 was enacted at the end of a five-year period during which Congress was moving quickly to pass and enforce laws to protect the constitutional rights of citizens and provide remedies for violations of those rights.

Prior to § 1983, the only option for redressing a violation of a constitutional right was through the common law, and those actions were heard in state court. Section 1983 allowed for these cases to be heard in federal court. From its enactment in 1871 until 1961, § 1983 lay virtually dormant—it was used in only 24 cases during this period. It has been argued that there are three reasons for its lack of use (Collins, 1997). First, § 1983 was rarely used because of a narrow interpretation and because the Bill of Rights did not apply to the states until the Warren Court of the 1950s and 1960s began in earnest the process of selective incorporation of rights through the Fourteenth Amendment's due process clause. Second, § 1983 was not used much because it was unclear whether actions of public officials that were not formally sanctioned by state law would amount to state action. Third, § 1983 may have been dormant due to a narrow application by the Supreme Court regarding the types of rights it was supposed to guarantee. For some time the Supreme Court held that common law liberty and property rights were secured by state law and not the Constitution (or § 1983). For example, a police chief in *Brawner v. Irvin* (1909) whipped an African-American woman primarily because of her race. The federal trial court held that the rights that were denied did not fall under § 1983, but rather under state law. The court also doubted seriously whether her rights had been denied under state law.

These three rationales seem to indicate the court's reluctance to realistically implement § 1983 for many years. There may have been other reasons for this reluctance as well. As a consequence, during its dormancy, citizens were primarily relegated to redressing their civil rights disputes against local officials in state court through state tort actions.

Resurrection of § 1983

Section 1983 was enacted by Congress for three main reasons: (1) to redress unconstitutional laws; (2) to provide a federal forum when there was no state court remedy on the books; and (3) to provide a federal remedy when the state court remedy was available in theory but not in fact. Section 1983 provides:

> *Every person who, under color of any statute, ordinance, regulation, custom, or usage, of any State or Territory or the District of Columbia, subjects, or causes to be subjected, any citizen of the United States or other persons within the jurisdiction thereof to the deprivation of any rights, privileges, or immunities secured by the Constitution and laws, shall be liable to the party injured in an action at law, suit in equity, or other proper proceeding for redress . . .*

This law has four important elements. First, a person filing suit must be a protected person within the meaning of the act. This means that anyone under the jurisdiction of the United States may bring suit under § 1983. Second, the defendant must have been acting under "color of law." This means the official must be acting within the scope of his or her authority at the time of the constitutional deprivation. Third, "every person" is interpreted to mean that every

individual public official and governmental entity may be liable for constitutional deprivations. Finally, a constitutionally protected right must have been violated. In order to prevail,
these elements must be established. These individual elements will be discussed in greater
detail later in this chapter.

For 90 years, § 1983 lawsuits were rarely filed against government officials, because they
were immune from suit. In two famous cases, however, the United States Supreme Court
began to expand its interpretation of who could be sued under § 1983. In *United States v.
Classic* (1941), the Supreme Court held that officials acting under color of law, as election officials were in Louisiana when they rigged an election, could be held liable for misuse of power
possessed by virtue of state law. Interpretation of § 1983 expanded in *Screws v. United States*
(1945), when the Court ruled that acting under color of law also meant acting under pretense
of law. In *Screws*, Robert Hall, an African-American, was beaten to death by officers who had
arrested him for theft. The officers were prosecuted under § 242 (criminal violation of civil
rights) and the Court stated that "acts of officers who undertake to perform their official duties
are included whether they hew to the line of their authority or overstep it."

The Supreme Court further expanded its interpretation of § 1983 in its landmark decision
of *Monroe v. Pape* (1961). Prior to this decision, it was extremely difficult to hold criminal justice officials liable under § 1983 due to the requirement of acting under "color of law." *Monroe*
broadened the language of this concept. Chicago police officers broke into Monroe's house in
the early morning and rousted him and his family out of bed, made him stand naked in the living room, and ransacked the house. He was arrested and detained at the police department for
10 hours and later released. Monroe was never prosecuted, but did file a § 1983 lawsuit based
on an illegal search and seizure and violation of his constitutional rights. The Court ruled that
the officers' actions, which were clothed in state law, constituted acting under color of law, and
that they misused their authority and power as police officers. The Court further concluded
that Monroe did not have to exhaust alternative remedies available in state court prior to
lodging his claim in federal court. In *Monroe* the Court dusted off the once-dormant law and
opened the door for future litigation against the police and correctional personnel. This decision, however, did not include liability against government entities, but only against individual
officers. Thus, the City of Chicago could not be sued (see Box 4.1).

Essential Elements of § 1983 Lawsuits

Monroe has become the cornerstone for police federal civil liability (Kappeler, 1997).
The law itself does not create substantive rights or jurisdiction in the federal courts (*Chapman
v. Houston Welfare Rights Organization*, 1979), and is therefore procedural. The plaintiff
suing under § 1983 must specifically plead federal jurisdiction under the appropriate statute
(*Monroe v. Pape*, 1961). Likewise, under *Monroe*, the plaintiff need not first bring separate
actions under state and federal law. There are several essential elements in understanding the
dynamics of § 1983 lawsuits.

BOX 4.1 *MONROE V. PAPE* (1961)

During early morning hours, 13 Chicago police officers broke into Monroe's house and ordered him and his six children out of bed and forced them to stand naked while they ransacked the house. He was then arrested and transported to the police station. He was held for 10 hours, not allowed to call an attorney, and was neither arraigned nor prosecuted. He filed a § 1983 lawsuit claiming that his Fourth Amendment protection against unreasonable search and seizure had been violated.

The United States Supreme Court granted certiorari to examine the issue of whether the Chicago police officers and the city should be liable under § 1983 for the officers' actions. The Court held that a plaintiff need not exhaust available state remedies prior to filing a § 1983 claim in federal court. The Court held that the officers' actions were "action under color of law" within the meaning of § 1983, even if what they did also happened to be in violation of state law. The Court concluded that the City of Chicago was not liable, because Congress did not intend to bring municipalities within the provisions of § 1983.

Justice Douglas's opinion was significant for several reasons. First, the decision dusted off the rarely used § 1983 after a lengthy period of disuse. Douglas stated that "Section 1983 makes a man responsible for the natural consequences of his actions." Prior to this decision, it was difficult to hold public officials liable for their actions under § 1983. Second, this is a seminal case because it literally opened up the floodgates of the courts, which have provided that citizens claiming that their constitutionally protected rights have been violated by a public officer's actions may now bring a civil suit against that officer. Third, the decision interprets the language in § 1983 that states: "every person acting under color of law, ... may be held liable." Every person is defined as "every officer." When officers perform their sworn duties by virtue of state law and misuse their authority, they may be held liable for the abuse of such power. Liability will attach under § 1983 when an officer misuses his or her authority and violates an individual's constitutionally protected right.

How Is "Person" Defined?

In *Monroe* the Court defined "person" within the meaning of § 1983 as individual officers. A government employee may be sued for money damages in his or her individual capacity for acts performed while discharging those duties. A suit against a state employee acting in his or her official capacity imposes liability against the entity that the employee represents and cannot be brought, because the Eleventh Amendment prohibits lawsuits against the state (*Brandon v. Holt*, 1985).

Further, the Supreme Court ruled in *Will v. Michigan Department of State Police* (1989) that state officials cannot be sued under § 1983 when they act in their official capacity. The Court emphasized that Congress did not intend to include states or state agencies within the definition of "person" for purposes of § 1983 liability. Plaintiffs may, however, sue a state and state agencies for prospective injunctive relief under § 1983 (*Kentucky v. Graham*, 1985).

The Supreme Court further expanded the definition of "person" to include local governments and their employees in *Monell v. Department of Social Services of the City of New York* (1978). Prior to *Monell*, local governments were immune from § 1983 liability based on the rationale that they were not "persons" as defined by law. The Dictionary Act (enacted in 1871 and originally codified at 16 Stat. 431) allowed the word "person" to be applied to political bodies. Based on the history of § 1983 and relying on the Dictionary Act, the Supreme Court concluded in *Monell* that municipalities, as well as other governing bodies, are "persons" within the meaning of § 1983. The Court in *Monell* held that governmental bodies may be held liable when an officer acts pursuant to a custom or official policy of the agency and it violates an individual's constitutional rights. Plaintiffs may now sue and recover damages against county, city, municipal, and other units of local governments for the actions of their officers. A complete discussion of supervisory liability will be presented in Chapters 5 and 6.

How Is Acting Under "Color of Law" Defined?

For liability to attach, a person must be acting under "color of law." This phrase normally means that an officer or official misused his or her official powers granted by law in the office he or she was sworn to uphold (*Monroe v. Pape*, 1961). In *West v. Atkins* (1988), the United States Supreme Court further stated that employees who carry out their official responsibilities act under color of state law and are state actors even when they act in violation of state law. The courts have broadened this phrase to include actions taken under the auspices of state and local laws, ordinances, and agency rules. Actions that exceed the law and the scope of authority constitute acting under "color of law." For example, assaulting a prisoner after a prison disturbance would constitute action outside the scope of the officer's authority.

Actions taken under color of federal laws by federal employees are excluded. *Bivens* actions are not incorporated under § 1983. The off-duty actions of an officer cannot be the basis of litigation unless the officer uses police equipment or uses his or her authority as an "official" employee.

Inquiries by the courts to determine what constitutes acting under color of law require a determination of the "nature of the officer's act, not simply his duty status" (Vaughn & Coomes, 1995). Using the "totality of circumstances" analysis, courts determine whether an officer was acting under color of law by examining whether criminal justice personnel invoke power if they discharge duties routinely associated with their work, or if they use their authority to lure plaintiffs into compromising positions. Further, courts hold that officers act under color of law if they wear their uniforms, draw their firearms, identify themselves as law enforcement or correctional officers, place suspects under arrest, detain and confine them, file official reports, and otherwise hold themselves out as official personnel for a government agency (Vaughn & Coomes, 1995).

For example, in *Ousley v. Town of Lincoln* (2004), the court found that an off-duty officer was acting under color of law when he arrested a youth for assault and disorderly conduct and malicious damage of property. Officer Kevin Harty of the Lincoln Police Department was off duty when he stopped his personal vehicle after observing Ousley fighting with his girlfriend in the middle of the street. Ousley shouted "Go ahead and hit me!" and pounded on the hood of Harty's car with his fists. Harty, not in uniform, exited his car and an altercation occurred between Ousley and himself. Ousley claimed that Harty chased, beat, and strangled him. Witnesses claimed that they saw Harty chase Ousley, that they heard Harty yell that he was the police and that someone should call the police. Harty's version was that he had a brief "encounter" with Ousley and that he returned to his car and waited for the police. Prior to the police arriving, Harty called the Lincoln Police Department and requested backup.

Responding police observed an obvious altercation between Harty and Ousley. Harty's shirt was torn and he had abrasions on his body. Ousley was covered in blood. The police filed three criminal charges against Ousley. The judge dismissed all but the malicious damage of property charge, ruling that Harty was not a credible witness. Ousley filed a civil lawsuit, claiming that his constitutional rights had been violated.

At trial, the court ruled that, based on the "totality of circumstances" surrounding the incident, Harty acted under color of state law. The court examined the circumstances of this incident and noted that Harty did not wear police attire, did not use any type of police weapon, and the location of the incident, all of which pointed in his favor. The court, however, found that Ousley presented compelling evidence that Harty not only announced that he was a police officer, which several witnesses' testimony verified, but also that he was acting in his official capacity as an officer at the time of the altercation, and requested backup from the department. The court concluded that such evidence showed that Harty was acting as a "police officer" at the time of the incident and ruled in favor of Ousley.

With some frequency, off-duty conduct emerges as a matter for the courts to consider in determining whether the concept of "color of law" should apply. *In Errico v. Township of Howell* (2008), the lower court addressed this question. Officer Moore was engaged in a pursuit of Errico that exceeded speeds of over 100 miles per hour. During the pursuit two additional officers joined officer Moore but Errico was able to elude them. Officer Storrow had ended his shift and was driving his personal vehicle home when he heard over the radio that the pursuit was nearing his vicinity. Storrow pulled into a store parking lot to assist in the possible intercept of Errico. After several minutes Storrow learned that the officers had lost sight of Errico and decided to proceed home. Storrow continued to listen to his police radio and learned that Errico was now on the same road that he was traveling and within several seconds Errico's vehicle collided with Storrow's. Errico died as a result of injuries sustained in the collision.

Errico's estate filed a lawsuit claiming that Storrow's action caused Errico's death. Errico's estate theorized that Storrow was acting in his personal capacity at the time of the accident and not in his official capacity as a police officer. They further argued that when Storrow left the parking lot and headed home in his personal vehicle, he was no longer concerned with the pursuit, and thus was not acting under color of state law. Storrow claimed that his department required him to be ready to assist on-duty officers and to be prepared to respond to any situations that he might encounter by himself. He asserted that he was acting in his official capacity consistent with his department's policy. The court agreed and granted summary judgment holding that Storrow was acting under color of law at the time of the incident.

What Is the Focus of the Complaint in a § 1983 Lawsuit?

The plaintiff must show that the conduct of the defendant resulted in the violation of a constitutional right or federal law that can be enforced in accordance with § 1983. Section 1983

BOX 4.2 SELECTED CONSTITUTIONAL AMENDMENTS

First Amendment: "Congress shall make no law respecting an establishment of religion, or prohibiting the free exercise thereof; or abridging the freedom of speech, or of the press; or the right of the people peaceably to assemble, and to petition the government for a redress of grievances." If criminal justice personnel violate First Amendment rights in their official capacity, they are subject to § 1983 litigation (*Alliance to End Repression v. City of Chicago*, 1982; *Hutchings v. Corum*, 1980).

Fourth Amendment: "The right of the people to be secure in their persons, houses, papers, and effects, against unreasonable searches and seizures, shall not be violated, and no Warrants shall issue, but upon probable cause, supported by Oath or affirmation, and particularly describing the place to be searched, and the persons or things to be seized." This amendment restricts the state and its officers (*Wolf v. Colorado*, 1949).

Fifth Amendment: "Nor shall any person be subject for the same offense to be twice put in jeopardy of life or limb; nor shall be compelled in any criminal case to be a witness against himself, nor be deprived of life, liberty, or property, without due process of law; . . ." State and local officers must follow this requirement (*Benton v. Maryland*, 1969).

Sixth Amendment (in part): "In all criminal prosecutions, the accused shall enjoy the right . . . to have the assistance of Counsel for his defense." This provision binds the states, as do other requirements in this amendment (*Gideon v. Wainwright*, 1962).

Eighth Amendment: "Excessive bail shall not be required, . . . nor cruel and unusual punishments inflicted." Another restriction that is binding on the states (*Robinson v. California*, 1962).

The Fourteenth Amendment (in part): "No state shall make or enforce any law which shall abridge the privileges or immunities of citizens of the United States; nor shall any state deprive any person of life, liberty, or property, without due process of law; nor deny to any person within its jurisdiction the equal protection of the laws." This amendment, by its terms, applies to the states (*Powers v. Lightner,* 1987).

---

creates no rights, but is a vehicle to redress violations of the Bill of Rights and certain federal statutes. Mere negligence is not actionable as a § 1983 claim—such claims must be brought in state court (*Daniels v. Williams*, 1986). Further, violations of city ordinances or state laws are not actionable under § 1983.

Box 4.2 identifies the primary constitutional amendments that form the basis of § 1983 actions. Criminal justice personnel must be familiar with these amendments, because they regularly make decisions that involve rights that are protected by these amendments. Violating these rights can lead to civil liability. Officers' actions may also lead to litigation against their agency. Therefore, criminal justice officers need to know the law, their legal responsibilities, and their department's policy and procedure manual. They also must be aware of how these amendments apply to the status of offenders in the criminal justice system.

Remedies Under § 1983

Filing a § 1983 lawsuit allows the plaintiff a range of remedies should he or she prevail. A prevailing plaintiff may be awarded monetary damages and injunctive or declaratory relief. As ordered by a court, injunctive relief prohibits a certain practice that a government entity may be performing, which violates a constitutionally protected right of another. Declaratory relief, in the court's opinion, may determine that a regulation or practice is unconstitutional without necessarily requiring any remedial action.

Another benefit of filing a lawsuit in federal court is that the process of discovery (obtaining documents from the defendant) is more simplified than in state court. Plaintiffs filing a § 1983 lawsuit are not required to exhaust state remedies prior to filing in federal court. Since 1976, prevailing plaintiffs' attorneys may be awarded attorney's fees. These features make filing a § 1983 lawsuit attractive and more likely that plaintiffs and their attorneys will file § 1983 lawsuits against criminal justice personnel.

Section 1983 authorizes any citizen in the United States to file a federal civil lawsuit. Corporations are excluded. Section 1983 has also been interpreted to mean that aliens legally in the United States may also file suit under § 1983 (*Graham v. Richardson*, 1975). Some courts have extended the Fourteenth Amendment due process and equal protection clauses in § 1983 cases to apply to illegal aliens. Pretrial detainees, probationers, convicted prisoners, and parolees may also file § 1983 lawsuits.

A plaintiff may file a § 1983 lawsuit in either state or federal court simultaneously, although a majority are filed in federal court (*Maine v. Thiboutot*, 1980). Plaintiffs are subject to statutes of limitations when filing a § 1983 lawsuit. Statutes of limitation are laws that stipulate a certain period for the action to be filed in court from the date the incident giving rise to the action occurred. In *Wilson v. Garcia* (1985), the Supreme Court determined that § 1983 cases are "personal injury" cases, and that statutory periods used in state courts be used. Generally speaking, the statutory period is three years.

The same types of damages awarded in state tort claims are available in § 1983 litigation: nominal, compensatory, and punitive. Damages are awarded for injuries, pain and suffering, loss of earnings, emotional distress, medical expenses, and loss of property (*Carey v. Pipus*, 1978). Punitive damages may be awarded for particularly blameworthy conduct on the part of the defendant. In *Smith v. Wade* (1983), the Supreme Court held that actual malice is not necessary to recover punitive damages—reckless or callous indifference to constitutional rights is sufficient (see Box 4.3).

As discussed in Chapter 1, Ross and Bodapoti (2006) found in a 15-year study of 150 police agencies that the average compensatory award granted by the court in 25 categories of police civil lawsuits was slightly more than $100,000 per case, excluding attorney fees. Generally criminal justice personnel prevail in a majority of civil actions, but when the plaintiff prevails, compensatory awards can be significant. For example, a review of custodial suicide litigation trends reveals that the average compensatory award granted to the estate is approximately $200,000 (Ross, 2010). This figure is comparable to the figures reported by O'Leary (1989)—$200,000— and the Americans for Effective Law Enforcement (AELE, 2008)—$225,000—regarding suicide litigation award trends.

For example, in *Woodard v. Correctional Medical Services of Illinois* (2004), the Seventh Circuit Appellate Court upheld a lower court's award of $1.75 million in the custodial suicide of a state prisoner. The award was based on a claim of an alleged custom of failing to follow proper procedures with mentally ill prisoners. Further in *Sisk v. Manzanares* (2003), the court

---

BOX 4.3 *SMITH V. WADE* (1983)

Prisoner Wade was voluntarily placed in protective segregation in a youth correctional facility in Missouri because he complained of physical abuse by other prisoners. Classification Officer Smith placed Wade in a cell with another prisoner and later placed a third prisoner, who had a history of fighting, in the same cell. Smith was aware of the third prisoner's assaultive history, ignored it, and failed to determine whether other cells were available. Wade later was sexually assaulted and filed a § 1983 claim against Smith, other officers, and correctional officials, asserting that his Eighth Amendment rights were violated. Wade prevailed and was awarded $25,000 in compensatory damages and $5,000 in punitive damages. The appellate court affirmed the decision and Smith appealed the punitive damage award to the United States Supreme Court.

The Supreme Court examined the issue of whether a jury could award punitive damages against an officer who acts with reckless disregard of or indifference to the safety of a prisoner and his or her protected constitutional rights. The Court affirmed the decision. The Court concluded that a jury is permitted to assess punitive damages in a civil action in which an officer's action is motivated by malicious intent and if the defendant acted with callous indifference to, or reckless disregard of, a prisoner's rights. Punitive damages may be awarded for particularly egregious and blameworthy misconduct marked by evil intent or motive, as demonstrated by the defendant.

This case is significant because in awarding punitive damages, the jury is sending a message that such actions are outrageous and that it intends to punish the officer for such actions. Punitive damages may be awarded when a defendant's actions are motivated by malicious intent and when the defendant acted in a callous, reckless manner, without regard for the safety or rights of the prisoner. This decision makes it less difficult for a plaintiff to recover punitive damages.

---

reduced a jury award of $10 million to $225,000 for failing to prevent a prisoner's suicide due to the state statutory limit on wrongful death awards.

In *King v. Marci* (1993), the court upheld a malicious prosecution award of $75,000 for two months in detention and emotional distress. Punitive damages for false arrest and excessive force were also proper. The court in *Franklin v. Aycock* (1986) assessed $5,000 each in punitive damages against three detention officers. They had repeatedly kicked a prisoner who was shackled in bed.

Plaintiffs filing § 1983 lawsuits may also seek declaratory and injunctive relief. When awarding a declaratory judgment, the court may declare that a state statute or regulation is unconstitutional. Declaratory relief in federal court is discretionary, as the court may award compensation for rights violations. For example, a court may examine a correctional department's use-of-force policy and declare it unconstitutional and require the department to rewrite it in accordance with constitutional provisions. When authorizing injunctive relief, a court goes further in providing redress to the plaintiff. The court could prohibit defendants from engaging in certain unconstitutional conduct in the future or require that they take certain steps to avoid further violations of the Constitution.

Compensatory and punitive damages were awarded to a prisoner who sustained injuries after a use-of-force altercation with correction officers. In *Jackson v. Austin* (2003), officers instructed Jackson to stand in line for the prison medical clinic and Jackson attempted to explain that he was there for treatment of his knee. Jackson explained that he could not stand for long periods and needed to sit. The officer refused to examine the prisoner's medical restriction orders signed by a physician. He grabbed Jackson and pushed him to the floor and handcuffed him. A second officer on the scene did not participate in the action, but failed to intervene in the actions of the first officer.

Jackson filed a §1983 lawsuit and the court rejected a motion for qualified immunity from the officers. The court held that the prisoner did not have to prove that he sustained significant or permanent injuries and that the officers used excessive force in restraining him. The court ruled in favor of Jackson and assessed $15,000 in compensatory damages and $30,000 in punitive damages against both officers. The court also noted that the prisoner was 60 years old and that the officers were aware that he had a knee injury.

Under the Federal Tort Claims Act, monetary damages may also be awarded to a plaintiff. In *Limone v. U.S.* (2009), released prisoners, after their convictions had been overturned, and representatives of prisoners who died in prison, brought a *Bivens* action against the U.S. government, asserting claims that governmental agents framed them. In a bench trial, the court found in favor of the plaintiff's and the government appealed the decision. The First Circuit Court of Appeals affirmed the lower court's decision. The circuit court held that the FBI's conduct of cultivating witnesses' false testimony, which led to wrongful convictions, was extreme and outrageous supporting a claim of intentional infliction and emotional distress and violated due process under Massachusetts law and the Federal Tort Claims Act. The court awarded $1 million per year of wrongful incarceration in the plaintiff's action. Further, the court ruled that the FBI agents engaged in malicious prosecution; agents engaged in a coercive conspiracy and intentionally inflicted emotional distress on the prisoners; supervisors were negligent in the supervision of the agents' activities; and loss of consortium damages were awarded to the prisoners' wives and children.

Injunctive relief may be granted in the form of a temporary restraining order, a preliminary injunction, or a permanent injunction. Courts can grant a broad range of injunctions in § 1983 cases. The Supreme Court in *Los Angeles v. Lyons* (1983) determined that the plaintiff could not sue for injunctive relief. The plaintiff, who had been a victim of a choke hold, sued, asking the court to enjoin the future use of choke holds by the Los Angeles Police Department. The choke hold had resulted in the deaths of 16 people, many of whom were African-American males like the plaintiff. The Court ruled that the plaintiff had not shown with certainty that he would have another encounter with the police. Even if he could make such a showing, he could not establish that the choke hold would be applied specifically to him. In an effort to limit federal court intrusion into the state's operation of prisons and jails after a finding of unconstitutional conditions in a facility, the courts have normally given officials the opportunity to develop a plan to bring conditions into compliance with the Constitution (*Lewis v. Casey*, 1996).

In *Chester v. Beard* (2009), prisoners on death row brought a class action lawsuit under § 1983 against Pennsylvania Department of Corrections officials, seeking an injunctive relief against claims of violations of their right to be free from cruel and unusual punishment and their right to due process arising from Pennsylvania's use of the lethal injection execution method. The court rejected the defendant's motion to dismiss. The court held that the prisoners had standing to bring the § 1983 claim to the state's use of the lethal injection method, requesting a permanent injunction, even if they were not under active death warrants. The court noted that being sentenced to death row supported the fact that the prisoners had sufficient personal stake in the action to satisfy the standing requirements. The court agreed with the prisoners indicating that they showed that the lethal injection method exposed them to the risk of extreme pain and suffering because the state failed to train personnel who were assigned with conducting the execution.

Can Attorney's Fees Be Assessed?

Section 1983 does not on its face require the awarding of attorney's fees. Awarding of attorney's fees is discretionary on the part of the court. Congress modified the American rule in the Civil Rights Attorney's Fees Awards Act of 1976 (42 U.S.C. § 1988). The rule is a tradition at common law that each party pays his own attorney's fees, win or lose (*Alyeska Pipeline Service Co. v. Wilderness Society*, 1975). The statute provides a financial incentive to bring lawsuits that might not otherwise attract attorneys, either because only injunctive relief is sought, or because the likelihood of substantial damages is uncertain. The Attorney's Fees Act states in part:

> . . . *the court, in its discretion, may allow the prevailing party, other than the United States, a reasonable attorney's fee as part of the costs, except that in any action brought against a judicial officer for an act or omission taken in such officer's judicial capacity such officer shall not be held liable for any costs, including attorney's fees, unless such action was clearly in excess of such officer's jurisdiction.*

In order for an attorney to recover attorney's fees, the plaintiff must obtain at least some actual relief on the merits of his or her claim. Plaintiffs who proceed in a § 1983 lawsuit pro se (on their own behalf) are not entitled to attorney's fees even when they prevail. Further, the Supreme Court has held that prevailing plaintiffs, not prevailing defendants, sued under § 1983, should recover attorney's fees (*Hughes v. Rowe*, 1980). There does not have to be a trial in order to recover attorney's fees. In *Maher v. Gagne* (1980), the Supreme Court ruled that the plaintiffs were entitled to attorney's fees even though the case was settled through a consent decree agreement. This ruling is significant for conditions-of-confinement suits that are settled under a consent decree. This may also be of significance to law enforcement agencies that settle under consent decrees in the future.

In determining the appropriate amount to award an attorney under § 1988, the Supreme Court in *Hensley v. Eckerhart* (1983) established a figure known as the "lodestar." This figure is computed by multiplying the number of hours reasonably expended on the litigation by a reasonable hourly rate. This computation is completed at the end of the litigation. The following factors are normally considered in calculating the lodestar figure: (1) the time and labor required; (2) the novelty and difficulty of the questions presented by the case; (3) the skill required to perform the legal service properly; (4) the preclusion of other employment by the attorney due to acceptance of the case; (5) the customary fee for similar work; (6) whether the fee is fixed or contingent; (7) time limitations imposed by the client or the circumstances; (8) the amount in dispute and the results obtained; (9) the experience, reputation, and ability of the attorney; (10) the "undesirability" of the case; (11) the nature and length of the professional relationship with the client; and (12) awards in similar cases. In 1996, however, Congress placed a cap on the hourly rate used under § 1988 in prisoner rights litigation. In accordance with 42 U.S.C. § 1997e(d)(3), the hourly rate used in determining the fee by federal judicial courts cannot exceed $112.50.

In *Knopp v. Johnson* (1989), experienced attorneys sought fees up to $190 per hour. The 35-day trial in a prison conditions case led to attorney's fees of more than $200,000. In *Spell v. McDaniel* (1987), a particularly egregious case, the court assessed $900,000 for compensatory and punitive damages and $325,000 in attorney's fees. A police officer kicked a restrained and compliant arrestee in the groin. The injury required surgical removal of a testicle, which resulted in sterility.

Prisoners prevailed in a § 1983 lawsuit and were awarded $12 million when they contested an unconstitutional policy and practice of performing suspicionless strip searches in *Bynum v. District of Columbia* (2006). The court ruled that the prisoners who were confined from 2002 to 2005 and were strip-searched illegally, had been deprived of their due process rights, resulting in a large damages award. Several prisoners shared in the award. The court conducted a hearing to determine whether the award was reasonable and affirmed the award. The court also awarded attorney fees in the amount of $4 million or 33 percent of the award and noted that such an amount was reasonable based on the complexity of the legal issues contained in the case.

In *Drumgold v. Callahan* (2011), the question of whether attorney's fees were excessive was asked in a case where withholding exculpatory evidence resulting in conviction of an innocent man. In 1988 Shawn Drumgold was arrested and charged with murdering a 12-year-old girl who was killed during a gang-related shooting. Detective Callahan investigated the murder and learned that a homeless man, Roy Evans, had information about the murder. Evans was also a witness of a crime against his cousin. Callahan moved Evans and his family into a hotel for eight months and paid him cash for his testimony. One of the assistant prosecuting attorneys was aware of the accommodations but the prosecuting attorney who litigated the case was unaware. During the trial Evans testified that he saw Drumgold in the area at the time of the murder and was asked by Drumgold's attorney if he had received anything in return for his testimony, and Evans replied, "no." Drumgold was convicted of first degree murder and sentenced to life in prison without parole.

In 2003, Drumgold moved for a new trial based on evidence that exculpatory information had been withheld during his trial. The court granted the new trial and Evans along with several other witnesses recanted their previous testimony. The prosecutor, however, declined to retry the case and Drumgold was released in 2004. Drumgold filed a § 1983 lawsuit against the parties claiming he did not receive a fair trial and a jury agreed and recommended that he be paid $14 million in damages for intentionally or recklessly withholding material exculpatory evidence that directly caused Drumgold to be convicted. Drumgold also moved for attorney's fees in the amount of $2,305,585 and costs of $100,399. Callahan opposed the motion on the basis that it was untimely, the amount was excessive, the time records lacked the required degree of specificity and detail, and the records reflected hours spent on unsuccessful claims.

Using the lodestar method the court agreed that the attorney's fees and costs were reasonable and were consistent with rates charged by other attorneys with comparable experience and competence, although the court did reduce the attorney's fees to $1,613,846.50 and costs to $51,631. The court noted that the litigation was "extraordinarily difficult," which further justified the rate. The court further stated that $14 million is the largest jury award for wrongful conviction in the history of Massachusetts and any further reduction, considering the nature of the victory, would be unfair to the attorneys whose skill and effort resulted in such an award. Further, the court ruled that the FBI agents engaged in malicious prosecution; agents engaged in a coercive conspiracy and intentionally inflicted emotional distress on the prisoners; supervisors were negligent in the supervision of the agents' activities; and loss of consortium damages were awarded to the prisoners' wives and children.

Who Pays for the Damages?

Criminal justice personnel in a civil lawsuit usually have legal representation provided by their employing agency. Law or written policy in most state agencies provides for representation through the state attorney general's office. As long as the officer acted within the scope of his or her authority and was held liable, the state will pay part or all of the award.

Lawsuits against local law enforcement officers and county sheriff's departments are handled differently. The city or county attorney's office usually will defend a civil lawsuit filed against an officer or government agency. In many jurisdictions, local departments participate in a risk management pool and retain legal counsel through it. Still other departments retain their own attorneys to defend department personnel. Most agencies will provide an attorney for the officer, but it is a decision made by local administrators on a case-by-case basis. This may be addressed in the department's policy manual, and officers should be aware of the policy in their department. If the agency decides not to provide an attorney, it will be necessary for the officer to retain his or her own attorney.

Should an officer lose a civil lawsuit, generally his or her employing agency will pay the damage award. Many states provide indemnification for state employees, although the amount varies. Most agencies will not indemnify blatant or outrageous actions outside the officer's authority. If the court awards more than the indemnification, the officer pays the difference. Indemnification also varies in local agencies. If punitive damages are awarded, the individual officer must pay them. Payment by the agency would be contrary to public policy. Criminal justice personnel should be aware of how their agency provides legal representation in the event of a civil lawsuit and how damages awards are paid should the officer be held liable.

In *Cabral v. U. S. Dept. of Justice* (2009), the nurse of the jail brought a § 1983 action against the sheriff for retaliation, barring her from entering the facility to do her job, and her right to freedom of speech when she informed the FBI of alleged prisoner abuse within the jail. The sheriff filed a motion for summary judgment and the court rejected it and a jury found in favor of the nurse. Further, the First Circuit Court of Appeals affirmed the lower court's decision. The court held that there was sufficient evidence to support the jury finding in favor of the nurse and evidence supporting her claim. The court found that the sheriff barred the nurse from the facility with a conscious indifference to her free speech rights, as was necessary to support an award of punitive damages to the nurse in the amount of $250,000. The court noted that the award was not excessive, where the sheriff's conduct was reprehensible and the award could have been more.

Mechanics of a § 1983 Lawsuit

Figure 4.1 illustrates the mechanical framework of a § 1983 lawsuit. With some exceptions, this basic process is followed. All § 1983 lawsuits originate with an incident (i.e., arrest, search, pursuit, use of force) in which a criminal justice officer acts under color of law in the performance of his or her duties. Depending on the situation, the act may or may not be within the scope of the officer's duties. The plaintiff may allege that the officer violated his or her constitutional rights as a result of the incident. In the case of jails and prisons, a prisoner may file a § 1983 lawsuit alleging that a rule or regulation has violated his or her constitutional rights, in addition to filing a complaint about an incident in which an officer violated his or her protected rights. As previously discussed, the plaintiff must file the suit within the statute of limitations. The plaintiff may file the lawsuit with legal counsel or may act as his or her own attorney (pro se).

The plaintiff will usually name individual officers who were involved in the incident, and also those in the chain of command—supervisors, administrators, and government entities. This is known as the "deep pockets" theory (del Carmen, 1991). This theory encourages the plaintiff to name multiple defendants in the lawsuit in an effort to find culpability with as many as possible—the idea being the more defendants named within the hierarchy of the agency, the more likely the award will be higher should the plaintiff prevail. Officers may have only limited resources with which to pay, but the city or the county might be better able to pay the award.

The plaintiff files a complaint with the court, outlining and describing the nature of the constitutional rights that allegedly were violated. All involved parties are named, and the complaint describes each defendant's liability. Each defendant receives a copy of the complaint. The attorney for each defendant also receives a copy of the complaint. Counsel meets with the defendants to discuss the alleged incident. Pertinent documents, such as the officer's incident report, policies and regulations, as well as any evidence, are reviewed. Defense counsel normally files a written response to the court denying the allegations or claiming immunity from the lawsuit.

Shortly after receiving the complaint, the defense counsel may file a motion to dismiss the case. A motion to dismiss asks the court to throw out the plaintiff's lawsuit because it is without merit, is not founded in law, or fails to state a valid legal claim. The judge may agree and dismiss the case, or may allow the plaintiff to amend the complaint.

If the plaintiff's case survives the motion to dismiss, the discovery period begins. Discovery is a process by which one party gains information held by another party (Franklin, 1993). It is a period established by the court to allow the plaintiff and the defendant to explore one

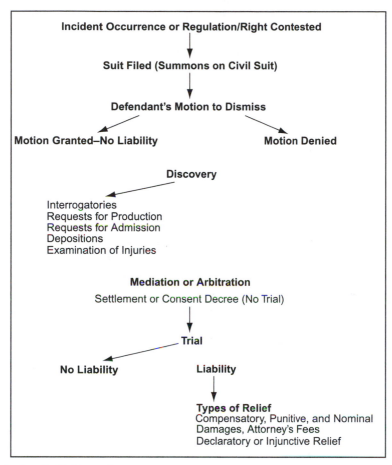

FIGURE 4.1 Mechanics of a Civil Lawsuit.

another's cases. Discovery provides for full disclosure prior to trial. It also allows the parties to examine evidence that may be useful in their case that may not be obtained through other means or sources. All jurisdictions provide for discovery.

There are five basic tools allowed in discovery:

1. Interrogatories
2. Requests for production
3. Requests for admission
4. Depositions
5. Examination of physical evidence

Interrogatories are written questions intended to solicit written or verbal responses. Interrogatories are commonly used and inexpensive. Under the Federal Rules of Civil Procedure, the number of questions is limited to 30. Named parties in the lawsuit sit down with their counsel and, under oath, answer each question. Second, documents known as requests for production are filed. This tool gives the requesting party the opportunity to obtain and examine physical evidence in the possession of the responding party. Documents may include departmental policies and procedures, incident reports, photos, audio and video recordings, drawings, personnel files, investigative reports, autopsy reports, and medical reports.

A third type of discovery tool is a request for admission. This document is a statement of fact under law asking the responding party to admit or deny the statement. If the issue in question is admitted to be true, it will be settled prior to trial. If the issue is contested it must be determined at trial. Both parties may use requests for admission. This can be helpful in settling issues prior to trial.

The fourth type of discovery tool is a deposition, which is out-of-court testimony given under oath and transcribed. This can be the most costly form of discovery. Both parties may take depositions of the other's clients. Although it is an informal questioning process in which the deponent answers verbally, rules of evidence still apply, and the responses are transcribed by a court reporter. Video and telephone depositions may be performed and used in conjunction with the transcribed document at trial. Deposition responses may be researched as to their accuracy and read to the jury at trial. Although used infrequently, the defendant may be asked to submit a written affidavit describing his or her actions in the incident. This, too, is taken under oath.

Finally, defense counsel will have the opportunity to examine the physical or mental injuries claimed by the plaintiff. This examination will be performed by a physician.

The discovery period is set by the court and may be extended at the court's discretion. Discovery may last as long as several months or years, depending on the complexity and magnitude of the lawsuit. At the conclusion of discovery, defense counsel may file a motion for summary judgment, asking the court to decide the case based on all evidence obtained through discovery. The court has several options: It can deny the motion; accept portions of the motion, requiring it to move to trial on those portions; or grant the motion. If the case involves both § 1983 claims and state tort actions, the federal court may dismiss the constitutional claims and remand the case to state court to deal with the remaining state issues.

If the defense counsel filed the motion for summary judgment, the plaintiff has the right to respond. The idea that each side is entitled to its "day in court" makes many courts reluctant to grant summary judgment. The court may hold that the issue is a matter for the jury to decide, and the case will move to trial. If the court grants summary judgment, the losing party has a right to appeal.

Due to the burgeoning court dockets across the country, many parties now attempt to find alternatives to going to trial. The predominant alternative methods are known as mediation and arbitration. Mediation is the more common of the two and involves the parties in dispute and a disinterested third person coming together in order to settle the case. The mediator does not have the authority to order the parties to settle the case. The mediator facilitates discussion and keeps the talks going in an attempt to work toward a resolution.

Arbitration, however, takes a more powerful judicial role in the dispute. The arbitrator listens to all the arguments from each side, weighs the evidence, and, based on the evidence, makes a recommendation. With mediation and arbitration, both parties must agree to the alternative method in reaching the resolution.

If the case goes to trial, jury selection begins. The judge and attorneys interview prospective jurors from a jury pool to determine who is qualified to serve as a juror. Individuals who cannot participate in an impartial manner are excused from duty. Once the jury is empaneled, the trial begins. The trial starts with opening statements, which provide an overview of the facts from the plaintiff and the defendant. Because the plaintiff has the burden of proof, his or her case is presented first. Once the plaintiff presents his or her witnesses and evidence, the defense presents his or her case. When both parties are finished presenting their evidence and witnesses, they make closing arguments to the jury. Both parties attempt to persuade the jury to find in favor of their client.

After closing arguments, the judge will instruct the jury about the law and their deliberations. The jury will take a period of time to deliberate the outcome of the case. The standard of proof used in civil cases is a preponderance of the evidence. The losing party may appeal the verdict. Should the jury find in favor of the plaintiff, the judge could issue a directed verdict in favor of the defendant officers. The plaintiff may still appeal such a verdict. If the plaintiff prevails, he or she would recover damages as discussed earlier and may be awarded attorney's fees.

This brief description of the mechanics of a § 1983 lawsuit is provided in order to illustrate the normal path of a civil case. Depending on the complexity and legal issues of the case, it can take years to complete. It will take even longer if the verdict is appealed. Many of the original complaints and allegations may never make it to court, due to rulings by the court and motions made by both parties. Prolonging the case with extensions and motions is sometimes a strategy in an effort for evidence to be lost, memories to fade, and witnesses to retire or die. Civil litigation is costly and can be highly stressful for those involved.

Summary

Section 1983 lawsuits are the most common type of litigation filed against criminal justice personnel. Students and practitioners alike should be aware of their potential liability under its provisions. Since the early 1960s, the courts have been inundated with civil rights cases. Section 1983 cannot be used by citizens or prisoners seeking to hold federal officials liable. It allows citizens, pretrial detainees, prisoners, and legal or illegal aliens to seek redress in federal court for alleged constitutional rights violations by officers acting under color of law. Commonly, acting "under color of law" is interpreted as meaning that the officer acted outside the scope of his or her sworn authority. Such actions taken by an officer may be while on duty or off duty, depending on the "totality of circumstances." Criminal justice personnel are encouraged to review their agencies' policies regarding conduct while off duty.

The mechanics of a § 1983 case and the process for working its way through the court system were provided. Discovery has significant importance to the criminal justice officer being named in the lawsuit. Discovery allows counsel of the plaintiff and the defendant to obtain information relevant to the litigation. Criminal justice practitioners should be prepared to respond to a variety of legal requests that indicate their knowledge or participation in the case. Defendants should also be prepared for a potentially lengthy process that can be disruptive to personal and job-related activities. Officers and supervisors named in a lawsuit are encouraged to meet with their legal counsel early in the proceedings. Moreover, defendants should be prepared to answer numerous questions at depositions or at trial by meeting with their attorney in advance of these proceedings.

During discovery the officer may have to complete interrogatories, give a deposition, and perhaps complete a written affidavit. Section 1983 lawsuits may be filed simultaneously in state and federal courts. Plaintiffs using § 1983 seek to hold state and local criminal justice personnel liable for causing a violation of constitutional rights and may be awarded compensatory and punitive damages, as well as attorney's fees. However, the fact that a § 1983 lawsuit has been filed does not necessarily mean that an officer's conduct was improper.

References

Americans for Effective Law Enforcement (2008). *Prisoner suicide (1973-2007)*. Chicago, IL: *AELE Law Library of Case Summaries*. www.aele.com.

Collins, M. G. (1997). *Section 1983 litigation*. Egan, MN: West Publishing.

del Carmen, R. V. (1991). *Civil liabilities in American policing: a text for law enforcement personnel*. Englewood Cliffs, NJ: Prentice-Hall.

Eisenberg, T., & Schwab, S. (1987). The reality of constitutional tort liability. *Cornell Law Review, 72*, 641-695.

Franklin, C. J. (1993). *The police officer's guide to civil liability*. Springfield, IL: Charles C Thomas.

Gressman, E. (1992). The unhappy history of civil rights legislation. *Michigan Law Review, 50*, 1323-1358.

Kappeler, V. E. (1997). *Critical issues in police civil liability* (2nd ed.). Prospect Heights, IL: Waveland Press, Inc.

O'Leary, W. D. (1989). Custodial suicide: evolving liability considerations. *Psychiatric Quarterly, 60*, 36-71.

Ross, D. L. (2010, March/April). The liability trends of custodial suicides. *American Jails*, 37-47.

Ross, D. L. (2008). Examining the liability trends of custodial suicides in jails, lock-ups, and prisons. Paper presented at the annual meeting of the Academy of Criminal Justice Sciences, Cincinnati, OH.

Vaughn, M. S., & Coomes, L. F. (1995). Police civil liability under section 1983: when do police officers act under color of law? *Journal of Criminal Justice, 23*, 395-415.

5

Defenses to Civil Litigation and Risk Management

OVERVIEW

The procedures for filing civil litigation against criminal justice personnel have been discussed. Plaintiffs may file civil actions either in state court under state tort law or § 1983 and in federal court under § 1983. In this chapter, the legal concepts of immunities and defenses will be presented. The chapter will conclude with a discussion of reducing liability exposure by examining basic principles of risk management and a few examples of best practices. It is critical that criminal justice personnel understand the defenses available, as well as their implications. Defenses in both state and federal court will be addressed, including official immunities and the good faith defense.

Official Immunity

A state cannot be a defendant under § 1983. States are not "persons" within the meaning of § 1983. The doctrine of sovereign immunity associated with the Eleventh Amendment prohibits private individuals from filing a lawsuit in federal court against a state without its consent. States, therefore, cannot be sued in federal or state court under § 1983. This, however, does not mean that an individual cannot sue an appropriate state official in order to compel the official's compliance with constitutional requirements. Moreover, sovereign immunity and statutory prohibitions on suing states apply only to the state itself and not to state agencies. Local governments, such as cities, counties, and other political subdivisions do not possess sovereign immunity. State officers are not protected by sovereign immunity when performing duties in their official capacity.

Sovereign Immunity

The origin of the doctrine of sovereign immunity is debatable. The doctrine has roots in both Roman and English common law and is based on the concept that the "king can do no wrong." The doctrine has shielded the government from being sued by a citizen. It was considered inappropriate for a citizen to file a lawsuit against the one who created and performed duties within the government. The legal effect of this doctrine is to prohibit a citizen from filing a lawsuit against the state or one of its subdivisions for an injury sustained by that person that was caused by the state, unless the state consents to the suit (Robinson, 1992). If consent is granted, it would normally take the form of a statute, defining the type of claim that may be filed.

In order to avoid citizens filing lawsuits against the states, Congress passed the Eleventh Amendment to the Constitution. Ratified in 1795, it states:

The judicial power of the United States shall not be construed to extend to any suit in law or equity, commenced or prosecuted against one of the United States by citizens of another state, or citizens or subjects of any foreign state.

The effect of this amendment was to eliminate the use of federal courts as an entity through which individuals could file claims against the states. Moreover, in *United States v. Clarke* (1834), the Supreme Court held that sovereign immunity also applied to the federal government. The concern was about the prospect of hindering public service and safety should the state be sued by citizens.

The United States Supreme Court ruled in *Hans v. Louisiana* (1890) that in accordance with the Eleventh Amendment and Article III of the Constitution, sovereign immunity of the states barred lawsuits from being brought by individuals against the states in federal court without their consent. Hans attempted to sue the state of Louisiana for not making good on interest payments on state-issued bonds. The Supreme Court held that sovereign immunity prohibited such lawsuits in the federal courts.

The Supreme Court, however, did not conclude that constitutional provisions were unenforceable against states and their officials. In *Ex parte Young* (1908), the Court emphasized that state officials threatening the enforcement or implementation of unconstitutional statutes and actions could be enjoined in federal court without running contrary to the Eleventh Amendment. In *Young*, the attorney general of Minnesota was sued in his official capacity for allegedly enforcing unconstitutional statutes involving railroad rate schedules. The Court stated that Young was an individual threatening to engage in tort-like behavior who could be enjoined without regard to sovereign immunity. The Court found that although it was improper to sue a state's attorney general for monetary damages, it was proper to enjoin his actions because he was acting unconstitutionally. The Court reasoned that the actions of the attorney general were carried out in his official capacity, and such an illegal act could be enjoined.

Types of Immunities

Because citizens are barred from suing the government due to sovereign immunity, the only legal recourse for individuals is to sue the government official responsible for their injury. Government actions are carried out by government employees, and the courts recognizing this have established some protections, as long as employees are acting within the scope of their authority. At issue are what types of immunities or defenses are available to criminal justice personnel and what degree of immunity they possess.

State Tort Law Immunity

State tort law immunity originates in common law principles. Officers are protected from liability if sued under state tort law. Today only a small number of states maintain sovereign immunity under state tort law. Because of the Eleventh Amendment immunity provision, a state cannot be sued under § 1983. Most states have waived state tort immunity. A state official can be sued, however, and he or she can be held liable for his or her actions in office.

Absolute Immunity

Immunity doctrine originates from late nineteenth-century common law. Immunity in civil rights litigation is a defense in damages actions, but not in suits seeking equitable relief. In reality, absolute immunity means no liability at all. A lawsuit would be dismissed by the court.

The United States Supreme Court in *Cleavinger v. Saxner* (1985) reiterated that absolute immunity flows not from rank or title or "location within the Government," but from the nature of the responsibilities of the individual official. The Court denied absolute immunity to a prison disciplinary board that had punished a prisoner for violating prison rules, because they lacked attributes of the judiciary (see Box 5.1).

BOX 5.1 *CLEAVINGER V. SAXNER* (1985)

Prisoners from a Federal Bureau of Prisons facility filed a *Bivens* action against three members of a disciplinary committee who had found them guilty of violating prison regulations. The prisoners claimed that their rights under the Fifth Amendment were violated, and they were awarded $4,500 each in compensatory damages. An appellate court affirmed, and the United States Supreme Court granted certiorari to examine whether the members of the disciplinary committee were entitled to absolute or qualified immunity.

The Court held that the disciplinary committee members possessed qualified immunity. The Court identified the positions that are granted absolute immunity: judges, the president, parole board, and prosecutors. The Court reasoned that past case decisions have demonstrated that immunity analysis rests on functional categories, not on the status of the defendant. Absolute immunity flows not from rank or title or "location within the government," but from the "nature of the responsibilities of the individual official." The Court further held that they did not perceive the committee's function to be a "classic" adjudicatory function.

This case is significant because the Court identifies the criteria that distinguish absolute and qualified immunity. The Court ruled that members of the committee were not professional hearing officers, nor independent like a judge or administrative judge, as they worked for the warden. Thus, they were entitled to only qualified immunity. This decision applies to all public officers and officials, such as police officers, correctional officers, probation and parole officers, juvenile officers, and supervisory and administrative personnel.

In theory, absolute immunity examines the degree of discretion that the official has in policymaking and implementing action. The higher the level of the official, the higher the degree of immunity (*Bradley v. Fisher*, 1872). Thus, absolute immunity is available to judges, legislators, prosecutors, and members of the parole board. Absolute immunity has been reserved primarily for those involved in the judicial process. In *Pierson v. Ray* (1967), the Supreme Court held that absolute immunity shielded a municipal judge who was sued under § 1983 by clergymen who asserted that he had convicted them unconstitutionally for a peaceful protest against racial segregation. The Court emphasized that such immunity was critical to protect the integrity of the judicial process. The Court also held that absolute immunity did not apply to the arresting police officers.

There are three reasons American courts have supported absolute immunity for judicial, legislative, and executive duties: (1) public officials have a duty to the public to make complex decisions about matters pertaining to society, and mistakes are inevitable and it would be unfair to hold them liable; (2) the threat of liability poses a two-pronged consequence—it would discourage decisionmaking and discourage individuals from seeking public office; and (3) defending against lawsuits by public officials would severely deplete their time, energy, and money, rather than performing their official duties (*Harlow v. Fitzgerald*, 1982). The courts, therefore, have continued their support for immunity, not from a legal or historical philosophy, but more from a practical standpoint in operating the government.

Absolute immunity, however, is only a defense to damages actions and not claims for equitable relief (Silver, 2010). Even judges may be successfully sued for injunctive or declaratory relief, and attorney's fees will be available to prevailing plaintiffs (*Supreme Court of Virginia v. Consumers Union of the United States*, 1980). The Supreme Court, however, ruled in *Forrester v. White* (1998) that under the functional approach, a judge's employment decisions are administrative acts that are not protected by absolute judicial immunity.

Generally, law enforcement officers do not possess absolute immunity. At times, police officers may be protected by absolute immunity when they are carrying out court orders, because they are performing an essential judicial function (*Apostol v. Landau*, 1992). In this case, officers who were merely present during the service of a court order, which was valid, were immune, even on a claim of illegal execution. Police officers in *Jacobs v. Dujmovic* (1990), who executed a valid writ based on a landlord's lien, were absolutely immune, regardless of whether the writ was obtained correctly. In *Conner v. Alston* (1988), absolute immunity attached to a parole officer's adjudicative duties involving the parole revocation of a parolee arrested and charged with robbery.

Courts have granted absolute immunity on one occasion to police officers (and perhaps correctional personnel). In *Brisco v. Lahue* (1983), the Supreme Court determined that police officers could not be sued under § 1983 for giving perjured testimony against a defendant in a state criminal trial. Under common law, trial participants, such as judges, prosecutors, and witnesses, were granted absolute immunity for actions related to the trial. Police officers therefore possess absolute immunity when testifying, even though it may constitute perjury. A word of caution is needed here. Should the officer's testimony be false, the prosecutor may criminally charge and prosecute that officer for perjury.

Qualified Immunity

Criminal justice personnel in general are granted a different form of immunity, known as *qualified immunity*. Under this doctrine, governmental officials cannot be held individually liable for federal civil rights violations unless their conduct violated a "clearly established right of which a reasonable person would have known" (Stone & Berger, 2009). Qualified immunity is based on the performance of discretionary acts. Discretionary acts are activities that require deliberation or judgment. This includes numerous tasks, but the courts determine the functions in which officers possess immunity. Discretionary actions, for example, may include the decision to arrest a drunk driver or cite a speeding motorist. In most situations, discretionary actions are applied to an agency administrator, who is responsible for policy decisions and implementation.

Criminal justice personnel are not immune from acts that involve ministerial duties. These duties amount to job functions in which the officer has no discretion. For example, in many jurisdictions, an officer who responds to a domestic violence disturbance and observes evidence of assault does not have the discretion to deliberate about whether an arrest is mandatory. In these types of cases, and in most jurisdictions, the officer must make an arrest.

There are two reasons for granting qualified immunity. First, without such immunity there would be a disincentive for officers to act in areas of constitutional uncertainty, even though their acts may later be judged constitutionally permissible. Fear of boldly crossing an ambiguous legal line would hinder officers in aggressively enforcing the law. Granting qualified immunity encourages reasonable officers to enforce the law vigorously within constitutional boundaries. Of course, acting outside the boundaries of the constitution de-immunizes the officer.

Second, immunity for criminal justice personnel is provided to avoid trial and even discovery in some cases. This is premised on the philosophy that immunity issues should be resolved prior to trial. The problem that frequently emerges, however, is whether an officer's actions were reasonable under the circumstances, or if they violated the plaintiff's constitutional rights. For example, whether a search is reasonable or unreasonable under the circumstances, and a reasonable officer would know that it is unreasonable, may influence the court to allow a jury to determine the issue at trial.

In *Scheuer v. Rhodes* (1974), the issue of immunity for a state governor and ultimately, high-level executives, emerged. The issue arose from Ohio's governor dispatching the Ohio National Guard onto the campus of Kent State University during student protests and disturbances regarding the United States' role in the Vietnam conflict. Soldiers opened fire and killed four unarmed students. The estates of the deceased students filed a lawsuit against the governor and he claimed absolute immunity from the lawsuit. The Supreme Court had previously opined that the *Young* decision allowed the state to invoke its sovereign immunity protection. But in *Scheuer* the Court concluded that neither sovereign immunity nor absolute immunity applied and that the governor and high-level executives could claim only qualified immunity. The Court reasoned that qualified immunity would apply according to the scope of the discretion exercised, the responsibility of the office, and the circumstances as they reasonably appeared at the time of the action in question.

A government official performing discretionary functions is entitled to qualified immunity in his or her individual capacity if his or her conduct does not violate constitutional standards in light of clearly established law at the time of the alleged violation. Qualified immunity is a government official's entitlement to not stand trial or face the other burdens of litigation as long as his or her conduct conforms to the law at the time. Implicit in the doctrine of qualified immunity is the recognition that police and correction officers, acting reasonably, may err (*Scheuer v. Rhodes*, 1974).

After *Scheuer*, the United States Supreme Court concluded in *Procunier v. Navarette* (1978) that state prison officials who were sued under § 1983 for alleged unconstitutional interference with a prisoner's mail could assert the qualified immunity defense. Prison officials may prevail on such a defense unless they violate "clearly established statutory or constitutional rights of which a reasonable person would have known."

The precedent-setting case that gives qualified immunity to criminal justice personnel is *Harlow v. Fitzgerald* (1982). The Supreme Court determined that the sole inquiry into whether an officer would be entitled to qualified immunity is whether the officer knew or should have known that he was violating the constitutional rights of the plaintiff (Box 5.2).

BOX 5.2 *HARLOW V. FITZGERALD* (1982)

Senior aides to President Nixon—Harlow and Butterfield—were accused of violating Fitzgerald's constitutional rights by having him dismissed from the Air Force. Fitzgerald asserted that they conspired to remove him from his post in retaliation for his blowing the whistle on purchasing practices within the Air Force. The lower court and the appellate court denied summary judgment to the two aides and they appealed. The United States Supreme Court granted certiorari to examine the issue of the type of immunity the two aides may possess as advisors to the president when acting in their official capacity.

The Court ruled that the two aides performed discretionary functions and when governmental officials perform such actions they are entitled to qualified immunity as long as their conduct did not violate an individual's constitutional rights.

This case is significant because it established new guidelines for determining how to assert a defense for "acting in good faith." To assert a good faith defense, the defendants must show that they were acting in accordance with the law at the time of their actions, based on training and experience. Acting in good faith is an affirmative defense and must be firmly supported by the defendant by showing that he or she did not violate constitutional rights of which a reasonable person would have known. The decision applies to § 1983 civil lawsuits and pertains to all criminal justice officials, such as police officers, correctional/detention officers, probation/parole officers, juvenile officers, and supervisors and administrators. The Court stated:

> . . . we conclude today that bare allegations of malice should not suffice . . . We, therefore, hold that government officials performing discretionary functions generally are shielded from liability for civil damages insofar as their conduct does not violate clearly established statutory or constitutional rights of which a reasonable person would have known.

With this decision, qualified immunity is provided to protect public officers in decisions in which the parameters of a person's constitutional rights are unclear. This may occur when: (1) a decision is made, and it is not clearly established that a constitutional right exists; or (2) the right was clearly established but the officer could not reasonably know that this decision or conduct was unlawful, thereby violating the constitutional rights of the plaintiff. Based on these two fundamental issues, the court must determine whether the officer is immune from civil liability. If the court concludes that the law was not clearly established and that the officer acted reasonably, the officer would be granted immunity.

Determining the reasonableness of an officer's actions can be problematic. This issue was answered in *Anderson v. Creighton* (1987). In *Anderson*, police officers and a Federal Bureau of Investigation agent conducted a warrantless search of the plaintiff's house. Although mistaken, the officers believed that a bank robbery suspect was hiding in the home. The officers entered the home with firearms drawn, assaulted the plaintiff's daughter, and knocked the plaintiff to the ground. The plaintiff was arrested and detained overnight in jail, although no charges were filed. The plaintiff filed suit and the FBI agent filed a motion for summary judgment based on probable cause to enter the home. The lower court granted summary judgment, but on appeal, the Court of Appeals reversed, holding that Anderson was not eligible for summary judgment. The Supreme Court reversed the appellate court's decision and held that Anderson was entitled to qualified immunity. In a 6-to-3 decision, the Court held that the principles of qualified immunity require that Anderson be permitted to argue that he is entitled to summary judgment if in light of the clearly established principles governing warrantless searches, he could, as a matter of law, reasonably have believed that the search of the Creightons' home was lawful. It should first be determined whether the alleged actions are actions that a reasonable officer could have believed lawful. If they are, then dismissal prior to discovery is required. If they are not, and if the actions Anderson claims he took are different from those alleged and are not reasonable, then limited discovery may be necessary.

The *Anderson* decision is important because it underscored the test of the "reasonable" officer developed in *Malley v. Briggs* (1986). In *Malley*, the plaintiff claimed in his § 1983 suit that his constitutional rights were violated when a state trooper obtained a warrant to arrest him based on an intercepted phone conversation that was part of a drug investigation. The charges were dropped and the plaintiff sued for unlawful arrest. The trooper claimed that he was entitled to absolute immunity. The Court rejected this defense, determining that the officer was entitled to qualified immunity. The Court examined whether a reasonable officer could believe entry into the home was justified by assessing the officer's actions in accordance with "objective reasonableness," and took into account the specifics of the law and the facts known to the officer. The standard used by the courts is "whether a reasonably well-trained officer in the same position would have known that his affidavit failed to establish probable cause and that he should not have applied for the warrant." When an arrest warrant lacks probable cause, liability is proper in accordance with the *Harlow* decision.

The principle of "reasonableness" is illustrated in *Tarantino v. Baker* (1987). Baker, a detective in a North Carolina sheriff's department, received an anonymous tip that Tarantino was growing marijuana in the general store. Baker went to the store at night and found a padlock on the front door and the windows covered. He went to the back door and knocked and did not receive a response. Baker shined his flashlight into a crack of the door, based on the "plain view doctrine," and observed marijuana plants inside the store. Tarantino was later arrested. At trial, the evidence was suppressed, as the court determined that Baker had exceeded the scope of a permissible "plain view" search. Tarantino filed a lawsuit claiming that his Fourth Amendment rights had been violated. The Fourth Circuit Court of Appeals dismissed the lawsuit, finding that a reasonable officer in Baker's situation would not know that his conduct violated the plain view rule. From this decision, it appears that when an officer's actions are close to going over the constitutional line, the courts will not hinder an officer from performing his or her duties.

The United States Supreme Court further addressed the issue of qualified immunity for police officers in *Saucier v. Katz* (2001). Katz was protesting a speech of then-Vice President Al Gore at a military base. He was approaching the podium when two military police officers grabbed him and escorted him away and into a van. Katz complained that the officers used excessive force, although he sustained no injuries. He filed a civil rights claim, asserting that his Fourth Amendment rights had been violated. The officers asserted a defense of qualified immunity. The U.S. District Court for the Northern District of California granted summary judgment, but on appeal the Ninth Circuit Court of Appeals denied qualified immunity for the officers. The Ninth Circuit held that qualified immunity and a constitutional violation issue should be treated as one issue before the trier of fact. The Supreme Court granted certiorari to address the requisite analysis in determining qualified immunity in situations involving excessive force and reversed the appellate court's holding.

The Supreme Court re-emphasized that the doctrine of qualified immunity protects government officials performing discretionary functions from liability as long as their conduct does not violate the constitutional rights of another. The Court restated that qualified immunity is a defense, but added that a ruling for qualified immunity requires an analysis not susceptible of fusion with the question of whether unreasonable force was used in making an arrest. Issues centering on qualified immunity must be taken in proper sequence and based on the merits of each case.

The question of the appropriateness of qualified immunity is whether a reasonable officer understood his powers and responsibilities to be, when he acted, under clearly established standards. To address this question, the Supreme Court in *Saucier* established a two-part test for determining whether qualified immunity applies. First, in the initial inquiry, the court must consider the "threshold question": taken in the light most favorable to the party asserting the injury, do the facts alleged show that the officer's conduct violated a constitutional right? If the facts as alleged by the plaintiff fail to establish a violation, then immunity applies. On the other hand, if the alleged facts sufficiently demonstrate a constitutional violation, the court must determine whether the right was clearly established. In making this determination, the court must assess whether the right claimed must be more than a merely a generalized right, it must be clearly established in a particularized sense so that a reasonable official in the defendant's position knows that his or her actions violate that right. If the court determines that these two components are met in a motion for summary judgment, the court will grant such a motion. If, however, the court finds questions regarding these two components, the court will deny the motion and the case may proceed to trial or may be settled out of court.

This decision further supported the Supreme Court's decision in *Anderson* (1987). The Court concluded that the officers' conduct did not violate Katz's constitutional rights, because they only used force to protect the Vice President's safety and were entitled to qualified immunity.

While the *Saucier* case sheds additional light on the legal principle of qualified immunity and requires a two-part test to determine how a court will assess an assertion, its application is often problematic and complicated. In an effort to further apply the tenets of *Saucier* and to provide further elaboration on what constitutes qualified immunity, the United States Supreme Court granted certiorari to review the facts in *Brosseau v. Haugen* (2004). Responding to a 911 call of two men fighting, officer Brosseau approached the two men. The officer's arrival caused a momentary distraction and Haugen attempted to flee the area. Brosseau requested backup and Haugen hid himself in the neighborhood. Back-up officers responded with a canine to help track Haugen. Brosseau also learned that Haugen was a suspected felon with a no-bail warrant out for his arrest. The man that Haugen was fighting and a third man were instructed by officer Brosseau to stay in a pickup truck parked in the driveway. Haugen's girl-friend, along with her three-old daughter, was also on the scene and the officers instructed her to remain in her car.

An officer who was looking for Haugen down the street radioed that a neighbor had seen Haugen in her backyard. As Brosseau approached the area, Haugen quickly appeared and ran toward the parked vehicles in a driveway. Brosseau chased Haugen, and Haugen jumped into a Jeep parked in the driveway. Believing that Haugen was going to retrieve a weapon, Brosseau unholstered her weapon, pointed it at him, and ordered him to get out of the vehicle. Haugen ignored her commands and started the vehicle. Brosseau tapped on the window with her gun several times and the window shattered. Brosseau attempted to grab the keys and struck Haugen on the head with her gun. Haugen placed the car in gear and began to move. Brosseau jumped back and to the left, and fearing for her safety and the safety of other officers, and citizens in the area, fired one shot through the rear of the driver's side window, hitting Haugen in the back.

Haugen proceeded down the street in the Jeep and after about a half a block realized that he had been shot and stopped the vehicle. He suffered a collapsed lung and was airlifted to a hospital. He survived the shooting and subsequently pleaded guilty to the felony of "eluding." He later filed a § 1983 action, claiming that officer Brosseau used excessive force. The District Court granted summary judgment to Brosseau after finding she was entitled to qualified immunity. Haugen appealed and the Ninth Circuit Court of Appeals reversed, holding that Brosseau had violated Haugen's Fourth Amendment right to be free from excessive force and that the right violated was clearly established and thus Brosseau was not entitled to qualified immunity. The United States Supreme Court reviewed the case to further assess the application of qualified immunity and not the issue of excessive force per se.

The Court reversed the appellate court's decision, finding that Brosseau's actions were reasonable within the "backdrop of the established law at the time of the conduct." If the law at the time did not clearly establish that the officer's conduct would violate the Constitution, the officer should not be subject to liability or, indeed, even the burdens of litigation. The inquiry must focus on the "specific context of the case, not as a broad general proposition."

In supporting his argument in opposition to qualified immunity, the plaintiff cited *Tennessee v. Garner* (1985), *Graham v. Connor* (1989), and several lower court decisions. While the Court acknowledged the standard for using reasonable force in their *Graham* decision, the Court noted that liability did not attach in any of the lower court cases, finding that, like Brosseau, the litigated officers had probable cause to believe deadly force was justified. The Court also noted that the "cases" cited by the plaintiff in support of his opposition to qualified immunity by no means clearly established that Brosseau's conduct violated the Fourth Amendment.

Brosseau is instructive as it further directs a lower court in determining the application of qualified immunity. The Court underscored the two-part test established in *Saucier* by noting that qualified immunity operates "to protect officers from liability." If an officer had fair notice that his or her conduct was unlawful and this was clearly established through case decisions, that conduct must be viewed within the context of the law and the facts and circumstances that faced the officer at the time of the conduct. If the law is not clearly established at the time of the officer's conduct, the officer should not be subject to liability. Thus, qualified immunity would be granted to the defendant officer or agency. The Court noted that while *Garner* and *Graham* provide standards of review when assessing claims of excessive force, the standard is general and may apply to varying circumstances. According to the Court, the shooting in the *Brosseau* case did not "clearly" underscore established law of shooting a "fleeing suspect in a vehicle" that would preclude granting qualified immunity. The Court held that the shooting is far from the obvious one where *Graham* and *Garner* offer a basis for such a decision. Because the plaintiff could only show a "handful" of cases relevant to the shooting, the Court held that the cases by no means "clearly established" that Brosseau's conduct violated Haugen's Fourth Amendment rights.

The United States Supreme Court reexamined the qualified immunity doctrine in their assessment in *Pearson et al. v. Callahan* (2009). After Pearson's conviction was overturned by the Utah Court of Appeals for possession and distribution of drugs, which he sold to an undercover informant in his house, he brought a § 1983 allegation asserting that his Fourth Amendment rights had been violated by supervising officers of the informant. The officers did not obtain a search warrant, but Pearson voluntarily admitted the informant into his house. The federal district court granted qualified immunity to the officers under the "consent-once-removed" doctrine, which allows a warrantless police entry into a home when consent to enter has already been granted. The court concluded that the officers were entitled to qualified immunity because they reasonably believed that the doctrine authorized their conduct.

Adhering to the procedure established in the *Saucier* decision (2001), the Tenth Circuit Court of Appeals denied qualified immunity for the officers, holding that the consent-once-removed doctrine was inappropriately applied given the facts of the incident. The court further held that the officer's conduct was unlawful because they had not first obtained a warrant, the respondent had not consented to their entry, and any entry by an informant did not apply to the officers.

The Court granted certiorari to address whether *Saucier* should be overruled in light of widespread criticisms. In a unanimous vote by the Court, Justice Alito delivered the opinion. The Court ruled that *stare decisis* does not preclude them from determining whether the *Saucier* procedure should be modified or abandoned. Re-examining a precedent is appropriate where a departure would not upset past decisions. In reviewing the *Saucier* protocols the Court stated that they were beneficial but should not be regarded as mandatory in all cases. The Court determined that the *Saucier* protocols frequently hamstring judicial resources and make it more difficult for a party to appeal a decision. The Court modified its past decision and authorized more flexibility for judges in the lower courts to determine the facts of each case and to determine the order of decisionmaking that will best facilitate the fair and efficient disposition of each case. The Court's decision does not prevent lower courts from still applying *Saucier*; rather, it recognizes that they should have discretion to decide whether the procedure is worthwhile in a particular case.

Finally, the Court held that the officers were entitled to qualified immunity because it was not clearly established at the time of the search that their conduct was unconstitutional. The Court maintained that the consent-once-removed doctrine had been accepted by two state supreme courts and three federal appellate courts and none of the courts had issued a contrary decision.

Good Faith Defense

The good faith defense is not authorized in state tort claims and is commonly used in civil liability lawsuits by defendant officers. The defense can be asserted by public officials, but not by government agencies, if the plaintiff can show that the injury can be linked to a policy or custom.

Good faith is an affirmative defense based on a subjective standard that is closely tied to the trial court's discretionary powers. The term has been mistakenly referred to as acting without intent to do wrong, or a lack of evil intention on the part of the officer. More precisely, asserting a good faith defense has nothing to do with the intentions of the officer, but asserts the actions of an officer to be "acting in good faith" in accordance with the law at the time of the incident. Linked to the *Harlow* decision, the standard that emerges is whether the officer, at the time the act was committed, violated a clearly established statutory right of which a reasonable person would have known. There are several factors the court will consider when scrutinizing the officer's actions: (1) whether the officer's actions were based on departmental policy and regulations; (2) whether the officer was acting pursuant to a valid law that was later invalidated by a court; (3) whether the officer was acting on the orders of a supervisor and believed the order to be valid; and (4) whether the officer was acting on the advice of legal counsel and believed the advice was valid (del Carmen, 1995).

The plaintiff bears the burden of pleading a good faith defense in § 1983 lawsuits (*Gomez v. Toledo*, 1980). Thus, the plaintiff need not assert in the complaint that the officer acted in bad faith. All the plaintiff needs to prove is that the injury resulted from a violation of constitutional rights or illegal acts. To establish this, the defendant officer must show that he was acting in good faith at the time. To put it differently, the officer must show that he acted in the reasonable good faith belief that the action taken was legal. It becomes imperative that police administrators keep their officers apprised of changes in the law and update their policies and regulations in accordance with these changes.

Aczel v. Labonia (2004) provides an example of how the court determines whether an officer's conduct merits qualified immunity through invoking a good faith defense. Acting on what they believed was probable cause, officers of Danbury, Connecticut, arrested Aczel for allegedly sexually assaulting female tenants in Aczel's apartment building. A witness observed the officers strike him in the head after he was handcuffed. The witness further stated that the officers caused Aczel to fall to the ground and heard him screaming afterward, although he did not personally observe the officers push him to the ground. The witness took a better position and observed Aczel on the ground in the fetal position, heard the officers yell at him to stop resisting, although he was just lying on the ground. He further observed the officers pepper-spray Aczel.

Aczel filed a § 1983 lawsuit and the lower court concluded that there were questions of fact that needed to be determined before the officers were entitled to qualified immunity. The officers appealed and the appellate court denied their motion for qualified immunity. The court reasoned that the there were too many discrepancies between their story and the witnesses' and Aczel's accounts to grant qualified immunity. The court reasoned that the law was clearly established on what constitutes proper conduct when making an arrest. Further, the court ruled that the officers gave conflicting accounts as to who initiated the use of force, how much force was used, and whether Aczel was actually reaching for one of the officers' weapons. Moreover, the court noted that the officers on appeal did not show that they were acting in good faith as they failed to argue any independent reason why they should be entitled to qualified immunity. It is not enough to "merely" assert that the officers were acting in good faith, there must be supportive documentation that accompanies such an assertion.

Probable Cause and Qualified Immunity

This is a narrow defense arising out of alleged illegal searches and seizures, false arrests, and false imprisonment. It is available to officers in both state tort actions and § 1983 litigation asserting that their actions were taken in good faith in accordance with the law at the time. Plaintiffs claiming that officers violated their Fourth Amendment rights by conducting an illegal search or seizure must show that the officer lacked probable cause. Immunity can be given to the officer if he or she can show that he or she had probable cause at the time.

Recall that in *Malley* the Supreme Court held that immunity would be denied where no reasonable officer could have believed that he or she had probable cause to obtain a warrant. Defendants seeking immunity based on probable cause have followed the Supreme Court's decision in *Anderson* rather than *Malley*. In *Gooden v. Howard County, Maryland* (1992), officers were granted immunity when they investigated screaming coming from an apartment. The officers removed the plaintiff, who admitted that she had made a loud noise in order to receive a psychiatric consultation. Qualified immunity applied because the investigation was objectively reasonable. In *Chew v. Gates* (1990), using a dog to search, despite the fact that it bit the suspect, did not violate clearly established law. The action was objectively reasonable because the crime was serious and the officer's safety was in peril.

Limits to qualified immunity involving a search without probable cause arose in *Schwab v. Wood* (1991). Attempting to obtain identification although he observed no criminal activity, an officer met verbal resistance and profanity. Reasonable suspicion was absent and the subsequent search and arrest were illegal. The plaintiff was acquitted of the charge of resisting detention. The plaintiff was granted summary judgment because "no reasonable jury could determine that a reasonably well-trained officer would believe that his actions were lawful under the circumstances."

Searches under a warrant are often upheld in accordance with a good faith defense. Section 1983 lawsuits based on deficiencies in the warrant itself rarely prevail. *United States v. Cancelmo* (1995) provided a close question as to probable cause. Officers drew up a drug search warrant based on conversations interpreted as using "coded" drug language and other conjectural circumstances. One person was a known drug dealer who frequently used coded language. Based on this information, a warrant was obtained and a reliable informant purchased cocaine at the plaintiff's house. Additional drugs found at the scene were held to justify a search of the entire residence. The Supreme Court upheld the search and stated that "hindsight, always perfect, does not render a search reasonable or unreasonable." Officers' failure to discover drugs was irrelevant.

The United States Supreme Court further addressed qualified immunity and the issue of probable cause in *Groh v. Ramirez* (2004). Groh, an agent of the Bureau of Alcohol, Tobacco, and Firearms, applied for a warrant to search Ramirez's ranch, where it was reported by an informant that there was a stockpile of weapons on the ranch, including automatic weapons, grenades, a grenade launcher, and a rocket launcher. Groh applied for a warrant to a magistrate judge. In an affidavit supporting the application, Groh listed the weapons to be searched on the ranch and the court found probable cause for the search and signed the warrant. The application described the objects and items to be searched and seized, but the warrant did not. Groh was required to report those items but he failed to provide a description of the ranch. Neither the application nor the affidavit was attached to the warrant and the warrant did not incorporate either of those documents by reference.

Groh and other agents conducted the search at the ranch the next day. Ramirez was absent from the home but his wife and children were there. Groh informed Ramirez's wife that he had a warrant to search the premises and also spoke to Ramirez on the phone, informing him that he was going search his residence. The search was not fruitful and Groh left a copy of the warrant with Ramirez's wife, although he did not give her a copy of the application or affidavit. Later the police faxed a copy of the application to Ramirez's attorney. Ramirez sued Groh and the other officers, claiming that they had violated his Fourth Amendment rights. The trial court found in favor of Groh, holding that the warrant was valid and that even if it was invalid, he was entitled to qualified immunity. Ramirez appealed the decision and the appellate court reversed the decision. Groh appealed to the United States Supreme Court to address the issue of qualified immunity.

Groh argued that although the warrant lacked the requisite information, the search was reasonable because it did not exceed the scope contemplated in the warrant application. However, because the particular items described in the application were not included in the warrant, there was no written assurance the magistrate had actually found probable cause to search for and seize every item listed on the application. The Court found that the warrant was invalid because it did not describe with specificity the items to be seized. The warrant was deficient and Ramirez had been denied information that outlined the scope of the search.

The Court held that, under the Fourth Amendment, absent certain exigent circumstances (which did not apply in the present case), the police had to obtain a warrant before searching a person's home, and the warrant had to be unambiguous. The Court ruled that any reasonable officer would have known that the warrant to search the ranch was invalid. The Fourth Amendment provides for the right to be free from unreasonable searches and seizures and the Court regarded the search as "warrantless."

Groh had a duty to ensure that the warrant was properly construed. The duty was to ensure that the warrant conformed to the constitutional requirements, not to simply proofread the document. The Court denied qualified immunity to Groh, stating that such immunity applied when a reasonable officer could have believed the warrant plainly complied with the Fourth Amendment's particularity requirement. The existence of the ATF's policy on invalid warrants proved to be detrimental to Groh. The Court stated that he should have known that he could not execute a patently defective warrant. Even a cursory review would have revealed a glaring deficiency that any reasonable police officer would have known was unconstitutional. A law enforcement officer had no right to qualified immunity if it would have been clear to a reasonable officer that his conduct was unlawful.

Qualified immunity applies to the discretionary functions of officers and is available on an individual basis. It is an affirmative defense made by an officer through his or her counsel. As these cases show, the court will make its decisions on a case-by-case basis. The key to being awarded qualified immunity includes being proactive prior to performing the duties of a police or correctional officer. When asserting a claim of qualified immunity, the officer must show that he or she was following the established law at the time of the incident. This suggests that officers actually are knowledgeable about state and constitutional law. Officers must show that their actions were reasonable under the circumstances and that a reasonably trained officer would know that the conduct was constitutional or unconstitutional, depending on the conduct. These factors should be addressed in agency policy and procedures, as demonstrated in the *Groh* decision. Officers need to be trained on a regular basis and evaluated in the performance of their duties to ensure they are complying with policy and that their conduct conforms to constitutional mandates. When performing their sworn duties, officers should clearly and completely document their actions and reasons for acting in a particular manner. Adhering to these few elements will assist in being granted qualified immunity with more success.

Principles for granting qualified immunity to police officers were further described by the United States Supreme Court in *Messerschmidt v. Millender* (2012). Shelly Kelly reported to the police that her boyfriend, Jerry Bowen, assaulted her. Kelly decided to end a romantic relationship with Bowen and move out of her apartment. Kelly had been assaulted by Bowen previously and he had an extensive criminal history and associations with a local gang. Kelly requested police protection during the move and several officers responded while she gathered her belongings but they had to leave to respond to an emergency call. Bowen suddenly appeared after the police left, grabbed Kelly, screamed at her never to call the police on him, attempted to throw her over a second floor railing but Kelly resisted. Kelly managed to free herself from Bowen and ran to her car. Bowen was able to retrieve a sawed-off shotgun and ran in front of Kelly's car and threatened to kill her if she left. Kelly accelerated the car, Bowen fired the shotgun five times, which blew out the tires of the vehicle, but Kelly managed to escape. Kelly reported the assault to the police, provided a photo of him, and advised the police that he was active member of the Mona Park Crips, a local street gang.

Detective Messerschmidt interviewed Kelly and she provided information about the assault, provided information about Bowen's association with the gang, informed him that Bowen may be residing at his foster mother's house (Millender), and provided the address. Messerschmidt performed a background check on Bowen and found that he had been arrested 31 times; nine of these arrests were for firearms-related offenses, six for violent crimes, including three arrests for assault with a deadly weapon. Further, the background check revealed that Bowen had ties to two local gangs and confirmed his residence at Millender's address.

Detective Messerschmidt prepared two search warrants to search the Millender residence. The first affidavit detailed detective Messerschmidt's extensive law enforcement experience, his previous training, his experience on a "specialized unit" investigation of gang-related crimes and behaviors, and his specialized training in the field of gang-related crimes and shootings. The second affidavit, integrated with the first, described the components of probable cause that supported Messerschmidt's belief to authorize the search. The second affidavit specified the details of the search at the Millender's residence, descriptions of Bowen's assault on Kelly, and the background check information that was performed on Bowen; that Bowen had gang ties and an extensive criminal arrest history; and that the search included weapons that were detailed in the warrant. The affidavit also detailed the concern for the safety of the community based on Bowen's previous criminal history and possessions of firearms, and requested a nighttime search. Prior to submitting the affidavit, Messerschmidt had the documents reviewed by his sergeant, his lieutenant, and the assistant district attorney, who approved it. The magistrate authorized the search warrant and the nighttime search.

The warrants were served two days later by Messerschmidt and members of the Emergency Response Team. Mrs. Millender, in her seventies, met the officers at the door with her grandson and daughter. Bowen was not at the residence. The search resulted in confiscation of Millender's shotgun, a California Social Security Services letter addressed to Bowen, and a box of 45-caliber ammunition. Millender legally possessed the shotgun. Bowen was arrested two weeks later when he was found hiding under a bed in a motel room.

Millender filed a § 1983 lawsuit claiming that the search was overbroad by requesting to search for all weapons, that the incident stemmed from a domestic violence dispute, that the search lacked probable cause, that Bowen was suspected of possessing a sawed-off shotgun, and that Millender had nothing to do with the incident. The lower district federal court found that the warrant was valid, Messerschmidt's conduct was reasonable, and that there was probable cause to believe that Bowen was at the residence, supporting a nighttime search. Millender appealed and the appellate court for the Ninth Circuit agreed with Millender that Messerschmidt lacked probable cause for the search warrant and that he was not entitled to "qualified immunity" because any officer would have known that probable cause did not exist beyond the gun used in the assault and that there was no evidence linking the domestic violence investigation with the search. The circuit court remanded the case back to the lower court with new instructions and Messerschmidt appealed to the United States Supreme Court and they granted certiorari.

The Court addressed the issue of whether a police officer is entitled to qualified immunity when he or she obtains a valid warrant to search for firearms, firearm-related materials, and gang-related items in the residence of a gang member and felon who had threatened to kill his girlfriend and fired a sawed-off shotgun. They ruled in favor of Messerschmidt and overturned the Ninth Circuit. Chief Justice Roberts wrote the opinion of the Court. In a five-to-four decision (the other Justices were Scalia, Kennedy, Thomas, Alito, and Breyer, who wrote a short concurrence), the Court held that the officers were entitled to qualified immunity as to both the firearms and gang-related materials sought in the warrant. Regarding the former, Justice Roberts rejected the notion that the officers were limited to seeking only the sawed-off shotgun because it was known to be the one used in the crime. Given all the facts set out in the warrant—including Bowen's gang membership and his attempted murder in public of someone because she had called the police on him—an officer would not be unreasonable in concluding that the sawed-off shotgun was not the only firearm Bowen owned. Moreover, the fact that California law allows a warrant to be issued for items possessed with the intent to commit a public offense further supported the search for all firearms and firearm-related materials. The Court's conclusion regarding the firearms was joined by seven Justices, with only Justices Sotomayor and Ginsburg dissenting.

The Court further held that the officers were entitled to immunity for the search for gang-related material, though on that point Justice Kagan parted ways and joined the other two dissenters. Chief Justice Roberts first rejected the notion that the officers were unreasonable in believing that Bowen's gang membership had anything to do with the crime, dismissing the dissenters' reliance on the officers' later deposition testimony as both subjective and beyond the scope of the affidavit and warrant. The Court found compelling the fact that the officers sought and obtained approval from a police superior and deputy district attorney, and that a magistrate had approved the warrant. The Court criticized the Ninth Circuit's refusal to credit that conduct, and the lower court's imposition on the officers of an independent duty to ensure at least a colorable basis for probable cause, as a misreading of *Malley*.

The Court distinguished this case from their decision in *Groh v. Ramirez* (2004), in which a "nonsensical" warrant was so plainly deficient that even a cursory reading would have shown that it failed the Fourth Amendment's particularity requirement, rendering the cases "not remotely similar." Summarizing the issue as to whether the magistrate here so obviously erred in approving the warrant that the officers should have recognized the error, Chief Justice Roberts affirmed that such situations are "rare," and that this was not one of them. The Court concluded that a reasonable officer could have believed that additional guns as well as gang-related material would be found at the location and that an objectively reasonable officer may conclude that it was objectively reasonable to search for such items based on the information provided.

The Court's decision in *Messerschmidt* reveals several core principles in the criminal and civil law. First, the Court has established a series of eight cases in which the fundamental principles and components of qualified immunity are described that can be granted to criminal justice personnel. An officer who makes a "reasonable mistake in judgment" will be protected from liability compared to the officer who knowingly violates the law. Second, the Court reminds officers that the Fourth Amendment requires probable cause based on articulable rationale in order to obtain a legitimate search warrant. Officers who fully document their belief and adhere to their training, experience, and document this in their affidavit, will with a high probability ensure that a magistrate will authorize the warrant. Third, and simultaneously, officers will ensure that they are protected from liability and will subsequently enhance the probability that a court will grant them qualified immunity from civil liability should a plaintiff file a lawsuit when they follow the contours of legal precedents.

Other Strategies for Reducing the Risk of Civil Liability

Criminal justice personnel have been successful in asserting qualified immunity as a defense in civil lawsuits. Invoking qualified immunity is, however, a "reactive" approach. The focus of criminal justice administrators and officers alike in the future should be toward developing proactive strategies and protection from lawsuits in order to reduce their frequency. Lawsuits may never be totally eliminated. However, understanding and implementing key elements of risk management and risk control can help to design a system to control some of the risk and protect the agency and its personnel.

What Is Risk Management?

Methods for managing risks associated with law enforcement functions are a concern not only for insurance carriers. Risk management is a process that also includes basic managerial functions: planning, organizing, and leading, as well as controlling agency losses at a reasonable cost. It uses accepted managerial techniques in order to preserve the assets of an organization or entity (Ashley & Pearson, 1993; Michigan Municipality Risk Management Authority, 2011; Narvaez, 2011) and helps to control risk while managing costs. Risk management is a process of identifying and analyzing potential hazards, exposures, and undesirable events and carrying out decisions that minimize, control, or eliminate their effects on an organization.

The risk management process is comprised of two important elements. Risk financing involves varying methods from which an agency can choose to pay for potential losses. This element is most likely beyond the control of agency administrators and left to government officials. The second area, risk control, is within the influence of administrators, supervisors, trainers, and agency personnel. It is both a managerial and line-level function, because it seeks to promote a proactive approach to efficient organizational operations and to decrease risk exposure. Risk control involves several key factors: (1) identifying potential risk exposures of the organization; (2) examining the alternatives available to either eliminating potential risks or mitigating the effects of those that cannot be eliminated; (3) selecting the best alternative or combination of alternatives to deal with each exposure; (4) implementing the chosen techniques; and (5) monitoring the process in order to alter or improve the program based on observed results. These factors can serve as multiple layers of protection.

Integrating these factors into an agency's operating system can reduce the risk of future litigation. They also assist in developing a systematic framework of protection against liability. Risk management is controlling the risks inherent in performing criminal justice agency functions, which produces a net outcome of managing liability. This is a full-time, ongoing responsibility of criminal justice administrators as well as line personnel, and not a one-time task.

Managing liability can be problematic, as it requires assessing, planning, forecasting, and monitoring. Managing and controlling risk can be associated with hurricane preparation, which has taken on new, sophisticated measures in recent years. States along the Gulf of Mexico and the Atlantic coast have experienced their share of destructive hurricanes. Hurricanes Andrew (1993), Floyd (1999), and Katrina (2005) wreaked havoc, costing billions in property damage and taking numerous lives. As a result, the National Weather Service has developed more sophisticated technology with which to forecast and warn of future hurricanes. However, despite new technology, it is still difficult to predict with pinpoint accuracy how many hurricanes may occur in a season and where they may strike. Yet this weather phenomenon is still somewhat predictable, as history reveals that they are likely to occur with some frequency between June and November. Therefore, based on this assessment, as well as forecasting, the weather service and residents living in these states must take proactive steps to prepare for the risk of a hurricane, knowing that a hurricane is likely to occur during this period.

Managing the risk of liability in a criminal justice agency is similar to predicting the occurrence of a hurricane. It is obvious that civil lawsuits are likely to be filed against criminal justice personnel for a variety of reasons, but it is difficult to predict with certainty. Because the risk of liability is foreseeable, personnel must take a proactive approach in assessing, forecasting, monitoring and, to the extent possible, controlling the degree of risk associated with the tasks and functions that are most likely to give rise to potential lawsuits. Like hurricanes, not all lawsuits can be predicted or eliminated. Yet criminal justice agencies must be prepared to defend against such risks. It requires administrative and line-level personnel to work together to implement risk-control practices. These practices should not be another fleeting "administrative program." Risk management requires building a system of protections that can reduce the number of lawsuits and more successfully defend those that will be filed.

Elements of Managing Risk

Job Assessment

The first layer of protection is to conduct a job assessment. Prior to working on reducing or controlling risks, a thorough assessment of job functions should be performed. A job task analysis is a formal study of the job and examines the functions of line officers and supervisors. The job assessment will identify the numerous tasks that personnel perform. Once the tasks are identified, they should be examined further in terms of their frequency of occurrence and "severity," or criticality (see Figure 5.1).

The National Weather Service predicts hurricanes based on past occurrences and present climatic conditions. Rating job tasks by their frequency and severity helps to evaluate past and

Job Task Assessment
(frequency, severity, and foreseeability)

↓

Job Descriptions ⟶ (performance evaluations)

↓

Risk Control Program

↓

Policy Development/Revision

↓

Risk Reduction Strategies
(risk avoidance, loss prevention, loss reduction,
resource segregation, and risk transfer)

↓

Training of Employees

↓

Field Implementation
(monitoring, compliance, and evaluation)

↓

Net Benefits
(risk reduction, efficient operations, improved performance,
administrative function, and liability defense)

FIGURE 5.1 Risk Management in Criminal Justice Agencies.

present dimensions of the job in order to respond to future job tasks. By reviewing tasks in this fashion, it will become evident which functions are performed frequently and which tasks are severe or critical in nature.

Frequency can predict severity/criticality, and an inverse relationship usually exists between the two. Incidents that occur more frequently tend to be less severe in nature. Conversely, the most severe incidents occur with less frequency. Another important element to consider is that of foreseeability. A question to ask while assessing the frequency and severity/criticality of a task is "What is the foreseeability or likelihood of the officer performing the task as it relates to the frequency and severity of the task?" If the task or incident is foreseeable, occurs with some frequency, and is highly critical, then the task/incident should be addressed by a risk management program. For example, it is foreseeable that an officer may have to use his or her firearm in the line of duty. The severity or criticality of a police officer firing his or her duty weapon is extremely high, but the frequency of this occurring is generally low. Officers may go through their whole career without ever firing their weapon in the line of duty; yet due to the severity/criticality of firing a weapon, they must be fully prepared to know when to use lethal force, as well as being competent in using the firearm. Further, the frequency of riots occurring within a correctional institution is low, but when a riot occurs, history reveals that severity may be high. Correctional personnel may never experience a riot in their facility but must be prepared to respond, should the need arise.

A job assessment that examines the frequency and severity of core job tasks is the first step toward controlling risk. Other considerations in assessing job tasks are also helpful in determining critical dimensions of the job. In analyzing the nature of the job, other factors of frequency should be considered, such as citizen and prisoner complaints, officer incident reports, new equipment and technology, officer misconduct, internal/external investigations, officer accidents, workers' compensation claims, past financial losses (property/personnel), trends in past liability claims (department, region, state, etc.), calls for service, and costs in liability defense. In addition to the job assessment, these factors can be useful in pinpointing additional critical components of the job that can be used to strengthen the framework for risk control and, ultimately, liability reduction. Performing a job assessment can also be beneficial in providing information with which to update or create new job descriptions that can be essential in directing supervisors in more meaningful performance evaluations of employees. A job assessment forms the foundation for a risk control system within the agency.

Policy and Procedure Development

Once a job assessment has been conducted, the next step is to develop or revise policies and procedures for the foreseeable incidents officers encounter. Developing and revising policies and procedures is an administrative function and comports with legal requirements addressed in the Supreme Court's holding in *Monell v. Department of Social Services* (1978). Administrators can incur liability for failing to direct officers, which can be interpreted as a lack of direction and guidance through written policies and procedures.

It is acknowledged that not every situation an officer faces can be predicted, and therefore policies can never be developed that would cover all aspects of the job. Policies and procedures that target the frequent core tasks of the job should be developed in line with constitutional and state requirements. Policies clarify statutory and constitutional requirements for officers and should be written and updated to reflect recent changes in the law. They provide direction for responding to many situations the officer may encounter. Policies also help to keep personnel accountable for performing their duties in a reasonable and professional manner (*Los Angeles Co. v. Humphries* (2010); *City of Ontario, CA v. Quon* (2010); see Chapter 7). Policies and procedures are at the core of the criminal justice agency and provide a layer of protection against assertions of liability for failure to direct. Policies and procedures should be reviewed annually and revised as the nature of the job changes and as the law changes.

Risk Control Strategies

Once the job assessment and policy development have been accomplished, the next step is to select a strategy or combination of strategies for controlling the risk of liability. The risk control strategies are: (1) avoidance; (2) prevention of losses; (3) reduction of losses; (4) segregation of resources; and (5) transference of risk. Depending on the foreseeability of an incident and its frequency and severity, the approach may be to use one or a combination of strategies. Many factors may emerge that will influence the selection of a strategy, such as number of depart-ment personnel, size of the jurisdiction, budget constraints, resources, facility constraints, legal requirements, and accreditation stipulations. These factors should be kept in mind when determining which strategy to use. Moreover, when considering a specific strategy, criminal justice personnel must consider their respective agency, available resources, and requirements that may preclude a particular strategy.

Risk Avoidance

The luxury of voluntarily avoiding a task or function regardless of its frequency is nonexistent in many jurisdictions. Providing 24-hour operations in corrections or policing is required. Thus, there is no option to avoid performing job duties. From the job assessment, however, some functions may emerge that can be curtailed or refined in order to decrease the frequency in participating in an activity. For example, some police departments have instituted a no-chase policy, based on the high degree of risk of property damage, injury, and death involving the officer and the public. Other police departments have instituted a practice of not provid-ing escort services for funerals due to the risk of vehicle accidents and injuries. Some agencies limit the firing of a weapon from or at a moving vehicle unless the officer's life is in imminent peril. The practice in a majority of detention centers is to require medical clearance from a physician prior to admitting a prisoner with obvious physical injuries.

Loss Prevention

Loss prevention involves instituting measures prior to an incident. This is undertaken to pre-vent a loss from occurring. Examples include the creation and implementation of policies and procedures, in-service training, authorizing and issuing proper equipment, keeping equip-ment current and operational, equipping transport vehicles with screens, and facility design. The primary objective of loss prevention is to prevent the frequency of the loss-causing events.

Loss Reduction

Loss reduction is different from loss prevention in that it attempts to minimize the loss, rather than preventing the loss. In prisons or detention centers, physical and sexual assaults between prisoners sometimes occur. Instituting proper classification practices and regular personal security checks may not totally prevent such assaults, but may help to reduce the number of assaults within the facility. In policing, requiring a minimum of two officers to respond to domestic violence calls may help to reduce injuries to the officers and individuals involved. Additionally, some agencies permit only two vehicles to engage in high-speed pursuits and may also place a ceiling on the maximum speed of the police vehicles.

Segregation of Resources

Segregating resources consists of maintaining department resources in separate locations so that no single event significantly depreciates the use of equipment. This involves duplication of equipment (maintaining more than one), such as vehicles, back-up vehicles, spare equipment, restraints, facilities, and perhaps overlapping shifts during critical periods. It would also include separating resources or using multiple facilities, such as precincts or satellite centers, for overflow or efficiency purposes. Resource segregation is intended to reduce the severity of potential losses, because the agency will still be able to function.

Risk Transfer

Transferring risk involves strategies that move, or transfer, risk from one party to another. In policing this could mean a policy that requires officers to transport a mentally impaired person to a mental health facility in order to obtain psychiatric clearance prior to transporting him or her to a detention center. In a detention center this could involve requiring mental health professionals to evaluate a suicidal prisoner in the jail at initial reception or upon discovering suicidal behaviors. This strategy controls risks by identifying situations in which the officer or agency can transfer risk to another before incurring a loss. This is closely related to risk avoidance and loss prevention.

Training

Training is an essential managerial responsibility. The Supreme Court ruled in *City of Canton v. Harris* (1989) that training is to be provided for recurring job tasks. Thus, performing a job assessment not only identifies frequent and core job tasks, but also can be instrumental in directing training efforts.

All personnel should receive ongoing training commensurate with their duties and in the proper implementation of policy. High-profile or high-liability areas should be addressed regularly. For example, empty-hand control techniques are frequently used by police and correctional officers. Many lawsuits have been filed that assert that the officer used excessive force during arrest or when subduing a combative person. Subject control training should be provided regularly, along with training in the department's use-of-force policy. Personnel must be competent in deciding when and how much force to use in various situations, and must do so within the boundaries of policy and the law.

Training today is not a luxury. It must be the goal of each criminal justice executive to provide regular, ongoing training to all personnel. The nature of business in criminal justice agencies requires officers to have the latest information pertaining to the legal issues of performing their job. Training in legal and liability issues should be provided annually. Changes in societal conditions, offender characteristics, treatment strategies, crime prevention approaches, and improvements in technology require updated training for all personnel.

As new policies and procedures are developed or revised, all employees should receive a personal copy of the policies as well as training on the new policies. Testing employees' comprehension of policies is suggested. This strategy for disseminating policies and procedures can assist in proper implementation at the line level and illustrates that there is a level of understanding of how the policy is to be followed. Supervisors should also receive a copy of the policy and appropriate training as well. Administrators should seek many methods for training their personnel, such as classroom presentations, simulation training, roll-call training, on-the-job training (field training), agency videotapes of incidents, interactive computer-based training, seminars, conferences, and training through the Internet. Training and documentation of training are key elements in risk control and are required by the courts. They provide an important layer of protection against liability (Ryan, 2008).

Field Implementation

It is an understatement to say that supervisory personnel are critical in any organization. Supervisors, as an extension of management, are an important component in reducing liability. There are two primary responsibilities of supervisors: (1) implementing policies and procedures, and (2) enforcing them. Historically, in many criminal justice agencies, supervisors received little attention in management training and the proper methods for implementing policy and personnel evaluations. Many organizational and liability problems can be corrected through proper training of supervisory personnel.

To avert and reduce liability, supervisors must be prepared to fulfill their responsibilities. The Field Training Officer (FTO) program in policing and corrections has provided new officers with a more efficient transition between the training academy and assuming the roles and responsibilities of an officer. Criminal justice administrators should also consider adopting or creating a similar program for newly promoted supervisors. After successfully completing such a program, administrators must remain committed to providing ongoing training for supervisors. Supervisors need to be trained in management philosophies, strategies for dealing with a diverse work group, legal and liability issues of management, administrative law, criminal law updates, policies and procedures updates, planning and goal setting, leadership skills, motivating the contemporary employee, managing stress, and evaluating employee performance. Maintaining a commitment to providing training to supervisors provides another layer of liability protection for the agency and all personnel.

Supervisors must also understand the disciplinary process within their departments. When personnel have violated policy, supervisors must respond appropriately based on the situation. They are the overseers and enforcers of policy and must ensure that personnel perform their duties in a professional and legal matter. Where there is a cavalier discipline philosophy, allegations of failure to supervise expose the department to litigation. As a matter of course, supervisors must be familiar with disciplinary procedures and the legal issues surrounding their responsibilities.

Administrators are encouraged to consider maintaining close contact with their risk management provider if they are a member of a risk management pool. A myriad of services are routinely provided by these entities, which can assist an agency in averting the risk of lawsuits and increasing officer safety. For example, risk management providers can provide agency risk assessments, audits of policies and procedures, model policies, training for agency personnel, and training videos on high-liability areas. The Michigan Municipal Risk Management Authority provides risk management services for law enforcement and detention agencies in Michigan. During the last 20 years they have performed liability assessments for their constituents in which they have developed model policies, training videos, and training on a variety of legal and officer safety issues, which have assisted in reducing the number of lawsuits and effectively defending cases that are litigated.

Similarly, the Legal and Liability Risk Management Institute (LLRMI, 2004) provides training, legal publications, and services for law enforcement and correctional agencies. Underscoring the importance of policy and procedure and officer performance in the field, they have assembled a *Quick Reference Legal Guide for Law Enforcement* (Ryan, 2005), which provides a brief overview of United States Supreme Court and lower court decisions. Highlights of each decision are noted, providing easy access to the focus of the decision, which can underscore agency policy and serve as guidance for officers in the field when they are faced with making decisions on various matters. Further, they have designed decision-making checklists for officers of frequently performed tasks that are addressed by policy and case decisions. For example, vehicle searches are performed with some frequency and carry the potential of a high risk of civil liability. Based on several United States Supreme Court decisions underscoring the Fourth Amendment and vehicle searches, LLRMI has designed a checklist that officers may refer to which incorporates policy, case law, and focus points to consider prior to conducting a search. The checklist includes components to developing probable cause, ordering occupants out of the vehicle, search incident to an arrest, and an inventory search, just to mention a few. These checklists embody significant sections of a working policy, can be used in training, and are used in the field when performing a task.

These two illustrations provide examples of how agencies can access their risk management provider, who can assist in risk control through the integration of case law, policy, and training through the design of checklists. These checklists provide a tool that can guide an officer in decisionmaking in high-liability areas. They represent a framework with which to assess an incident, make a decision, and later provide an explanation to justify the decision. Such assistance to officers assists in controlling risk in decisionmaking and can avert cases of liability. Even if an agency is not a member of a formal risk management program, an agency may replicate the process by researching high-liability areas and applicable case decisions, develop or revise policy accordingly, develop the checklists, and provide training for their officers. Such endeavors underscore proactive risk management techniques and illustrate risk control techniques.

Monitoring and Evaluating Risk Control

Once these risk control procedures have been instituted, supervisory personnel should monitor them. Policies that create new programs should be monitored to ensure proper implementation. Monitoring the process is essential in successful implementation and can ensure accountability with all personnel. Supervisory personnel are responsible for working closely with line personnel as they integrate policy with action. When problems emerge in implementing the policy, supervisors need to evaluate the problem and work toward its resolution. Rather than ignoring problems or resorting to old methods, a quick response to emerging problems will provide for more efficient line operations and decrease the risk of liability.

After a reasonable period of monitoring a policy, program, or new activity, constructive evaluation should occur. Line officers and supervisors should collectively evaluate the successes and problems associated with the activity. Modifications in responsibilities of personnel may result and should be worked out accordingly. Evaluation helps to measure the success and impact of the policy. Many criminal justice agencies embark on new programs or systems and do little or nothing to monitor and evaluate the outcome. Evaluation is necessary to determine the future activities of those who are participating so that changes may be made as warranted. Identifying problems early can help make needed changes, assist in reducing risk, and possibly reduce liability.

Net Benefits

Although adopting and developing risk management strategies can create more work for all employees in an organization, it has several positive management and line-level benefits. First, one of the primary goals of all employees is to work toward reducing the exposure of risk to personnel or property loss. Officer safety issues in corrections and law enforcement should be of utmost concern to administrators and line officers. An ongoing commitment to achieving this can be accomplished through risk management approaches. Second, developing and maintaining risk management techniques will create more efficient agency operations and simultaneously improve performance of all personnel. Street-level and cell block management efforts can be significantly improved. Work-related accidents can be decreased, as well as workers' compensation claims. Citizen and prisoner complaints can decrease as officers work to resolve problems at the root level. Analyzing the job can pinpoint revision or development of critical policies and procedures that will in turn help to focus ongoing training for all personnel. Third, developing and maintaining a risk management program are administrative functions. Risk management techniques are at the center of basic management. Management is responsible for the activities of the organization and how employees accomplish them. This can be achieved through planning, forecasting, controlling, communication, budgeting, staffing, supervising, training, and directing the tasks of all employees. All command personnel should work toward acceptable methods to achieve organizational goals by minimizing the risks associated with the job. Gaining the compliance of all personnel to work toward ways to reduce the risks of the job can also help keep employees accountable.

Finally, maintaining a risk management program will significantly assist in defending lawsuits that may arise. A risk management program should not be implemented primarily out of concern about being named as a defendant in a lawsuit. Establishing an ongoing process of risk management should be undertaken for the reasons listed above. By adhering to these risk management principles, an agency will place itself in a much better position to defend a lawsuit. Thus, a risk management program serves as a proactive management system that increases the ability of the organization to operate more efficiently, control foreseeable risks, direct employees in the performance of their duties, and work toward reducing identifiable job-related risks. In this way, should a lawsuit be filed against the department, management has a foundation on which to assert a legal defense. Adopting this proactive approach is preferable to attempting to build a reactive defense against a legal challenge after a high-profile incident. Maintaining a risk management system can show that the department and employees are acting in good faith in accordance with the law and professional industry practices. It also provides a mechanism whereby the agency can assert a more likely defense of qualified immunity. To successfully invoke a defense of qualified immunity, an agency must have a management system in place that illustrates that constitutional mandates are in place and are followed. Creating and maintaining such a system can be most helpful in persuading a court that the agency should be granted qualified immunity.

Examples of Best Practices

Best practices is a method or technique that has consistently shown results superior to those achieved with other means and is used as a benchmark. Best practices is a superior method or innovative practice that contributes to the improved performance of an organization, usually recognized as "best" by other peer organizations. It implies accumulating and applying knowledge about what is working and not working in different situations and contexts, including lessons learned and the continuing process of learning, feedback, reflection, and analysis (what works, how and why; Narvaez, 2011). The following are examples of police agencies that have instituted principles of risk management that illustrate best practices.

Michigan Municipal Risk Management Authority (MMRMA) has been providing risk management services to municipalities and counties in Michigan since 1981. Among the many services offered, MMRMA provides model policy development, training programs, and training DVDs for constituent law enforcement agencies including police officers, deputies, detention officers, and administrators. MMRMA has been successful with these agencies in implementing risk management strategies through policy implementation and training programs that have reduced the risk of liability claims in several topic areas. In 2009 MMRMA was recognized for its achievements by the national association of risk management, Public Risk Management Association, for developing two programs that serve as best practices in the industry.

In the first program, MMRMA provided financial assistance to over 125 law enforcement agencies to purchase Tasers. A model program was designed, which incorporated the following components: certification of instructors within the agency, development of a model policy that identified protocols for deploying the Taser, training in the policy for all personnel, training in associated legal and medical issues, and training on using the device. Further, if an officer deployed a Taser during an incident, a report of the encounter is required, the report is reviewed by a supervisor, and all incidents are reviewed. A database was developed to analyze the incidents where the Taser was deployed in order to measure trends of field use. During a five-year review from 2003 to 2008, MMRMA (2011) reported the following results of 1,000 filed activations of the Taser: subject injuries decreased by 80 percent, officer injuries decreased by 65 percent, and excessive force claims declined by about 60 percent.

In the second program, MMRMA developed an eight-hour training program designed to improve police officer's, detention officer's, and supervisor's response to violent restraint encounters where the restrained individual suddenly died in custody after restraint. Similar to the Taser program, MMRMA first conducted an instructor program and certified instructors to travel around the state to conduct eight hours of training in Sudden Deaths in Custody. The program is designed to teach officers how to recognize common signs and symptoms associated with these deaths, protocols for appropriate response, how to respond to special needs populations, recommended use of force strategies, legal issues regarding officer response, medical care and response issues, report writing and documentation of the incidents, and investigation protocols. Since the implementation of the program, over 800 officers and supervisors have been trained, agency policies have been revised, and five cases have been documented where officer response has prevented a sudden custodial death. MMRMA (2011) reported that between the two programs, claims of excessive force have declined by 66 percent and payouts or losses in claims have declined from $2.7 million to $192,300, a decline of about 80 percent.

Revising policy, practices, and training of officers has led to other models of best practices in law enforcement. Police officers and detention officers with regularity confront individuals with a mental illness. The Memphis, Tennessee, police department formed a partnership with mental health professionals and designed a training program and policy in 1988 on how to respond to the mentally ill and entitled it the Crisis Intervention Team (CIT). CIT is one of several models of collaboration between law enforcement and mental health. Specifically, CIT is a police-based specialized police response. Other strategies are police-based mental health responses, in which the police department hires mental health consultants to assist with mental health crisis calls, and mental health–based specialized responses, which are typified by mobile crisis units. Based on the success experienced by the Memphis Police Department, the program is being employed by numerous law enforcement agencies and is considered by many to be the most rapidly expanding and promising partnership between law enforcement and mental health professionals. The Bureau of Justice Assistance estimates that there are more than 400 CIT programs operating in the United States (Reuland & Schwarzfeld, 2008).

Compton, Bahora, Watson, and Oliva (2009) reviewed 14 published studies on agencies using the CIT program. They found that the Memphis model is serving as the prototype (best practices) for large police departments across the country. These departments have revised their policies and procedures for responding to the mentally ill and provide 40 hours of training to selected officers in response to protocols and how to work with mental health professionals. The researchers reported that CIT implementation appears to be associated with decreased use of high-intensity police units such as Special Weapons and Tactics (SWAT) teams, a lower rate of officer injuries, and increased referral of individuals with mental illnesses to treatment facilities by law enforcement officers. Further, they reported that officers are more likely to use less-lethal force equipment in lieu of firearms in a majority of incidents, that officers transported arrestees to the hospital rather than the jail, and that officers spent an average of 70 minutes at the hospital per incident.

Overall the research shows support for the notion that the CIT model may be an effective component in connecting individuals with mental illnesses who come to the attention of police officers with appropriate psychiatric services. Research indicates that the training component of the CIT model may have a positive effect on officers' attitudes, beliefs, and knowledge relevant to interactions with such individuals, and CIT-trained officers have reported feeling better prepared in handling calls involving individuals with mental illnesses. On a systems level, CIT, in comparison to other pre- and post-diversion programs, may have a lower arrest rate and lower associated criminal justice costs. The goals of CIT can be viewed from different perspectives: some see it as an officer safety program, others as an officer educational in-service training, and yet others as a community safety effort, a risk management program, or a type of jail diversion, among other viewpoints. Regardless of the view, CIT is more than a training program because it promotes a community effort and partnership between the police and community mental health to provide the best intervention response based on the needs and behaviors of the person.

While many more illustrations could be cited, these examples portray best practices that can minimize the risk of litigation. These three examples illustrate that agency managers can reduce the risk of costly liability by applying core risk management principles of policy development/revision, training, and follow-up implementation and monitoring in the field by supervisors. The examples also illustrate that beyond reducing litigation risks, officer safety concerns are also enhanced. The multipurpose of risk management serves as a holistic method to enhance the standards and operations of the agency in the most efficient manner. This assists in making the agency more accountable to the communities they serve (Martenilli & Shaw, 2011).

Summary

This chapter has explored two primary components for responding to civil lawsuits filed in accordance with § 1983. First, law enforcement officers do not have absolute immunity, but rather qualified immunity. They may assert such a defense by demonstrating that they should be immune from such liability because they were acting in good faith. In order to successfully prevail with such a claim, criminal justice personnel must show that they were acting in accordance with the current status of the law at the time, and within accepted training and policy provisions. Acting in good faith has been a successful defense in the past.

Qualified immunity can protect an officer from many of the risks associated with civil liability for alleged constitutional right violations (Stone & Berger, 2009). To maximize the benefit of this doctrine, officers should pay close attention to performing their duties within the guidelines of the law; being knowledgeable of their agency's policies and procedures; and performing their duties in accordance with their training. Keeping current in the legal aspects of the job and reviewing agency policies will not only assist an officer in adhering to agency standards, but can also be used to successfully defend against a constitutional rights claim resulting from citizen-officer contact.

Second, in order to reduce litigation and provide a proactive approach to risk management, risk-control strategies were presented. Criminal justice agencies should strive to incorporate risk reduction strategies throughout the organization as identified through an ongoing process of risk assessment. This means that officers and supervisors participate together in identifying the frequency and severity of risks specific to job tasks that officers perform routinely. Once the risks have been identified, implementing elements of risk control should be considered in designing a risk control program so that managers and line-level employees may work toward more efficient agency operations in an effort to reduce the risk of liability in the future.

It is not possible to completely eliminate liability for police or correctional agencies. Therefore, criminal justice agencies must strive to be proactive in reducing such risks. Combining the two components of immunity and risk management can place the criminal justice agency in a viable position to defend future claims of liability. Criminal justice managers should closely examine these strategies and incorporate them as needed. Implementing risk management strategies remains one of the most important mechanisms in insulating a department from needless civil litigation. A majority of the consent decrees filed under § 14141 stipulate that police agencies undertake a system of risk management. Thus, managers should voluntarily incorporate these strategies into the overall operations of the department. In doing so, mangers show a good faith effort in taking proactive measures to perform their sworn duties within the framework of the law.

References

Ashley, S., & Pearson, R. (1993). *Fundamentals of risk management.* Livonia, MI: Meadowbrook Insurance Group.

Compton, M. T., Bahora, M., Watson, A. C., & Oliva, J. R. (2009). A comprehensive review of extant research on Crisis Intervention Team (CIT) programs. *Journal of the American Academy of Psychiatry and the Law, 36,* 45–55.

del Carmen, R. V. (1995). *Criminal procedure for law enforcement personnel* (3rd ed.). Monterey, CA: Brooks/Cole.

Legal and Liability Risk Management Institute (2004). *Guide to motor vehicle searches—Fourth Amendment.* Rochester, MN: Legal and Liability Risk Management Institute.

Martinelli, T. J., & Shaw, L. E. (2011, March). Updating ethics training: policing privacy series, managing risk by reducing internal litigation. *Police Chief,* 60–62.

Michigan Municipal Risk Management Authority (2011). Safe guarding our members, *Annual Report,* pp. 1–16, Livonia, MI.

Narvaez, K. (2011). *Success stories: public entities adopt ERM best practices.* Fairfax, VA: Public Entity Risk Institute.

Reuland, M., & Schwarzfeld, M. (2008). *Improving responses to people with mental illness: strategies for effective law enforcement training.* Washington, DC: Bureau of Justice Assistance, U.S. Department of Justice. <www.ojp.usdoj.gov.BJA>.

Robinson, C. D. (1992). *Legal rights, duties and liabilities of criminal justice personnel* (2nd ed.). Springfield, IL: Charles C Thomas.

Ryan, J. (2005). *Quick reference: legal guide for law enforcement.* Rochester, MN: Legal and Liability Risk Management Institute.

Ryan, J. (2008). Managing law enforcement liability risk. *PATCE Newsletter, 3,* 1–5.

Silver, I. (2010). *Police civil liability.* New York, NY: Matthew Bender & Co.

Stone, M. P., & Berger, M. J. (2009). The scope of federal qualified immunity in civil rights cases. *AELE Monthly Law Journal, 2,* 501–508.

6 ▪▪▪
▪▪▪
▪▪▪

Administrative and Supervisory Liability

OVERVIEW

Criminal justice administrators and supervisors, like other organizational executives, are responsible for planning, controlling, organizing, budgeting, staffing, directing, reporting, and supervising employees. Additional responsibilities include managing emergencies, establishing priorities, knowledge of day-to-day operations, community and institutional issues, technology, the political process, and managing people. One major area of concern is knowledge of legal and supervisory liability issues. The developing case law in this field strongly suggests that administrators and supervisors need to know the limits of their jobs and need to be aware of their subordinates' competence and performance.

Managing people is central to the effective operation of any organization. Criminal justice personnel exercise legal authority over citizens and prisoners. Therefore, they must exercise a high degree of skill in using their authority and discretion when executing department policy and enforcing the law. Legal actions against personnel frequently result from decisions in which they have implemented a specific policy that violated the constitutional rights of another. For example, a policy directs police officers to use a roadblock to stop a fleeing motorist and officers place a semi-truck with a trailer just over the crest of a hill at night. The fleeing motorist hits the roadblock with his car and dies. This could be considered an unwarranted use of excessive force. Other civil litigation may result from allegations of officers failing to perform their legally assigned duties, performing their duties negligently, misusing their authority, using excessive force, or depriving an individual of his or her constitutional rights.

Criminal justice administrators and supervisors face potential liability that arises out of supervising their employees. Because administrators are responsible for many managerial functions, these duties frequently expose administrators to liability. Any employee action that allegedly deprives an individual of a protected right may in turn expose the administrator to liability. This often places administrators in a position to explain why they should not be held responsible for the employee's conduct. Such situations are often difficult to defend and make the administrative chain of command more vulnerable to liability, as well as heightening the potential for organizational liability.

Virtually every action taken by an administrator in dealing with citizens, prisoners, and employees involves potential liability and legal consequences. Administrators must manage within the context of legal supervisory responsibilities.

This does not suggest that managerial decisionmaking be impeded by paranoia—rather, it implies that the efficient operation of the contemporary criminal justice agency be maintained within working guidelines of potential supervisory liability issues. The duty of supervisors is to know their own potential for liability when they perform their basic managerial functions. Carrying out a supervisor's responsibilities requires not only developing the competency (directing, planning, budgeting, evaluating, etc.) to lead the organization, but also requires that administrators concomitantly continue to develop competency in hiring, training, supervising, and firing, to reduce their own risk as well as reducing the risk of the organization to litigation. A thorough understanding of the fundamental liability issues will equip the administrator to accomplish this objective.

Supervisory Liability Issues

Basis for Liability

Every criminal justice administrator and supervisor should be familiar with Title 42 United States Code § 1983 (see Chapter 3). Since 1978, this has been the primary vehicle by which administrators have been sued for violations of constitutional rights resulting from their management responsibilities. It is used to apply the rights guaranteed by the U.S. Constitution to the everyday decisions and policies of state and local government agencies. Administrators and supervisors must be familiar with the law and agency policies in order to avoid liability for violating an individual's constitutional rights.

Section 1983 lawsuits often name the supervisor along with the officer. This practice is based on the theory that the officer acts for the agency and, therefore, what is done reflects agency policy and practice. As a legal strategy, the plaintiff includes the agency and supervisors, because the higher a position the employee holds, the closer the plaintiff gets to the deep pockets of the county or state agency. Chances of monetary recovery are increased if supervisory personnel, by virtue of their position, are included in the lawsuit. Moreover, naming administrative and supervisory personnel may also create a conflict of interest in the legal strategy for the defense, thus strengthening the plaintiff's claim against one or more defendants.

Policymaker

The United States Supreme Court has held that supervisors can be held responsible for acts of their employees (*Monell v. Department of Social Services*, 1978). *Monell* expanded the meaning of the "every person" clause in § 1983 to include government entities. The supervisor is not liable because an employee violated the individual's constitutional rights, but may be liable for failing in his or her supervisory responsibilities when the failure results in a violation of constitutional rights (see Box 6.1).

BOX 6.1 *MONELL V. DEPARTMENT OF SOCIAL SERVICES OF THE CITY OF NEW YORK* (1978)

Female employees of the New York Department of Social Services filed a § 1983 claim asserting that a policy requiring pregnant employees to take unpaid leaves of absence before they were medically necessary violated their constitutional rights. The claim sought injunctive relief and back pay. The department changed the policy prior to the decision and the lower court denied the request for back pay. The Court of Appeals affirmed and the employees appealed to the United States Supreme Court.

The Court granted certiorari to assess the issue of whether a municipality or local government entity could be held liable under § 1983 when the government's policy or custom violated a person's constitutional right. The Court rejected the idea that a government entity could be held liable under *respondeat superior*. The Court did state that a government entity could be held liable under § 1983 when an alleged unconstitutional action is the result of a policy or custom. The Court also expanded the "every person" language of § 1983 to include local governments.

This case is significant because local governments, along with their officers, can be held liable under § 1983 when their policy is the "moving force" that created a constitutional injury. Government entities are no longer immune from § 1983 litigation. *Monell* provides that the officer, the city, the county, and the government entity may be sued and held liable for monetary damages and injunctive and declaratory relief. Policies and procedures should be in writing and direct officers' actions within the preview of the law.

Under § 1983, the doctrine of *respondeat superior* (a Latin phrase meaning "let the master answer") does not form the basis of liability (*Polk County v. Dodson*, 1981). Under the common law doctrine of *respondeat superior*, the master is responsible for the actions of the servant. It does not, however, apply to public employment, because public officials are not the "masters" of their employees; they serve the government agency. This has been the case for much of our national history, as municipal and county employers of criminal justice agencies were not held liable on this theory. To attach liability would move into the realm of sovereign immunity. In addition, police officers acted as agents of the law sworn to uphold the law, not as employees of their agency. *Respondeat superior* only held an employer liable, not superior officers. Under other theories of liability, however, superior officers could be sued, for example, if they participated in or ratified the tortious actions of their subordinates (*Wilkins v. Whitaker*, 1983).

The *Monell* decision established governmental liability for the behavior of criminal justice personnel when they implement or execute promulgated or adopted policies or regulations, or conduct that results from a "custom" even though the custom has not received approval through formal channels. To establish governmental liability, the plaintiff must prove that a policy or custom existed, and that it was the moving force behind the officer's violation of a person's constitutional rights. The courts have not specifically defined the type of involvement that creates supervisory liability, but they have suggested several potential theories in which liability may be incurred under § 1983 against a supervisor, if the supervisor: (1) directly participated in the action; (2) after learning of the violation through a report or complaint, failed to remedy a wrong; (3) created a policy or custom under which unconstitutional practices occurred or allowed such a policy or custom to continue; and (4) was grossly negligent in managing the subordinates who caused the unlawful condition or event (del Carmen, 1991; Kappeler, 1997).

To prevail on a policy or custom issue, the plaintiff must actually establish that a policy existed and that executing it or failing to execute it caused the constitutional violation. For example, in *Jenkins v. Wood* (1996), liability did not attach against officials for alleged excessive use of force while search warrants for a residence were being executed, in the absence of evidence of a municipal custom or policy of encouraging or tolerating the use of excessive force while executing search warrants or the execution of illegal search warrants. Likewise, the plaintiff's claim in *Graham v. District of Columbia* (1992) that police officers used excessive force against him pursuant to official policy was dismissed. The plaintiff failed to identify any specific policy or any factual basis for a policy allowing excessive force. Conversely, in *McConney v. City of Houston* (1989), the municipality was held liable and paid out $25,000 for an unconstitutional policy of detaining a diabetic arrestee without a warrant for four hours even after determining he was not intoxicated.

The plaintiff must establish an affirmative causal link between a supervisor's inaction and the harm suffered (*Rizzo v. Goode*, 1976). In *Wilson v. City of North Little Rock* (1986), the court ruled that neither the chief nor other officials were liable for prior threats and harassment against a business catering to African-Americans. There was no evidence that linked the chief to actions of his officers, nor was there evidence that he knew of such threats or harassment. Generally, the issue consists of whether an action or omission of the supervisor caused an officer to violate the constitutional rights of another.

In *Los Angeles County California v. Humphries* (2010), the United States Supreme Court, with an 8-0 decision (Justice Kagen recused), reaffirmed their former opinion in *Monell* regarding the issue of policy and custom. The Humphries were charged with child abuse but were exonerated. By California law, their names were added to the sex offender Central Index and would remain on the index for 10 years. Neither the statute nor the County had established any policy or procedure to challenge the validity of the index. The Humphries filed a § 1983 lawsuit seeking damages, an injunction, and a declaration that State of California and Los Angeles County officials had deprived them of their constitutional rights by failing to create a mechanism through which they could contest inclusion in the Index. The District Court granted the defendants summary judgment, but the Ninth Circuit disagreed, ruling that the Fourteenth Amendment required the state to provide those on the list with notice and a hearing, and thus respondents were entitled to declaratory relief. The court also held that respondents were prevailing parties entitled to attorney's fees, including $60,000 from the county. The county objected, claiming that as a municipal entity, it was liable only if its "policy or custom" caused the deprivation of a plaintiff's federal right. The Ninth Circuit found that respondents could prevail against the county on their claim for declaratory relief because *Monell* applied to prospective relief claims.

The county appealed the decision to the United States Supreme Court claiming the statute was created by legislature and was not county policy under *Monell*, and asserted that *Monell* addressed policy and custom claims seeking monetary damages and not prospective relief. The Court examined the question of whether *Monell* provided a prevailing plaintiff with all the available types of relief. The Court affirmed the Ninth Circuit's holding, ruling that the primary issue of their decision in *Monell* is that a governmental entity may be held liable if their policy or custom was the driving force behind the constitutional deprivation. Further the Court held that consistent with *Monell* there is no bifurcation of relief that may be provided to a plaintiff. The decision means a prevailing plaintiff may be awarded monetary and/or prospective relief when claiming the governmental agency's policy or custom created the constitutional deprivation in accordance with *Monell.*

Official Policymaker

The question of who is considered an "official" policymaker arises frequently. Not all supervisors fall into this category. In *Monell* the Supreme Court stated that a policy can be created by those whose edicts or acts may fairly be said to represent official policy. On two occasions the Court has ruled on the issue of who is a policymaker for liability purposes. In *Pembaur v. City of Cincinnati* (1986), the Court held that public officials who have final policymaking authority can render an agency liable under § 1983. Acting at the direction of the county prosecutor, sheriff's deputies entered a medical clinic and arrested two individuals not named on the arrest warrant. The owner of the clinic, a doctor, sued under § 1983 and the Court found the county liable under *Monell.* This decision underscored *Monell* in that policy could be made by those who may fairly be said to represent "official policy," as the prosecutor in this case did.

In *City of St. Louis v. Praprotnik* (1988), the Supreme Court held that a government entity may be held liable where authorized policymakers "approve a subordinate's decision and the basis for it." The Court further added that the determination of who is the official policymaker for liability purposes is to be made by examining state law. Generally, criminal justice administrators would fall within this category. In *Marchese v. Lucas* (1985), the court found the sheriff to be the official agency policymaker and assessed $125,000 against him for failing to train and discipline correctional officers when they beat a prisoner. In *Ware v. Jackson County, Missouri* (1998), the jail director was determined to be the final policymaker as it related to the discipline of detention officers, even though other county officials could review and overturn his decisions. There was no systematic review process of his broad authority to discipline errant officers.

In determining who is the official policymaker in county law enforcement, the United States Supreme Court ruled, however, in *McMillian v. Monroe County, Alabama* (1997), that an Alabama sheriff, in his law enforcement capacity, was a state rather than a county official. In Alabama the governor and the attorney general normally have authority over the sheriff's office and not the county, because Monroe County had no law enforcement authority. Thus, when there is no authority to make policy in the area of law enforcement, no liability will attach.

Liability can be imposed against supervisors if they establish or enforce a policy or custom that causes a constitutional deprivation. But liability generally cannot be based on a single incident of misconduct. *In City of Oklahoma City v. Tuttle* (1985), the United States Supreme

Court determined "that proof of a single incident of unconstitutional activity is not sufficient to impose liability. . . . unless it was caused by existing unconstitutional municipal policy, which can be attributed to a municipal policy maker." Generally, the plaintiff must establish that the deprivation was a result of continuing agency policy and that the policy was the moving force behind the deprivation.

Factors that may strengthen a plaintiff's claim of agency practices of constitutional abuses include:

1. Frequency of the violation;
2. The extent to which the practice was routinized by employees;
3. The extent to which the practice was accepted by supervisors;
4. The extent to which the action represented shared beliefs of employees;
5. Retention of, failure to discipline, or failure to investigate the violating employee;
6. Failure to prevent future violations (del Carmen & Kappeler, 1991).

Gaines v. Choctaw County Commissioners (2003) provides a prime example of how a sheriff's policy was actionable and how personal liability attached due to his participation in a constitutional violation. At the time of the arrest, the detainee was a patient in the hospital where he was being treated for acute renal failure and pneumonia. Over the protests of hospital physicians, the sheriff personally removed the detainee from the hospital and confined him at the jail. His condition deteriorated to the point where he was unable to walk or feed himself. On several visits the family of the detainee found his condition worsening and eventually paid other detainees to bathe and feed him. According to the family, detention officers refused to dispense medications to the detainee because the sheriff's policies did not require them to do so. The sheriff did transport the detainee to a medical clinic and an attending physician recommended that he be admitted to a hospital. The sheriff refused. The family contacted the state human resources agency, which intervened and caused the detainee to be admitted to the hospital. Upon admission he was found to be malnourished and dehydrated. He died two days later.

The estate of the detainee filed a lawsuit claiming that the sheriff and county denied the detainee medical care while confined. The court found no liability for failing to train the officers or the sheriff. The court also stated that the county did not have a duty to appoint a physician, but merely had the authority to do so; the county had the authority to act and its failure to do so could be construed as a county policy. The court agreed with the estate, holding that a Fourteenth Amendment violation was substantiated against the sheriff in his individual capacity, based upon on his direct participation and policies, which contributed to the death of the detainee.

Further, the court's decision in *Murphy v. Franklin* (2007) demonstrates how a sheriff's policies and procedures may create a constitutional violation of prisoners' rights. A pretrial detainee brought a § 1983 claim against the sheriff and jail administrator, alleging that he was subjected to punitive, degrading, and inhumane treatment. The detainee alleged that he was shackled, hand to feet, to the toilet in an isolation cell, and, on another occasion, shackled to a cot. The detainee asserted that he was shackled several times for no apparent reason in a "lockdown" cell for almost 12 days in a position with his hands and feet connected and fastened to the toilet and was not released to allow for urinating or defecating. He was not provided clean clothing, nor personal hygiene items, nor bedding. The court held in favor of the detainee, ruling that the sheriff was responsible for promulgating all policies and procedures in the county jail and the complaint was sufficiently specific to state a valid § 1983 claim. According to the court, the collective action of these practices condoned by the sheriff served no legitimate penological purpose other than to mistreat detainees in violation of their constitutional rights.

Supervisors on the Scene or Commanding Officers Causing a Violation

Liability will attach for a supervisor on the scene who actually participates in or fails to prevent a violation from occurring. In *Masel v. Barrett* (1989), a sergeant who was supervising six officers monitoring a political demonstration was found liable when he stood by and watched the officers use excessive force on the demonstrators, as well as beating one of them. The claim of supervisory liability is valid unless the failure to intervene is proven to be negligent.

Liability can also attach even if the supervisor was not actually on the scene but directed or led the actions of the officer and it caused a violation. In some cases in which a supervisor decides to act or not act, or selects a tactic or type of equipment to use in an operation, it may increase the supervisor's liability. In *Morrison v. Washington County* (1983), a sheriff responsible for administering a jail was held liable because he was consulted about the decision to arrest an intoxicated individual (who later died in the jail) for public drunkenness. The sheriff had received information from officers in the field regarding the situation, and rather than being transported to the hospital, the arrestee was brought to the jail.

The Supreme Court in *Hudson v. McMillian* (1992) found two correctional officers and a prison lieutenant liable for the beating of a compliant restrained prisoner. The two officers were escorting the prisoner to a segregation cell and began hitting him in the face and kicking him in retaliation for an earlier argument. A lieutenant on the scene observed the beating but merely cautioned the two officers "not to have too much fun." The supervisor was held liable for failing to properly intervene, supervise, and control the officers.

For liability to attach against a supervisor, a plaintiff must establish a "causal connection" between the incident and the supervisor's failure. Generally, one incident does not show a practice of failing to intervene with officers. In *Warner v. City of New Orleans* (2004), Warner was arrested and claimed that the arresting officer used excessive force in violation of the department's policy on use of force and a policy regarding a special task force that was designed to actively patrol certain sections of the city. Warner filed a § 1983 lawsuit against the arresting officer for excessive force, against the chief of police for failing to supervise his officers and promoting unconstitutional policies and procedures, although he was not on the scene at the time of the arrest.

The District Court found that the arresting officer did not use excessive force. The court ruled that the chief was not personally liable because there was no evidence that he had a legal duty to prevent an officer's misdeeds or that his failure to prevent such conduct amounted to a violation of Warner's constitutional rights. Further, the court stated that the chief's official duty was to make departmental policy and that the plaintiff failed to show evidence of any "persistent widespread practice of tolerating either false arrest or excessive force, or any failure to properly supervise the officers in the department. The court noted that the chief was not on the arrest scene at the time and was not involved in the incident. Thus, the plaintiff failed to establish evidence that would show that the alleged chief's failures as a supervisor were connected to Warner's alleged rights violations. The court further stated that the chief had taken proactive measures to lead his department and such measures were not "unwanted, wanton, or otherwise unconstitutional."

Theories of Supervisory Liability

Deliberate Indifference

Some ambiguity exists among federal courts regarding the level of culpability required for finding liability with supervisors under § 1983. The courts have used the standard of gross negligence on occasion but more commonly use the standard of deliberate indifference.

This standard was first established in *Estelle v. Gamble* (1976), when a prisoner sued correctional officials for denial of medical treatment and improper medical treatment of a back injury he sustained while working on the prison farm. The Court stated in *Estelle* that deliberate indifference involves a conscious intentional decision or choice to inflict unnecessary and wanton pain on a prisoner. In *Stokes v. Delcambre* (1983), the Court upheld an award of $250,000 against a sheriff, $105,000 in punitive damages against a correctional officer, and $70,000 in compensatory damages against both defendants for ignoring repeated screams from a prisoner who was being sexually assaulted by other prisoners. The Court determined that there was sufficient evidence to support deliberate indifference to the safety of the prisoner and that the officers were wanton and oppressive in their actions toward the prisoner.

The concept of deliberate indifference has been expanded over the years by the United States Supreme Court in several correctional cases (*City of Canton v. Harris*, 1989; *Wilson v. Seiter*, 1991; *Farmer v. Brennan*, 1994). The standard has not been specifically defined, but applied on a case-by-case basis. It generally means that the actor disregarded a known or obvious consequence of his or her actions, consciously chose a course of action with disregard for the harmful outcome, and disregarded a risk of harm of which he was aware. The Court in *Farmer* stated that officials must possess knowledge that a substantial risk of harm existed by evidence of their actions or failures to act.

Deliberate indifference may be demonstrated by either actual intent or reckless disregard. An administrator acts recklessly by "disregarding" a substantial risk of danger that is either known to the administrator or that would be apparent to a reasonable person in the administrator's position. Mere negligence is insufficient to support a § 1983 claim. Administrators are not liable if they can show that they responded reasonably to known risks.

There are many forms of administrative actions that in their totality may create evidence of deliberate indifference to constitutionally protected rights. Case law reveals seven general theories from which potential administrative liability emerges: (1) negligent hiring, (2) negligent assignment, (3) negligent entrustment, (4) failure to direct, (5) failure to supervise, (6) failure to discipline, and (7) failure to train. These theories are not mutually exclusive, meaning that the plaintiff may allege several theories in the lawsuit against the administrator. For example, it is not uncommon for the plaintiff in an excessive force claim against an officer to assert a failure by the administrator in directing, supervising, and training the officer. A discussion of each theory will follow, with the exception of failure to train, which will be addressed in Chapter 7.

Negligent Hiring

An emerging area of administrative liability is negligent hiring. Claims citing this deficiency generally assert that the constitutional violation would not have occurred had the administrator properly performed a thorough screening of the errant officer prior to hiring him or her. Liability stems from claims that the administrator failed to conduct a complete background investigation of the employee prior to employment. Liability emerges when an employee is unfit for appointment, such unfitness was known to the employer or should have been known through a background check, and the employee's act was foreseeable.

Hiring deficiencies led to liability in *Jones v. Wittenburg* (1977) and the sheriff was ordered by the court to train and psychologically test the staff. In *Brown v. Benton* (1978), the court found that termination of an officer was reasonable based on results of background checks. Liability attached in *Parker v. Williams* (1988) when evidence supported the plaintiff's claim against a sheriff for promoting a policy or custom of not conducting reasonable background checks on prospective employees. A former prisoner had been kidnapped and raped by the chief jailer. In *Benavides v. County of Wilson* (1992), the court concluded that the sheriff had complied with state requirements when hiring candidates for the position of correctional officer. Allegations of deliberate indifference for improper screening of employees were not supported, even though the prisoner sustained an injury during his confinement.

There is potential for administrative liability in failing to test and evaluate officer candidates for psychological deficiencies. The plaintiff in *Bell v. City of Miami* (1990) prevailed in a § 1983 action brought against the municipality for failing to adequately screen police officer candidates prior to employment. Allegations of an illegal entry and excessive force were upheld pursuant to a policy of failing to psychologically test police officer candidates and a failure to review complaints. A widespread pattern and practice of this failure was established. In *Stokes v. Bullins* (1988), the court held that a failure to use the National Crime Information Center (NCIC) by a small-town police department to check the background of a police officer candidate was not actionable. Even when the candidate had admitted to being arrested for a minor crime and a further check would have revealed 15 prior arrests, some including offenses involving violence, it failed to rise to a level of gross negligence. The candidate had lived in the community for many years, had not posed a problem, and the admitted arrests were investigated.

The United States Supreme Court decided a case involving hiring practices in law enforcement for the first time when it reviewed *Board of Commissioners of Bryan County v. Brown*

BOX 6.2 *BOARD OF COMMISSIONERS OF BRYAN COUNTY V. BROWN* (1997)

Respondent Jill Brown and her husband drove from Texas into Oklahoma, and soon after crossing the state line they noticed a police checkpoint. Mr. Brown turned his vehicle around, and a deputy and a reserve deputy pursued the Browns' vehicle at high speeds. The Browns finally stopped and the deputies approached their vehicle. The reserve deputy approached the passenger side and ordered Mrs. Brown out. She refused and he used an "arm bar," pulling her from the vehicle and forcing her to the ground. Mrs. Brown sustained a knee injury and underwent corrective surgery. She sued under § 1983, claiming excessive force and that the sheriff improperly hired the reserve deputy by ignoring his background of misdemeanor charges for assault and battery, resisting arrest, and traffic charges. The District Court found in favor of Mrs. Brown and the county appealed. The appellate court affirmed.

The United States Supreme Court granted certiorari to determine the issue of whether the county was properly held liable for the respondent's injuries based on the sheriff's decision to hire. In a 6-to-3 decision, the Court found in favor of the sheriff's decision to hire the reserve deputy. Mrs. Brown asserted the "but for" test, claiming that the sheriff ignored the deputy's past and, but for a more thorough review, he would not have hired him. The Court rejected that theory and stated that a court must test the link between a policymaker's decision and a particular injury. The plaintiff must prove a deliberate indifference to the risk that a violation of the Constitution will follow that decision. Only when the policymaker deliberately ignores "painfully obvious" information in the background of an applicant and makes a decision to hire where a constitutional right has been violated can the plaintiff claim deliberate indifference. In Oklahoma, a history of misdemeanors does not preclude one from being hired into law enforcement.

This decision is important because it was the first time the Court applied the deliberate indifference standard to hiring decisions. Applying the standard of deliberate indifference to hiring decisions creates a high barrier for a plaintiff to overcome. It is recommended that administrators develop and adhere to adequate hiring procedures, continue to conduct thorough and complete background checks, and require psychological examinations when making hiring decisions.

(1997). This case (Box 6.2) involved an excessive force claim made against a deputy after he engaged in a pursuit. The plaintiff alleged that the sheriff was deliberately indifferent to the constitutional rights of citizens because he ignored an alleged violent history of the deputy and, therefore, the hiring practices were unconstitutional. The deputy had one misdemeanor arrest while in college, several years prior to employment, for an assault that occurred during a fight. The plaintiff asserted that this incident, of which the sheriff was aware, should have placed the sheriff on notice of the deputy's proclivity toward violence.

The Court ruled in favor of the sheriff, stating that the hiring policy was not the moving force behind the incident or the plaintiff's injury. While the Court did state that one incident could trigger liability, they were reluctant to impose liability for one isolated incident involving the hiring process. Emphasizing this reluctance, the Court noted, "every injury suffered at the hands of a municipal employee can be traced to a hiring decision in the 'but for' sense: but for the hiring of the employee, the plaintiff would not have suffered the injury. A court must carefully test the link between the policy maker's inadequate decision and the particular injury alleged."

The Court further stated:

> . . . *a finding of culpability simply cannot depend on the mere probability that any officer inadequately screened will inflict any constitutional injury. Rather, it must depend on a finding that this officer was highly likely to inflict the particular injury suffered by the plaintiff. The connection between the background of the particular applicant and the particular constitutional injury must be strong.*

The Supreme Court opined that the deputy's background did not make his use of excessive force in making the arrest a plainly obvious consequence of the hiring decision. "Only where adequate scrutiny of the applicant's background would lead a reasonable policy maker to conclude that the plainly obvious consequence of the decision to hire the applicant would be the deprivation of a third party's federally protected right can the official's failure to adequately scrutinize the applicant's background constitute 'deliberate indifference.'"

The implication of this decision is that administrators should ensure that they conduct adequate background investigations and use psychological examinations prior to hiring employees. There is no magic legal formula for hiring prospective employees, but failing to institute adequate measures and take reasonable steps in employee selection or ignoring information regarding the unfitness of a candidate can increase the risk of liability. Hiring procedures must be instituted, state standards must be met, and the law must be followed. In these cases the Supreme Court has created a high barrier for the plaintiff to overcome. The plaintiff must show that the employee's background made the specific constitutional violation a "painfully obvious consequence" of his or her being hired.

In *Morris v. Crawford County* (2002), a claim that the sheriff failed to properly conduct an adequate hiring investigation was dismissed by the court and the appellate court affirmed. A detainee confined in the jail claimed that, during booking, an officer assaulted him after he refused to take a Breathalyzer test. The detainee was arrested and confined in jail for disorderly conduct and driving while intoxicated. The detainee began banging on his cell and four officers responded. The detainee claimed that the officers dragged him out of his cell, beat him, and one officer used a knee drop on him that severed his intestine. The detainee claimed that this conduct violated his constitutional rights and that the sheriff knew of such violent tendencies at the time he hired the officer but ignored them, and that such knowledge was the direct cause of his injury.

The appellate court held that the detainee failed to show a strong causal connection between the officer's background and the specific constitutional violation. The court noted that the only violent act in the officer's background was an incident in which he slapped a detainee, although protective orders were obtained against the officer by his ex-wife and girlfriend. The court ruled that the sheriff and the county were not liable under § 1983 on the theory of deliberate indifference in the hiring of the officer.

Since the Supreme Court's decision in *Brown*, a plaintiff must show a strong connection between the background of the particular applicant and the specific violation alleged. Thus, plaintiffs cannot prevail merely because there was a probability that a poorly screened officer was highly likely to violate their rights. Rather, they must show that the hired officer was highly likely to inflict the particular type of injury suffered by them.

In *Hardmen v. Kerr County, Texas* (2007), the county hired an officer who would have regular contact with female prisoners. The officer raped a female prisoner and she filed a lawsuit claiming that the county failed to conduct a thorough background check that would have resulted in a decision not to hire him. The court agreed that Kerr County should have performed a better job in screening the officer. That the officer omitted answers to key questions during his interview, such as whether he had previously been fired, should alone have been cause for alarm. Also, had the county contacted the past employer, it is likely that they would have learned that he was fired for making improper advances toward female students. Such knowledge may have prompted the county to reconsider hiring him for a position that would place him in close proximity with female prisoners on a regular basis. The court ruled, however, that even if the county was negligent in hiring the officer, it was insufficient to hold the county liable for any constitutional violation. There are no grounds to find that the rape in question was a plainly obvious consequence of hiring him. Even if the county had performed a thorough job of investigating the officer's history, there was absolutely no history of violence, sexual or otherwise, to be found. While being fired from a prior employment was troubling, the court held that it requires an enormous leap to connect improper advances towards female students to the sexual assault at issue in this case.

In *Macon v. Shelby County Government Civil Service Merit Bd.* (2009), Macon was employed as a detention officer with the Shelby Sheriff's Department. Macon was arrested for driving under the influence and speeding, and lodged in a county jail in Arkansas. The Shelby Sheriff's Department was informed of the arrest and detective Bartlett went to the jail and spoke to the arresting officer. The arresting officer informed Bartlett that Macon stated he was a convicted felon and Bartlett was unaware of this conviction. Back at the Shelby department an internal affairs investigation was performed on Macon. A review of Macon's personnel file revealed that a background check was performed before he was hired, which used the National Criminal Information Center database and no criminal records were found. Bartlett used the National Law Enforcement Telecommunications System to further check Macon's background and found that message stating, "Record No Longer On File-Expunged." Bartlett followed up and was informed that Macon had pled guilty to a felony drug charge of manufacturing, possessing, and delivery of a controlled substance. The case had been sealed several years before his employment at the Sheriff's Department.

Bartlett examined Macon's application form and found that he marked "no" to questions regarding past arrests, convictions, or indictment on any criminal charges. Macon also left blank a question regarding whether a charge was expunged. Bartlett interviewed Macon and asked him if his employment application was accurate and he stated yes, except where the form asked about a prior conviction. Macon stated that he was told not to answer that question by an unnamed person, that it would not show up, and that the department would most probably not find out. Macon was charged with falsifying his employment application and violating Departmental Rules and Regulations. After a due process hearing Macon was terminated and he appealed to the County Civil Service Merit Review Board. At the hearing Macon admitted that he had been convicted of a felony charge prior to his employment and that he indeed answered no to the question regarding a felony conviction. Macon maintained that he was not required to answer further questions on the application form as the charge was expunged and that he did inform the training lieutenant during his academy training. The Board affirmed the termination and Macon filed a wrongful termination lawsuit. The district court upheld the termination and Macon appealed the decision.

The Appellant Court rejected the appeal, upholding the termination. The court reasoned that the county's application form was not flawed in requiring applicants to answer questions regarding past charges, convictions, and expungment of any convictions. The court held that the county's policy and practices used for conducting preemployment background checks were reasonable and properly followed, and Macon's own conduct was the reason for the termination.

Hiring an applicant is one of the most important decisions administrators must make. Failing to conduct a thorough and complete investigation can heighten the risk of civil liability in the future. Investigators need to be trained in how to perform background investigations in order to ensure that the most qualified person is hired. To ensure that background investigations are performed properly, consider the following recommendations (Brushway, 2004):

1. **Provide applicants with a personal history packet.** This packet should be distributed to applicants and should specify what forms need to be completed, by what date, and provide clear instructions. The packet should require all education and employment information, including names, addresses, phone numbers of supervisors, co-workers, and reference information.

2. **Obtain a notarized waiver.** Ensure that the language of the waiver allows the investigator the ability to access all aspects of the applicant's past. Records can show the character of the applicant. Make certain the waiver contains language that stipulates that negative information will remain confidential. Include a release of liability of the investigatory agency and a disclaimer that all information and materials are the property of the investigating agency.

3. **Conduct an "initial interview" to go through the personal history statement of the applicant.** Open-ended questions should be used to elicit information necessary for the investigator to begin the investigation. Creating a timeline can be helpful in cross-referencing information provided by the applicant with information the investigator discovers during the investigation.

4. **Follow up on reference information.** In addition to reviewing reference comments, follow up by making personal contacts with references and others who may have relevant information regarding the applicant. Avoid relying solely on reference letters, but rather speak with neighbors, friends, supervisors, past educators, military, etc.

5. **Learn from the past.** Avoid making the same mistakes that have occurred in other departments. Departmental investigators should be trained in all aspects of performing background checks and keep abreast of legal and liability issues affecting the hiring process in their state. Make certain to follow the required state hiring standards as well as the departmental policy on hiring candidates. The use of psychological assessments by trained and qualified individuals should be considered and used if required by the state.

These components can assist in performing adequate hiring investigations. They will be very useful in defending against claims that the hiring agency failed to conduct a less than thorough investigation or ignored information that should have been reviewed when making the hiring decision.

Negligent Assignment

Negligent assignment is assigning an employee to a job without ascertaining his or her competence, or retaining an employee on a job who is known to be incapable of performing the job. Examples include assigning a reckless driver to transport prisoners or assigning an officer who has in the past demonstrated mental or physical instabilities to a prison gun tower. The administrator has an affirmative duty not to assign a subordinate to, or leave in a position for which the subordinate is unfit. In *Moon v. Winfield* (1974), liability attached for failure to place a police officer who was unfit for his regular assignment into a non-sensitive position. The court held the supervisor liable because he had the authority to assign or suspend the officer, but failed to do so. The supervisor had received five separate misconduct reports within a two-week period, as well as a warning that the officer had been involved in a series of incidents that indicated mental instability.

In *L.W. v. Grubbs* (1992), an appellate court found supervisors liable when a prison nurse filed a claim for improperly assigning her to work with young violent prisoners when the supervisors knew of their previous violent histories. The court found that the supervisors created a dangerous situation when they assigned the nurse to work by herself with these prisoners, and, when left alone with them, she was raped by one prisoner.

An example of assigning an unfit person to perform the duties of a police officer is provided in *Grancid Camilo-Robles v. Diaz-Pagan* (1998). The plaintiff prevailed in an action against the superiors of a known mentally impaired police officer who was under psychological care for failing to remove him from assigned duties as a police officer. The plaintiff was arrested at gunpoint, slapped in the face, and held in a lockup by the officer for three hours for parking in an unauthorized parking zone at the courthouse. The officer had a history of 18 disciplinary infractions for bizarre behavior and brandishing his weapon at citizens. He was committed to a psychiatric hospital after being diagnosed with schizophrenia and was released three months later. A police psychiatrist recommended that the officer be terminated, and the agency director discharged him. The officer appealed the decision and was reinstated. A psychiatrist reevaluated him, cleared him for full duty, and he returned to duty fully armed. One day later, he became engaged in a deadly force encounter and shot two people, killing one of them. He was assigned to desk duty, psychologically evaluated again, and again returned to regular duty by the department. He later threatened to kill a fellow officer, and the department terminated him. The officer eventually pleaded guilty to voluntary manslaughter and was sentenced to a prison term. In the subsequent civil action, the director was found liable for having foreknowledge of the officer's mental unfitness for duty and deliberate indifference to his condition by reassigning the officer to active duty, where a known and foreseeable harm and death occurred. The court maintained that the director acquiesced in his administrative capacity in assigning him duties for which he was clearly unfit. The court also held that the director failed to take preventive or training measures to control the known violent tendencies of the officer.

Frequently, in determining liability, the court will examine whether there exists a pattern of policy violations by improperly assigning officers who previously heightened liability exposure for a department that has been instrumental in violating the constitutional rights of citizens. In *Hogan v. City of Easton* (2006), the plaintiff prevailed because he was able to show the court that officers used excessive force in his case and had a history of unjustifiably firing their weapons over 10 years, resulting in substantial monetary settlements. The city operated an Emergency Response Team (ERT) and assigned several officers to perform the related duties. Prior to the standoff and shooting in the Hogan incident, several members had accumulated an extensive record of excessive force claims and settlements which the court ruled amounted to deliberate indifference in assigning officers to such responsibilities without supervisory remedy. The plaintiff researched the personnel records of assigned ERT officers and discovered that six team members had accumulated a total of 46 excessive force claims over a period of 10 years prior to the special assignment, which resulted in significant monetary settlements. After the Hogan shooting, the grand jury reported that the city had no code of conduct, written safety rules, or recognized manual of policies, and the command structure failed to identify and remedy obvious safety deficiencies. The court held that, based upon a pattern of an obvious disregard by the city to discipline officers for engaging in a pattern of abuse of authority in using force, for ratifying a practice of assigning officers to a high liability duty without more rigorous selection criteria, that the plaintiff established the existence of a policy and custom of deliberate indifference to the use of excessive force by ERT members.

Administrators must pay careful attention to complaints and adverse reports against subordinates. They must be investigated and properly documented. Further, administrators must generally be aware of the strengths and weaknesses of subordinates and not assign them to perform tasks for which they lack skill or competence.

Negligent Entrustment

Negligent entrustment involves the supervisor's failure to properly supervise or control an employee's custody, use, or supervision of equipment or facilities entrusted to him or her (del Carmen, 1991). This theory of liability is different from negligent assignment in that negligent entrustment goes beyond employee incompetence in carrying out his or her duties to incompetence in the use of equipment entrusted to the employee. For example, legal claims may emerge for failing to direct the proper use of an impact weapon in a disturbance situation that later results in the serious injury or death of a prisoner. In *Roberts v. Williams* (1971), a county farm superintendent had given an untrained trustee guard a shotgun and the task of guarding a work crew. The supervisor was held liable because the shotgun went off, seriously wounding a prisoner.

In *Slaken v. Porter* (1984), a jury awarded a prisoner $32,000 when evidence supported a claim of excessive force by correctional officers after they used high-pressure hoses, tear gas, and billy clubs to subdue him while he was in a one-man cell. The officers and supervisory personnel were found to be deliberately indifferent to the prisoner's constitutional right to be free from a known risk of harm. Supervisors were found liable because they should have been aware of the officers' propensities and because they had the duty to ensure that instruments of control were not misused. In *Norris v. Detrick* (1996), the court found that prison officials properly administered two doses of chloracetaphenone (CN) gas when confronted by a prisoner with known martial arts skills who refused to return to his cell after numerous orders to do so. The court noted that whether the use of gas is constitutional depends on the totality of circumstances, including provocation, the amount of gas used, and the purposes for which the gas was used. In *Pereira-Gonzalez v. Lopez-Feliciano* (1990), police supervisors were held liable for failing to confiscate the duty weapon of an officer who had a history of spouse abuse. The officer shot his wife after asking supervisors to take the weapon.

Negligent entrustment need not only include the misuse of equipment or weapons. Sanctioning or condoning the misuse of physical force may also increase the risk of liability for superiors. A sheriff was liable in *Duckworth v. Whiesnant* (1996) for tacitly condoning the use of excessive force. The sheriff condoned the practice of kicking arrestees in the groin. In this case the deputy admitted to kicking the plaintiff in the groin while he was handcuffed. The court concluded that the county had "entrusted" this practice to officers and that it amounted to deliberate indifference.

In some claims plaintiffs attempt to show that an administrator failed to equip department officers with the proper equipment which, if accessible, may have resulted in a different outcome. This type of claim is generally conjecture by a plaintiff and is asserted to demonstrate that an administrator deliberately made a decision that resulted in violating a citizen's constitutional rights. In *Estate of Larsen v. Murr* (2006), the plaintiff alleged that at the time of Mr. Larsen's death, the city engaged in a custom of not arming officers with less-lethal weaponry. An officer shot and killed a suspect whom he believed would have killed him if he had not fired his duty weapon. In 2000, a city committee was studying whether to entrust officers with Tasers, less-lethal shotguns, and pepper balls. These weapons were available to the department, but the decision to provide them to patrol officers was not made until 2003. The court concluded that there was no deliberate decision made by the city not to deploy less-lethal weapons prior to the incident. Assuming, however, that there was such a decision that would support a custom or policy, the plaintiff presented no evidence that the officer would have acted any differently had he been equipped with a less-lethal weapon. The court stated that it would not speculate that if the officer had been issued a less-lethal weapon, he would have chosen to use it under the circumstances. The court concluded that the failure to issue less-lethal weapons did not cause the decedent's death.

The test of liability is that of deliberate indifference. The plaintiff must prove that the officer was incompetent, inexperienced, or reckless, and that the supervisor knew or had reason to know of this. The defense for the supervisor is that the use and custody of equipment were properly supervised, but despite adequate precautions, the incident still occurred.

Failure to Direct

A significant responsibility of any administrator is to develop and implement agency policies and procedures. Policies and procedures put into operation the statutory requirements of criminal justice personnel. They provide direction to officers in the proper performance of their duties. Policies guide officers in making decisions about how to legitimately respond in different situations, particularly when a supervisor is not immediately available.

Failing to direct refers to a failure to inform employees of the special requirements and limits of the job to be performed. This is frequently interpreted as the failure of an administrator to promulgate policies and procedures that direct personnel in the specific tasks of the job. In *Ford v. Brier* (1974), the court ruled that failing to establish adequate policies gives rise to civil liability. Examples include the supervisor failing to inform employees of the proper procedures for dispensing medication to prisoners or the limits of using force to restore order during a fight.

In police work some of the more obvious examples of failing to develop policies and guidelines include making arrests, using force, engaging in high-speed pursuits, performing searches on arrestees, and responding to the mentally impaired. For example, in *Garris v. Rowland* (1982), liability existed for failure to establish a policy of informing officers when an arrest warrant had been quashed. A practice of not informing officers of the status of arrest warrants had developed.

In *Rivas v. Freeman* (1991), liability attached against a sheriff for failing to develop sufficient and appropriate procedures and policies regarding identification of arrestees, warrantless searches, and computer checks for information. Although the sheriff was not personally involved in the arrest of the plaintiff, the court found that he formulated the policies and customs that resulted in the violations of the plaintiff's constitutional rights. The lack of established policies and procedures caused the plaintiff's arrest, his unnecessary six-day incarceration, and resulting humiliation. The evidence at trial supported a claim that the officer's actions showed that the sheriff failed to establish policies that would properly direct them in the performance of their duties.

In *Women Prisoners v. District of Columbia* (1994), the district court found prison officials liable for violating the rights of female prisoners who were subjected to sexual harassment. The court held that the harassment was the result of a government custom and practice and that officials failed to properly train employees in the area of sexual harassment. A federal district court in *Estep v. Dent* (1996) granted injunctive relief to a prisoner based on a claim that the prison policy that required him to cut his earlocks violated the Religious Freedom Restoration Act. Requiring the prisoner to cut his earlocks would substantially violate the tenets of his Jewish faith. The court found that prison officials were deliberately indifferent and failed to establish that the policy was the least restrictive means of furthering its interests in maintaining security.

A federal appellate court in *Vineyard v. County of Murray* (1993) found that the county was deliberately indifferent to the rights of prisoners who had been beaten by deputies. The court stated that the county's policy of condoning such behavior was the moving force behind the violation of the prisoner's constitutional rights. In *Valencia v. Wiggins* (1993), liability was assessed against jail officials who acted outside the boundaries of established policy. A prisoner was awarded $2,500 in damages and $27,000 in attorney's fees when the jury found that officers used excessive force against him in a jail disturbance. The officer struck a handcuffed, nonresisting prisoner and placed him in a choke hold. The jury found that the force and choke hold violated the jail's policy and constituted malicious and sadistic harm.

The court rejected a motion of summary judgment filed by the City of Yakima, Washington, in *Richards v. Janis* (2007). The Yakima Police Department adopted the use of the Taser and implemented a policy for its usage. In part, the policy directed officers to: "use extra caution when considering its use on juveniles under 16 years of age; pregnant females, elderly subjects, handcuffed persons; and persons in elevated positions." Officer Cavin arrested Richards, who did not resist arrest and was handcuffed. Without provocation, Officer Cavin applied the Taser and Richards filed a lawsuit, claiming that the city's Taser policy was unconstitutional as well as the use of excessive force. The chief interpreted the department's policy as allowing the Tasering of subjects who are handcuffed as long as they are standing. Officer Cavin could not recall any policy restrictions on applying the Taser on handcuffed individuals. The chief did not conduct an internal investigation of officer Cavin's use of force but received numerous witness statements reporting that Richards did not resist arrest and that the officer's behavior was generally abhorrent. The court held that the plaintiff sufficiently presented evidence showing that the city had a policy and custom serving as the moving force behind officer Cavin's Taser usage. The plaintiff presented records of officer Cavin's Taser use in which the court determined that the city acquiesced in enforcing the policy and concluded that the police department had a well-settled policy serving as the moving force behind officer Cavin's excessive Taser use. With this information the court concluded that the Yakima police department failed to conduct an internal investigation, which demonstrated that it condoned and ratified the officers' misconduct.

The best defensible position for administrators is to establish and maintain a current, comprehensive, and constitutional written policy manual. Policies should be reviewed and revised annually, in order to reflect the current status of the law. The written policy should reflect not only the theory, but also the actual practice of the department. Agency procedures should mirror written job descriptions. Employees should be trained and tested in their comprehension of policy content. Each employee should have an individual current copy of the policy manual and it should be inspected periodically. Supervisors must be familiar with and enforce all policies.

The importance of implementing and enforcing departmental policies was further emphasized in the Court's decision in *City of Ontario, California v. Quon* (2010). The city signed a contract with a private company for 20 pagers specifically to be used by the Emergency Response Team (ERT), which included 20 officers. The city limited the number of messages for each officer on a monthly basis and informed them that the pagers would be treated like their work computer. The city provided each member of the ERT with a policy on the use of the pager, addressed the policy with all team members, informed each officer that there was no expectation of privacy in using the pager, and that the messages on the pager would be monitored periodically. Each officer signed documents acknowledging his or her comprehension of the policy. Sergeant Quon exceeded the number of authorized messages and a lieutenant counseled him about the overages. Sergeant Quon agreed to pay for the overages but after two months failed to do so. The chief of police instructed internal affairs to investigate further and they performed a search of the pager and found that sergeant Quon made 456 messages, of which 57 were not work related, and many involved sexually explicit content. Quon was later disciplined.

Sergeant Quon filed a § 1983 lawsuit claiming that the chief ordered a search of his pager, which violated his Fourth Amendment rights. The district court ruled that Quon had an expectation to privacy but determined that the search of the pager was reasonable. Quon appealed to the Ninth Circuit Appellate Court and they reversed holding that the search was unreasonable.

The City of Ontario appealed the decision to the United States Supreme Court and the Court granted certiorari to examine privacy expectations in communications made by employees on electronic equipment provided by an employer. The Court addressed three questions: Did Quon have a privacy expectation? Did the review of the pager messages constitute a search? Do searches of electronic equipment have the same protection as physical property at the workplace? The Court reviewed the background of an expectation of privacy and reasonable searches under the Fourth Amendment. The Court, however, made a distinction about searches of employer property assigned to employees at the workplace. The Court ruled employees have a right to privacy but there are exceptions. At the workplace, "special needs" in regard to work-related misconduct is a justified exception and a warrantless search is allowed. In this case there were justifiable grounds for conducting the search of the pager. The city had a legitimate interest in ensuring that employees were not being forced to pay out of their own pockets for work-related expenses, or on the other hand that the city was not paying for extensive personal communications.

As for the scope of the search, reviewing the transcripts was reasonable because it was an efficient and expedient way to determine whether Quon's overages were the result of work-related messaging or personal use. The review was also not "excessively intrusive." The Court reasoned that Quon as a law enforcement officer would or should have known that his actions were likely to come under legal scrutiny, and that this might entail an analysis of his on-the-job communications. Under the circumstances, a reasonable employee would be aware that sound management principles might require the audit of messages to determine whether the pager was being appropriately used. Quon was not given any assurances of an expectation of privacy regarding the search of the pager. Indeed the police department provided the officers with a policy on the use of the pager, informed them to treat it as a work computer, to expect periodic monitoring of the pager, and each officer signed a supportive policy document. The Court determined that the search was reasonable in its scope, was not intrusive, and did not violate Quon's Fourth Amendment rights against an unreasonable search.

Because the search was motivated by a legitimate work-related purpose, and because it was not excessive in scope, the search was reasonable. The employer had a legitimate reason for the search, and that the search was not excessively intrusive in light of that justification—the Court also concluded that the search would be "regarded as reasonable and normal in the private-employer context." The Court reversed the Ninth Circuit Appellate Court's decision.

Ostensibly the Court's ruling gave deference to workplace management who has a responsibility to ensure employees adhere to workplace policies. The decision serves to remind administrators to ensure that policies are implemented that address all electronic equipment, its work-related usage, and articulate that the equipment will be monitored periodically to maintain integrity of the equipment. Administrators are encouraged to address the policy with all employees through training, provide a copy to each employee, and require each employee to sign that they have read and received training in the policy. Finally, administrators and supervisors should work to enforce the policy in order to maintain accountability by all employees.

Failure to Supervise Subordinates

A fundamental responsibility of criminal justice supervisors is to provide adequate supervision and control over the activities of subordinates. Allegations of failing to supervise employees involve abdication of the responsibility to oversee employee activities. Failing to supervise employees properly can result in litigation for failing to know about employee behavior. Examples include tolerating a pattern of physical abuse of arrestees or prisoners, racial discrimination, and pervasive deprivation of individual rights and privileges.

Permitting unlawful activities in an agency may constitute deliberate indifference, giving rise to liability. The key issue relates to a policy or custom of inadequate supervision of employees. The plaintiff must show that the agency failed to supervise its personnel or that such failures resulted in deliberate indifference. The usual standard is whether the supervisor knew of a pattern of behavior but failed to act on it. The question becomes "What constitutes knowledge of a pattern of behavior among employees?" Many courts have established that actual knowledge is required, while other courts state that knowledge can be inferred if a history of violations is established and the administrator had direct and close supervisory control over the employee committing the violation. In *Johnson v. Cannon* (1996), the court found a sheriff liable for failure to provide proper supervision and control of a deputy. Over a period of several months, a deputy had stopped female motorists for traffic violations and forced them to have sexual intercourse with him. The failure to properly supervise the deputy rose to a level of deliberate indifference.

Courts hold that a supervisor must be "causally linked" to the pattern of constitutional violations by showing knowledge of it, and that this failure to act amounts to approval and thus tacit encouragement for the pattern to continue. In *Shaw v. Stroud* (1994), the estate of the deceased failed to connect an alleged failure to supervise with a North Carolina state trooper's history of excessive force claims in a situation in which he used deadly force. The trooper stopped a motorist in front of his house and attempted to arrest him for driving while impaired. During the arrest a struggle ensued, and the driver took the trooper's metal flashlight and struck him on the head. The driver came at the trooper again and struck him a second time, and on a third attempt the trooper fired his duty weapon several times, killing the driver.

The trooper, his sergeant at the time, and a former sergeant were sued by the family. The former sergeant had supervised the trooper for approximately five years but had transferred 18 months prior to the shooting. The trooper had accumulated more than 25 complaints from citizens alleging excessive force. A district court judge had also voiced concern to the trooper's supervisor regarding the number of "injured" defendants who appeared in his courtroom after being arrested by this trooper. The Fourth Circuit Court of Appeals dismissed the claim of inadequate supervision against the current supervisor because he had responded to complaints by sending other supervisors to monitor court cases and by riding with the trooper to evaluate his conduct during arrests. The court, however, remanded the case to the lower court with regard to the first supervisor's inaction, because the court held that he failed to investigate the many complaints lodged against the trooper, constituting a failure to supervise. The jury in the lower court found that the trooper responded correctly by shooting the motorist. Therefore, because the jury found in favor of the trooper, the supervisor could not be held liable.

The severity of an employee's constitutional violation must be sufficient in order to justify a verdict of failing to properly supervise an employee. In *Atchinson v. District of Columbia* (1996), a police officer confronted a man carrying a machete on the street. The officer shouted "Freeze!" one time and did not give another warning before using deadly force. The appellate court ruled that even a single incident of such use of force was adequate to support a complaint of inadequate supervision and training of police in the use of force. Conversely, in *Singleton v. McDougall* (1996), a sheriff was not liable for alleged inadequate supervision when an officer used deadly force in an arrest situation. The evidence showed that there had been "numerous" (although the number was not specified) incidents in which deputies had previously used deadly force. The plaintiff's contention was that such incidents proved that the sheriff failed to supervise his subordinates in the proper use of firearms and thus was deliberately indifferent to the rights of the citizenry. Despite previous lawsuits alleging the use of excessive force or wrongful use of deadly force by deputies, there had been no single case in which the courts had ruled that department personnel had violated a clearly established right in this area. The court concluded that the sheriff was entitled to qualified immunity, as the evidence failed to show that a reasonable person in the sheriff's position would know that the unresolved lawsuits established a right requiring corrective action.

In *Williams v. White* (1990), the Eighth Circuit Court of Appeals found that a prison superintendent may be liable for operating a prison with unsanitary and inhumane conditions and may be directly liable when he fails to train, supervise, or control his subordinates. In *Treadwell v. Murray* (1995), a prisoner asserted that correctional officials failed to oversee officers and medical personnel when the officials deprived him of an unsafe rehabilitative environment and initial inappropriate medical classification. The prisoner claimed that the physician's improper classification prevented him from being eligible for "different types of incarceration," such as halfway houses, work-release programs, or road camps. According to the prisoner, the director of corrections abdicated his supervisory responsibility by failing to oversee the actions of his employees, which ultimately resulted in a constitutional deprivation. The court found that the prisoner failed to state a claim of deliberate indifference under § 1983 based on supervisory liability. The court further concluded that the prisoner failed to substantiate any wanton, obdurate, or offensive acts by the director of corrections in his supervisory capacity, nor could he point to any single incident, or isolated incident, in which the director created any pervasive risk of harm that deprived the prisoner of a constitutionally protected right.

In *Giroux v. Sherman* (1992), a prisoner was awarded $36,000 in punitive damages, claiming on four occasions that at least eight correctional officers beat and tormented him without provocation. Due to the beatings, he aggravated an old injury, which required hospitalization. While in the hospital, he was also beaten and sustained kidney and throat injuries. Supervisory liability was also found when the court stated that supervisors failed to identify and correct their behavior.

In *Campbell v. City of New York* (2004), the court found that supervisors of an arresting officer were liable for failing to supervise and failing to discipline officer misconduct. Campbell requested police assistance when he was assaulted by his ex-wife's son. Officer Buckley responded, but did not arrest the son. The police received a second call from Campbell six months later, asking for assistance in enforcing a restraining order that allowed him to visit his children, who were in his ex-wife's custody. Officer Buckley responded and learned that Campbell's ex-wife had a protection order against him, and Campbell was arrested. Campbell served time in jail but the charges were later dropped. Campbell filed a citizen complaint for false arrest. Detectives investigated the complaint and informed Campbell that his ex-wife had called the NYPD reporting that he had threatened to kill her. Campbell's ex-wife signed an affidavit stating that Campbell made threats to her and he was arrested a second time. These charges were later dropped and Campbell filed a lawsuit claiming that supervisors of the NYPD failed to adequately supervise and discipline the officers involved in the case.

The court ruled in favor of Campbell, holding that the officers caused a formation of a custom, practice, and policy that was detrimental to Campbell's rights. The court found that supervisors failed to adequately supervise the involved officers and allowed a practice of officer misconduct. The court agreed with Campbell's claim that failing to supervise officers ostensibly encouraged other officers to retaliate against citizens who filed complaints. The court, however, dismissed the false arrest claim filed regarding the first arrest as there was a lawful protection order against him.

This decision not only questions the officer's decision-making ability, but questions a department's level of supervision with their officers. Supervisors can insulate themselves from allegations for failure to supervise by ensuring that officers follow through with all investigations in a timely manner and reminding investigators of the importance of remaining impartial in their review of citizen complaints. In addition, supervisors must show that they have taken proactive measures to properly supervise their officers when misconduct occurs. For example, supervisors were held liable in *Neris v. Vivoni* (2003) when it was shown that the supervisors had actual knowledge of employees' unconstitutional conduct and took no steps to remedy the situation. Failure to take remedial intervention measures in the face of such knowledge rose to a level of supervisory deliberate indifference.

In *Estate of Brutsche v. City of Federal Way* (2007), the plaintiff brought claims against several municipalities for failure to supervise Emergency Response Team (ERT) members and for developing unconstitutional policies. Several cities joined in a mutual aid agreement to form an ERT and an executive board was responsible for formulating the policies of the team. The ERT served a "high-risk" warrant of Brutsche's property based on a number of factors, one of which was a high risk of violence by Brutsche. During the execution of the warrant Brutsche was injured and he sued the municipalities, claiming that the policies and customs of the ERT caused his injuries and that the supervisors of team members failed to properly supervise officers, ratifying their unconstitutional use of excessive force. The municipalities filed a motion for summary judgment.

The court noted that the municipalities were persons within the meaning of § 1983 and were subject to a lawsuit. Brutsche argued that the officers of the team followed an unconstitutional policy of the departments, which resulted in a violation of his Fourth Amendment rights. He argued that policies of the team to execute high-risk warrants caused the team to use unreasonable force. He also argued that such policies, when executed and resulted in excessive force and an injury, also supported a claim of failure to supervise team members in the proper techniques that would minimize the use of force. The court granted summary judgment because Brutsche could not provide any supporting evidence that showed that the team's execution of the warrant resulted in a sustainable injury. The court found that the policy used to classify warrants as high risk could not be considered the cause of Brutsche's injuries. The court also noted that officers had been directed personally by supervisors in the execution of the warrant and the techniques used in implementing the policy in the field, and found no evidence that officers were improperly supervised in the performance of their duties.

It is imperative that administrators not shut their eyes to, or tolerate, improper employee conduct. Performance should be evaluated periodically, as well as informal appraisals of employee conduct to encourage proper conduct. Supervisors should review employee performance firsthand and review all incident reports. All complaints of improper conduct by officers must be investigated and appropriate discipline should be provided. Remedial correction of unsatisfactory employee performance should be documented, and employees who chronically fall below the accepted standard should be put on notice that employment is based on adherence to policy and proper conduct in the workplace. This strategy can assist in reducing potential supervisory liability.

The issue of what level of supervisory behavior would lead to liability was further examined in *Ashcroft v. Iqbal* (2009). After the attack on the World Trade Center in New York City (September 11, 2001), Iqbal was held in a Detention Center as a "person of interest" along with 183 others. Iqbal was placed in a segregation housing unit and released from his cell for one hour daily. Iqbal pled guilty to Fraud of the United States and after serving his sentence he was transported back to Pakistan. He subsequently filed a Federal Torts Claim (*Bivens* action) against the Director of the Federal Bureau of Investigation, Robert Mueller, and United States Attorney General John Ashcroft, who supervised Director Mueller. Iqbal asserted that Mueller implemented an unconstitutional policy developed by Ashcroft, which included harsh treatment in the segregation unit that violated his religious rights as a Muslim. The complaint asserted that petitioners designated the respondent a person of high interest because of his race, religion, or national origin, in contravention of the First and Fifth Amendments to the Constitution. The complaint alleged that "the [FBI], under the direction of Defendant Mueller, arrested and detained thousands of Arab Muslim men . . . as part of its investigation of the events of September 11." It further alleged that "[t]he policy of holding post-September-11th detainees in highly restrictive conditions of confinement until they were 'cleared' by the FBI was approved by defendants Ashcroft and Mueller in discussions in the weeks after September 11, 2001." Lastly, the complaint alleged that petitioners "each knew of, condoned, and willfully and maliciously agreed to subject" the respondent to harsh conditions of confinement "as a matter of policy."

Ashcroft's motion for summary judgment was rejected by the lower court and the Second Circuit Appellate Court since both courts held that Iqbal's complaint was adequate to allege petitioners' personal involvement in discriminatory decisions, which, if true, violated clearly established constitutional law. The Court granted certiorari to examine the issue of whether a supervisor may be held liable when an employee implements policy that allegedly discriminates against the plaintiff in violation of his constitutional rights.

The Court ruled that because vicarious liability is inapplicable to *Bivens v. Six Unknown Fed. Narcotics Agents*, 403 U.S. 388 (1971) and § 1983 suits (see *Monell v. New York City Dept. of Social Servs.*, 1978), the plaintiff must plead that each government-official defendant, through his own individual actions, has violated the Constitution. Purposeful discrimination requires more than "intent as volition or intent as awareness of consequences"; it involves a decision-maker's undertaking a course of action "because of," not merely "in spite of," the action's adverse effects upon an identifiable group. The Court ruled that Iqbal must plead sufficient factual matter to show that petitioners adopted and implemented the detention policies at issue not for a neutral, investigative reason, but for the purpose of discriminating on account of race, religion, or national origin.

Several of his allegations—that petitioners agreed to subject him to harsh conditions as a matter of policy, solely on account of discriminatory factors and for no legitimate penological interest; that Ashcroft was that policy's "principal architect"; and that Mueller was "instrumental" in its adoption and execution—are conclusory and not entitled to be assumed true. Moreover, the factual allegations that the FBI, under Mueller, arrested and detained thousands of Arab Muslim men, and that he and Ashcroft approved the detention policy, do not plausibly suggest that they purposefully discriminated on prohibited grounds. Given that the September 11 attacks were perpetrated by Arab Muslims, it is not surprising that a legitimate policy directing law enforcement to arrest and detain individuals because of their suspected link to the attacks would produce a disparate, incidental impact on Arab Muslims, even though the policy's purpose was to target neither Arabs nor Muslims. Even if the complaint's well-pleaded facts gave rise to a plausible inference that Iqbal's arrest was the result of unconstitutional discrimination, that inference alone would not entitle him to relief. Iqbal's claims against Ashcroft rested solely on their ostensible policy of holding detainees categorized as "of high interest," but the complaint does not contain facts plausibly showing that their policy was based on discriminatory factors.

Iqbal argued that, under a theory of "supervisory liability," petitioners can be liable for "knowledge and acquiescence in their subordinates' use of discriminatory criteria to make classification decisions among detainees." This meant that Iqbal believed that a supervisor's mere knowledge of his subordinate's discriminatory purpose amounts to the supervisor's violating the Constitution. The Court, however, rejected the argument. The Court held that in a § 1983 suit or a *Bivens* action—where masters do not answer for the torts of their servants—the term "supervisory liability" is a misnomer. Absent vicarious liability, each government official, his or her title notwithstanding, is liable only for his or her own misconduct. In the context of determining whether there is a violation of clearly established right to overcome qualified immunity, purpose rather than knowledge is required to impose *Bivens* liability on the subordinate for unconstitutional discrimination; the same holds true for an official charged with violations arising from his or her superintendent responsibilities.

Iqbal's claims against Ashcroft rested solely on their ostensible "policy of holding post-September-11th detainees" in the ADMAX SHU once they were categorized as "of high interest." To prevail on that theory, the complaint must contain facts plausibly showing that petitioners purposefully adopted a policy of classifying post-September-11 detainees as "of high interest" because of their race, religion, or national origin. The Court concluded that the complaint failed to support the allegation.

The application of the majority's decision to supervisory liability in local law enforcement cases is best evidenced by the Court noting that the clearly established precedent that supervisors cannot be held liable under § 1983 or *Bivens* based upon *respondeat superior* liability; in other words, simply because they supervise the person who committed the wrongful act. The Court went on to assert: "because vicarious liability is inapplicable to *Bivens* and § 1983 suits, a plaintiff must plead that each Government–official defendant, through the official's own individual actions, has violated the Constitution. The factors necessary to establish a *Bivens* [or § 1983] violation [against the supervisor] will vary depending on the constitutional provision at issue. Where the claim is invidious discrimination in contravention of the First and Fifth Amendments, our decisions make clear that the plaintiff must plead and prove that the defendant [supervisor] acted with a discriminatory purpose."

The Court held: "In the context of determining whether there is a violation of clearly established right to overcome qualified immunity, purpose rather than knowledge is required to impose *Bivens* liability on the subordinate for unconstitutional discrimination; the same holds true for an official charged with violations arising from his or her superintendent responsibilities."

In cases involving allegations of discrimination, such as racial profiling allegations, it will not be enough for a plaintiff to show that a supervisor knew of and acquiesced in the racial profiling but instead will have to show that the supervisor had a purpose to discriminate. A plaintiff must show plausible facts showing a policy was based on discrimination factors.

The case will likely have an impact where there is some state of mind requirement such as use of force in jails and prisons. It may not in those cases be enough to show that the supervisor knew of and acquiesced to the force; a plaintiff may be required to prove that the supervisor had the requisite malicious and sadistic intention related to the use of force (Ryan, 2009).

Negligent Failure to Discipline/Negligent Retention

Failure to discipline involves the administrator's failure to investigate complaints about employees and take appropriate action as warranted. Allegations can also result from the supervisor failing to take action against an employee in the form of suspension, transfer, or termination when the employee has demonstrated unsuitability for the job. Claims of retaining errant officers after they have repeatedly engaged in misconduct can also result in supervisory liability.

The supervisor has an affirmative duty to take all necessary and proper steps to discipline or terminate a subordinate who is obviously unfit for employment. Unfitness may be determined either from acts of prior gross misconduct or from a series of prior acts of lesser misconduct that indicate a pattern (del Carmen, 1991). Courts have imposed liability for inaction when a supervisor had actual knowledge that the employee had previously engaged in unlawful conduct and did nothing to correct the behavior. In *Hogan v. Franco* (1995), the chief was found liable for failing to discipline, supervise, and train errant officers in the proper use of force. In this case the plaintiff sustained major nerve damage to his arm, wrist, and back from the improper use of handcuffs and misapplication of an impact weapon (a baton) by the arresting officer. Evidence was confirmed that the chief knew of a history of officers physically abusing prisoners or mishandling arrest situations. Trial testimony confirmed more than 10 successful lawsuits won by plaintiffs for similar complaints made against the department. The chief was aware of at least one officer who had a propensity for violence and beating arrestees. The chief was held liable for tolerating the failure to investigate, discipline, or correct violations, which suggested the adoption of a policy supporting such violations. Such persistent failure to discipline amounted to an inference of an unlawful policy of ratification of unconstitutional conduct within the meaning of *Monell* and rose to a level of deliberate indifference. The plaintiff was awarded $200,000 in compensatory damages against the chief and the officer.

The *Hogan* case illustrates how the courts make a connection between official policy and a failure to discipline in cases of known officer misconduct. In essence, failing to identify officer misconduct or tolerating known misconduct creates a de facto policy creating liability on the part of the administrator as the official policymaker of the department. It can rise to a level of deliberate indifference if the administrator or supervisor was aware of the misconduct and chose to ignore the misconduct or did not take measures to prevent it. In *Diaz v. Martinez* (1997), summary judgment was denied because the chief failed to discipline and maintain accurate records about a rogue officer or recommend remedial training. This demonstrated supervisory indifference. Moreover, in emphasizing the association between failing to discipline and official policy, the court held in *Grandstaff v. City of Borger* (1985) that the police chief was the sole policymaker, and therefore his failure to discipline several officers involved in an egregious shooting, in which a person was killed, was evidence of a municipal policy of ignoring constitutional rights violations.

In *Vann v. City of New York* (1995), the court determined that deliberate indifference was evidenced by an abusive officer who had been the subject of numerous complaints, disciplined several times, and placed on restricted duty. He was returned to regular duty and committed additional assaults. Prior to his return to regular duty, a psychological evaluation noted that the officer had a personality problem that escalated minor situations into violent incidents. In returning him to regular duty, the chief failed to monitor the problem officer's conduct despite prior "red flag" incidents of violent behavior. After his return to regular duty, the officer continued to receive citizen abuse complaints that were not investigated by the chief.

Deliberate indifference was determined by a pattern of ignoring complaints in which the need to discipline was obvious.

A fundamental requirement of all supervisors is to enforce their own legitimate regulations and follow through with appropriate discipline as necessary. A correctional officer's rights were not violated when the department of corrections required him to wear an American flag patch on his uniform shirt (*Troster v. Pennsylvania State Department of Corrections*, 1995). In *Flynn v. Sandahl* (1995), the warden did not violate a correctional officer's due process rights by ordering him to submit to a psychiatric examination after co-workers complained that he had threatened them with physical harm. Any privacy interest of the officer was outweighed by requirements of maintaining a stable prison workforce.

In several cases, supervisors have been held liable for promulgating policies that discourage investigation of police misconduct, and failing to discipline, which encourage constitutional violations. In *Bastia v. Rodriguez* (1983), the court ruled that the persistent failure to discipline subordinates who violate constitutional rights could give rise to an inference of ratification. In *Skevofilax v. Quigley* (1984), a police chief was held liable for continually failing to discipline or control subordinates in the face of knowledge of their propensity to use force improperly. This created an official custom or de facto policy that was actionable under § 1983. In *Haynes v. Marshall* (1989), a prisoner brought a valid claim against a prison superintendent for having a policy of using force against prisoners to enforce rules.

In *Beck v. City of Pittsburgh* (1996), a "custom" of failing to discipline officers created liability for the police chief. It was determined that investigative policies requiring a complainant to produce evidence other than his or her word, not considering prior complaints against an officer, not having a tracking system for prior complaints and dispositions, eschewing standards for reporting patterns, and a practice of not reviewing recommendations for no discipline, were sufficient to establish deliberate indifference. Also, in *Nolin v. Town of Springville* (1999), the court found sufficient evidence of deliberate indifference on the part of the chief for failing to discipline and train officers. In a five-person department, numerous cases involving claims of excessive force had been settled out of court during a relatively short period. It was determined that all members of the department, including the chief, would have known of such claims. After each claim, the chief neither disciplined the officer nor required retraining. This pattern of settling claims in a small department, without disciplinary action being taken, or requiring retraining of officers in the use of appropriate force, rose to a level of deliberate indifference and liability attached.

Administrative liability will be avoided when supervisors fulfill their basic functions of properly enforcing security practices and institutional policies. A prison official's termination of a correctional officer found sleeping on the job after taking medication for an arthritic knee was not found to be arbitrary or capricious (*Nebraska Department of Correctional Services v. Hansen*, 1991). Correctional officials were not liable when they took prompt effective disciplinary action after a female employee complained of alleged sexual harassment by a correctional officer (*Hirschfeld v. New Mexico Corrections Department*, 1990).

If the agency's disciplinary system is deficient, supervisory liability may attach. In *Gutierrez-Rodriguez v. Cartagena* (1989), the court held the police administrator personally liable, as it found the disciplinary system to be grossly deficient, reflecting a reckless and callous indifference to the rights of citizens. Several officers in the department had accumulated numerous civilian complaints that had gone uninvestigated. Additionally, supervisors exhibited a pattern of failing to discipline officers. In this case the plaintiff was shot by four officers. They had approached his vehicle with guns drawn and the plaintiff, noticing the four in plain clothes, attempted to speed away. The plaintiff was parked off the road with his girlfriend and was not a "wanted" person. One round hit him in the back, causing him to drive into a ditch. The car landed on its side and the plaintiff sustained a back injury, leaving him a paraplegic.

The chief knew the histories of these officers but failed to take remedial or preventive measures. Failing to do so amounted to deliberate indifference and, as a result, the incident above occurred. The chief was found liable and the plaintiff was awarded $4.5 million. The disciplinary system existed in name only. The court found the following procedures inadequate:

1. Officers investigated could refuse to testify or give a statement.
2. The agency did not have any provision for remedial training as one of the disciplinary options.
3. The withdrawal of a complaint closed the internal investigation without the agency doing anything about it.
4. The immediate supervisors of the officers were not involved in the disciplinary process.

In another case the disciplinary system was so faulty that the court awarded summary judgment to the plaintiff. In *Cox v. District of Columbia* (1993), the civilian review board (which exclusively ruled on excessive force allegations) chronically delayed decisions and ignored statutory deadlines. The court considered that these "flagrant" violations deprived citizens of their constitutional rights and amounted to deliberate indifference on the part of the administration.

Properly following departmental procedures when considering discipline or termination of an employee is important in defending a claim that an officer was wrongfully discharged. Documenting past occasions of discipline is critical in justifying a supervisor's decision to pursue more severe sanctions or termination of the employee. In *Peterson v. Civil Service Commission of Cedar Rapids* (2005), the appellate court upheld the decision of the chief of police of Cedar Rapids, Iowa, when he terminated an officer for an incident of excessive force. Officer Peterson attempted to stop a motorist for speeding. Peterson activated his lights and siren as the motorist exited the highway, but the motorist ignored them. The motorist proceeded to his residence and pulled in the driveway. Peterson stopped behind him and activated his in-car video camera. The motorist exited his car and ignored Peterson's commands to stop and keep back from the car. Peterson was joined by several back-up officers and informed the motorist that he was under arrest. The motorist resisted arrest and the officers forced him to the ground to control and handcuff him. Two of the responding officers informed a supervisor that Peterson used excessive force during the confrontation by kneeing him in the head as they pinned him to the ground. Peterson informed a lieutenant that he only used his knee to pin the motorist's shoulder for control purposes, which was an authorized technique. The lieutenant, however, informed Peterson that he thought discipline was warranted. After an internal affairs investigation and an administrative hearing, the chief fired Peterson for excessive use of force. Peterson appealed the decision and the civil service commission upheld the termination.

Peterson filed a lawsuit and the court overturned the termination, holding that the videotape of the incident did not support the chief's decision to fire him. The court ruled that the use of force was inadvertent and not excessive, and ordered that Peterson be reinstated. The civil service commission appealed the decision. The appellate court reviewed the videotape, witness statements, and the officers' testimony, and found that Peterson had used excessive force in response to the motorist's behavior. The court also examined Peterson's personnel file and noted that he had a prior suspension for a similar traffic stop. In that incident, Peterson pointed his firearm and taunted a driver for failing to follow his commands. The court noted that the department had implemented policy and practices for responding to employee misconduct and had followed them in the past. Thus, the court ruled that the chief had the authority to suspend, demote, or fire for misconduct that was detrimental to the public interest. Given the prior suspension, the severity of the sanction was appropriate as the next step in progressive discipline.

In contrast, however, an appellate court overturned the termination of an officer who was cited for excessive use of sick leave and lying during an internal affairs investigation. In *Atchison v. Monroe Municipal Fire and Police Civil Service Board* (2011), officer Atchison appealed her termination to the court after she learned that several officers in the department had not been disciplined or terminated for the same conduct in which she was terminated. The lower court rejected her appeal holding the Board's decision was based on good faith and upon cause, and she appealed the lower court's decision.

The Appellate Court reviewed the case. The record reflected that Atchison committed 27 violations of the sick leave policy, failed to call to log out for an off-duty job, and lied about the charges during the investigation. The chief testified that Atchison was an exemplary employee for the first three years of employment but for the past several years her performance went downhill. She had never been the subject of disciplinary proceedings during her seven-year employment. The chief also testified that in previous internal investigations other officers had lied and some of them had been terminated. The chief believed he acted in good faith.

The appellate court determined that the termination was excessive punishment in response to Atchison's infractions and disproportionate to the punishment handed out to other officers in similar circumstances. The court noted that the purpose of punishment was to correct the behavior of officers whose conduct was affecting the department's morale, and Atchison had not received warnings or been disciplined previously before being terminated. The court further held that the sick leave policy was ambiguous and some of the charges against Atchison were refutable. Also, the zero tolerance policy against lying was ambiguous as it had frequently gone unenforced in the years following its development. The court found that Atchison had received commendations on multiple occasions in addition to her clean disciplinary record. The court overturned the termination and amended the penalty to a 90-day suspension without pay or benefits.

Clearly, administrators and supervisors must have workable disciplinary procedures that are adequate and legal. They must protect the rights of both the employee and the complainant.

Steps of progressive discipline must be outlined and employees must be made aware of the consequences of misconduct. Supervisors must be trained in implementing appropriate disciplinary procedures in order to remediate or correct employee performance. Complaints about employees should be investigated, and proper procedures for conducting the investigation should be implemented. Supervisory documentation of the investigation and the results should be kept in the employee's personnel file. Steps toward termination should be followed as policy and investigation warrant as noted in the *Peterson* case.

In *Castagna v. City of Seal Beach* (2005), supervisors prevailed in a lawsuit when an officer claimed he was fired contrary to department policy and law. Officer Castagna became involved in a probate matter and forged a document. The conduct came to the attention of the department captain and he began an investigation. The investigation revealed that officer Castagna introduced a forged document, lied under oath, and lied to investigators, although the prosecutor declined to file charges. The department issued Castagna a "Notice of Intent to Discipline," advising him that the chief was considering terminating his employment. Officer Castagna was informed of his rights, notified of a pre-disciplinary hearing, and given copies of the forged documents. He was placed on administrative leave pending the results of the internal affairs investigation. Several months later, Castagna received a copy of the investigation's findings, concluding that he indeed engaged in misconduct. The notice did not specify any type of proposed discipline but did stipulate that he was to respond to the notice. Rather than respond he filed suit, claiming that the department failed to complete the investigation according to state law within one year and failed to outline any proposed discipline. He claimed wrongful discipline and requested a temporary order prohibiting the department from disciplining him. The officer was subsequently fired.

At trial the court refused the request for a temporary order and also held that the department followed the proper protocols for conducting an investigation and notifying him of such an investigation. The firing was also upheld by the court. Officer Castagna appealed and the appellate court affirmed the lower court's decision. The appellate court noted that the department followed the law and policy by conducting a timely investigation once they learned of the misconduct, that officer Castagna was properly notified, and afforded him with his rights while on administrative leave, and that the termination was lawful.

Administrators who adhere to their department's policy in disciplining officer misconduct are likely to prevail in a lawsuit and will avoid claims of negligent retention. In *Day v. Civil Service Commission of Borough of Carlisle* (2008), Corporal Day attended a supervisors' meeting where the chief of police explained the policy for properly reporting a complaint against a fellow officer. Later, Day violated the policy when he accused a detective of holding a gun to the head of the detective's girlfriend, falsifying time records, and taking money and drugs from an investigation. Day also accused the chief of knowingly covering up these incidents. The chief performed an investigation and found that the claims were unsubstantiated and initiated discipline against Day. The chief informed Day by letter and verbally that he was filing charges against him and that any repetition of such conduct would result in termination. A few days later Day made the same allegations against three different officers and the chief conducted a second investigation, finding that Day's claims were unsubstantiated. As a result, Day was terminated. Day appealed his termination to the commission and over the course of a year and several hearings the commission upheld his termination. Day appealed this decision to the court.

The lower court found in favor of the commission and the appellate court affirmed. Day argued that he was terminated for other reasons and not for violating departmental policy. The court found no evidence to support his claims and because his conduct was a direct act of insubordination, the commission was within its rights to recommend termination of his employment.

First Line of Defense

Critical components of administration include planning, controlling, directing, budgeting, and supervising subordinates. Administrators must also be concerned with the ever-present liability component, which may emerge from fulfilling their basic supervisory functions. The first line of defense against litigation begins with the administrator making a firm commitment and concerted effort to transform administrative functions into a proactive risk management program to minimize future lawsuits (as discussed in Chapter 5). Administrators and supervisors represent the best protection against liability, but the basics must be in place first.

Liability Risk Reduction

By integrating the fundamental components of management with risk reduction elements, administrators create a strategy that allows the organization to operate effectively and demonstrate a good faith effort toward reducing liability potential. Criminal justice agency administrators have a duty in assessing their risk management priorities to minimize or alleviate the potential for all types of costly internal litigation (Martinelli & Shaw, 2011).

The basic elements of a risk reduction program include the following:

1. Performing an analysis of agency incidents, complaints, audits, and lawsuits in order to identify problems specific to agency needs. After an assessment has been conducted, supervisors should obtain the assistance of legal counsel to determine the latest court decisions (state and federal) that affect prisoner and employee rights.
2. Based on the outcome of the internal assessment, outdated policies should be revised and new policies should be developed. Revising existing policy and procedure manuals is essential to complying with court rulings and changes in the law. Once policies are revised or newly developed, administrators should keep supervisors updated on the revisions and the administrative interpretations of the revisions. This will ensure proper implementation and enforcement. It is recommended that agency policies be reviewed annually and revised accordingly. Correctional officials are encouraged to maintain up-to-date policies and procedures, developed in accordance with state and professional correctional standards.
3. All supervisors and employees should receive training in the policy manual on a regular basis. Moreover, all employees should be trained regularly in the legal dimensions of the job and in frequently performed tasks. All employees should receive regular competency-based training in the types of weapons and equipment that correspond to their duties.

4. Administrators and supervisors must provide proper direction, supervision, and reinforcement of training objectives to ensure that the mission of the agency is being carried out. Administrators must investigate complaints and follow established agency disciplinary procedures as necessary.

5. Written documentation of training, complaints, investigations, and employee disciplinary actions by administrators and supervisors is essential to corroborate management's role in supervising subordinates. Written documentation provides a record of events and incidents and establishes a process of reasonable actions taken. It will provide protection for the individual and the agency in civil litigation.

Summary

This chapter has examined the basis of supervisory liability under § 1983. While administrative liability under § 1983 started with the *Monell* decision, it is still developing, and has emerged as a primary source of litigation for supervisors. Case examples indicate that this area of litigation will continue, and it is incumbent upon administrators to keep abreast of the legal standards imposed upon them. Through court decisions, the days of unfettered supervisory discretion have been replaced with several theories of supervisory liability. Judicial intervention has created a mixed blessing for the administrator.

Management theories and practices indicate that administrators should be competent in directing the organization, as well as in planning, budgeting, staffing, decisionmaking, controlling staffing, reporting, and supervising employees. Since the *Monell* decision, administrators must also develop and maintain a managerial competency in understanding that their actions or omissions may expose them to a heightened risk of liability under § 1983. This chapter examined six of the seven areas in which supervisors may be named as defendants for allegedly failing in their administrative functions: (1) negligent hiring, (2) negligent assignment, (3) negligent entrustment, (4) failure to direct, (5) failure to supervise, and (6) failure to discipline/ negligent retention (failure to train is addressed in Chapter 7). The legal standard of review in these types of allegations is that of deliberate indifference, which is a high standard for the plaintiff to prove.

Court intervention relative to administrative functions has created a legal arena that requires administrators to be more proactive in working with employees and managing the operations of their organization. Court intervention, however, has also helped administrators to acquire more or new resources and facilities, which have improved overall operations and employee performance. Thus, administrators need to become more proactive in developing their knowledge of the law and the liability dimensions of their jobs. Developing and implementing risk reduction strategies as discussed in this chapter and Chapter 5 can assist administrators in operating an organization that works toward reducing the risk of supervisory liability, thus making it more efficient. Moreover, administrators should be committed to further educating their employees in the legal nature of their responsibilities. This combined approach will assist in reducing the number of lawsuits filed, as well as placing the agency in the best position to successfully defend against a lawsuit.

References

Bushway, S. (2004). Background investigations of police candidates: one of the most important investigations you'll ever conduct. *Police Disciplinary Bulletin, 12*, 1–3.

del Carmen, R. V. (1991). *Civil liability in American policing: A text for law enforcement personnel.* Englewood, NJ: Prentice-Hall.

del Carmen, R. V., & Kappeler, V. E. (1991). Municipal and police agencies as defendants: liability for official policy and custom. *American Journal of Police, 10*, 1–17.

Kappeler, V. E. (1997). *Critical issues in police civil liability* (2nd ed.). Prospect Heights, IL: Waveland Press, Inc.

Martenelli, T. J., & Shaw, L. E. (2011, April). Updating ethics training—policing privacy series: managing risk by reducing internal litigation. *Police Chief, 78*, 112–118.

Ryan, J. R. (2009). United States Supreme Court raises significant issues with respect to supervisory liability: legal updates. *Legal, Liability and Risk Management Institute,* <www.LLRMI.com>.

7 ⬛

Liability for Failure to Train

OVERVIEW

Since the United States Supreme Court decision in *City of Canton v. Harris* (1989), the plaintiff in the majority of civil lawsuits cites as a secondary claim that the errant officer was inadequately trained (Box 7.1). Several scholars estimate that actions for failure to train and failure to supervise are the two most common types of claims brought against police administrators (Barrineau, 1994; Kappeler, 1997; del Carmen, 1991; Staff, 1990). Although tremendous strides have been made in mandating pre-service police training throughout the United States and the number of hours of in-service training for veteran officers is increasing (Flink, 1997), failure-to-train allegations are still a concern for the police administrator.

Because failure-to-train claims represent a majority of supervisory liability actions, this chapter addresses this critical managerial responsibility. Criminal justice administrators can be held liable if inadequate or improper training causes injury or the violation of an individual's constitutional rights. Ongoing training is critical for avoiding civil litigation (Gallagher, 1990) and in structuring a defense to legal assertions (Vaughn & Coomes, 1995).

Liability Framework for Failure to Train Under *Canton*

Supervisory Liability

Following *Monell v. New York City Department of Social Services* (1978), numerous § 1983 lawsuits have been filed against criminal justice departments on the basis that the incident involved misconduct that was motivated by the agency adopting a policy or custom of inadequate training or supervision of the officers. These cases generated considerable judicial disagreement regarding the appropriate standard with which to assess these actions. Standards applied ranged from ordinary negligence to willfulness. Disagreement as to the type of evidence required to prove inadequate training produced a great deal of debate in the federal courts. Much of the uncertainty was resolved in the Supreme Court's 1989 decision in *Canton*.

Expansion of the Deliberate Indifference Standard

The Supreme Court ruled that a local government can be held liable under § 1983 if an officer injures a person due to a deficiency in training. Inadequate training may serve as a basis for § 1983 liability where the failure to train amounts to "deliberate indifference" to the rights of persons with whom the police may come into contact. The degree of fault is fundamentally related to the policy requirement noted in *Monell* (Silver, 2010). Moreover, *Monell* will not be satisfied by a mere allegation that a training program represents a policy for which the city is responsible. The Court stated that "in light of the duties assigned to specific officers or

---

BOX 7.1 *CITY OF CANTON V. HARRIS* (1989)

Harris was stopped for speeding and was arrested after she became uncooperative with the officer. She was transported to the police station in a patrol wagon and upon arrival was found sitting on the floor. She was brought inside for processing where she collapsed to the floor two times. The officers left her on the floor for approximately one hour during processing and failed to summon medical attention. Court testimony revealed that the shift commander was responsible for determining the medical care of arrestees but did not receive training with which to make medical decisions. She was released into the care of her family whereupon she was taken to a hospital by an ambulance summoned by her family. She was diagnosed as suffering from emotional stress reaction, anxiety, and depression. She was hospitalized for a week and received outpatient medical care for about one year. She sued the city for a variety of claims, but most notable were the claim of denial of medical care while in custody, and training deficiencies of officers in medical care for arrestees. Harris prevailed and was awarded $200,000 in damages. The city appealed to the Sixth Circuit Court of Appeals, which ruled that a municipality could be held liable for failure to train when a plaintiff could prove intentional, reckless, or gross negligence on the part of the municipality. An error was made by the court in explaining jury instructions and a retrial was ordered. Prior to retrial, the city sought review by the Supreme Court and they granted certiorari to determine the issue of whether a municipality could be held deliberately indifferent to the training needs of its officers.

The Court concluded that the standard with which to examine claims of failing to train is deliberate indifference. Deliberate indifference can mean a callous disregard of known risks and failing to take steps to abate them, or a conscious choice from among several alternatives. While the Court ruled that a municipality must provide ongoing training for recurring job tasks an officer encounters, the justices did not state how frequently training must be provided nor the duration of the training. On remand the appellate court reversed its former decision, based on deliberate indifference.

This case is significant because the Court has expanded the standard of deliberate indifference to claims against administrators for failing to train their officers. Deliberate indifference is a higher standard for a plaintiff to prove in court. Officers must receive realistic ongoing training to "obvious" recurring job functions. The decision also applies to correctional officials.

---

employees, the need for more or different training is so obvious, and the inadequacy so likely to result in the violation of constitutional rights, the policy makers of the city can reasonably be said to have been deliberately indifferent to the need."

The former standard of gross negligence used by many lower federal courts was rejected by the Supreme Court, and the higher standard of deliberate indifference was adopted. This standard was first established in a Texas prison case, *Estelle v. Gamble* (1976). Deliberate indifference was expanded in *Canton* and requires proof of much more than negligence. Over the years, the Supreme Court has established that deliberate indifference resides on a continuum between "mere negligence and something less than acts or omissions for the very purpose of causing harm or with knowledge that harm will result" (Vaughn & del Carmen, 1995). "Deliberate" means that a particular course of action has been chosen from among several alternatives, and "indifferent" means there has been some conscious disregard for a person's rights (Plitt, 1997). Only where failure to train reflects a "deliberate" or conscious choice by a municipality can a city be liable for such a failure under § 1983. Liability may not attach for failure to train or improper training without some proof that the department was, or should have been, aware of the need and then made a deliberate choice not to provide training, or not to review and/or improve the training provided.

Factors Necessary to Establish Deliberate Indifference

The Court's opinion provides a framework for litigating failure to train under the deliberate indifference standard. Actionable cases of inadequate training rest with the plaintiff proving the following factors. First, it must be established whether a training program is adequate to the tasks that the particular employee must perform, and if it is not, whether such inadequate training can justifiably be said to represent "city policy." Second, the identified deficiency must be directly related to ultimate injury. The failure to train must have been the cause of harm. Third, it is not necessary for a policy regarding training to be unconstitutional in order for liability to attach. A valid policy may be unconstitutionally applied, and when the training in how to apply the policy is deliberately indifferent, liability may attach. Fourth, in general, one incident of improper training will not result in liability. A pattern or history of problems or incidents that can be related to improper training will normally be the key to liability. Fifth, the focus of training must address regular and ongoing tasks that officers routinely face. The Court noted that the use of deadly force is one such area requiring regular training. The plaintiff must prove that these known needs were left unattended by the municipality. Finally, the degree of training required need only be adequate to address a particular matter. The Court acknowledged the need for a department to evaluate its needs and allocate appropriate resources, but rejected the idea that training must be the most modern available. The standard established by the Court clearly makes it more difficult for plaintiffs to prevail in a § 1983 lawsuit.

After 22 years of the *Canton* decision, the United States Supreme Court took occasion to further elaborate on the issue of training in *Connick v. Thompson* (2011). Thompson was found guilty of attempted robbery and murder in separate incidents and was sentenced to the death penalty. After 18 years in prison, 14 years on death row, and one month prior to his execution, undisclosed evidence was discovered. Thompson's private investigator discovered the crime lab report from the armed robbery investigation in the files of the New Orleans Police Crime Laboratory. Thompson was tested and found to have blood type O, proving that the blood on the swatch was not his. Thompson's attorneys presented this evidence to the district attorney's office, which, in turn, moved to stay the execution and vacate Thompson's armed robbery conviction. The Louisiana Court of Appeals then reversed Thompson's murder conviction, concluding that the armed robbery conviction unconstitutionally deprived Thompson of his right to testify in his own defense at the murder trial.

Thompson then brought this action against the district attorney's office, Connick, Williams, and others, alleging that their conduct caused him to be wrongfully convicted, incarcerated for 18 years, and nearly executed. The only claim that proceeded to trial was Thompson's claim under § 1983 that the district attorney's office had violated *Brady* by failing to disclose the crime lab report in his armed robbery trial (*Brady v. Maryland*, 1963). Thompson alleged liability under two theories: (1) the *Brady* violation was caused by an unconstitutional policy of the district attorney's office; and (2) the violation was caused by Connick's deliberate indifference to an obvious need to train the prosecutors in his office in order to avoid such constitutional violations. Before trial, Connick conceded that the failure to produce the crime lab report constituted a *Brady* violation. Accordingly, the District Court instructed the jury that the "only issue" was whether the nondisclosure was caused by either a policy, practice, or custom of the district attorney's office or a deliberately indifferent failure to train the office's prosecutors.

Prosecutors testified that office policy was to turn crime lab reports and other scientific evidence over to the defense. They also testified that, after the discovery of the undisclosed crime lab report in 1999, prosecutors disagreed about whether it had to be disclosed under *Brady* absent knowledge of Thompson's blood type. The jury rejected Thompson's claim that an unconstitutional office policy caused the *Brady* violation, but found the district attorney's office liable for failing to train the prosecutors. The jury awarded Thompson $14 million in damages, and the District Court added more than $1 million in attorney's fees and costs. The Fifth Circuit affirmed by an equally divided court. The United States Supreme Court granted certiorari and reversed the appellate court's decision. The Court examined whether a district attorney's office may not be held liable under § 1983 for failure to train its prosecutors based on a single *Brady* violation.

The Court reaffirmed its decision in *Canton* and stated that deliberate indifference in this context requires proof that city policymakers disregarded the "known or obvious consequence" that a particular omission in their training program would cause city employees to violate citizens' constitutional rights. It further reiterated that a pattern of similar constitutional violations by untrained employees is "ordinarily necessary" to demonstrate deliberate indifference. In a 5-to-4 decision, Justice Thomas wrote the opinion and determined that a single incident created liability.

Thompson mistakenly relied on the "single-incident" liability contending that the *Brady* violation in this case was the "obvious" consequence of failing to provide specific *Brady* training and that this "obviousness" showing can substitute for the pattern of violations ordinarily necessary to establish municipal culpability.

In *Canton*, the Court theorized that if a city armed its police force and deployed them into the public to capture fleeing felons without training the officers in the constitutional limitation on the use of deadly force, the failure to train could reflect the city's deliberate indifference to the highly predictable consequence, namely, violations of constitutional rights. Thomas found that failure to train prosecutors in their *Brady* obligations did not fall within the narrow range of *Canton*'s hypothesized single-incident liability. The obvious need for specific legal training present in *Canton*'s scenario—police academy applicants are unlikely to be familiar with constitutional constraints on deadly force and, absent training, cannot obtain that knowledge—was absent. Attorneys are trained in the law and equipped with the tools to interpret and apply legal principles, understand constitutional limits, and exercise legal judgment. They receive training before entering the profession, must usually satisfy continuing education requirements, often train on the job with more experienced attorneys, and must satisfy licensing standards and ongoing ethical obligations. Prosecutors not only are equipped but are ethically bound to know what *Brady* entails and to perform legal research.

Taking a narrow perception of the *Canton* decision, Thomas opined that recurring constitutional violations are not the "obvious consequence" of failing to provide prosecutors with formal in-house training. The nuance of the allegedly necessary training also distinguished the case from the example in *Canton*. The prosecutors were familiar with the general *Brady* rule. Thus, Thompson could not rely on the lack of an ability to cope with constitutional situations that underlies the *Canton* hypothetical, but must assert that prosecutors were not trained about particular *Brady* evidence or the specific scenario related to the violation in his case. That sort of nuance failed to support an inference of deliberate indifference. Contrary to the holding below, it did not follow that, because *Brady* has gray areas and some *Brady* decisions are difficult, prosecutors will so obviously make wrong decisions that failing to train them amounts, as it must, to "a decision by the city itself to violate the Constitution." Connick argued that he was entitled to judgment as a matter of law because Thompson did not prove that he was on actual or constructive notice of, and therefore deliberately indifferent to, a need for more or different *Brady* training, and the Court agreed.

The decision shows that the Court made a distinction between legal training for attorneys and criminal justice practitioners. Training for law enforcement and corrections personnel should be conducted consistent with the Court's requirement of providing them with ongoing training to tasks that they encounter on a regular basis. The Court also maintained its former principle, that a successful plaintiff must show a pattern of violations before imposing liability, unless one incident is particularly egregious. Further, the decision confirms that the standard of deliberate indifference is difficult to overcome before liability will attach.

Application of Deliberate Indifference

Although the Court resolved the long-debated controversy about inadequate training issues, it also created many questions regarding how lower courts should interpret and apply the deliberate indifference standard. Questions pertaining to failure-to-train issues include: (1) What constitutes a policy of inadequate training? (2) Can a municipality be liable for the single act of an officer? (3) Will liability attach for an occasional officer mistake? (4) Who has the responsibility to train officers? and (5) Who determines whether the training was adequate?

Answers to these questions are far from clear, but cases can provide general trends in how courts have applied the deliberate indifference standard in claims of deficient training. The mere fact that an incident occurred and a constitutional right may be involved does not automatically indicate that there is a training deficiency. The failure to train must first be linked to some specific policy relative to the training. In order for supervisory liability to attach, the burden of proof rests with the plaintiff to show that the policy was the moving force behind the constitutional violation (*Polk County v. Dodson*, 1981). A policy exists only when a course of action is established by the official responsible for final policy with respect to the subject matter involved (*Pembaur v. City of Cincinnati*, 1986). Application of these two Supreme Court cases is illustrated in *Vineyard v. Murray County of Georgia* (1993). The plaintiff brought claims of excessive force, failure to train, and failure to supervise against the sheriff. The claims arose from several deputies beating a restrained arrestee in a hospital bed. The deputies beat him repeatedly on the head and chest. He sustained a broken jaw and other injuries. Applying *Canton* to the policy and training issues, the federal district court found that the sheriff was deliberately indifferent to the needs of the arrestee. The Eleventh Circuit Court of Appeals determined that the county had inadequate polices for training, supervision, and discipline, as well as inadequate procedures for following up on citizen complaints. The manner in which the sheriff investigated the incident evidenced a policy of deliberate indifference and a manual of policies and procedures did not exist. The plaintiff was awarded $175,000 in compensatory damages and $60,000 in punitive damages. The court determined, however, in *Robinson v. City of St. Charles* (1992), that in order to prevail in a policy/training claim for excessive force, the plaintiff must show that the city had notice that its police training was inadequate and that it deliberately chose not to remedy the situation.

Can training liability be imposed for actions stemming from a single incident? The general answer to this question is no, but with an exception (*Oklahoma City v. Tuttle*, 1985). The Supreme Court, deciding a case about the fatal shooting of an unarmed individual, gave a qualified ruling, holding that claims of failure to train and supervise stemming from a single unconstitutional activity is insufficient to impose liability unless it was caused by an existing unconstitutional municipal policy, which policy can be attributed to a municipal policymaker. This holding is important because it rejects liability based on a single incident, but allows for an exception: if the incident was caused by an existing, unconstitutional policy (del Carmen, 1991). The exception was applied by the Court in *Pembaur v. City of Cincinnati* (1986). The county prosecutor was the "official policymaker" and directed officers to make a warrantless, forceful entry into a house with axes. The deputies were attempting to arrest two doctors who failed to attend a grand jury hearing. The Court ruled that the City of Cincinnati could be held liable on one occasion for a Fourth Amendment violation, because the prosecutor's decision to direct officers to enter the house constituted official policy or custom.

Liability was imposed in a single incident of failure to train and supervise in *Atchinson v. District of Columbia* (1996). The plaintiff, who was carrying a machete, was shot by an officer after receiving nothing more than a warning to "freeze," adequately asserted a claim against the District of Columbia for inadequately training and supervising officers in the use of deadly force. The federal appeals court held that even a single incident of such use of force was sufficient to support the complaint of inadequate training and supervision.

Determining the adequacy of a training program can be difficult. In *Canton*, the Court did not specify the subject matter or the number of hours required for officers to attend. In an effort to avoid federalism and to avoid second-guessing municipal training programs, the Court took the position that training be afforded to officers in order to "respond to usual and recurring situations with which they must deal." In resolving this question, the Court focused on the training program in relation to the tasks that the particular officers must perform. "That a particular officer may be unsatisfactorily trained will not alone suffice to attach liability on the city, for the officer's shortcomings may have resulted from factors other than a faulty training program." According to the Court, liability will not attach for a sound program that has been negligently administered. Neither will it suffice to impose liability for an officer making a mistake or avoiding an accident because he should have received more or better training—"[a]dequately trained officers can make mistakes." Liability can only attach when the city's failure to train reflects deliberate indifference to the constitutional rights of citizens. The deficiency must be closely related to the ultimate injury. Training should be designed to correspond directly to the recurring tasks of police work (*Jones v. City of Chicago*, 1989).

The nature of the police function is such that in all responsibly managed police departments officers are required to undergo training prior to being assigned patrol work. The court used the topic of lethal force as an example to demonstrate the need for adequate training. In *Zuchel v. City and County of Denver, Colorado* (1993), the city was found to be deliberately indifferent in regard to providing adequate training in the use of deadly force. The training consisted of only a lecture and a film and did not include "live" shoot/don't shoot practice training. In *Houck v. City of Prairie Village, Kansas* (1996), however, failure to have a detailed training program on problems of taking suicidal or mentally disturbed police officers into custody was not deliberate indifference to a known problem. The chief was not liable for failing to take custody of a suicidal officer who fired his gun within his residence. While not a deadly force case, the court in *Dorman v. District of Columbia* (1989) held that the need for specific training in suicide prevention, beyond what the officers had received, was not so obvious that the city's policy in not providing it could be characterized as deliberate indifference.

The standard of review in failure-to-train litigation is deliberate indifference. When analyzing assertions of inadequate training, the court will determine three critical components: (1) whether a constitutional right was violated; (2) whether there was a failure to train or the training was inadequate; and (3) whether there was deliberate indifference to the need for training.

In *Griffith v. Coburn* (2005), a federal district court of Michigan examined the question of whether officers should receive additional training beyond academy training. Officers attempted to serve an arrest warrant on Arthur Partee and met resistance in his house. Partee had exhibited bizarre behavior at home, had a history of mental impairment, and his mother asked that the police take him into custody. At the house, the officers met resistance as they attempted to take control of Partee. Partee lunged off of a couch at the officers and struggled with them. During the struggle, Partee managed to unsnap one of the safety snaps on an officer's holster and began to pry on it. The officer placed him in a lateral vascular neck restraint for about two to three seconds and they fell to the floor. Partee became unresponsive and resuscitation efforts by emergency medical personnel on scene failed to revive him.

Partee's estate filed a § 1983 lawsuit against the officers for excessive force. A claim was also filed against the chief of police for being deliberately indifferent to the training needs of the officers who used the neck restraint. The court granted summary judgment to the officers, finding that the neck restraint was not excessive force. The court assessed the failure to train claim within the framework of two components: "(1) 'failure to provide adequate training in light of foreseeable consequences that could result from the lack of instruction'; and (2) 'failure to act in response to repeated complaints of constitutional violations by its officers.'" Documentation was presented that showed that the officers received more than adequate training in the Pressure Point Control Tactics (PPCT) lateral neck restraint. Such training was approved by the state of Michigan's police training standards council.

The court ruled that the plaintiff failed to show that the need for post-academy training on the neck restraint was so obvious that the police department would be acting with deliberate indifference if they failed to conduct further training. The court also noted that the plaintiff failed to show evidence that the chief inadequately trained his officers and that the department was on notice by complaints from the community that officers misused the neck restraint. Absent such evidence the court granted summary judgment to the chief, concluding that the chief was not on notice that the training was inadequate.

Status of Failure-to-Train Liability

What has been the impact of the *Canton* decision on police training? In answering this question, Ross (2000) conducted a 10-year analysis of 1,500 published § 1983 federal court decisions citing the administrator for failure to train. Case analysis revealed that 64 percent of the litigation involved municipal police departments, 29 percent involved county sheriff's departments, five percent involved state police agencies, and two percent involved transit authority police agencies. All 1,500 cases arose from police officer actions, followed by claims of inadequate training (100%), failure to supervise (45%), failure to discipline (30%), and failure to direct (25%). Analysis indicates that failure to train and failure to supervise were combined as managerial liability issues in 54 percent of the cases. For example, an officer may have decided to engage in a high-speed pursuit and, as a result, the fleeing suspect killed an innocent third party. The estate of the deceased filed a § 1983 claim against the officer for deciding to pursue, and as a secondary claim filed a failure-to-train action against the administrator.

Table 7.1 identifies the 10 most frequently litigated training categories. Police administrators prevailed in slightly less than two-thirds of the litigation, or a two-to-one ratio. Nonlethal force and lethal force (i.e., excessive force claims) combine to be the most litigated areas asserting a failure to train officers (25%). Seventy-five percent of allegations asserting inadequate training in nonlethal force cases pertain primarily to physical force techniques and the use of equipment. Five of the categories (50%) involve issues of citizen deaths or injuries (lethal and nonlethal force, detainee suicide, pursuits, and medical care issues). Four of the categories (40%) involved high compensatory awards to the plaintiffs (pursuits, lethal/nonlethal force, and medical care issues). Three of the categories (30%) pertain to potential officer safety issues (nonlethal/lethal force and pursuits).

The data show that the standard of deliberate indifference is a high hurdle for the plaintiff to overcome when asserting a training deficiency. Despite this, the plaintiffs prevailed in approximately one-third of the cases overall, and the average award was significant, amounting to more than $450,000. Lethal force and emergency vehicle operations categories skewed the average award due to claims that stemmed from wrongful death lawsuits. Claims asserting the denial of medical care and nonlethal force also account for high average awards granted to the plaintiff. Attorney's fees averaged slightly more than $60,000.

Determining accurate award trends in police civil liability cases is problematic. These figures must be read with caution, because the courts do not document the award or the amount of attorney's fees assessed in every published case. Moreover, the figures do not reflect the cost

Table 7.1   Top Ten Categories in Police Training Litigation Since *Canton*

Topic	Plaintiff Prevailed % (#)	Police Prevailed % (#)	Average Award	Average Attorney Fee
Nonlethal Force	44 (99)	55 (126)	$351,219	$79,592
Physical (55%)				
Baton (20%)				
Restraints (17%)				
Aerosols (6%)				
Taser (2%)				
False Arrest/Detention	37 (69)	63 (116)	$155,100	$35,300
(n = 185)				
Search and Seizure	35 (60)	65 (110)	$148,000	$34,800
Residence (44%)				
Personal (23%)				
Vehicle (19%)				
Strip (14%)				
Failure to Protect	38 (60)	62 (100)	$185,000	$39,400
Detainee Suicide	37 (57)	63 (96)	$231,000	$73,600
Lethal Force	42 (64)	58 (88)	$1,212,567	$96,100
Emergency Vehicle	39 (57)	61 (88)	$1,389,789	$95,900
Medical Care	38 (52)	62 (86)	$472,789	$100,500
Police as Plaintiff	19 (19)	81 (81)	Not reported	Not reported
Other	16 (15)	84 (82)	$289,678	Not reported
Total	36 (552)	64 (973)	$492,794	$60,680

or the time that officers, administrators, or counsel spent in preparing to defend or try the case. Therefore, these figures are only presented to show limited trends in these categories and to reveal categories in which higher awards are more likely to occur, should the plaintiff prevail.

Implications of Failure-to-Train Litigation

Each litigated category in Table 7.1 represents the most fundamental and critical tasks that police officers routinely perform, yet deficiency in training is frequently asserted. The prevailing ratio indicates two important factors of the deliberate indifference standard. First, the standard is difficult for plaintiffs to establish. Second, a majority of police departments appear to be providing training and successfully defending these allegations in a significant number of cases. Despite the prevailing record, the potential for liability still exists as the following discussion of cases illustrates.

Lethal and Less-Lethal Force

These two categories represent critical issues for police agencies and exhibit high-risk areas for liability. Further, both categories represent high awards granted to prevailing plaintiffs. Police administrators are encouraged to ensure that their use-of-force policies reflect the *Graham v. Connor* (1989) and *Tennessee v. Garner* (1985) decisions, and provide ongoing refresher training for all officers in competently using their firearms, empty-hand control techniques, restraints, other control equipment, and the constitutional limits of using force. These two cases provide the standards for examining claims of excessive force by police officers. In *Davis v. Mason County* (1991), a jury awarded four plaintiffs $528,000 in compensatory damages, $225,000 in punitive damages, and $323,559 in attorney's fees in an excessive force case involving four deputies. For approximately four months these deputies had illegally stopped, beaten, and illegally arrested citizens. It was discovered that the deputies had little or no training, and at least one deputy did not attend a police academy. The court determined that the county exhibited deliberate indifference to the training needs of the deputies in the constitutional limits of force. In *Bordanaro v. McLeod* (1989), the plaintiff was awarded $5.3 million for deliberate indifference due to a "practice of breaking down" doors without a warrant. A lack of continuing training after the academy was found to have risen to a level of deliberate indifference involving deadly force, searches and seizures, and pursuits. The court found that the department was "ill-prepared and ill-equipped to perform the obvious and recurring duties of police officers." The department was operating under policies established in 1951 and no supervisory training was provided. The court in *Walsweer v. Harris County* (1990) awarded $6.3 million to a man rendered paraplegic after he was shot five times by the police. The county was held liable for inadequately training officers in the use of deadly force and maintaining deficient policies regarding force. Conversely, in *Mateyko v. Felix* (1990), the court held that providing three to four hours of training in the use of a Taser was adequate, even if officers did not know its full physical effects.

Frequently a plaintiff will automatically assume that an unreasonable use of force verdict will support a claim of failure to train. Such a presumption is not automatic, as the courts generally use the following criteria to review claims of failure to train: (1) the training program was adequate for preparing the officers to perform the tasks they encounter; (2) the training program was adequate in addressing the subject matter under question; and (3) whether the inadequacies of a training program contributed to or actually caused the injury.

In *Ciminillo v. City of Cincinnati* (2006), such an issue was appealed to the Sixth Circuit Court of Appeals. A crowd attending a party moved the "party" to the street and many of the participants became rowdy, by shouting, setting fires, and throwing bottles at other nearby residents. Officers responded wearing riot gear and the rowdy party crowd began throwing bottles at them. The plaintiff, who was not participating with the crowd, attempted to leave the area by exiting through the backyard of a nearby house. The homeowner stopped him in the yard and threatened him with a bat. As the plaintiff was moving away from the yard, he claimed that he observed a kneeling police officer firing "bean bags" at the crowd and he approached the officer with his hands raised, in a non-threatening and compliant manner. Ciminillo claimed that the officer discharged a bean bag at him, striking him in the chin and chest while he was attempting to leave the area at the request of the officer. He claimed that he sustained injuries to the chin and chest (requiring stitches in his chin), bruised lungs, and permanent facial scars.

The officer who fired the bean bag had a different version of the incident. The officer claimed that he gave several orders for Ciminillo to stop, but he kept advancing toward him while he was in the act of throwing an unknown object in his direction. Ciminillo filed a § 1983 lawsuit, claiming that the officer used excessive force in violation of his Fourth and Fourteenth Amendment rights, and also filed state tort claims for assault and battery. He also filed a claim against the City of Cincinnati for failing to adequately train the officer.

The lower court granted summary judgment on behalf of the officer and the city, and the plaintiff appealed the decision. The appellate court addressed the issue of whether the plaintiff was seized and how that may affect the use of force. The court ruled that the use of a bean bag resulting in an injury equates to a seizure. The court reasoned that a seizure occurs when a person becomes the deliberate object of an officer's exertion of the use of force. Using the criteria established in *Graham v. Connor* (1989), the court found that Ciminillo was attempting to comply with the officer, approached him with his hands up, was not threatening the officer, and was not committing a crime. The court reversed summary judgment on behalf of the officer, determining that shooting a non-threatening person with a less-than-lethal device was unreasonable force.

The appellate court affirmed the lower court's ruling that the city did not fail to adequately train the officer. According to the court, the plaintiff failed to provide evidence consistent with the three previously mentioned criteria. The plaintiff failed to show that there was a connection between the injuries sustained and a failure to train officers or an inadequacy in the training program. Further, the court held that the plaintiff could not produce evidence that revealed that the use of bean bags had not been misused on past occurrences. Summary judgment for the city was affirmed.

A common strategy of the plaintiff when asserting failure to train is an attempt to show that the agency adopted a practice or policy of training that violates a person's constitutional rights. In *Luke v. Brown* (2007), the plaintiff argued that the practice of training officers to shoot twice in rapid succession (double-tap) when confronted with a suspect who is wielding an edged weapon in a threatening manner from a distance of 21 feet or less was unconstitutional. The plaintiff presented an expert who opined that the accepted standard in police work is to train officers to "Evaluate and Shoot, Evaluate and Shoot," and argued that the lack of a period of evaluation between shots rises to a level of deliberate indifference. The court awarded summary judgment and ruled that the plaintiff failed to cite any precedent establishing that the firing of a second shot immediately after the first shot renders the second shot unconstitutional under the circumstances. The court agreed that officers need to be trained in the constitutional provisions of using lethal force, and acknowledged that it was undisputed that Dekalb County did train its officers accordingly. The court noted that the plaintiff did not present any evidence of a prior incident in which a county officer caused an injury to another by excessive force because of the double-tap method. Thus, adopting a practice of training the double-tap method of firing a weapon was not unconstitutional.

In *Escobar v. City of Houston* (2007) the issue of training regarding firearms handling was asserted by the plaintiff. The court examined two issues: (1) whether an officer received proper instruction on indexing his weapon before a decision to shoot was made; and (2) whether the officer's training was inadequate 17 months after graduating from the police academy and was the cause of the *Escobar* suit. The city argued that its training requirements met and in some respects exceeded the standards set by the state of Texas. The city maintained that no amount of training can eliminate the possibility of an accident and that no amount of indexing training will ensure that an officer will properly index his finger each time his weapon is drawn. Evidence was shown that the chief conducted an internal affairs investigation into each incident. The city also presented comparison evidence showing that in the numerous daily contacts between the police and the public, accidental discharges of a weapon were statistically unlikely.

The court, however, rejected the city's arguments, stating that meeting the state standard did not equate to finding no constitutional violation. Further, the court rejected the comparison argument regarding officers and the public contact with no accidental discharges. Rather, the court focused on whether examining prior incidents showed a "pattern" of deficient training that is obvious and obviously likely to result in a constitutional violation. According to the court, evidence of 26 similar incidents of accidental discharges over five years, combined with memos and letters from the chief regarding firearms training, the inconsistent evidence as to what training officers actually received on firearms indexing, and the obviousness of the risk created if officers were not trained on indexing, showed deliberate indifference to officer training, thereby precluding summary judgment.

In *Swofford v. Eslinger* (2009), deputies pursuing two felony car burglary suspects encountered a property owner, armed, on his own property, and shot at him. In a lawsuit by the property owner, the sheriff failed to offer any evidence concerning how officers were trained on the proper use of deadly force, and admitted that the decision to use firearms was completely up to the deputies. The sheriff was denied summary judgment by the court. The need to train officers in the proper use of deadly force is so obvious that the failure to do so can be characterized as deliberate indifference to constitutional rights. Deliberate indifference was also found in the sheriff's failure to provide proper supervision and training for K-9 teams.

Failure to Protect

The police have a duty to exercise reasonable care toward arrestees. This duty commences at the time of arrest and continues until release from custody. The Supreme Court, however, in *DeShaney v. Winnebago County Department of Social Services* (1989) held that police generally are not liable for failure to protect individuals from harm inflicted by third parties, but may be liable for an injury inflicted by law enforcement officials (del Carmen, 1991). An increasing number of actions have been successful when the lawsuit has proven that there was actual failure to protect, and when there are facts and circumstances that make the harm or injury that occurred different from a risk faced by the general public. The plaintiff may claim that he is different from the public in general and that the police had knowledge of him and his situation. Training of police officers in this area is a policy concern for administrators, because liability may attach for the city when a lawsuit is filed for failing to protect an arrestee from himself or from actions by officers. Potential training and policy issues in this area include equal protection concerns of racial bias under the Fourteenth Amendment, domestic violence situations, and discrimination violations under the Americans with Disabilities Act (ADA). In *Barber v. Guay* (1995), a mentally impaired arrestee prevailed in a deliberate indifference claim to training under the ADA when he alleged that the arresting deputy denied him proper police protection and fair treatment due to his psychological and alcohol problem. The City of Chicago was liable for failing to protect a wife from domestic violence at the hands of her husband, who was a police officer in the department (*Czajkowski v. City of Chicago*, 1993). The husband's partner was found liable because he failed to intervene and assisted the officer in attempting to cover up the abusive incident. It was determined that the department had a custom of failing to take action and was deliberately indifferent to officer training.

In *Wilson v. Maricopa County* (2006), a prisoner was fatally assaulted by another prisoner and the county filed for summary judgment. The court ruled that the sheriff was deliberately indifferent for failing to properly train and supervise officers in providing a safe environment for prisoners. The court also found that the sheriff was deliberately indifferent in fostering and knowingly encouraging a climate of condoning brutality among the prisoners and indifference to proper supervision. According to the court, a supervisor could be found to be deliberately indifferent to the safety of prisoners if he knew that not having an officer on the ground in the yard posed a risk of violence among the prisoners.

Emergency Vehicle Operations

Of the 10 most commonly litigated training areas, police vehicle operation is the most frequently performed police function. The Ross study (2000) revealed that these lawsuits represent the highest awards granted to prevailing plaintiffs. Researchers have documented the need for policy development and ongoing training in operating the police vehicle in emergency situations (Alpert, 1997; Beckman, 1987; Falcone et al., 1994; Gallagher, 1989; NIJ, 1998). Legal allegations that plaintiffs frequently assert include being deliberately indifferent in training to policy concerns; decision making to pursue or to terminate; the use of spikes, roadblocks, and ramming; failure to use emergency equipment; improper use of the vehicle in a risky environment; and wrongful deaths of citizens. Based on a review of more than 250 pursuit-type cases, Kappeler (1997) found that generally one factor alone is insufficient to establish a valid claim, but as the number of factors increases, so does the likelihood of liability.

Past case rulings reveal conflicting trends in court decisions. In *Frye v. Town of Akron* (1991), a passenger was killed after a high-speed pursuit involving a motorcycle. The court held that police pursuits may violate due process and that failure to train in the mechanics of hot pursuit can be characterized as "deliberate indifference." In *Fulkerson v. City of Lancaster* (1992), the court determined that there was no "obvious need" for specialized training in high-speed pursuits beyond what was given in the academy. The court found that a single incident was insufficient to impose liability in a pursuit case where the city had not developed policy, but rather allowed the officer to use his discretion whether to pursue or not (*Dismukes v. Hackathorn*, 1992). According to the court, the pursuit was not objectively unreasonable and there was no evidence that the department had a history of pursuits that resulted in damage or injury.

The Supreme Court in *County of Sacramento v. Lewis* (1998) established that the standard for reviewing police actions in pursuits is "shocks the conscience." A deputy with the Sacramento County Sheriff's Department engaged in a high-speed pursuit of two youths on a motorcycle, at speeds of more than 90 miles per hour. Smith violated the department's policy by operating his vehicle in excess of 80 miles an hour. The chase ended after the motorcycle tipped over and Smith skidded into the motorcycle, causing the death of Lewis, a passenger on the bike. The District Court granted summary judgment to Smith and the Ninth Circuit Court of Appeals reversed. The United States Supreme Court reviewed the case in order to determine what standard should be applied in police pursuit cases.

Rejecting the deliberate indifference standard, the Court determined that conduct that shocks the conscience in accordance with the Fourteenth Amendment is the proper standard to apply in police pursuit situations. The Court reasoned that in the circumstances of a high-speed chase aimed at apprehending a suspected offender, where unforeseen circumstances demand an instant judgment on the part of the officer who feels the pulls of competing obligations, only a purpose to cause harm unrelated to the legitimate object of arrest will satisfy the "shocks the conscience" test. In chases in which there is no intent to harm an offender physically or to worsen his or her legal plight there is no liability.

Since the *Lewis* decision, the lower courts have had the opportunity to review legal actions surrounding police pursuits and training. In failure-to-train claims, the courts apply the *Monell* and *Canton* decisions in determining administrative liability. Generally, the *Lewis* decision has made it extremely difficult for a plaintiff in prevail in failure-to-train claim as the plaintiff must first show that the named officer intended to harm the suspect in the pursuit, which rises to a level of "shocking to the conscience." For example, the defendants in *Philebaum v. Myers*, *Ridenour v. City of Portland, Oregon* (2006), *McCoy v. City of Monticello* (2005), *Sanders v. City of Union Springs et al.* (2005), *Herman v. City of Shannon, Mississippi* (2004), and *Grazier v. City of Philadelphia* (2003) were granted summary judgment. Each case involved a pursuit that ended either in an injury or death to the suspect and claims were filed against the officer for violating his or her constitutional rights and against departmental supervisors for failure to train. Regardless of the jurisdiction, the courts consistently have ruled that a plaintiff must first prove the *Lewis* test. The courts agree that the plaintiff must show that the officer engaged in the pursuit with the intent to cause physical harm to the plaintiff or worsen his or her legal plight. Failing to do so does not give rise to liability. Absent such evidence, claims of failure to train fall. The courts consistently hold that police training must be so obviously inadequate that it amounts to deliberate indifference to the constitutional rights of citizens and that the inadequacy was the "moving force" behind the alleged constitutional violation. There must be a direct link between a failure to train and the alleged injury. The courts have maintained that comprehensive policies and training should be provided for officers who engage in pursuits, but until a plaintiff can successfully overcome the *Lewis* test, failure-to-train claims will normally fail.

In *Labar v. Alercia* (2011) a police officer gave chase of a felony suspect. While driving, the suspect struck the vehicle of Jolene Labar and she died as a result of the crash. Mr. Labar filed suit against the municipality on a claim that they implemented a policy of Emergency Response Driving-High-Speed Motor Vehicle Pursuit and asserted that the Palmer Township police department failed to train their officers with respect to high-speed pursuits. Labar further claimed that the Township maintained a policy of failing to reprimand officers involved in misconduct, failed to require in-service training or retraining of officers known to engage in unsafe acts, police misconduct, or who were known to encourage or tolerate the same, and failed to require police officers to be adequately trained in the pursuit policy. The township filed for a motion for summary judgment and the court granted the motion.

The court held that Labar failed to demonstrate that there was an "official policy" in which administrators implemented and enforced that tolerated police misconduct representing well settled law. The court ruled that a claim questioning the level of training or supervision of agency personnel in accordance with § 1983 requires a showing that the failure amounted to deliberate indifference to the rights of persons with whom those employees will come into contact. The failure to train may amount to deliberate indifference where the need for more or different training is so obvious, and inadequacy highly likely to result in violation of consti- tutional rights. The court noted that the Township indeed maintained a constitutional policy addressing high-speed pursuits and officials had provided officers training on the policy and driving skills on a regular basis. Based on these factors the court held that there was no obvious or a lack of training likely that would have resulted in a constitutional violation.

False Arrest/Unlawful Detention

Taking a person into custody, charging him or her with a crime, and detaining him or her is certainly a recurring circumstance for police officers. It occurs more than 296 million times per year (BJS, 2005). False arrest and detention can be the basis for liability under § 1983. Both are considered intentional torts and the individual is restrained or deprived of freedom without legal justification (del Carmen, 1991). The plaintiff may allege that the administrator failed to properly instruct officers in the laws of arrest and detention or that the department practiced a custom of allegedly arresting and detaining people. In *Clipper v. Takoma Park, Maryland* (1989), the city was found liable for inadequate training in an improper arrest coordinated by the lieutenant who was in charge of the detective bureau and by the department's training coordinator. The investigating officer did not receive training materials giving typical examples of arrests properly based on probable cause. The arrestee was mistakenly arrested for a bank robber, who was videotaped. The court held that this evidence met the deliberate indifference standard and the plaintiff was awarded $304,355. In *Tilson v. Forrest City Police Department* (1994), the city was not held liable for failing to train regarding detention of arrestees. The arrestee was in a county jail for 14 months without being formally charged with a crime. The mere fact that the chief knew the plaintiff had been arrested and that written procedures for conducting criminal investigations were lacking illustrated insufficient grounds for impos- ing liability. In *Rivas v. Freeman* (1991), the sheriff was found liable for inadequately training deputies and detention officers in the mechanics of arrest and detention. The plaintiff sued for wrongful detention because he was misidentified as a probation violator and detained for six days. He was awarded $100,000.

In *McCollum v. Doe* (2011) plaintiff McCollum filed a § 1983 claim alleging that officers from the Philadelphia police department stopped him on the highway for speeding after a short pursuit. He claimed that unidentified officers threw him to the ground, assaulted him, sprayed silicone in his mouth, rummaged through his belongings, and threatened to kill his daughter and rape his wife if he were to say anything about the incident. McCollum alleged that his car was towed and he was left unconscious on the side of the road. In this lawsuit he claimed that the officers should be held liable for assaulting him and for false imprisonment. He also asserted that the city should be held liable for failing to train, supervise, and discipline police officers, which resulted in physical injuries and constitutional injuries.

McCollum maintained that the city had a formal policy that through inaction condoned and tolerated unconstitutional conduct by its officers. He further claimed that the city was deliberately indifferent to the patterns, practices, customs, and need for more of different training and supervision in the areas of abuse of police powers, the failure for police to follow policies and procedures regarding probable cause for arrest, the use of physical abuse against detainees, the identification of officers who engage in physical abuse, and the failure of officers to deter fellow officers from committing unlawful conduct. The city moved for summary judgment arguing that McCollum failed to provide evidence that the city engaged in a pattern or practice that officers routinely violated the constitutional rights of citizens nor did he provide evidence that the city's policy or custom caused his harm, or evidence that the city failed to provide training to their officers amounting to deliberate indifference.

The court agreed with the city ruling that McCollum failed to set forth any specific facts showing a genuine issue for trial. The court found no evidence presented by McCollum showing that the city failed to train its officers regarding a requirement that officers intercede when other officers engage in constitutional violations. Absent a showing that the city maintained an official policy and practice condoning constitutional violations by police officers, the court granted the city's motion.

In *Battiste v. Sheriff of Broward County* (2008), the plaintiff challenged whether a police chief provided adequate training in forming probable cause sufficient to make valid arrests. Union activists were conducting an allegedly peaceful protest in downtown Miami, Florida. They claimed that deputies from a county sheriff's department detained them without probable cause while being supervised by the local police department. The plaintiffs alleged that the chief failed to adequately train the deputies and that a report established that he had notice of prior "widespread" unjustified arrests by police during protests. The court ruled that the chief was entitled to qualified immunity based on his role as a supervisor. Further, the court ruled that it found no prior case law establishing that a police chief, based on alleged past unjustified arrests by his officers, had an obligation to conduct training for "borrowed" officers regarding when to make arrests.

Medical Care

The Supreme Court has ruled that the police do not specifically owe a duty of medical care to an individual citizen, absent a "special relationship" (*City of Revere v. Massachusetts General Hospital*, 1983). The due process clause of the Fourteenth Amendment requires a government agency to provide medical care to people who have been injured while being apprehended by the police. This is frequently a major allegation in excessive force claims, pursuits, arrests of intoxicated or mentally impaired individuals, and injuries sustained while in detention. The plaintiff will likely assert that the government entity was deliberately indifferent to the needs of the arrestee and failed to properly train officers in summoning medical care, observing symptoms of medical or psychological distress, and how to properly respond to such situations.

This study revealed the third highest award granted to plaintiffs in this category. In *Burkhart v. Washington Metro Area Transit Authority* (1996), the plaintiff was awarded $109,000 in damages, based on a claim that the transit authority inadequately trained officers in how to respond to disabled patrons, particularly the hearing impaired. The court in *Vine v. County of Ingham* (1995) held that the police agencies were not deliberately indifferent to the medical needs of arrestees. An arrestee who was under the influence of methyl alcohol died while in police custody. At booking in the city lockup, the intake officer placed the detainee in an observation cell, because he was belligerent and had attempted suicide during past confinements. The detainee passed out on the floor and was visually checked by officers periodically. Nearly six hours later officers noticed he was unresponsive and found he had choked on his mucus vomit. He was transported to the hospital and later died. The court determined that because deputies had received academy training and in-service training, despite not rendering medical treatment at booking, the sheriff was immune from liability.

The court underscored the fact that the police agency had provided minimal training in responding to the medical needs of arrestees, such as first aid and when to summon medical assistance. The officers were not required to have detailed training in medical treatment.

In *Thomas v. Sheahan* (2007), the special administrator of the estate of an individual who died at the jail from meningitis and pneumonia filed a lawsuit against the county, the sheriff, the president of the county board, correctional officers, and a medical technician. The special administrator asserted that jail officials violated the prisoner's rights on theories of wrongful death, survival action, and intentional infliction of emotional distress. The court rejected the county's motion for summary judgment, holding that the prisoner's illness was an objectively serious medical need and the medical technician and correctional officials were aware of his serious medical symptoms. The court found that the county was deliberately indifferent to its widespread practice of failing to train its employees on how to handle prisoner medical requests.

Arrestee/Detainee Suicide

Suicides and attempted suicides of arrestees present a significant problem for criminal justice practitioners. There has been a proliferation of cases brought against agencies and millions of dollars awarded to plaintiffs during the past 25 years. These actions normally allege that the agency and its employees failed to take steps to prevent a suicide attempt or a suicide, and allegations of inadequate training are typical of such cases. Under § 1983, plaintiffs allege that the city violated the constitutional rights of the person to be free from self-injury, failure to protect, and frequently for deficient building and policies. In *Farmer v. Brennan* (1994), the Supreme Court held that deliberate indifference must be established in prisoner safety and health cases, based on a showing that the official was subjectively aware of the risk and made no effort to reduce it. This still places some responsibility on administrators to ensure minimal safeguards when placing arrestees in detention. Legal standards require that policies and training be reasonably adequate to address the particular subject or problem. The courts in *Wallace v. Estate of Davis* (1994, $1.4 million awarded), *Hare v. City of Corinth, Mississippi* (1994), *Bragado v. City of Zion Police Department* (1993), *Elliot v. Chesire County* (1991), *Burns v. City of Galveston* (1990), and *Simmons v. City of Philadelphia* (1991) found the government entity to be deliberately indifferent to training methods, screening procedures, and the protection of suicidal arrestees. Each case dealt with deficiencies in minimum training guidelines and policies surrounding the foreseeable needs of arrestees exhibiting intoxication, mental impairment, and the stress associated with detention.

In *Harvey v. County of Ward* (2005), an arrestee committed suicide in the jail after he accumulated some of his medications. The decedent's estate claimed that jail officers had information (provided by the detainee's wife) that he was storing his medication so that he could later commit suicide. The family also filed a claim against the sheriff for failing to train his officers and implement policies that would lessen the likelihood of detainee suicide.

The court granted summary judgment for the sheriff and the officers in the absence of any evidence that either of them was aware of a conversation with the detainee's wife regarding his medication. The court also found that the sheriff's suicide prevention policy was reasonable and that the county was not deliberately indifferent to training its officers in suicide awareness. The fact that the policy had not been updated recently, and that the jail was not accredited by the American Correctional Association, did not alter the result when the policy contained a detailed listing of factors for the identification of possibly suicidal prisoners, procedures for screening detainees, and required that officers receive ongoing training in suicide intervention.

Compare, however, *Howard v. City of Atmore* (2004). A detainee committed suicide in a city lockup and his sister filed a civil lawsuit claiming that the officer failed to follow his training and policy in making security checks. The rules and policies of the facility required officers to make security checks twice an hour. Evidence revealed that the officer had not followed his training and policy, which led to the detainee's death. The court ruled that the officer was not entitled to summary judgment and liability attached. The chief of police however, was granted immunity by the court, as he had developed and implemented procedures, as well as training on the procedures concerning the identification and handling of potentially suicidal detainees.

In *Branton v. City of Moss Point* (2007), the court examined the issue of officer training and detainee suicide. The decedent was arrested for drunk driving and during booking, an officer asked whether he had attempted suicide or was thinking about it now, and the decedent responded "no." The decedent was placed in a cell for combative prisoners with a bed sheet and committed suicide two hours later. The decedent's estate filed a § 1983 lawsuit, alleging that the city should be held liable for failing to properly train officers in prisoner screening, failing to train officers concerning suicidal prisoners, and failing to furnish medical care to prisoners in need. The court denied summary judgment for the city, holding that there was sufficient evidence to show that officers were improperly trained and that there was evidence that the booking officer possessed actual knowledge that the detainee exhibited a substantial risk of suicide.

In *Mombourquette v. Amundson* (2007), the court determined that the county was deliberately indifferent to training detention officers regarding suicide prevention strategies. The court found an affirmative link between the failings in the detention facility and the failure to prevent the plaintiff from committing suicide. First, the court held that there was a lack of training and a lack of clear delineation of authority with respect to assessing the risks associated with suicide. Second, the court ruled that officers were inadequately trained in communicating a detainee's medical needs with other officers working in the facility, stating that effective communication was sorely lacking. According to the court, these failures in adequate training amounted to deliberate indifference to the risk that the plaintiff would seriously harm himself.

In *Wilson v. Taylor* (2009), the decedent prisoner was housed in solitary confinement and hung himself. His estate filed a § 1983 lawsuit against correctional officials claiming a failure to protect, a failure to train officers on measures to prevent suicide, wrongful death claims, and unconstitutional policies and procedures regarding supervising prisoners in their cells. Correctional officials filed a motion for summary judgment and the federal district court denied it. The court found that the prisoner had attempted suicide previously during his confinement and that the officials were deliberately indifferent to taking steps to prevent it once they became aware of his behaviors. The court determined that correctional officials maintained unconstitutional policies and customs underscoring the failure-to-train claim. Further, the court determined that officers acted recklessly and with wanton indifference when several officers threw the prisoner against a bench by grabbing his throat and threatening to harm him further. The court held that correctional officials and their officers acted with outrageous disregard and with deliberate indifference to the prisoner's rights and to the rights of other prisoners supporting the § 1983 claims.

Search and Seizure

Police officers frequently search and seize citizens' vehicles, property, dwellings, and businesses, as well as their persons. Plaintiffs alleging that the police improperly conducted a search and improperly seized property are more likely to file a lawsuit under § 1983 because they pertain to a violation of Fourth Amendment rights. Police administrators must ensure that officers routinely receive updated training that is commensurate with the law. A $6.1 million judgment was granted to the plaintiff in *Doe v. Calumet City* (1990) because the officers strip-searched females during traffic and misdemeanor arrests without probable cause. The city had adopted a policy that prohibited such searches, but failed to distribute it to officers and failed to conduct training explaining the policy. In *Hufford v. Rodgers* (1990), a sheriff was held liable for inadequate training and supervision of a deputy who seized a child from a mother pursuant to papers supplied by her former husband erroneously implying that he had a right to the child. The City of North Reading, Massachusetts, was held not deliberately indifferent to the rights of the plaintiff during a personal search in *Swain v. Spinney* (1997). During booking at the lockup, the plaintiff was strip-searched for possible drug possession and claimed emotional trauma after her eventual release. The city produced a policy and training manual developed by a statewide risk management group specifying when strip searches are warranted. The city had also provided training to officers. The plaintiff in *Wall v. Gwinnett County* (1993) settled out of court for $9.8 million relating to six site searches of his business and residence. More than 100 boxes of financial records were seized through the searches. The suit claimed that the search warrants were obtained by misrepresentation and that the searches were intended to damage the plaintiff's business. Allegations of inadequate training/supervision and emotional distress emerged.

The legality of a search poses critical concerns for police officers, and new cases are frequently decided. Like many other tasks, this requires administrators to conduct ongoing training. A case in point is the Supreme Court's decision in *Wyoming v. Houghton* (1999), which involved the search of a motor vehicle passenger's purse. The Court analyzed the situation as if the purse were a container in the car. The Court determined that when officers have probable cause to search a car, they may inspect a passenger's belongings found in the car if the container could conceal the object of the search.

Officer as Plaintiff

An emerging area of litigation is police officers as plaintiffs. They are filing claims against citizens for injuries or wrongs committed against them and the department for failing to train. In *Carlson v. City of Tonawanda* (1995), the deceased officer's estate prevailed when the deputy was fatally shot attempting to arrest a suspect. The estate sued the city on the basis of deficient policies and regulations and inadequate training policies, which created additional risks to those ordinarily faced by officers arresting a suspect. The court ruled in *Darrow v. Schumacher* (1993) that the mere failure to adopt a special training policy for special events could not be the basis of liability when there was no showing that any failure was the direct cause of an injury. The court held in *McCormick v. City of New York* (1991) that the city's failure to provide officers with a newer type of vest could not make the city liable for the shooting death of the officer, nor could a claim of failure to train be valid. In *Collins v. City of Harker Heights, Texas* (1992), the court ruled that federal civil rights law does not provide a remedy for a municipal employee fatally injured during employment because of the city's customary failure to train or warn its employees to know about hazards in the workplace.

Over the years, academy and in-service training instructors have moved to using more scenario-based training, in response to the Supreme Court's decisions for criminal justice agencies to provide realistic training. As such, the courts have begun accepting claims that allege an unsafe training environment. In *Cole v. State of Louisiana Department of Public Safety and Corrections* (2002), the court found in favor of a plaintiff correctional officer who sustained injuries requiring extensive hospitalization and treatment during an in-service scenario-based training exercise portraying a prison disturbance. The simulation training was designed for officers to role-play riotous prisoners so that the tactical unit of the prison could practice using techniques, equipment, and tactics to quell and control such a disturbance in the future. The simulation training called for five exercises and the morning exercises were conducted without incident. In the morning exercises, protective gear was worn by all personnel and those playing the role of officers used batons wrapped in foam. In the afternoon, Cole and other officers assumed the role of angry prisoners. The officers role-playing as "prisoners" wore helmets and the "officers" used unpadded batons. At trial, Cole testified that he had never participated in this type of role-play exercise in his previous seven years of employment and since being a member of the tactical unit. He stated that the training exercise turned into a "free for all." He reported that someone grabbed him and started hitting him on his left arm with full force several times. He yelled out "red," the code word which was supposed to stop the activity, but he continued to be struck with the unpadded batons. At some point the exercise was stopped and Cole was transported to a hospital. He sustained numerous injuries from being struck with the baton six times and being tackled to the ground, including a serious head injury resulting in brain damage, and general injuries to his neck, left shoulder, arm, and back.

Cole filed a lawsuit claiming that his injuries were sustained from an intentional tort of battery resulting from an unsafe training exercise conducted by his employer. At trial, a video was shown of the simulated training exercise. Photographs of Cole's injuries were also shown. The video showed that unpadded batons were used and that the helmet Cole wore came off while he was being struck. Administrators in charge of the training testified that tactical training is very physical, that officers could reasonably expect to get scuffed up and might incur bruises, but they would not sustain significant injuries. They also testified that they "try to avoid any significant injuries to the extent they can, but it is just a physical type of training."

After weighing the evidence and testimony, the trial court found that Cole had established that the Department of Corrections was liable for his injuries and awarded him $1.8 million, including $675,000 in general damages, $175,000 in future medical damages, $914,390 in lost wages, and $105,000 for loss of consortium to his family. The department appealed the case and the Louisiana Supreme Court upheld the finding. The court held that striking someone with an unpadded baton is harmful or offensive conduct intending harm to result from such contact, and that Cole met the elements of proving an intentional tort. Further, the Court ruled that there was overwhelming evidence that the force used in the training was "unnecessary and unanticipated" in order to complete the goals of the training exercise. The Court upheld the damages awarded by the lower courts but reduced a portion of the medical compensation amount, without specification.

In *Hayes v. University of Southern Mississippi and Ted Socha* (2003), the court took occasion to assess the safety of training at a police academy. Hayes attended academy training in the Police Corps Academy at the University of Mississippi. The program was started by the United States Congress and gave oversight to the Department of Justice. During the fourth day of training during a 22-week course, Hayes participated in a mandated realistic, scenario-based training exercise that used various safety precautions. The exercise was performed in the gym on padded mats and the role-players as well as the training cadet officers wore protective gear, including headgear, mouthpiece, knee and leg protection, and groin protectors. Further, there were four academy personnel on-site, including a safety instructor who would oversee the exercise and stop it at the end of two minutes or if a problem occurred. The goal of the exercise was to assess the candidate's response to an unexpected physical reaction from a suspect who the candidate was questioning about suspicious behavior. The role-player was trained in what to do, what to say, and how far to take the scenario. During the exercise, Hayes was forced to the mat and rolled on her knee, sustaining an injury. The safety instructor immediately stopped the training, allowed Hayes to catch her breath, and escorted her off the mat. The instructor provided remedial medical attention to Hayes and then transported her to the hospital where she received treatment for an injured tendon in her knee. She returned to the academy and a month later, while completing a mandated test, was observed to be cheating by an instructor. After an investigation she was allowed to submit a letter of resignation. She filed a lawsuit claiming that the academy was indifferent in planning and operating an unsafe training exercise with unsafe conditions, assault, and delayed medical care, which directly led to her knee injuries. She requested payment of damages, compensation of medical bills which amounted to $43,000, and reinstatement into the academy.

At trial, academy personnel testified that the training scenario was planned out in advance and safety measures were implemented. As soon as an injury was observed the exercise was discontinued, and medical care was provided at the academy and at the hospital. The academy paid for the medical treatment at the hospital. An expert witness for the academy testified that the training exercise was properly planned and performed like other scenario-based training used across the United States and agreed that proper safety measures were in place and followed by academy instructors. The court agreed with the defendants and found the purpose of the training exercise was appropriate for the circumstances and in accordance with the Police Corps Academies and that the exercise was conducted with the degree of care ordinarily and customarily exercised in its performance.

The issue of an instructor providing safe and proper training was addressed in *Hamilton v. Martinelli & Associates* (2004). The plaintiff was a probation officer and her duties required her to restrain violent youthful offenders and that she receive commensurate subject control training. She was required to wear a uniform and carry pepper spray. During mandatory training, certified by the State Board of Corrections Standards and Training Commission, she sustained injuries to her neck and back while performing a physical control technique. She sued the instructor for negligence and an intentional tort. As a result of the injuries, she was not able to perform the job as a probation officer or police officer.

The lower court ruled against Hamilton, concluding that the doctrine of primary assumption of the risk barred her claim, and granted summary judgment to the instructor. She appealed and the appellate court affirmed. The appellate court concluded that Hamilton assumed the risk of her injuries in the training course. The court dismissed the fact that the instructor failed to provide a written disclaimer warning or consent form to students at the beginning of the training. The instructor did ask all participants to identify prior injuries and sensitive areas of their bodies by placing silver tape on the identified areas before the class started. The instructor also demonstrated the techniques to the participants before they practiced them. The court noted that this certified training enabled her to perform her employment duties and that by participating in an employer-required training course, she assumed the risk that she would be injured while attending training to restrain a violent youthful offender. The court finally concluded that she failed to offer evidence that the instructor exceeded the boundaries of the normal risks associated with this type of training.

Issues of whether an administrator failed to provide training and created a hostile work environment were asserted in *Hawkins v. County of Oneida, New York* (2007). A black plaintiff officer alleged that he was not properly trained in firearms necessary to function as a gun tower officer and that he was not provided emergency response team training, which amounted to a pretext for race discrimination and failure to provide training constituted a Title VII rights violation. He also asserted that he was wrongfully terminated from his position. The court granted summary judgment for the county on the failure-to-train claims, because it was determined that the officer, who was a probationary employee, was ineligible for such training. Probationary employees were not assigned to the gun towers or assigned to emergency team assignments. Further, the court denied summary judgment on the officer's claims of a hostile work environment. The court found that the county permitted a widespread custom of race discrimination within the sheriff's department, which included persistent intimidation, racist and racially charged remarks, ridicule, insults, and discriminatory conduct by officers and supervisors sufficient to show that an abusive and hostile work environment was tolerated, and violated the officer's rights.

In *Hennagir v. Department of Corrections* (2009) a health care worker for the department filed a legal claim alleging disability discrimination and retaliation in violation of the Americans with Disabilities Act in connection with the department's refusal to allow the employee to continue in her position without completing the required physical safety training. The appellate court affirmed summary judgment of the lower court in favor of the department of corrections. The court concluded that successful completion of the required training was an "essential job function" for the employee, and that allowing the employee to continue with identical job duties, by eliminating the essential job function of completion of the required physical safety training was not a "reasonable accommodation." The court reasoned that the department required all employees who had prisoner contact to complete the training and that the safety training was an essential job function. The court held the potential consequences of a prisoner attacking any employee was incredibly severe and such training was designed for employee protection.

Emerging Topics

Case analysis reveals additional areas that appear to be emerging as training concerns for administrators. Police officers are frequently asked to respond or to intervene with individuals suffering from alcohol and drug dependence or mental illness. A litigation trend has emerged as plaintiffs or estates of deceased individuals assert that the police responded improperly due to policy and training deficiencies. Intervention with this special needs population can heighten the liability risk for the officer and the local government. In *Young v. City of Atlanta* (1995), the court found the city liable for inadequately training officers in the city lockup to recognize arrestees with mental problems and dispensing prescribed medication during detention. In *Russo v. City of Cincinnati* (1992), the city was held liable for failing to train officers in how to respond to "disturbed individuals." Officers shot and killed a schizophrenic man who was in possession of two knives when he charged at them. An investigation revealed that the training of new and in-service officers was virtually nonexistent regarding the handling of mentally disturbed individuals. The court held the chief liable in *Roy v. Inhabitants of Lewiston* (1994) on the grounds that he failed to adequately train officers in nonlethal alternatives for subduing dangerous but intoxicated persons.

Issues of custodial deaths after a violent struggle and restraint with individuals under the influence of a chemical substance or suffering from mental impairment are emerging as a training concern, as the courts have recognized that these interventions occur with some frequency for police officers (*Brown v. Gray*, 2000). In the cases of *Cruz v. City of Laramie, Wyoming* (2001), *Johnson v. City of Cincinnati* (1999), *Gutierrez v. City of San Antonio et al.* (1998), *Kinneer v. Gall* (1996), *Animashaun v. O'Donnell* (1995), and *Elmes v. Hart* (1994), officers were forced to restrain highly combative individuals who were under high levels of intoxicants or were exhibiting signs of psychosis. After restraint, the subject suddenly died in police custody. The government entities were all found liable for inadequate policies and training in directing officers in how to respond to, restrain, and provide medical care to arrestees. Conversely, no liability attached in *Harris v. District of Columbia* (1991), *Estate of Phillips v. City of Milwaukee* (1996), *Cottrell v. Caldwell* (1996), *Melendez v. Howard County Government* (1997), *Guseman v. Martinez* (1998), and *Young v. City of Mount Ranier* (2001) for claims of inadequate policy or training in the restraint of intoxicated or mentally impaired individuals. All of these entities had provided policy direction and training for their officers in how to properly intervene and control such persons.

In *Lewis v. Board of Sedgwick County Commissioners* (2001), a detainee brought an action against the county alleging that jail officers used excessive force against him and that the county failed to adequately train its officers. The detainee became disruptive and detention officers used pressure point control tactics to control and subdue him, and then secured him in a restraint chair. The detainee alleged that such use of force violated his due process rights. A jury returned a verdict in favor of the detainee and awarded him $500,000 and the county requested a new trial or judgment as a matter of law. The court agreed and found that there was no evidence that the officers used excessive force or that the county was deliberately indifferent to the training needs of their officers. The court held that the county provided training on use-of-force techniques at the correctional academy and on the job. The county provided a training manual and policies outlining their force techniques and under what circumstances they authorized these techniques. The court noted that the county had encountered only 22 complaints of excessive force in its jail from approximately 90,000 detainees who were admitted into the jail.

Contrast, however, the decision in *Swans v. City of Lansing* (1998). After assaulting an arresting officer and assaulting a sergeant in the detention facility, a violent schizophrenic arrestee was "maximally" restrained and placed in a cell for observation. The arrestee unexpectedly died in custody. The estate filed suit and claimed a failure on the part of the police chief to train officers in the proper use of restraints. The jury found in favor of the plaintiff. The judge noted a policy and custom of using maximum restraint and that the officers were not trained regarding the manufacturers' warnings about the dangers of using the restraint system. The estate was awarded $12.9 million and the city later settled for $10 million. This area and the many variables associated with it, such as issues of force, restraints, responding to special needs populations, medical/psychological care, and transportation concerns, suggest considerations for training and potential policy revision.

An emerging trend in failure-to-train claims directed at criminal justice agencies are allegations that question how officers have been trained to respond to the mentally impaired. Police response to the mentally ill has been an ongoing complex societal issue since the 1970s, due to the closing of many mental health facilities and the increased usage of antipsychotic medications. In some communities, police contact with the mentally impaired may be increasing, necessitating varying response strategies and training. Plaintiffs' attorneys have begun to bring § 1983 actions against police departments based on the Americans with Disabilities Act (ADA, 1990). Title II § 12132 of the ADA provides that "no qualified individual with a disability shall, by reason or such disability, be excluded, or be subjected to discrimination by any such entity." In passing the Act, Congress's main purpose was to eliminate discrimination against individuals with disabilities. The Act applies to governmental entities such as criminal justice agencies, and it guarantees disabled persons full access to all of the "services, programs, or activities of a public entity." The Act applies to "all" core functions of government, including the lawful exercise of police powers, including the proper use of force by officers acting under color of law. The ADA is a remedial statute, designed to eliminate discrimination against the disabled in all facets in society. The question emerges as to whether police administrators have enacted policies and training that prepare their officers to respond to the mentally impaired or other disabled persons in accordance with the ADA.

This question was addressed in *Schorr v. Borough of Lemoyne, Pennsylvania* (2003). Schorr had been diagnosed with bipolar disorder. His condition deteriorated and his family was granted a request for an involuntary commitment order under the Pennsylvania Mental Health Procedures Act. A crisis intervention worker of the hospital issued the order and requested that the police assist in executing the commitment order. Two officers responded, placed him in custody, and transported him to the hospital. He was placed in a "high security room" to wait for an evaluation. He escaped from the hospital when a crisis intervention worker entered the room. Schorr fled to his apartment and at the request of the family, two officers responded. A violent confrontation occurred and Schorr was shot and killed by one of the responding officers. The family filed a § 1983 lawsuit, claiming excessive force in violation of the Fourth Amendment. They also filed allegations of unconstitutional policies and procedures for dealing with mentally ill persons and failing to train officers to properly respond to the mentally ill under the provisions of the ADA. The District Court granted judgment in favor of the plaintiffs. The court reasoned that while the ADA does not apply to "on the street exigent circumstances decisions" facing the safety of officers or others, it does apply to claims of failure to train. The court ruled that the ADA applies in cases in which the agency failed to properly train its officers in properly responding to situations involving the mentally impaired. The court determined that noncompliance with the requirements of the ADA occurred well before the encounter with Schorr. Such a failure occurred when the policymakers of the department failed to institute policies to accommodate disabled individuals such as Schorr by giving officers the tools and resources to handle the situation peacefully.

While not binding on other federal court jurisdictions, this decision is instructive. In light of the *Schorr* decision, police administrators should review their procedures and revise them accordingly and provide their officers with appropriate training when interacting with disabled persons. Persons with disabilities can include a number of conditions and such procedures should be established to properly address the requirements. In *Miami-Dade County v. Walker* (2002), the county successfully defended such a claim. Officers attempted to arrest Walker, who had been diagnosed with schizophrenia. Walker was seriously injured in a violent struggle with the officers and the family filed a § 1983 lawsuit alleging that the county failed to train its officers. The court granted summary judgment to the county, holding that it did provide training for its officers as outlined in its policies and in a training document titled *How to Handle the Mentally Ill.* The court concluded that the county was not deliberately indifferent to the rights of the mentally ill.

Claims for failing to properly train police officers in properly responding to the mentally impaired were lodged against the chief in *Estate of Sowards v City of Trenton* (2005). Neighbors of Sowards saw him threaten another man with a knife and called the police. Sowards was diagnosed with paranoia schizophrenia but the responding officers were unaware of this fact. After speaking with the victim, two officers went to Sowards' apartment door, but Sowards refused to open it. He began yelling and cursing the officers, informing them that he had a surprise for them. The officers summoned back-up and a corporal and other officers responded. Unable to persuade Sowards to exit the apartment after some time, the corporal decided to use force. The corporal did not have a warrant, nor did he know that the occupant in the apartment was indeed Sowards, or whether he possessed a weapon. The officers kicked the door and dislodged it about a foot. The officers observed the barrel of a gun pointed at them and one officer yelled "gun." The officers dove for cover and called for an ambulance. Simultaneously, one officer began firing at Sowards through the door and the corporal also began firing. Other officers began firing and 39 rounds were fired in total. The Special Response Team also responded and the team entered the apartment and found Sowards dead on the floor. An investigation was performed and it was discovered that Sowards had not fired any rounds.

The estate filed a § 1983 lawsuit under the Fourth and Fourteenth Amendments, claiming excessive force, entering the apartment without a warrant, and also sued the city for failing to adequately train the officers on handling a barricaded gunman/hostage situation and failing to train officers to properly respond to the mentally impaired. The district court granted summary judgment and the Sixth Circuit Court of Appeals affirmed. The appellate court concluded that the officers' use of force was consistent with criteria set forth in the *Graham* decision and that entry into the apartment was necessary given the totality of circumstances, despite the outcome and that Sowards suffered from a mental illness. The court also ruled that the training of the officers was not the proximate cause of the shooting or the entry into the apartment, and summary judgment was also granted on claims of failure to train in responding to persons with a mental illness, as the officers had received such training.

Claims of failing to train officers regarding handling mentally ill individuals and ADA issues emerged in *Wolfanger v. Laurel County, Kentucky* (2008). A deputy used a control technique during the arrest of a mentally ill person and he sustained minor injuries. The plaintiff filed a lawsuit alleging excessive force and his expert opined that the county was deliberately indifferent for failing to provide deputies with specialized training in using force when responding to mentally ill or suicidal persons. The court rejected the argument, holding that a plaintiff's allegations of inadequate training will not activate a § 1983 claim unless the situation causing the injury is recurring, such that a court may impute prior knowledge and deliberate indifference. In this case the plaintiff could not show evidence that similar circumstances had occurred previously, let alone occurred with frequency. The court also noted that the plaintiff failed to show that the arresting deputy had a history of using excessive force against mentally ill persons.

Similarly, in *Morrison v. Board of Trustees of Green Township* (2007), the court granted summary judgment to officers on a claim that supervisors failed to provide specialized training in using force with mentally ill persons. The plaintiff argued that officers were not trained to avoid unnecessary physical force during such encounters, particularly when the contact resulted in an injury. The court held that the plaintiff failed to present any evidence that showed a history of constitutional violations or an obvious likelihood that such violations were likely to occur absent better training. Thus, the court ruled that the plaintiff failed to demonstrate that the county consciously chose not to provide adequate training, amounting to deliberate indifference.

Conversely, in *Estate of Harvey v. Jones* (2006), summary judgment was denied by the court when two officers testified that they never received any training on how to interact with mentally disturbed persons or persons under the influence of drugs. One of the officers stated that he came into contact with "a lot" of mentally ill people on the streets. The plaintiff also submitted information that the city failed to train officers in a prior incident involving a mentally ill person who died in custody, which had occurred 10 years earlier. The court determined that such evidence constituted deliberate indifference because the likelihood that an officer would contact a mentally ill person required necessary training.

Since 2000 over 8,000 criminal justice agency officials have provided their officers with a Taser (Taser International, 2012). As the device has been employed numerous times in the field, questions have emerged about the liability for failure to train on a specific piece of equipment (Scarry, 2011).Questions of whether officers have been properly trained to apply the Taser have emerged as the device is being used more in the field. In *LeBlanc v. City of Los Angeles* (2006), an officer contacted a narcotically intoxicated suspect who resisted arrest, and applied the Taser. The person filed a legal action claiming that failure to train on the proper use of the Taser with intoxicated persons violated his constitutional rights. Testimony revealed that agency training materials on the use of the Taser provided no guidance on how and whether the Taser should be used on intoxicated persons. The court ruled in favor of the plaintiff, holding that the failure to instruct officers on Taser use against intoxicated persons amounted to deliberate indifference and a constitutional violation. The court further held that the city was liable for failing to supervise or audit Taser use by officers. The court's decision was influenced by an officer's testimony that he would respond in the same way in the future if confronted with similar resistance and was not reprimanded for such conduct, which amounted to deliberate indifference in the view of the court.

In *Ellis v. Country Club Hills* (2012), officers responded to a 911 call that Ellis's stepfather was beating his mother. On location the officers learned that Mrs. Ellis was suffering a sickle-cell attack, had not been taking her medication, and refused the officers' offer to provide her with medical assistance. The officers were asked to leave but they informed Mr. Ellis that an ambulance had been summoned.

Mr. Ellis claimed in a § 1983 lawsuit that the officers activated the Taser several times while it struck him the bicep. Mr. Ellis alleged that the officers continued to deploy the Taser while he lay on the ground and then the officers struck him several times with a collapsible baton on his arm, back, legs, shoulder, neck, and the back of his head. Mr. Ellis further claimed that the officers carried him out of the bedroom, ran his head into a wall, and kicked him in the groin and in the head several times. Mr. Ellis claimed that the officers used excessive force and that the city failed to train the officers in the proper use of the Taser and force techniques.

The training lieutenant of the department testified that he was a certified Taser instructor; provided eight hours of training for officers who were assigned the Taser, including drills, discussions on fact patterns on when to deploy the Taser; and administered a 25-question written examination to each officer after the training. Further, the lieutenant testified that he instructed officers to announce the use of the Taser prior to using it and that the department, by policy, followed a use of force continuum. The city had adopted a policy that all officers receive training in the use of Taser and other force measures annually. The named officers in the lawsuit testified that they indeed received training in the use of the Taser, the policy, and the continuum, consistent with the lieutenant's testimony. The city filed a motion for summary judgment asserting that Ellis could not demonstrate that the officers' use of force was excessive and he failed to show a failure to train officers with the proper use of the Taser.

The court granted summary judgment for the city. The court opined that Ellis failed to demonstrate how the city's training violated his constitutional rights and failed to show how the city's training program was deficient. The court opined that the focus must be on adequacy of the training program in relation to the tasks officer must perform. Further, the court ruled that there was no evidence to demonstrate that the city maintained an inadequate training program but contrarily stated that a system of training was implemented.

Failure to Train in Corrections

Lawsuits alleging a constitutional injury resulting from a department's policy of failing to provide training to correctional employees are common. Prior to the *Canton* decision, several cases ordered jail and prison administrators to train their personnel or improve their training programs (*Jones v. Wittenburg*, 1971; *Miller v. Carson*, 1975; *Owens v. Haas*, 1979). In *Owens*, the Second Circuit Court of Appeals held that while a county may not be liable for merely failing to train employees, it could be liable if its failure was so severe as to reach the level of gross negligence or deliberate indifference. In *Hays v. Jefferson County* (1982), the Sixth Circuit Court of Appeals ruled that a supervisor may be held liable "only where there is essentially a complete failure to train. . . . or training was so reckless or grossly negligent that future misconduct is almost inevitable, or would be characterized as substantially certain to result."

Since *Canton*, several correctional administrators have been found liable in lawsuits alleging a failure to train. Using the deliberate indifference standard, a federal district court in *Coleman v. Wilson* (1995) determined that custodial staff were inadequately trained in signs and symptoms of mental illness, which supported allegations that disciplinary and behavior control measures were used inappropriately against mentally ill prisoners. The three-hour training course attended by all new officers and additional in-service training at the institutional level was insufficient to prevent some officers from using punitive measures to control prisoners' behavior without regard to cause of the behavior.

The Ninth Circuit Court of Appeals ruled in favor of prisoners in *Madrid v. Gomez* (1995) on several issues, including failure to train, excessive force, constitutionally inadequate mental health services, and deficient medical care. The court held that staffing levels were insufficient, training and supervision of medical staff were almost nonexistent, and screening for communicable diseases was poorly implemented. Prisoners frequently experienced significant delays in receiving treatment, there were no protocols or training programs dealing with emergencies or trauma, and there were no procedures for managing chronic illness. Prisoners established prison administrators' deliberate indifference, showing that they knew that unnecessary and grossly excessive force was routinely being used against prisoners by officers and that these practices posed a substantial risk of harm to prisoners. The court also held that prison officials had actual subjective knowledge that conditions of isolation presented a substantial excessive risk of harm for mentally ill and other vulnerable prisoners and that the officials acted wantonly in violation of the Eighth Amendment.

Prison officials were found liable in *Gilbert v. Selsky* (1994) when they failed to train hearing officers in prison disciplinary proceedings. The district court found that prison supervisory personnel were personally involved with violations of prisoners' constitutional rights.

Conducting regular training of correctional personnel and fully documenting that training can assist in defending against allegations of inadequate training. In *Vine v. County of Ingham* (1995), the district court held that the sheriff and the county were not deliberately indifferent to a prisoner who died in their custody after consuming methyl alcohol prior to arrest. The court ruled that the sheriff had provided the necessary training to his officers commensurate with state law, and they had also received substantial in-service training. The court noted that such claims would apply only if the conduct represents usual or recurring situations officers must deal with.

Prison officials successfully defended a failure to train claim in *Tucker v. Evans* (2002). A prisoner was attacked and killed by a fellow prisoner. The estate of the deceased prisoner brought a § 1983 action, claiming that prison officers failed to protect the prisoner and that they failed to properly train correctional officers. The district court denied summary judgment and on appeal the appellate court reversed the decision. The court reasoned that correctional officers had no prior warning that the prisoner was at risk because he did not know about an argument between the two prisoners. The court found that correctional officials did not show callous indifference to the prisoner and were entitled to qualified immunity because they did not violate the Eighth Amendment by failing to train their officers. According to the court, correctional officials provided officers with six weeks' training at the state's correctional academy and they also provided subsequent on-the-job training.

In some failure-to-train claims, the plaintiff has attempted to hold the governmental entity to national standards developed by associations regarding suggestions for training. In *Smith v. Board of County Commissioners of County of Lyon* (2002), county officials successfully defended such a claim. A county jail detainee brought a § 1983 lawsuit, claiming under the Eighth Amendment that he failed to receive adequate medical care for a spinal cord injury that he sustained during a fall at the jail. He also claimed that officials had failed to adequately train correctional officers. The detainee alleged that officers failed to provide treatment for his injuries and failed to provide clean bedding and clothing to him as he suffered from incontinence on five occasions.

The court granted summary judgment for the officers as they presented evidence that once they were aware that the detainee required medical attention they immediately took him to the jail medical unit for treatment. The detainee alleged that there were systemic and gross deficiencies in training detention officers. He claimed that county officials failed to follow certain national training standards, but failed to show that the county had any duty to follow the standards. The court granted summary judgment for the county on the training claims as well, holding that the minimum standards for the operation of county jails are established in state law, rather than by national standards.

Prisons and jails admit prisoners with a wide range of medical needs and the question in many lawsuits involves the adequacy of training provided for facility employees. In *Wakat v. Montgomery* (2007), the estate of a prisoner who died in a county facility brought a § 1983 claim against the county, the facility's physician, and officers. The court granted summary judgment in favor of the county. The court ruled that the county complied with training standards of the state, provided officers with training in the basics of correctional health care, and periodically provided in-service training on prisoner medical care issues. Further, the court determined that the physician did not act with deliberate indifference in providing medical care for the prisoner while confined. The court did not find any evidence that showed a pattern or a recurring situation of tortious conduct by inadequately trained employees.

Summary

Case review reveals that deliberate indifference is a difficult standard for plaintiffs to establish in asserting claims of inadequate training. The trends and the margin for winning civil lawsuits by the police illustrate this point. As several case examples have shown, police administrators should note specific training categories that may apply to their respective departments. Administrators are encouraged to review the following recommendations in an effort to shore up potential agency deficiencies to insulate the agency, supervisors, and officers from civil liability.

First, consistent with the decisions in *Canton* and *Iqbal*, administrators must provide training to their employees on a regular basis. While deliberate indifference is a high standard to overcome, a plaintiff may prevail if the following can be demonstrated: (1) a policy that consciously ignores providing training that whereby causes a constitutional deprivation, (2) a widespread practice that reveals a custom of failing to train to recurring tasks, and (3) an allegation that the constitutional injury was caused by a person with final policymaking authority. A plaintiff must show that the governmental entity failed to provide adequate training in light of foreseeable consequences or failure to act in response to repeated complaints of constitutional violations by officers.

Second, each administrator should conduct an internal assessment of routine and recurring tasks that officers and supervisors perform. Incident reports, calls for service, citizen/ prisoner complaints, disciplinary actions, and changes in job requirements spanning a three-year period should be assessed based on the criticality and frequency of the activity.

As changes in the law affect job functions, appropriate training should be developed. Based on this assessment, regularly scheduled training should be provided to all officers and supervisors in those activities. At a minimum, each category identified should be a priority addressed through training on a recurring basis.

Third, once a training assessment has been finalized, administrators are encouraged to revise the policies and procedures that parallel training topics. For example, the use-of-force policy should be reviewed annually and revised to accompany the training. As use-of-force laws and authorized restraint techniques and equipment change, training that addresses the policy change should be performed. Moreover, a policy of annual/biannual training that outlines the topics to be covered and by what time interval the training will be conducted should be established by the administrator. It is recommended that training in high-liability areas requiring physical skills and competency be provided on an annual basis. Minimally, this would include lethal and nonlethal force (and equipment), emergency vehicle operations, arrest, and search and seizure laws. Officers should be provided with realistic, incident-based training in these areas. Training for officers in their constitutional requirements in these high-liability areas is also suggested. In the past 30 years, search and seizure laws and laws of arrest have been most likely to change. This affects officers' and supervisors' Fourth Amendment duties; therefore, annual training is recommended in these areas. Administrators are encouraged to provide training that comports with the standards as specified by the training and standards council for their respective states. Correctional administrators should likewise address training issues surrounding the First, Fourth, Eighth, and Fourteenth Amendments.

Fourth, to avert future failure-to-train liability and to maintain occupational professionalism, supervisory training should be instituted. This should include pre- and post-promotion training, conducted at least biannually, concentrating on supervisory duties and including policy interpretation, implementation, and enforcement, as well as performance evaluation of subordinates. Supervisors should also receive regular training that emphasizes managerial responsibilities in risk management and the reduction of administrative liability. A commitment to ongoing training for supervisors is essential for the efficient operation of the department.

Fifth, it is critical that all training be documented and accurate training records be maintained. Several computer programs have been designed to track training, and administrators should use the programs that are appropriate for their needs. Training records for each officer and administrator should be maintained and inspected at least twice a year to ensure their completeness. Administrators should monitor and evaluate current and future training needs annually. It is also recommended that police administrators review their Field Training Officer (FTO) program in light of the research findings. Training scenarios for FTOs could be developed from these high-liability areas, placing the new officer in positions in which he or she will be evaluated. This would be most beneficial in reinforcing appropriate decisionmaking and future behavior. Administrators are encouraged to enlarge their roll-call training with documentation and consider providing training through teleconferencing, interactive computer-based training, and training available via the Internet.

Sixth, scenario-based training has become popular with many criminal justice departments as well as training academies. Such training frequently utilizes contextual learning components

(Severginin and Ross, 2012; Ross, 2011). Contextualization is a style of adult learning that seeks to tie in new information with existing knowledge and real-life situations. It acknowledges that skills and knowledge are integrated into actual field applications. Using such training methodologies underscores the central component in the *Canton* decision, which addressed providing "realistic" training for officers. As agencies provide more scenario-based training, they should ensure that the scenarios are designed to meet the types of encounters that officers routinely face, that the scenarios are scripted out in advance, that all role-players are pre-trained, and that measures are taken to reduce the risk of injury to all participants, provide safety equipment for all participants, videotape the training, and thoroughly document the training. Such training can assist in defending the next allegation of failing to train.

Further, to increase performance under stress, simulation training should be provided on an ongoing basis to improve decisionmaking and to enhance expertise and the experience of officers (Ross, 2011). In order to obtain a clearer picture of the human factors influencing perceptions researchers have recommended that police officers receive stress-induced training through a force simulator or simmunitions training (Klinger and Brunson, 2009; Engel and Smith, 2009; Novak, 2009). Simulators can provide realistic training for officers by immersing them in field-type confrontations. Using a virtual force simulator designed by the Meggitt Corporation, Ross, Murphy, Hazlett, and Burnell (2009) placed 150 veteran police officers in lethal force scenarios and exposed them to various stress inoculation components. The objective was to measure whether the scenarios, designed with various stressors (visual, lightening, tactical, and auditory) would activate the sympathetic nervous system (SNS) in order to assess the officers' perceptions of stress, other physiological factors, and psychological dimensions. The results of the research showed that the officers truly believed that the scenarios were "realistic" such that the brain triggered significant measurable SNS discharges in each officer. Recommendations from the findings showed that officers should routinely be provided with virtual simulator training with stress immersion strategies to enhance the human factors involved in stressful lethal force encounters.

Stress inoculation and dynamic scenario-based training is highly useful in exposing officers to recognize a level of threat, exposing them to the effects of perceptual narrowing problems at combat distance, and enhancing forced decisionmaking. Such "intensity" factors complement the "frequency" factor necessary in the use of force training. This type of training enhances the ability to build expertise in field performance and maximizes proper decisionmaking. It keeps the brain in the training mode, which is essential for officer field performance. Realistic-scenario-based training should be structured around dynamic encounters where the instructor has previously trained the officer to recognize a threat level with response options consistent with the threat cue (Ross et al., 2009). Exposing officers to anticipated/unaccepted threat cues in spontaneous lethal force encounters, where the officer can experience the effects of SNS activation, are important in managing stress and perceptions. Integrating stimulus response training and building dynamic scenario-based training around the four components of reaction time (perception, analyze, formulate a strategy, and motor response) would be useful.

Section 12132 under the Americans with Disabilities Act is emerging as a component of legal actions filed against the criminal justice administrator. The criminal justice agency's response to the mentally ill should be coordinated with professionals from the courts, mental health, police, and detention facilities in order to provide a comprehensive approach to addressing the associated societal issues. Administrators should develop and/or revise policies and procedures, and provide training to officers consistent with state standards. This will go a long way toward defending allegations that the department was deliberately indifferent to the needs of the mentally impaired.

Since the Canton decision, police and correctional personnel have prevailed in a majority of civil lawsuits, and continued strides are being made toward providing regular training for criminal justice personnel. Administrators should continue to maintain the commitment to providing and expanding regular training in order to avert future lawsuits alleging inadequate training.

References

Alpert, G. P. (1997). Pursuit driving: planning policies and action from agency, officer, and public information. *Police Forum, 7*, 1–12.

Barrineau, H. E. (1994). *Civil liability in criminal justice* (2nd ed.). Cincinnati, OH: Anderson Publishing Co.

Beckman, E. (1987). Identifying issues in police pursuits: the first research findings. *Police Chief*, July, 57–63.

Bureau of Justice Statistics (BJS) (2005). *Sourcebook of criminal justice statistics*. Washington, DC: U.S. Department of Justice.

del Carmen, R. V. (1987). *Criminal procedure for law enforcement personnel*. Monterey, CA: Brooks/Cole.

del Carmen, R. V. (1991). *Civil liabilities in American policing: a text for law enforcement personnel*. Monterey, CA: Brady.

Engel, R. S., & Smith, M. R. (2009). Perceptual distortion and reasonableness during police shootings: law, legitimacy, and future research. *Criminology and Public Policy, 8*, 141–151.

Falcone, D. N., Charles, M. T., & Wells, E. (1994). A study of pursuits in illinois. *The Police Chief*, July, 59–64.

Flink, W. L. (1997). *1997 Executive summary of the sourcebook*. Phoenix, AZ: International association of directors of law enforcement standards and training.

Gallagher, G. P. (1989). Managing the risks of police pursuits. *Governmental Risk Management Reports*, December, 1–6.

Gallagher, G. P. (1990). Risk management and police administrators. *The Police Chief, 57*, 18–29.

Kappeler, V. E. (1997). *Critical issues in police civil liability* (2nd ed.). Prospect Heights, IL: Waveland Press, Inc.

Klinger, D. A., & Brunson, R. K. (2009). Police officers' perceptual distortions during lethal force situations: informing the reasonableness standard. *Criminology and Public Policy, 8*, 117–140.

National Institute of Justice (NIJ) (1998). *Pursuit management task force*. Washington, DC: U.S. Department of Justice.

Novak, K. J. (2009). Reasonable officers, public perceptions, and policy challenges. *Criminology and Public Policy, 8*, 153–161.

Plitt, E. A. (1997). *Failure to train liability*. Chicago, IL: AELE: *Americans for Effective Law Enforcement Police Civil Liability Manual*.

Ross, D. L. (2000). Emerging trends in police failure to train liability. *Policing: An International Journal of Police Strategies and Management, 23*, 169–193.

Ross, D. L. (2011, December). Liability for failure to train in use of force. *Journal of Law Enforcement Executive Forum, Special Edition*, 59–79.

Ross, D. L., Murphy, R. L., Hazlett, M., & Burnell., B. (2009). Virtual training systems and survival humanistic factors. *Interservice/Industry Training, Simulation, and Education Conference (conference proceedings)*, 1–10.

Scarry, L. (2011). Failure to train. *Law Officer*. <www.lawofficer.com>.

Severginin, V., & Ross, D. L. (2012, March). Best practices in police use of force training. *Journal of Law Enforcement Executive Forum*, 25–38.

Silver, I. (2010). *Police civil liability*. New York, NY: Matthew Bender & Co.

Staff, H. (1990). *Canton v. Harris* determines standard for training liability cases. *The Police Chief, 57*, 37.

TASER International, Inc. (2012, April). <www.taser.com>.

Vaughn, M. S., & Coomes, L. F. (1995). The liability of moonlighting: are police officers employed as security guards acting under color of law? *Police Liability Review, 6*, 6–9.

Vaughn, M. S., & del Carmen, R. V. (1995). Civil liability against prison officials for inmate-on-inmate assault: where are we and where have we been? *Prison Journal, 75*, 69–89.

8 ▪▪▪

Operating Criminal Justice Agencies Under a Consent Decree

OVERVIEW

Beyond civil litigation filed by citizens or prisoners in state or federal courts, there are additional methods by which criminal justice personnel are scrutinized about performing their sworn duties. Congress has passed significant legislation authorizing the Department of Justice to initiate investigations and pursue litigation against correctional and police entities. In 1980, Congress passed the Civil Rights of Institutionalized Persons Act (CRIPA), Title 42 U.S.C. § 1997, which addresses investigations relating to conditions of confinement. In 1994, Congress promulgated Title 42 U.S.C. § 14141 as part of the Violent Crime Control and Law Enforcement Act, which prohibits government authorities or those acting on their behalf (including law enforcement officials) from engaging in a pattern or practice of conduct that deprives people of their constitutional rights.

The purpose of this chapter is to describe how these two pieces of legislation operate and affect criminal justice agencies. The issue of police misconduct and prisoner abuse is clearly a matter of social policy and legislation requiring assessment. These laws have had a significant impact on the criminal justice system and represent a major federal government intervention into the operations of criminal justice agencies. Legislation affects policy, and administrators and officers should be aware of the mechanics of these two statutes and address changes in their agency's operations as appropriate.

Section 14141

High-profile incidents, such as the Rodney King arrest (1991), the Amadou Diallo (1994) and Abner Louima (1997) incidents in New York, and the riots in Cincinnati after a police officer shot and killed an African-American youth (2001) have raised concerns about how the police treat citizens. In addition, the 2000 Rampart precinct scandal in Los Angeles, where a veteran officer, Rafael Perez, stole one million dollars' worth of cocaine only serves to convince the public that police corruption is rampant as well. These, among other incidents, have become popular examples that police pundits point toward in order to prove their contention that the police are corrupt and require federal regulation (U.S. Commission on Civil Rights, 2000).

These and other examples are frequently cited by police critics who make sweeping indictments alleging that the police profession is corrupt, that it hides behind the "blue curtain" of cover-up, and that it chronically uses excessive force. There is no question that acts of police misconduct have occasionally occurred and that excessive force has been used in some circumstances. There is no empirical evidence, however, to support claims that excessive force or officer misconduct occurs with statistically significant frequency (Ross, 2005). In his analysis, Ross found in 65 published articles on the police use of force from 1968 to 2004, including two Department of Justice national studies (1996 and 2001) and an International Association of Chiefs of Police independent national study (2001), that the use of any type of force is rare in police contacts with citizens. Moreover, he found that excessive force accusations, in contrast to public perception, were even rarer.

The United States Supreme Court has addressed proper police conduct in a series of landmark cases since the 1960s. The Court's interpretation of the "due process" rights of citizens has played a significant role in shaping social policy. For example, the Court's decisions in *Mapp v. Ohio* (1961) (which established the exclusionary rule) and *Terry v. Ohio* (1968) (which established standards for investigatory detentions and weapons pat-downs) placed restrictions on police in conducting searches and seizing evidence, and required police officers to follow legal procedures. These procedures are intended to properly guide officers and curb police misconduct. As shown in previous chapters, since the 1960s, citizens have used Title 42 U.S.C. § 1983 as the primary civil remedy for asserting legal claims against the police for alleged constitutional violations (Kappeler et al., 1993; Vaughn & Coome, 1995; Worrall, 2001; Ross, 2003a,b; Silver, 2010). While § 1983 remains a viable mechanism to redress alleged governmental intrusions on citizens' rights, some scholars argue that it has only been partially successful in deterring or curbing police abuse of authority (Silveria, 2004; Walker, 2003; Kim, 2002; Levenson, 2001; Livingston, 1999). This argument, however, has been considerably weakened after the Court's decision in *Groh v. Ramirez* (2004), when it denied qualified immunity to an officer who relied on an invalid warrant that he had prepared, even though it was approved by a magistrate. The decision further warns against police abuse of power and sends a message to the police community regarding judicial intolerance of such misconduct.

Despite police reforms and commission reports about police practices over the past 50 years, advances in police practices, and court decisions, police misconduct still occasionally occurs. Seeking to remedy the issue, Congress enacted § 14141 of Title 42 as part of the Violent Crime Control and Law Enforcement Act in 1994. Section 14141 grants authority to the Department of Justice (DOJ) to pursue equitable and declaratory relief against police engaged in a "pattern and practice" that deprives individuals of their constitutional rights. Section 14141 does not authorize compensatory damage awards to citizen complaints, but rather gives the DOJ the power to initiate police reform by essentially dictating future management practices in that police entity (Silveria, 2004). In an initial assessment of the application of § 14141, Livingston (1999) argued and agreed with some police scholars that police reform will be most effective when reform involves not only simple adherence to the rules, but also a wholehearted embrace of change in organizational values and systems.

Section 14141 specifically authorizes the DOJ to bring a lawsuit against a police organization rather than individual officers. Beginning in 1996 and through 2011, the DOJ has performed investigations of 47 police departments. One investigation was dropped. The DOJ is currently investigating seventeen police departments (DOJ, 2012).

Background of § 14141

Provisions of the Act

As a result of the Rodney King incident, Congress passed the Violent Crime Control Act in 1994. As part of this legislation, Congress gave authority to the United States Attorney General to investigate allegations of "patterns and practices" of police misconduct. Section 14141 substantially enhances the Department of Justice's statutory basis for intervening into the affairs of police departments. This provision allows the Special Litigation Section of the Civil Rights Division to investigate and bring a civil lawsuit against a police department when the Attorney General believes that constitutional violations based on patterns and practices have occurred. The fundamental purpose of § 14141 is to remedy systemic police abuse.

In establishing a claim, § 14141 requires the DOJ to demonstrate that a municipality or police department engaged in a "pattern or practice" of conduct by law enforcement officers that has deprived individuals of their constitutionally protected rights. Congress provided no explicit guidance nor has there been any judicial interpretation of § 14141, and defining a "pattern or practice" of misconduct can be problematic. There are, however, two components that shed light on the interpretation. First, the United States Supreme Court suggested in developing Title VII language that the term "pattern and practice" can mean "denoting something more than the mere occurrence of isolated or accidental or sporadic unlawful acts" (*Int'l Brotherhood of Teamsters v. United States*, 1977). In the police context, this can mean that a "pattern or practice" of conduct by police officers that violates constitutional rights would likely show that such conduct is a practice or custom that occurs frequently or regularly (Livingston, 1999). With such regularity of occurrence, a court could conclude that such abusive conduct is the *regular* practice rather than the *unusual* practice. The Supreme Court has also ruled in *Hazelwood School District v. United States* (1977) (a case predating § 14141) that a plaintiff can make a prima facie case of "pattern or practice" of discrimination simply through the introduction of statistical evidence. Because statistical evidence was sufficient proof of a "pattern or practice" of discrimination (in an educational setting), a plaintiff need not prove any overt institutional practice to satisfy the definition.

Second, in the predecessor to § 14141, the Judicial Committee Report in 1991 suggested that establishing a "pattern or practice" need not be based on extensive evidence of systematic repeated violations (H.R. Rep. 102). The report cited acts or omissions that constituted patterns and practices in illustrating the potential applicability of § 14141 to situations in which relief was formerly unavailable. For example, the Committee cited the Ninth Circuit Appellate Court's holding in *Mason County v. Davis* (1991). Affirming the lower court's decision, the appellate court determined that a § 1983 claim was valid when four separate plaintiffs showed a pattern of excessive force stemming from unconstitutional traffic stops performed by deputies over a period of nine months. Such a pattern of abuse demonstrated the inadequacies of training provided by the department for its officers.

Consent Decree

Once allegations of constitutional violations emerge, the DOJ conducts a preliminary inquiry to determine the nature of the allegations. The DOJ may notify the agency or the municipality that it will be conducting a formal investigation. If the investigation reveals evidence of a pattern or practice of abuse, the DOJ may release a letter of general findings to announce its discovery, or it may simply walk away, stating that there is no evidence to support a claim.

There are several options available to the DOJ when a "pattern or practice" is established, in its opinion, under § 14141. First, the DOJ may file a lawsuit against the police agency, which may involve a lengthy litigation process. Second, a lawsuit may be filed with the expectation that the city will settle the case through a consent decree or settle it through a memorandum of agreement (MOA). While both are settlements, there are distinctions between them. Consent decrees serve as court-ordered and court-enforceable settlements. A federal judge provides oversight of the consent decree, which normally lasts five years (Livingston, 1999). When an MOA is used to settle the DOJ claim, there is no judicial oversight. A municipality agrees in writing to comply with recommendations made by the DOJ, which threatens a future consent decree or litigation if the agency fails to comply with the agreement. Ostensibly, a consent decree is an MOA with teeth (Silveria, 2004). A Special Monitor is appointed by the court to serve as an independent auditor in consent decrees and MOAs. The Special Monitor reports on each defendant's compliance on a quarterly basis.

Investigation Trends of § 14141

Trends

Considering the lack of congressional guidance on the definition of a "pattern or practice," policy patterns of § 14141 have differed significantly from the Clinton administration to the Bush administration. Under the Clinton administration, the first investigations occurred in 1996. Pittsburgh, Pennsylvania, and Steubenville, Ohio, were the first cities the DOJ investigated for practices and patterns of police misconduct. Both investigations resulted in five-year consent decrees commencing in 1997 and both cities successfully completed the period of judicial monitoring (Livingston, 1999). The third and final police agency placed under a consent decree during the Clinton administration was the New Jersey State Police in 1999. The consent decree specifically addressed racial profiling and methods to remedy such allegations (DOJ, 1999). Prior to 2001 and the George W. Bush administration, the DOJ had initiated an investigation of the Los Angeles Police Department (LAPD), but they were placed on a consent decree during the first year of the Bush administration.

During the first three years of the Bush administration, more § 14141 investigations were completed than in the six years after its passage under the Clinton administration. Section 14141 investigations by the DOJ have increased under the Bush presidency. From 2001 to 2005, the DOJ conducted 18 § 14141 investigations. As a result, four agencies agreed to consent decrees, six agreed to MOAs, eight are still under investigation or monitoring, and the DOJ dropped the lawsuit in the Columbus, Ohio, investigation (DOJ, 2006). Investigations are still being conducted in accordance with § 14141, but the trends had shown that under the Bush administration the investigations were slightly more likely to result in a MOA.

Table 8.1   Trends of Consent Decrees, MOAs, and Investigations of Law Enforcement Agencies: 1996–2011

Investigations	Settlements	Consent Decrees	MOA	Court Decisions
47 (17 ongoing)	9	7	9	5

Under President Obama's administration, investigations of police departments have continued. Since 2009 there have been 21 police departments investigated in accordance with § 14141. Of these investigations 17 are ongoing and four resulted in settlement agreements (DOJ, Special Litigation Section, 2012).

The trends of consent decrees and MOAs filed by the DOJ from 1996 to 2011 are shown in Table 8.1. The DOJ has conducted 35 investigations involving one state police agency, 18 municipalities, and 11 county sheriff's departments (DOJ, Special Litigation Section, 2012).

These investigations have resulted in seven consent decrees and nine MOAs. Cases resulting in a settlement account for nine of the investigations and there have been five investigations resulting in litigated court decisions. Under a settlement agreement, the department voluntarily agrees to make recommended changes in applicable practices, operations, policies, and training. On average the completion of a five-year consent decree is estimated at a cost of $45 million to the governmental entity. Thus far, Columbus, Ohio, is the first city to challenge a § 14141 action in court. The city filed a motion to dismiss the action, claiming that § 14141 constituted an abuse of the government's power to enforce the Fourteenth Amendment (*United States v. City of Columbus*, 2001). Denying the motion, the federal district court held that § 14141 creates congressional oversight to prevent violations of the Fourteenth Amendment. The case continued to drag on for several more years and the DOJ decided to drop the case under the Bush administration. This decision is important because it demonstrates an aggressive, adversarial approach to § 14141 enforcement (Silveria, 2004). A review of the contents of the MOA suggests a more "cooperative" strategy and policy approach to the enforcement of § 14141.

Types of Allegations Made Under § 14141

Section 14141 allows the DOJ to file a lawsuit against a police entity for allegations of "pattern or practice" of police misconduct. The allegations must show that an individual's constitutional rights were violated. While such allegations may include a variety of claims, analysis of the consent decrees and MOAs reveal several levels of claims.

The first level of claims regarding police officer misconduct is a natural outgrowth of Code of Practice (COP) as it is the officer or officers who initiates the contact with the citizen. Common complaints typically include: using excessive force; false arrest and false imprisonment; and improper traffic stops, searches, and seizures of people. The second level of claims concerns practices condoned by departmental administrators. Common allegations may include: supervisors who condoned officer abuses; failed to implement or enforce policies; failed to train, supervise, and discipline officers; failed to investigate officer misconduct or citizen complaints; and failed to implement a risk management system that could assess officer practices of abuse.

The number of complaints and investigations conducted by the Special Litigation Section of the Department of Justice has increased slightly over previous years. From 2005 to 2011, 25 investigations were performed (DOJ, 2012). Common complaints investigated include the following topics: use of force involving Tasers, less-lethal equipment, and canines; use of force policies; multiple applications of the Taser; discipline practices; medical care; training of officers and supervisors; response to the mentally ill; conducting internal investigations of critical incidents; and incorporating early warning/risk management systems.

Principal Components of § 14141 Consent Decrees

Each consent decree addresses unique and specific abuses identified by the DOJ investigation of a particular police entity, and forms the basis for the claim of a "pattern or practice" of police misconduct. While not every consent decree requires the police agency to address the same issue or the same number of issues, analysis of the six consent decrees reveals a total of 94 factors that have been addressed during the monitoring period. Many of these factors required by the DOJ during the duration of the consent decree were derived from the DOJ's report on *Good Policing* (DOJ, 2003).

Consent decrees mainly call for the revision or development of policies and procedures. Common policy areas generally include: use of force, citizen complaints, in-car video camera usage, conducting investigations, performing arrests, searching and obtaining warrants, conducting traffic stops, foot pursuits, and racial profiling.

The second general factor of each consent decree is the establishment of a data-driven information management system. These systems are designed to provide useful information about the activities of all officers and supervisors in the department in order to establish accountability measures. The data management system is comprised of six separate elements, including: a risk management database and analysis; officer and supervisor database; citizen complaints; and an early identification system for problem officers. A separate tracking system must be designed and maintained that documents: police and citizen contacts, police use of force, traffic stops, citizen arrests, police misconduct, and police response to the mentally impaired. Each database requires an involved officer to complete and submit designated forms and reports documenting his or her actions in a given incident.

The use of a reporting system is a core component in the consent decree actions (Walker, 2003). It is integrated into the data-tracking/reporting system, the revised policy, the early identification system, investigation protocols, and the risk management assessment system. In many agencies this has meant a total revamping of their entire system.

The early identification system is designed to identify potential problem officers so supervisors can provide those officers with early intervention, normally through counseling or additional training by a supervisor. The system is integrated into the other database systems described above. The system provides supervisors with greater flexibility in addressing performance problems (Walker et al., 2000). The concept is supported by research that suggests that in any law enforcement agency a small number of officers are involved in a disproportionate percentage of problem incidents, such as citizen complaints, use-of-force incidents, civil lawsuits against the department, and other indicators of performance problems (Walker, 2001).

Another factor addresses establishing varying agency programs. Such programs can include: field officer training, in-service training, police response to the mentally impaired, community outreach, and employee assistance programs. Training is a core component in consent decrees and MOAs. Generally, the decrees do not stipulate the content of such training. Common training subject areas include: use of force; search and seizure laws; response to domestic violence, hostage and barricade situations; emotionally impaired persons; vehicle pursuits; communication skills; and training on racial, gender, and religious differences of community citizens. Supervisors must also attend the training.

Performing investigations represents the fourth major factor of the consent decree, and topic areas can include: criminal, civil, citizen complaints, disciplinary complaints, and internal affairs investigations. A majority of many of the decrees contain the requirement of performing use-of-force investigations. Citizen complaint investigations also must be addressed. After investigations are concluded, a report must be submitted that shows how the investigation was conducted and the evidentiary basis of the findings of the investigation. These provisions are designed to correct specific problems that are unique to a department's failure to conduct investigations or past failure to perform a thorough and complete investigation.

The fifth factor addresses administrative oversight of the entire consent decree. For each agency, an independent monitor is assigned by the court to provide quarterly monitoring progress of how the agency was complying with the components of the consent decree.

All reports must be entered into a database that tracks the unique components of each consent decree. Supervisors must dedicate time to analyze trends and patterns of officer activities that were identified in the previous sections. Supervisors must periodically monitor the documents that are to be part of the ongoing assessment of officers, including annual performance evaluations (Livingston, 1999). Quarterly reports must be prepared by supervisors documenting these assessments. Certain steps must be taken when an officer accumulates a number of use-of-force incidents, citizen complaints, or other incidents that may reveal conduct outside authorized policy requirements. For example, if an officer accumulates more than three citizen complaints within two years, he or she must be counseled and attend refresher training in the subject matter consistent with the complaint. More severe sanctions may be assessed depending upon the severity of the complaint. Documentation of the remediation must be entered into the early intervention system and the database. Supervisors must perform annual evaluations of every officer under their command.

Memorandum of Agreement

Since 2001, DOJ investigations have increasingly resulted in memorandums of agreement (MOAs). MOAs are more conciliatory than consent decrees. They do not involve judicial monitoring as do consent decrees. While stipulations from consent decrees and MOAs may be similar, MOAs are more likely to address three primary topic areas beyond officer training and developing an early intervention warning system with all officers: (1) policy and procedure; (2) citizen complaints; and (3) data collection.

The first area addressed in an MOA is policy and procedure for performing investigations within the police department. All of the departments are required to revise their policies pursuant to the findings of the DOJ investigation.

Perhaps the most fundamental difference in the MOA is a change in the use-of-force policy. While police agencies today provide their officers with a use-of-force policy, revisions may have to be made, such as restricting the use of certain force techniques or equipment, reporting procedures, or tracking and analyzing force incidents. The Washington, DC, MOA required the department to completely overhaul their use-of-force policy and bring it into compliance with applicable law and professional standards (DOJ, 2003). The City of Cincinnati was required to develop policy language that limited the use of pepper spray, the use of canines, and the use of the choke hold (DOJ, 2001). The Cleveland Police Department was required to address their procedures for using detainee holding cells and was also required to revise its lethal force policy (DOJ, 2002).

Previous complaints have been made that police frequently do not enforce their departmental policies. The problem may be that the officer in question is being investigated by his or her immediate supervisor, resulting in a less than thorough investigation. Thus, investigations into officer actions contrary to the policy are required in all MOAs to ensure the integrity of, and public confidence in, the investigation. The subject matter of investigations generally includes: use of force, citizen complaints, traffic stops, and searches and seizures. In Cincinnati, the MOA requires an investigation when an officer uses force. The officer must first notify his immediate supervisor, the supervisor must respond to the scene, and an investigator from internal affairs must respond to the scene of "serious" force incidents. The investigator may neither ask leading questions nor show preference to statements made by the officer, nor may they disregard a witness's or the arrestee's statement of the incident.

Another major component addressed in most of the MOAs is the handling of citizen complaints. Modifications to complaint procedures are required. The goal is to enhance citizen satisfaction in the outcome of the complaint process by providing more transparency in the process. In many of the MOAs, officers are required to carry complaint forms in their patrol vehicles and are required to inform citizens that they have a right to file a complaint about the officer's response. Investigations of citizen complaints must be performed and documented, and a report of the nature of the disposition and description of the evidentiary grounds used to determine the outcome of the investigation must be completed.

Data collection is also addressed by most MOAs. Data is required to be collected, analyzed, and assessed in a variety of topic areas, but is focused on traffic stops. This requirement has emerged from allegations that police have engaged in racial profiling practices during traffic stops. When an officer makes a traffic stop, he or she is required to submit a lengthy form documenting the nature of the stop. That information is submitted to a supervisor for review. The information is then entered into the database system for further analysis and it is also entered into the early intervention database.

An example of an investigation and settlement agreement between the Department of Justice and a municipality is noted in the investigation of the Warren, Ohio, Police Department (WPD) (DOJ, 2012). The investigation focused on whether the WPD engaged in unconstitutional or unlawful policing through the use of excessive force, and the WPD cooperated throughout the investigation. The investigation involved an in-depth review of WPD documents, as well as extensive community engagement. The DOJ reviewed thousands of pages of documents, including written policies and procedures, training materials, and internal reports; data; video footage; and investigative files. DOJ attorneys and investigators also conducted interviews with WPD officers, supervisors, command staff, and city officials, and conducted interviews with community members and local advocates. The DOJ found reasonable cause to believe that the WPD engaged in a pattern or practice of excessive force in violation of the Fourth Amendment of the U.S. Constitution and the Violent Crime Control and Law Enforcement Act (VCCLEA) of 1994. The DOJ, WPD, and City of Warren officials reached an agreement that, once implemented, will resolve the DOJ's investigation. To create sustainable reform, the agreement requires the WPD to continue to develop and implement:

- new use of force policies and protocols;
- systems to ensure that uses of force are documented and evaluated;
- systems to track citizen complaints and ensure they are investigated promptly; and
- officer training on conducting effective and constitutional policing.

Civil Rights of Institutionalized Persons Act

The Civil Rights of Institutionalized Persons Act (2012), 42 U.S.C. § 1997 et seq. (CRIPA) was passed by Congress in 1980 and is similar to § 14141. CRIPA authorizes the United States Attorney General to conduct investigations and litigation relating to conditions of confinement in state or locally operated institutions (excluding private facilities). Under the statute, the Special Section of the Civil Rights Section investigates covered facilities to determine whether there is a "pattern or practice" of violations of residents' federal rights (the Section is not authorized to represent individuals or to address specific individual cases). The intent of Congress in passing CRIPA, as identified in § 1997g, is to correct deplorable conditions and abuses of the use of force in institutions that amount to deprivations of rights protected by the United States Constitution.

Section 1997a grants discretionary authority to the Attorney General. Under this provision, whenever the Attorney General has reasonable cause to believe that any state or political subdivision of a state, official, employee, or agent thereof, or other person acting on behalf of a state or political subdivision of a state is subjecting persons residing in or confined to an institution to egregious or flagrant conditions that deprive such persons of rights protected by the Constitution, or that causes that person harm, may institute an investigation or civil action in a federal district court for equitable or declaratory relief. The legislation does not provide for monetary awards. Section 1997b stipulates that prior to performing an investigation at a facility, the Attorney General must provide notification in writing to the governor or chief executive officer that an investigation will be taking place. The announcement must also identify the allegations and supporting facts warranting the investigation.

Section 1997a of the Act defines *institution* as: "any facility or institution which is owned, operated, or managed by, or provides services on behalf of any State or political subdivision

Table 8.2   DOJ Investigations from 1997 to 2011

Facility	Investigations	Court Decisions	Consent Decrees	Settlement
Prison/Jail	40 (6 ongoing)	12	5	17
Juvenile	42 (5 ongoing)	9	8	20

of a State." There are five types of "institutions" addressed under CRIPA: (1) jails and prisons, (2) juvenile correctional facilities, (3) mental health facilities, (4) developmental disability facilities, and (5) nursing homes. In accordance with CRIPA, the DOJ reviews complaints, conducts investigations, litigates civil actions that demonstrate a "pattern and practice" of abuse, enforces and monitors court orders, and monitors the progress toward compliance in consent decrees and settlements. The discussion in this chapter only addresses issues pertinent to jails, prisons, and juvenile facilities.

CRIPA enforcement has been a priority with the DOJ since 1997 and there have been 82 investigations performed involving jails, prisons, and juvenile facilities. From 1997 to 2011, the DOJ (2012) has reported trends with respect to these facilities as shown in Table 8.2.

Of the adult facilities, jails accounted for 45 percent of the investigations in accordance with CRIPA. All total, 17 states were involved with the investigations involving jails and prisons, and investigations of juvenile facilities were performed in 20 states. Settlement of the action is the most common method for resolving a CRIPA action in the three confinement facilities while a consent decree was used less frequently. There are 11 investigations in various stages being performed by the Department of Justice.

Similar to § 14141, an investigation under CRIPA can result in a consent decree. Investigations into alleged "patterns or practices" that result in a consent decree generally address the following topics regarding prisoner rights: medical and mental health care (including suicide prevention); prisoner supervision and failure to protect (including population management); classification and prisoner discipline; policies and procedures; abuses of the use of force by officers/staff; food services; officer and supervisor training and performance evaluations; the process of conducting investigations of prisoner complaints; and quality of administrative management of the facility.

If an institution decides to enter into a consent decree after the DOJ investigation, a federal court will oversee the stipulations of the agreement and monitor the progress of the compliance with the orders, like § 14141 actions. Many of the consent decrees include an array of the above-described factors that the correctional entity must change, which would be specific to that institution, based on the DOJ's investigation. Failure to comply with the consent decree can result in extending federal oversight for a period of time determined by the court. The DOJ may also bring a civil action against the entity in federal court. Special monitors are appointed, as in § 14141 actions, to monitor the progress toward completion of the stipulations. The institution must provide periodic progress reports.

In 2011, the Lake County Jail facility (Indiana) agreed to settle a legal action with the Department of Justice out of court. Complaints by numerous detainees regarding the medical and mental care provided by jail officials violated their rights. Additional complaints included protection from other prisoners (prisoner safety), deficient suicide prevention practices by correctional officers, force measures used by correction officers, environmental hazards and jail sanitation conditions, and fire safety hazards. The investigation by the Department of Justice found the complaints were legitimate and filed a suit against the facility. The facility agreed to make the recommended changes and settled the legal action. In total over 50 policy changes with associated training were required, quarterly reporting of all duties performed was required, and the facility was required to hire a new jail administrator with additional correction officers (DOJ, 2012).

The court's decision in *United States v. Terrell County, Georgia* (2006) provides an example of the federal government enforcing CRIPA. The federal government brought a legal action in accordance with CRIPA against a county, county sheriff, and other county officials, seeking a determination that county jail conditions were grossly deficient in violation of the Fourteenth Amendment. The district court granted the government's motion for summary judgment. The court held that the sheriff and other officials were deliberately indifferent to the jail's gross deficiencies in the areas of medical and mental health care for prisoners, protection of prisoners from harm, environmental health and safety of prisoners, and fire safety, in violation of the due process clause. The court remarked that the lack of funds is not a defense to, nor legal justification for, unconstitutional conditions of a jail, for the purpose of analyzing a deliberate indifference claim under the due process clause. Even if a defendant argued that it is planning or working toward construction of a new jail to remedy the unconstitutional conditions at the current facility, the failure to implement interim measures to alleviate those conditions demonstrates deliberate indifference.

Discussion

These two statutes address the ongoing challenges of reforming criminal justice entities. Reforms have been attempted numerous times over the years. Formally, there have been two primary methods that have addressed abuses and misconduct. First, there have been several commission reports since the 1960s. Typically, incidents of alleged misconduct or riots generate an investigation, followed by "blue ribbon panel" reports calling for sweeping changes in the criminal justice agency involved. These reports have been successful in highlighting abuses, but they have not been successful in providing lasting solutions.

The second reform attempt has come through the judicial system. Title 42 U.S.C. § 1983 created a remedy for citizens and prisoners to challenge alleged constitutional rights violations by an officer and his or her supervisor. The United States Supreme Court, beginning with its decisions in *Monroe v. Pape* (1961) and *Monell v. Department of Social Services* (1978) has upheld this remedy. Numerous lawsuits have been filed during the last 40 years and the results of these lawsuits show that plaintiffs have been modestly successful in prevailing in civil rights actions (Kappeler et al., 1996; Ross, 1997). Critics complain, however, that the judicial system has been inconsistent in awarding claims on behalf of plaintiffs and that state laws generally indemnify the officers in the majority of punitive damage awards (Levenson, 2001; Silveria, 2000). Such claims, however, are not fully supported. At least two studies have found that plaintiffs have prevailed in civil lawsuits against the police in 48 percent of cases (Kappeler et al., 1996; Ross, 1998) in 45 percent of cases in correctional litigation.

The courts have fashioned other remedies to curb or punish officer misconduct. The exclusionary rule, developed by the United States Supreme Court in *Mapp v. Ohio* (1961), requires that police officers comply with the requirements of the Fourth Amendment (search and seizure) as well as the Fifth and Sixth Amendments (self-incrimination). It provides that evidence obtained unlawfully by police officers may not be used in a criminal proceeding. The Court ruled that it is the law that sets a criminal free—nothing can destroy a government more quickly than its own failure to follow the law.

It has been argued that exceptions to the exclusionary rule have weakened its ability to deter police abuse (Livingston, 1999; Walker, 2003). This argument, however, has been shown to be misleading. Davies (1985) and Orfield (1987) conducted independent studies that concluded that the exclusion of evidence in cases involving murder, rape, and other violent crimes is exceedingly rare. Orfield also noted that the more serious the crime, the greater the officer's desire to follow the legal procedures, thereby showing the deterrence effect of the exclusionary rule. The American Bar Association (1998) found in a study of police officers and prosecutors that since the *Mapp* decision, police officers generally follow the procedures of the rule and that it has enhanced professionalism. Levenson (1999) observed that there is no evidence and no reason to believe that a police officer will be any less motivated to lie in an administrative hearing, where his reputation and job position are at risk, than in a criminal proceeding where the court threatens to exclude evidence.

There are a variety of laws on the books (i.e., obstruction, perjury, planting evidence, etc.) that allow criminal prosecution of officers who engage in misconduct that rises to the level of criminal behavior. For example, the United States Department of State (2005) chronicles a selection of 18 criminal prosecutions as examples of police and correctional officers sentenced for crimes of abuse from 1999 to 2005. While any law or court standard directing officer conduct can be violated, the ultimate responsibility lies with the individual officers, supervisors, prosecutors, and the courts to ensure that the rule is followed. Prosecutors have the absolute discretion to refuse to prosecute cases if they suspect police misconduct. *Brady v. Maryland* (1963) requires the prosecutor to disclose evidence that may exonerate a defendant and that could be used to impeach a government witness, so a prosecutor has greater motivation to "look behind the curtain." For more than 40 years, however, the exclusionary rule has generally served as a successful spur toward professionalizing the police and curbing abuse (Kamisar, 2003). For example, two officers were convicted and sentenced to prison on federal charges for the Rodney King beating (Levenson, 2001), even after acquittal on state charges. Officer Rafael Perez of the Rampart Precinct of the Los Angeles Police Department was also sentenced to state prison for his participation in the scandal (Boyer, 2001).

Undermining Democratic Accountability

Consent decrees in general, and operating a criminal justice agency by consent decree, in particular have a profound effect on public policy. "Policy," wrote Kaufman (1960) "is enunciated in rhetoric, and is realized in action." With its passage of CRIPA and § 14141, Congress has ushered in a new model of attempting to curb abuses or misconduct without fully considering the consequences of its handiwork. Management by consent decree represents the new paradigm of attempting to address misconduct and accountability at a federal level, rather than at the local or state levels. There is no question that police and correctional officers are human and abuses have occurred. Officer misconduct cannot be condoned and guilty officers should be held accountable. But the question emerges as to whether § 14141 and CRIPA represent the appropriate social mechanism by which to address allegations of abuse. After years of DOJ investigations and consent decrees, it remains questionable as to whether such federal intervention is effective in bringing lasting reforms to criminal justice agencies. There are several reasons for caution and skepticism about forcing consent decrees on police and correctional agencies and whether it represents legitimate social policy.

One question that begs to be answered is whether every solution should be a federal solution in a country that is founded on the principle of federalism. Federalism is defined as a political system in which power is divided and shared between the national/central government and the states (regional units) in order to limit the power of government. Policing by decree undermines that accountability of government to its constituents and therefore it becomes less responsive (Sandler & Schoenbrod, 2003).

Consent decrees by their intrinsic nature are settlements negotiated behind closed doors, although they become public record upon filing in the court proceedings. It has been suggested that because a potential consent decree requires the cooperation of the police entity in crafting equitable relief, such an agreement does not implicate a "strong" degree of federalism (Kim, 2002). When such important policy decisions are made behind closed doors under threat of a major lawsuit by the federal government, officials become indebted to them and to a minority of community constituents. This represents a policy consequence that results in the government failing to represent the public as a whole. A major power shift occurs when policy-making responsibility is stripped from the local or state government and transferred to the federal government and to the federal courts. Such an action violates the principle of limited government and turns the judiciary into a super-legislature. Subsequently, this frequently leaves governments less capable of responding to the legitimate desires of the public and makes elected officials less accountable to the public. Rabkin (1989) suggests that "the more government is accountable to private litigants, the less it can be accountable to anyone else. Limiting the choices of government officials limits their responsibility, for they cannot be responsible for choices they are not allowed to make."

Entering into a consent decree shifts power from the affected government to the DOJ and the courts. Neither the United States Constitution nor state constitutions allow one legislative body to bind the next, by either contract or budgetary appropriation (McConnell, 1987). Governments may not contract away the power to change policy. Citizens who may have legitimate concerns with governmental policies are unable to approach employees of the DOJ and the federal judge, neither of which are elected officials. Moreover, a consent decree is shifted away from the concerns of local voters to the specific concerns of technocrats (Sandler & Schoenbrod, 2003). Consent decree investigations can take years to conduct and conclude.

Police agencies essentially lose their rights to a speedy judicial process. Once the contents of the decree are issued, police executives are bound by the stipulations.

Undermining Police Executive Leadership

Consent decrees have been used as a remedy in the United States during the past 40 years in a majority of prison and jail condition cases in an attempt to reform the prison and jail system. Jails and prisons have been subject to consent decree accountability for longer than their police counterparts. It is debatable whether these decrees have brought lasting reforms to correctional institutions, because the decrees have not accomplished all of their objectives (Sandler & Schoenbrod, 2003). DiIulio (1990) observed in his review of prison consent decrees that successful accomplishments were accounted for by small incremental advances and compromises rather than full-scale assaults. What this means is that when judges act like legislatures, they are more likely to succeed. This, however, exceeds the boundaries of judicial responsibility and allows the judge to assume the role of a super-legislature. Ironically, Congress restricted the use of consent decrees in corrections and limited judicial intervention when it passed the Prison Litigation Reform Act (PLRA, 1996), which ostensibly reduces the filing of "frivolous" prisoner lawsuits and terminates existing consent decrees of correctional facilities. Yet despite the passage of the PLRA, the DOJ continues to pursue investigations into correctional institutions.

A major consequence of consent decrees is that they cannot ensure effective leadership within the agency that is necessary for ongoing reforms to be accomplished, and may even undercut opportunities for such leadership to emerge (Livingston, 1999; Walker, 2003). Glazer (1979) remarked that court orders that are aimed at restructuring public institutions normally result in a decline in staff morale, an increase in staff turnover, and an increase in the unruliness of clientele groups, which undermines police authority by the entire consent process. Wilson (1989) noted that consent decrees aggravate the unfortunate tendency of bureaucracies to focus on counting things rather than helping people. Such appears to be the case with the new paradigm of performing criminal justice responsibilities by decree.

In the only study conducted to date on the impact of police consent decrees, the Vera Institute of Justice (Davis et al., 2002) surveyed a sample of police officers, supervisors, and community leaders in the City of Pittsburgh regarding their perceptions about the outcome of the decree. Generally, community leaders (40%) perceived that the police treated citizens better than before the consent decree, that the decree was a useful tool in improving police practices and accountability, and that they had greater confidence in the police. Citizen complaints declined by 50 percent overall. Supervisors reported that community-oriented policing efforts were detrimentally affected. Their concern emerged from the fact that they were strapped with a great deal of paperwork that kept them from spending quality time with their officers and providing leadership. Although a majority of supervisors reported that the early warning intervention system assisted in identifying problem officers sooner, discipline of officers declined by 45 percent.

The most significant negative impact of the decree was felt by line officers. They commented that their morale had been detrimentally affected, that they were more reluctant to use force and reluctant to make traffic stops. While the use of sick time declined slightly, there was an increase in officers leaving the department. Generally, officers reported that they were less likely to engage in proactive policing strategies. During the five years, arrests declined by 40 percent, clearance rates of arrests declined by 35 percent, traffic summonses declined by 35 percent, and arrests of African-American suspects dropped by 15 percent. There was no noticeable change in the occurrence of Part I or Part II crimes.

Costs

Start-up and maintenance costs linked with successful compliance with consent decrees are enormous. It is estimated that the LAPD consent decree may cost between $30 and $50 million annually, meaning that over five years, they could pay out more than $250 million (Levenson, 2001). The Cincinnati consent decree cost approximately $13 million in start-up costs and more than $20 million annually to ensure compliance with the stipulations (Walker, 2003). Without financial assistance from either the state or the federal government, municipalities will be unable to implement or maintain the requirements of the consent decree. Correctional departments have experienced the same problem in funding the associated costs with making the necessary changes consistent with the consent decrees. State and county budgets have had to be realigned and other funding priorities have been neglected in order to comply with a consent decree.

The financial problem is a congressional one. Congress has repeatedly been criticized by state governors for creating unfunded mandates for the states. The United States Supreme Court determined in *Printz v. United States* (1997), in overturning a portion of the Brady Handgun Violence Prevention Act, that by requiring state governments to absorb the financial burden of implementing a federal regulatory program, Congress can take credit for solving problems without having to ask their constituents to pay for the solutions and without raising taxes. Even when the municipalities are not forced to absorb the implementation costs, they are still put in a position of taking the blame for its burdensome effects. Having shifted the blame to local and state officials, Congress is not compelled to consider the negative consequences of its mandate.

Conversely, it is costly for the DOJ to conduct investigations. Since the 1990s, conducting investigations into allegations of misconduct in criminal justice agencies has been a major priority of the DOJ (Department of State, 2005). While costs for conducting such investigations have not been published, the following questions arise: "Does it make sound public policy to spend millions in conducting these investigations?" and "Does it make good public policy for DOJ attorneys to spend their time and budget conducting these investigations?" Clearly these are important questions that require detailed assessment if future investigations are performed.

Summary

It remains debatable whether operating correctional institutions or policing under a consent decree will prove to be effective in bringing about lasting reforms to the criminal justice system (Ross & Parke, 2009). As a matter of practice, patterns of police abuse of citizens or prisoners should not be condoned and an organizational culture that allows such misconduct should be held accountable. Police and correctional officers must be accountable for following the law and proper procedures in performing their duties. Governments cannot be above the law, but federal intervention fails to provide the appropriate social policy to bring about long-term and lasting reforms. The incremental gains are not justified by the immense costs and the long-term threat to our system of democracy.

There are lessons to be learned from the consent decrees, and criminal justice managers should take these lessons into consideration. Administrators are encouraged to voluntarily undertake the following proactive strategies in order to increase their accountability. These strategies align with risk-management principles discussed in Chapter 5 through Chapter 7.

Because consent decrees require a monitor to review the compliance and progress toward the stipulations, administrators should first create a compliance officer position to oversee departmental activities. The compliance officer should report to the chief executive of the department (Schmidt, 2004; Ross, 2003a,b). This position could be a supervisor who would be responsible for ensuring that policies and practices are implemented properly and tracks and assesses pertinent departmental information. Second, administrators should consider instituting a data tracking system designed to record information about the performance of officers and supervisors. Systematically collecting and assessing data about calls for service, arrests, use of force, traffic stops, and pursuits can be instrumental in providing police supervisors with valuable information to use in leading the organization and provide early warning of marginal officer performance. The same type of system could be used to track pertinent information in correctional institutions as well.

Third, administrators should voluntarily review and revise policies and procedures on a regular basis. As the law changes, policies should also be changed in order for officers and supervisors to perform their duties within legal parameters. Fourth, intersecting the data tracking system with the early intervention system has the potential to transform the organizational culture and department. It can raise the standard of officer conduct and supervisory accountability in maintaining proper officer performance and identifying problem employees early. The system provides supervisors with more flexibility in addressing appropriate intervention strategies to keep officer conduct from progressing further, thus requiring more severe sanctions. It serves to maintain accountability of officers and supervisors and assists in reducing allegations of failure to supervise or discipline officers.

Fifth, in compliance with the United States Supreme Court decision in *City of Canton v. Harris* (1989), administrators should endeavor to provide their officers with ongoing training commensurate with their duties and in accordance with state requirements. Training should be documented in the data tracking system and designed to address frequently occurring situations, agency policies, and high-profile topics, such as: use of force, pursuits, arrests with or without warrants, domestic violence calls, traffic stops, ethical behavior, and conducting felony arrests. Correctional agencies should also address high-profile subjects as: use of force, responding to special needs prisoners, searches, disturbance control, special threat group management, escapes, medical and psychological care issues of prisoners, transportation of prisoners, and security functions, to mention a few. Sixth, agencies should ensure that investigations into citizen and prisoner complaints and incidents of officer use of force are performed properly, pursuant to policy and the appropriate legal standard. Administrators should consider using an external agency to perform investigations when high-profile cases occur.

The compliance officer should perform regular inspections and audits to ensure that departmental regulations are being followed to prevent any patterns of abuse from occurring. Implementing and maintaining such a system provides a proactive framework with several benefits. Administrators as agency leaders must set the tone for proper conduct and create a department culture that protects constitutional rights of citizens. Public education about such efforts could help to improve public confidence in police and protect it from frivolous complaints. This assures the public that officers are adhering to departmental policies and that supervisors are enforcing them properly, underscoring accountability. It demonstrates to the community that the department has voluntarily undertaken a system of self-governance without being threatened by a lawsuit or judicial intervention.

A fundamental component of the criminal justice profession is that administrators have the responsibility and the right to manage their own departments as other professions do. Criminal justice agencies in the United States have made significant changes since the 1960s, but the new era of consent decrees overshadows and discounts these accomplishments. Rather than the decree stipulations becoming the "standard," leaders of criminal justice agencies will be well served to study the stipulations and work toward making appropriate changes in their department as warranted. Voluntarily incorporating these features and changing agency practices as needed exhibits a policy that underscores professionalism, proactive leadership, and ensures that the agency can be accountable without forced federal intervention. Information provided by the Department of Justice shows a trend of such investigations and resulting consent decrees to be decreasing slightly. Proactive efforts by administrators based on lessons learned from past investigations appear to be affecting these declining trends. Administrators are encouraged to review these investigations and to continue to manage their departments in ways that place them in the best position to defend against complaints of misconduct.

References

Boyer, P. J. (2001, May 21). Testimony on police misconduct ignited the biggest scandal in the history of L.A.P.D.: Is it the real story? *The New Yorker*, 60.

Civil Rights of Institutionalized Persons Act (2012), Title 42 U.S.C. § 1997. http://www.DOJ.gov. Civil Rights Special Litigation Division, accessed March, 2012.

Davies, T. Y. (1985). A hard look at what we know (and still need to learn) about the costs of the exclusionary rule: the NIJ study and other studies of lost arrests. *American Board Foundation Research*, 610–645.

Department of Justice (2012). *Settlements and consent decrees (1997–2011)*. Washington, DC: Special Litigation Division of the Civil Rights Division. <www.doj.org>.

DiIulio, J. J., Jr. (1990). *Courts, corrections and the constitution*. New York, NY: Oxford University Press.

Glazer, N. (1979). The Judiciary and social policy. In L. J. Theberge (Ed.), *The judiciary in a democratic society*. Lexington, MA: Lexington Books.

Kamisar, Y. (2003). In defense of the search and seizure exclusionary rule. *Harvard Journal of Law and Public Policy, 1*, 119–138.

Kappeler, V. E., Kappeler, S. F., & del Carmen, R. V. (1996). A content analysis of police civil liability cases: decisions of the federal district courts, 1978–1990. *Journal of Criminal Justice, 21*, 325–337.

Kaufman, H. (1960). *The forest ranger: A study in administrative behavior.* Baltimore, MD: Johns Hopkins University Press.

Kim, E. (2002). Vindicating civil rights under 42 U.S.C. 14141: Guidance from procedures in complex litigation. *29 Hastings Constitutional Law Quarterly, 767*, 1–34.

Levenson, L. L. (1999). Administrative replacements: How much can they do? *26 Pepperdine Law Review*, 879–881.

Levenson, L. L. (2001). Police corruption and new models for reform. *35 Suffolk University Law Review, 1*, 1–41.

Livingston, D. (1999). Police reform and the department of justice: An essay on accountability. *Buffalo Criminal Law Review, 2*, 817–859.

McConnell, M. W. (1987). Why hold elections? Using consent decrees to insulate policies from political change. *University of Chicago Legal Forum*, 295.

Orfield, M. W., Jr. (1987). Comment: The exclusionary rule and deterrence: An empirical study of Chicago narcotics officers. *54 University of Chicago Law Review*, 1015–1055.

Prison Litigation Reform Act (1996). Public L. No. 104–134, Statute 1321, Codified at 18 U.S.C. § 3626.

Rabkin, J. A. (1989). *Judicial compulsions: How public law distorts public policy.* New York, NY: Basic Books.

Ross, D. L. (1997). Emerging trends in correctional civil liability cases: A content analysis of federal court decisions of title 42 United States code section 1983: 1970–1994. *Journal of Criminal Justice, 25*, 501–515.

Ross, D. L. (2003a). *Civil liability in criminal justice* (3rd ed.). Cincinnati, OH: Anderson Publishing Co.

Ross, D. L. (2003b). Emerging trends in police failure to train liability. *Policing: An International Journal of Police Strategies and Management, 2*, 169–193.

Ross, D. L. (2005). A content analysis of the emerging trends in the use of non-lethal force research in policing. *Law Enforcement Executive Forum, 5*, 121–149.

Ross, D. L., & Parke, P. (2009). Policing by Consent decree: An analysis of title 42 U.S.C. section 14141 and the new model for police accountability. *Police Practice & Research: An Interdisciplinary Journal, 3*, 199–208.

Sandler, D., & Schodendbrod, D. (2003). *Democracy by decree.* New Haven, CT: Yale University Press.

Schmidt, W. (2004). Criminal justice compliance officer. *Journal of Law Enforcement Executive Forum, 5*, 1–14.

Silver, I. (2010). *Police civil liability.* New York, NY: Matthew Bender & Co.

Silveria, M. J. (2004). An unexpected application of 42 U.S.C. 14141: Using investigative findings for 1983. *52 UCLA Law Review, 601*, 1–30.

U.S. Commission on Civil Rights (2000). *Revisiting who is guarding the guardians?: A report on Police Practices & Civil Rights in America.* Washington, DC: Author.

U.S. Department of Justice (2003). *Principles of good policing: Avoiding violence between police and citizens.* Washington DC: United States Department of Justice.

U.S. Department of Justice Web site (2012). www.DOJ.gov. Civil Rights Special Litigation Division. html. Accessed March, 2012.

United States Department of State (2005). *Second periodic report of the United States of America to the committee against torture.* Washington, DC: U.S. Department of State.

Vaughn, M. S., & Coomes, L. F. (1995). Police civil liability under section 1983: When do police officers act under color of law? *Journal of Criminal Justice, 23*, 395–415.

Walker, S. (2001). Early warning systems for police: Responding to the problem police officer: *Research in brief.* Washington, DC: U.S. Department of Justice.

Walker, S. (2003). New approaches to ensuring the legitimacy of police conduct: The new paradigm of police accountability: The U.S. Justice Department "pattern or practice" suits in context. *22 Saint Louis University Public Law Review, 3,* 1–43.

Walker, S., Alpert, G. P., & Kenney, D. J. (2000). Early warning systems for police: Concept, history, and issues. *Police Quarterly, 2,* 132–152.

Wilson, J. Q. (1989). *Bureaucracy: What government agencies do and why they do it.* New York, NY: Basic Books.

Worrall, J. L. (2001). Culpability standards in section 1983 litigation against criminal justice officials when and why mental state matters. *Crime & Delinquency, 47,* 28–59.

9

Personnel Issues and Liability

Liability and Sexual Harassment

Sexual harassment has become one of the most potentially critical management problems faced by the administrator. The Equal Employment Opportunities Commission has annually reported on the outcome of claims of sexual harassment in the workplace. The trends of outcome of claims filed from 1997 through 2011 are shown in Table 9.1 (EEOC, 2012).

Over the period the total number of claims filed has declined by 3 percent, averaging 13,690 claims annually, and 48 percent of the claims are found "no reasonable cause" in a legal proceeding. No reasonable cause means the court found the claim was unsupported by the evidence presented. Claims filed by males have increased by 3 percent and account for 15 percent of all claims. Cases settled out of court account for 10 percent of the resolved cases and the trend has increased by 4 percent. The average annual total payout is about $50 million, which accounts for an increase of one percent from 1997.

Claims of sexual harassment fall within the purview of Title VII of the Civil Rights Act of 1964 under the general prohibition of sexual discrimination in the "terms, conditions, or privileges of employment." Title VII prohibits employment discrimination based on gender, race, national origin, or religion. Failure to act appropriately not only has adverse effects for the agency, but also may result in supervisory liability and disciplinary action.

The courts are increasingly reviewing sexual harassment cases, and several have emerged in corrections. In *Speed v. Ohio Dep't of Rehabilitation and Correction* (1994), the court awarded a female correctional officer $7,500 in damages for invasion of privacy based on a male supervisor's observation of her from the ceiling of a prison restroom. In *Holland v. New Jersey Department of Corrections* (2001), the court awarded $3.74 million to correctional employees who alleged racial and sexual harassment and discrimination in the workplace. Conversely, in *Spicer v. Commonwealth of Virginia Department of Corrections* (1995), the Court of Appeals found correctional officials not liable for employees who made sexual remarks about a female employee's breasts when the department made a prompt and effective response to remedy the situation after she complained. In addition, the Missouri Department of Corrections settled four sexual harassment cases over 18 months totaling $177,500 (Associated Press, 2004). The cases involved four female correctional officers who had been harassed by male officers and supervisors. Collectively, the cases showed a departmental culture of policies and practices that condoned harassment and tolerated a "code of silence." The DOC reported that it disciplined 22 employees for sexual harassment over three years: three were fired, one was reprimanded, and the rest were suspended for varying amounts of time.

Claims of sexual harassment have also emerged in policing. Ross (2000) reported in a review of more than 1,500 § 1983 published decisions from 1989 to 1999 that "police as plaintiff" is an emerging liability area that cites administrators for failure to train officers. Throughout the 1990s,

Table 9.1   Sexual Harassment Charges: FY 1997–2011

Factor	1997	2011	% Change	Average
Claims filed	15,889	11,364	–3	13,690
By males	11.6%	16.3%	+3	15%
Cases settled	6.8%	12%	+4%	10%
No reasonable cause	41%	53%	+2%	48%
Reasonableness	5%	6.1%	+0.2%	6%
Court closure	40%	21%	–48%	28%
Payout (millions)	$49.5	$52.0	+1%	$50.0

a significant number of claims alleging sexual harassment were filed primarily by female officers against their supervisors and fellow male officers. Vaughn, Cooper, and del Carmen (2001) found, in a survey of 849 Texas police chiefs, that 12 percent of the respondents had incurred a lawsuit from an officer within the preceding three years. These chiefs reported that they lost 41 percent of the cases. They also reported that they are commonly sued for allegations of: sexual harassment (25%), disciplinary actions (24%), employment discrimination (13%), overtime/compensation/pay issues (10%), race discrimination/reverse discrimination (7%), and disability discrimination (4%).

The City of Los Angeles, California, was ordered to pay $1.7 million for Los Angeles police employees claiming sexual discrimination and racial harassment (Associated Press, 2000a). A total of 24 women and four men alleged acts of discrimination, sexual harassment, or retaliation while serving on the force in cases filed from 1994 to 2000. The lead plaintiff claimed that she was subjected to racist remarks, sexist comments, and on one occasion was grabbed by a fellow officer while other officers watched and laughed. It was alleged that female officers who complained about sexual harassment were subjected to death threats and left stranded without backup in emergencies. One female officer settled out of court for $175,000. Other cases involved male employees who said their supervisors harassed them. Two officers claimed that they faced retaliation after their wives sued the LAPD.

Other examples include two separate sexual harassment claims that were settled by the FBI in 1993 and in 2000. The Associated Press (1993) reported that a former female agent was awarded $300,000 because she claimed that her superior harassed her for 10 years. This was the first sexual harassment case brought against the FBI. In the 2000 case, the Associated Press reported that another former female FBI agent had settled a sex discrimination claim for $150,000. She claimed that she had been harassed by co-workers and her supervisor over a period of many years, denied equal job treatment, and was punished when she complained.

The Louisiana Department of Public Safety settled a claim of sexual harassment for $50,000 (Associated Press, 2012). A civil action filed by the subjected woman claimed that while working in the office as an administrator for the department's Probation and Parole district office in Thibodaux, harassment escalated from inappropriate comments and touching to sexual assault. The Justice Department found at least four other department employees, including a part-time internal affairs investigator, knew about her harassment but didn't report it. Department of Public Safety and Corrections spokesperson reported that agency officials were quick to act once the woman's allegations were reported to them. As part of the settlement, the department agreed to modify its sexual harassment policies and training.

Sexual Harassment Defined

The Equal Employment Opportunity Commission (EEOC) guidelines on sexual harassment (29 C.F.R. § 1604.11, 1995), define sexual harassment as "unwelcome sexual advances, requests for sexual favors, and other verbal or physical conduct of a sexual nature." These factors constitute sexual harassment when: (1) such conduct is made a term or condition of employment; (2) such conduct is used as a basis for employment decisions affecting the person; and (3) such conduct has the purpose or effect of interfering with an employee's performance, or creates an intimidating, hostile, or offensive work environment. In *Anthony v. County of Sacramento Sheriff's Department* (1994), a female deputy stated a cause of action for sexual harassment claiming a hostile work environment and inadequate training in department policy. In *Farmers Insurance Group v. County of Santa Clara* (1995), the county settled out of court in a sexual harassment claim for $1,283,000 for failing to train and develop policy on sexual harassment. A male deputy's sexual harassment of three female deputies, including one for whom he had training responsibility, was not within the scope of his employment.

Types of Sexual Harassment

Sexual harassment claims have been separated into two categories. The first, *quid pro quo* sexual harassment, occurs when a supervisor conditions an employment benefit or continued employment on the employee's acquiescence in sexual behavior. The liability associated with this term is limited to circumstances in which a "tangible economic action" has been taken with respect to the employee.

The second type is known as "hostile or offensive work environment" sexual harassment. No employment benefits need be gained or lost, and this type of harassment may be engaged in not only by managers or supervisors, but also by co-workers or persons who are not even employed by the employer. This type of sexual harassment occurs when sexual jokes, graffiti, suggestive remarks, cartoons, physical interference with movement such as blocking or following, or sexually derogatory comments create a hostile work environment. Thus, if a supervisor said to an employee, "Go out with me and you will do well in the organization," this would be considered *quid pro quo* sexual harassment, even if nothing detrimental (or positive) actually occurred. If no "tangible economic action" resulted, such a comment would be considered part of a hostile work environment.

Evans v. Leelanau County Sheriff's Department (1994) is illustrative of both types of sexual harassment. Evans, a female correctional officer, was the victim of sexual harassment from the sheriff, her sergeant, and several correctional officers over a period of 18 months. The sheriff told her that she should lose weight, wear her uniform so that it would outline her "figure" better, and that she had a nice set of "jugs." The sheriff would summon Evans to his office, where he would have open in plain view a lingerie catalog and state that he would "enjoy seeing her in one of those outfits." The sheriff would occasionally brush up against her in the hallway, and pat and stroke her hair. The department primarily employed males and there was only one restroom. Male employees left pornographic magazines opened in the restroom and would also leave them opened on the booking counter, dispatch area, officers' control room, and virtually any area to which officers had access. Pictures of nude women were pinned on several of the walls in the control room. Evans complained to her sergeant and later to the sheriff, but nothing changed. There was no policy against sexual harassment within the department. She filed a lawsuit asserting hostile work environment sexual harassment. The county settled out of court for an undisclosed amount.

Plaintiffs have also filed legal actions alleging retaliation because they reported or filed a sexual harassment complaint. In *Barth v. The Village of Mokena* (2004), a female police officer prevailed when she sued on a claim of retaliation. Barth claimed that the chief customarily condoned a work climate of harassment. She alleged that she was subject to ongoing incidents of harassment and because she reported the incidents to supervisors, she was treated differently. She claimed that she was denied assignments, subjected to unwarranted and disproportionate disciplinary action, denied backup, and denied compensation for training time. Further, she claimed that the chief discriminated against women because of gender and that the chief, as the policymaker, created and perpetuated a hostile work environment. The chief denied the claims and filed a motion with the court for a dismissal.

The court rejected the chief's motion and held that he violated Barth's constitutional rights as he was the official policymaker. In that capacity, the court concluded that his actions expressed a widespread practice and official policy that was well settled, amounting to a custom of official conduct, creating a hostile work environment. Barth did not have to be any more specific with her claims to demonstrate examples of retaliation for reporting sexual harassment.

United States Supreme Court Decisions

In three landmark decisions, the United States Supreme Court set the standard for administrative liability in cases alleging sexual harassment. The cases of *Faragher v. City of Boca Raton* (1998) and *Burlington Industries, Inc. v. Ellerth* (1998) established the rule that an administrator is responsible for the misdeeds of an employee when that employee uses the agency relationship to accomplish the misbehavior. The Court in *Ellerth* declared that a tangible employment action was a "significant change in employment status, such as hiring, firing, failing to promote, reassignment with significantly different responsibilities, or a decision causing a significant change in benefits." The supervisor's action must inflict some direct economic harm. If the harassment does not result in a tangible job detriment, an employer still may be liable for hostile work environment sexual harassment engaged in by managers or supervisors. The Court stated that in such instances, the employer may affirmatively avoid liability if it can show that: (1) it used reasonable care to prevent and correct harassment (such as having a policy on the subject), and (2) the employee unreasonably failed to make a complaint under the policy or to avoid harm otherwise.

Justice Souter noted that the primary purpose of Title VII "is not to provide redress but avoid harm." In keeping with Congress's intent to prevent sexual harassment, the Court decided to model its rule on the premise that an administrator should be rewarded for making an effort to stop harassment. Along with the administrator's responsibility to thwart sexual harassment, the Court also recognized the victim's responsibility to avoid harm by using the agency's antiharassment policy.

In a third case, the Court further expanded employer liability under Title VII. In *Oncale v. Sundowner Offshore Services, Inc.* (1998), the Court held that sexual harassment includes same-sex harassment. Oncale worked for Sundowner on an oil rig as a "roustabout" with an eight-man crew. He alleged that he was subjected to sex-related, humiliating actions against him by members of the crew, including his supervisor. On more than one occasion, he alleged he was physically assaulted in a sexual manner and threatened with rape. He finally filed suit against the company after repeated complaints to management were ignored. The district court and the Fifth Circuit Court of Appeals found in favor of the company. Oncale appealed to the United States Supreme Court and they granted certiorari.

The Court examined the issue of whether same-sex harassment is actionable under Title VII. The Court held that same-sex sexual harassment is clearly actionable. The Court ruled that "when members of one sex are exposed to disadvantageous terms or conditions of employment to which members of the opposite sex are not exposed," such conduct is actionable. Moreover, the Court explained that Title VII is not a "civility" code designed to remedy all interpersonal problems in the workplace. It forbids only objectively offensive conduct that alters the conditions of the victim's employment. The Court cautioned courts and juries to distinguish this type of conduct from ordinary socializing in the workplace, such as "intersexual flirtation" or "male-on-male horseplay," which are not within the scope of the antidiscrimination law.

The decisions in *Burlington* and *Faragher* emphasize that if an employer shows that it acted reasonably to prevent and correct sexual harassment, and that the employee unreasonably failed to avoid harm, it can successfully avoid liability. If, however, the employer fails to satisfy the Court's requirements, liability will attach (Collins & Vaughn, 2004). In some cases in which the employer is unable to avoid liability completely, the affirmative defense may be used to mitigate damages if the employee could have avoided some but not all of the harm that occurred.

Gonzales v. New York State Department of Corrections (2002) provides an instructive example of an employer failing to take action when there was knowledge. A female correctional officer brought suit under Title VII on allegations of sexual harassment and a hostile work environment. The court ruled in favor of the officer, finding that she been subjected to a hostile work environment for more than a year and that the department failed to take any action after she had repeatedly reported it to supervisory personnel. The court found that she had incurred a pattern of offensive behaviors almost daily, which included male officers using derogatory terms such as "nigger" and "spic" in her presence, and calling her and other female officers "bitches." The court concluded that such unchecked behavior amounted to a hostile work environment in accordance with Title VII and awarded her $100,000.

In *Pennsylvania State Police v. Suders* (2004), the United States Supreme Court examined the issue of sexual harassment and constructive discharge in a police department for the first time. Suders was a communications operator for the Pennsylvania State Police (PSP) and claimed that from the beginning of her employment male supervisors harassed her. Suders claimed that the harassment continued throughout her employment, which eventually led to her quitting the job. She alleged that supervisors would talk about having sex with animals, would talk about how to "satisfy" a man orally, and would make obscene gestures in her presence. She complained to the EEOC in Pennsylvania but did not receive any relief. In retaliation, she was arrested by the PSP on false charges and before they could officially file the charges, she resigned.

She filed a Title VII claim, alleging sexually harassment and claimed that she was constructively discharged from her job. The lower court granted judgment for the department, stating that Suders never gave the department a chance to respond to her complaints. The court did not address her claim that she was forced to resign because of the hostile work environment. She appealed and the appellate court reversed the lower court's decision. The court determined that the lower court should have addressed her constructive discharge claim and that constructive discharge was a tangible employment action, thereby making the department automatically (and strictly) liable for the supervisors' actions in the event Suders proved her sexual harassment claim. The Supreme Court reviewed the case to determine whether the employer could be held liable. The appellate court's decision that a constructive discharge was always a tangible employment action was too limiting.

In an 8-to-1 decision, the Court reversed the decision and remanded the case to the lower court for further proceedings. The Court reasoned that an employee's decision to quit could be construed as a constructive discharge where the abuse endured was so "intolerable" that resignation was deemed a "firing response." The employer, however, would have a defense to such a claim when it could prove: (1) it had a "readily accessible and effective policy" in place for reporting and resolving sexual harassment complaints and (2) the employee failed to take advantage of the employer's policy. The Court also held that the employer would not have a defense, however, if the employee could demonstrate the decision to quit resulted from "an employer-sanctioned adverse action," which resulted in an official change in employment status or situation, e.g., humiliating demotion, severe pay cut, or transfer to a position where the employee would be faced with unbearable working conditions.

In *Jurgens v. City of North Pole* (2007), a female dispatcher complained to the chief that officer Jurgens had made sexual advances toward her and other dispatchers. Such offensive advances negatively affected her work performance and created an intimidating, hostile, and offensive work environment. The chief performed an investigation and determined that Jurgens's conduct amounted to sexual harassment and he was fired. He appealed the termination to the hearing board and the board upheld the termination and he filed a civil lawsuit.

The police department's policy indicated that sexual harassment refers to both the conduct and the effect of the conduct. Conduct will be considered sexual harassment when it has the purpose or effect of unreasonably interfering with an affected person's work performance or creating an intimidating, hostile, or offensive work environment. The court found that Jurgens's conduct created a hostile and offensive work environment supporting a claim of sexual harassment, and affirmed the board's termination. The court ruled that the dispatchers' testimony supported their claims that Jurgens's conduct made them feel unsafe, was unrelenting, and adversely affected their work performance.

Sexual Misconduct by Correctional Employees

A related and emerging area for correctional supervisors is claims of sexual misconduct by correctional staff with female prisoners. Correctional employee-on-prisoner misconduct involves a range of behaviors, ranging from lewd comments to voyeurism to assault and rape. Since 1999, the federal government, 41 states, and the District of Columbia have passed laws criminalizing some types of staff sexual misconduct (GAO, 1999). Supervisors must be diligent in investigating prisoner complaints about correctional officer sexual misconduct.

To investigate this emerging problem, researchers from the Government Accountability Office (GAO, 1999) conducted a study of female prisoners and sexual misconduct by correctional staff. The study examined 506 allegations of sexual misconduct between 1995 and 1998 in four jurisdictions: California Department of Corrections, the Federal Bureau of Prisons, the Texas Department of Corrections, and the District of Columbia. Only adult female institutions were studied and not detention facilities. Of the 506 claims filed, 18 percent were sustained in which a high percentage of staff resigned or were terminated. All four jurisdictions were involved in at least two civil lawsuits. Allegations ranged from verbal harassment, improper surveillance, improper touching, and/or consensual sex. Allegations of rape or other types of forced sexual assault were relatively rare. None of the jurisdictions had a tracking system in place that readily made available comprehensive data on the topic.

The GAO also reported that at least 23 departments of corrections had faced class action or individual damage suits related to sexual misconduct. During the 1990s, the Justice Department filed civil lawsuits alleging systemic sexual misconduct by male correctional staff in womens' prisons in two states (Arizona and Michigan). Both suits were filed in 1997 under the Civil Rights of Institutionalized Persons Act of 1980, which is designed to protect the rights of people housed in state and local government institutions. In 1999 the state of Arizona and the Justice Department entered into a settlement agreement, which requires Arizona to revise employee and prisoner training, strengthen investigative techniques, and requires male officers to announce their presence prior to entering female housing units, when feasible. Moreover, the state of Michigan also entered into a similar settlement with the Justice Department regarding male officers working in female housing units.

The court in *Women Prisoners v. District of Columbia* (1994) found a pattern of sexual harassment by employees, including assaults, a lack of response and, at times, an inadequate response. Part of the harassment involved unjustified invasions of privacy by male officers. Medical examination policies were not followed and illnesses were not responded to. Prenatal care of pregnant prisoners was grossly inadequate, as were general prison conditions. The evidence revealed a level of sexual harassment that was so malicious that it violated the Eighth Amendment.

Although the GAO study focused on adult prison systems, county detention facilities have incurred civil liability for officer sexual misconduct. In *Ware v. Jackson County* (1998), widespread and condoned misconduct of jail employees created county liability when "rampant sexual misconduct" toward female prisoners was proven. Refusal to terminate an assaultive employee, to monitor him after a termination recommendation had been made, or to investigate several incidents demonstrated deliberate indifference. Compare, however, *Thomas v. Galveston*

County (1997), in which liability did not attach against the county. A female prisoner alleged that a male detention officer sexually assaulted and harassed her during the three months she was confined in the jail. She did not complain to the officer's superiors, because he threatened her until after the final assault. She notified a supervisor and an investigation began immediately. The investigation revealed that several officers had assaulted the plaintiff and other female prisoners. Based on the investigation, the officers were disciplined and one officer was terminated and criminally prosecuted. The county was granted summary judgment because there was no evidence that the county knew about the officers' conduct and disregarded it. Female prisoners did not inform officials until after the last assault, and the investigation revealed the officers' misconduct. The county had policies in place, and once they were informed of the misconduct they promptly investigated, disciplined the officers, and terminated one officer.

Likewise, consistent discipline with officers by supervisors rebuffed claims of sexual assault in *Hegenmiller v. Edna Mahan Correctional Institution for Women* (2005). Two female prisoners alleged that a correctional officer sexually assaulted them over a two-year period of their confinement. When a captain learned of the allegations, he reported the allegations to his superiors and an investigation led to the termination and prosecution of the officer. Further investigation revealed that another officer was involved and the first officer had covered for his participation in the repeated assaults. The second officer was also fired.

Prior to the assaults, the prison had instituted policies and training for the officers that prohibited sexual contact with prisoners. Further, administrators verbally informed officers that they would be investigated, fired, and prosecuted if they had sexual contact with prisoners. Prior to the firing of the two officers, there were six incidents involving six officers for such assaults on female prisoners. Five were fired and prosecuted. The prisoners claimed that the administration knew of other incidents of sexual assault but failed to investigate them and filed a lawsuit, claiming deliberate indifference to the risk of assaults. They also claimed that the administration failed to provide training to officers and failed to implement adequate policies on prisoner and officer contacts. The lower court granted summary judgment to the prison administration and the prisoners appealed. The appellate court affirmed the lower court's decision, concluding that the administration was not deliberately indifferent to sexual assaults in the prison. Moreover, the court ruled that the administrators did not fail to train the officers. The prisoners failed to show that the administration's actions were linked to the conduct of the officers who were fired. They also failed to show that they faced a substantial risk of harm to which the administration acted with deliberate indifference. The court underscored the fact that the administration vigorously enforced its own policy; had investigated, fired, and prosecuted officers in the past, as well as in this incident. The court failed to find any evidence that the administration looked the other way or tried to intervene on behalf of any officer who violated the no-contact rule.

In *Boxer X v. Harris* (2006), a male prisoner brought a civil rights action against a female officer who allegedly made him strip and masturbate for her enjoyment. The prisoner claimed that the female officer threatened reprisal if he did not perform the act. The district court dismissed the case and the prisoner appealed. The appellate court reversed, holding that the prisoner stated a valid § 1983 claim for violation of his privacy rights but it did not give rise to a claim of cruel and unusual punishment under the Eight Amendment. The officer was terminated from her position.

A female detainee brought a § 1983 claim against a deputy whom she alleged sexually assaulted her in *Kahle v. Leonard* (2007). The detainee claimed that on three different occasions the deputy entered her cell after lockdown and forced her to perform intercourse with him. She alleged that after reporting the assault the county failed to investigate the claims. The deputy filed a motion for summary judgment and the court denied it. The court held that jail officials were aware of the deputy's conduct, which created a substantial risk of serious harm from the deputy and exhibited deliberate indifference to the risk by not addressing the misconduct. The court ruled that in 2002 (the year of the incidents), the law, for qualified immunity purposes, was clearly established and that a supervisor who was deliberately indifferent to a substantial risk of such an assault could be held liable under § 1983.

In *Heckenlaible v. Virginia Peninsula Regional Jail Authority* (2007), a female prisoner sued a correctional officer and the regional jail authority, seeking to recover damages for injuries suffered as a result of an alleged nonconsensual sexual encounter between her and the officer. The prisoner alleged that the jail authority should have been aware of the officer's propensities for sexual assault and should have never hired him or allowed him to supervise female prisoners. The court agreed that the officer's conduct was unacceptable but ruled in favor of the jail authority on the liability claims. The court held that absent any evidence indicating that the officer was known by anyone to have a propensity to commit sexual assault at the time he was hired, or evidence indicating that some testing would have revealed that the officer would pose a risk of danger to prisoners, the jail authority was not liable. The court noted that the jail authority never received any complaints from prisoners about the officer, and once they learned of the misconduct, swiftly investigated the matter and took appropriate action. The court granted summary judgment.

In *Chao v. Ballista* (2009) a female prisoner confined in a Massachusetts correctional facility filed a § 1983 claim against correctional officials, asserting that the officials failed to properly investigate and protect her from sexual abuse from a correction officer. The prisoner alleged that during her incarceration she was subjected to numerous incidents of sexual misconduct by the officer and it continued even after the officer's assignment was changed. Legal counsel for the department moved to have the claims dismissed and the federal district court rejected them and found in favor of the prisoner. The court found that the Prison Litigation Reform Act was not subject to the prisoner's claims requiring remedy of the allegations through institutional means. The court held that the correction officer and the prisoner engaged in 50 to 100 sexual encounters, that the officer had sexually abused a second female prisoner, that the officer continued the sexual relationship even after being reassigned, and that a prison nurse placed the prisoner on oral contraceptive pills during her incarceration. The excessive amount of claims, severity of the abuse, and the numerous warning signs alleged by the prisoner more than sufficiently supported a § 1983 claim.

Supervisory Liability

While some claims of sexual harassment against co-workers have been cited, a significant number have been filed against the employee's supervisor or administrator. An administrator is generally liable for sexual harassment of his or her employees when the harassment results in a "tangible employment action," such as termination, demotion, or unwarranted transfer; and the harassment results in a severe or pervasive hostile work environment created by the supervisor. Regarding conduct between co-workers, an employer is responsible for acts of sexual harassment in the workplace when the employer knows, or should have known, of the harassment. Supervisory liability will not attach when the supervisor can show evidence of acting reasonably to prevent harassment by acting promptly to correct the behavior. In *Williamson v. City of Houston, Texas* (1998), a police officer repeatedly complained to her sergeant that a male officer was sexually harassing her by commenting on her body, pulling her hair, sticking his tongue in her ear, and trying to look up her skirt and down her neckline. The female officer then asserted that after she complained, the sergeant retaliated against her by criticizing and taunting her, giving her a written reprimand, and transferring her to a less desirable position. Rejecting the city's claim that it should not be held liable because it did not have proper notice of the harassment, the Fifth Circuit Court of Appeals held that when the officer first complained to the sergeant, a supervisor, the city was placed on notice.

In *Wright v. Rolette County* (2005), an appellate court reversed a lower court's decision on a sexual harassment and constructive discharge claim. Wright complained that she was subjected to sexist and offensive language daily and was embarrassed that men in the department called her a "big-breasted Canadian secretary," "a dizzy [expletive]," and "Canadian bacon." The sheriff admitted that he participated in the name-calling in front of others, including at a peace officer's meeting. The sheriff also implied that there was a camera in the female restroom, so she began using the restroom designated for female prisoners. The sheriff allegedly made vulgar comments about Wright's anatomy and requested a sexual favor. Wright claimed that she objected to these comments but they were ignored. While she attended correctional officer training, she completed sexual harassment training but did not make a formal complaint, fearing she would lose her job. She did complain to a county commissioner but he stated that there was nothing that he could do. She also complained to the county attorney, but the county did nothing to remedy the situation.

A week later, Wright was diagnosed by her physician with high blood pressure, anxiety, depression, and he prescribed her medication. Wright gave notice a few days later, alleging that the sheriff's behavior caused a hostile work environment. Wright was placed on paid leave pending an investigation, after which an attorney concluded the comments were inappropriate but not unwelcome. Wright returned to work and quit three months later, claiming she was constructively discharged. She sued, alleging sexual harassment and the sheriff requested qualified immunity; the lower court refused, and he appealed.

The sheriff was not immune on Wright's harassment charges, but the court did grant immunity on the claims of constructive discharge. According to the court, the sheriff's conduct could be considered sexual harassment even if he did not touch Wright or make sexual advances toward her. Wright's allegations showed a violation of her constitutional rights, requiring her to seek medical treatment. Because the sheriff received complaints from Wright and did nothing to address the allegations, liable attached. The court, however found that Wright failed to show that she was constructively discharged because of the harassment, and the sheriff was granted qualified immunity. Wright failed to demonstrate that the working conditions were intolerable for a reasonable person as it appeared that the harassment stopped after she returned to work.

Responding with an investigation to a claim of sexual harassment and following through with appropriate discipline was useful in defending such a claim. In *Rudd v. Shelby County* (2006), Rudd, a deputy sheriff, filed a complaint of sexual harassment with her superior and an investigation was conducted by internal affairs. Rudd reported that a sergeant handcuffed her in a bent-over position, to a file cabinet. She also reported that the sergeant rubbed himself against her, draped a chain around her neck, and asked her over the intercom, if it was "too hot in the kitchen for her." During the investigation Rudd was allowed to work in a separate facility to avoid contact with the sergeant. Within a month, the department reprimanded two of Rudd's supervisors. The sergeant was demoted to patrol officer, suspended for 30 days, and placed on probation for six months. The sergeant ultimately retired under a settlement agreement. Rudd left her job within two weeks of the harassment and sued, claiming that the sergeant's actions constituted sexual harassment, gender discrimination, and a hostile work environment under federal and state law. The court denied the county's motion for summary judgment and a jury awarded her $1 million in compensatory damages, back pay, and lost future wages.

The county appealed the award and the appellate court reversed the judgment. Because the sergeant was Rudd's co-worker and not her supervisor, Rudd had to show that her employer knew or should have known of the harassment and failed to take prompt action. The court agreed that the sergeant's conduct was shocking, but because the county responded with good faith to safeguard Rudd, liability did not attach. The court determined that Rudd did not prove that the county failed to take prompt action. Within several weeks the sergeant was disciplined and the county followed through with the discipline.

In *McCurdy v. Arkansas State Police* (2004), the court examined whether a single incident of supervisor harassment was enough to hold the employer strictly liable. McCurdy was a dispatcher for the Arkansas State Police (ASP) and within a short time of her employment her supervisor began harassing her. The one-time incident occurred in the dispatch room and McCurdy quickly left the room following the action, where there was offensive touching. McCurdy informed another dispatcher but would not report the episode until a higher-ranking supervisor responded. A subsequent investigation found that McCurdy's supervisor had violated departmental policy against sexual harassment and was subsequently disciplined. McCurdy filed a lawsuit claiming a hostile work environment and sexual harassment. The court rejected the claim and granted judgment for the department. The court concluded that there was no tangible employment action that occurred and because the department followed the principles in the *Suders* case by promptly investigating and disciplining the harasser, liability could not attach.

In *Erickson v. Wisconsin Dept. of Corrections* (2006), a prisoner raped a female payroll clerk and she filed a lawsuit, claiming sexual harassment. Erickson worked in payroll and had limited contact with prisoners. The only prisoners allowed in the building were trustees who performed janitorial duties. Prior to allowing prisoners to work as trustees, a file check was performed and prisoner Spicer was cleared despite being classified as high risk.

One evening Erickson worked late and Spicer began intimidating her and she immediately left. Erickson reported the incident to the warden and she promised Erickson that nothing like that would happen again. Two weeks later Erickson worked alone again and Spicer raped her and escaped in her car. Erickson sued the warden for sexual harassment. At trial, the jury found the warden liable and she appealed. The appellate court affirmed, holding that the warden created a hostile work environment. The court held that Erickson provided her employer enough information to trigger liability if the employer did not act to prevent or correct the potentially harassing behavior. According to the court, once Erickson informed her employer of the first complaint she did nothing to correct the situation and was on notice about the complaint. The warden did not investigate the situation, did not interview any other employees, and did not question or remove Spicer from the position. The court held that the warden failed in her duty to prevent and correct the incident from occurring.

In *Briggs v. Waters* (2007), a former employee of a county sheriff's department sued the county sheriff and others, claiming to have been subjected to quid pro quo sexual harassment and was fired in retaliation for spurning the sheriff's advances. The defendants moved for summary judgment and the district and appellate courts denied the motion. The court held that the female employee showed that the conduct of the sheriff was unwelcome, as required for a Title VII action and under § 1983 when she initially offered an excuse when asked to accompany him on business trips and did not respond to a follow-up email, and by shrugging away when the sheriff hugged her. The court denied summary judgment as the sheriff terminated the officer, who had been convicted of obstructing justice in an unrelated matter and was appealing the decision, as a pretext for termination based on her rebuff of his sexual advances. The court held that the officer established a prima facie case of disparate discipline, in violation of Title VII and her equal protection rights, by showing that she was terminated following her conviction for obstructing justice, while two male officers convicted of drunk driving were not terminated.

In *Smith v. City of Chattanooga* (2007), a female police officer filed a sexual harassment claim against her supervising sergeant. Smith was assigned to work with Sergeant Grace and they got along well. Smith later married and she alleged that Grace began to treat her differently. Smith asserted that Grace would frequently pull her off of patrol duty to perform computer data entry and he would sit in the room with her. Smith also asserted that Grace began to spread rumors that she was having an affair with a fellow officer. Smith denied the affair, claiming that the officer was a friend. Grace continued to spread the rumor throughout the department, particularly when Smith and the other officer were present. Smith filed a sexual harassment claim against Grace. Grace was placed on administrative leave during an investigation. Grace was later reinstated and ordered to attend sexual harassment training. Although Smith and Grace did not work with each other, Smith claimed that she felt hostility from Grace in the station house and filed a sexual harassment lawsuit. The court found in favor of Grace and Smith appealed.

The appellate court found that Grace could not be held liable individually and upheld the lower court's verdict. The court also upheld the courts' ruling against the city. The court opined that the city responded appropriately by placing Grace on administrative leave when Smith complained, investigated the claim, and mandated that Grace complete sexual harassment training. The court concluded that the city responded appropriately and exercised reasonable care to prevent and promptly correct any sexually harassing behavior.

In *Reed v. Cedar County* (2007), the jail administrator, who was female, filed a legal action against the county and the sheriff in his individual and official capacity, alleging that she was subjected to sex discrimination and sexual harassment in violation of Title VII. She alleged that the sheriff repeatedly made sexual advances toward her after she informed him to stop. The court found that the county had implemented reasonable anti-sexual harassment policies, along with its reporting procedure and county-wide mandatory employee training program. The jail administrator was fully aware of the procedures and had on many occasions provided training to county personnel on the policies. The court also held that the jail administrator provided sufficient evidence to hold the county and the sheriff liable for his conduct. The court stated that the jail administrator complained about the sheriff's conduct on five occasions to the chief deputy and county supervisors, who failed to investigate or take any corrective action in violation of Title VII.

In *Miller v. State Dept. of Public Safety* (2011), Diana Miller experienced several occasions of sexual harassment during her employment with the Delaware State Police (DSP). In 2004, Miller was supervised by Lieutenant Taylor in Troop 2 and Captain Laird. Not long after her arrival in Troop 2, Taylor began regularly throwing small pieces of paper and candy wrappers down her blouse and stated that Miller should be his Kent County "girl." This type of behavior continued on and off through early 2007. In February 2007, the DPS underwent reorganization and Miller reported directly to Captain Laird. With frequency Laird would enter Miller's office and stare at her for long periods of time and from his office, which was in direct line of sight of Miller's desk. In March 2007, Laird began making sexual advances toward Miller and visited her home in uniform when she was on medical leave and while medicated. Laird began groping Miller's breasts and attempted to kiss her. Several days later Laird texted Miller with sexually suggestive messages. Laird informed Taylor to instruct Miller's boyfriend to end the relationship with her or he would experience problems at work.

When Miller returned to work from her medical leave, she was informed that several complaints had been made against her by several employees and she believed this was a result of the preferential treatment she was receiving from Laird. During her 2006 annual performance evaluation she had received a superior review overall. An investigation was performed and it was ruled "not substantiated." During the investigation Laird spoke up for her and his wife befriended Miller. The friendship began to intensify between Miller and Laird's wife to the point where the Lairds would visit Miller's house for dinner and later ending with sleep overs. As the relationship continued the Lairds became more controlling of Miller and Mrs. Laird convinced Miller to sleep with her husband (Captain Laird) as he was the only one who spoke on her behalf during the investigation. Miller consented as she believed that if she refused she may lose her job. Miller attempted to transfer out of Troop 2 to end the relationship with the Lairds but it was denied. Later, on a trip with the Lairds, Miller had nonconsensual sex with Captain Laird. When the three returned to work Miller decided to end the relationship with the Lairds, and Captain Laird contacted Miller and indicated that it would not be good if she exposed the relationship.

In 2007, Miller filed a complaint against Taylor and Laird for sexual harassment and she was transferred to the Delaware State Police Training Academy upon her own request. Laird filed for retirement during the investigation and at a hearing it was determined there was sufficient evidence to support Miller's sexual harassment claims. Liard retired just before the conclusion of the investigation prior to any discipline being implemented. In 2008, Miller filed a legal action claiming sexual harassment and stated that she did not report Taylor's or Laird's behaviors as she was intimidated by the two and that she feared she would be fired. Theresa Schneider (who also had sexual relations with Taylor and Laird) testified at a deposition that there was general hostility against women in the DSP in the male-dominated agency and an "old school culture" of retaliation existed if any woman made a complaint about gender-based discrimination. Miller further claimed that she also suffered from stomach pains while the alleged harassment was occurring.

The Delaware Superior Court reviewed the allegations based on three forms of harassment under Title VII: hostile work environment, quid pro quo sexual harassment, and retaliation. The court found that Miller's claim against Taylor failed as his behavior had ceased in 2006. On the second claim of quid pro quo, the court found sufficient evidence against Laird to support a classic allegation. The court noted that Laird was in a position to utilize Miller's vulnerable position to make her believe he could save her job if the internal investigation against her did not go well, and he used his employment status to manipulate and coerce her. On the third claim of retaliation, the court granted summary judgment to the DSP as Miller voluntarily requested transfer to the Training Academy and did not experience any adverse employment action.

The Supreme Court has sent a clear message that Title VII requires employers to try to prevent sexual harassment in the workplace and to provide appropriate discipline as warranted. These cases require administrators not only to have a sexual harassment policy, but the agency must also aggressively enforce that policy by promptly correcting any sexually harassing behavior (Rossi, 1998; Box 9.1) Supervisors must be familiar with the agency's sexual harassment policy and provide periodic training to all employees.

BOX 9.1 PROCEDURES TO FOLLOW WHEN INVESTIGATING HARASSMENT CLAIMS

- Fully investigate all complaints
- Ensure that investigators are well trained
- Upon receiving the complaint, do not delay the investigation
- When practical, reassign employees involved in the complaint
- Use an impartial investigator
- Remain neutral with the individual you are interviewing
- Keep the investigation confidential
- Interview all potential witnesses
- Stay in touch with the complainant, accused, and witnesses
- Take action, regardless of the investigation outcome
- Take advantage of the opportunity to re-educate the department about harassment

When the supervisor is on notice of sexual harassment, Title VII requires the administrator to take some action to stop the harassment. This still is not sufficient to avoid liability. The administrator must prove that the complainant unreasonably failed to prevent or correct the problem by taking advantage of the sexual harassment policy or by correcting the problem in some other way. To meet this component of the defense, administrators must encourage their employees to take advantage of the policy by promptly investigating and documenting all complaints and by preventing retaliation against those who do complain. Further, in accordance with the Supreme Court's decision in *Suders*, if an employee can prove that she or he resigned as a result of prohibited conduct by a supervisor, while the supervisor acted under his or her official capacity, the employer will be automatically liable for that supervisor's conduct, i.e., the employer will not have a defense to a constructive discharge claim.

As shown in the *Miller v. State Dept. of Public Safety*, behavior in the workplace and after-hours can be severe enough to substantiate a claim of sexual harassment. Additionally, the ongoing decisions in claims of sexual harassment by the courts routinely show that in a claim of hostile work environment resulting from harassment a plaintiff employee must show that he or she suffered intentional discrimination, the discrimination was pervasive and regular, the discrimination detrimentally affected the plaintiff, and the discrimination would detrimentally affect a reasonable person of the same gender in that position. Administrators are encouraged to critically assess their current sexual harassment policy, assess how sexual harassment claims are handled, and provide periodic documented training on policy and prevention strategies.

Americans with Disabilities Act

The Americans with Disabilities Act (ADA) was signed into law on July 26, 1990, and applies to agencies with at least 15 employees. The Act is codified at 42 U.S.C. §§ 12101–12213 and provides that employers may not discriminate in employment against qualified individuals with disabilities. The ADA protects individuals with disabilities from discrimination in public services and accommodations. The Act does not repeal Title VII of the Rehabilitation Act of 1973, nor does it preempt any statute or federal law that establishes a higher standard of protection. The courts have the final opinion on ADA disputes. In its relatively short existence, the courts have increasingly examined cases to interpret the meaning of the statute.

Practices and Activities Covered by the ADA

The ADA prohibits discrimination in all employment practices, including job application procedures, hiring, firing, promotion, compensation, training, as well as other terms, conditions, and privileges of employment. It applies to recruitment, advertising, tenure, layoff, leave, fringe benefits, and all other employment-related activities.

Persons Protected by the ADA

Employment discrimination is prohibited against "qualified persons with a disability." This includes applicants for employment and employees. An individual is considered to have a "disability" if he has a physical or mental impairment that substantially limits one or more major "life activities," has a record of such an impairment, or is regarded as having such an impairment.

Commonly recognized physical impairments that may interfere with the performance of life activities include blindness, deafness, muscular dystrophy, cerebral palsy, and cardiac problems. Any mental or psychological disorder generally recognized by medical authorities, such as schizophrenia or bipolar disorder, that interferes with an individual's performance or major life activities is a disability (*Sutton v. United Airlines, Inc.,* 1999). Individuals discriminated against because they have a known association or relationship with an individual with a disability are protected.

A "qualified person with a disability" is one who meets legitimate skill, experience, education, or other requirements of an employment position that she or he holds or seeks, and who can perform the essential functions of the job with or without reasonable accommodation. Requiring the ability to perform "essential" functions assures that an individual with a disability will not be considered unqualified simply because of inability to perform marginal or incidental job functions. If the individual is qualified to perform essential job functions except for limitations caused by disability, the employer must consider whether the person could perform those functions with a reasonable accommodation. If written job descriptions have been prepared in advance of advertising or interviewing applicants for a job, this would be considered as evidence, although not conclusive evidence, of the essential functions of the job.

The term "major life activity" means activities like walking, sitting, standing, seeing, hearing, breathing, performing manual tasks, caring for oneself, learning, and working. The inability to work at one job may not count, because it is not substantial enough a limitation on the ability to work. A person with a disability must also be "qualified." This means someone who "satisfies the requisite skill, experience, education, and other job-related requirements of the job and who, with or without reasonable accommodation, can perform the essential functions of the job."

"Essential functions" means job tasks that are fundamental and not marginal. Thus, if a person with a disability can do the essence of the job despite having a disability, the employer cannot discriminate against that person because of the disability. The employer must also reasonably provide accommodations for the disabled person that do not create an undue hardship for the employee. This means doing things like making facilities accessible to persons with disabilities, restructuring nonessential parts of the job, altering work schedules, modifying equipment or machinery, and providing someone to aid the disabled worker. An accommodation is not reasonable if it imposes an "undue hardship" on the agency's work by requiring "significant difficulty or expense."

The ADA does not protect individuals because of homosexuality, bisexuality, transvestitism, transsexualism, pedophilia, exhibitionism, voyeurism, gender identity disorder not resulting from physical impairments, compulsive gambling, kleptomania, pyromania, or psychotic substance use disorders resulting from current illegal drug use. An alcoholic is protected, but not if his or her current use of alcohol interferes with performance of the job or poses a direct threat to property or the safety of others.

Enforcement of the ADA

The Equal Employment Opportunities Commission (EEOC) is charged with enforcing the provisions of the ADA. An individual with a disability who believes he or she has been discriminated against may file a complaint with the EEOC, after which an investigation will be conducted. The EEOC has broad investigatory authority, including subpoenaing witnesses and evidence. After the investigation, the commission will state its findings and can compel an agency to comply with the provision by hiring the person. The commission and/or the complainant may submit civil actions against the agency. In cases of a political subdivision, the statute reserves the decision to pursue remedies to the Attorney General (Colebridge, 2000). Compensatory and punitive damages may be available in cases of intentional discrimination or when an employer fails to make a good faith effort to provide a reasonable accommodation.

The ADA and Job Descriptions

Although it is a prudent management strategy to have current job descriptions and to revise them periodically, the ADA does not require employers to do so. Written job descriptions that are prepared prior to advertising a position or interviewing applicants for a job will be considered as evidence along with other relevant factors. Job descriptions should be reviewed to make sure they accurately reflect the actual functions of a job. Job descriptions should focus on outcomes or results of a job function, not solely on the way it is customarily performed.

It is important that management specify essential job functions. The courts have been instrumental in identifying the essential functions of police officers. Case law has established that firing a weapon and making forcible arrests are essential job functions of a police officer (*Davoll v. Webb*, 1999). Driving a police vehicle is also essential (*Gonzalez v. City of New Braunfels, Texas*, 1999), as is collecting evidence (*Holbrook v. City of Alpharetta*, 1997). This does not totally quantify or exhaust other essential functions of the job, but specifying core tasks can avert claims of discrimination under the ADA (see Box 9.2).

The EEOC suggests that when considering essential job functions, an employer should consider written job descriptions, the amount of time spent performing the function, the consequences of not requiring performance of the job, collective bargaining agreements, and the experience of the job incumbent or incumbents in similar positions.

Must Employers Give Preference to a Qualified Applicant with a Disability?

An employer is free to select the most qualified applicant available and to make decisions based on reasons unrelated to a disability. For example, an essential function in corrections is to be able to walk for extended periods and climb stairs in a housing unit. Two people apply for a correctional officer position and the employer administers a mandatory physical step test for five minutes and provides a reasonable accommodation for the person with a disability. The person without the disability obtains a better score on the performance test. The employer can hire the applicant with the better score.

BOX 9.2 ESSENTIAL JOB FUNCTIONS OF LAW ENFORCEMENT OFFICERS

- Effect an arrest, using force if necessary, and restraints
- Physical aspects—running, climbing, jumping, swimming, rescuing, standing for prolonged periods, searching, and investigating in various environments. Subdue resisting subjects with control tactics. Pursue suspects on foot in different types of terrain. Lift, carry, and drag objects and people.
- Communicate effectively, give directions/commands, give information, listen to people, and testify in court
- Conduct visual and audio surveillance for extended periods
- Enter and exit vehicles quickly. Operate motor vehicles under normal and emergency conditions, during day or night
- Exercise independent judgment within legal requirements
- Gather information in criminal investigations by conducting interviews
- Load/unload and fire different types of weapons from varying positions
- Use other equipment such as batons, aerosol sprays, flashlights, cones, etc.
- Direct traffic for extended periods
- Prepare written reports and other documents and perform mathematical computations
- Read and comprehend laws, rules, regulations, and policies
- Manage interpersonal conflicts to maintain order and restore peace

---

Limitations on Medical Examinations Prior to Employment

An employer may not ask or require a job applicant to take a medical examination before making a job offer. The employer cannot make any preemployment inquiry about a disability or the nature or severity of a disability. An employer may ask if an applicant has a driver's license or can drive but may not ask questions regarding a visual impairment. An employer may, however, ask questions about the ability to perform specific job functions and may, with certain limitations, ask a person with a disability to describe or demonstrate how he or she would perform these functions.

An employer may condition a job on the satisfactory result of a post-offer medical examination or medical inquiry if this is required of all entering employees in the same job category. A post-offer examination or inquiry does not have to be job-related and consistent with business necessity. If the person is not hired after the medical examination, the reason or reasons for not hiring must be job-related and consistent with business necessity. The employer must show that no reasonable accommodation was available that would enable the person to perform the essential job functions, or that accommodations would impose an undue hardship. An "undue hardship" refers to an accommodation that would be unduly costly, extensive, substantial, or disruptive, or that would alter the operation of the business. A post-offer medical examination may not disqualify an individual with a disability who is currently able to perform essential job functions because of speculation that the disability may cause a risk of future injury.

Tests for illegal use of drugs are not medical examinations under the ADA and are not subject to the restrictions of such examinations. Information from all medical examinations and inquiries must be kept apart from general personnel files as a separate, confidential medical record, available only under limited conditions.

Alcoholics and the ADA

While a current illegal user of drugs is not protected by the ADA if an employer acts on the basis of such use, a person who currently uses alcohol is not automatically denied protection. An alcoholic is a person with a disability and is protected by the ADA if he or she is qualified to perform the essential functions of the job. An employee may be required to provide an accommodation to an alcoholic. An employer, however, may discipline, discharge, or deny employment to an alcoholic whose use of alcohol adversely affects job performance or conduct. Moreover, an employer may prohibit the use of alcohol in the workplace and can require that employees not be under the influence of alcohol.

Requirements to Make Reasonable Accommodation

An employer is only required to accommodate a "known" disability of a qualified applicant or employee. The requirement generally will be triggered by a request from an individual with a disability, who frequently will be able to suggest an appropriate accommodation. Accommodations must be made on an individual basis, because the nature and extent of a disabling condition and the requirements of a job will vary in each case.

The ADA and Performance Standards

An employer can hold employees with disabilities to the same standards of performance as other similarly situated employees without disabilities for performing essential job functions, with or without reasonable accommodation. An employer also can hold employees with disabilities to the same standards of performance as other employees regarding marginal functions unless the disability affects the person's ability to perform those marginal functions. If the ability to perform marginal functions is affected by the disability, the employer must provide some type of reasonable accommodation, such as job restructuring, but may not exclude an individual with a disability who is satisfactorily performing a job's essential functions.

Criminal Justice Cases Involving the ADA

The Ninth Circuit Court of Appeals rejected an ADA challenge to a correctional officer who challenged a policy of assignment rotation in *Kees v. Wallenstein* (1998). The union sued on behalf of four Seattle correctional officers to block officer rotation policies. One officer had a neck and back injury and could suffer paralysis if reinjured. Another officer had residual injuries from a prisoner assault. A third officer had a toe amputated and a fourth officer had a displaced vertebra. The district court found that the plaintiffs were not "qualified" for their employment because of their "no prisoner contact" medical restrictions. The court of appeals agreed. The court held that the "ability to restrain prisoners during an emergency is critical to jail security," and jail safety is jeopardized by the plaintiff's inability to respond to emergencies. The court also noted that the bargaining agreement provided that correctional officers were expected to rotate among several positions, most of which require prisoner contact.

In *Miller v. City of Springfield, Missouri* (1998), the Eighth Circuit Court of Appeals upheld the use of the Minnesota Multiphasic Personality Inventory (MMPI) for testing of police applicants. A woman who had served as a police officer for 10 years moved to Springfield, Missouri, where she was hired as a dispatcher. After twice failing the police officer agility test, she passed that portion, but scored a 66 on the MMPI-2, indicating above-normal depression. She sued under the ADA, claiming that management perceived her as disabled, and challenging the MMPI as not job-related. The appellate court held she presented no evidence that she was disabled, and the fact she was hired as a dispatcher meant the city did not perceive her as disabled. Regarding the MMPI, the court held that it was appropriate as a psychological screening mechanism, is job-related, and consistent with business necessity where the selection of individuals to train for the position of police officer is concerned.

Two police officers and the union in New Jersey challenged a 12-year-old policy requiring officers of all ranks to be psychologically tested every three years in *PBAL-319 v. Township of Plainsboro* (1998). One of the officers was later directed to participate in counseling for anger management. The officers filed suit, claiming they were forced to reveal personal and private information that was unrelated to work performance and their fitness for duty as police officers; the process violated their right to due process; and the screening caused humiliation, embarrassment, emotional distress, anguish, and harm to their personal reputations. The court dismissed the case, concluding that periodic psychological screening is constitutional, provided that management provides for the privacy of officers' files and records and respects their rights to due process. No appeal was filed.

In *Williams v. Philadelphia Housing Authority* (2004), a 24-year veteran challenged his termination by the department based on his mental instability. Near the end of his employment, Williams' behavior became erratic—yelling at co-workers and threatening them. PHA suspended him without pay and two days later they ordered him back to work and he called in sick daily for several days. The PHA ordered Williams to undergo a psychological exam with the departmental psychologist and he went on medical leave for two months. The chief informed Williams that he would be exhausting his sick leave and annual benefits within a month and that if needed additional leave, he needed to request a medical leave of absence or it would be deemed a voluntary resignation. Prior to the end of the sick leave, the psychologist cleared Williams to return to work on restricted duty, provided he would be prohibited from carrying a weapon. The chief contended that he could not accommodate him because there were no non-firing bearing positions open at the time, although there was one position open in the radio room. The chief again asked Williams to seek a medical leave of absence to in order to keep his job. Williams did not respond and the department fired him. Williams filed several claims against the PHA, including an ADA claim for failing to accommodate his disability. The federal court granted judgment to PHA, finding that Williams was not disabled within the meaning of the ADA.

Williams appealed and the court reversed the decision. The court reasoned that Williams met the definition under the ADA. Although Williams agreed that he should not carry a weapon, he argued that he could do other jobs at the police department, like working in the radio room. The court looked to the EEOC regulations for guidance. EEOC regulations stated that working was substantially limited where one was significantly restricted in the ability to perform either a class of jobs or a broad range of jobs in various classes as compared to the average person having comparable training, skills, and abilities. Testimony at court revealed that Williams' disability did not preclude him from working in a "broad range of jobs." Williams requested the accommodation and the court agreed that he should be allowed to work in the radio room in accordance with the provisions of the ADA.

In *Almond v. Westchester County Dept. of Corrections* (2006), a probationary officer who was terminated after she displayed hysterical behavior and underwent psychiatric assessment following training in disturbance control and use of a baton, brought a civil action against the Department of Corrections alleging wrongful discharge in violation of the ADA. She complained that the exercises were too hard and asserted that she had been exhibiting nervous and erratic behavior throughout the day, crying and complaining that the training was too tough. The Department of Corrections moved for summary judgment and the court granted the motion. The court held that the officer failed to establish a bona fide claim of disability discrimination under the ADA, on the theory that the employer perceived her to be either a drug addict or mentally ill. She did not prove that the employer considered her to be a drug addict despite her statement that she had overmedicated herself, her admission to taking some sort of drug on the day of the training incident, and her supervisor's order that a drug test be administered, and assuming that the employer perceived her to be mentally ill. The court concluded that she did not show that the employer believed she was impaired from working or from performing some other major life activity.

In *Van v. Miami-Dade County* (2007), a county detention officer with diabetes sued the county seeking damages for discrimination pursuant to the ADA and the Florida Civil Rights Act. The county required a physical examination of employees. At the examination, the physician concluded that the officer's diabetes was not under control and that he would not be allowed to perform the safety-sensitive duties of a correctional officer and would be placed on restricted duty. The physician informed the officer that he would be released to full duty as soon as he was able to provide a He-Alc test result showing that his sugar level was 8.0% or less. The officer filed a lawsuit claiming discrimination and the county moved for summary judgment. The court awarded summary judgment and held that the officer was neither disabled nor regarded as disabled, thus defeating his discrimination claims under the ADA and the Florida Civil Rights Act, even though he was regarded as unable to fulfill the correctional officer position. According to the court, the position of correctional officer was a single, particular job, which could not constitute a substantial limitation of the major life activity of working, and the county did not view the employee's impairment of uncontrolled diabetes as a substantial limitation on his ability to work in a broad class of positions. The court also ruled that the ADA did not require the county to create a long-term or permanent restricted duty position for an allegedly disabled correctional officer suffering from diabetes and thus the county was not required to alter its policy of six months' restricted duty followed by compulsory leave in order to reasonably accommodate the employee.

In *Johnson v. Sedgwick Sheriff's Department* (2012), Johnson filed a claim under the Americans with Disability Act asserting that he was fired from his position as a detention officer for repeatedly sleeping on the job. He filed a pro se complaint for damages in the United States District Court for the District of Kansas, raising claims under Title VII. He alleged that the Department fired him because he was black and has attention-deficit hyperactivity disorder (ADHD), and that other employees who were not black or disabled slept on the job but were not fired. He alleged that his ADHD caused him to "become distracted, bored, and drowsy in the midst of boring, repetitive tasks," and that he asked several times "to work in the lobby."

The undisputed facts showed that Mr. Johnson was found sleeping on the job three times in 2007, and had two suspensions and one counseling report in 2006 for three additional incidents of sleeping on the job. On each occasion in 2007 he denied having been asleep. At the time of his termination Mr. Johnson was in the "reckoning period" for five separate disciplinary violations, a period in which he was expected to remain offense-free. Any of the three sleeping violations in 2007 would have been his fourth offense during the reckoning period, and department policy allowed for dismissal after a third violation in a reckoning period. Department records showed that between 2001 and 2010, 30 detention deputies had been disciplined for sleeping. None had been terminated, but none had more than three reported incidents. Moreover, Johnson had received a "marginal" performance rating in 2007 and was on a 90-day probation period at the time of his firing.

The district court ruled against Johnson concluding that he had failed to meet his burden to show that the defendant's reason for firing him was a pretext for racial discrimination and he appealed. The Tenth Circuit Appellate Court affirmed the lower court's decision. In analyzing an ADA claim, the court stated that an ADA claimant "must show that he (1) was disabled; (2) was qualified, that is, could perform the essential functions of the job in question, with or without accommodation; and (3) suffered adverse employment action because of the disability." The court determined that there was no evidence that Johnson's ADHD qualified as a disability under the ADA, as he had simply alleged that he had the condition but provided no evidence that it substantially limited a major life activity.

Alternatively, the court concluded that even if Johnson's ADHD qualified as a disability under the ADA and that his propensity to fall asleep was a symptom of his ADHD, he had failed to provide any evidence that a reasonable accommodation would have enabled him to perform the essential functions of a detention deputy, which, among other things, requires visual monitoring of inmates and hence the ability to stay awake. The court rejected Johnson's argument that rather than monitoring inmate pods, he could have been assigned to a light-duty position in the jail lobby. The lobby position is one of many duty assignments that detention deputies must be able to perform on a rotating basis, and the position is sometimes used when a deputy needs a temporary light-duty assignment. Department officials provided evidence that creating a permanent lobby position would interfere with its use as a temporary assignment, and that rotating deputies through a number of positions avoids a variety of problems. The court noted that a temporary lobby assignment might have been feasible, but creating a new, permanent lobby position was unwarranted because the ADA does not require an employer "to accommodate a disabled worker by modifying or eliminating an essential function of the job."

The court addressed the racial-discrimination claim, and found that Johnson's wholesale failure to provide any admissible evidence, such as affidavits or other sworn testimony, in support of the contentions in his response brief that he was treated differently from other deputies who slept on the job. In particular, it concluded that there was no evidence of disparate treatment holding that he had failed to meet his burden to show that defendant's reason for firing him.

Should Consider in Light of the ADA

Employers should be proactive in order to minimize potential exposure to litigation to reduce the claims filed under ADA. First, an agency should review its Equal Employment Opportunity and discrimination and harassment policy statements to ensure that they include statements to the effect that discrimination on the basis of disability will not be tolerated. Second, employers should provide training for their human resources personnel as well as their first-line supervisors regarding the ADA, particularly with respect to accommodation issues. Third, employers should review and update (or prepare new) job descriptions to ensure that they include all the essential functions of a particular position.

Moreover, these statements should be amended to include an explanation about a disabled individual's right to request accommodations. Managers should review all mandatory fitness standards applied to applicants to ensure compliance with the ADA. Further, managers should ensure that medical information is retained in a separate file from other nonconfidential information.

While the ADA does not require maintenance of job descriptions, identifying essential job functions is critical in determining whether an applicant or employee is a qualified individual with a disability entitled to the protections of the ADA. It is a prudent management practice to develop and revise job descriptions regularly. From job descriptions, all employees learn what the job requirements are and performance evaluations should be based on these requirements. Managers should identify the core job functions of each employee and categorize them as "major," "essential," or "critical" duties and "other" duties or responsibilities. Employers should review their recruiting programs and particularly the notices and advertisements placed for individual jobs to ensure that they accurately reflect essential job functions.

Employers should revise their application forms, and hiring and interview processes. Employers cannot ask direct questions on an application about whether the applicant is disabled or has a disabling condition. During an interview the applicant cannot be asked such questions about a disability. A review of all interview forms and revisions should be made as warranted. Interviewers should be trained to ask questions related to the essential functions of the job.

An employer may be held liable under ADA for discrimination as a result of the use of a standardized test, whether of physical or mental aptitude capabilities. In order to avoid liability for what appear to be neutral testing programs, an employer must make sure that the testing used is: (1) job-related, and (2) consistent with business necessity. In other words, employers should review any testing programs to determine that the testing is designed and administered to measure actual ability to do the essential functions of the job in question.

Wrongful Termination

Employment-at-Will

The law generally examines employment as a matter of contract and the legal status of the employee will dictate the legal requirements of supervisors' interactions with employees. When issues of employment law emerge, the first question to be analyzed is whether the relationship involves employment or another kind of contractual relationship. In most, if not all, criminal justice agencies, the employer has the right to control what the employee does, when the employee does it, and how it is accomplished. This type of situation is considered an employment relationship.

In the public sector, when an employer hires a person, the legal presumption that governs their working relationship is that the employment is "at will." This means that the employee works at the pleasure of the employer and the employer may dismiss the employee at any time without explanation or legal penalty. This is known as the "American rule." In seventeenth-century England, there was a presumption that employment was for one year unless otherwise stated. The United States courts adopted the one-year rule after the American Revolution. The courts reexamined this philosophy at the end of the nineteenth century as individual freedom to contract expanded. The courts adopted the rule that an employee without a definite term of employment was an employee at-will and may be discharged without reason (Avery, 1997).

Employment-at-will has, over the years, meant that the employer could terminate an employee for no cause, good cause, or even for "causes morally wrong" (*Hutten v. Waters*, 1915). An example of this is illustrated in many sheriffs' departments after an election. A newly elected sheriff enters office and fires employees for no cause other than he wants to hire employees whom he believes will work best with his goals. The terminated employees basically had no recourse or protections.

The example above is not completely accurate today, because there are no true employment-at-will situations. The concept has been eroded by Congress and state legislatures, which have passed laws restricting employers from terminating at-will employees. Federal statutes that modify employment-at-will include the Civil Rights Act of 1964, which prohibits discharge for discriminatory reasons; the Age Discrimination in Employment Act, which prohibits discharge solely on the basis of age; and the Rehabilitation Act of 1973, which bars dismissal of an otherwise qualified handicapped employee when reasonable accommodation of the handicap can be made (Allred, 1995). State legislatures have also passed similar antidiscrimination laws that protect employees as well as civil service commissions. Antidiscrimination laws, both state and federal, also generally prohibit retaliation. Thus, workers cannot be fired for filing discrimination charges against their employers. Nor can they be discriminated against for other reasonable actions taken in opposition to discrimination by their employers.

Employment today is protected in many ways. In many states, employees are represented by unions and collective bargaining agreements with employers. Employees who have bargained for individual contracts of employment or who are covered by employer policy manuals or other manifestations of promises that the workers have job security are generally protected.

Many employees are covered by their state personnel act, which stipulates that an employee may not be fired for reporting improper government activities. Whistle-blowing statutes protect employees from retaliation if they report improper activity. Most states provide that a career employee cannot be fired for failing to meet job performance requirements without first showing prior written warnings documenting poor job performance. The system provides for hearings to ensure that due process rights are guaranteed. Other exceptions to the employment-at-will rule include formal written contracts, personnel handbooks, and implied good faith. Violations of these standards can subject employers to civil litigation.

In *Lee v. City of Detroit* (2008), an inspector for the Detroit police department was demoted for whistleblowing. Inspector Lee had received numerous promotions during his 25-year tenure at the police department, had received various awards and commendations, while only receiving one disciplinary suspension. He was the supervisor of the Gang Enforcement Section. In a meeting regarding the deployment of officers to various schools used as voting precincts for Election Day in 2004, Lee's commanding supervisor directed him to deploy officers to specific schools in order to obtain funding from Homeland Security. This direction was contrary to what Lee desired to do, as he was going to assign officers to schools that were designated as polling locations. In the meeting, Lee's supervisor interrupted Lee and grabbed his arm and shouted, "Look nigger, assign the officers to specific schools." Both Lee and his commanding officer are black. One other inspector (who was white) was also in the room. Lee wrote a memo to the deputy chief, informing him of the incident, hoping that it would be investigated. Lee also was prepared to make a complaint with United States Equal Employment Opportunity Commission and possibly file a lawsuit.

Information regarding Lee's memo was posted on a web site, which angered the chief. One month later Lee was transferred from the Gang Enforcement Section to the Records division. Lee believed that the transfer was punishment for the memo and with the transfer lost the opportunity to work holidays and make triple pay. Lee reported that several supervisors came to him, informed him to drop the complaint and to not pursue legal action or his career would be destroyed and his chances for promotion to commander were in jeopardy. A meeting was convened to resolve the complaint, but several of the commanders stated that they knew nothing of the memo and the request to investigate it. Lee then filed a lawsuit in federal court alleging violations of the Whistleblower's Protection Act. After he filed the lawsuit, Lee was demoted to lieutenant and lost tangible benefits. At a hearing regarding the lawsuit the chief stated that she transferred Lee to the Records division because he failed to demonstrate competency and ability as the supervising officer of the Gang Enforcement Section. The deputy chief stated he knew nothing about the memo, the complaint, or Lee's transfer. Lee retired shortly thereafter.

The City of Detroit moved for summary judgment and the court granted it and Lee appealed. The appellate court denied the appeal and stated that Lee failed to bring a legitimate Whistleblower Act claim. The court describe the rules governing the Act, and stated a party must: (1) show that he was engaged in protected activities as defined in the Act; (2) the party was subsequently discharged, threatened, or otherwise discriminated against; and (3) that a causal connection existed between the party's protected activity and the discharge, threat, or discrimination. The court further explained that the party must report a complaint to an outside body. The court concluded that Lee failed to plead his case to an outside party as he directed his case to the deputy chief.

It is improper to say today that a public employer can simply discharge an employee for any reason. It is most accurate to hold that employment-at-will has been significantly modified.

Due Process and Discharge

Many courts recognize an exception to the employment-at-will rule based on the tort of wrongful discharge. This holds that an employer may not discharge an employee in violation of a public policy contained in a statute (*Brockmeyer v. Dun & Bradstreet*, 1983). In its broadest sense, an employer may not discharge an employee for reasons of malice, bad faith, or retaliation, because to do so contravenes public policy. Public policy has generally been defined as no citizen can lawfully do that which has a tendency to be injurious to the public or against the public good. Some have held that this principle implies a contract, including at-will employees, and good faith. A bad faith discharge would breach the stipulations of the contract and conceivably result in a civil lawsuit (Allred, 1995).

Wrongful termination lawsuits emerge when an employee believes the employer has terminated her or him for no legitimate reason in violation of his or her constitutionally protected rights secured under the Fourteenth Amendment. The Fourteenth Amendment protects individuals from being deprived of property or liberty without due process of law. This language has been linked to a property interest in employment matters (*Cleveland Board of Education v. Loudermill*, 1985). Property interests arise when a public employer demonstrates a reasonable expectation of ongoing employment, because the employer has created a binding policy that discharge will occur only for stated reasons, such as for just cause.

Property interests or rights in employment are created by acts of the employer. Property rights are established by state laws, local ordinances, or statutes, not by the Constitution (*Board of Regents v. Roth*, 1974). If one of these items protects the public employee against discharge except for just cause, the employee will automatically have a property interest in employment. Employee handbooks, policy manuals, and contracts normally create property interests for employment purposes. If a claim of wrongful discharge emerges, the court will examine state laws to decide whether the employee has a valid claim to employment. The United States Supreme Court stated in the *Roth* decision that "for the proposition that to demonstrate a property right in employment, the employee clearly must have more than an abstract need or desire for it. He must have more than a unilateral expectation of it. He must, instead, have a legitimate claim of entitlement."

It is important to recognize that a property interest only applies to continued employment. A right to a particular position or duties is nonexistent. Management may reassign employees to new responsibilities or duties without infringing on the property rights of their employees (Avery, 1997).

Employers may not infringe on the property rights of vested employees without first ensuring due process of law. Vested employees are those who have successfully completed the probationary status of the department. Probationary employees do not have a property interest.

Employers may not discharge employees with property interests without first providing due process. The central feature of due process is a hearing. In *Cleveland Board of Education v. Loudermill* (1985), the United States Supreme Court held that the "root requirement of the due process clause is that an individual be given an opportunity for a hearing before he is deprived of any significant property interest." Loss of property interests can involve disciplinary actions such as suspensions, severe disciplinary actions, and dismissal. This means that a hearing must be conducted prior to the termination of employment. This protection is to ensure that employees with property interests are granted the essence of fundamental fairness. This provides a balance to the interest of the employee in retaining his or her job and the employer's interest in simultaneously reducing the risk of error.

A hearing is required, but it need not be formal. The Court in *Loudermill* stated "that a pre-termination hearing, though necessary, need not be elaborate. The formality and procedural requisites for the hearing can vary, depending upon the importance of the interests involved and the nature of the subsequent proceedings." Due process also requires that advance notice be given to the employee before the hearing and the notice should be given in writing at least 24 hours prior to the actual hearing. The charges should be conveyed to the employee prior to the hearing. There is no requirement that an attorney be allowed during the hearing or that the employee be given the right to consult with one during the hearing. Any investigatory reports that have been submitted should be given to the employee. Documentation of the hearing and transcripts should be recorded. Other proactive strategies for administrators to consider are identified in Box 9.3.

After a discharge, the employee must be granted a full hearing before an impartial decision-maker. This can be someone inside or outside the department. Legal representation and cross-examination of witnesses should be allowed. The final decision should be placed in writing and the employee informed that he or she may file an appeal. These procedures will be useful in ensuring that the employee is provided with the requirements of due process and will place the employer in a more defensible position should the employee file a civil lawsuit for wrongful discharge.

In *Garner v. Gwinnet County* (1999), the court upheld the discharge of a mentally unstable police officer. A police officer's performance began to deteriorate and he developed suicidal thoughts and a vivid fantasy of killing the chief. The chief had him examined by three different doctors, who determined that he was unsuited for police work. One doctor stated that he was burned out and should not be on the street carrying a weapon. The chief demoted him to animal control officer. The officer demanded reinstatement and filed an EEOC complaint. The officer's behavior deteriorated further and the chief fired him after giving him a hearing. The officer filed a legal action demanding reinstatement and sought damages for emotional injuries from observing animals being euthanized.

The court found in favor of the chief, holding that he had competent medical evidence that the officer posed a threat to himself and others. The chief's actions were proper, the court ruled, because it would have been reckless to reinstate an employee whom defendants perceived posed a threat to the community.

In *Spades v. City of Walnut Ridge* (1999), a police officer attempted suicide by shooting himself in the head. Because of his "violent use of a firearm" and the city's exposure to liability, he

---

BOX 9.3 PROACTIVE STRATEGIES FOR AVOIDING WRONGFUL DISCHARGE CLAIMS

- Develop employee handbooks that describe at-will employment
- Develop written guides and statements regarding discipline and termination policies
- Develop and maintain a progressive disciplinary system and consistently enforce it
- Distribute discipline statements to all employees
- Train all supervisors and investigators in the disciplinary process
- Performance appraisals should be candid and should reflect the employee's actual job performance
- Progressive discipline that is properly documented provides evidence that a good faith effort was made to give an employee an opportunity to correct performance
- Provide a reasonable opportunity for an employee to meet agency expectations
- When practical, suspend employees pending an investigation by an impartial supervisor— thoroughly investigate any dispute prior to taking action
- Discharge decisions should have a second review by another person
- Document all complaints, investigations, and supervisory actions with an employee
- If possible, allow an employee to resign instead of being fired
- When feasible, resolve disputes through arbitration or mediation

---

was terminated. After receiving counseling, medication, and treatment for his physical and psychological injuries, he sought reinstatement. When rejected, he filed a civil action claiming that he was wrongfully discharged, and filed a claim under the ADA. He alleged that he was illegally terminated because of his disabling depression and that management failed to grant him federally mandated medical leave.

The court found that the city had a legitimate reason for terminating the officer. The court reasoned that increased potential liability associated with an employee's past behavior is a legitimate concern of the city, particularly when there is a known violent history. Claims of improper hiring, supervision, and retention loom large in the minds of employers and their lawyers. Liability did not attach because the court held that the city articulated a nondiscriminatory reason for his termination.

The question of providing a presuspension hearing was examined by the U.S. Supreme Court in *Gilbert v. Homar* (1997). A campus police officer was charged with felony drug possession and suspended without pay pending an investigation. The officer filed a civil action claiming that his property interest rights and his Fourteenth Amendment due process rights were violated because the university failed to give him a presuspension hearing. The Court held that the due process clause of the Fourteenth Amendment does not require a formal or informal hearing prior to a temporary deprivation of an officer's property interest. The Court did hold that a post-suspension hearing was required within a reasonable period.

In *Pittman v. Wilson County* (1988), the county had adopted a personnel resolution to govern employment decisions. The resolutions regarding employment were placed in an employee handbook and distributed to all employees. A central feature of the resolution dealt with disciplinary procedures for errant employees, and it stated that an employee may be dismissed by a department head or the county manager. The clause also stipulated that employees could be dismissed only for causes related to poor job performance after three prior warnings. The policy did allow for a predismissal conference between the supervisor and the employee.

Dispatcher Pittman of the Wilson County Sheriff's Office was accused of misconduct by her supervisor. Instead of being fired, she agreed to resign. Three days later she contacted her former employer and complained that she was coerced into resigning and demanded a discharge hearing. The county refused and she filed a civil action claiming that her Fourteenth Amendment rights were violated in that she was denied a predismissal hearing before an impartial official.

The District Court found in favor of the county, holding that Pittman had no property interest in her job and that she had not been wrongfully discharged from her job as a dispatcher. She appealed and the Fourth Circuit Court of Appeals affirmed, holding that she was an at-will employee with no property interests in continued employment, citing *Roth*. Central to the court's holding was the county's resolution on disciplinary actions. The court concluded that resolutions under North Carolina law were not binding, because they were not in an ordinance or a state statute.

The United States Supreme Court affirmed a city's termination of a police officer in *City of San Diego v. Roe (*2004). Roe was a police officer with the San Diego police department. He made a video showing himself taking off a police uniform and engaging in a sexual act. He sold the video on eBay, which was discovered by his supervisor. Internal affairs conducted an investigation and found that Roe's conduct violated the department's policies. The chief ordered him to cease displaying, manufacturing, distributing, or selling any sexually explicit material or engaging in any similar behaviors. Roe ignored the orders and he was fired for disobedience of lawful orders. Roe sued, claiming the firing violated his First Amendment right to free speech. The district court granted summary judgment to the city but the appeals court reversed, finding Roe's conduct was protected as citizen commentary on matters of public concern because his conduct took place off duty and was unrelated to his job.

The city appealed to the United States Supreme Court and they reversed the appellate court's decision. The Court concluded that Roe's conduct was not a matter of public concern. Public employees had a First Amendment right to speak on matters of public concern, which were typically matters concerning government policies of interest to the public. However, Roe's expression did not qualify as a matter of public concern because his actions did nothing to inform the public about any aspect of the department's operation, workings, or functions. Moreover, even though Roe's actions occurred off-duty, his expression was linked to his official status as a police officer and was designed to exploit his image as an employee. Therefore, there was no basis for finding that Roe's expression was of concern to the community, so his speech was not protected by the First Amendment.

The levels of punishment and the termination of detention officers who abused a juvenile detainee were examined in *Stroud v. Shelby County Civil Service Commission* (2006). Thomas and Stroud were investigated for using excessive force against two juvenile detainees in the jail and were fired. It was also determined that they were untruthful during the investigation. Both officers appealed to the civil service board. After the hearings, the board concluded that both officers used excessive force and had been untruthful during the investigation, warranting their dismissal. The officers appealed the termination and filed a lawsuit for wrongful discharge. The court found that there was evidence to support the claim that the officers were untruthful during the investigation, but found no evidence to support the excessive force claim against Stroud. The court found that the board treated the officers differently from other employees who had received lesser sanctions for similar conduct. The lower court sent the matter back to the civil service board. After a hearing, the board reinstated their earlier decision and the officers appealed again. The lower court overturned the board's decision and found that the officers were treated differently from officers in the past and should receive a 30-day suspension without pay.

The civil service board appealed and the appellate court reversed the lower court's decision, upholding the board's decision to terminate Stroud. The court found that there was sufficient evidence to support the charge that Stroud used excessive force and his termination was warranted under the county's rules. There was a video showing Stroud using excessive force, as well as statements from fellow officers. The investigation report verified the claims, and the officer was found to be untruthful.

In *McKee v. City of Hemingford Village Board of Trustees* (2008), the chief of police challenged his termination for insubordination and brought a legal action against the city. The police department consisted of three employees, including the chief. The chief requested vacation time well in advance and the city board approved it. Between the time of the approval and the date of the chief's vacation, two of the officers resigned. The city board met and canceled the chief's vacation and informed him he would be terminated if he did not report for work. Another board meeting was held and the chief was asked if was going to comply or take his vacation. The chief responded by stating that was in the process of finding officers to cover for him while he took his vacation. The board took a vote to terminate the chief, it was approved, and the next day the chief received a letter of termination from the board.

The chief requested a hearing to appeal the termination decision. The board granted the hearing appeal, hired an independent attorney to hear the appeal, and the chair of the board who wrote the letter excused himself. The board met and rejected the chief's appeal and he filed a civil lawsuit. The chief argued that he was denied sufficient due process during the time prior to his actual termination. The city argued that the chief was only entitled to a more limited process, including oral or written notice of the charges against him, an explanation of the city's evidence, and an opportunity to present his side of the story. The court noted that the chief received oral notice of the charges against him at two different Board meetings and was allowed to present his side of the story at the second meeting with the Board. The court upheld the Board's termination decision, ruling that the chief was provided with sufficient due process as he met with the Board on two meetings and the Board also provided him with an opportunity to appeal the decision.

In *Vaughn v. City of Puyallup* (2008), officer Vaughn was fired for leaving the scene of an arrest, failing to follow department policies, and lying. Vaughn was an eight-year veteran with the police department and responded to a shoplifting call at a Sears store. At the store Vaughn failed to perform a criminal history check of the detained shoplifter and informed his supervisor that he was leaving the store, leaving the suspect in the custody of store security. Vaughn's sergeant responded to the store and performed a check and learned that the suspect had an active warrant out for his arrest on several violent charges. The sergeant filed a report to his supervisor indicating that Vaughn violated department policies by leaving the scene and lying to him. Vaughn was notified that an internal investigation was being conducted to determine whether he had violated policy regarding his handling of the Sears call. After the investigation, a hearing was provided for Vaughn and he submitted a written statement about the incident but refused to answer any questions. The hearing officer informed Vaughn that he would be provided with the decision in a few days. However, internal affairs continued to investigate the incident and provided a second hearing that Vaughn did not attend. He did submit a written protest stating that the second hearing was biased and unfair. At this time Vaughn and other officers sent confidential letters to city council and the mayor calling into doubt the leadership ability of the chief and accusing the chief of being biased and using unfair retaliation against officers.

The chief learned that one of the letters had been submitted by Vaughn and reopened the Sears store investigation. The IA investigator concluded that Vaughn violated policy and recommended to the city attorney that Vaughn be terminated for mishandling the incident. The chief informed Vaughn of a third hearing and the possible discipline measures that might result. Vaughn chose not to attend the hearing but submitted a written statement. The chief issued a memo to Vaughn informing him of his termination and Vaughn appealed to the city's civil service commission. The commission held a four-day hearing, found that Vaughn committed inappropriate actions during the Sears incident, but concluded that termination was inappropriate and recommended suspension, with a demotion and a decrease in pay. The chief agreed and Vaughn resigned after the suspension. Vaughn then filed a legal civil action alleging that the city denied him proper due process during the time of the disciplinary hearings.

The city requested summary judgment. Vaughn primarily argued that he was deprived of a meaningful forum to present his side of the story. He claimed that although he was given three hearings (in accordance with *Loudermill*) those hearings were meaningless because the chief and others were biased and could not provide him with a fair proceeding. The court stated that in order to determine whether a city employee was given due process in a disciplinary hearing, a court must balance the interest in retaining the employee against the risk that the employee might be erroneously terminated. The court found Vaughn's arguments unpersuasive and held that he had not presented any evidence to show that he would be unfairly treated had he represented himself at the hearings he chose not to attend. The court ruled that the city properly investigated the incident, afforded Vaughn the proper due process through three hearings, and rejected his arguments, granting the city's motion for summary judgment.

In *Staub v. Proctor Hospital* (2011), the United States Supreme Court granted certiorari to determine the issue of supervisor liability regarding the wrongful discharge of an employee who was a military reservist. Staub was employed by Proctor Hospital as a technician and was also serving in the United States Army Reserve. His immediate supervisors were hostile to his military obligations, which required him to be away from the hospital intermittently. Staub was placed on a period of corrective action for poor work performance and one of the supervisors determined that Staub failed to improve in accordance with the corrective plan. The Director of Human Resources, Buck, reviewed Staub's personnel file and decided to fire him. Staub filed a grievance against Buck claiming that one of the supervisors fabricated the allegation underlying the corrective action out of hostility toward his military obligations, but Buck adhered to her decision. Staub sued Proctor under the Uniformed Services Employment and Reemployment Rights Act of 1994 (USERRA), which forbids an employer to deny "employment, reemployment, retention in employment, promotion, or any benefit of employment" based on a person's "membership" in or "obligation to perform service in a uniformed service," and provides that liability is established "if the person's membership . . . is a motivating factor in the employer's action." He claimed that the two supervisors were motivated by hostility to his military obligations, not Buck, and that their actions influenced Buck's decision. Staub filed a legal action and a jury found Proctor liable and awarded Staub damages, but the Seventh Circuit Appellate Court reversed, holding that Proctor was entitled to judgment as a matter of law because the decision-maker had relied on more than the supervisors' advice in making her decision.

Staub appealed the decision to the Supreme Court and in an 8–0 decision the Court found in favor of Staub (Justice Kagan abstained). Writing for the Court, Justice Scalia opined that if a supervisor performs an act motivated by antimilitary animus that is intended by the supervisor to cause an adverse employment action, and if that act is a proximate cause of the ultimate employment action, then the employer is liable under USERRA. In construing the phrase "motivating factor in the employer's action," the Court started from the premise that when Congress creates a federal tort it adopts the background of general tort law. The Court ruled that the Seventh Circuit erred in holding that Proctor was entitled to judgment as a matter of law. Both supervisors acted within the scope of their employment when they took the actions that allegedly caused Buck to fire Staub. There was also evidence that their actions were motivated by hostility toward Staub's military obligations, and that those actions were causal factors underlying Buck's decision. Finally, there was evidence that both supervisors had specific intent to cause Staub's termination.

The decision of the Court demonstrates that tort law requires a showing of intent and specific consequences of a supervisory decision that adversely impacts an employee's continued employment. Further, when such actions are underscored with malicious intent by supervisors acting within the scope of their employment duties, liability will attach. While this decision targets stipulations in accordance with USERRA, the philosophy of the legal principles described in the case holding may be applied to similar supervisory decisions.

The Eleventh Circuit Court affirmed the lower court's finding of summary judgment when an African-American female officer, Summers, claimed that she was wrongfully discharged for discrimination. In *Summers v. The City of Dothan, AL* (2011) police officer Summers was discharged for violation of department policy involving two incidents. In the first incident, Summers arrested and lodged a detainee for outstanding trespass warrants for 104 days but failed to complete the necessary paperwork and filing it with the magistrate. The second incident occurred a year later when Summers wrote traffic tickets on a motorist and failed to submit them pursuant to agency policy. The failure was discovered when the motorist attempted to pay the associated fines. After her annual review, which followed the second incident, she was terminated. Summers complained to the chief that she was being discriminated against and was not being treated equally, due to her gender and race, and not due to her conduct. Summers filed an Equal Employment Opportunity claim and the termination was sustained.

Summers filed a lawsuit for discrimination and wrongful discharge. The court maintained that in order to prevail in a claim of discrimination Summers would have to show other employees and incidents were not punished as harshly as she, despite violating the same rules or policies. These incidents would have to be nearly identical. She asserted that other officers in the department had failed to submit proper paper work on arrests and confinement of detainees. During discovery Summers proffered several examples in which officers were not disciplined but the court found that they were not sufficiently identical to her conduct and did not provide evidence of disparate treatment equaling discrimination. The court found that Summers did not establish a prima facie case of retaliation and held that it was not an error for the lower court to award summary judgment to the city. Further, the court stated that the city had established an applicable policy and enforced it appropriately.

Fair Labor Standards Act

Background

During the Great Depression, the Fair Labor Standards Act (FLSA) was enacted to ensure that employers complied with federally mandated minimum wage, equal pay, and overtime standards. Child labor restrictions are also addressed in the Act (Allred, 1995). The provisions of the Act are stipulated in 29 U.S.C. §§ 201–219 and it is enforced by the U.S. Department of Labor. Over the years, the Act has undergone many amendments, and since 1974 it has applied to both private and public employment.

The FLSA and its requirements have been examined by the United States Supreme Court on two occasions. In *National League of Cities v. Usery* (1974), the Court held that the federal government did not have the power under the Tenth Amendment to interfere with "traditional" functions of state and local governments, including the power to decide wage rates to be paid to their employees. The Court reversed its prior decision in *Garcia v. San Antonio Metro Transit Authority* (1985). It ruled that the FLSA could be entirely applied to state and local governments and did not violate the Tenth Amendment. The *Garcia* decision prompted Congress to help the states by enacting Public Law 99–150 in 1986, which gave the states relief from having to pay overtime and provided compensatory time off instead of monetary payments.

Work Time/Overtime

The FLSA provides that salaried executive, administrative, and professional employees are exempt from its minimum-wage and overtime provisions (§ 213). Work time is defined by the Act to mean all hours an employee is engaged in work, including waiting to be engaged in work, or actually at work, authorized or not. Beyond actual hours worked, provisions of the Act define "work time activities" to include actual job-related duties, requiring an employee to wear a pager and refrain from consuming alcoholic beverages, maintaining vehicles when required by the agency, testifying in court, attending mandatory training sessions, and preparing for an employee grievance. Work time does not include attending training that is not mandated, maintenance of physical fitness and preparing for work, outside employment, or uninterrupted mealtime lasting for at least 30 minutes.

The normal work week is established at 40 hours per week during a seven-day period. Work time above this standard is to be compensated at a rate of time and one-half. Section 207k of the FLSA provides an overtime provision. Police officers are paid straight time on an hourly basis. Should they exceed 171 hours in a 28-day period, they would qualify for overtime pay for all hours beyond this period. Sleep time may be excluded from this provision.

In *Jeter v. Montgomery County* (2007), a black employee brought a civil action against a county, alleging denial of earned wages, retaliation, and race discrimination. The employee asserted that after she complained about her lack of overtime pay, her home detention verification program was canceled, her workload increased, and she was informed by her superiors that she was not a team player. The county moved for summary judgment. The court held that the employee's claim of being denied overtime was sustained in violation of FLSA as she worked more than 40 hours per week without additional compensation. The court also held that her claim alleging an equal protection violation due to race-based discrimination in pay was sustained where she was treated differently, based on her race, from a similarly situated white employee.

Compensatory Time

The FLSA allows compensatory time to be accrued by public officials. In lieu of overtime pay, the FLSA accrual provisions permit up to 480 hours of compensatory time at a rate of one and one-half hours for each hour of overtime. As long as the time off does not conflict with work duties, compensatory time must be granted when an employee requests it. Policy statements should address such a provision. When an employee retires or resigns, cash must be paid.

The use of compensatory time creates a potential financial liability for an agency (Brooks, 2004). Pursuant to Title 29 U.S.C. § 207, when employees leave the department, they must be paid for accumulated compensatory time based upon their salary when they leave or their average salary over the previous three years, whichever is greater. Accordingly, an agency may want to "force" employees to take compensatory time when it is advantageous to the department. In *Christensen v. Harris County* (2000), the United States Supreme Court ruled that the FLSA permits a public employer to order an employee to take compensatory time off whenever the employer chooses to do so.

This, however, raises another question: Can an employee demand to be allowed to take compensatory time off whenever the employee wants to take the time off? The law on this issue is not as clear. The FLSA (Title 29 U.S.C. § 207) provides that an employee who has earned compensatory time by working overtime must be allowed to take such time off within a reasonable time of the request unless doing so would cause an "undue disruption" to operations. In *Houston Police Officers' Union v. City of Houston* (2003), the Fifth Circuit Court of Appeals addressed the Houston Police Department's policy that placed an inflexible cap prohibiting more than

10 percent of the force being scheduled off on a particular day for such things as annual leave and compensatory leave. Thus, an officer who requested to use compensatory time on a day when 10 percent already had scheduled time off would have that request denied. The court found the policy in compliance with the FLSA, stating that the statute only requires that an agency permit an employee to take compensatory time within a "reasonable" period after the request.

Violation Claims

An employee claiming a violation of the FLSA minimum-wage and overtime requirements may file a civil suit in federal or state court. Moreover, the Department of Labor may file lawsuits on behalf of employees. Employers found to have violated the act are liable for unpaid minimum wages or unpaid overtime compensation.

Police officers and other employees of the Greenville, North Carolina, Police Department won a settlement of $660,000, including $255,000 in attorney's fees and costs, in a lawsuit regarding overtime issues (*Daily Reflector*, 2000). The federal suit, initiated in 1999, alleged that officers were not paid for time spent responding to off-duty pages and phone calls; arriving early for their scheduled shift or staying late; cleaning their department-authorized weapons and assigned vehicles; preparing for court; and reviewing files and completing paperwork. The settlement did not reflect payment for time employees said that they spent "on-call" and "on-standby," but it did release the city from further claims on these issues.

In *Stachowski v. Town of Cicero* (2005), a police officer's termination was upheld for falsifying overtime claims. Stachowski was a 21-year veteran police officer who was accused of making false overtime claims of nearly $53,000.00. He was suspended without pay and the town board initiated termination proceedings. The board denied Stachowski's request for a hearing, noting that the severity of the charges justified his termination, and they fired him. He applied for and received retirement benefits and sued the town for denial of due process and equal protection rights. The lower court dismissed his claims, finding that the board's termination was justified and that he could have appealed the decision. His equal protection claim was also dismissed because he failed to allege that similarly situated officers were treated differently.

Stachowski appealed and the appellate court affirmed the lower court's decision. His claims were dismissed as state law provided that a town's board had the final authority to terminate an employee's employment. The court stated that Stachowski did have the right to appeal the board's decision under state law and because he did not, such failure did not give rise to a due process violation. Further, the court stated that his equal protection claim was meritless because Stachowski was not similarly situated to other officers who retired with untarnished records.

Beyond providing protections regarding overtime and compensatory pay, the FLSA also includes employee protections against discrimination and retaliation by an employer when an employee submits a work-related complaint. In *Kasten v. Saint-Gobain Performance Plastic Corp.* (2011), the United States Supreme Court examined whether an oral complaint, rather than a written complaint made by an employee, is protected under the FLSA. Kasten made a complaint to his supervisors that he was not paid for putting on and taking off his protective clothing required to perform his job. Kasten alleged that the process of putting on the protective gear caused him to be late in "clocking in and clocking out" in a timely matter. The process did not provide time credit for employees, which violated the provisions of the FLSA. Rather than submit a formal written complaint about the problem he orally notified his supervisors several times in accordance with the company employee handbook and policies. He further made several complaints to the Director of Human Resources and the operations manager. Over a period of time Kasten was dismissed, and claimed that he was fired for making the complaints. The company denied that Kasten made any complaints and stated that they fired him for poor performance and chronically clocking in late, which violated company policy.

Kasten filed a lawsuit for retaliation and wrongful discharge and the Seventh Circuit affirmed the lower court's decision, ruling that oral complaints made by employees are not protected under the FLSA. The Court granted certiorari to examine whether "an oral complaint of a violation of the FLSA" is "protected conduct under the [Act's] anti-retaliation provision." With a 6-to-2 decision (Justice Kagen abstaining), the Court reversed the lower court's decisions. The Court took a broad perspective, holding that Congress, in passing the FLSA, intended that the antiretaliation provision covered written and oral complaints, and that both are protected. The language of the provision, "making a complaint," is not bound to just written complaints but also included oral complaints made by employees. The Court opined that Congress intended that the FLSA protect employees from retaliation and protects an employee from the fear of bringing a complaint to an employer in order to improve labor conditions. The Court stated that the FLSA encourages employees and the employer to work together in enforcing work-related standards. The Court ruled that the Secretary of Labor has consistently held the view that "filed any complaint" covers both oral and written complaints. The Equal Employment Opportunity Commission has set out a similar view in its Compliance Manual and in multiple briefs. These views are reasonable and consistent with the Act.

The Court ruled the method of the complaint is not at issue, rather the FLSA provisions are met when an employee makes the complaint. Once the complaint is made the employer is placed on notice and reasonable accommodations must be provided. Administrators are therefore encouraged to keep employee handbooks and policies current and to adhere to the agency's grievance procedures. Further, administrators are encouraged to train all supervisors to all policies and the employee handbook in order to respond to employee complaints appropriately, which can result in averting labor-related problems. Agency administrators should maintain a work climate that encourages employees to work in harmony with supervisors, which serves to effectively resolve prospective work problems.

In *Anderson v. City of Los Angeles* (2011), police officer Anderson was charged with several counts of misconduct in which she violated agency policy by failing to request compensation after working overtime, for failing to identify other officers whom she instructed to do the same thing, and for making a false statement in a deposition in which she claimed that other officers and supervisors knew that she had violated department policy. During a hearing of the policy violations, Anderson plead guilty to the first count only and the board found her guilty on all counts and terminated her employment of 19 years. Anderson filed suit pursuant to the FLSA and the lower court held that it doubted that the employer has ever communicated to police officers that they may be fired simply for working overtime and not requesting reimbursement, and reinstated her employment. The department appealed and provided documents supporting that employees indeed had been informed to submit reimbursement.

The appellate court affirmed the lower court's decision. The court found that the documents submitted by the department prohibited employees from working overtime without authorization and not for neglecting to request compensation after working overtime, which involved the complaint for which she was terminated. The court ruled that although Anderson admitted to failing to request compensation for working overtime, the department defendants failed to show a statute, rule, or regulation that makes it an act of misconduct for a police officer to work overtime, whether authorized or unauthorized, and not ask to be compensated for it.

Employee Drug Testing
United States Supreme Court Decisions

The prevalence of substance abuse in our society has caused concern about public officials' fitness for duty. Screening or testing employees for drug use is an evolving area of the law. Because public employees operate equipment and machinery, and make decisions about the liberty of citizens, employers must have the public's as well as the employees' interests in mind and be familiar with the legalities of conducting drug searches with employees.

The Fourth Amendment protects persons from unreasonable searches and seizures. The United States Supreme Court has held that searches without consent or a valid search warrant are unreasonable except in certain specific circumstances (*O'Connor v. Ortega*, 1987). When special needs exceed the normal need in law enforcement, a search may be reasonable even though performed without probable cause. When a special need exists, the court must evaluate and balance the need for the search and the person's Fourth Amendment protected right against an unreasonable intrusion.

Balancing the need to conduct a search against employee privacy was the essential issue before the United States Supreme Court in *Skinner v. Railway Labor Executives Association* (1989). Following a major train accident, a federal regulation authorizing blood and urine testing of employees who violate safety rules by the Federal Railroad Administration (FRA) was implemented. The regulation was prompted by evidence that the accident was a result of widespread drug use by employees working for the railroad. Employees of the union challenged the searches, claiming that they violated their Fourth Amendment right to be free from unreasonable searches.

In a 7-to-2 decision, the Court upheld the regulation as constitutional. The Court determined that drug testing through blood and urine was a search, and the necessity of conducting such searches required neither probable cause or individualized suspicion. The Court found that a compelling government interest to perform such searches outweighed any employee right or privacy interest. The FRA drug testing program withstood constitutional scrutiny based on special needs of the government.

Using the balancing test between the interests of the government and the privacy rights of the individual, the Court again upheld a regulation requiring mandatory drug testing of United

States Customs Service employees in *National Treasury Employees Union v. Von Raab* (1989). The Customs Service implemented a drug-screening program requiring urinalysis of service employees seeking transfer or promotion to positions having direct involvement in drug interdiction, requiring the incumbent to carry firearms, or handling "classified" material. Customs employees challenged the drug testing requirement, claiming it was a violation of their Fourth Amendment rights. The District Court agreed and enjoined the program. The Court of Appeals vacated the injunction, holding that the requirement did not violate the Fourth Amendment.

Using the same analysis as in the *Skinner* decision, the United States Supreme Court upheld the requirement that workers seeking such positions within the Customs Service must undergo urinalysis. The Court stated that in view of the fact that the drug problem in society is pervasive, caused primarily by drug smuggling, the government has a compelling interest to ensure agents are physically fit to perform their job functions, particularly agents who carry firearms. The Court ruled that these interests outweigh the privacy interests of those seeking promotion to such positions, and a warrant is not required. The Court further stated that government employees do not have the same privacy expectations as private citizens.

From these two cases, the Court recognized employment issues and drug testing as "special needs" that provide for an exception to the warrant requirement under the Fourth Amendment and individualized suspicion of a particular employee is not required by the Constitution. Moreover, it is not necessary that a documented drug problem exist within the particular workplace to justify such testing. The Court specified three governmental interests that could justify mandatory testing in the absence of individualized suspicion. First, the government has an interest in maintaining the integrity of the workforce. Second, the government has a legitimate interest in maintaining and enhancing public safety. Finally, the government has an interest in protecting sensitive information, and in some situations suspicionless testing of individuals whose jobs involve access to these classified documents. The public safety rationale adopted by the Court in *Von Raab* and *Skinner* outweighs any privacy expectation of the individual governmental employee. Administrators should keep abreast of changes in the law and develop and maintain testing policies that underscore this principle.

Lower Court Decisions

Testing job applicants for drug use may be required after a conditional offer of employment has been made. The ADA neither supports nor abolishes such testing, because they are not medical examinations. An applicant cannot be required to provide medical information prior to a conditional offer of employment. The California Supreme Court upheld the screening of police applicants, but struck down such tests as a condition for promotion with veteran officers in *Loder v. City of Glendale* (1997). Likewise, in *Feliciano v. City of Cleveland* (1993), the Sixth Circuit Court of Appeals upheld a surprise test of police academy cadets and the dismissal of two who tested positive.

A controversial drug testing issue is that of mandatory and random drug testing of public officials, such as police and correctional officers. Conducting random searches has generally been upheld when there is individualized suspicion. Random testing of police officers with notice was upheld in New York in *Clark v. New York City Housing Unit Authority* (1990). A federal district court upheld random testing of prison employees who are issued or given access to firearms in *AFGE Council 33 v. Barr* (1992). The New Jersey Supreme Court upheld mandatory urinalysis of officers on an articulated, individualized suspicion of drug use in *Rawlings v. Police Department of Jersey City* (1993). Officers who are under custodial arrest are still subject to testing requirements for administrative purposes.

In *Brown v. City of Detroit* (1989), police officers challenged the city's random drug testing program. A Michigan state court issued a temporary restraining order on the strip-search portion of the program. In court, the plaintiff officers argued that *Von Raab* was intensely fact-specific to Customs agents and not applicable to police officers. The court rejected this argument and observed that both positions have the power of arrest and the right to use deadly force. The city's drug testing program was upheld by the court, but the city could not search body cavities for hidden urine absent a reasonable suspicion. Compare, however, *Guiney v. Police Commissioner of Boston* (1991). The Massachusetts Supreme Court struck down random testing of Boston police on state constitutional grounds.

A California appellate court examined a policy on police officers reporting to work with the odor of alcohol on their breath in *Hinrichs v. County of Orange* (2004). Hinrichs reported to work and a supervisor smelled alcohol on her breath and called her to his office. She reported to the office and another supervisor was also in attendance. Sergeant Schmutz informed her that he smelled alcohol on her breath and she responded that she had two beers at lunch several hours earlier and that she was taking Nyquil. The sergeant asked her to take a Breathalyzer test and she agreed, but no test was administered. Henrichs was reassigned for the day and her weapon was taken from her. Sergeant Schmutz submitted a report documenting the incident and the department obtained a statement from a witness who reported that she smelled medicine on Hinrichs' breath. Internal affairs notified her that they were conducting an investigation for the use of alcohol. Her attorney demanded a copy of the report that the sergeant filed and the department stated that if discipline higher than a reprimand was issued they would grant the request. A month later, the department issued a reprimand to Hinrichs for violation of the rules which stipulated that "the odor of an alcoholic beverage on the breath will be considered presumptive evidence of a violation." She appealed the reprimand to the captain and he denied her appeal. She filed an administrative appeal with the human relations department. She also filed a lawsuit claiming that she was denied her right to be informed of the nature of her initial interrogation and her right to obtain copies of the non-confidential reports and witness statements. She also claimed a violation of due process and that the rule was non-specific and overly broad. The lower court denied her lawsuit, stating that her administrative appeal had not been resolved.

Hinrichs appealed and the appellate court reversed the lower court's decision. The court disagreed with her that Sergeant Schmutz did not follow proper procedure in confronting her regarding the smell of alcohol, as this did indeed place her on "notice." The court agreed, however, that she was denied the sergeant's report and witness statement, and that the department had a duty to provide the documents. The court also determined that the rule was not unconstitutional, but that it was inapplicable in this situation. The letter of reprimand made no reference that Hinrichs' ability to perform the job was compromised, but stated that she could not perform her duties due to the smell of alcohol on her breath. According to the court, the department could not justify how the smell of alcohol impaired her performance and the department admitted that she was not impaired or under the influence, and there was no certain connection between the regulation and the purported violation.

In *Diaz v. City of El Centro* (2005), officer Diaz was terminated for possessing marijuana, other drugs, and drug pipes against departmental rules and policies. Officer Diaz had been recognized in numerous performance evaluations as one of the department's best training officers. His live-in girlfriend reported to Diaz's supervisors that he had physically abused her by striking her in the head. Two officers went to his home and Diaz denied the accusation, stating that she was jealous because he was dating another woman. Later that day, Diaz's girlfriend called the department and reported that she found drugs in the home. An officer responded to the house and the girlfriend gave him a box that contained marijuana, marijuana pipes, a knife, bullets from a .38 special, and other drugs. She reported that the box was found in Diaz's bedroom closet. The department conducted an investigation and Diaz admitted the box and the contents were his, but denied using drugs while working on duty. He stated that the box was "found property" that he discovered in an abandoned house, and used the items for training. Departmental rules required him to report the items, and he admitted that possessing marijuana was illegal and was against departmental rules.

The chief fired him and Diaz appealed to the personnel appeals board. The board found that there was no illegal search of his home producing the drug and other items. Diaz argued that he did not use drugs and his exemplary performance at the department should be considered in determining a less severe punishment for violating departmental rules. The board upheld the termination. Diaz filed legal action in the state court and the lower court reversed the board's ruling, finding that the city had to show convincing evidence that the officer's warrantless search of the boxes was justified. The court also found that the termination hearing lacked fairness and that the termination was too harsh. The city appealed.

The appellate court upheld the hearing board's decision to terminate Diaz as there was substantial evidence to support its decision. The court concluded that administrative agencies had broad discretion to determine discipline, and the courts should not interfere unless there is a clear abuse of discretion. Further, the court held that the exclusionary rule did not apply to civil and administrative proceedings involving public employee discipline. The department did not conduct the search; rather, Diaz's girlfriend discovered the boxes, opened them, and turned them over. Finally, the court found that the punishment was reasonably justified as Diaz knew that possessing drugs was illegal and the termination was appropriate, due to the loss of trust in such an exemplary officer.

In *Rice v. Belfiore* (2007), an officer who was a member of the bomb squad was fired for failing a random drug test. Rice worked as a member of a six-member bomb squad, which required that he be on call 24 hours a day, seven days a week. Pursuant to department policy, a random drug test was administered and Rice tested positive for marijuana. Rice was notified that a disciplinary hearing would be conducted for possession and use of drugs, engaging in conduct unbecoming an officer, and failing to maintain a drug-free workplace. He was advised that possible sanctions may include: dismissal from service, demotion in grade and title, suspension without pay for a period of time not exceeding two months, and a fine not exceeding one hundred dollars, or a reprimand. After the hearing, the hearing officer recommended that Rice be terminated. The Police Advisory Board agreed and Rice was terminated. Rice filed a lawsuit arguing that the policy adopted by the department on a drug-free workplace and the practice of the department was to encourage rehabilitation. He argued that this was his first violation and requested that he be reinstated.

The court denied Rice's claim and held that there was nothing preventing the department from terminating him based on his failed drug test. Contrary to Rice's claims, the department had a written zero-tolerance policy that required it to initiate disciplinary proceedings with the goal of terminating any police officer who tested positive for drug use. The court concluded that while rehabilitation was a goal of the policy, termination of employment for violating a zero-tolerance policy was not unreasonable for such behavior and upheld the discharge.

The courts continue to uphold department rules on random drug testing of police officers. In *Goldin v. Kelly* (2010), officer Goldin of the New York Police Department submitted his hair for a random drug test. He tested positive for cocaine with a level four times the level indicating more than inadvertent use. The department had changed its practice from using urinalysis to testing hair samples. At a department hearing the commissioner found him guilty and dismissed him from the department. Goldin filed a lawsuit and the lower court granted summary judgment and he appealed.

The New York Appellate Court agreed with Goldin that changing the drug testing method to hair testing was an improper practice counter to the Collective Bargaining Agreement but denied his request to render the results of the test as unlawful. The court rejected Goldin's claim that the level of cocaine detected was the result of passive ingestion due to intimate sexual contact with his cocaine using girlfriend and not due to intentional ingestion. Moreover, the court found no merit in Goldin's assertion that the practice of using hair samples was a violation of former collective bargaining agreements and upheld his termination from the department.

Administrative Considerations

Administrators must balance the need to initiate and carefully maintain a drug screening policy with the privacy rights of employees. This area of the law is unsettled and can be fraught with complex liability issues. State and federal laws must be examined for embarking on such an endeavor. This topic is an obvious area for policy development and enforcement. Numerous issues concerning such a program include whether to mandate testing, proper protocols, what if employees refuse, what system is in place to handle such concerns, what laboratory should be used, how should false positives be handled, how should retesting be processed, what information do supervisors need before a program begins, and will such testing invade employee privacy? These and other questions must be researched and considered prior to establishing a program.

If a program is already in place, administrators must keep abreast of changing state and federal laws to ensure that agency rules are consistent with the law. Review and revision of regulations already in place should be conducted regularly and as laws change. Consistent enforcement of the agency's drug-screening regulations is essential. Instituting or failing to institute a drug-screening program can increase the liability of administrators from employees or an innocent third party injured by an employee. Therefore, criminal justice managers are encouraged to seek assistance through legal counsel and risk management services as they implement and maintain their programs.

Summary

This chapter has highlighted several key areas that may further expose administrators of criminal justice agencies to civil liability. During the past several years, it has become more common for police and correctional officers to become plaintiffs. Supervisors must be familiar with many aspects of personnel legal issues. Contemporary managers can be sued under Title VII of the Civil Rights Act of 1964 for claims of sexual harassment and discrimination based on race, gender, color, religion, and national origin. Claims of sexual harassment against supervisors and co-workers have been emerging with more frequency than other areas, and the United States Supreme Court has issued three decisions regarding this topic since 1998. The Americans with Disabilities Act provides another avenue of potential supervisor liability that affects hiring and firing aspects of the job. The Fair Labor Standards Act has been examined by the United States Supreme Court on two occasions and stipulates the requirements for proper wages, overtime, and compensatory time. Employee drug testing also emerged as a significant legal area in the early 1980s and requires employers to adhere to essential provisions of the FLSA when performing such searches.

These issues and others are continuing to evolve. Criminal justice managers should keep abreast of these changes in the law and implement the necessary policy and administrative systems that follow the mandatory requirements. Training for mid-level and first-line supervisors, as well as line-level employees, is essential to producing a healthy work environment. Further, adhering to the laws and agency policy on these subjects assists in communicating to all employees and the community that management will not tolerate infringement of protected employee rights in the workplace.

In light of the developments surrounding the issues of sexual harassment, administrators must ensure that their policies on the subject matter are consistent with the *Suders* decision. Sexual harassment and constructive discharge can be linked together if the plaintiff can show that such a climate caused him or her to resign. Training for all personnel should be provided and claims of sexual harassment claims must be investigated promptly and appropriate sanctions implemented as warranted. Case law examples indicate that supervisors should be trained and all investigations and sanctions should be thoroughly recorded. The same consistency and thoroughness should be followed in claims of sexual assaults and decisions to discharge an employee. Supervisors should ensure that they are familiar with their own disciplinary procedures and practices. Such proactive measures can assist in defending claims of unconstitutional supervisory practices. Administrators are also encouraged to research and be familiar with their own state's laws on personnel practices.

Moreover, due to the complexity of the rules regarding the FLSA, administrators should study the issues carefully and comply with contractual terms and state statutes that deal with the same issues. The costs to an agency for failure to adhere to the rules can be minimized when administrators take proactive measures to ensure that employees are treated fairly. As administrators have questions in this area, they are encouraged to contact the Department of Labor.

In Chapters 6 through 8, various administrative liability issues were addressed and in Chapter 9 additional special litigation components were examined. These chapters have highlighted the continuing themes and patterns of litigation focused against administrators since the *Monell* decision in 1978. Based on the case examples and the discussion on risk management presented in the latter portion of Chapter 5, criminal justice managers are encouraged to review their administrative strategies and strive to implement components of the bureaucratic management principles as appropriate in order to insulate their agencies from successful litigation.

It has been argued that civil liability in the criminal justice system may result from "poor management" and "administrative disorganization" (DiLulio, 1987; Useem and Kimball, 1989; Vaughn, 1996). It has also been argued that where more structure, accountability, and restricting of officer discretion is implemented by administrators, through following the principles of the bureaucratic model, civil liability may be reduced (White, 2001; Blumberg, 1989). Still others maintain that in a contemporary criminal justice agency, administrators should consider combining a blend of bureaucratic, human relations, and contingency style of management to overcome some of the authoritarian and hierarchal aspects of management comprised by the bureaucratic model (Dias and Vaughn, 2006; Zaho, 1996). In light of the continued litigation trends in which administrators are cited as being deliberately indifferent to a citizen's, prisoner's, and/or an employee's constitutional rights, administrators are encouraged to review the following components of the management model and incorporate them into their style of management:

- A delineation of hierarchy of authority and division of labor;
- Clear structure of command and span of control;
- Formal and informal communications with agency personnel;
- Implementation and enforcement of written current policies and procedures;
- Provision of ongoing training for all personnel, consistent with their assigned duties and full documentation;
- Maintenance of a robust field training officer (FTO) for newly hired employees and a similar program for new supervisors;
- Appropriate delegation of tasks and responsibilities with employees and keeping job descriptions current;
- A process of regularly supervising, monitoring, and formally assessing field performance of all employees;
- Thoroughly investigated practices of alleged misconduct and discipline personnel as warranted;
- Implementation of a system of early identification and intervention with marginal employees; and
- Keeping all personnel accountable and compliant with Professional Ethics, agency policy, and the law.

To motivate and lead agency personnel, administrators are encouraged to consider incorporating various principles from the human relations model. To reduce the risk of potential of civil liability, however, administrators should shore up their management approaches to incorporate the principles identified in the previous items, which align with many of the fundamental principles of the bureaucratic model of management. Improvements in supervision strategies, increased training, keeping employees accountable, and enforcing agency policies and procedures have been shown to reduce the potential of civil litigation (White, 2001; Hughes, 2001; Vaughn, Cooper, & del Carmen, 2001). As illustrated, criminal justice managers may be sued in their individual capacity and the supervisor plays a critical responsibility in ensuring that the risk of civil litigation for the agency is minimized. Learning from the case examples presented in the previous chapters, and applying the components previously discussed, combined with risk management strategies, will assist in placing the agency in the best position to defend against the next lawsuit.

References

Allred, S. (1995). *Employment law: a guide for North Carolina public employers* (2nd ed.). Chapel Hill, NC: Institute of Government, University of North Carolina.

Associated Press (1993, June 5). FBI agrees to pay out $300,000 to settle sexual harassment suit. *Daily Reflector*, 3.

Associated Press (2000a, October 4). City to pay 1.7 million to Attorneys in L.A. Police employee harassment cases.

Associated Press (2004, December 19). State prison system settles four sex-harassment cases in 18 months. *USA Today*, 4.

Associated Press (2012, February 15). Louisiana settles federal Lawsuit over sexual harassment. <www.NOLA .com>.

Avery, I. T. (1997). *Legal aspects of police supervision*. Incline Village, NV: Copperhouse Publishing Company.

Blumberg, M. (1989). Controlling police use of deadly force: assessing two decades of progress. In R. G. Durham & G. P. Alpert (Eds.), *Critical issues in policing* (pp. 442–464). Prospect Heights, IL: Waveland Press.

Colebridge, T. D. (2000). The Americans with disabilities act. *FBI Law Enforcement Bulletin*, September, 26–31.

Collins, S. C., & Vaughn, M. S. (2004). Liability for sexual harassment in criminal justice agencies. *Journal of Criminal Justice*, *32*, 531–545.

DiLulio, J. S. (1987). *Governing prisons: a comparative study of correctional management*. New York: Free Press.

Dias, C. F., & Vaughn, M. S. (2006). Bureaucracy, managerial disorganization, and administrative breakdown in criminal justice agencies. *Journal of Criminal Justice*, *34*, 543–555.

Government Accountability Office (GAO) (1999). Women in prison: sexual misconduct by correctional staff. Report Number: GGD, 99–104.

Hughes, T. T. (2001). Police officers and civil liability: the ties that bind? *Policing: An International Journal of Police Strategies and Management*, *24*, 240–263.

Ross, D. L. (2000). Emerging trends in police failure to train liability. *Policing: An International Journal of Police Strategies and Management*, *23*, 169–193.

Rossi, A. M. (1998). Twelve considerations when investigating discrimination or harassment complaints. *Police Department Disciplinary Bulletin*, May, 2–5.

U.S. Equal Employment Opportunities Commission (EEOC) (2012). Litigation statistics. *Sexual Harassment Charges—EEOC and FEPAs Combined—FY 1997–2011.* <www.eeoc.gov>.

Useen, B., & Kimball, P. (1989). *States of siege: U.S. prison riots, 1971–1977.* New York: Oxford University Press.

Vaughn, M. S. (1996). Police civil liability and the First Amendment: retaliation against citizens who criticize and challenge the police. *Crime and Delinquency, 42,* 50–75.

Vaughn, M. S., Cooper, T. B., & del Carmen, R. V. (2001). Assessing legal liabilities in law enforcement: police chief's views. *Crime and Delinquency, 47,* 3–27.

White, M. D. (2001). Controlling police decisions to use deadly force: reexamining the importance of administrative policy. *Crime and Delinquency, 47,* 131–318.

Zaho, J. (1996). *Why police organizations change: a study of community-oriented policing.* Washington, DC: Police Executive Research Forum.

10

Use of Force in Law Enforcement and Corrections

OVERVIEW

Law enforcement and correctional personnel have legal authority to use force in the performance of their duties. The police frequently use force to effect lawful arrests, in self-defense, and to overcome unlawful resistance. Correctional personnel frequently use force in self-defense, breaking up fights, maintaining security and order, and quelling disturbances or riots. When using force, criminal justice personnel must justify the type and degree of force used in any situation and are required to use force within a framework of legally prescribed guidelines. Agency procedures guide officers in their use of force. Using force outside these guidelines can give rise to civil liability if a citizen or prisoner alleges that the officer violated his or her constitutionally protected rights by using unreasonable force.

Use of force by criminal justice practitioners is one of the most controversial aspects of the legal authority granted to them. Frequently, in incidents in which force was used, claims of excessive force arise and numerous questions emerge, such as: What constitutes excessive force? What is reasonable force? Was the amount or type of force used by the officer appropriate and necessary? What is the appropriate standard with which to evaluate the use of force? Did the officer violate the constitutional rights of the plaintiff? These and many more questions will be raised by a plaintiff seeking to win monetary damages. This chapter examines the liability issues surrounding claims of excessive force in police and correctional work. This topic is of critical importance to officers, because they must be aware of how the courts have established standards with which to evaluate such claims. Moreover, supervisory personnel must understand their role in training officers in proper use-of-force decisionmaking and use-of-force procedures, developing policy guidelines for agency personnel, and investigating claims of excessive force. Allegations of excessive force and brutality will be addressed and legal precedents will be presented.

What Is Known About the Use of Force by Criminal Justice Personnel?

Studies on Police Use of Force

Research studies that evaluate police use of force as well as legal decisions were limited prior to the 1980s. Hopkins (1931) reported on a study of the New York Police Department and found in 166 cases (23% of the cases examined) that some type of physical force was used against citizens. Common methods of force used were strikes (67 cases), rubber hose (19 cases), blackjack (12 cases), and one suspect was hung out of a window. The Wickersham Commission (National Commission on Law Observance and Enforcement, 1931) also reported such police use-of-force practices.

More recently, however, police use-of-force measures have become fertile ground for scholarly research. Past researchers have focused their efforts on deadly force and firearms issues primarily because of their high profile and potential for liability, and because of more complete recordkeeping, which makes data collection less problematic (Alpert, 1989; Binder & Fridell, 1984; Binder & Scharf, 1980; Bloomberg, 1982; Chevigny, 1969; Fridell, 1989; Fyfe, 1978, 1988; Geller, 1985; Horvath, 1987; Jacobs & Britt, 1979; Lester, 1984; Matulia, 1982; Milton et al., 1997; Pate & Fridell, 1993; Reiss, 1971; Schultz & Service, 1981; Waegel, 1984). In comparison, less research has been conducted on the nature and extent of nonlethal force used by police, although a body of research is emerging. Most empirical research on nonlethal force by police has been based on data collected through the observation of officers on patrol (Reiss, 1971; Friederich, 1980; Sykes & Brent, 1983; Bayley & Garofalo, 1989). These studies indicate that force used by the officer is infrequent in citizen and police encounters and is generally a result of antagonistic behaviors of the citizen. Other studies have reviewed use-of-force reports filed by police (Croft, 1985; Croft & Austin, 1987; NIJ, 1999; Garner et al., 1996; Greenfeld et al., 1997; Greenleaf & Lanza-Kaduce, 1995; McLaughlin, 1992). These studies indicate that police use of force is a complex issue, frequently revolving around the changing situational dynamics of the arrest environment, and is rare in occurrence, given the number of citizen and police contacts and the number of arrests that are made annually. It is also recognized that continuing research on the situational dynamics of police-citizen encounters is needed to further improve our understanding of the police use of force (Mastrofski & Parks, 1990; Ross, 1999; Alpert & Dunham, 1999).

The Violent Crime Control and Law Enforcement Act of 1994 (VCCLEA) illustrates congressional concern about allegations of police use of excessive force. Part of the Act (§ 14141) authorizes the Civil Rights Division of the Department of Justice to initiate civil actions against police agencies when, among other conduct, their use of force reaches a level constituting a pattern or practice of depriving individuals of their constitutional rights. Since 1999 the Department of Justice has performed 49 investigations of police departments. As a result of these investigations, seven police departments have entered into consent decrees, which stipulate federal intervention for five years. Memorandums of agreements have been entered into with six agencies and the DOJ is currently conducting investigations of nine police departments (DOJ, 2011).

The Department of Justice has been researching contacts between the police and citizens since 1996 after the passage of the VCCLEA. Citizens age 16 and older have been surveyed and about half of the survey addresses police contact that results in the police threatening or using varying force measures. Table 10.1 displays comparisons of survey results for the years 2002, 2005, and 2008 in which force was threatened or used by the police during the contact (Durose, Schmitt & Langan, 2005, 2007; Eith & Durose, 2011).

Over the reporting period about 43 million contacts occurred on average between the police and citizens and in 1.5 percent of the contacts force was threatened or used by the police. Contacts where the police used or threatened force decreased by 14 percent from 2002 to 2008. While citizens believed that the contact was legitimate, about 78 percent believed the force

Table 10.1 Force Used in Police Contacts with Citizens: 2002, 2005, 2008

Component	2002	2005	2008
Total contacts	45.3 mil	43.5 mil	40 mil
Citizen felt contact legitimate	84%	80%	81%
Threatened/used force by officer	664,500 (1.5%)	707,520 (1.6%)	574,000 (1.4%)
Traffic related	50%	48%	59%
Reported crime to police	26%	20%	21%
Suspicious behavior	18%	24%	20%
Investigate crime	18%	21%	19%
White citizen	56%	53%	54%
Black citizen	26%	28%	28%
Hispanic citizen	15%	13%	13%
Other citizen	3%	6%	5%
Male	78%	77%	75%
Average age of citizen	28	27	28
Curse, insult/verbal threat to officer	23%	22%	22%
Disobeyed the officer	34%	14%	15%
Attempt to elude officer	4%	5%	4%
Resist handcuffing	6%	5%	6%
Active resistance	24%	—	26%
Pushed/grabbed by officer	42%	55%	60%
Struck by officer	8%	9%	17%
Gun pointed by officer	19%	15%	26%
Aerosol used by officer	5%	3%	6%
Conducted Energy Device applied	—	5%	8%
Handcuffed	30%	41%	54%
Arrested	38%	30%	40%
Citizen believed force excessive	75%	83%	74%
Injury sustained to citizen	14%	15%	19%
Citizen filed complaint/lawsuit	19%	13%	14%

used by the police was excessive, even though about 15 percent on average filed a complaint or lawsuit. A significant number of the contacts emerged from incidents involving the following: traffic related, reporting a crime to the police, responding to suspicious person/behaviors, and investigating a crime. During the contact police encountered the following types of resistance: verbal insults, cursing, and threats; noncompliance to officer commands; attempts to elude the officer; active resistance; and resistance during handcuffing. While not shown in Table 10.1, the behavior of citizens reported in about 25 percent of the contacts provoked a force response from the police. Over 50 percent of the use of force contacts were against a white citizen with an average age of 28 for all groups.

Responding officers used empty hand control techniques in over 50 percent of the contacts. Officers used intermediate weapons in about 8 percent of the contacts and pointed their firearm at a citizen in about 20 percent. The citizen was arrested in about 42 percent of the contacts and they were handcuffed in about 36 percent. Citizens sustained an injury in about 16 percent of the contacts where force was used.

The International Association of Chiefs of Police (IACP) studied the use of force by police (2001) and reported that 564 police departments submitted incident report data regarding 45,913,161 calls for service, which included county, state, municipal, and federal agencies. These calls for service resulted in 177,215 use-of-force incidents and 8,082 citizen complaints. A baseline figure of the police use of force was 3.61 for every 10,000 dispatched calls for service. This resulted in a rate of the police using force in less than one percent. Arrests (39%) accounted for the most frequent circumstance in which force was used, followed by disturbance calls (21%), traffic stops (14%), domestic incidents (11%), drunk/disorderly calls (9%), and investigations (6%). The prevalence of excessive force was estimated by examining force incident complaints and the number sustained, equaling 0.42 percent of the time. Expressed differently, excessive force was *not* used in more than 99 percent of the incidents. Intoxication significantly influenced the use of force during traffic stops, as they reflect 46 percent of the force incidents. Male drivers were almost 10 times more likely to use multiple types of force against the officers in traffic stops, requiring officers to use physical and chemical force (52%). Subjects did not incur an injury in 60 percent of the incidents, minor injuries accounted for 38 percent, major reported injuries accounted for less than one percent and five subject deaths occurred. Officers sustained an injury in only 13 percent of the incidents, minor injuries were sustained in 12 percent, and in less than one percent of the incidents was an officer injured. Citizen complaints for the use of physical force generated the majority of complaints, followed by impact weapons, pepper spray, and firearms.

Ross (2005) performed a content analysis of 43 published police use-of-force studies in the United States from 1969 to 2003 in order to assess the trends and patterns of the studies' findings. He found that 15 studies used incident reports, 14 used surveys, 11 used field observations, and three used citizen complaints to study the police use of force. Highlights of the studies showed that the police used any force in about three percent of the arrests and excessive force was used in less than one percent of the arrests. The police primarily used any type of mechanical restraints and physical control techniques in 85 percent of the incidents, used pepper spray in about 10 percent and used multiple types of force techniques/equipment in 88 percent of the incidents. Subjects resisted the police efforts of arrest or control in 88 percent of the confrontations and used multiple types of physical and verbal resistance against the officer in 90 percent of the circumstances. The subject displayed behaviors consistent with intoxication of any substance in 65 percent and suspects used a weapon against the officer in four percent of the incidents. The police encountered resistance requiring the use of force in situations of: felony arrest (44%); traffic stop (24%); disturbance call (12%); and domestic calls (12%). The combined findings of these studies revealed that police use of force is rare, given the millions of annual citizen contacts and that the use of excessive force was estimated to be less than one percent of the incidents where force was used or threatened.

Hickman et al. (2008) performed a comparative analysis of the findings of 36 published studies regarding the nature of the police use of less-lethal force covering a period from 1980 to 2008. They also combined the use of force data from the 2002 Police-Public Contact Survey (PPCS) and the Survey of Inmates in Local Jails (SILJ) to develop estimates of the type of force used or threatened during a police and citizen contact. The researchers concluded that the police use of force is rare in citizen contacts, which reinforce prior study findings reported since the 1960s (1 to 2%). The likelihood that police will use any force increases to 20 percent during the course of effecting an arrest. Correlates of the use of less-lethal force involve gender, age, race, and subject levels of resistance, which have been reported for 40 years. The primary finding of their research supported previous research that the suspect's level of resistance is the strongest predictor for determining the level of force used by the police. Attempts to escape from the officer and active levels of resistance by the suspect were the strongest factors related to the severity of the police use of force. Also, as the severity of the subject's level of resistance escalated, so did the level of the officer's use of force techniques, which led to an estimated injury potential to the suspect in about 24 percent of the incidents of arrest. The research, however, did not provide measures for estimating the police use of excessive force.

Although these studies reported that force used by the police is infrequent, use-of-force incidents have precipitated numerous civil litigation actions against the police for excessive force. Limited research has been conducted regarding the nature and trends of civil litigation relative to excessive force claims. A publication group (LRP, 1992) researched police shootings and found that plaintiffs prevailed in 63 percent of the cases and that the average award was $1,327,927. Kappeler et al. (1993, updated in 1996) conducted a content analysis of published § 1983 claims against the police from 1978 to 1994, and identified the 20 most prevalent topics of litigation filed against the police. They reported that excessive force claims ranked sixth out of 20 categories in which plaintiffs (56%) are likely to prevail in a § 1983 lawsuit. They also found that the average award in excessive force claims amounted to $178,878. Ross (2000) reported that from 1989 to 1999, claims for failing to train in nonlethal force is the most litigated topic area filed against administrators. Police prevailed in 57 percent of failure-to-train claims involving nonlethal force, and 60 percent in lethal force allegations.

Studies on Use of Force in Corrections

Physical encounters between prisoners and correctional personnel are intrinsic to the institutional environment. Working as a correctional officer can be a dangerous job, and deciding to use force is an extremely critical issue. The decision to use force in corrections has resulted in riots, disturbances, death and injury, property damage and, of course, civil liability.

Research studies specifically analyzing force used by correctional officers are virtually nonexistent. A handful of studies have examined prisoner assaults on correctional officers (Kratcoski, 1987; Light, 1991; Ross, 1996; Rowan, 1996). Camp and Camp (2003) reported that from 1994 to 2001, prisoner assaults averaged 14,000 annually against prison correctional officers and 4,000 annually against detention officers. The Department of Justice (2003) reported that prisoner assaults on officers increased more than 28 percent in prisons and 15 percent in jails from 1995 to 2001. Prior studies reveal that a majority of prisoner assaults occur while the officer is performing routine tasks, such as enforcing facility rules, breaking up fights, and supervising prisoners. These studies suggest that prisoner assaults on officers are often unprovoked and spontaneous, with prisoners losing control and lashing out at officers as the nearest symbol of authority.

Ross (1990) conducted a national examination of the status of use-of-force policies in state and federal adult institutions (41 states and Federal Bureau of Prisons). He reported that 90 percent of the respondents had a use-of-force policy that was written within three years of the survey. Hemmens and Atherton (1999) conducted a study on use of force in corrections for the American Correctional Association. They surveyed officials in state adult correctional institutions (46 states, two military prisons, and the Federal Bureau of Prisons), 30 jails, eight institutions in Canada, and 39 juvenile institutions. They reported that the American and Canadian prison systems have a written policy on the use of force, and 97 percent of the jails and juvenile institutions have written policies. All respondents were less likely (45%) to have a policy covering specialized applications of force (special response teams and use of specialized equipment and restraint techniques). More than 80 percent of the agencies allow officers to use chemical agents on prisoners in a variety of situations, and less than 45 percent allow the use of stun guns. Firearms use is authorized in more than two-thirds of U.S. correctional institutions and jails, and in only 17 percent of the Canadian institutions and 11 percent of the juvenile departments. Forty-three percent of respondents revealed that they did not sustain an "excessive force" incident in 1997. Approximately 51 percent, however, indicated they had incurred between one and 25 incidents of "excessive force," and 94 percent reported that they had disciplined the officer.

Ross (2008) conducted a use-of-force study in 15 county detention facilities for the Michigan Municipal Risk Management Authority (MMRMA). All of the agencies were insured by MMRMA and were dispersed throughout the state of Michigan, including the Upper Peninsula. He analyzed 949 use-of-force incidents between 2003 and 2005. A statistical review of the incidents where detainees resisted the officers, requiring a level of force, revealed that 40 percent of the incidents occurred in the booking area; that officers had to use force as result of performing a basic job function, such as a search, an escort, and supervising detainees; officers were three times more likely to encounter a use-of-force situation while conducting a personal search than in a self-defense situation; officers encountered a resistive detainee who was intoxicated in 32 percent of the incidents—18 percent were mentally impaired; detainees exhibited verbal and physical assault resistance more than other types of resistance, while lethal force used by detainees only accounted for five percent of the detainee assaults; in 35 percent of incidents, detainees wrestled with officers on the floor; detention officers primarily employed verbal control to dissuade detainees, but also used physical force measures more frequently than other forms of force; multiple officers generally responded to a use-of-force encounter as opposed to only one officer responding; and officers and prisoners rarely sustained injuries from these encounters.

This brief review of the use-of-force literature reveals the topic to be a paramount issue for the public and criminal justice personnel. In response, the United States Supreme Court has established guidelines for determining the components of excessive force and has established standards of review when considering allegations of excessive force (*Tennessee v. Garner*, 1985; *Whitley v. Albers*, 1986; *Graham v. Connor*, 1989; *Hudson v. McMillian*, 1992). While not easily defined, these standards outline how claims of excessive force in police work and corrections are examined. The United States Supreme Court has developed different standards for examining use of force, and the appropriate standard is based on the status of the individual. Therefore, the remaining discussion will describe how the courts specifically apply use-of-force standards in policing, in detention facilities, and in prisons.

Lower Court Use-of-Force Decisions

Claims alleging the use of excessive force by criminal justice personnel that violate the constitutional rights of an arrestee or prisoner may be filed in state court using state tort laws or in federal court under § 1983. The major distinction between the two court systems is the component of a constitutional deprivation. To be successful in a federal action, the plaintiff must prove that the officer's actions caused the deprivation of a constitutionally protected right (Kappeler, 1997). Excessive force lawsuits are filed in state court as torts for assault and battery or wrongful death. Existing tort law or statutes will govern the examination of such claims. Most claims of excessive force are filed in federal court under § 1983.

"Shocks the Conscience" Test (Fourteenth Amendment)

Prior to the United States Supreme Court's decisions on the use of force, lower courts (*Skinner v. Brooks*, 1944; *Stein v. State*, 1976; *Fobbs v. City of Los Angeles*, 1957; *Hostin v. United States*, 1983) had authorized criminal justice personnel to use reasonable and necessary force in the following circumstances: to effect an arrest and overcome unlawful resistance, in self-defense, in defense of a third party, and to prevent an individual from harming himself. Before the *Garner* (1985) and *Graham* (1989) decisions, there was considerable controversy in the lower federal courts about which doctrinal approach should be used in excessive force claims. Some courts held that excessive force claims should be viewed as deprivations of liberty without due process of law. This approach was premised upon the notion that individuals have a substantive due process right under the Fourteenth Amendment to be free from the unreasonable and unwarranted violation of their physical integrity by police officers, even in the course of an otherwise valid arrest (*Screws v. United States*, 1945; *Brazier v. Cherry*, 1961; *Monroe v. Pape*, 1961; *Johnson v. Glick*, 1973; *Shillingford v. Holmes*, 1981). For many years, a majority of courts used Judge Friendly's decision in *Johnson v. Glick* (1973), employing the "shocks the conscience" test. This "test" originated in *Rochin v. California* (1952), in which Justice Frankfurter stated that due process prohibits governmental actions that "shock the conscience." Under that formulation, the due process standard has generally been construed to incorporate subjective factors, such as the intent or motivation of the government actor. In use-of-force cases, the question usually turns on whether the type and degree of force was designed to "punish" an individual rather than to accomplish a legitimate law enforcement goal, such as maintaining or restoring control. Using Justice Frankfurter's "shocks the conscience" test, the court in *Glick* established four factors for evaluating the actions of the officer: (1) the need for the use of force; (2) the relationship between the amount of force needed and the amount that was used; (3) the severity of the injuries sustained by the plaintiff; and (4) whether force was applied in good faith or maliciously and sadistically for the purpose of causing harm.

Although the *Glick* standard originated from a use-of-force incident in a detention facility, it was applied by many courts to police and correctional situations. Uniform application of the "shocks the conscience" test was not universally accepted by the courts. The test created judicial disagreement as to what actions actually constitute significant bodily injury before the plaintiff could prevail in a § 1983 action. Some courts held that only "serious" or "severe" injuries are actionable under § 1983 (*Raley v. Fraser*, 1984; *Owens v. City of Atlanta*, 1985; *Gumz v. Morrissette*, 1985). These courts strictly applied the test, concluding that not every tort committed by a police officer violates a person's rights guaranteed by the Fourteenth Amendment. In *Raley*, a choke hold was placed on the plaintiff by a police officer four times during an encounter. His arms were bruised and his face was scraped, handcuffs on his wrists caused welts, and he suffered a sore throat and a hoarse voice for weeks following the incident. These injuries were not permanent, and although the plaintiff's resistance was minimal, the court concluded that the officer's use of "draconian measures" was not disproportionate between the officer's actions and the plaintiff's resistance. The court of appeals affirmed. In *Owens* an arrestee died from positional asphyxia as a result of being placed in a "stretch" hold position known as the "mosses crosses" in a jail cell. The court concluded that the method of restraint did not violate the decedent's constitutional rights.

Fourth Amendment Interpretation

Other courts, however, did not require a showing of a severe injury to prevail in the legal action. Some courts emphasized the second factor of the *Glick* test, using juries to determine whether the amount of force was justified given the facts (*Shillingford v. Holmes*, 1981; *Hall v. Tawney*, 1980). Moreover, during this period, other courts analyzed excessive force claims as Fourth Amendment violations if the incident resulted from an unreasonable search and seizure (*Kidd v. O'Neil*, 1985; *Gilmere v. City of Atlanta*, 1985; *Martin v. Gentile*, 1988). Judge Phillips' opinion in the *Kidd* case reveals the court's reasoning regarding principles of examining the use of force. He explained that the constitutionally protected interests that citizens have in personal security may be invaded in various contexts due to countervailing governmental interests. The issue is always what degree of force is justified by those interests in the circumstances of a particular case. The court emphasized that it is not the severity of the force used, standing alone, that is the measure of whether a constitutional violation has occurred.

Use-of-Force Standards Established by the Supreme Court

From 1985 to 1992, the United States Supreme Court developed several standards for evaluating claims of excessive force. These standards can be somewhat confusing and difficult to apply. The following case illustrates this point:

> After booking and fingerprinting an intoxicated arrestee, a police officer attempted to transport him to the county jail 20 miles away. The arrestee was handcuffed, with cuffs behind his back, and placed in the backseat of a patrol car (not seatbelted), which had a protective Plexiglas screen. Approximately five miles into the transport, the arrestee

reached through the open window of the screen, threatened to kill the officer or himself, and grabbed the steering wheel, causing an accident. The arrestee crawled through the window into the front seat and choked the officer. The officer and arrestee exited the vehicle and the arrestee continued to choke the officer. The officer attempted to use his pepper spray, but accidentally sprayed himself, disabling him considerably. A passerby stopped and assisted the officer and placed the violently resisting arrestee in a "chokehold" on two separate occasions. After the second application, the arrestee appeared to submit, but became unresponsive and subsequently died on the way to the hospital in an ambulance. The estate filed a § 1983 claim of excessive force under the Fourth Amendment. The defendant filed for summary judgment under the Fourteenth Amendment, and the court granted summary judgment to the officer.

This case (*Proffitt v. City of Pana, Illinois*, 2000) illustrates the problem of which standard of review should apply in a use-of-force situation. The arrestee was legitimately arrested, booked, and transported to jail. However, he was not formally lodged in a detention facility. Should the Fourth or Fourteenth Amendment apply? The court, granting summary judgment, applied the Fourteenth Amendment ("shocks the conscience" test), because the arrestee had been booked and fingerprinted. This type of question emerges routinely, and Table 10.2 illustrates the varying Supreme Court standards and their appropriate application. The matrix in Table 10.2 provides a brief depiction of the appropriate precedent case and the appropriate standard of review (Brave, 2011).

In order to determine the appropriate standard that applies in a claim of excessive force, the status of the individual must be distinguished. A police officer's use of force is reviewed in accordance with the Fourth Amendment, and the objective reasonableness test or standard is applied as depicted in the second column. The six criteria applied in the review are identified on the bottom of the column and the perception of the officer is also taken into consideration. The *Graham* decision is the controlling case for police officer use of force.

A person arrested and confined in a jail is referred to as a pretrial detainee and has not been convicted of the charge. Generally the person is awaiting arraignment, trial, or sentencing. Use of force in the jail setting is reviewed in accordance with the Fourteenth Amendment and the courts generally apply the four criteria listed in the third column of the matrix. As shown in the last column, convicted prisoners bring a claim of excessive force against correctional officers under the Eighth Amendment (cruel and unusual punishment). In accordance with the *Hudson* decision, courts will review claims in accordance with whether the officer's use of force was based on malicious and sadistic purposes or in good faith to restore order.

The following discussion provides an assessment of how the United States Supreme Court applies different standards to claims of excessive force.

Lethal Force

With the *Tennessee v. Garner* decision (1985), the Supreme Court provided its interpretation of the constitutional guidelines on the use of deadly force against a fleeing felon. Prior to this

Table 10.2   Use of Force Status Matrix*

Force Recipient	Free Person		Pre-Trial Detainee	Incarcerated and Convicted Person
	Seized Person—Fourth Amendment	Not Seized Person Under Fourth Amendment		
Constitutional Amendment	Fourth Amendment		Fifth Amendment—Federal Officers Fourteenth Amendment—State Officers	Eighth Amendment
Use-of-Force Standard	Objective Reasonableness Test		Due Process Clause "Shocks the Conscience" Test	Cruel and Unusual Punishment
Leading Cases	*Graham v. Conner*, 490 U.S. 386, 104 L. Ed.2 d 443, 109 S. Ct. 1865 (1989); *Tennessee v Gamer*, 471 U.S. 1, 105 S. Ct. 1694, 85 L. Ed. 2d 1 (1985); *Brower v. County of Inyo*, 489 U.S. 593, 109 S. Ct. 1378, 103 L. Ed. 2d 628 (1989); *Chew v. Gates*, 27 F.3d 1432 (9th Cir. 1994); *Saucier v. Katz*, 533 U.S. 194 (2001); *Brosseau v. Haugen*, 543 U.S. 194 (2004); *Scott v. Harris*, 127 U.S. 1769 (2007). Seizure = no freedom of movement by means applied (*Brower*)	Seizure = no freedom of movement by means applied (*Brower*)	*County of Sacramento v. Lewis*, 523 U.S. 833,118 S. Ct. 1708, 140 L. Ed.2d 1043 (1998); *Johnson v. Glick*, 481 F.2d 1028 (2d Cir. 1973), *cert denied*, 414 U.S. 1033, 94 S. Ct. 462, 38 L. Ed. 2d 324 (1973); *Bell v. Wolfish*, 441 U.S. 520, 99 S. Ct. 1861, 60 L. Ed. 2d. 447 (1979); *Rochin v. California*, 342 U.S. 165, 72 S. Ct. 205, 96 L. Ed. 2d 183 (1952). *See also Brothers v. Klevenhagen*, 28 F.3d 452 (5th Cir. 1994); *Valencia v. Wiggins*, 981 F.2d 1440 (5th Cir.), *cert denied*, 509 U.S. 905,113 S. Ct. 2998, 125 L.Ed. 2d 691 (1993).	*Hudson v. McMillian*, 503 U.S. 1, 112 S. Ct. 995, 117 L. Ed. 2d 156 (1992); *Wilson v Seiter*, 501 U.S. 294, 111 S. Ct. 2321, 115 L. Ed. 2d 271 (1991); *Whitley v. Albers*, 475 U.S. 312, 106 S. Ct. 1078. 89 L. Ed. 2d 251 (1986); *Estelle v. Gamble*, 429 U.S. 97, 97 S. Ct. 285, 50 L. Ed. 2d 251 (1976); *Hope v. Pelzer*, 536 U.S. 730 (2002); *Wilkins v. Gaddy*, 559 U.S. __ (2010).
Use-of-Force Test—Parameters	—Are the officers' actions "objectively reasonable" in light of the facts and circumstances confronting them, without regard to their underlying intent of motivation? **Totality of circumstances encountered?** —Reasonableness is determined by balancing the nature and quality of the intrusion with the countervailing governmental Interests. **Must consider officer "perception at the moment."**		*County of Sacramento v. Lewis*—A police officer does not violate substantive due process by causing death through deliberate or reckless indifference to life in a high-speed automobile chase aimed at apprehending a suspected offender. Holding-in such circumstances, "only a purpose to cause harm unrelated to the legitimate object of arrest will satisfy the element of arbitrary conduct shocking to the conscience, necessary for a due process violation."	*Whitley* held that only an "unnecessary and wanton infliction of pain" and "actions taken in bad faith and for no legitimate purpose" are a cruel and unusual punishment. *Hudson* stated that the *Whitley* standard applies in both prison-riot and non-riot contexts. *Hudson* also held that **all** excessive force claims must show malice, sadism, and intent to cause harm. *Hudson* also held the 5th Circuit's "significant injury" requirement was improper under the 8th Amendment analysis.

Table 10.2   Use of Force Status Matrix*

—Reasonableness contemplates consideration of the facts of the incident, including: **1.** Is the suspect an Immediate threat to officers and/or others? **2.** Is the suspect actively resisting seizure? **3.** Are the circumstances tense, uncertain, and/or rapidly evolving? **4.** What is the severity of the crime(s) at issue? **5.** Is the suspect attempting to evade seizure by flight? **6.** Dangerousness of flight?	*Johnson v. Glick*—four-part "shocks the conscience" test: **1.** The need for the use of force; **2.** The relationship between that need and the amount of force that was used; **3.** The extent of the injuries inflicted; and **4.** Whether the force applied was in good faith or maliciously and sadistically for the purpose of causing harm.	*Wilkins* reaffirmed the "malicious and sadistic" standard established in *Hudson*.

*Reprinted with the permission of Liability Assessment and Awareness International, Inc., Eau Claire, WI.

decision, the *Glick* standard was applied in most excessive force cases. Further, guidelines directing officers in the use of deadly force were found in state law or agency regulations. In *Garner*, the Supreme Court for the first time established a standard of review for evaluating claims of excessive force arising from deadly force incidents. This decision also initiated a separation for the evaluation of use-of-force cases in policing and in corrections, an issue lower courts had been struggling with for years.

The justification of using deadly force to prevent the escape of a suspect was first defined in *Tennessee v. Garner* (1985). Two Memphis police officers responded to a call about a prowler inside a building at 10:45 P.M. Once at the scene, the officers observed a 15-year-old burglar attempting to flee. One officer noticed the youth and believed he was unarmed, but shot him as he was scaling a fence to prevent him from escaping. The officer used deadly force in accordance with a state fleeing statute that authorized officers to use such force to prevent suspects from escaping.

The youth died and his father filed a § 1983 lawsuit for alleged violations of the Fourth, Fifth, Sixth, Eighth, and Fourteenth Amendments. The family petitioned the United States Supreme Court to review the "fleeing felon" deadly force rule. The Supreme Court held that the rule was unconstitutional and served no important governmental function. The Court held that it is not permissible to use deadly force to prevent the escape of a felony suspect under all circumstances.

Moreover, the Court maintained that "apprehension" by the use of deadly force constitutes a seizure subject to the Fourth Amendment's reasonableness requirement. Conversely, the Court stated that if an officer has "probable cause to believe that the suspect poses a threat of serious physical harm, either to the officer or to others, it is not unconstitutionally unreasonable to prevent escape by using deadly force." The police must have probable cause to believe that the suspect is dangerous.

The *Garner* decision is significant, because for the first time the U.S. Supreme Court applied the Fourth Amendment to claims of excessive force arising from a deadly force incident, not general principles of due process of law. The primary issue, therefore, in excessive force claims becomes the matter of seizure under the Fourth Amendment. A court must balance the need for the seizure against the nature and quality of the seizure to determine whether the seizure was reasonable. Obviously, not all seizures require the use of lethal force. Reasonableness depends on when a seizure is made and how it is performed. The decision in *Garner* therefore provides:

1. An officer must have probable cause to believe that the suspect poses a significant threat of death or serious injury to officers or citizens.
2. Lethal force may be warranted to prevent an escape or protect a citizen.
3. Lethal force may be used only when a felony has been committed. The felony must be dangerous, involving violence or the threat of violence.
4. A suspect is dangerous if he threatens the officer with a weapon or the officer has probable cause to believe the suspect committed an offense in which he inflicted or threatened to inflict serious physical injury.
5. When practical, an officer should give a warning prior to using lethal force.

Lethal Force Actions

Liability trends of published § 1983 lethal force case decisions have been reported in two studies. Lee and Vaughn (2010) examined 86 cases and assessed the organizational factors that may contribute to an unreasonable shooting. In the case decisions where a plaintiff prevailed on claims of defective policies and procedures and a failure to train claims (about 25%), the researchers hypothesized that a breakdown in basic management may contribute to excessive use of lethal force. Lee and Vaughn recommend that a primary concern of police administrators and supervisors should be to ensure solid managerial principles and administrative practices are implemented, which can assist in reducing the potential of an unreasonable use of force.

Ross (2012) examined 1,000 (18%) of 5,534 § 1983 lethal force case decisions published by the courts from 1989 to 2011. The police were awarded summary disposition in 84 percent of the cases. Cases proceeded to trial in 26 percent and the police prevailed in 88 percent. Appellate courts in the Second, Fourth, Sixth, Seventh, Ninth, and the Eleventh Circuits accounted for 77 percent of the decisions. Court decisions noted that officers formed the belief that the plaintiff presented an immediate threat in 65 percent of the incidents and 35 percent believed the plaintiff presented an imminent threat. While the total time of an incident may occur over several minutes to several hours, the average reaction (response) time to shoot was less than two seconds. The case decisions all involved circumstantial and environmental factors, suspect behaviors, and human factors impacting the officers' perceptions and decisionmaking to fire their weapon. The collective totality of these variables significantly assisted the court and a jury in finding in favor of the police in a high number of cases.

Many cases hinge on the issue of whether the arrestee presented an immediate or imminent threat of harm to the officer or others. Plaintiffs will most likely litigate such cases from the perspective of hindsight. This strategy ignores the fundamental holdings of both *Garner* and *Graham* in that the use of force will be judged at the moment it is required, from the perspective of the officer, and the rapidly evolving events of the situation—not from hindsight, regardless of the outcome. Moreover, the perceived danger must only be apparent, not actual, in order to justify the use of lethal force (McGuiness, 2009). The use of lethal force by police underscores these principles as the following cases illustrate.

An officer in *Fraire v. City of Arlington* (1992) shot and killed the driver of a truck he was attempting to stop for driving while impaired. When the driver attempted to run over the officer, he fired one shot into the oncoming truck. The court held that the officer acted in self-defense because the driver placed him in imminent danger, and therefore the officer had used reasonable force. The court concluded that objective reasonableness is measured by the established law at the time of the incident.

Compare, however, a similar incident with a different decision by the court in *Smith v. Cupp* (2005). An officer arrested Smith for making several harassing phone calls from a Waffle House. The officer cuffed Smith, searched him, placed him in the back seat of the patrol car, and radioed for a tow truck. The officer's patrol car did not have a protective screen separating the front and back seats. The officer left the patrol car running, along with the air conditioning. As the officer met the tow truck operator, Smith climbed into the front seat of the patrol car, put the car in gear, and rapidly accelerated the car directly at the officer. The officer fired four rounds at the car as it came at him, barely missing him. Three of the rounds hit the car and one round hit Smith in the ear. The car traveled a few yards and collided with a tree. Smith died and his family filed a § 1983 action claiming excessive force.

The district court denied summary judgment, holding that the officer's use of deadly force was constitutionally unjustified. Anticipating that the officer would file an interlocutory appeal, Smith sought certification for an immediate appeal. The Sixth Circuit Court of Appeals affirmed the lower court's decision. The court reasoned that Smith had been compliant and arrested for a non-violent offense, and although there was some danger to the public from Smith's driving off in a stolen police car, the danger was not so grave as to justify the use of deadly force. The court further concluded that no person at the scene was ever in danger. According to the court, although Smith had possession of a dangerous "weapon," he was not threatening the lives of those around him when he was fatally shot. Finally, the court held that this type of situation did not present a "perceived serious threat of physical harm to the officers or others in the area from the perspective of a reasonable officer," and such deadly force was unconstitutional. This case is instructive as it applies to the facts of this situation. The decision does not alter the factor of the "perception of the officer" in examining the choice to use a level of force, but addresses the immediacy of the need to use force in self-defense.

Determining how the courts interpret the appropriate standard in lethal force shootings can be problematic. In *Gutierrez-Rodriguez v. Cartagena* (1989), the court held that four officers acted with "reckless and callous indifference" in firing their weapons and rendering the plaintiff a paraplegic when they shot him in the back. Four undercover officers approached the plaintiff's vehicle, in which he and his girlfriend were seated. Seeing the officers, the plaintiff began to drive away and the officers opened fire on the car. The jury awarded $4.5 million in compensatory and punitive damages, which was upheld by the court, agreeing that the officers deprived the plaintiff of his protected liberty interests.

Courts acknowledge that events occur rapidly during an arrest, and decisions pertaining to the degree of force must be made quickly and often occur under adverse conditions. In *Pittman v. Nelms* (1996), two officers stopped a vehicle driven by a suspected drug dealer. The officers approached the vehicle from opposite sides, and one officer leaned into the window on the driver's side. The driver quickly accelerated the car and the officer's arm became trapped inside. The car dragged the officer 25 to 30 feet. The officer's partner fired his weapon into the back seat as the car was dragging his partner. The round hit the driver and the vehicle stopped. The driver later filed suit for excessive force, claiming that the officer should not have shot, because his partner was thrown away from the car after traveling only 10 to 15 feet, he was not seriously hurt, and the incident lasted only a few seconds. The court ruled in favor of the officers, stating that the officer was in serious danger and the situation was tense, uncertain, and rapidly evolving. The officers did not use excessive force, as a reasonable officer faced with this type of danger could have believed his decision to fire was justified. The same standard of review was applied in *Nelson v. County of Wright* (1998); *Radecki v. Barlea* (1998); *Medeiros v. Town of Dracut* (1998); and *Colston v. Barnhart* (1997). In each of these cases, the officers were under immediate assault and in imminent personal danger during the arrest. The officers discharged their firearms but only wounded the arrestee. The confrontations lasted less than three minutes, were tense, and escalated rapidly. The court held that a reasonable officer could have believed that the use of deadly force would not be excessive or in violation of clearly established law, which required an objectively reasonable response.

It appears that there are divergent court decisions regarding lethal force and when it may violate departmental policy. In both *Sigman v. Town of Chapel Hill* (1998) and *McRae v. Tena* (1996), police fired their weapons and killed an arrestee who threatened the officers with a weapon. The court determined that reasonable force must be viewed by the perception of the officer at the moment it is required, despite the language of the department policy restricting the officer's use of force. The policy is irrelevant when officers are faced with immediate danger. In both *Wallace v. Estate of Davis* (1997) and *Russo v. City of Cincinnati* (1992), officers shot and killed a mentally impaired person who was suicidal and threatened officers with weapons. The court found that the officers acted unreasonably and violated their policy on dealing with the mentally impaired. The men had not actually pointed the weapons at the officers, and the courts concluded they did not pose a serious threat to the officer.

The court also concluded that the force was unreasonable, and therefore violated department policy, when an officer held a gun to the head of a nine-year-old child, threatening to pull the trigger during the search of her home (*McDonald v. Haskins*, 1992). The child posed no threat to the officer and did not resist, attempt to flee, or assault anyone. The facts in the case stated a valid excessive force claim. Lethal force will be evaluated on the likelihood that the officer perceived a serious risk of harm to himself, based on the circumstances at the time, and force must be tailored to its necessity. The court in *Mathieu v. Imperial Toy Company* (1994) held that the officers who shot nine times at a mentally impaired man who held a toy gun used unreasonable force under the circumstances. The court opined the officers approached the man in an open area, with no available cover or backup, and allowed for no alternative but deadly force if the individual made any movement.

The Ninth Circuit Court of Appeals (*Cruz v. Escondido*, 1997) and a U.S. District Court in Kansas (*Guseman v. Martinez*, 1998) have defined the parameters of lethal force. Neither of these cases involved officers using their weapons, but in *Cruz* a police dog was deployed to restrain the plaintiff, who sustained injuries that required lengthy hospitalization and surgery. In *Guseman* the plaintiff died as a result of positional asphyxiation due to her wrists and ankles being restrained. The question for the courts in these two cases focused on how likely death must be in order for the force used to be considered deadly force. In *Cruz* the court rejected the Model Penal Code definition of force that causes or creates a substantial risk of causing death or serious bodily injury. Rather, the court interpreted both *Garner* and *Graham* to mean that a plaintiff must present evidence that the force used, in the circumstances under which it was used, posed more than a remote possibility of death. The court concluded that lethal force is force that has a reasonable probability of causing death. In *Guseman* the court concurred with the Ninth Circuit's definition of lethal force, commenting that almost any force can cause death in aberrant circumstances. Deadly force under the Fourth Amendment applies only to that force that is reasonably likely to cause death. In both cases, officers were exonerated.

Officers responded to a silent alarm at a liquor store where a mentally impaired man threatened to harm two employees with a concealed axe in *Isom v. Town of Warren, Rhode Island* (2004). The employees were able to escape from the store and informed the responding officers that the suspect had an axe in his hands. Back-up officers responded, and entered the store taking various tactical positions, and began talking with Isom. He told the officers that he was going to die today and raised the axe slightly over his head. From positions of cover, the officers continued to talk with Isom but he became non-responsive. A detective entered the store and decided to spray Isom with pepper spray so that the other officers could subdue and control him. The detective instructed Isom to drop the axe and when he did not comply he sprayed him. The spray did not affect him and Isom turned, raised the axe above his head, and charged the officers. From about 10 feet away from Isom, two officers fired their weapons. He fell to the floor and later died. The department's use-of-force policy authorized officers to use force in self-defense or defense of another, to preserve the peace, to overcome resistance, to perform searches, to prevent self-injury or suicide, and to prevent an escape from custody. The policy authorized the use of pepper spray to protect an officer or another, to subdue a person resisting arrest, or to deter persons engaged in riotous conduct.

Isom's estate filed a § 1983 lawsuit alleging that the officers used excessive force in violation of the Fourth Amendment and also filed claims of a wrongful death. The lower court granted summary judgment for the officers and the estate appealed. The appellate court affirmed the decision, ruling that the officer acted within his discretion when he decided to use the pepper spray and did not breach his duty of care. The court held that there was no evidence that the officers acted unreasonably and framed their assessment of the officers' actions within the criteria established by the United States Supreme Court in *Graham*. The court ruled that the situation was "fraught with hazard," as Isom was committing a crime, posed an immediate threat to the safety of the officers and others, and was actively resisting arrest. The claim of wrongful death also failed, as the court ruled that the officers followed the department's use-of-force policy, which gave them broad discretion when using force.

In conjunction with § 12131 of the Americans with Disabilities Act (1990) and allegations that an officer used excessive force in the shooting of a family member, in *Sudac v. Hoang* the family brought a legal action under the Fourth Amendment (2005). Sudac was diagnosed with bipolar disorder. His condition worsened and he began tearing up the house and threatened his mother and sister with a knife. Fearing that they would be killed, his mother and sister left the house, retreated to a neighbor's house, and called the police. Sudac left the house and threatened a neighbor with the knife as two officers from the Kansas City, Kansas, Police Department responded. As the officers exited their patrol vehicles, Sudac fled down an alley and the officers followed him. Sudac stopped and the officers maintained a distance of about 10 to 15 yards, drew their weapons, and asked him to drop the knife. Sudac began walking backward down the alley and the officers followed him. Sudac abruptly stopped and one officer sprayed him with pepper spray, which had no effect. Sudac continued walking backward as the officers followed and occasionally he would extend his hand with the knife at the officers. The officers had their weapons pointed at him and instructed him to stop and to drop the knife, but he ignored their requests. While Sudac was walking, the officers noticed that a couple was getting out of a car and, fearing that they would be harmed, closed the gap between themselves and Sudac to about eight feet. Sudac stopped, raised the weapon above his head and quickly lunged at one of the officers. The officer fired four rounds, killing Sudac.

Sudac's mother filed suit, claiming that the officer deprived her son of his Fourth Amendment right to be free from an excessive use of lethal force. She also claimed that the officer used force without recognizing that her son was a mentally disabled person in violation of his constitutional rights. The district court granted summary judgment to the officer, holding that the officer properly perceived that there was probable cause to believe that his life was in immediate jeopardy. The court stated that the law does not require officers to utilize "alternative, less intrusive means if their conduct is objectively reasonable," even though they did attempt other means to control Sudac. Officers may use deadly force in self-defense and it is not constitutionally unreasonable. Finally, the court ruled that under the totality of circumstances, the officer used objectively reasonable force and was entitled to summary judgment. Claims alleging that the officers violated the ADA also failed.

The issue as to whether an officer may use lethal force against an unarmed suspect was addressed in *McKinney v. Duplain* (2008). After leaving a bar, McKinney, a college student, who had been drinking, ended up at the wrong residence at 3:30 A.M., and attempted to gain entrance through the back door. Believing that McKinney was attempting to enter the house, the owner called 911, hung up during the call, and public safety officers of the college responded as they were the closest units available. The college officers had an agreement with the city police department to respond to calls for service in the communities that were near the campus. Because the caller had hung up in the middle of the call, officers had reason to believe the suspect had entered the residence.

Officer Duplain responded and observed that two other Ball State University (BSU) officers had already begun to proceed around the east side of the house and he headed around the west side to the backyard with his duty weapon unholstered. As officer Duplain entered the back-yard, he observed a subject (McKinney) about 15 feet from him standing near a tree, with his hands in his coat pockets (McKinney had not entered the residence but had banged on the door several times and yelled to be let in). Duplain gave several commands for the suspect to show his hands as he pointed his weapon at him. McKinney looked to his left and then his right, and with his hands in his coat pockets rapidly charged the officer. Duplain fired four rounds and McKinney fell to the ground and died at the scene. Duplain had only been in the backyard for several seconds before McKinney charged him and all four rounds were fired within two seconds. There was a low level of lighting available in the backyard from a porch light that cast several shadows in the yard and near the tree. McKinney did not have a weapon in his possession.

The family of McKinney filed a § 1983 claim against officer Duplain, alleging that he used excessive lethal force. Duplain filed a motion for summary judgment and the federal district court denied it. The case proceeded to trial and after a two-week trial, the jury returned a directed verdict in favor of officer Duplain. Next-door neighbors were awakened to McKinney banging on the back door and from their second-story bedroom window had a view into the backyard of the residence. They observed and testified in court that McKinney was in the backyard, that Duplain entered the backyard with his weapon drawn, heard his commands, observed McKinney charge the officer with his hands in his coat, and observed Duplain fire his weapon, shooting McKinney. The plaintiff argued that officer Duplain should not have entered the backyard but once he confronted McKinney he should have used empty-hand control techniques to control him, as he was unarmed. The defense argued that officer Duplain had to make a split-second decision about the degree of force to use, consistent with the *Graham* criteria, that the situation rapidly escalated, that the suspect had his hands in his pockets, and Duplain would not know whether McKinney was unarmed and, without warning, rapidly charged the officer. Based on the circumstances and the neighbors' testimony the jury agreed that Duplain's decision to use lethal force had been made without the luxury of time, that he would not know whether McKinney was armed or not, and such a decision to shoot was objectively reasonable regardless of whether McKinney was unarmed. The jury agreed that the officer was not required to use the least intrusive amount of force possible when the suspect was charging him and posed an immediate threat to him.

Plaintiffs have brought § 1983 excessive force claims against officers who used lethal force against a person who had either lunged at the officer while holding a cell phone or while pointing it at the officer. In *Hudspeth v. City of Shreveport* (2008), officers were involved in a vehicle pursuit with Hudspeth for about five minutes when he pulled into a convenience store parking lot. Hudspeth exited his vehicle, holding a small, silver cell phone, and walked away from responding officers. As he walked he would turn slightly and point the phone at the officers. Hudspeth tussled with one officer, who had his duty weapon drawn, and he pulled away. Hudspeth then turned slightly toward the officer, pointing the cell phone at him, and the officer fired two rounds. Hudspeth continued to walk toward the entrance of the store and rapidly turned toward the officers and pointed the cell phone at an officer with both arms outstretched, as if he was aiming a handgun. The officer crouched and Hudspeth was shot in the back as he turned away from the officers and he later died. The incident was captured on the in-car camera of one of the officers' patrol cars and was posted on the Internet.

Hudspeth's wife filed a § 1983 claim against the officers on a claim of excessive force. The court awarded summary judgment to the officers and noted that it supported the officers' perception of the incident and provided indisputable evidence of what transpired. Relying on the *Graham*, *Brosseau*, and *Garner* decisions by the United States Supreme Court, the lower district court found that the officers' actions and decision to shoot were objectively reasonable. The court ruled that Hudspeth fled from the officers in his car, resisted their efforts of arrest in the parking lot, pointed a cell phone in their direction, continued to elude them, and his actions of resistance were captured on the videotape, supporting the officers' perception of danger. The court stated that the officers had an articulable basis to believe Hudspeth was armed and could reasonably have perceived him as posing a threat of serious bodily harm, consistent with the *Garner* decision. Further, the court determined that it was irrelevant that Hudspeth was unarmed and that his back was toward the officers when they fired their weapons, explaining that events leading up to the moment force is used are what is relevant, as they set the stage for what follows.

An emerging trend associated with a number of shootings is the use of a suspect's vehicle as a deadly force instrument used against the officer justifying the use of lethal force. In *Thomas v. Durastanti* (2010), an agent of the Bureau of Alcohol Tobacco and Firearms (ATF) shot a suspect who drove his vehicle at him. The Appellate Court of the Tenth Circuit noted that a court considering the issue of summary judgment on the basis of qualified immunity must ordinarily consider disputed facts from the perspective most favorable to the plaintiff. That was not true, however, when there is clear contrary video evidence of the incident. The man who drove by the ATF agent had been an occupant of a vehicle transporting crack cocaine for a planned sale, and the confrontation, which involved ATF agents dressed in plainclothes, as well as a uniformed state trooper, occurred in a parking lot. The occupants attempted to drive off, at one point placing one of the agents in possible danger. The driver was shot in the head and the plaintiff suffered a gunshot wound to his leg. The appeals court noted that the use of lethal force is justified when an officer is threatened by a weapon, which may include a vehicle attempting to run over an officer, as occurred in this case.

The agent argued that the car was accelerating toward him and that he had no way to escape, justifying the use of lethal force. While there was a dispute about the speed of the car, this could be observed on the marked patrol car's videotape. While the plaintiff claimed that the car slowed or perhaps even stopped, the court found that this was contradicted by the video evidence. Indeed, the vehicle did strike the agent. Under these circumstances, the officer's use of lethal force was reasonable. The court rejected the plaintiff's argument that the vehicle occupants were "harmless" individuals who had merely been stopped for a routine traffic violation, since the driver engaged in an assault on the agents, narrowly missing one with his car and actually striking the other.

Similarly in *Terrell v. Smith* (2012) the court granted summary judgment to an officer who shot and killed the driver of a vehicle endangering his safety. Officers stopped a vehicle driving down a street late at night without its headlights on. Inside the car, two friends were high on crack cocaine. They exited the vehicle and were ordered to kneel down. One complied, but the other hopped back in the car and drove off. An officer managed to place himself in the open doorway of the car, as the driver attempted to make a U-turn in his direction. The officer continued to run alongside the vehicle as it moved forward, repeatedly warning the suspect to stop the car. The vehicle's door and frame struck the officer's body. After multiple warnings, the officer fired two shots, killing the driver. A federal appeals court found that the use of lethal force by the officer was reasonable under these circumstances. The driver was using his vehicle in a manner endangering the safety of the officer.

Compare however, in *Rodriguez v. Passinault* (2011), a deputy who fired 12 shots at a truck he claimed was coming toward him and his partner, killing the driver, was not entitled to qualified immunity in an excessive force and unreasonable seizure lawsuit brought by a passenger in the vehicle who was not shot. The plaintiff claimed that the driver was not moving his truck toward the officers, but toward the only exit available to him, eight feet from any officer. She claimed that the deputy continued firing shots after the truck went by him. The appeals court noted that by shooting the driver, the deputy intended to stop the car, effectively seizing everyone in the vehicle, including the passenger, who was injured when the car crashed.

Further, the courts are likely to deny summary disposition in lethal force incidents (and others) when the need to use force has subsided. For example in *Brockington v. Boykins* (2011) and *Sanchez v. Fraley* (2010), the courts determined that the use of lethal force was excessive since officers continued shooting when the suspect posed no threat. In each case, officers justifiably shot the suspect when he posed an initial threat but that continuing to shoot the suspect on the ground when the suspect was unarmed and incapacitated, several more times, was unjustified and unreasonable.

The *Graham* Decision and Objectively Reasonable Force

Objective Reasonableness Standard

With its decision in *Graham v. Connor* (1989; see Box 10.1), the United States Supreme Court put to rest the debate about how to examine claims of excessive force during an arrest. *Graham* applies only to persons at liberty. The Court established that excessive force claims arising out of arrests, investigatory stops, or other seizures of "free citizens" are properly analyzed under the Fourth Amendment's objective reasonableness standard. Deciding whether the force used in a given instance is "reasonable" under the Fourth Amendment requires a careful balancing of the nature and quality of the intrusion on the arrestee's Fourth Amendment interests against the countervailing governmental interests. The Court emphasized that the overriding function of the Fourth Amendment is to protect an individual's personal privacy and dignity against unwarranted intrusion by the state. This principle parallels the *Terry v. Ohio* (1968) decision, in which Justice Warren broadly characterized the personal security and privacy interests protected by the Fourth Amendment.

The Court held that the Fourth Amendment governs all use of force against persons at liberty, and this corresponds with its former decision in *Garner*. The Court also extended this principle beyond deadly force cases to all excessive force cases in which the person is a "free" citizen. *Graham* would suggest that the use of any significant force against an unresisting arrestee is unreasonable.

BOX 10.1 *GRAHAM V. CONNOR* (1989)

Graham, a diabetic, asked his friend Berry to drive him to a convenience store to purchase orange juice to counteract the onset of an insulin reaction. Once in the store, he observed a long line at the checkout counter, decided to put the juice container down, and ran out of the store. Graham requested that his friend drive him to another friend's house for assistance.

Officer Connor of the Charlotte, North Carolina, police department observed Graham hurriedly exiting the store and conducted an investigatory stop. During the stop, Berry informed the officer of Graham's condition, and the officer ordered Berry to wait while he performed a check and summoned backup. During the check, Graham exited the vehicle, ran around it twice, and passed out. Several officers responded, and one rolled the unconscious Graham over and secured him with handcuffs. Berry attempted to explain that Graham was experiencing an insulin reaction, but officers ignored him. One officer thought Graham was drunk and needed to be locked up, while another officer stated "ain't nothing wrong with him, I've seen a lot of diabetics that never acted like this." The officers picked Graham up and slammed him headfirst into the hood of the car. The officers shoved him into the police car, where he sustained a broken foot, cuts on his wrists, a bruised forehead, and an injured shoulder. Berry attempted to give some orange juice to Graham while in the squad car, but the officers refused to let him have it. Later, Officer Connor returned to the store and found that no crime had taken place and the officers drove Graham home.

Graham filed suit, claiming that the officers used excessive force during the arrest. Relying on the *Glick* test, officers prevailed at trial and the Fourth Circuit Court of Appeals affirmed. The Supreme Court granted certiorari and found that the lower courts had improperly applied the appropriate standard in determining the excessive force claim. The Court remanded the claim to the district court for reconsideration under the Fourth Amendment standard. The jury, using the Fourth Amendment reasonableness standard, found in favor of Graham. The officers' use of force was unreasonable, because Graham was unconscious when apprehended. This was further compounded by his medical condition, as officers failed to acknowledge warnings by Berry that Graham was experiencing an insulin reaction.

This case is significant because the Court ruled that the appropriate standard of review of excessive force claims arising from an arrest is "objective reasonableness" in accordance with the Fourth Amendment. The Court established the following factors of legal review: the severity of the crime at issue, whether the suspect is actively resisting arrest, whether the suspect is attempting to evade the arrest by flight, and whether the suspect is an immediate threat to the officer or others. The Court noted that officers are often forced to make split-second decisions regarding force and that the reasonableness of such decisions must be based on the perception of the officer and not through hindsight. Determining whether reasonable force was used will be made by courts on a case-by-case basis, in light of the facts and circumstances the officer faced at the time force was required.

Equally important, the Court stressed that the government's primary interest is in the apprehension of criminal suspects as it relates to excessive force claims. That interest is jeopardized whenever a suspect forcibly resists arrest or attempts to avoid detention by fleeing. The government is also concerned about the health and safety of police officers confronted by an armed or otherwise dangerous suspect during the course of an arrest or investigatory stop.

In *Chimel v. California* (1969), the Court stated that it is entirely reasonable for a police officer to "search the person in order to remove any weapons that the arrestee might seek to use in order to resist arrest or effect his escape." Otherwise, the officer's safety might be endangered, and the arrest itself frustrated. Moreover, the government has an interest in preventing arrestees from concealing or destroying evanescent evidence during arrest. In *Graham* the Court recognized that the right to make an arrest or investigatory stop necessarily carries with it the right to use some degree of physical coercion or threat to effect it. The Court's deference to varying degrees of physical coercive police conduct derives from and comports with the common law tort principle that police officers are privileged in making forcible arrests.

The Court established several criteria with which to evaluate excessive force claims. Noting that there is no precise or mechanical application possible for this test of reasonableness, the Court requires that careful attention be paid to the facts and circumstances of each case, including the severity of the crime at issue, whether the suspect poses an immediate threat to the safety of the officers or others, and whether the suspect is actively resisting arrest or attempting to evade arrest by flight. The Court emphasized that reasonableness must be judged from the perspective of a reasonable officer on the scene, not hindsight, and should take into account the fact that police officers are often forced to make split-second decisions about the degree of force to use in a particular situation. The Court also noted that an assessment of an excessive force claim will be judged on the totality of circumstances. The Court endorses a "reasonableness at the moment" standard that requires fact finders, when assessing the reasonableness of a particular seizure, to take into account the unpredictable and rapidly evolving dynamics of the arrest environment. The question in each case is whether the officers' actions are objectively reasonable in light of the facts and circumstances confronting them, without regard to their underlying intent or motivation (Klotter, 1999).

For example, in *Smith v. Freland* (1992), a police officer acted reasonably when he shot and killed a motorist who had fled from him at speeds in excess of 90 miles per hour when the officer reasonably believed he was in imminent danger or citizens were imminent danger. The motorist attempted to run the officer down and went through a roadblock. When the officer had him cornered in a cul-de-sac, he turned around on a lawn and drove right at the officer, at which point the officer fired his duty weapon. The officer's use of deadly force was measured against the facts at the time the force was used, as opposed to what may have been done or what was possible by way of hindsight. The court concluded that the officer fired in self-defense and prevention of the motorist's escape, as it presented a threat to others.

It therefore follows that when the crime is minor and the individual neither resists nor attempts to flee, the use of force may be constitutionally excessive, depending upon the facts of the incident. If the person peacefully submits to an arrest, only the amount of force required to secure that person in handcuffs would be appropriately reasonable. Even minimally physically intrusive police conduct may offend a person's Fourth Amendment rights when the government's interests are not justified under the circumstances. This may occur after a suspect has been subdued and is restrained and compliant, and an officer uses unnecessary physical force.

This point was illustrated in *Hogan v. Franco* (1995), in which the jury returned a verdict in favor of the plaintiff for excessive force on the part of three officers. The plaintiff was arrested after resisting the confiscation of alcohol at a public fireworks display. After he was hand-cuffed, an officer threw him against a fence so forcefully that the handcuffs tightened around his wrists. During transport to the station in a police van, the officer drove in a reckless manner, causing the arrestee to be thrown about. At the station, an officer beat the restrained arrestee with a baton before placing him, injured, in a holding cell. The plaintiff requested medical attention but was denied, and an unidentified officer struck him with a baton. The next day, the plaintiff was taken to the emergency room at the local hospital and was treated for lacerations of the leg and severe bruising of the head and chest from the baton strikes. He also sustained severe nerve damage to his wrist and lower back from being handcuffed.

The court concluded that the actions of the arrestee were nonviolent and the arrest was for an ordinance violation (open container), not a misdemeanor. The plaintiff was not a threat to any officer, no officer was ever in danger, and he was not a flight risk. Because there was no reasonable explanation for his injuries, the officers were held liable. The plaintiff was awarded compensatory damages amounting to $200,000.

Application of *Graham*

Ross (2002) conducted a 10-year study of the lower court's application of the *Graham* standard. Using a content analysis methodology, he took a random sample of 1,200 cases from 4,800 published § 1983 cases (25%) from 1989 to 1999. These cases represent legal actions litigated in court claiming excessive force on the part of law enforcement officers. Four force categories and prevailing trends emerged from the analysis: (1) the use of empty-hand control techniques accounted for 36 percent of the cases (including wrist locks, pressure points, control holds, takedown techniques, and neck restraints) with officers prevailing in 65 percent of the actions; (2) the use of mechanical restraints accounted for 27 of the cases and officers prevailed in 68 percent of the claims; (3) lethal force actions represented 18 percent and officers won 80 percent of the time; (4) use-of-equipment claims accounted for 19 percent; and (5) officers prevailed in 83 percent of the lawsuits.

While the study reveals that officers prevail on average in slightly more than 70 percent of the claims that are litigated in court, there is a divergent perspective of how the lower courts apply the standard of "objective reasonableness." Generally, the majority of the lower courts interpret objectively reasonable force based on the manner of the officer's intrusion, the scope of the intrusion, the need to perform official duties, justification of the intrusion, facts and circumstances of each situation, and the degree of resistance the officer encountered, including the threat and/or the use of weapons. The lawfulness of the officer's decision to use force will turn on the facts and circumstances known to the officer at the time the force was used. What was determined or discovered after the force was used cannot be used to justify the use of force and would not normally be admissible evidence. This trend is underscored by the generally held principle known as the "one plus one theory" of control in which, generally, officers may use one level of force higher than the level of resistance they encounter (Silver, 2005). The officer's use of force does not have to be the least intrusive amount available. Courts have permitted the police to use somewhat greater amounts of force that inflicted or threatened to effect an arrest, because such force may be required to subdue the assailant.

Other courts, however, have attached additional criteria in assessing claims of excessive force by requiring a plaintiff to prove that he sustained: (1) a significant injury that (2) resulted directly and only from a use of force that was clearly excessive and (3) the excessiveness was objectively unreasonable. The injury must be significant—minor harms and transient distress do not constitute significant injuries. The fact that the force may have been excessive does not allow recovery for injuries that would have occurred absent the excessive nature of the force. A few courts, in contradiction of the *Graham* standard, have added that the injury sustained from the use of force must be severe and that the officer's actions were initiated with "malicious intent" (*Ortega v. Schram*, 1991).

Although the decision in *Graham* established the standard by which to review claims of excessive force arising out of arrests, a lack of uniform application of the standard exists within the courts. In this section, several use-of-force topics are discussed, illustrating how the courts have applied the objective reasonableness standard.

Restraint Equipment Claims

The common law has recognized, and the *Graham* case emphasized, that an officer need not retreat when confronted with resistance to a lawful arrest. Police officers are entitled to use "objectively reasonable" force to overcome resistance in effecting an arrest. Applying the reasonableness standard to use-of-force situations, however, can be problematic and is open to interpretation.

Although the Supreme Court held in *Graham* that a "severe" injury resulting from an application of force was not an element required in determining reasonable force, the Fifth Circuit Court of Appeals has created a seemingly hybrid standard by combining components of the Fourth and the Fourteenth Amendments. In *Johnson v. Morel* (1989), the court, sitting en banc, held that in order to prevail on an excessive force claim under § 1983, a plaintiff must prove that he sustained a significant injury, which resulted from force disproportionate to the need, and the excessiveness of which was objectively unreasonable. Johnson (an African-American) was driving across a bridge with other African-American passengers when his car stalled. A police officer happened by and began pushing the stalled vehicle with his squad car while shouting racial epithets. On the other side of the bridge, Johnson complied with an investigatory stop and exited his vehicle. The officer continued shouting at him and, after a check, discovered that Johnson's driver's license had expired. The officer arrested Johnson and handcuffed him so tightly that it caused severe lacerations on his wrists and left permanent scars. Johnson filed a § 1983 lawsuit and the district court found in favor of the officer. Johnson appealed and the appellate court concluded that an officer's use of excessive force does not give constitutional import to minor harms. The Fifth Circuit held that a jury must determine whether Johnson's injuries were constitutionally significant.

The Fifth Circuit Court of Appeals dismissed an excessive force claim against a deputy sheriff in *Wisniewski v. Kennard* (1990) on the grounds that the plaintiff had not sustained "significant injuries" during the arrest. The plaintiff had escaped custody while being transported to jail. Once the deputy found him, he handcuffed his wrists tightly, stuck his duty weapon in his mouth, threatened to blow his head off, and punched him three times in the stomach. The district court found in favor of the deputy, and the Fifth Circuit affirmed, concluding that the injuries were not significant. However, in *McCrory v. New Orleans* (1990), a district court found in favor of the plaintiff when an officer handcuffed his wrists, fracturing his hand. The officer had arrested the plaintiff for intoxication and for disturbing the peace. The plaintiff was uncooperative and attempted to pull his arm away during handcuffing. As a result, the plaintiff sustained a fractured hand and filed a lawsuit claiming that excessive force was used. The court found in favor of the plaintiff, but also stated that he contributed to his own injury in resisting being handcuffed.

Not all courts have followed the Fifth Circuit's interpretation of significant injury in handcuffing cases. The Second Circuit, underscoring *Graham*, held in *Calamia v. City of New York* (1989) that excessive force claims arising out of an arrest should be heard by a jury according to the Fourth Amendment standard. The plaintiff had been handcuffed during arrest, but no permanent injury was sustained. The plaintiff contended that the officer placed the handcuffs on too tightly and forced him to sit in an uncomfortable position for several hours. The court made no mention of a threshold of injury requirement. Similarly, in *DeGraff v. District of Columbia* (1997), *Bond v. Queen* (1999), *Trout v. Frega* (1996), *Smith v. Mattox* (1997), and *Taft v. Vine* (1995), the courts concluded that the use of handcuffs was reasonable, given that a valid arrest was made and that officers followed proper procedures during their application. There was no standard of a significant injury considered by the courts, despite the claim that officers fractured the plaintiff's wrist in *Trout*, and that an officer handcuffed a female plaintiff to a mailbox for a short period in *DeGraff*. The standard applied in these cases was that of objective reasonableness in accordance with *Graham*.

In *Carter v. City of Wyoming* (2007), officers responded to a jewelry store regarding a possible theft by a female shopper. An officer responded to the store and placed Carter under arrest (it was later acknowledged that the officer arrested the wrong person). The officer grabbed Carter's arm and forcibly pulled her hands behind her back and placed the handcuffs on her wrists extremely tightly. Carter claimed that she began screaming in pain. She also claimed that the officer did not loosen the tightness of the cuffs, but slammed her into the patrol car trunk, further injuring her shoulder from a recent surgery. She was transported to the jail.

Carter filed a lawsuit alleging that the officer used excessive force. She also presented a medical report that showed that her hands were injured from the use of the handcuffs and that her shoulder was also re-injured from the officer pushing her down onto the trunk. The court denied the officer's motion for summary judgment. The court held that the officer used excessive force when he grabbed Carter's arm and shoved her into the patrol car secured in handcuffs. The court reasoned that Carter did not pose an immediate safety threat to the officer, the public, nor did she actively resist arrest. The court found that rather than check the tightness of the handcuffs, the officer ignored her complaints of pain by shoving her into the car, rising to a constitutional rights violation.

Empty-Hand Control Techniques

Police officers frequently must resort to an empty-hand control technique to control a resisting arrestee. These techniques may include joint locks, takedown techniques, control holds, pressure points, hand/leg strikes, and neck restraints. Claims in this category are filed more frequently because of their more common use during arrest.

The Ninth Circuit, in contrast to the Fifth Circuit, has maintained a framework of excessive force claims review by considering the totality of circumstances. In *Forrester v. City of San Diego* (1994), approximately 100 sit-in demonstrators refused to comply with verbal commands by officers to move as they were trespassing and blocking an entrance to a medical building. Demonstrators ignored warnings from the police that they would use pain compliance techniques to move them. The officers administered pain compliance to the wrists and arms of the demonstrators and moved them out of the way of the building. Complaints of injuries were asserted by the demonstrators, including bruising, pinched nerves, and one broken wrist. Several of the demonstrators filed suit, lost in district court, appealed, and the appellate court affirmed. The Ninth Circuit Court of Appeals concluded that police officers are not required to use the least intrusive degree of force possible. Rather, the question is whether the force used was reasonable in effecting a particular seizure. The court found that the officers' application of pain compliance techniques was not excessive.

Other circuits appear to follow this same line of analysis. In *Wallace v. City of Shelby* (1997), a federal district court determined that the use of a leg sweep to control a resisting arrestee during handcuffing was reasonable force. The plaintiff repeatedly refused to place her hands behind her back during an arrest for domestic violence. After the plaintiff disobeyed several verbal instructions by the officer to cooperate, the officer used an authorized leg sweep, which caused him to lose his footing on the ice, and he and the arrestee fell to the ground. The plaintiff's face was injured and she filed suit. The court reviewed the circumstances and ruled that the officer did not violate the plaintiff's rights. The facts supported the case, and the court held that the officer's motive in applying force was irrelevant. The Fourth Circuit Court of Appeals in *Hart v. Rogers* (1998) held that the use of a bear hug to control a resisting and intoxicated arrestee did not violate his constitutional rights, despite a minor head injury. As the officer was attempting to place the plaintiff in the patrol car, he pushed the officer and began to run from the officer. Being intoxicated, he stumbled and the officer placed his arms around his upper torso. The plaintiff resisted and they fell to the ground, slightly injuring the plaintiff's head. A lawsuit was filed and the lower court found in favor of the officer. The appellate court affirmed. The appellate court held that the officer encountered a larger, intoxicated, resisting citizen, who shoved the officer and was attempting to flee. In light of the circumstances, wrapping his arms around the plaintiff and taking him to the ground was objectively reasonable.

In *Mahone v. Palazzo* (1999), the court ruled that the use of a wristlock was reasonable despite the fact that the resisting plaintiff suffered a fractured wrist. It was unclear whether the officer injured the wrist during controlling the plaintiff prior to handcuffing or whether the plaintiff injured it earlier during a fight with his wife when he had struck her in the face. The court reasoned that using a wristlock was necessary to remove the plaintiff from a residence, and had he not attempted to pull away from the officer during arrest, the officer would not have applied it. Likewise, in *Smith v. Mattox* (1997), the Eleventh Circuit Court of Appeals affirmed the use of an armlock in the course of effecting an arrest after the plaintiff had threatened the officer with a baseball bat. When confronted by the plaintiff with the bat, the officer ordered him at gunpoint to drop it. He complied, ran from the officer, and after a short time fell prone to the ground as instructed. The officer knelt on the plaintiff's lower back to handcuff him. The plaintiff resisted as the officer brought his hand back for handcuffing, and in so doing the plaintiff's arm was broken. The court concluded that the officer's use of force was reasonable because the arrestee had moments earlier posed a threat of safety to the officer by threatening him with a bat and attempting to flee.

The Tenth Circuit Court of Appeals, however, ruled in *Paul v. The City of Altus* (1998) that placing an officer's knee on the neck of a prone arrestee during handcuffing could be considered excessive force. The plaintiff was not resisting, and the officer had been trained not to place his knee on the neck during handcuffing. The court found in favor of the plaintiff because the officer was "deliberately indifferent" to the safety of citizens. Similarly, in *Matasic v. City of Campbell* (1997), the Sixth Circuit Court of Appeals ruled that an allegation of placing a foot on the plaintiff's neck was not excessive. Officers attempted to stop the plaintiff's vehicle because they thought he was stealing a car. The plaintiff attempted to elude the officers and a pursuit took place. Once the plaintiff stopped, the officers wrestled him to the ground and handcuffed him. The plaintiff sustained a one-centimeter laceration and some abrasions. The court concluded that the force used by the officers was reasonable because the officers thought they faced a dangerous fleeing felon.

Compare, however, the court's ruling *in Garcia v. City of Chicago* (2003). While waiting to pick up his cousin at his uncle's restaurant, Garcia noticed an officer drive by who had gang affiliations. The officer had threatened to beat him up over a photo that showed the officer flashing gang signs. The police department had a strict prohibition against officers affiliating with gangs. Two other officers joined the first officer and demanded that Garcia turn over the picture. Garcia attempted to move away from the officers but they pushed him on the ground. The officers punched and kicked him numerous times, head butted him, and slapped him in the face. Garcia sustained a broken nose, which caused disfigurement, and incurred a tumor on his hip where he was kicked.

Garcia filed a lawsuit against the officers for excessive force. He also alleged that the city had a custom and practice of not adequately investigating, disciplining, or prosecuting misconduct by officers. At trial, Garcia produced 72 citizen complaints about police misconduct between 1999 and 2001. According to Garcia, these complaints supported his allegation of a pattern and practice. The jury awarded Garcia $1 million in compensatory damages and the city appealed. The court decided to lower the award to $250,000. The court agreed that the attack was brutal and was borne out of "passion and prejudice."

In *Feldman v. Community College of Allegheny* (2004), the court agreed with arresting officers that they appropriately used a straight-armbar takedown technique. A student at the college had an ongoing dispute with a computer lab instructor and refused to leave the lab. The instructor called security, who in turn summoned the police to remove him. Two officers responded and directed the student to leave, but he refused and actively resisted their efforts of control. The student claimed that the officers wrestled him to the ground and kicked him in the head. The officer's account was that one officer used a trained straight-armbar technique and took him to the ground because he refused to leave and resisted their efforts of control.

The student sued the college, the officers, and the city police department, alleging false arrest and excessive force. The arrest charges were dropped. The court granted summary judgment and the student appealed. The Third Circuit Court of Appeals affirmed the lower court's decision, agreeing that the officers used objectively reasonable force. The court agreed that the student needed to be controlled before being placed in handcuffs and that the technique used was proportionate to the resistance confronted.

In an objectively reasonable use-of-force incident, an allegation that the officer caused an injury to the suspect will fail as the *Graham* standard addresses reasonable force and not whether an injury resulted. But if an officer is disciplined for using excessive force, will such administrative sanction be used to determine liability later in court? In *Dunn v. Mattatall and Porter* (2007), Dunn failed to stop his vehicle and led officer Mattatall on a high-speed pursuit through residential areas at speeds over 50 miles per hour at 2:30 A.M. Dunn ran through three stop signs, two red lights, and for about a mile drove his vehicle in the opposite direction of oncoming traffic. Officer Mattatall activated his overhead lights and siren and radioed for back-up. After about a five-mile pursuit, Dunn stopped his vehicle. From his vehicle Mattatall instructed Dunn to roll down the driver's side window, to throw the keys onto the payment, and to keep his hands outside the window. With his duty weapon drawn and flashlight in the other hand, Mattatall approached Dunn's vehicle, briefly examined the vehicle as he approached the driver's side door, and holstered his weapon. The incident was videotaped from Mattatall's patrol car.

Mattatall opened the driver's side door and instructed Dunn to exit the vehicle. Mattatall held onto Dunn's wrist to remove him from the car and officer Porter arrived. Dunn began to struggle with Mattatall and shouted that the seatbelt was preventing him from exiting. Porter, with his weapon pointed at Dunn, ordered him to come out of the car, to which Dunn replied that he was trying, and finally the seatbelt was unbuckled. Porter holstered his weapon and the officers pulled Dunn from the vehicle. Due to Dunn's resistance, Mattatall and Porter lost their grip and Dunn pulled free. Dunn twisted and spun on his left foot, lost his balance, and fell hard on his right side on the payment. Officers handcuffed Dunn and he began complaining that he was a sick man and that the officers broke his hip and ankle. The officers summoned an ambulance and he was treated at the scene and then transported to the hospital where he was treated for a fractured femur. Dunn filed a § 1983 claim against the officers for excessive force in violation of his Fourth Amendment rights.

The department conducted an investigation into the incident, reviewed the video, and interviewed the officers. Based on the findings of the investigation, the chief disciplined officer Mattatall. The court, however, granted summary judgment on the legal action, finding that the use of force was objectively reasonable. The judge commented that the touchstone of any excessive force allegation is the reasonableness of the officers' actions and the question before the court is whether the officers' actions are objectively reasonable in light of the facts and circumstances, without regard to their underlying intent or motivation. The judge disagreed with the plaintiff's claim that the officers' conduct amounted to gratuitous force. Rather, the court determined that the video clearly showed that Dunn posed a threat to the community while fleeing from the officers. Further, the court ruled that Dunn did struggle and resisted being taken from the car by the officers, and the level of force that was used to force him to the ground caused his injury. Nonetheless, the court determined that the officers used reasonable force under the circumstances. The force applied was not gratuitous, punitive, or disproportionate, given the situation facing the officers. According to the court, to find otherwise would be second-guessing the officers who are required to act. Thus, such actions of the officers failed to deprive Dunn of his constitutional rights.

Perhaps one of the most controversial empty-hand control techniques used by police officers is the neck restraint. Improper application of the technique has led to several deaths. Conversely, proper application has assisted in controlling violent suspects and reduced the need for the officer to use lethal force. A policy of using neck restraints was the subject of concern for the United States Supreme Court in *Los Angeles v. Lyons* (1983). During a traffic stop the plaintiff had been rendered unconscious as a result of a police "choke hold." He did not offer resistance. He sued for an injunction regarding the practice of using the neck restraint, because the hold had been used in similar situations and 15 deaths had occurred. The Court refused to issue an injunction, because Lyons could not prove that he would be subject to such a hold in the future.

The Fifth Circuit Court of Appeals concluded that an officer allegedly grabbing an arrestee around his throat on two separate occasions during an arrest, for suspicion of having cocaine in his mouth, failed to show evidence of an injury (*Williams v. Bramer*, 1999). The court concluded that a physical confrontation inevitably occurred when an officer searched the detainee. The plaintiff's alleged injuries of fleeting dizziness and temporary loss of breath and coughing were not cognizable injuries rising to the level of a constitutional violation.

In two neck-restraint cases decided in the Tenth Circuit, the courts found in favor of the plaintiffs (*DeCorte v. Robinson*, 1998; *Franklin v. City of Kansas City, Kansas*, 1997). The courts agreed that the officers' use of the "carotid hold" was unreasonable in light of the minimal resistance encountered during arrest. The Ninth Circuit, however, in *Nova v. City of Dublin* (1997), declined to order an injunction prohibiting the use of the neck restraint, which would force the police department to revise its policy on using neck restraints. In *Mosier v. Robinson* (1989), the court also concluded that using a choke hold on a restrained, intoxicated arrestee at the police station was excessive and unreasonable.

In *Coburn v. Benton Township et al.* (2005), a federal district court of Michigan examined whether officers used excessive force when they applied a vascular neck restraint on an actively resisting person during arrest. Officers attempted to serve an arrest warrant on Griffith and met resistance. Griffith had exhibited bizarre behavior at home, had a history of mental impairment, and his mother requested that the police take him into custody. At the house the officers met resistance as they attempted to take control of Griffith. He lunged off of a couch at the officers and struggled with them. During the struggle Griffith managed to unsnap one of the officer's safety snaps on his holster and began to pry on it. The officer placed him in a lateral vascular neck restraint for about two to three seconds and they fell to the floor. Griffith became unresponsive and resuscitation efforts by emergency medical personnel on scene failed to revive him.

The family filed a § 1983 lawsuit against the officers for excessive force. They also filed a claim against the chief of police for being deliberately indifferent to the training needs of the officers who used the neck restraint. The court granted summary judgment on behalf of the officers, finding that the neck restraint was not excessive force. The court agreed that the officers are permitted to use a degree of force in effecting the arrest of an individual who is actively resisting arrest. The court determined that there was evidence to show that Griffith reached for the officer's weapon during the struggle. Such behavior, the court ruled, posed a threat of serious physical harm to the officer and to others, and his actions accordingly justified the use of deadly force. If the officer was justified in using deadly force, then he could certainly use the neck restraint, which the court ruled was not deadly force. Finally, the court held that the use of the vascular neck restraint under the circumstances was not objectively unreasonable. Accordingly, the defendants were entitled to qualified immunity, thereby dismissing the excessive force claim.

In *Chapman v. Martinez* (2008), the plaintiff brought a § 1983 claim against three officers of the Omaha, Nebraska, police department, alleging excessive force that resulted from the application of Lateral Vascular Neck Restraint (LVNR). The arresting officer brought Chapman to the police department after an arrest and during a Breathalyzer test he became assaultive and struck an officer in the face. Other officers responded to subdue him, including detention supervisor Morris who applied the LVNR (the incident was videotaped). Chapman was not rendered unconscious, but the technique assisted in controlling him and he was placed on the floor, handcuffed, and escorted to a holding cell. Once in the holding cell Chapman became combative, kicking the officers as they began removing the handcuffs, and pressure point applications (infra-orbital and mandibular angle) were applied. The officers were able to control him, removed the handcuffs, and exited the cell. Chapman did not sustain observable injuries but was offered the opportunity to be examined by medical staff. He refused on three occasions. Chapman was charged with assaulting an officer and released on his own recognizance the next day. After his release Chapman visited the hospital and was instructed to take medication for sore muscles.

Chapman filed a lawsuit alleging that officers used excessive force, maliciously assaulted him through the application of the LVNR and the pressure points, and denied him medical attention. The case proceeded to trial. The federal district court applied the Fourth Amendment to the allegations, even though Mr. Chapman was held at the detention area of the police department. The court reasoned that Mr. Chapman had not been completely booked into or turned over to the custody of the detention officers at the time that he assaulted the officer in the Breathalyzer room and applied the *Graham* standard. After a week trial the jury returned a no cause verdict on behalf of the officers. The plaintiff argued that the application of the LVNR amounted to lethal force and that the officers sexually assaulted Mr. Chapman in the holding cell. He also argued that he was denied medical attention although he could not document in court that he sustained a treatable injury. He claimed that he was denied medical assistance. The jury rejected the plaintiff's arguments and determined that based on his assault of the officer, the application of the LVNR without rendering him unconscious and using pressure points in the holding cell were objectively reasonable.

In *Harris v. City of Circleville* (2009), arresting officers were in the process of admitting the arrestee into the jail. During booking, one of the officers grabbed the arrestee, pulled on the arrestee's necklace, kicked his leg out from under him, and used a takedown technique to ground him. On the ground the officer kicked the arrestee in the ribs, fracturing several of them. The arrestee sustained several injuries and medical care was delayed because of his African-American race. The arrestee filed suit and the lower court rejected summary judgment and the appellate court affirmed the decision. The court determined that the arrestee was not offering resistance and the officer's unprovoked use of force was excessive and unreasonable.

Graham Applied to High-Speed Pursuits

The United States Supreme Court applied the *Graham* holding to police pursuits in *Scott v. Harris* (2007). The Court held that an officer's use of the Precision Intervention Technique (PIT) to ram a fleeing suspect's vehicle and thereby rendered the driver quadriplegic was objectively reasonable under the circumstances. Deputy Scott attempted to stop Harris, who was driving recklessly at speeds over 100 miles per hour in an attempt to elude him. Scott obtained authorization from his supervisor to apply the PIT maneuver and bumped the back of his car, causing it to crash into a ditch, leaving Harris a quadriplegic. Harris filed a civil action claiming that Scott used excessive force by using lethal force contrary to the decision in *Tennessee v. Garner* (1985). The appellate court affirmed the lower court's decision to reject qualified immunity and Scott appealed to the United States Supreme Court.

The Court granted certiorari and in an 8-to-1 vote reversed the appellate court's decision. Harris argued that Scott had used lethal force contrary to the *Garner* decision, theorizing that the actions of Scott constituted deadly force. Moreover, Harris argued that Scott did not possess probable cause to believe he presented an immediate threat of serious physical harm to the officer or others and that Scott failed to first provide him a warning. Scott did activate his overhead lights and siren.

A videotape captured the pursuit and, after viewing it, the Court rejected Harris's argument and granted qualified immunity to officer Scott. The majority noted that Harris created the risk of imminent threat to himself, the public, and the officers by driving recklessly. The videotape convincingly showed the dangerousness of Harris's eluding conduct as he crossed the center line numerous times and failed to stop, placing innocent passing motorists and officers at risk. The Court found such active eluding behaviors compelling evidence that Harris posed a serious risk of harm to others.

For the Court, all that mattered was whether Scott's actions were reasonable. Endorsing the objective reasonableness standard established in *Graham*, the Court focused on Scott's actions in relation to the risk of harm and danger posed by Harris's actions and distinguished a car chase from an unarmed foot pursuit, commenting that car chases are much more dangerous. Based on Harris's dangerous behaviors, the Court applied the *Graham* criteria to the rapidly evolving circumstances and determined that Scott's actions were constitutionally justified.

In assessing Scott's actions as objectively reasonable, the Court has added a new component criterion in assessing the use of reasonable force, that being "dangerousness of flight." The danger that flight poses cannot be mechanically measured because each case is different. The police cannot mechanically calculate the degree of risk that a suspect will take or the degree of harm that a suspect will invoke to elude capture. A person deciding to flee forecasts to police the likelihood of dangerousness and uncertain conduct presenting a threat of danger to the police and innocent bystanders. Indeed, fleeing in a vehicle becomes a lethal weapon increasing the risk of serious injury or death to innocent bystanders and the police. Framed within the *Graham* criteria, the type of force Scott used was appropriate and reasonable. Had Scott not taken reasonable measures to terminate the pursuit, innocent people might have been harmed.

Police Equipment

In an attempt to minimize the need for police to use lethal force, various types of equipment have been developed to help officers effect arrests. These types of weapons can include impact weapons, flashlights, and aerosol sprays. As officers have used these instruments, claims of excessive force have emerged.

The First Circuit's decision in *Bordanaro v. McLeod* (1989) found that officers from two police departments violated citizens' constitutional rights. Six police officers beat unarmed patrons in retaliation for a fight between an off-duty officer and a guest at a bar. The officers beat the patrons with clubs, bats, a fire axe, and nightsticks. As a result, one patron died. This unconstitutional practice of excessive and abusive use of weapons resulted in an award against the municipalities of more than $5,000,000. The Ninth Circuit Court of Appeals in *Davis v. Mason County* (1991) found that sheriff's deputies used excessive force on four separate occasions during illegal arrests. Three different deputies misused their stun guns and batons, and pointed weapons at compliant citizens while conducting traffic stops. The jury award against the individual deputies was $320,000. The court ruled that the deputies' conduct was driven by evil motives or intent and that they exhibited reckless and callous disregard for the constitutional rights of the citizens.

The question of the officer's objectively reasonable use of force is usually left for the jury to decide, but must be judged in light of the information and situation facing the officer at the time the force was used. A police officer need not suffer a brutal or serious injury prior to using serious force on a citizen. The force need only be reasonable under the circumstances. In *Cotton v. Busic* (1992), the officer got into a scuffle with an arrestee who had earlier been throwing rocks at houses. During handcuffing, a second officer thought the arrestee was reaching for his partner's weapon and struck him in the head with an impact weapon, while the first officer struck him in the head with a flashlight. The arrestee sustained bumps, bruises, and lost one eye. In light of the facts, the court determined that the force was reasonable. In *Mathis v. Parks* (1990), an officer was attempting to persuade a drunk individual at a bar to leave with his brother, when an argument developed. The officer retrieved his impact weapon as the drunk individual continued to argue, and the officer then struck him in the head with the baton, causing cuts and bruises. A second officer arrived on the scene and attempted to handcuff him. He resisted and the officer kneed him with full force in the stomach. As the officers were transporting him, they noticed that he was having a heart attack, and he died prior to arriving at the hospital. The court ruled on behalf of the plaintiff, stating that although he was drunk, he was only trespassing and not physically resisting or being aggressive.

In contrast to the above court decisions, in *Carver v. Bullock* (1999), the Fourth Circuit Court of Appeals ruled in favor of an officer who struck an arrestee as he attempted to run from him after a vehicle pursuit. Once the officer caught the citizen, the citizen began kicking the officer.

The officer had his flashlight in his left hand (the encounter took place at night) and struck him one time on the head. The court concluded that the circumstances created a dangerous and tense situation and that the officer's use of force was reasonable. In *Radecki v. Barlea* (1998), the Tenth Circuit Court of Appeals used the "shocks the conscience" standard in evaluating another officer's use of his flashlight as an impact weapon. During an arrest, the arrestee attempted to grab the officer's weapon. A second officer yelled to the officer under attack to hit him with his flashlight. The officer did, causing him to release his grip on the weapon. The individual began to run from the scene, and the second officer shot and killed him. The lower court determined that the deputy's conduct did shock the conscience and found him liable for using excessive force. The deputy appealed and the appellate court reversed the verdict, finding that he did not use force that shocked the conscience, because he was confronted with an explosive emergency situation when the arrestee suddenly grabbed for his weapon.

Summary judgment was denied to officers in *Landis v. Cardoza* (2007). Officers confronted an agitated suspect off the highway in a thickly wooded area that included bogs of water. The suspect actively resisted their efforts at empty-hand control and attempted to escape from the officers. Unable to fully control the suspect, officers applied a Taser five times, struck him with an impact weapon (baton) numerous times, and held him in a position that submerged his head in water, causing him to drown. The court ruled that the unwarranted use of force precluded summary judgment. The court further determined that officers should have known that it is almost always an excessive use of force to restrain an arrestee in a manner that places his head under water for a long period of time while also striking him with baton.

Police have been using various forms of pepper spray when faced with arrestee resistance since the late 1980s. As the police have increasingly used these products, several claims citing excessive force have been filed. Most courts have ruled that the use of pepper spray is reasonable force. In *Darnell v. Carver* (1998), *Omokaro v. Whitemeyer* (1998), *Monday v. Oullette* (1997), *Sappington v. Bartee* (1999), *United States v. Holloway* (1995), and *Lester v. City of Rosedale* (1991), the courts agreed that in light of the circumstances during arrest and the degree of resistance offered by the arrestee, it was reasonable to use an aerosol in order to control the person. In *Monday*, an officer sprayed a 300-pound mentally impaired man who was refusing to be transported to the hospital for admission. No injuries were sustained and the man was controlled and handcuffed. In *Holloway*, the court determined that it was reasonable and not outrageous to spray an arrestee in order to remove crack cocaine from his mouth.

In *Omokaro* (1998), the plaintiff resisted officers' efforts to control him. He would not comply with orders of arrest and officers sprayed him. He fell to the ground, but kept kicking and thrashing. The officers used their baton for pressure on the shin and applied pressure point techniques under his jaw. When these techniques failed, one officer was able to control him by applying a lateral vascular neck restraint. His hands and legs were restrained as he attempted to kick and bite the officers. Within a matter of minutes he was observed to be unconscious, CPR was administered, and Omokaro was revived and transported to a hospital. He sued, claiming excessive force, but judgment was granted in favor of the officers. The court stated that the officers used objectively reasonable force relative to the severity of the crime at issue, the threat posed by the arrestee, and how actively he resisted arrest.

Conversely, in *Lamb v. City of Decatur* (1996) and *McCartt v. Keyes* (1999), the courts held that the use of pepper spray was unreasonable force. In *McCartt*, the arrestee had allegedly been trespassing on a private beach. During arrest, the responding officer attempted to place handcuffs on the plaintiff, and he backed away. When the officer warned that he would be sprayed, the person was still defiant. The officer sprayed and immediately restrained him with handcuffs. A lawsuit was filed claiming use of excessive force. The lower court ruled in favor of the plaintiff, and the Sixth Circuit Court of Appeals affirmed. The court concluded that the plaintiff was illegally arrested, did not display any risk of aggression, was not attempting to flee, and was not a danger to officers. In *Lamb*, the plaintiff and other demonstrators filed a class action lawsuit alleging excessive force as the police sprayed them twice to break up a "peaceful" union protest. The court ruled that using force against people who were exercising their First Amendment rights of assembly and free speech was clearly unconstitutional, and declared the force unreasonable. The court also stated that there is no value in the First Amendment if demonstrators could be dispersed or intimidated by the unnecessary use of force.

Survivors of an arrestee who died during an altercation filed a § 1983 lawsuit in *Wagner v. Bay City, Texas* (2000), claiming excessive force and deliberate indifference to medical needs. The arrestee actively resisted arrest by striking officers with his fists. The officers sprayed the arrestee with pepper spray, placed him on the ground with one shin across his back, and handcuffed him. They transported him to the jail and the arrestee was heard moaning. At the sally port (a secure jail entrance area), the officers found the arrestee to be unresponsive and summoned medical personnel, who attempted to treat him but were unsuccessful. The federal district court denied summary judgment for the officers and the appeals court reversed the decision, granting judgment for the officers. The court ruled that the officers were not deliberately indifferent to the medical needs of the arrestee, and used reasonable force to control him. The court also noted that decontamination of pepper spray could effectively be done in the jail and the officers believed the arrestee was still breathing during transport.

As indicated earlier, previous studies on police use of force show that officers use multiple types of force in about 88 percent of altercations. *Stewart v. Prince George's County* (2003) provides an example of how the courts review such cases. Employees of a Target store asked a customer, Stewart, to leave the store and not return, because he had threatened a female employee. He left but returned several times. Security called the police but they did not respond. Several hours later Stewart returned to the store and began throwing items at the cashier. An officer responded and found Stewart at a nearby store. Corroborated by a video camera, the officer walked Stewart to the store, side-by-side, to apologize to the employee and warned him not to return to the store. Within several minutes, Stewart returned to the store a third time and security summoned the same officer, who responded. Again the videotape showed the officer speaking with Stewart, who became agitated, threatened the officer, and refused to leave. A struggle ensued and the officer radioed for backup. The tape showed another officer responding and the two officers wrestled with Stewart. The second officer sprayed Stewart with pepper spray several times and struck him with his collapsible baton several times. The officers were finally able to control him and placed him in handcuffs. As they escorted him out of the store, Stewart collapsed and died en route to the hospital of cardiac arrest.

Stewart's family filed a § 1983 lawsuit against the officers, the police department, and Target. The defendants requested summary judgment and the family demanded a trial. The court agreed that a trial was necessary and the defendants appealed. The Fourth Circuit Court of Appeals concluded that the defendants were entitled to summary judgment as they had used objectively reasonable force. The court determined that the officers correctly and appropriately escalated their use of force in response to Stewart's active resistance. The court further noted that Stewart was given ample opportunity to leave the store but became defiant and actively resisted efforts of arrest. The officers had used verbal control without success; and the use of pepper spray, batons, and handcuffs was not unconstitutionally unreasonable given the totality of circumstances. The videotape also showed that the officers used force proportionately in response to Stewart's behavior.

In *Piasek v. Southfield* (2007), an officer made a traffic stop of a motorist who exceeded the posted speed limit by 30 miles per hour and was driving erratically on a busy highway. After the stop, a second officer joined the first officer and they began performing sobriety tests on the driver. The driver smelled of alcohol, failed to recite the ABCs, and failed to walk a straight line without stumbling. When asked to blow in an alcohol tube, he slapped the device from the officer's hand and attempted to run down an embankment. One officer was able to grab the driver's wrist and forearm and pushed against a patrol car. The driver went to the ground and started to crawl toward the lane of traffic. The officers were able to move him back onto the shoulder area, but had difficulty handcuffing him. One officer delivered a knee strike to the motorist's upper thigh, which was partially ineffective. The second officer sprayed one short burst of his pepper spray into the face of the motorist and this assisted in subduing him, allowing the officers to secure the handcuffs. The incident was videotaped on the officer's in-car camera. The motorist was later convicted of driving under the influence and obstructing and resisting arrest.

The motorist filed a § 1983 lawsuit claiming that the officers used excessive force by applying the pepper spray and knee strike, although he claimed no injuries. The case proceeded to a jury trial and the jury delivered a no-cause verdict. During trial the jury viewed the videotape and observed how dangerous the traffic was on the night of the arrest and the active nature of the motorist's resistance. The jury concluded that the officers had a responsibility to make the arrest safely in order to prevent the motorist from running into oncoming traffic. The jury determined that it was objectively reasonable to use empty-hand control techniques and an aerosol to effect the arrest and to gain the compliance of the resisting motorist. The jury concluded that the force used by the officers was objectively reasonable under the circumstances of the arrest environment and the resistance level demonstrated by the motorist.

Officers sometimes use canines in effecting arrests and such cases have resulted in lawsuits claiming excessive force. In *Jarrett v. Town of Yarmouth* (2003), officers engaged in a high-speed pursuit of Jarrett, who was observed to be speeding. Officers radioed for a canine officer as Jarrett crashed his vehicle and fled the area. For about 20 minutes the canine officer tracked Jarrett and spotted him in the middle of the road about 50 yards away. The officer yelled for Jarrett to stop or he would release the dog. Jarrett fled and the officer instructed his dog to locate Jarrett and hold him. The dog was trained in the "bite and hold" technique and within 30 seconds the dog found Jarrett. He bit Jarrett on the leg, held him until the officer instructed him to "release," and the dog complied. Jarrett was transported to the hospital by ambulance, treated for his injuries, received stitches, and was released from the hospital after two weeks. Jarrett was charged with two misdemeanor offenses. He filed a lawsuit claiming that the officers used excessive force by releasing the dog on him, alleging that such actions constituted deadly force.

The jury found in favor of Jarrett, awarding him $50,000 in punitive damages. The officers appealed and the appellate court reversed the verdict. The court concluded that the use of force must be assessed from the perspective of the officer on the scene. The court held that releasing the dog was not deadly force and that the "bite and hold" method was not unconstitutional. Further, the court held that the officer's decision to release the dog was objectively reasonable under the circumstances.

In *Mann v. Yarnell* (2007), officers responded to a family disturbance call. Mann's wife informed officers that her husband had assaulted her earlier that day, that he was irrational, that he had been continuously using methamphetamines for the last five days, and that he was threatening suicide. Mann shot at the responding officers and fled toward his house to escape from the officers. The officers met Mann at a fence and ordered him to go to the ground on his stomach and to place his hands behind his back. Mann failed to comply and an officer instructed his canine to engage him. The canine bit and held Mann's left calf for about 15 seconds and other officers attempted to handcuff him. Mann was able to break free, knocked the handcuffs away, and grabbed the barrel of an officer's shotgun. The officer applied a brachial stun technique to the side of Mann's neck several times until it immobilized him. Other officers were able to control him and handcuff him. Mann was transported to the hospital and his injuries were treated. Mann filed suit, claiming excessive force.

The district court ruled in favor of the officers and the appellate court affirmed. The court reviewed Mann's claims (and the video) by examining the severity of the crime, whether he posed a threat of harm, and whether he was actively resisting arrest. The court concluded that Mann's level of resistance forced the officers to rapidly make decisions on the types of force required and granted summary judgment in their favor. The court ruled that the videotape contradicted Mann's allegations and held that the use of the canine in a bite-and-hold maneuver on his leg could not be considered unreasonable force. The canine was at all times on its leash and under an officer's direction. The use of the stun to the neck was considered reasonable given the violence and the level of resistance demonstrated by Mann.

In *Phillips v. Community Insurance Corporation* (2012), officers deployed an SL6 Baton Launcher at Ms. Phillips for failure to exit her vehicle. The device is a shoulder-fired, semiautomatic firearm that fires polyurethane bullets with a force equivalent to a .44 magnum pistol. Its use has been deemed "less lethal" by the police department's use of force policy, and is considered tantamount to using a bean-bag shotgun or a hand baton. The "target area" for an SL6 is below a person's belly button, excluding the groin. The officers testified that the SL6 is designed to be used against persons exhibiting resistive, assaultive, or other dangerous behavior.

Officers received a call that a vehicle was being driven erratically and that the driver was possibly intoxicated. The make and color of the car was similar to one that had been reported stolen. Further, dispatch information provided to officers was found later to be incorrect, however. Within several minutes of the dispatch, officers found the vehicle parked on a sidewalk with the driver's side door open, a female sitting in the driver's side, and the car was parked against a hedgerow. The lights of the vehicle were on and the officers thought the vehicle might be still running. Responding officers radioed for backup, treated the situation as a "high risk stop." Seven units responded, surrounded the vehicle with their headlights on, and observed the female moving around in the front seat. Officers identified themselves and instructed the driver to place her hands outside the car window and to step out numerous times over a 10-minute period. She refused, lit up a cigarette, and placed her legs out the car door window. Officers continued to instruct Phillips to exit the car and she refused. From about 40 to 50 feet from the Phillips car, officer Hoffman shot one projectile as a warning shot, and hit the side of the car, denting it. The officers waited, instructed Ms. Phillips to exit, and rather than comply, she leaned back onto the front seat with her legs stretched out and feet on the ground. Officers fired a round and it struck Ms. Phillips in the leg but she remained in the car and cried out in pain. After 15 seconds a second round was fired from the SL6 and it struck her legs and she still remained in the car. A third round was fired, after several seconds had passed and officers instructed her to exit, which struck her in the leg, and she did not move. After several more seconds, and instructions to comply, a fourth round was fired, striking her leg. Ms. Phillips exited the car and knelt down on the ground. Officers instructed her to stand, walk back toward them, with her arms up, and she complied. The officers controlled and arrested her. Ms. Phillips sustained welts to her thigh area of both legs and a wound to her ankle requiring 30 stiches as the flesh was torn from the bone. Ms. Phillips could not walk for a week or perform her job as a personal trainer. She filed a § 1983 lawsuit claiming excessive force was used by the officers.

The case resulted in two trials; in the first, the jury was deadlocked and the court ruled a mistrial, and in the second trial the court found in favor of the officers. Ms. Phillips appealed to the Seventh Circuit Court of Appeals and claimed that the use of the SL6 was excessive given the facts of the case. The officers argued that the degree of force used was reasonable given the threat of safety to the officers and the dispatch information initially provided (intoxicated person in a stolen car who would not comply with orders to exit).

The court reversed the lower court's decision and remanded the case back to the lower court to determine damages. The court opined that while Ms. Phillips resisted instructions several times to exit the car, she did not present an immediate threat to the officers, was not actively resisting, did not verbally threaten the officers, and three rounds fired from the SL6 was excessive given her passive noncompliance. The court held that permitting substantial escalation of force in response to passive noncompliance would be incompatible with the excessive force doctrine and would likely bring more injured citizens before the courts. Under the totality of the circumstances, the court concluded that the force used surpassed the level permissible under the Fourth Amendment to effectuate Ms. Phillips' arrest.

Conducted Energy Weapons

The use of electrical devices has become more prominent in policing and corrections since the late 1990s. Such devices have commonly been referred to as Conducted Energy Devices (CED), Conducted Energy Weapons (CEW), Electro-Muscular Devices (EMD), stun guns, or Electronic

Control Device or Weapon (ECD or ECW). For convenience's sake, this discussion will refer to these devices as Tasers® (Thomas A. Swift Electric Rifle), which is manufactured by TASER International.

According to Taser International, Inc. (2012), 16,700 public agencies in 107 countries are using the Taser and it has saved 86,000 lives from potential deaths or serious injury. Tasers are considered less-lethal devices and an intermediate or medium use of force designed to momentarily incapacitate a resisting person in order for an officer to control him or her with little or no resultant injury resulting to either the person or the officer (*Bryan v. McPherson*, 2009; Zigmund, 2007). As police and correctional agencies have implemented the use of Tasers during incidents requiring force, other less-lethal devices have been decreasing (Smith et al., 2007; Hougland et al., 2005). For example, the use of impact weapons and the use of aerosols have significantly declined as many police agencies are deploying Tasers in the field more than other types of less-lethal technology (Taser International, Inc., 2012).

Alpert et al. (2010) reported in a study performed for the National Institute of Justice that using pepper spray and Tasers decrease suspect and officer injuries, whereas using physical control techniques are more likely to increase injury rates to the suspect and officer. Both products minimize physical struggles that are likely to injure officers and suspects. The researchers report that the medical research shows that death or serious harm associated with their use is rare and both are safe. They also report that agency administrators using Tasers and pepper spray need to ensure that their policy on using force articulates the appropriate use of all force measures, and to continue to provide ongoing training to officers. The injury-related findings also align with other studies performed on the use of the Taser during a use of force confrontation (Bozeman et al., 2008; Ho et al., 2009; Laub, 2011).

Like other types of police equipment, however, Tasers have been the subject of litigation (Brave & O'Linn, 2010; Daigle, 2012; Ferrell, 2012; Farber, 2007, 2010). Smith et al. (2007) examined 53 published § 1983 case decisions regarding the use of the Taser from 1990 to 2007, with a majority of the cases decided after 2000. They reported that the courts rarely deny summary judgment for the officers when they apply the Taser. Specifically, they reported that the courts dismissed motions for summary judgment in 15 percent of the decisions, awarded summary judgment in 84 percent, and in *McKenzie v. City of Milpitas* (1990) the court ruled against a municipality for failing to guide officers' use of the Taser by policy. They reported that the courts are more likely to dismiss a motion for summary judgment when the suspect fails to demonstrate resistance requiring any level of force.

In *Mateyko v. Felix* (1991), a district court in California ruled against an officer's use of a Taser during an arrest. An officer had stopped an individual for jaywalking. As the officer was issuing a citation, the citizen resisted and the officer radioed for assistance. The responding officer used the Taser to restrain the arrestee, who later sued, claiming excessive force. The court held that the use of a Taser did not constitute deliberate indifference to the arrestee's rights under § 1983. The court determined that he resisted, was convicted of resisting arrest, and therefore the force used was reasonable under the circumstances.

In *Draper v. Reynolds* (2004), the officer used a Taser during a traffic stop. Meeting Draper behind his truck, the officer asked that he retrieve documents from the cab five times, but he refused to comply. Draper became agitated, began yelling and cursing at the officer, stating that he was harassing him and blinding him with his flashlight. The officer used the Taser as a stun device one time and was able to control and handcuff Draper. Draper sued, claiming that the officer used excessive and disproportionate force.

The court granted summary judgment, agreeing with the officer that the arrest circumstance was tense, rapidly evolving, and uncertain. Because Draper continued to refuse the verbal commands of the officer, the court held that additional commands of arrest were not necessary, and had the officer attempted to handcuff him, an unnecessary struggle would have ensued, leading to serious injury. Based on the totality of the circumstances, the use of the Taser was proportional to the tense situation, and the officer did not violate Draper's constitutional rights.

Citing *Draper*, the court in *Stanley v. City of Baytown, Texas* (2005) granted summary judgment to the officer who used a Taser to effect an arrest. Officer Elizondo responded to assist paramedics and fire rescue personnel in controlling Stanley so that they could provide medical treatment for him. Stanley was highly agitated and combative, having previously taken steroids. Stanley was dressed in only boxer shorts, was sweating profusely, and actively resisting, making it difficult to control him. The paramedics and rescue personnel abandoned their efforts to treat Stanley, fearing for their safety. Stanley was unresponsive to their verbal attempts to calm him down. Elizondo arrived on the scene and spent several minutes trying to calm him down but was unsuccessful. Elizondo decided to use his Taser in the "push/stun mode," and applied a two-second application of the Taser. The Taser application was successful, Stewart calmed down, was treated by medical personnel, and did not receive any injuries. Stanley filed a lawsuit claiming that the officer used excessive force. The district court granted summary judgment for the officer, commenting that Elizondo's use of the Taser was not unreasonably disproportionate to the need to use force. In fact, the officer's decision to use the Taser may well have prevented much greater harm to Stanley and other people. Further, the court emphasized that the officer's intervention was reasonable and in keeping with his community caretaking function and therefore did not constitute an unlawful seizure.

An emerging question regarding the application of the Taser is whether multiple applications on a subject increases an officer's liability. In *Buckley v. Haddock* (2008), a deputy stopped a speeding motorist at night on a busy highway. The motorist became agitated about receiving a ticket and refused to sign it after the deputy repeatedly asked him to do so in accordance with Florida law. The deputy warned the motorist that he would be arrested and the motorist replied, "So arrest me." The deputy handcuffed the motorist and while being escorted to the patrol car the motorist dropped to the ground, began crying, crossed his legs, and refused to stand up and walk to the patrol car. The deputy instructed the motorist several times to stand up and warned that he would use his Taser if he did not comply. The deputy also stated to the motorist that he needed to stand up so that the oncoming traffic would not hit him, to which he replied, "my life would be better off if I was dead." After several warnings and attempting to lift him up unsuccessfully, the deputy used the Taser in the Drive-Stun mode three times. Finally, the motorist did stand up, was placed in a patrol car, and transported. The incident was videotaped. The arrestee filed a § 1983 claim for excessive use of the Taser and the lower court denied summary judgment for the officer.

The appellate court reviewed the case and overturned the lower court's decision, granting qualified immunity to the officer. The appellate court reasoned that the motorist posed a hazard to oncoming traffic when he sat down and chose to resist the officer's instructions, resisted the officer's efforts to lift him up, and refused to comply when warned that the Taser would be used. The court concluded that under the circumstances the use of the Taser was reasonable and a moderate use of non lethal force. The court further stated that the deputy gradually used varying levels of force, culminating with his repeated (but limited) use of the Taser, to move the plaintiff to the patrol car, and such force was not unconstitutionally excessive. Moreover, the court held that "we do not sit in judgment to determine whether an officer made the best or a good or even a bad decision in the manner of carrying out an arrest. The government has an interest in arrests being completed efficiently and without waste of limited resources, police time, and energy that may be needed elsewhere at any moment. We also reject the district court's rationale that had the deputy simply waited for back-up, two officers could have lifted and carried the plaintiff to the car without any application of force. A single officer in the deputy's situation confronting a non-compliant arrestee like the plaintiff need not—as a matter of constitutional law—wait idly for back-up to arrive to complete an otherwise lawful arrest. That an officer has requested more police assistance does not make the use of force before reinforcements arrive unreasonable."

In *Beaver v. City of Federal Way* (2007), an officer attempted to subdue a fleeing residential burglary suspect. The officer warned the suspect to stop or he would use the Taser, but he continued to flee. The officer deployed the Taser and it slowed the suspect slightly. He continued to run and the officer activated the Taser four more times for a five-second duration on each application. The officer activated the Taser five times over an 85-second period. The suspect was finally taken into custody and later filed a § 1983 lawsuit, asserting excessive use of the Taser in violation of his constitutional rights. The court granted summary judgment, noting that the law concerning excessive force claims involving the use of Tasers would not clearly indicate to a reasonable officer that multiple uses under the circumstances violated the arrestee's rights.

In *Bryan v. McPherson* (2009), officer McPherson stopped Bryan for a seatbelt violation. Bryan, who was 21, did not respond to McPherson's questions, hit the steering wheel, and began cursing at the officer. Bryon exited the vehicle, claiming he did not hear the officer instruct him to remain inside the vehicle. Bryan was agitated, was yelling gibberish, began hitting himself, and was dressed in boxer shorts and tennis shoes. Bryon remained about 20 to 25 feet from McPherson, did not threaten him, did not advance toward the officer, and did not attempt to flee. The officer, however, testified that Bryan did advance toward him. While Bryan stood facing away from McPherson, the officer activated his Taser without warning. The Taser immobilized Bryan causing him to fall forward landing on his face, causing facial contusions and fracturing four teeth. One probe was surgically removed in the emergency room. Bryan filed an excessive force claim under the Fourth Amendment and the district court denied summary judgment and the Court of Appeals for the Ninth Circuit affirmed.

Using the core factors for reviewing a claim of excessive force established in the *Graham* decision, the court concluded that Bryan did not pose an immediate threat of harm to officer McPherson and the use of the Taser under the circumstances was not reasonable. The court further considered additional factors beyond the *Graham* factors, including: (1) Bryan's mental status and behaviors, (2) the officer's failure to consider less-intrusive techniques and force alternatives, and (3) the officer's failure to provide a warning prior to deploying the Taser. In forming their decision, the court determined that Bryan was stopped for a seat belt violation; was not a dangerous felon; was not a flight risk; did not offer resistance; was not an immediate threat and did not threaten the officer; was, at most, disturbed; and was facing away from the officer when he deployed the Taser.

The court further noted that there are not two tracks of an excessive force analysis, one for the mentally ill and one for serious criminals. The court, however, stated that the emotional state of the person who is not a threat to the officer diminishes the degree of force that is necessary. The court determined that the Taser can play an important role in defusing dangerous situations from a distance, protecting officers, bystanders, and the suspect. But the court added that the Taser and other similar devices are considered an intermediate level of force, which is justifiable by a strong governmental interest that compels the employment of such force.

This case serves as a reminder for officers considering the use of the Taser. First, the court made its decision on the specific fact patterns of the incident and recognized that the use of a Taser is an important device to assist officers in effectuating an arrest. Further, the court noted that in examining a claim of excessive force, a court should consider all the relevant arrest circumstances. Second, the Taser causes pain, is not risk free, and officers need to consider the risk of secondary injuries after activation. Third, the application of the Taser is considered an "intermediate or medium" use of force and each activation must be justified as a separate use of force. Fourth, the totality of circumstances must be considered, particularly whether the person poses an immediate threat to the safety of the officer or others and is actively resisting arrest or evading efforts of arrest and control. Fifth, as feasible the officer should provide a warning prior to deploying the Taser and assess whether the person heard the warnings, giving him or her reasonable time for volitional compliance. Sixth, officers should respond based on the behaviors of the subject and in accordance with their agency policy for using the Taser and their training (Brave & O'Linn, 2010).

Compare however, the court's holding in *Mattos v. Agarano* (2010). Officers responded to a domestic dispute call and Jayzel Mattos's husband, Troy, was sitting on the front stairs. He smelled of alcohol and was muscular. The officers requested to see Jayzel to determine her status and they followed Troy into the house. Inside the house Troy began yelling at the officers to leave and they asked Jayzel to step outside to speak with them. Before Jayzel could step outside, another officer informed Troy that he was under arrest. Jayzel reached for Troy but an officer brushed against Jayzel's chest causing her to extend her arms to protect herself and in the process bumped an officer. Without warning, an officer deployed the Taser at Jayzel for one five-second cycle and she fell to the floor. The officers arrested Troy, and charged Jayzel with obstruction, but the charges were later dropped, and she filed a § 1983 lawsuit claiming excessive force. The lower court found in favor of the officers and Jayzel appealed.

The Ninth Circuit Court of Appeals examined the case in the light most favorable to Jayzel, and noted that her actions in obstructing the officers, although inappropriate, did not constitute a serious crime. Jayzel herself may have posed little threat, but any interference she caused only heightened the danger Troy represented. Jayzel's actions "exacerbated an already tense and rapidly escalating situation." On balance, Jayzel's actions were not a serious crime, but carried the potential for a far more serious crime—assault on an officer. The court next considered the threat to the officers' safety. The court viewed the officers' safety as "the most important of the three *Graham* factors." Given the dangerous nature of domestic violence situations, the close quarters in which the officers and the Mattoses were contained, Troy's intoxicated state, and the contact made between Jayzel and the officer, there was the risk of immediate threat to the safety of the officers. This factor significantly influenced the court's decision in favor of the officers.

Further, the court considered whether the "suspect was actively resisting arrest or attempting to evade arrest by flight." The court distinguished the case from the *McPherson* ruling, holding that officers in *Mattos* encountered a threat and danger in a restrictive environment. With all the participants in close contact in a small room, there was real danger that if Troy could not be subdued then someone—including Jayzel—might be injured. In such circumstances, the officers had an important interest in obtaining immediate control. The officers used the Taser only once in a domestic violence situation that could have quickly become much more dangerous to everyone involved. The court concluded that the force used against Jayzel was reasonable within the meaning of the Fourth Amendment.

Post-Arrest Use of Force

As discussed, the *Graham* standard of using force applies to "free" citizens. The question then emerges of what standard applies to post-arrest situations and pretrial detainees. This question creates confusion about when the Fourth Amendment protection ends and due process protection under the Fourteenth Amendment begins. Additional questions arise as to when the Eighth Amendment prohibition against cruel and unusual punishment regarding the use of force applies. These questions are more than academic, because the status of the arrestee will help a court determine which amendment is appropriate and which standard will be applied in a use-of-excessive-force case. This becomes important, as the outcome of an excessive force case will depend on the standard used by the court. In *Henson v. Thezan* (1988), an arrestee who was charged with child molestation, rape, and attempted murder alleged that he was pushed down a flight of stairs, beaten during transport, and beaten at the police station. The court applied the Fourth Amendment because the arrestee had not yet appeared before a judicial officer.

The court in *Valencia v. Wiggins* (1993), however, found that a pretrial detainee's beating in a detention facility was not governed by the Fourth Amendment standard. Rather, the court applied the *Whitley* and *Hudson* (Eighth Amendment) standard, because it was impractical to draw a line between convicted prisoners and pretrial detainees for the purpose of maintaining security in the facility.

The standard generally applied to post-arrest force situations in detention facilities is the "shocks the conscience" standard previously discussed in the *Johnson v. Glick* case (1973) under the Fourteenth Amendment due process clause (see Table 10.2). The evaluation of use-of-force claims under due process is fundamentally different from the objective reasonableness standard, in that it focuses on the state of mind or motivation of the officer. If it can be shown by the plaintiff that the force used by the officer was unnecessary, inflicted an injury, and was for sadistic and malicious purposes rather than to restore order, liability will most likely attach. Application of the "shocks the conscience" standard is applied on a case-by-case basis.

For example, in *McClanahan v. City of Moberly* (1998), a pretrial detainee alleged that she was the victim of excessive force in connection with her transfer from a police department to a county jail. The district court granted summary judgment for the defendants, finding that the detainee's allegations of being slapped three times, without any evidence of a resulting injury, was at most a slight injury that did not implicate the due process clause of the Fourteenth Amendment. In *Riley v. Durton* (1997), a pretrial detainee brought a § 1983 action and claimed that an officer used handcuffs, inserted the tip of a pen into the detainee's nose, threatened her, and slapped her across the face. The appeals court affirmed the lower court's summary judgment for the officer, finding that the Fourth Amendment did not extend protection from excessive force to pretrial detainees and the alleged use of force did not violate the Eighth Amendment. The court held that the officer's use of force did not violate due process where an injury suffered by the detainee was minimal.

The estate in *Brothers v. Klevenhagen* (1994) brought a § 1983 claim against the county and the sheriff, alleging the use of excessive force. The deceased, an unarmed pretrial detainee, attempted to escape during transport from one holding cell to another. The deputies fired at the detainee only as a last resort to prevent an escape, and he would have escaped if the deputies had not fired at him. The appeals court affirmed the lower court's summary judgment for the county. The court found that the due process clause of the Fourteenth Amendment, rather than the Fourth Amendment, provided the appropriate constitutional standard for evaluating the deputies' use of force. The sheriff's department policy allowed deadly force only when immediately necessary to prevent escape and was designed in a good faith effort to maintain or restore discipline, and not maliciously and sadistically for the purpose of causing harm.

Claims of brutality against detainees emerge within the context of excessive force. One particularly egregious example is illustrated by *Mathis v. Fries* (1996). While confined as a pretrial detainee, Mathis claimed that the facility's director of security sexually abused him. The district court entered summary judgment for the detainee, finding sufficient evidence to support claims that the director repeatedly sodomized the detainee while he was handcuffed to pipes in the security office. Finding that these acts violated the detainee's due process rights, the court rejected a petition for qualified immunity and awarded the detainee $250,000 in compensatory damages and $500,000 in punitive damages. The court called the director's action an outrageous abuse of power and authority. The court in *Casaburro v. Giuliani* (1997) found that egregious physical misconduct toward an arrestee may violate the Eighth Amendment if it was a punishment. An allegation of handcuffing a detainee for seven hours while in a holding cell would qualify, absent a legitimate reason. Tight handcuffing for the sole purpose of causing harm was actionable because it was "grossly disproportionate" to the need and the misdemeanor charge against the arrestee.

In *Fennell v. Gilstrap* (2009), a pretrial detainee brought an excessive force claim under the Fourteenth Amendment against a detention officer in the jail. The detainee assaulted another detention officer and five other officers responded and the detainee continued his assault against them. The responding detention officer kicked the detainee as he struggled with the other officers who were unable to control and restrain him. The kick, targeted for the detainee's arm/shoulder, missed and the kick struck him in the face, and he sustained a fracture. The lower court granted summary disposition for the officer and the appellate court affirmed. The appellate court noted that the detainee assaulted the officer, would not comply, and continued to resist being controlled and grabbed another officer. The kick was not excessive given the behaviors of the detainee.

Post-Conviction Use of Force

The United States Supreme Court has established different standards of excessive force review when such claims originate in a prison setting. The explicit language of the Eighth Amendment prohibits the imposition of "cruel and unusual punishments." According to the Court, this language was designed to protect those convicted of crimes. The Court noted in *Ingraham v. Wright* (1977) that the clause applies after the state has complied with constitutional guarantees associated with criminal prosecution. Therefore, applying the Eighth Amendment standard to convicted persons should not be problematic.

Whitley v. Albers (1986)

Following the *Garner* (1985) decision, the Supreme Court in *Whitley v. Albers* (1986) reviewed a deadly force incident that occurred during a prison riot. The Court established how the Eighth Amendment prohibits cruel and unusual punishment, including allegations of excessive force asserted by prisoners. In *Whitley*, Oregon prison officials were confronted with a disturbance by prisoners who had killed another prisoner and taken a correctional officer hostage. Threats to kill the hostage and other prisoners were made by prisoners, should force be used by officials. Officials ultimately decided to use force to free the hostage and retake the cellblock. Prisoner Albers was shot in the left knee after several warnings to release the hostage had failed and after a warning shot had been ignored. He filed suit against prison officials, claiming that his Eighth and Fourteenth Amendment rights had been violated.

The Supreme Court reversed the appeals court's decision, which had found in favor of Albers. The Court ruled that the infliction of pain in the course of a prison security measure is only an Eighth Amendment violation if it is inflicted "unnecessarily and wantonly." The standard of deliberate indifference was rejected by the Court as not sufficiently broad enough to be used in analyzing deadly force claims associated with prison riots. The Court held that whether the force used inflicted unnecessary and wanton pain and suffering ultimately turns on whether the use of force was applied in a good faith effort to maintain or restore discipline, or whether it was applied maliciously and sadistically for the purpose of causing harm. This language is taken from the fourth component outlined in the *Glick* (1973) decision.

The Court held that liability would attach in deadly force situations if the prisoner could show that such force manifested "obduracy and wantonness." "Obdurate" can be defined as "hardened feelings," or "without remorse." "Wantonness" can be defined as "malicious," "without regard," "inhumane," or "merciless." For example, in *Austin v. Hopper* (1998), an onerous and barbaric "security" measure was condemned when it was determined that there was no immediate threat to security or an attempt to restore order was present. A practice of compelling prisoners to stand for hours shackled to a "hitching post," spread-eagled, without the ability to stretch or move in direct sunlight caused great pain, heat exhaustion, dehydration, and injury, for nondangerous rule infractions. This practice clearly violated the Eighth Amendment and exemplified the Court's definition of obduracy and wantonness.

The court in *Gravely v. Madden* (1998) found that a correctional officer who shot and killed an escaping prisoner did not act with obduracy and wantonness in violation of the Eighth Amendment. An appeals court reversed a lower court decision against the officer, because the court determined that he acted within the scope of his authority, the force was reasonable, and therefore he had qualified immunity. The prisoner had escaped from a minimum-security facility and was staying at a friend's residence. When the officer entered the house, the prisoner was twice instructed to stop and give up. The prisoner leaped off a porch and the officer fired one round, killing him.

Hudson v. McMillian (1992)

Using the *Whitley* standard, courts have ruled in favor of prison officials when the use of deadly force is warranted. This standard has mainly been applied to prisoner escapes and riot situations (*Duametef v. Fial*, 1996; *Kinney v. Indiana Youth Center*, 1991). The question emerges, however, of whether the *Whitley* standard applies to all use-of-force situations or cases involving only deadly force. For a time the courts were divided on this question. The Supreme Court's decision in *Hudson v. McMillian* (1992) resolved this controversy and held that all excessive force claims must show malice, sadism, and intent to cause harm (Box 10.2). In establishing this standard of excessive force review in corrections, the Court underscored its earlier standard of review in the *Whitley* decision: whether force was applied in good faith, in an effort to maintain or restore discipline, or maliciously and sadistically for the purpose of causing harm.

The *Hudson* case arose out of an incident in an Angola, Louisiana, prison where two correctional officers beat a compliant and handcuffed prisoner during an escort to another cell. As the officer punched Hudson, a supervisor observed the beating and merely cautioned the officers "not to have too much fun." Hudson sustained minor bruises and swelling of his face, lip, and mouth. A punch to the face also cracked his dentures and loosened his teeth. He filed a civil action claiming excessive force. A federal district court found in favor of Hudson, but an appellate court reversed. The U.S. Supreme Court granted certiorari to answer the question of whether the use of excessive physical force by correctional officers against a prisoner constituted cruel and unusual punishment. The Court responded by saying "yes," holding that an injury to a prisoner does not have to be "serious" or "significant" to constitute cruel and unusual punishment in violation of the Eighth Amendment. The Court held that the officers' actions did indeed violate Hudson's constitutional rights, despite the fact that he sustained only minor injuries.

BOX 10.2 *HUDSON V. MCMILLIAN* (1992)

After an earlier argument, two correctional officers at the state prison at Angola, Louisiana, handcuffed prisoner Hudson and removed him from his cell. While escorting Hudson to an administrative segregation cell, the officers punched and kicked him, even though he was compliant. The supervisor on duty observed the officers striking Hudson, but merely told them "not to have too much fun." The blows were strong enough to dislodge Hudson's dental plate, which broke when it hit the floor. Hudson also sustained minor bruises and swelling of his face, mouth, and lip. Hudson filed a § 1983 lawsuit, claiming excessive force in violation of his Eighth Amendment right to be free of cruel and unusual punishment. He prevailed in the lower court, winning $800.00. On appeal, the Fifth Circuit Court of Appeals reversed. Hudson appealed to the United States Supreme Court.

The Court examined the issue of whether the use of force against a prisoner constituted cruel and unusual punishment even if the prisoner did not sustain a serious injury. The Court held, in a 7-to-2 vote, that a prisoner does not have to sustain a serious injury in order to prevail in a civil action. A prisoner will prevail on a claim of excessive force when he can show that the officer used force "maliciously and sadistically" to cause harm. The severity of injury is not at issue. The Court established that the standard for the use of nonlethal force for correctional officers is whether the officer used force in a good faith effort to maintain or restore order, or maliciously and sadistically for the purpose of causing harm. The court concluded that the officers used force in a malicious and sadistic fashion, thereby violating Hudson's constitutional right to be free from cruel and unusual punishment. Hudson did not possess a weapon, was not threatening the officers, was secured in handcuffs, and was compliant.

The question to be asked in correctional use-of-force situations is: What level of force is needed and was the force used repugnant to the sensibilities? The standard established by the Court makes it easier for prisoners to prevail in excessive force actions.

For the first time, the Supreme Court held that in use-of-force cases, the extent of injuries sustained is irrelevant. The Court rejected the third component from the *Glick* decision (extent of injury sustained). The Court emphasized that when prison officials maliciously and sadistically use force to cause harm, contemporary standards of decency are violated, regardless of whether significant injury is evident. This clause becomes the standard to assess all excessive force claims—not just prison disturbances or riots. *Hudson* states that in order to establish a valid claim of excessive force under the Eighth Amendment, it must be shown that the defendant used force in a "malicious and sadistic manner for the purpose of causing harm."

The Court noted that not every push, shove, or injury leads to civil liability. They noted that the Eighth Amendment excludes from constitutional review *de minimis* (trifling) uses of physical force, provided that such force is not "repugnant to the conscience of mankind." A definitive meaning of this phrase remains unclear. Generally, the intent of the officer is examined along with the legitimate objective and rationale for the application of force. The standard is applied on a case-by-case basis depending on the circumstances of the incident.

For example, in *Samuels v. Hawkins* (1998), the court found that throwing a cup of water at a cuffed and shackled prisoner who had thrown a cup of urine at the correctional officer was not malicious and sadistic. Similarly, in *Stanley v. Hejiria* (1998), a videotaped cell extraction of a riot ringleader did not demonstrate sadistic or malicious conduct on the part of the response team and liability did not attach. Minor injuries were not constitutionally severe enough to be characterized as significant where force was reasonably necessary.

Moreover, in *Dennis v. Thurman* (1997), a prisoner brought a § 1983 claim alleging that 36 officers withheld water from him for 36 hours after a forced cell extraction. The prisoner had to be forcibly extracted from his cell in order for officers to search it, because they had learned he was planning to kill a correctional officer. Officers had to use a block gun, which shot rubber blocks at high velocity. The court held that the officers did not use excessive force against the prisoner in removing him from his cell. The court found that no officer acted maliciously or sadistically for the purpose of causing pain to the prisoner. Shutting off the water to his cell for an extended period did not violate his Eighth Amendment rights, because he had in the past used water to flood his cell, creating a dangerous condition for himself, other prisoners, and officers.

In *Campbell v. Sikes* (1999), an appellate court affirmed summary judgment for correctional officers and a doctor on a claim that the officers used excessive force by restraining a mentally impaired prisoner. The court found that using a straitjacket to restrain the prisoner failed to constitute excessive force, absent evidence that the force was applied maliciously and sadistically. The court noted that the prisoner posed a serious threat to herself and others, lesser restraints were ineffective, the restraints used caused no physical injury, and the prisoner's physical condition was carefully monitored.

Conversely, in *Giroux v. Sherman* (1992), a prisoner prevailed in an excessive force claim asserting that on four separate occasions eight officers beat and tormented him without provocation. For one beating, the prisoner was awarded $10,000. This beating was so severe that the prisoner was hospitalized with internal injuries. While in the hospital, other officers punched his kidneys, complicating his recovery. He was awarded additional damages amounting to $10,000 and punitive damages of $10,000. The prisoner was awarded additional damages resulting from two other attacks in which one correctional officer punched him in the throat and head without provocation, and another officer wantonly and without cause beat him in the kidneys, causing further injury and requiring surgery. The prisoner was awarded more than $38,000 in damages.

In *Madrid v. Gomez* (1995), the court found evidence of sadistic and malicious conduct of correctional officers who beat mentally impaired prisoners. Prisoners of the Pelican Bay State Prison in California brought a class action lawsuit citing numerous constitutional violations, including excessive force allegations. The court held that prisoners established that prison officials frequently used unnecessary and grossly excessive force against prisoners and that these practices posed a substantial risk of harm to prisoners. The court found that officials had an affirmative management strategy that permitted the use of excessive force for the purpose of punishment and deterrence. Such practices and actions of officers constituted wanton and malicious conduct in violation of the Eighth Amendment.

In *Estate of Davis by Ostenfeld v. Delo* (1997), a court held that officers, a supervisor, and the prison superintendent were liable for using excessive force when they forcibly removed a prisoner from his cell. The court found evidence to support the claim that the prisoner was struck in the face and head 20 to 25 times by several officers, while other officers held him down after he had complied with an order to lie face down. The prisoner sustained numerous injuries, and the court found that the officers used force maliciously and sadistically for the purpose of causing harm. After an investigation ordered by the superintendent, he failed to take corrective action against an officer who failed to submit a mandatory force report, was found to have sustained numerous complaints of excessive force in the past, and for whom recommendations were submitted for his termination. The superintendent was held liable, and the prisoner was awarded $70,000 in compensatory damages and $40,000 in punitive damages.

Assessment of *Hudson v. McMillian*

For more than 10 years the courts have applied the *Hudson* decision in prison use-of-force encounters in accordance with the Eighth Amendment. Ross (2004) conducted a content analysis of 4,010 published § 1983 cases filed against correction officers in prison to examine how the courts have applied the standard. A random sample of 1,025 (25%) cases decided from 1992 to 2002 was examined. As shown in Table 10.3, the sample revealed five common use-of-force categories.

As shown in Table 10.3, correctional officers prevailed in each category and during the reporting period, officers prevailed in more than 75 percent of the prisoner claims. Claims of physical force accounted for 44 percent of the actions, and include empty-hand control techniques, such as control holds, wristlocks, takedowns, pressure point, hand/leg strikes, and neck restraints. The use of restraints included handcuffs, leg restraints, straitjackets, four-point restraints, and the restraint chair. The use of aerosols accounted for 11 percent of the claims and included chemical agents and pepper spray. Force devices included the use of batons, Tasers, stun guns, and sting ball grenades, and accounted for nine percent of the cases studied. The use of a firearm accounted for only one percent of the actions. Use-of-force claims involving combinations of the above categories accounted for 58 percent of the cases (excluding firearms).

Case analysis also revealed four plaintiffs' allegation levels in asserting a claim of excessive force. The first level alleged that the responding officers overreacted by using the degree of force he or she employed. Claims at this level generally asserted that the officers recklessly

Table 10.3 Trends of Use-of-Force Claims in Corrections by Type (1992 to 2002)

Claim Type	Number Studied (%)	Prisoner Prevailed (%)	Officer Prevailed (%)
Physical force	455 (44)	90 (20)	365 (80)
Restraints	355 (35)	77 (19)	278 (78)
Aerosols	110 (11)	26 (26)	84 (76)
Force devices	100 (9)	22 (22)	78 (78)
Lethal force	5 (1)	0	5 (100)
Total Number	1,025 (100)	215 (21)	810 (79)

misused physical control techniques and/or force equipment, and failed to follow their training and the department's use-of-force policy. A frequent secondary claim alleged that the plaintiff suffered some type of injury as a result of the excessive force, and that timely and adequate medical care was denied or delayed. The third claim level asserted that supervisors failed to adequately train, supervise, and direct officers in the constitutional limits of force and failed to keep officers proficient in force tactics and equipment. The final level of allegations generally claimed that supervisory personnel failed to investigate excessive force claims and failed to discipline officers, thereby tolerating a "pattern and practice" of excessive force. The cases below provide examples of these levels of claims and how the lower courts have applied the *Hudson* standard.

In *Marquez v. Gutierrez* (2003), a prisoner brought a § 1983 lawsuit claiming that an officer's use of deadly force was excessive, in violation of his Eighth Amendment rights. While the plaintiff prisoner was assaulting another prisoner, the correctional officer assigned to a security tower shot the attacking prisoner in the leg, causing severe injury. The district court ruled that the officer used excessive force. It denied summary judgment and the officer appealed. The appellate court reversed the lower court's decision, concluding that a reasonable correctional officer could have believed that shooting one prisoner in the leg to stop an assault that could have resulted in a serious injury or death of another prisoner was a good faith effort to restore order, and was therefore lawful.

In *Jackson v. Austin* (2003), a prisoner who was severely beaten by correctional officers did not have to show that he sustained a significant or permanent injury in order to prevail. While waiting to see the prison physician, a prisoner with a knee condition sat down in the medical clinic. Officers ordered him to stand and the prisoner attempted to explain that he was permitted to sit because his knee injury prevented him from standing for long periods. Refusing to look at the prisoner's written medical restriction, the officers forcefully pushed him to the floor and handcuffed him. The prisoner did not sustain an injury and the court awarded the prisoner $15,000 in compensatory damages and $30,000 in punitive damages. The court also found liable an officer who did not participate in the altercation, but failed to intervene. The court noted that the prisoner was 60 years old and that the officers were aware that he had a knee injury.

As indicated in Table 10.3, the use of restraints accounted for about one-third of the claims. The United States Supreme Court addressed a unique application of restraints in *Hope v. Pelzer* (2002). The Alabama prison system instituted a restraint process for disruptive prisoner conduct known as the "hitching post." As a punitive measure, a recalcitrant prisoner would be restrained to the post with his hands extended above shoulder level for several hours, usually outside in the sun. While restrained to the post a prisoner would have little mobility to move his arms, the handcuffs would cut into his wrists, causing pain. Frequently, the prisoner's ankles would also be shackled.

Prisoner Hope was restrained to the hitching post for fighting and disobeying orders to work on two occasions. During the first incident, Hope was restrained to the post for two hours, and was offered water and a bathroom break every 15 minutes. On the second occasion, Hope was restrained to the post for several hours without a shirt, provided with water but not permitted bathroom breaks. He claimed that one officer taunted him about his thirst. He filed a § 1983 lawsuit alleging excessive force against three officers. The district court granted summary judgment to the officers and Hope appealed. While the appellate court found that the hitching post constituted cruel and unusual punishment in violation of the Eighth Amendment, the court granted qualified immunity to the officers. Hope appealed to the United States Supreme Court and they agreed to review the case. Reversing the appellate court's decision, the Court determined that restraining a prisoner in such a manner established an Eighth Amendment claim and exhibited cruel and unusual punishment. The Court held that the restraint process constituted an "unnecessary and wanton" infliction of pain for reasons "totally without penological justification." Further, the Court stated that a reasonable officer would have known that using a "hitching post" as alleged by the prisoner was unlawful.

In *Wilkins v. Gaddy* (2010) the United States Supreme Court affirmed its decision in *Hudson v. McMillian* (1992) holding that a prisoner does not have to suffer a serious injury to support a claim of excessive force that amounts to cruel and unusual punishment under the Eighth Amendment. Wilkins claimed that officer Gaddy acted maliciously and sadistically without any provocation when he slammed him to the ground for requesting a grievance form. Wilkins claimed that on the ground, Gaddy kicked, punched, and choked him until another officer arrived and removed him from Wilkins. Wilkins alleged that he received numerous injuries, back pain, psychological trauma, and mental anguish from the assault.

The Court ruled that the lower court and the appellate court for the Fourth Circuit erred by granting summary judgment to officer Gaddy. The Court noted that the Fourth Circuit had strayed from the clear holding in *Hudson* and its decision was not defensible. The Court reversed and remanded the case back to the lower court, instructing it to review the allegations within the standard of "whether force was applied in a good faith effort to maintain or restore discipline, or maliciously and sadistically to cause harm." Finally, the Court reemphasized that when prison officials maliciously and sadistically use force to cause harm, contemporary standards of decency are always violated.

Using force control techniques for the purpose of punishment by correctional officers or supervisors will heighten exposure to potential liability. In *United States v. Miller* (2007), an appellate court upheld the lower court's denial of summary judgment for a supervisor who used excessive force. The appellate court held that there was sufficient evidence that a supervisor acted maliciously and sadistically toward a prisoner in violation of the Eighth Amendment prohibition against cruel and unusual punishment. The evidence the court reviewed showed that the supervisor kicked and stomped a prisoner who was lying on the ground when there was no legitimate reason to do so. The court noted that to inflict greater injuries upon a prisoner does not make an attack any less malicious or sadistic for the purpose of the Eighth Amendment prohibition against cruel and unusual punishment.

In *Reid v. Wakefield* (2007), Reid was a state prisoner and claimed that, during an escort to the showers by officers, he was assaulted by them. He claimed in his civil action that during the escort his hand slipped through a handcuff and he informed one of the officers, holding his hand in the air. He alleged that the officer grabbed him, slammed him against a gate, and then slammed him to the floor, where a second officer choked him, and responding officers began kicking him. Reid stated that he sustained injuries requiring medical treatment. After the incident he stated that he was placed in a strip cell with no mattresses, blanket, or clothing, because he allegedly assaulted the officers. Later Reid stated that he wrote to the warden indicating that he feared for his safety and he was transferred to another facility. Reid filed a legal action alleging excessive force and unconstitutional confinement conditions against the officers and the warden.

The defendants moved for summary judgment and the court granted it. The warden was not liable because he was not in the housing unit when the alleged use of force took place. The court also found that the officers used reasonable force only to protect themselves and in order to control Reid. It was determined that Reid began to use the handcuff as a weapon against the officers and would not stop resisting after the officers instructed him several times to stop. Reid struggled with the officers on the floor and sustained minor injuries that were treated by medical personnel. The court also denied his claim of cruel and unusual living conditions as he failed to show evidence that he was denied basic human needs such as food, clothing, medical care, shelter, and personal safety from physical assault. The court found that Reid could not produce any evidence that he was the victim of any physical assault by a prisoner or an officer during his placement in the strip cell or after his transfer to the other correctional facility.

Aerosols are commonly used in prison in order to control a combative or insubordinate prisoner. Aerosols are considered a less-than-lethal use of force and have been successful in reducing the risk of injury to prisoners and the officers who are attempting to control prisoners. In *Treats v. Morgan* (2002), a prisoner brought a § 1983 action against the officers, alleging that officers used pepper spray excessively in violation of his Eighth Amendment right. The prisoner failed to obey the commands of correctional officers and did not threaten them or anyone else. An officer administered a burst from the canister in the prisoner's face and a supervisor placed him on the ground and handcuffed him. The court denied the officers' request for summary judgment and the appellate court affirmed. The appeals court ruled that the spraying a prisoner who only disobeyed an order and was not threatening prison security or other persons precluded summary judgment.

Similarly, in *Danley v. Allyn* (2007), officers who sprayed a prisoner with pepper spray over a dispute regarding access to toilet paper were denied summary judgment. The prisoner requested toilet paper for his cell and when he asked a second time an officer sprayed him with pepper spray. The prisoner filed a § 1983 lawsuit, claiming that he was subjected to excessive force and then denied medical treatment. The officers filed a motion for summary judgment. The lower court denied the motion and the appellate court affirmed. The court held that the officers were not entitled to qualified immunity, noting that the officers had fair warning that to employ pepper spray as punishment, or for the sadistic pleasure of the sprayers, as distinguished from what reasonably necessary to maintain prisoner control, was constitutionally prohibited.

The need to restrain violent prisoners has increased the need to develop humane methods. The restraint chair was developed and designed to safely immobilize a combative prisoner in a seated position so that the prisoner may calm down while being monitored by correctional officers and medical personnel. The prisoner's wrists, lap, shoulders, and ankles are secured with straps, restricting the ability to self-harm or harm others. As with other types of equipment, lawsuits have been filed by prisoners alleging that use of the restraint amounted to excessive force, constituting cruel and unusual punishment.

The Iowa Ombudsman's office issued a report on a study of the restraint chair in five counties in Iowa (Angrick, 2009). The report revealed that while no prisoners died while restrained in the chair, there were several standards violated by officers using it and several lawsuits were filed after its use. The report provided several suggestions for using the restraint chair properly.

In *Johnson v. Wright* (2005) officers were denied summary judgment regarding allegations that they beat a prisoner in his cell and continued the beating while restrained in a restraint chair. The prisoner alleged that the officers entered his cell without provocation and began striking and kicking him. He covered his stomach and face to ward off the blows and the officers continued to kick him in the back. The officers secured him in handcuffs and moved him from the cell and secured him in a restraint chair. While in the restraint chair and still secured in handcuffs, two of the officers continued to strike the prisoner in the face and stomach. The court reasoned that the prisoner secured in handcuffs and in the restraint failed to present a risk of harm or threat to the officers and such conduct amounted to sadistic and malicious use of force, contrary to any legitimate penological objective.

In *Roush-Dean v. Murrary, Paige, and Kucharek* (2008), the court examined the constitutionality of whether officers could apply a Taser to a prisoner who was secured in a restraint chair. The court reviewed the case to determine whether such force amounted to unnecessary and wanton infliction of pain and punishment. Prisoner Roush-Dean became combative in her cell. Officers secured her in handcuffs and placed her in a restraint chair. After 20 minutes, two officers and a supervisor approached her to remove the handcuffs. The supervisor instructed her to remain calm while the officers removed the handcuffs and warned her that if she failed to comply, the Taser would be used. As one handcuffed was removed, the prisoner quickly raised her arm to strike an officer. The supervisor delivered one application of the Taser in the Drive-Stun mode for a five-second cycle to her upper chest/lower shoulder area. The prisoner's resistance subsided and she was secured with the straps of the restraint chair. She was examined by medical staff and monitored for two hours while secured in the restraint chair. She was released back to her cell and medical staff examined her again. A slight burn mark was observed on her shoulder area but it did not require medical attention.

Prisoner Roush-Dean filed a § 1983 suit claiming that her rights had been violated and that the placement in the restraint chair amounted to punishment. The court awarded summary judgment to the officers. The court concluded that in the context of the situation, the use of the Taser in the Drive-Stun mode amounted to a minimal amount of force. The court, however, stipulated that using a Drive-Stun does not equate to a minimal use of force, but rather the supervisor's decision to use the Taser in the Drive-Stun mode minimized the type and level of force applied, and that the supervisor could have chosen to select other alternative forms of force. The Taser was used as a compliant measure that was painful, but was not used for punishment or for sadistic purposes. The court ruled that the officers knew that the prisoner was combative, posed a threat of harm to herself and others, and placing her in the restraint chair for her own protection was reasonable. The court also noted that the supervisor did instruct the prisoner to calm down during the removal of the handcuffs and did warn her not to resist or the Taser would be used. Such instructions and warnings were reasonable and the application of the Taser did not amount to a wanton or sadistic use of force to inflict harm.

Similarly, the court in *Birdine v. Gray* (2005) granted summary judgment to officers who placed a prisoner in a restraint chair and applied the Taser to him twice. Like the *Roush-Dean* case, officers placed the prisoner in a restraint chair to protect him from harming himself in his cell. He had been tearing up the cell and had threatened officers. As he was being placed in the restraint chair, the prisoner began kicking and thrashing and an officer applied the Taser twice, which aided in calming him and securing him in the restraint chair. The court found that the prisoner was monitored on a regular basis, was offered to be released from the chair when acting appropriately, and the chair was not used for punishment but only for the purpose of restoring order and protecting the prisoner. Such force was reasonable and related to institutional safety and security.

Like their police counterparts, correctional officers are using Tasers in a variety of situations on a more frequent basis. Claims of excessive force have been filed by prisoners in these incidents. In *Montoya v. Board of County Commissioners* (2007), the court awarded summary judgment to officers who applied the Taser one time when a prisoner refused to be transferred to a segregation cell after violating the rules of the facility. The court held that the Taser was not used for punishment nor in retaliation for violating rules, but rather was merely applied as a compliance measure that reduced the need to use other force options. Conversely, in *Vasquez v. Raemisch* (2007), the court ruled in favor of a prisoner who was Tasered for failing to comply with a body cavity search. The prisoner was subjected to three body cavity searches within a short period on the same day and did not display any resistance or threat. On the third search, the officers made contact with the prisoner's genitals as a means of obtaining sexual gratification or humiliating him and one officer applied the Taser in the Drive-Stun mode. The court found that other officers on the scene should have intervened and the use of the Taser was not applied for legitimate security interests but rather for sadistic and malicious purposes.

In *Lewis v. Downey* (2009), the Seventh Circuit Appellate Court overturned the lower court's summary judgment when a correction officer deployed a Taser on a prisoner who ignored instructions to get out of his bed. The prisoner alleged that being shot with a Taser amounted to cruel and unusual punishment in violation of the Eighth Amendment. The court found that an officer who stood by while the officer deployed the Taser on the prisoner was not liable as he did not have a realistic opportunity to stop the officer from using the Taser. The court held that the officer was not entitled to qualified immunity from liability for his use of a Taser against the prisoner, where at the time of the conduct, the prisoner was allegedly prone on his bed, and the prisoner allegedly did not have enough time to respond to the officer's order to get out of bed. Such actions demonstrated that the officer acted maliciously and sadistically to cause harm.

Summary

Several factors should be evident from this discussion. The use of force by police and correctional officers is a critical topic in civil liability and is of fundamental importance. Understanding how the courts examine claims of excessive force is essential. Officers can never justify their use of force for punishment or revenge rationales. Legitimate force used by officers must be within the framework of standards established by the United States Supreme Court. The Court has established three standards of review, depending on the status of the individual. The use of force in policing requires a Fourth Amendment review under the standard of "objective reasonableness" established in the *Graham* decision. The Court identified five factors for analyzing claims of excessive force. These factors underscore the ideology that the suspect dictates the degree of force that an officer applies and officers should make certain to articulate them when justifying their force decisionmaking.

As an arrestee's status changes to that of a pretrial detainee, the courts use the "shocks the conscience" standard of review as articulated in the *Glick* decision. Examining allegations of excessive force in this category appears to create the most confusion as to when the Fourth Amendment applies, when the Fourteenth Amendment applies, and when to consider the Eighth Amendment. Generally, the Fourteenth Amendment due process clause applies to pretrial detainees, although from time to time courts have been known to apply the Eighth Amendment.

Third, the *Hudson* ruling underscores that the excessive force claims arising out of the prison context will be evaluated in accordance with the Eighth Amendment. The applicable standard of using force in good faith and not maliciously or sadistically for causing harm aligns with the cruel and unusual punishment clause of the Eighth Amendment. Severe or significant injury need not occur for a valid excessive force claim to be made. The court affirmed and reemphasized this standard in its decision in *Wilkins*.

While the general trend of contemporary rulings by the Supreme Court has been to substantively limit a plaintiff's ability to prevail in civil rights actions, the *Graham* and *Hudson* decisions have opened the door to increased § 1983 use-of-force litigation. Prior to *Graham*, under the Fourteenth Amendment standard, plaintiffs were protected from egregious police behavior that caused severe injuries (*Wise v. Bravo*, 1981). In contrast, the *Graham* standard of objective reasonableness is more restrictive, protecting individuals from police conduct that is objectively unreasonable (*Maynard v. Hopwood*, 1997).

The Fourth Amendment reasonableness assessment requires a fact finder to examine only one question: Was the force used by the police officer objectively reasonable based on the totality of the circumstances? An unreasonable seizure itself crosses the constitutional boundary of whether the plaintiff sustained severe injuries. Therefore, proper application of the Fourth Amendment should stress the reasonableness of a seizure rather than focusing on the extent of a plaintiff's physical injury.

In *Graham* the Supreme Court commented that there is no precise definition of objective reasonableness and cannot be mechanically applied, but must be evaluated by the totality of circumstances, the perspective of the officer, and within the framework of the five-part test.

There is, however, divergent interpretation and application of these factors. Generally, it can be concluded that the majority of the lower courts primarily interpret "objectively reasonable force" as being based on the manner of the officer's intrusion, the scope of the intrusion, the need to perform official duties, justification of the intrusion, facts and circumstances of the situation, and the degree of resistance the officer encountered, including the threat or the use of weapons. The lawfulness of the officer's decision will turn on the facts and circumstances known to the officer at the time the force was used. What was determined or discovered after the force was used cannot be used to justify the use of force and would normally not be admissible evidence. An officer's motivation in using force is irrelevant, and evil intent does not make an otherwise reasonable use of force bad and, likewise, the absence of evil intent does not make an objectively unreasonable use of force appropriate.

Finally, studies performed on case trends by the lower courts when applying the standards from the *Graham* and *Hudson* decisions show that officers are prevailing in a significant number of litigated cases. This also shows that officers are generally receiving sufficient training in use-of-force decisionmaking, using force within the law and policy, and adhering to legal precedents. Officers should continue to receive regular training on civil liability cases pertinent to their job duties when employing force techniques and force equipment. They also have more equipment options at their disposal than in previous years, which gives them a greater range of options to use when encountering resistance. As officers use varying less-lethal devices, equipment, and the restraint chair, they are reminded to use the device in accordance with the manufacturer's specifications.

Correctional officers are reminded that a prisoner does not have to show that he sustained an injury in order to assert a legitimate claim. The court only needs to determine that the officer used force maliciously, with the intent to cause harm. Police and correctional officers must be able to articulate their perception as to why they chose a certain course of action in justifying the type and degree of force they used. Officers are encouraged to submit thorough and detailed reports after a force incident.

Administrators and trainers should continue to review court decisions in their jurisdictions across the nation in order to more effectively design guidelines that provide officers with a range of options regarding the appropriate level of force in a given situation (see Box 10.3). Further, continuing training in the use of all equipment, including classroom training and practical application training, should be provided regularly. Supervisors should receive ongoing training in how to evaluate officers' incident reports on use of force and enforce departmental guidelines when unreasonable force is discovered. Supervisors play a significant role in determining whether reasonable force was used in arrest situations. Moreover, since the use of Tasers has increased, officers and supervisors are encouraged to review the court's decision and rationale for the reasonable deployment of the Taser in the *McPherson* case. The decision can be used as guidance to officers as arrest circumstance variables dictate. A continued commitment on the part of police administrators, trainers, and officers will help in developing a balance between the rights of citizens to be free of unreasonable seizures and the interests of society in maintaining legitimate law enforcement, while protecting police officers.

BOX 10.3 RESPONSE TO RESISTANCE POLICY CONSIDERATIONS

- Policy philosophy
- Definitions
  - Control
  - Resistance
  - Objectively reasonable force
  - Nonlethal force and lethal force
- Authority to use force
- Types of resistance (psychological intimidation, verbal, passive, defensive, active aggression, and aggravated active aggression)
- Levels of force
  - Officer presence
  - Verbal instructions
  - Empty-hand control (control holds, wristlocks, come-along holds, takedown tactics, pressure points, hand/leg strikes, stuns, and neck restraints)
  - Aerosols (pepper spray and other chemical agents)
  - Use of canine
  - Intermediate weapons (batons, flashlights, Tasers, stun guns, etc.)
  - Lethal force guidelines
- Description of authorized equipment (restraints, restraint chair, etc.)
  - Manufacturer's recommendations
- Escalation/de-escalation of force
- Medical considerations
- Force and restraint of "special needs" prisoners
- Transportation in restraints
- Reporting use of force
- Investigation of use-of-force incidents

References

Angrick, W. P. (2009). *Investigation of restraint device in Iowa's county jails.* Des Moines, IA: Iowa Citizen's Aide/Ombudsman Office.

Alpert, G. (1989). Police use of deadly Force: the Miami experience. In R. G. Dunham & G. P. Alpert (Eds.), *Critical issues in policing: Contemporary readings.* Prospect Heights, IL: Waveland Press, Inc.

Alpert, G., & Dunham, R. (1999). The force factor: measuring police use of force relative to suspect resistance: *Police use of force.* Washington, DC: National Institute of Justice.

Alpert, G., Smith, M. R., Kamiski, R. J., Fridell, L. A., MacDonald, J., & Kubu., B. (2010). *Police use of force, tasers and other less-lethal weapons.* Washington, DC: National Institute of Justice, Department of Justice.

Bozeman, W. P., Hauda, W. E., Heck, J. J., Graham, D. D., Martin, B. P., & Winslow, J. E. (2008). Safety and injury profile of conducted electrical weapons used by law enforcement officers against criminal suspects. *Annals of Emergency Medicine, 20,* 1–10.

Bayley, D. H., & Garofalo, J. (1989). The management of violence by police officers. *Criminology, 27,* 1–27.

Brave, M. (2011). *Use of force recipient status matrix*. Eau Claire, WI: Liability Assessment and Awareness International, Inc. Use of Force Training Materials.

Brave, M., & O'Linn, M. K. (2010, February). *Bryan v. McPherson*—A new standard for the use of electronic devices? *The Police Chief*, 1–5. International Association of Chiefs of Police, Washington, DC.

Binder, A., & Scharf, P. (1980). The violent police-citizen encounter. *Annals of the American Academy of Political and Social Science, 452*, 111–121.

Binder, A., & Fridell, L. A. (1984). *The use of firearms by police officers: the impact of individuals, communities, and race*. Albany: State University of New York. Doctoral dissertation.

Bloomberg, M. (1982). Issues and controversies with respect to the use of deadly force by police. In T. Barker & D. L. Carter (Eds.), *Police deviance*. Cincinnati, OH: Pilgrimage Press.

Camp, C., & Camp, G. (2003). *Prisoner assaults on correction officers*. Middletown CT: Criminal Justice Institute, Inc. *Corrections Yearbook*.

Chevigny, P. B. (1969). *Police power: police abuse in New York City*. New York, NY: Vintage Books.

Croft, E. B. (1985). *Police use of force: an empirical analysis*. State University of New York at Albany. Doctoral dissertation.

Croft, E. B., & Austin, B. A. (1987). Police use of force in Rochester and Syracuse, New York, 1984 and 1985, *Report to the New York State Commission on Criminal Justice and the Use of Force* (Vol. III, May). Albany, NY: New York State Commission on Criminal Justice and the Use of Force.

Durose, M. R., Schmitt, E. L., & Langan, P. A. (2005). *Contacts between police and the public, 2002*. Washington, DC: Bureau of Justice Statistics, Department of Justice.

Durose, M. R., Smith, E. L., & Langan, P. A. (2007). *Contacts between police and the public, 2005*. Washington, DC: Bureau of Justice Statistics, Department of Justice.

Eith, C., & Durose, M. R. (2011). *Contacts between police and the public, 2008*. Washington, DC: Bureau of Justice Statistics, Department of Justice.

Farber, B. J. (2007, March). Civil liability for use of tasers, stunguns, and other electronic control devices. *Americans for Effective Law Enforcement Monthly Law Journal, 3*, 101–108.

Farber, B. J. (2010, February). Taser, electronic control devices (CEDs): an "Intermediate" use of force? *Americans for Effective Law Enforcement Monthly Law Journal, 2*, 101–109.

Ferrell, C. E. (2012, December). What every police chief should know about electronic control devices. *The Police Chief*, 12–15. International Association of Chiefs of Police, Washington, DC.

Fridell, L. (1989). Justifiable use of force measures in research on deadly force. *Journal of Criminal Justice, 17*, 157–165.

Friederich, R. J. (1980). Police use of force: individuals, situations and organizations. *Annals of the American Academy of Political and Social Science, 425*, 82–97.

Fyfe, J. J. (1978). *Shots fired: An examination of New York City police firearms discharges*. Albany: State University of New York. Doctoral dissertation.

Fyfe, J. J. (1988). Police use of deadly force: research and reform. *Justice Quarterly, 5*, 165–205.

Garner, J., Buchanan, T., Schade, T., & Hepburn, J. (1996). *Executive summary: understanding the use of force by and against the police*. Washington, DC: National Institute of Justice.

Geller, W. A. (1985). Officer restraint in the use of deadly force: the next frontier in police shooting research. *Journal of Police Science and Administration, 13*, 153–171.

Greenfeld, P., Langham, A., Smith, S., & Kaminski, R. (1997). *Police use of force: collection of national data*. Washington, DC: Bureau of Justice Statistics. Research in Brief.

Greenleaf, R. G., & Lanza-Kaduce, L. (1995). Sophistication, organization, and authority-subject conflict: rediscovering and unraveling Turk's theory of norm resistance. *Criminology, 33*, 565–585.

Hemmens, C., & Atherton, E. (1999). *Use of force: Current practice and policy*. Lanham, MD: American Correctional Association.

Hickman, M. J., Piquero, A. R., & Garner, J. H. (2008). Toward a national estimate of police use of nonlethal force. *Criminology and Public Policy*, *7*, 563–604.

Ho, J., Dawes, D., Ryan, F. J., Lundin, E. J., Overton, K. G., Zeider, A. J., et al. (2009). *Catecholamines in simulated arrest scenarios*. Darwin, Australia: ACEM Winter Symposium.

Hopkins, E. J. (1931). *Our lawless police*. New York, NY: Viking Press.

Horvath, F. (1987). The police use of deadly force: a description of selected characteristics of intrastate incidents. *Journal of Police Science and Administration*, *15*, 226–238.

Hougland, S., Mesloh, C., & Henych, M. (2005 March). Use of force, civil litigation, and the taser: one agency's experience. *FBI Law Enforcement Bulletin*, 24–30.

International Association of Chiefs of Police (2001). *Police use of force in America*. Alexandria, VA: IACP.

Jacobs, D., & Britt, D. (1979). Inequality and police use of deadly force: an empirical assessment of a conflict hypothesis. *Social Problems*, *24*, 401–411.

Kappeler, V. (1997). *Critical issues in police civil liability* (2nd ed.). Prospect Heights, IL: Waveland Press, Inc.

Kappeler, V., Kappeler, S. F., & del Carmen, R. V. (1993, updated 1996). A content analysis of police civil liability cases: decisions of the federal courts, 1978–1990. *Journal of criminal Justice*, *21*, 325–337.

Kratcoski, P. (1987). The implications of research explaining prison violence and disruption. *Federal Probation*, *52*, 27–32.

Laub, J. (2011). *Study of deaths following electro muscular disruption*. Washington, DC: National Institute of Justice, Department of Justice.

Lee, H., & Vaughn, M. S. (2010). Organizational factors that contribute to police deadly force liability. *Journal of Criminal Justice*, *38*, 193–206.

Lester, D. (1984). The use of deadly force by police. *Police Journal*, *57*, 170–171.

Light, S. (1991). Assaults on prison officers: interactional themes. *Justice Quarterly*, *8*, 243–261.

LRP Publications, (1992). *Personal injury verdict reviews*. Horsham, PA: Author.

Mastrofski, S., & Parks, R. (1990). Improving observational studies of police. *Criminology*, *28*, 475–496.

Matulia, K. (1982). *A balance of forces*. Gaithersburg, MD: International Association of Chiefs of Police.

McGuiness, J. M. (2009, Spring). A primer on North Carolina and federal use of force law: trends in Fourth Amendment doctrine, qualified immunity and state law issues. *Campbell Law Review*, *3*, 1–71.

McLaughlin, V. (1992). *Police and the use of force: the Savannah study*. Westport, CT: Praeger Publishers.

Milton, C. H., Lardner, J. W., & Albrecht, G. L. (1997). Police use of deadly force. In H. W. More, Jr. (Ed.), *Critical issues in law enforcement* (4th ed.). Cincinnati, OH: Anderson Publishing Co.

National Commission on Law Observance and Enforcement (Wickersham Commission) (1931). *Report on lawlessness in law enforcement*. Washington. DC: U.S. Government Printing Office.

National Institute of Justice (1999). *Use of force by police*. Washington, DC: U.S. Department of Justice.

Pate, A., & Fridell, L. (1993). *Police use of force: official reports, citizen complaints, and legal consequences*. Washington, DC: Police Foundation.

Reiss, A. (1971). *The police and the public*. New Haven, CT: Yale University Press.

Ross, D. L. (1990). Study examines non-deadly physical force policies. *Corrections Today*, July, 64–66.

Ross, D. L. (1996). A national assessment of prisoner assaults on correction officers. *Corrections Compendium*, *25*, 1–8.

Ross, D. L. (1999). Analyzing patterns of citizen resistance during police arrest. *FBI Law Enforcement Bulletin*, June, 22–28.

Ross, D. L. (2000). Emerging trends in police failure to train liability. *Policing: An International Journal of Police Strategies and Management, 23*, 169–193.

Ross, D. L. (2002). An assessment of the *Graham v. Connor*, ten years later. *Policing: An International Journal of Strategies and Management, 2*, 294–318.

Ross, D. L. (2004). An analysis of *Hudson v. McMillian*: Ten years later. *Criminal Law Bulletin, 6*, 15–48.

Ross, D. L. (2005). A content analysis of the emerging trends in the use of non-lethal force research in policing. *Journal of Law Enforcement Executive Forum, 5*, 121–148.

Ross, D. L. (2008). Analyzing of detainee resistance and detention officer use of force in Michigan jails. *Law Enforcement Executive Forum, 4*, 107–128.

Ross, D. L. (2012, April). *Presentation on human factors and lethal force liability issues.* Chicago, IL: International Law Enforcement Educators and Training Association annual conference.

Rowan, J. R. (1996). Who is safer in male maximum prisons? *Corrections Today, 58*, 2–4.

Schultz, D., & Service, J. (1981). *The police use of force.* Springfield, IL: Charles C Thomas.

Smith, R. M., Petrocelli, M., & Scheer, C. (2007). Excessive force, civil liability, and the taser in the nation's courts: Implications for law enforcement policy and practice. *Policing: An International Journal of Police Strategies and Management, 30*, 398–422.

Sykes, R. E., & Brent, E. E. (1983). *Policing: a social behaviorist perspective.* Brunswick, NJ: New Rutgers University Press.

Taser International, Inc. (2012, March, 16). *Statistical Update on Taser Usage.* www.Taserinternational.com.

Waegel, W. B. (1984). The use of lethal force by police: the complaint. *Journal of Police Science and Administration, 8*, 247–252.

Zigmund, E. (2007). Electronic control devices: liability and training aspects. *AELE Monthly Law Journal, 5*, 501–509.

11

Section 1983 and Correctional Liability Issues

OVERVIEW

Justice White, writing for the United States Supreme Court in *Wolff v. McDonnell* (1974), stated that there is "no iron curtain drawn between the Constitution and prisons of this country, . . . a prisoner is not wholly stripped of constitutional protections when he is imprisoned for crime." Since the *Wolff* decision, prisoners have filed numerous lawsuits under § 1983, claiming deprivation of constitutional rights. Prisoners may file lawsuits in both federal and state courts under § 1983. Most prisoner litigation is filed in federal court *in forma pauperis* (Maahs & del Carmen, 1995; Ross, 1997). Section 1983 prisoner actions have included inadequate medical care, access to the courts, prison conditions, use of excessive force, failure to protect, and administrative deficiencies.

Prisoners commonly file § 1983 lawsuits seeking to gain some type of monetary award or equitable relief. In these lawsuits, the prisoner is generally complaining about the manner in which officials treated him or her, challenging the constitutionality of the treatment or conditions of confinement, or contesting a correctional practice or rule. Other prisoners may file lawsuits to break up the monotony of prison life. Frivolous lawsuits have been submitted to harass correctional officials or to seek an opportunity to leave the facility for a court appearance.

Court decisions concerning prisoner litigation have had a profound impact on the correctional system. Since the 1970s, court intervention through case decisions has directly affected a wide range of prison issues, including health care services, access to the courts, use of force, religious practices, disciplinary procedures, conditions of confinement, officer brutality, and administrative practices. As a result, both jail and prison operational policies and procedures have been significantly affected. This chapter will describe the liability issues most frequently raised by prisoners under § 1983 and examine the standard of review.

Application of the Deliberate Indifference Standard

The U.S. Supreme Court's holding in a particular case often results in establishing a standard or test with which to evaluate future claims. Arguably, one of the most common and far-reaching standards applied to correctional litigation developed by the Court is that of "deliberate indifference." This standard was established in the seminal case of *Estelle v. Gamble* (1976). In this Texas prison case, the prisoner sustained a back injury while on a work assignment and claimed that he was repeatedly denied or delayed medical care, despite 17 examinations by medical doctors, X rays, prescribed medication, and bed rest. The Supreme Court determined that the proper method for examining claims of denial of medical care under the Eighth Amendment is whether correctional officials were deliberately indifferent to the needs of the prisoner. The Court ruled that liability will attach when the actions of correctional personnel constitute cruel and unusual punishment in violation of the Eighth Amendment. In *Estelle* the Court found that the officials' response did not rise to a level of deliberate indifference.

Deliberate indifference is not easily defined, is difficult to apply, and difficult for a prisoner to meet (Bober & Pinals, 2007; Schlanger, 2003; Vaughn, 1996). The Court distinguished deliberate indifference from "negligence" and has ruled that an act of negligence is not enough to impose liability under § 1983 (*Daniels v. Williams*, 1986). Negligence is the failure to use care as a reasonable person and careful person may do under similar circumstances (*Black's Law Dictionary*, 2004). Since first enumerating this standard, the Court has held that deliberate indifference resides on a continuum between "mere negligence and something less than acts or omissions for the very purpose of causing harm" (*Farmer v. Brennan*, 1994). "Deliberate" means that a particular course of action has been chosen from among various alternatives, and "indifference" means that there has been some conscious disregard for a person's rights (Plitt, 1997; Vogt, 2000).

Deliberate indifference requires certain duties: (1) serious medical complaints, especially of a continuing nature, should not be ignored (whether correctional personnel regard them as false or exaggerated); (2) medically trained personnel should make medical judgments; (3) serious, chronic symptoms should receive attention; and (4) neither a blind eye nor a deaf ear should be tolerated regarding a prisoner's complaint where, with proper care, a correctional officer could have known about the complaint (Silver, 2008). Under the deliberate indifference standard, there is a general expectation that "adequate" or "reasonable" care will be provided to prisoners under the control of correctional personnel. A system that provides adequate medical and mental health care to prisoners at intake and throughout incarceration must be in place. Most, if not all, detention and prison facilities have instituted health care services to prisoners, despite continued claims of inadequate medical care. Prisoners generally have no right to be treated by a private physician (*Hawley v. Evans*, 1989).

Deliberate indifference can be manifested in a number of ways. The refusal of correctional or medical personnel to provide care, or a delay in providing such care, may be actionable under the deliberate indifference standard. A series of incidents that, if viewed in isolation, appear to involve only negligence, may give rise to deliberate indifference. Problems caused by understaffing, a lack of or deficient equipment, substandard facilities, and a lack of procedures may be so egregious that the ensuing inability to render adequate medical care is so evident that the failure to redress these problems is tantamount to "deliberate indifference" (Krantz, 1997).

Actions emerging from a pretrial detainee's claims of being deprived of needed medical care are examined under the due process clauses of the Fifth and Fourteenth Amendments rather than the Eighth Amendment. The courts have agreed that the cruel and unusual punishment clause of the Eighth Amendment does not apply to pretrial detainees, but the due process clause protects them.

Over the years, the Supreme Court has expanded the standard of deliberate indifference beyond health care services. The Court has extended the standard to other prisoner claims, including conditions of confinement (*Wilson v. Seiter*, 1991), failure to protect (*DeShaney v. Winnebago County Department of Social Services*, 1989; *Farmer v. Brennan*, 1994), failure to train (*City of Canton v. Harris*, 1989), claims emerging from supervisory deficiencies, and claims resulting from custodial suicides. The following discussion illustrates how the courts have applied this standard to correctional situations.

Deliberate Indifference and Health Care

Providing health care services to pretrial detainees and state prisoners is a fundamental responsibility. Today's detention and prison facilities confine prisoners with a variety of medical problems ranging from hypertension, asthma, obesity, cirrhosis, hepatitis, respiratory diseases, diseases like HIV/AIDS, and differing degrees of mental illness (Maruschak, 2010). Over the years, numerous types of civil liability claims alleging inadequate medical care have emerged. Ross (1997) found that in a 25-year analysis (1970 to 1994) of § 1983 litigation in jails and prisons, medical care claims were the most frequently filed by prisoners and correctional officials prevailed in approximately 55 percent of the cases.

In *Arnold v. Lewis* (1992), a prisoner filed a § 1983 claim against correctional officials for being deliberately indifferent to his mental health care needs. The district court ruled in favor of the prisoner, finding that the officials' actions constituted deliberate indifference to serious medical needs in violation of the Eighth Amendment. The officials had placed the prisoner in lockdown as a punishment for symptoms of her paranoid schizophrenia as an alternative to providing mental health care. The officials knew that the mental health program at the facility was deficient and were aware that the prisoner's mental condition deteriorated when she was locked down in a small cell without treatment, but failed to correct the grossly inadequate psychiatric care. Prison officials' actions warranted injunctive relief, ensuring that she would receive the appropriate treatment.

A lower district court granted summary judgment to correctional officials in a § 1983 action brought by a female prisoner in *Giron v. Corrections Corp. of America* (1998). After being raped by a correctional officer, the plaintiff alleged that correctional officials deliberately disregarded a substantial risk of harm to her and denied her psychological care. The court concluded that the official's awareness of two prior incidents of sexual misconduct by other officers was insufficient to establish that the officials must have drawn the inference that a substantial risk of harm existed. The court held that she was not deprived of necessary medical care after the sexual assault. The plaintiff was seen by a psychiatrist 18 times and a psychologist at least 100 times during a six-month period.

In *Tucker v. Randall* (1993) a pretrial detainee alleged inadequate medical care by detention officers of a sheriff's department. The appeals court affirmed the lower court's holding that the officers did not act with deliberate indifference to the medical needs of the detainee, even when they failed to treat him with ice and aspirin as instructed by a doctor, or delayed more than two months in having the injuries reexamined. A reasonable person would not have viewed the detainee's injuries as life-threatening or serious. The detainee was transported to a hospital prior to booking and the hospital doctor did not treat the injuries as serious or life-threatening. Further, the detainee did not complain of injuries to the booking officer upon arrival.

The duty to provide medical care is a continuing one, and delay of such care either at the onset or continuation of serious medical symptoms may be actionable. In *Lancaster v. Monroe County, Alabama* (1997), a sheriff and several of his detention officers were found to be deliberately indifferent to the serious medical needs of an alcoholic pretrial detainee who died from seizures brought on by withdrawal symptoms. The detainee was jailed for driving under the influence of alcohol and placed on a top bunk in a holding cell, because lower bunks were occupied. Detention officers were notified twice by the detainee's wife that he was an alcoholic and suffered from delirium tremens. The officers acknowledged the condition and promised to watch him. The detainee's father notified the sheriff of his condition, and the sheriff informed the father that the detainee would be taken to the hospital if he had a seizure. During the night, several prisoners stated that the detainee suffered from the "shakes" and a headache. At mid-morning, the detainee sat up in his bunk, began shaking, and fell out of bed, landing on his head. He was transported to the hospital, where he died three days later due to the head injuries. The pathologist determined that the detainee was having a seizure when he fell out of his bed. The detainee's wife filed a § 1983 action for wrongful death and deliberate indifference to the deceased's serious medical condition. The court found in favor of the plaintiff and determined that his inebriated condition progressed into seizures, constituting a serious medical condition. The evidence showed that the condition would worsen with delay and that the sheriff failed to plan for medical care until after the detainee had a seizure. The officers knew the deceased's condition was serious, yet allowed him to remain in the top bunk and failed to plan to obtain medical attention until after the seizure.

In *Reed v. McBride* (1999), an appellate court found in favor of a prisoner's Eighth Amendment claim of withholding food and life-sustaining medication from him while incarcerated. The court found that the prisoner's medical condition progressively worsened, making it serious, and supporting his claim of deliberate indifference. The court found that depriving a prisoner of food may be so objectively serious as to support a claim of cruel and unusual punishment under the Eighth Amendment, when the amount and duration of the deprivation is considered. The prisoner suffered from a variety of ailments, including paralysis, heart disease, Hunt's syndrome, high blood pressure, rheumatoid arthritis, and other crippling diseases. In *Gutierrez v. Peters* (1997), however, the appellate court affirmed judgment in favor of prison officials when a prisoner claimed that he received inadequate medical treatment for an infected cyst on his eye. The court acknowledged that the cyst was a serious medical condition, but failed to find that the officials acted with deliberate indifference despite isolated delays in treatment. The court found that a six-day wait to see the physician was not an unreasonably long delay for the condition in view of the fact that the physician had seen the prisoner one week earlier and had concluded the cyst was not infected, and the physician promptly prescribed a course of treatment.

Delay in providing medical care in a detention facility was addressed in *Blackmore v. Kalamazoo County* (2004). The Sixth Circuit Court of Appeals reversed the lower court's provision for summary judgment when a detainee filed a lawsuit claiming delay in medical attention. Blackmore was admitted into the Kalamazoo County jail for driving under a suspended license. He was booked, placed in a cell, and within an hour he began complaining of abdominal pain. Detention officers gave him antacids but did secure further medical care. Two days later he again complained of extreme abdominal pains and requested immediate medical care. The officers placed him the observation cell as Blackmore was vomiting the antacids given earlier. Later that day, a nurse examined him and determined that he was suffering from appendicitis. He was transported to the hospital and an appendectomy was successfully performed. Blackmore filed a lawsuit claiming that the officers violated his constitutional rights by denying him prompt medical attention. He also alleged that the sheriff failed to implement policies and to train officers to adequately respond to detainee medical needs.

In reversing the lower court's decision granting qualified immunity to the officers, the appellate court ruled that Blackmore proved that the officers demonstrated a "culpable state of mind" by being aware that Blackmore had a serious medical condition and yet failing to seek medical care until two days after he made the complaint. To be liable, a detainee must show that his medical needs posed a "substantial risk of serious harm." The court ruled that a serious medical need is one that has been diagnosed by a physician as mandating treatment or one that is so obvious that even a layperson would easily recognize the necessity for medical care. The court reasoned that Blackmore complained over two days that he had abdominal pains, filed several sick call requests asking for medical care, was observed to be vomiting, and the officers placed him in the observation cell. His condition was progressively deteriorating and officers were aware of his obvious need for medical care but did not seek medical attention until two days later. Thus, Blackmore sufficiently showed that his need for medical care was not addressed, violating his Eighth Amendment rights. The court also found that the county failed to implement policies on how to deal with prisoner illness and they also failed to adequately train the officers. Such failures supported a constitutional claim of deliberate indifference.

A detainee asserted that he was delayed medical care in *Rand v. Simonds* (2006). The detainee claimed that he asked to see a specialist pertaining to ongoing pain in his shoulder and was denied care amounting to deliberate indifference to his serious medical needs. The detainee alleged that he made numerous requests to the physician's assistant, the superintendent, and the assistant superintendent that he needed outside medical care for his shoulder injury. The detainee maintained that administrators of the detention center purposely delayed medical treatment so that they would not have to pay the specialist. The detainee did see the specialist several days after the repeated requests were made. The defendants filed a motion for summary judgment and the court granted it. The court held that the detainee was indeed examined by the orthopedic surgeon and the delay did not further complicate the injury in the shoulder nor did it cause him any additional pain. The specialist determined upon examination that the shoulder did not require surgery and that a delay in his assessment did not measurably increase any injury to the shoulder condition. The court concluded that the detainee's injury did not amount to a "serious medical need" amounting to deliberate indifference.

In *Foster v. Elyea* (2007) a special administrator, on behalf of a deceased prisoner, brought a § 1983 claim against prison officials, alleging that their failure to provide the prisoner with prescribed medication, treatment, diet, and exercise opportunities hastened his death or caused him great emotional distress. The defendants moved to dismiss and the court denied the motion. The court held that the allegations of the special administrator stated an Eighth Amendment claim that employees were deliberately indifferent to the prisoner's serious medical needs. The administrator alleged that the employees knew that the prisoner faced a risk of death if he did not receive his prescribed medication, treatment, diet, and exercise for his type 2 diabetes, high blood pressure, and congestive heart failure, but that department of corrections employees personally involved in delivering medical services to the prisoner failed to provide those things to him.

A detainee in a county jail brought a § 1983 claim against county officials and a physician, asserting that while confined her serious medical needs were deliberately ignored in *Goebert v. Lee County* (2007). The detainee gave birth to a stillborn infant in the jail. The court denied summary judgment to the officials noting that the jail commander was deliberately indifferent to the medical complaints of prisoners in the past and in this incident. The court found that the detainee's amniotic fluid leak constituted a serious medical need and that the jail commander's failure to provide the detainee with medical treatment supported a claim of deliberates indifference. According to the court, the jail commander responded to the detainee with disbelief that she was pregnant, required medical care, and that she could visit an outside physician if she could pay for it.

In *Jones v. Muskegon County* (2010), the estate of a detainee who died of cancer during confinement filed a wrongful death claim in accordance with § 1983 and the Fourteenth Amendment asserting that detention officers and medical professionals were deliberately indifferent to his deteriorating condition while incarcerated. Jones was confined in the Muskegon County Jail on a charge of second-degree murder. During admission into the facility he responded "no" to all health care questions minus one, that he had a sexually transmitted disease. From September 2004 through March 2005, Jones did not complain of any health care problems, but in March he mentioned to his attorney on a visit that he was not feeling well and an officer noticed that he was not eating his meals on a regular basis. The officer informed the jail nurse and she examined Jones, who had lost about 70 pounds since his admission. The doctor of the jail examined Jones and transferred him to the local hospital where he was diagnosed with abdominal cancer. Jones underwent surgery in April 2005 and was cleared to return to the jail by the surgeon about two weeks later. On May 5, 2005 he died in the medical unit of the jail. Jones' estate filed the lawsuit against 26 defendants, including jail officers, jail health care workers, the jail doctor, and administrators of the jail.

The federal district court applied the standard established under *Farmer* (1994) and *Estelle* (1976) requiring that the plaintiff must show that officers intentionally denied or delayed access to medical care for a serious medical need and that such medical condition posed a serious risk of medical harm. The court granted summary judgment in favor of the defendant county, even though the court did question the quality of medical care for prisoners housed at the jail. The Sixth Circuit Court of Appeals affirmed the lower court's decision. The court noted that once the need to provide medical care to Jones was observed, the correction officers referred him to the nurse who examined him within hours of the referral in the medical unit. Therefore, the court ruled that neither the officers nor the nurses or the doctor ignored that Jones needed medical care and that the plaintiff failed to submit any evidence that would prove otherwise. The court held that there was no widespread practice of abusing policies and procedures that applied to providing medical care to prisoners that could be directly linked to Jones' death. Malpractice claims against the jail doctor failed as the court ruled that it was the jail doctor who had Jones transferred to the hospital and did not have a role in returning him back to the jail.

In *Spears v. Ruth* (2009), city police officers arrested Ruth after a struggle. After restraint Ruth advised the officers that he had smoked crack cocaine and it was later asserted that the officers failed to mention the fact to responding paramedics. On the arrest scene, the decision was made to transport Ruth to the jail and he was admitted. At the jail Ruth was examined by nurses and they decided that he did not need to be transported to the hospital. A short time later Ruth began to hallucinate and acted violently toward himself and officers secured him in a restraint chair for his safety. Ruth was Tasered in order to relax his muscles and he remained in the chair for three hours where he calmed down but continued to hallucinate. Ruth was released from the restraint chair and later began to shake and spit up blood, and then became unresponsive. Ruth was transported to the hospital where he was diagnosed with respiratory and cardiac failure and multiorgan failure resulting from cocaine use. He lapsed into a coma and died 11 months later.

Ruth's estate filed a § 1983 lawsuit claiming the officers were deliberately indifferent to a serious medical illness. The district court rejected the officers' petition for summary judgment and they appealed to the appellate court for the Sixth Circuit who reversed the lower court's decision. The court ruled that Ruth's condition and need for medical attention was not so obvious to the officers to establish the existence of a serious medical need for the purposes of supporting a claim of deliberate indifference in violation of due process.

Deliberate Indifference and Psychological Care

The deliberate indifference standard also applies to the psychological needs of mentally impaired prisoners. Allegations generally revolve around appropriate treatment of the mentally impaired while incarcerated and involuntarily medicating a prisoner who manifests a mental defect. The United States Supreme Court has addressed this issue and the lower courts have on numerous occasions applied the standard of deliberate indifference.

In *Washington v. Harper* (1990), the United States Supreme Court ruled that involuntarily medicating a prisoner who has been diagnosed by a psychiatrist as suffering from a mental defect and who posed a significant risk of harm to himself and others did not violate the Fourteenth Amendment. Harper was diagnosed with bipolar disorder and refused to take his prescribed medication. In compliance with prison policy, two psychiatrists determined that he was "gravely disabled" and posed a danger to others and himself, and medicated him without his consent. He filed a § 1983 lawsuit challenging the decision to medicate him against his will.

The Court rejected his claim, holding that the state had a legitimate interest in the safety and security of the prison—for the safety of other prisoners, for Harper, and for the officers and staff in the institution. The Court ruled that involuntarily medicating a prisoner implies a due process component consistent with the Fourteenth Amendment and that a hearing must be conducted prior to administering medication without a prisoner's consent. Pursuant to the state of Washington's policy, such a hearing was in place and before involuntarily medicating Harper, he was provided with a hearing. The hearing outcome concluded that for the safety of Harper and the security of the institution, he be medicated without his consent. The Court ruled that such a policy and practice protected Harper's due process rights under the Fourteenth Amendment and affirmed the state of Washington's penological and therapeutic interest in medicating Harper against his will.

The nation was stunned in 1998 when a man walked into the Capitol building in Washington, D.C., and shot and killed two federal police officers when he was looking for "aliens" and the key to the innermost portions of the Capitol. In *United States v. Weston* (2002), the appellate court ruled that the Federal Bureau of Prisons could involuntarily medicate Weston. Prison psychiatrists concluded that Weston needed to be medicated, but he refused. His attorney filed a legal action requesting that officials be prohibited from medicating him without his consent. The appellate court affirmed the lower court's decision to involuntarily medicate Weston because the action was essential in order to render the prisoner nondangerous, based on medical/safety concerns.

The United States Supreme Court has further expanded its decision in *Harper* by examining whether the government can medicate a mentally impaired prisoner against his will so that he can be rendered competent to stand trial. The Court addressed this issue in *Sell v. United States* (2003). A federal criminal defendant with a long history of mental illness was initially found competent to stand trial for a criminal charge of fraud. He was released on bail but was later denied bail because his condition deteriorated. His attorney requested a reconsideration of his competence. After an examination at a medical center for federal prisoners, the defendant was found incompetent to stand trial and was hospitalized to determine whether he would attain competency to allow his trial to proceed. The defendant refused to take his antipsychotic medication and, after a hearing, a psychiatrist authorized that he be medicated involuntarily. A U.S. magistrate judge issued an order forcing the administration of drugs. The district court found no evidence that the defendant was dangerous, but upheld the order, finding that the involuntary medication was the only viable hope of rendering the defendant competent to stand trial in order to obtain an adjudication of his guilt or innocence.

The appellate court affirmed and the United States Supreme Court ruled that the Constitution allows the government to administer psychiatric drugs even against the defendant's will, in limited circumstances. The Court held that in order to administer such medication against the will of the accused defendant for trial purposes, four criteria must be met: (1) there are important governmental interests at stake, such as timely prosecution, bringing the defendant to trial, assuring the trial is fair, and the court's evaluation of the facts of each case; (2) involuntary medication will significantly further such governmental interests that the administration of drugs will likely render the defendant competent to stand trial: (3) involuntary medication is necessary to further such interests and any alternative and less intrusive treatments are unlikely to produce the same results; and (4) the administration of drugs is medically appropriate—that is, in the defendant's best medical interests in light of the defendant's medical condition.

The *Sell* decision was applied to a prisoner serving a sentence on death row in *Singleton v. Norris* (2003). Singleton was serving his sentence on death row and was being forcibly medicated. He sought an order that would stop the treatment. The state court denied the request and he filed a habeas corpus petition seeking a stay of execution of his death sentence. The district court denied the petition and the prisoner appealed. The appellate court affirmed, holding that a state does not violate the Eighth Amendment or due process by executing a prisoner who has regained competency through forced medication that is part of appropriate medical care.

In *Norris v. Engles* (2007), a detainee diagnosed with manic bipolar depression became combative and was restrained in his cell. He filed a § 1983 action asserting deliberate indifference to his mental health needs. The officials filed a motion for summary judgment and the court denied it. The officials filed an appeal and the appellate court reversed. The court found that restraining the detainee to a floor-grate in an uncomfortable manner for approximately three hours did not violate the detainee's substantive due process rights. According to the court, the officers' actions of restraining the detainee for three hours did not support a claim of deliberate indifference. The officers only restrained the detainee after she had threatened to pull out her own peripherally inserted central catheter (PICC) so that she would not bleed to death.

In *Estate of Rice v. Correctional Medical Services* (2012) a schizophrenic man arrested for an attempted bank robbery often refused to take his medication, bathe, or eat while in a county jail. Correction officers transported the prisoner back and forth between a number of mental health facilities and the jail on a number of occasions. While at the jail pending a transfer to a state psychiatric facility, he died from excessively drinking water (psychogenic polydipsia). During his confinement the prisoner refused medication on several occasions, which exacerbated his mental illness; fought with officers requiring the use of the restraint chair to calm him; and refused to eat, causing weight loss. His estate filed a lawsuit claiming that that jail officials, the nurses, and the jail doctor were deliberately indifferent to his mental illness, which contributed to his death. The appellate court for the Seventh Circuit agreed with the lower court that the prisoner died due to his own volitional self-destructive behaviors and not from a lack of intervention by jail officers and health care providers. The court concluded there was no basis that any of the defendants were liable for his death.

Deliberate Indifference, the Americans with Disabilities Act, and Prisoners

The Americans with Disabilities Act (ADA) was enacted in 1990 to protect qualified people with disabilities. The Act not only applies to free citizens but also applies to prisoners in state prisons and other correctional facilities (*Pennsylvania Dep't. of Corrections v. Yeskey*, 1998). In *Yeskey*, a prisoner who had been denied admission to a prison boot camp program due to his history of hypertension sued correctional officials under the ADA. The United States Supreme Court held that Title II of the ADA, prohibiting a "public entity" from discriminating against a "qualified individual with a disability," applied to prisoners in state prisons. As applied in the correctional environment, the ADA was instituted to protect disabled prisoners from discrimination under the Fourteenth Amendment and has primarily been applied to health care issues.

A district court let stand a jury verdict and monetary damages in the amount of $150,000 in a § 1983 action stemming from an ADA claim in *Beckford v. Irvin* (1999). The plaintiff prisoner had been confined to a wheelchair since 1984. In 1994 he was transferred from a psychiatric center to another correctional facility, where he was assigned to a Mental Health Observation Unit (MHOU). He was placed in the MHOU such that his wheelchair could fit within the cell. Shortly after the transfer, officials took away the wheelchair and denied him access to it for the majority of his time at the facility, despite his repeated requests. The jury concluded that the prisoner's rights had been violated because he was denied the use of his wheelchair, he was unable to participate in outdoor exercise or take a shower. The jury awarded damages against two supervisory officials for being deliberately indifferent to the prisoner's serious medical needs.

In *Hanson v. Sangamore County Sheriff's Dep't* (1998), failure to provide a known deaf arrestee with an interpreter or the physical means to make a telephone call was actionable under the ADA. A § 1983 claim based on a violation of the ADA was not defensible by qualified immunity. The district court rejected county officials' motion for summary judgment in *Roe v. County of Comm'n of Monongalia County* (1996), when a mental health patient brought an action under the ADA. The plaintiff was picked up on a mental health warrant and held in a padded cell, handcuffed, and shackled. He was not given proper treatment or a hearing and was not allowed to use a bathroom, change clothes, or eat without handcuffs. The court found that the prisoner stated a valid claim because he was unable to communicate with his family, was unable to attend to his personal hygiene, and was isolated in a manner that the ADA was designed to prevent.

Diabetic prisoners brought a class action under § 1983 against state correctional officials alleging violations of the Eighth Amendment and the ADA in *Rouse v. Plantier* (1998). The court denied summary judgment for the defendants on the issue of whether the prisoners' diabetes was a disability under the ADA. The court ruled that the prisoners might be substantially limited in the foods they could eat, in the exercise regime in which they could engage, and by numerous special complications that diabetes presented for them. If the prisoners' condition was considered without mitigating measures such as medicines, or assistive or prosthetic devices, the court found it was clear that they could be considered disabled.

Prisoners with disabilities have brought legal actions complaining that the use of restraints by correctional officers violates their constitutional rights. In *Williams-El v. McLemore* (2002), a prisoner sought equitable relief against a practice of using restraints on prisoners with disabilities. The prisoner alleged that correctional officers failed to provide him large handcuffs, rather than the standard handcuffs, for transportation purposes. The prisoner was diagnosed with a congenital deformity known as Kasabach Merrit Syndrome, which caused his right hand to be severely curled inward at the wrist and caused pain to his extremities when improperly positioned. The court barred summary judgment for the correctional officials, holding that they were deliberately indifferent to his disability needs by using handcuffs that did not accommodate his disability under the ADA, which caused him undue pain in violation of the Eighth Amendment.

The courts have also taken occasion to address ADA as it applies to parole decisions. In *Thompson v. Davis* (2002), a state prisoner who had a history of substance abuse brought a legal action against state parole board members, alleging a practice of denying parole to prisoners with substance abuse histories, in violation of the ADA. The lower court dismissed the case and the prisoner appealed. The appellate court found that, under the provisions of the ADA, a parole board may not categorically exclude a class of disabled people from consideration for parole because of their disabilities,. The court found that while the term "qualified individual with a disability" under the ADA does not include an individual who is currently engaging in the illegal use of drugs, the ADA protects individuals who have successfully completed, or are participating in, a supervised drug rehabilitation program and are no longer using illegal drugs.

In *Winters v. Arkansas Dept. of Health and Human Services* (2007), the family of a detainee who died of peritonitis while confined in jail filed a civil legal action against the sheriff and the Arkansas Department of Health and Human Services. The family sued under § 1983, the Americans with Disabilities Act (ADA), and the Rehabilitation Act. The appellate court affirmed the lower court's award of summary judgment. The court noted that the detainee was arrested for criminal trespass, and although he was not treated for his peritonitis due to his inability to communicate because of his mental illness the sheriff and jail officials sought immediate treatment for his mental illness, and attempted to transport him to a state hospital, but he was denied admittance due to a lack of available space. The court found that neither the county sheriff nor the Arkansas Department of Health and Human Services was deliberately indifferent to the serious medical needs of the detainee, nor was there a policy or custom to deprive mentally ill detainees of treatment. According to the court, the detainee died from a condition that neither defendant knew of or suspected, the sheriff and other jail officers attempted to get the detainee into a mental health treatment facility, but no facility would accept custody of him.

In *Herman v. County of York* (2007), the estate of a prisoner who committed suicide while confined in jail filed a § 1983 claim against the county, the administrator, and medical care personnel, and also filed a claim under the ADA in accordance with the Eighth Amendment. The defendants moved for summary judgment. The court found that the prisoner was not denied access to the county's jail programs or services because of his disability and any failure by the county to prevent his suicide thus was not discrimination in services, programs, or activities of a public entity in violation of the ADA. The prisoner denied thoughts of suicide, he informed a nurse that he did not wish to take antidepressant medications that had been prescribed for him, and a nurse told him to return to mental health services if necessary.

In *Brockman v. Tex. Dept. of Criminal Justice* (2010), a mentally ill prisoner diagnosed with bipolar disorder hung himself to death in his cell in a Texas prison. His mother filed a lawsuit, claiming that prison authorities had been deliberately indifferent to her son's condition, in violation of the Eighth Amendment. She further filed a disability discrimination claim under the Americans with Disabilities Act (ADA). She argued that he had been denied treatment for his condition, that he was denied medication or it was confiscated, causing manic episodes and extreme side effects. She also contended that prison employees missed clear signs that his mental health was deteriorating and that he was a suicide risk. At the time of his death, the prisoner was being housed in isolation, which was allegedly a violation of the standards issued by National Commission on Correctional Health Care (NCCHC), which direct that suicidal prisoners not be housed in isolation, unless under constant supervision. He was allegedly not closely monitored, and his mother argued that log entries showing the contrary had been fabricated.

The Fifth Circuit Court of Appeals upheld the lower court's summary judgment decision in favor of the defendants. The court noted that prisoners with disabilities have the same interest in access to the programs, services, and activities provided to the other inmates as individuals with disabilities outside of prison have to the counterpart programs, services, and activities. At a minimum, they have a due process right not to be treated worse than other inmates solely because of their disability. They determined that the lawsuit's federal civil rights clams against the state Department of Criminal Justice and prison officials in their official capacity failed to support an ADA claim, while all other federal civil rights and ADA claims were time-barred as they involved conduct that had occurred over two years ago.

Deliberate Indifference and AIDS

Since the 1980s, more prisoners entering correctional facilities have been diagnosed with HIV/AIDS. Between 1991 and 1995 (Maruschak, 1997) the number of HIV-positive prisoners grew at about the same rate (38%) as the overall prison population (36%). At year-end 1995, four percent of all female state prisoners were HIV positive, compared to 2.3 percent of male state prisoners. Maruschak and Beavers (2009) reported that in 2008, 5,174 prisoners reported being diagnosed with AIDS and they accounted for about 0.5 percent of the state and federal prisoner population. The rate of confirmed AIDS in prison is 2.5 times the rate in the U.S. general population. Since 1998, the cases of prisoners diagnosed with AIDS appear to be declining, although reporting definitions changed in 2003. About 70 percent of the prisoners were tested for HIV during their confinement. More men than women prisoners report being diagnosed with AIDS. From 1995 to 2008, prisoner deaths from AIDS accounted for about 2 percent of the prisoners' deaths.

Detention facilities have also seen a steady increase in prisoners being admitted with AIDS or HIV. This has posed a significant problem for correctional officials in terms of classification, housing, providing medical care, and privacy concerns. Liability issues under the Eighth Amendment have also emerged for correctional officials.

Testing prisoners for AIDS has resulted in litigation based on the notion that testing is unconstitutional, or conversely, that failure to test was compromising medical care to HIV-positive prisoners was not deliberately indifferent. Assisting a terminally ill prisoner was seen as therapeutic and isolation involved no deprivation of any constitutional right to privacy because institutional concerns outweighed any prisoner rights. Conversely, failure to mandatorily test all prisoners infected with HIV and segregate carriers was not deliberately indifferent where extensive educational programs and some testing were in place (*Meyers v. Maryland Div. of Corrections*, 1992).

Expanding the disabilities associated with the Americans with Disabilities Act, the United States Supreme Court ruled in *Bragdon v. Abbott* (1999) that HIV infection is a "disability" under the ADA, even when the infection has not yet progressed to the so-called symptomatic phase, as a physical impairment that substantially limits the major life activity of reproduction. A patient infected with HIV brought an action under the ADA against a dentist who refused to treat her at his office. The court held that when assessing the risk associated with treating or accommodating a disabled person under the ADA, the risk assessment must be based on medical or other objective evidence and not simply on a person's good-faith belief that a significant risk existed.

In *Polanco v. Dworzack* (1998), an AIDS-infected prisoner brought an action against prison medical personnel, alleging deliberate indifference to his serious medical needs. The district court granted summary judgment to the defendants, holding that the failure of medical personnel to provide the prisoner with a specific, name-brand dietary supplement he had requested was not deliberately indifferent to his serious medical needs. The court further noted that a prisoner does not have the right to the medical treatment of his choice, and therefore a mere disagreement with a doctor's professional judgment is not a constitutional violation. The prisoner had been maintaining steady weight, was given daily supplementary snacks, and medical personnel met with him whenever he requested a sick call.

The district court in *McNally v. Prison Health Care Services, Inc.* (1998) found that a pretrial detainee stated a valid claim that his constitutional rights were violated when he was denied his HIV medication. The court found that the jail's failure to provide him with medication was deliberately indifferent to his medical needs, causing him to suffer significant harm. The detainee was arrested by police and injured by arresting officers. The police took him to a hospital for treatment of cuts on his nose and a blackened eye prior to transporting him to the jail. Once at the jail, the detainee informed booking personnel that he had been diagnosed with HIV and was on a strict regimen of medication and needed his medication immediately because he had missed a dose earlier in the day. The detainee's physician confirmed this, but the detainee was denied his medication during his three-day confinement. Upon release from the jail, he was hospitalized for several days as a result of being deprived of his medication.

In *Rivera v. Alvarado* (2003), a prisoner's mother brought legal action claiming that correctional officials and doctors failed to adequately treat and provide medical care to her son in violation of the Eighth Amendment. Her son was diagnosed with AIDS and she claimed that the officials and doctors were aware of his serious medical needs and failed to provide proper treatment, which contributed to his death. The court dismissed the lawsuit, finding that the doctors were not deliberately indifferent to the health care needs of the prisoner. The court noted that the prisoner was admitted to the hospital in a timely manner, where the medical staff took X-rays and administered antibiotics, and that the doctors, a first-year resident and the attending physician in charge of the residents, did not play a significant role in the decisions regarding the prisoner's treatment.

In *Clark v. Williams* (2009), correction officials were sued on claims that assigning a prisoner to share a cell with another prisoner diagnosed with HIV and Hepatitis B, and failing to provide him with medical care when he contracted Hepatitis B violated his Eighth Amendment rights. The federal district court determined that the prisoner had no administrative remedy, and thus, the exhaustion requirement of the Prison Litigation Reform Act did not have to be met. The court precluded summary judgment for correctional officials noting that they were aware that one prisoner was infected and assigned another prisoner who contracted the infection, and failure to take adequate measures to reduce the risk, with full knowledge of the risk, supported a claim of deliberate indifference.

Deliberate Indifference and Environmental Hazards

It is common for inmates to smoke. Not only do prisoners smoke, but "squares" (cigarettes) also serve as part of the prison economy. Debts and favors are frequently paid with cigarettes. The United States Supreme Court has taken the opportunity to further apply the deliberate indifference standard to issues of environmental hazards in prisons and jails. The Supreme Court in *Helling v. McKinney* (1993) concurred with a prisoner who brought a § 1983 action claiming that his constitutional rights were violated because he was exposed to secondhand smoke. The prisoner was double-celled with a chain-smoking prisoner and claimed that the smoke endangered his health. Justice White emphasized that when prisoners are exposed to dangerous or unhealthy conditions, they need not wait until they suffer from a serious or life-threatening illness before asserting claims about improper conditions. The Court ruled that Helling did show that the correctional officials' actions under the Eighth Amendment supported a deliberate indifference claim, as he was exposed to high levels of environmental tobacco smoke (ETS) that posed an unreasonable risk of serious danger to his future health (Box 11.1).

Since the *Helling* decision, numerous correctional officials have enacted a smoking ban within prison living units, and lower courts have frequently rejected prisoner claims of ETS. In three separate cases (*Weaver v. Clarke*, 1997; *Scott v. District of Columbia*, 1998; *Caldwell v. Hammonds*, 1999), prisoners all claimed that correctional officials were "deliberately indifferent" to their medical needs because they were exposed to ETS. In *Caldwell*, the appellate court affirmed a prisoner's claim that he indeed was exposed to ETS. Prison officials had instituted a policy banning smoking within the prison. Cigarettes were still sold in the prisoner canteen and officers permitted smoking in cell blocks. The court found that pervasive unsanitary and unhealthy conditions in the prisoner's cell block were obvious to any observer. The director of corrections was aware of these conditions and was, therefore, deliberately indifferent to them, giving support to the prisoner's claim.

In *Weaver* and *Scott*, prison officials were not deliberately indifferent, because they had instituted reasonable measures to ensure that prisoners observed the no-smoking policy and had improved ventilation.

In *Atkinson v. Taylor* (2003), a prisoner filed a lawsuit claiming that his Eighth Amendment rights were violated by being exposed to ETS, which created a serious medical need that posed an unreasonable risk of harm. The prisoner stated that he was constantly exposed, over seven months, to a chain smoker who shared the same cell with him and that correctional officials were aware that tobacco smoke was dangerous. He complained that he suffered numerous symptoms

---

BOX 11.1   *HELLING V. McKINNEY* (1993)

Nevada state prisoner McKinney filed a § 1983 action, claiming that he was exposed to environmental tobacco smoke (ETS) from his cell mate, who smoked five packs of cigarettes a day. He asserted that being subjected to the smoke caused health problems in violation of his Eighth Amendment right to be free from cruel and unusual punishment. The lower court found no medical evidence to support his claim, that he did not have a constitutional right to a smoke-free environment, and that correctional officials were not deliberately indifferent to his rights. The prisoner appealed and the lower court reversed. Correctional officials appealed to the United States Supreme Court.

The Court assessed the issue of whether involuntary exposure to ETS and its potential of a health risk support a § 1983 lawsuit in accordance with the Eighth Amendment. The Court held that a sufficiently high risk of future harm stemming from a prisoner's conditions of confinement could give rise to an Eighth Amendment claim. In such claims, the prisoner must prove that he was exposed to high levels of ETS. The Court further held that a prisoner seeking damages must convince a court that being exposed to such a risk violates contemporary standards of decency. The Court also determined that deliberate indifference was the proper standard with which to evaluate such claims.

This case is significant in that prisoner challenges to such claims need not cause a current health problem in order for the condition to be actionable. The Court agreed that being exposed to secondhand smoke can create a health concern for prisoners and that smoking may be prohibited. This decision grants authority to officials to develop policies that prohibit smoking within prisons and detention facilities. Counterclaims filed by prisoners requesting the right to smoke during confinement are unlikely to prevail.

---

as a result of his exposure to ETS and that no change was made in his housing conditions when he asked to be moved. The appellate court agreed with the prisoner and affirmed the federal district court's decision in denying summary judgment. The court held that there was ample evidence to establish a legitimate claim that the prisoner was exposed to a future of risk harm.

Other claims have been brought against correctional officials in this category beyond issues of secondhand smoke. Several claims have been filed for asbestos exposure. A prisoner brought a pro se action to recover for exposure to asbestos in *Johnson v. DuBois* (1998). The district court ruled that although the prisoner could recover for asbestos exposure without actually suffering from asbestosis, cancer, or other physical injuries, the prisoner failed to establish that he was exposed to asbestos. Based on news articles, the prisoner alleged that almost all buildings erected prior to 1970 used asbestos as fireproofing material, which the court found to be insufficient evidence. The prisoner contended that he was exposed to asbestos while working on several correctional department work crews during his confinement, and that he was not provided with protective clothing or devices. Contrast this with the decision in *LaBounty v. Coughlin* (1998), in which a prisoner brought a § 1983 claim for asbestos exposure in prison. The appellate court overturned summary judgment granted by the lower court, finding that the prisoner stated an Eighth Amendment deliberate indifference claim based on allegations that he was exposed to asbestos while incarcerated, and that prison officials knowingly failed to protect him from such exposure.

Even with the *Helling* decision, some correctional facilities allow prisoners to smoke. Prisoners have challenged this practice, claiming a risk to their health. In *Williams v. District of Columbia* (2006), a prisoner filed a § 1983 action seeking damages for alleged exposure to secondhand tobacco smoke while he was confined in the jail. The district court denied summary judgment to jail officials. The court held that the prisoner's allegations—that while he was confined in the jail he was subjected to an intolerable level of environmental tobacco smoke (ETS), and that such exposure caused health problems at the time he was confined and posed a risk to this future health, and that the defendants were deliberately indifferent to his condition—were substantiated, as it was shown that prisoners and officers smoked tobacco in the jail, and that the housing unit did not have adequate ventilation or windows or doors that could be opened to remove the smoke, and his cellmate smoked five packs of cigarettes day.

In *Jackson v. Goord* (2009), a state prisoner filed a multiclaim lawsuit alleging that the conditions of confinement and a smoke-filled toxic environment violated his Eighth Amendment right to be free from cruel and unusual conditions of confinement. The federal district court granted summary judgment on the conditions confinement issue but denied summary judgment on the environmental claims. The prisoner was assigned to work in the prison auto body shop and exposure to the fumes from oils, gas, paint, and other toxic materials caused the prisoner headaches, nose bleeds, and nausea. The court determined that the prisoner stated a valid claim precluding summary judgment as it was also shown that he was exposed to asbestos for four to five hours a day and such exposure for a prolonged period of time created a risk to his health. The court further noted that correctional officials had consciously failed to take measures to reduce exposure to cigarette smoke within the prison and such failure amounted to deliberate indifference to a substantial known environmental health risk.

Deliberate Indifference and Prison and Jail Conditions

Prisoners have initiated numerous lawsuits claiming that the conditions of their confinement are substandard. Allegations emerging from conditions of confinement can include such issues as: poor sanitation, living environment, plumbing, ventilation, heating, hygiene, food, overcrowding, noise, and the "totality" of the conditions themselves. An example of these issues was illustrated in the classic case of *Holt v. Sarver* (1970), depicted in the 1981 film *Brubaker*. In this case, a class action claim was filed by Arkansas prisoners complaining of vermin-infested facilities, rampant sexual assaults by other prisoners, abuse of the trustee system, absence of meaningful rehabilitation programs, conditions of isolation cells, overcrowded living conditions, defective plumbing facilities, excessive use of corporal punishment by correctional officials, and corruption between officers and prisoners. When a lower federal court examined these issues, it ruled that in the "totality of the circumstances" (cumulative impact) the Arkansas prison system, through its deplorable conditions, violated the Eighth and Fourteenth Amendment rights of prisoners.

Prison officials have a responsibility to provide adequate living conditions for prisoners. The Constitution, however, does not mandate "comfortable prisons." "Discomfort in prison is not guaranteed," nor does the Constitution permit "inhumane prisons" (*Rhodes v. Chapman*, 1981;

BOX 11.2 *WILSON V. SEITER* (1991)

Wilson sought monetary damages and injunctive relief in a § 1983 action claiming that the conditions of confinement violated his Eighth Amendment right to be free from cruel and unusual punishment. He also brought an action under the Fourteenth Amendment. He asserted that the totality of conditions, including overcrowding, excessive noise, inadequate heating and cooling, improper ventilation, lack of storage space, unsanitary dining facilities, and housing with the mentally impaired violated his rights. The lower courts rejected Wilson's claim and he appealed to the United States Supreme Court.

The Court granted certiorari to assess the issue of whether the deliberate indifference standard applied to conditions of confinement in accordance with the cruel and unusual punishment clause of the Eighth Amendment. In a 5-to-4 decision, the Court held that if conditions of confinement deprive a prisoner of basic human needs, those conditions are not actionable unless the correctional official has acted with a sufficiently culpable state of mind in allowing those conditions to exist. The Court ruled that the appropriate standard to apply to such actions is that of deliberate indifference that satisfies the Eighth Amendment's state of mind requirement. The decision in *Estelle v. Gamble* (1976) dictated this decision.

This case is significant because it grants more authority to correctional officials in operating their facilities. It makes it more difficult for prisoners to prevail in such actions because they must prove that officials had a culpable state of mind—meaning that officials intended, through the conditions, to punish prisoners under the Eighth Amendment. Prisoners must show that correctional officials were deliberately indifferent to the conditions in question and intended harm to the prisoner as a result. It is unlikely that prisoners will prevail on such a claim.

Farmer v. Brennan, 1994). The United States Supreme Court expanded the application of the deliberate indifference standard to conditions-of-confinement cases with its decision in *Wilson v. Seiter* (1991). Wilson filed a § 1983 action against Ohio correctional officials, claiming that overcrowding, mixing of healthy and physically and mentally impaired prisoners, excessive noise, inadequate heating and cooling, and a lack of sanitation violated his Eighth and Fourteenth Amendment rights to be free from "cruel and unusual" punishment. The Court noted that "deliberate indifference" is the sole standard for evaluating allegations of inadequate prison conditions. The Court also stated that prisoners filing such claims must show a culpable state of mind on the part of the official. This means that prisoners must show that corrections officials had the "intent" to continue such deplorable prison conditions. The Court's decision is significant because it makes it more difficult for prisoners to prevail in such actions (Box 11.2).

A prisoner brought a pro se complaint against correctional officials alleging unconstitutional conditions of confinement in *Davis v. Scott* (1998). The appeals court held that the prisoner's three-day confinement in a crisis management cell, which he alleged had blood on the walls and excrement on the floor, did not constitute an extreme deprivation as to violate the prisoner's rights under the Eighth Amendment. The court noted that the prisoner had cleaning supplies available to him. In *Geder v. Godinez* (1995), an Illinois prisoner confined at Statesville Prison filed a claim for cruel and unusual conditions of confinement. He alleged that he was confined in conditions that included defective pipes, sinks and toilets, improperly cleaned showers, a broken intercom system, stained mattresses, accumulated dust and dirt, and infestation by rats and roaches. The district court granted summary judgment for the correctional officials. The court concluded that whether the conditions were viewed separately or cumulatively, they were insufficient to establish a deprivation of human needs sufficient to constitute a violation of the Eighth Amendment. The court further noted that there was nothing to show that prison officials knew of and consciously disregarded an excessive risk to prisoner health or safety. Prison conditions are not unconstitutional under the Eighth Amendment simply because they are restrictive or harsh.

In *Dixon v. Godinez* (1997), a prisoner brought a § 1983 action claiming that the conditions of his protective custody cell violated his Eighth Amendment right to be free from cruel and unusual punishment. The lower court granted summary judgment to correctional officials. On appeal, the court ruled that poor ventilation in the prisoner's cell during the summer did not violate the Eighth Amendment, because the cell had a window that opened, as well as an electric fan. The prisoner's claim that the rank air in the cell exposed him to diseases and caused respiratory problems was not supported by medical or scientific sources. Further, the appellate court affirmed a lower court's holding in *Beverati v. Smith* (1997) that conditions in an administrative segregation cell did not violate his constitutional rights. The court found that conditions within the segregation cell block were not atypical, although the cells allegedly were infested with vermin; smeared with human feces and urine; flooded with water; and unbearably hot. Additionally, there was cold food in small portions; infrequent receipt of clean clothing, bedding, and linen; inability to leave cells more than three or four times per week; denial of outside recreation; and denial of educational or religious services.

Conditions-of-confinement actions frequently contain multiple claims, alleging that the "totality" of prison conditions are cruel and unusual. In *Simpson v. Horn* (1998), a prisoner brought a § 1983 lawsuit against a correctional commissioner and other officials, claiming that the prison was overcrowded in violation of the Eighth Amendment prohibition on cruel and unusual punishment. He also asserted that the classification system for double-cell assignments violated the equal protection clause of the Fourteenth Amendment. The court found that the alleged deficiencies in the prison were not cruel and unusual punishment, and granted summary judgment to the correctional officials. The court noted that prison officials have the right, acting in good faith and in particularized circumstances, to take into account racial tensions in maintaining security, discipline, and good order in prisons and jails. The court found that housing two prisoners in a cell designed for one prisoner does not per se violate the Eighth Amendment proscription against cruel and unusual punishment, but it may if it results in deprivation of essential food, medical care, sanitation, or other conditions intolerable for human confinement. The prisoner had alleged that as a result of overcrowding, prisoners were not provided with adequate furniture, cleaning supplies, laundry service, ventilation, bedding, clothing, recreational equipment, or telephones. He also alleged that food was served cold 85 percent of the time and that the dining hall was not kept clean or free of vermin.

Detention centers holding pretrial detainees and sentenced offenders have been prime targets for litigation regarding inadequate jail conditions. In *Ingalls v. Floyd* (1997), severe jail conditions, including extreme overcrowding, continuous periods of sleeping on the floor, physical fights over toilet paper availability, frequent food contamination, and lengthy periods without outdoor exercise, warranted denial of qualified immunity to the sheriff. Moreover, a pattern of continued assaults by both officers and prisoners, including severe physical injuries during a riot and even a correctional officer poisoning a prisoner, which were known but not remedied, presented triable issues of deliberate indifference. A practice of double-celling pretrial detainees was found to be unconstitutional in *Newkirk v. Sheers* (1993). Despite the availability of cots, pretrial detainees were forced to sleep on mattresses on the floor and to sleep adjacent to small toilets for lengthy periods. Qualified immunity was denied and the court determined that the sheriff was deliberately indifferent to the needs of prisoners. Compare, however, *Hamilton v. Lyons* (1995), in which the court found that temporarily requiring pretrial detainees to sleep on the floor in a cold cell did not violate the Eighth Amendment. Absent the intent to punish, the presence of vermin was not actionable.

Conditions of confinement in which pretrial detainees were forced to endure the following were actionable in *Antonelli v. Sheahan* (1996). The court determined that pretrial detainees stated a claim when they asserted that the jail was serving rancid food, provided no exercise, failed to protect detainees from extreme cold, lacked sufficient lighting, and allowed incessant noise at night over a lengthy period. The court also noted that a pest infestation claim was not defensible by showing two pest control sprayings in 16 months where the problem was persistent and prolonged and resulted in physical harm. The court concluded by stating that the confinement of pretrial detainees must be related to a legitimate and objective goal and that there can be no intent to punish.

The Ninth Circuit Court of Appeals affirmed the lower court's decision not to enjoin correctional officials from placing mentally disturbed or suicidal prisoners in safety cells in *Anderson v. County of Kern* (1995). The court heard testimony that mentally disturbed and suicidal prisoners were violent and dangerous to themselves, requiring temporary placement in a safety cell. In some cases prisoners were so violent that it was necessary to shackle them to a toilet grate for protection against suicide. The court agreed, and also held that the deprivation of sinks, urinals, and beds for short periods during violent episodes was constitutionally justifiable because the prisoners were confined to safety cells only for short periods. Likewise, in *Robeson v. Squadrito* (1999), there was no Eighth Amendment violation for overcrowded jail conditions where the mattress on the dayroom floor was not unsanitarily maintained, minimal exercise did not threaten health, diet was minimally adequate, and there was no deliberate indifference to safety.

In *Jones v. Goord* (2006), prisoners filed a legal action against New York correctional officials challenging the double-celling policy at a maximum-security prison. Double-celling is a practice in which two prisoners are housed in the same cell designed for one prisoner. The prisoners complained that the practice was unconstitutional, created undesirable conditions, including the fact that prisoners were forced to sleep near a toilet, were exposed to cellmates' odors, and kept excess personal property in their cells, amounting to deliberate indifference to their welfare. The prisoners also asserted that such conditions created an unhealthy environment as they were exposed to excessive levels of secondhand smoke, increasing their risk of respiratory diseases in violation of their Eighth Amendment rights. The court noted that the Eighth Amendment does not guarantee prisoners freedom from any and all sorts of unsavory environs, and that to the extent that conditions are restrictive and even harsh, they are part of the penalty that criminal offenders pay for their offenses against society. The court found that the practice of double-celling and exposure to secondhand smoke did not create an unreasonable risk of serious damage to the prisoner's future health, in violation of the Eighth Amendment. The court noted that records of the prison showed that the practice of double-celling actually decreased the risk of violence and in the number of prisoner-on-prisoner assaults throughout the prison.

In *Greene v. Mazzuca* (2007) a prisoner brought a § 1983 action against prison personnel, alleging that his administrative confinement for participating in a riot violated his Eighth and Fourteenth Amendment rights. The prisoner complained that being confined 23 hours a day was excessive and amounted to cruel and unusual punishment. The court found the allegations—that the prisoner was confined in his cell 23 hours a day, that he was denied out-of-cell recreation, and that he demonstrated injuries from an objectively serious deprivation—for the purposes of his condition of confinement claim, supported a claim of deliberate indifference. The court held that the allegation that the prisoner was subjected to 24-hour illumination stated a claim for violation of his Eighth Amendment rights, although the prisoner did not allege that he suffered any adverse effects as a result of the lighting. According to the court, the lack of educational or rehabilitative programming while he was in administrative confinement did not, however, deny the prisoner minimal civilized measures of life's necessities, in violation of the Eighth Amendment.

In *Solomon v. Nassau County* (2011), the lower federal district court denied a county's motion to dismiss a federal civil rights lawsuit by a pretrial detainee at its jail seeking damages for injuries he suffered when a rat allegedly came out of a hole in his mattress and bit his penis, causing him sexual dysfunction and emotional distress. The prisoner argued that the county acted with "deliberate indifference to his health and safety in failing to adequately protect him from rodents." Evidence showed that the conditions of jail cells were deplorable and insects and rodents were rampant. There were allegedly eleven prisoner complaints about rodents in the two years prior to the incident, as well as 50 prisoners signing a petition requesting action against the presence of rodents, and the prisoners claimed that adequate corrective measures were not taken. The trial judge agreed that the allegations were sufficient to prohibit summary judgment.

Deliberate Indifference and Failure to Protect

Prisons and jails confine a diverse population. Many prisoners are mentally impaired, violent, depressed, chemically addicted, and assaultive. With this population, a variety of confinement behaviors are common, such as violent assaults, including sexual assaults; intimidation; extortion; homosexuality; suicides; and uncontrolled outbursts. Legal actions for failure to protect are often filed against correctional personnel. Correctional personnel must be prepared to respond to a variety of human behaviors. Liability concerns regarding failure to protect arise from three potential situations: prisoner-on-prisoner physical assaults, self-inflicted injuries, and prisoner-on-prisoner sexual attacks.

The United States Supreme Court further expanded the standard of deliberate indifference to claims of failure to protect in *Farmer v. Brennan* (1994). In a unanimous decision, the Court held that prisoners can prevail in suits against correctional officials for prisoner-on-prisoner assaults if they can show that officials knew of a substantial risk of harm and recklessly disregarded that risk. Farmer was serving a lengthy federal prison sentence for multiple crimes. He entered prison as a preoperative transsexual and possessed feminine traits. He was classified as a "biological male" and housed in a male correctional institution. His situation posed problems for a housing assignment by the Federal Bureau of Prisons. Prior to his assault, Farmer was housed in protective custody, away from the general population. After a disciplinary transfer to the U.S. Penitentiary in Terre Haute, Indiana, Farmer was placed in administrative segregation. He was later released to the general population. Approximately one week later he was raped and beaten in his cell after he rejected the sexual advances of another prisoner (Box 11.3).

BOX 11.3   *FARMER V. BRENNAN* (1994)

Farmer brought a *Bivens* action under the Eighth Amendment, claiming that correctional officials were deliberately indifferent to his constitutional right to be safe during his incarceration. Farmer acknowledged that he was a transvestite and suffered from a slight psychotic disorder. Prior to his confinement, Farmer submitted to an unsuccessful "black market" testicle removal surgery. Farmer's appearance resembled a female's, as he had undergone hormonal therapy. Due to his "condition," proper security placement of Farmer was difficult for officials. He was placed in segregation for disciplinary reasons and later released to general population without objection. Within two weeks, Farmer alleged that he was beaten and raped by other prisoners. He filed suit and the lower court and appellate court found in favor of the correctional officials. He appealed to the United States Supreme Court.

The Court examined the issue of whether prison officials may be held liable under the Eighth Amendment for unsafe conditions in prison when they know that prisoners face risks of harm and fail to take measures that would reduce or eliminate such risks. The Court held that the Constitution does not mandate "comfortable prisons," but prison officials do have a duty to protect prisoners from violence at the hands of other prisoners. The Court ruled that a prison official cannot be found liable under the Eighth Amendment unless the official knows of and disregards an excessive risk to the prisoner's health and safety. The Court stated that if the official possessed knowledge that a prisoner faced a substantial risk of serious harm and disregarded that risk by failing to take reasonable measures to alleviate or abate it, a violation under the Eighth Amendment would exist.

This case is significant because the Court applied the deliberate indifference standard to claims of failing to protect prisoners from attacks by other prisoners. This is a high standard for the prisoner to overcome, because he must prove that officials "knowingly disregarded an excessive risk of harm." To win such cases, prisoners must show evidence that a substantial risk of harm existed through long-standing, pervasive, and well-documented assaults that were noted by prison officials, and that they failed to recognize such risks and take steps to alleviate such conduct.

With its decision, the Court expanded the scope of "deliberate indifference" in claims for failure to protect by holding that deliberate indifference can mean "reckless" behavior (on the part of correctional officials) "only when a person disregards a risk of harm of which he was aware." This means that correctional officials are aware of facts from which the inference can be drawn that a substantial risk of serious harm exists and they must draw the inference that the risk exists. To prevail in a lawsuit asserting failure to protect a prisoner, the plaintiff must show that officials consciously and recklessly disregarded a substantial risk of harm to a prisoner.

In order to prove that correctional officials possessed knowledge of a substantial risk of harm, a plaintiff can use circumstantial evidence to show that the risk was obvious. The Court noted three situations in which a plaintiff may prevail: (1) if assaults were pervasive, long-standing, well-documented, and expressly noted by correctional officials; (2) if officials refused to verify underlying facts of such assaults; and (3) if prison officials declined to confirm inferences of risk that they strongly suspected to exist. Prison officials may be held liable if they know of a substantial risk of physical harm to a general class of prisoner but no harm has yet occurred. Prisoners do not have to first be assaulted before protective action is taken by correctional personnel. Moreover, correctional officials will not be held liable when they can show that they responded reasonably to known risks.

There are two levels of deliberate indifference (Silver, 2010). The first level involves a failure to protect from a pervasive risk at an institution. In *Matthews v. Armitage* (1999), the widow of a prisoner who was stabbed by another prisoner brought a civil rights action against prison officials, alleging Eighth Amendment violations. The district court granted summary judgment as a matter of law, holding that the officials did not act with deliberate indifference to the prisoner's health and safety and were entitled to qualified immunity. The court noted that the two prisoners had coexisted in each other's presence in the general population at least 50 times without incident and that there had never been a stabbing in the protective custody unit previously. In *Lopez v. Smith* (1998), a state prisoner filed a § 1983 action against correctional officials alleging violation of his civil rights by placing him in a cell with a dangerous cell mate, providing inadequate medical care, and placing him in a security unit. An appellate court affirmed the lower court's dismissal of the case, finding that the prisoner's 15-day confinement in the security unit while he awaited transfer did not violate his constitutional rights. The court held that officials were not deliberately indifferent for failing to provide the prisoner with a blanket and pillow, absent the prisoner's failure to produce any evidence that he was denied adequate warmth or heating, or that he suffered from the cold. The court further found that the prisoner failed to state a claim regarding his alleged placement in a cell with a dangerous prisoner who subsequently broke his jaw.

In *Saunders v. United States* (2007), a pretrial detainee brought an action under the Federal Tort Claims Act (FTCA) seeking to hold the United States liable for injuries he suffered during a fight at a state jail while in federal custody. The district court granted the defendant's motion to dismiss. The court held that the detainee's claim that the United States Marshal's Service acted with deliberate indifference by placing him in an unsafe state jail, and in failing to respond to his verbal concerns about his safety, involved a discretionary decisionmaking exception.

The court noted that there was no allegation that the Marshal's Service had any knowledge of unsafe conditions at the jail other than an apprehension expressed by the detainee himself.

In *Rigan v. County of Sullivan* (2007), a detainee filed a § 1983 claim against the county sheriff, jail administrator, and correctional officers, alleging that he was harassed and beaten by other prisoners while confined at the jail. The prisoner claimed that he was classified to the housing unit where the assault occurred, which amounted to deliberate indifference in violation of the Eighth Amendment. The defendants filed a motion for summary judgment and the court granted qualified immunity. The court noted that the classification procedures of the jail were properly followed and that the classification officer asked if the prisoner had any enemies in the general population. The prisoner did not provide any information that would place the officers on notice that another housing assignment should be provided. The court found that the security checks of the jail and prisoner cells by the officers were adequate and did not amount to deliberate indifference to the prisoner's safety. The officers made visual inspections from outside the cell tier every 15 minutes and conducted head counts. The prisoner never informed the officers of the harassment, and once the officers knew the prisoner was being assaulted, they immediately removed him from the tier and provided him with medical assistance. The court added that the Eighth Amendment does not guarantee an assault-free prison environment, but promises only reasonable good faith protection.

A prisoner attacked by other prisoners filed a § 1983 claim against the warden and the Indiana Department of Corrections alleging that the warden was deliberately indifferent to his safety in violation of the Eighth Amendment in *O'Brien v. Indiana Department of Corrections ex rel. Turner* (2007). The appellate court affirmed summary judgment on behalf of the correctional officials. The court found that the warden was not deliberately indifferent to a substantial risk of harm to the prisoner by placing the prisoner, who was a former prison officer, convicted of rape, in a protective unit where other at-risk prisoners were housed, even though the prisoner was assaulted. The court ruled that prison officials initially housed the prisoner in segregation for his own protection and, having considered the nature of the threat against him and the availability of placing him among other prisoners, officials decided to place him with other former police officers, correctional officers, and prosecutors—a course of action that had been followed in the past.

The second level of deliberate indifference involves a failure to protect a prisoner after a specific reported threat, irrespective of the dangerous nature of the prison. Correctional officials were denied summary judgment in *Dowling v. Hannigan* (1998) when a state prisoner brought a claim of failure to protect from other prisoners' assaults. The district court found that correctional officials abdicated their responsibility to protect prisoners from attacks by other prisoners. A correctional officer had received a note stating that one prisoner was going to attempt to kill or injure the plaintiff because he had informed authorities about a drug transaction. Prison officials failed to inform the plaintiff about the threat, and he was attacked with an edged weapon (a razor blade melted in a toothbrush). The court found that there were factual issues, precluding summary judgment, regarding the adequacy of the official's response. Likewise, in *Freeman v. Godinez* (1998), the court denied summary judgment for correctional officials, finding that the prisoner stated a claim arising from a physical attack by other prisoners. The court held that the prisoner need not exhaust administrative remedies prior to filing a § 1983 claim. The prisoner claimed that prison officials knew he was on a "hit list" and interrogated him about gang activities that may have put him in danger. He requested and was twice denied protection. He was later attacked by three prisoners and stabbed in the back, chest, and face, and beaten with pipes.

Failure to protect litigation has also emerged from situations in jails. In *Lopez v. Le Master* (1999), a pretrial detainee brought a § 1983 claim against the sheriff, asserting that he was beaten by fellow prisoners. The appellate court reversed the summary judgment granted by the lower court. The detainee was placed in a general population cell and later threatened by another prisoner. The prisoner notified a correctional officer about the threat, and the officer interviewed the prisoner in an office. The prisoner filed a written statement regarding the threat, and the officer placed him back in the cell. The plaintiff was later attacked and beaten by several prisoners. The plaintiff was taken to the hospital for treatment of his injuries, brought back to the jail, and released the next day. Upon his release he again went to the hospital and was diagnosed with postconcussion syndrome and a severe strain to the cervical, thoracic, and lumbosacral spine. The appellate court found that material issues of fact precluded summary judgment in that the sheriff was deliberately indifferent by failing to monitor prisoners, failing to protect prisoners, maintaining a policy of understaffing the jail, and failing to respond to the prisoner's medical needs.

The Eighth Circuit Court of Appeals affirmed a lower court's granting of summary judgment for detention officers and the sheriff in *Perkins v. Grimes* (1998). The plaintiff filed a § 1983 claim, alleging that he was raped by another prisoner. The appellate court ruled that neither the jailers nor the sheriff were deliberately indifferent to the detainee's safety when they housed him with a prisoner who later raped him. The court noted that although officers were on notice that the prisoner was easily provoked, they also knew that the detainee and the prisoner had previously been housed together without incident, and the officers neither knew, nor had reason to know, that the prisoner was a violent sexual aggressor. The plaintiff had been confined in a holding cell for public intoxication. Another prisoner, who was larger and heavier and confined for the same charge, was subsequently raped. The detainee alleged that a detention officer was aware of the assault and failed to intervene.

Special threat groups have emerged as a source of assaults, disturbances, escapes, and a threat to the security of prisons and jails. In *Palmer v. Marion County* (2003), a detainee who was severely beaten by other detainees brought a § 1983 claim against officers for failing to protect him and a claim against the county for deliberate indifference to the adequate training of officers and supervisors. The detainee alleged that jail officials were indifferent to the housing and classification of detainees by race and gang member status, who controlled the jail. The appellate court affirmed the lower court's decision to grant qualified immunity to jail officials. The court held that the affidavit filed by the detainee, who claimed that he observed the practice of segregating detainees by race, placing gang members with non-gang members, not segregating detainees who felt threatened, and not intervening to stop detainee fights in the cell blocks, was insufficient to show that the county had either a widespread practice of allowing detainees to fight or segregating them by race.

In *Rodriguez v. Secretary for Department of Corrections* (2007), an inmate in a Florida prison brought a § 1983 suit against two prison officials, asserting that they violated his Eighth Amendment right to be free from cruel and usual punishment. After his release from a segregation cell back to general population, the prisoner was assaulted by other prisoners. The prisoner had asked to be transferred to another institution or to be placed in protective custody. The court granted summary judgment to the chief prison security officer and the warden and the prisoner appealed. The appeals court reversed, holding that the officials had had subjective knowledge that the prisoner faced a substantial risk of serious harm from his former gang members. The court ruled that there was evidence that the prisoner informed the security chief that he was a former gang member who decided to renounce his membership, that gang members had threatened to kill him when he returned to the compound in retaliation for renunciation, and that the prison compound was heavily populated with gang members.

In *Clem v. Lomeli* (2009), a prisoner confined in a California prison was beaten by his cellmate and filed a §1983 claim for failure to protect him from the assault. Evidence showed that a correction officer heard the prisoner's screams and deliberately ignored the prisoner's pleas for assistance and did not take any measures to stop the assault. The lower court granted summary judgment in favor of the correction officer and the prisoner appealed. The appellate court reversed the lower court's decision holding that the evidence and medical treatment to the injuries sustained clearly supported the prisoner's claim of deliberate indifference. The court noted that when a correction officer knowingly ignores a substantial risk of harm posed to a prisoner and fails to act, a claim of deliberate indifference, as shown in this incident, will be supported.

The Prison Litigation Reform Act and the Antiterrorism and Effective Death Penalty Act

As evidenced by the above discussion, prisoners in both jails and prisons have filed numerous lawsuits over the years asserting the deprivation of various constitutional rights. While it is acknowledged that some lawsuits have assisted in bringing reform to corrections, many of them have been categorized as baseless and frivolous. The determining factor of what distinguishes a legitimate lawsuit from a frivolous lawsuit can be problematic. In an effort to constrain the surge in prison litigation and to more carefully define a legitimate lawsuit, Congress enacted the Prison Litigation Reform Act in 1996 (PLRA) and Title I of the Antiterrorism and Effective Death Penalty Act (AEDPA). It was signed into law as part of H.R. 3019, Omnibus Appropriations Bill, and codified at 18 U.S.C. § 3626. The PLRA pinpoints actions addressing conditions of confinement, and the AEDPA focuses on state and federal habeas corpus petitions.

The PLRA did not curtail the right of a prisoner to file a lawsuit. The purpose of the new legislation was to limit the ability of prisoners to complain about prison conditions and to limit the jurisdiction of the federal courts to issue orders relieving conditions of confinement that allegedly violated the constitutional rights of prisoners (Palmer & Palmer, 1999). The Act is also intended to grant more authority to the states to manage their correctional systems and, at the same time, to limit the federal courts' "hands-on" intervention of managing prisons from the bench. The days of the court holding correctional administrators accountable for requirements not mandated by the Constitution and continuing to maintain some level of oversight for many years may be ending. There are numerous sections of the PLRA; only five will be discussed.

Section 802 of the Act addresses appropriate remedies with respect to prison conditions and seeks to resolve these actions in the least intrusive means necessary to correct the violation. This section ostensibly pertains to consent decrees. A consent decree is a binding agreement made outside of court between two conflicting parties and is established with time limits. For example, correctional officials would agree to build more prisons to alleviate prison overcrowding within five years.

For years, many correctional systems have entered into consent decrees (sometimes involuntarily), primarily due to overcrowding problems, as one alternative to resolving a prisoner lawsuit. This provision terminates existing court-ordered consent decrees unless the court finds continuing constitutional violations. This section mandates that courts shall not enter or approve consent decrees unless they comply with correcting a harm found by the court and the court requires preliminary relief to correct such harm. This can be a double-edged sword. On the one hand, terminating a consent decree requiring a population cap on a crowded prison may appease the legislature. On the other hand, it may create a whole new set of problems for correctional personnel. The impact of this provision is viewed as violating the Constitution's separation of powers clause. At least one legal scholar states that consent decrees constitute final judgments that cannot be reopened by Congress (Alexander, 1996). It remains to be seen how this provision will be further implemented.

Section 803 of the Act states that lawsuits brought by prisoners alleging poor conditions of confinement may not be filed until available administrative remedies have been exhausted. This means that the grievance system within the institution must be exhausted first. Prior to enactment of § 803, the federal courts could require prisoners to pursue internal remedies if such a system was certified by the Department of Justice or a federal district court. There appear to be at least two potential problems with this provision. First, the U.S. Supreme Court held in *McCarthy v. Madigan* (1992) that federal prisoners need not exhaust the prison grievance procedures prior to filing a *Bivens* action for damages. The Court did not believe that policy reasons required judicial imposition of an exhaustion requirement. Moreover, the Court also held that a plaintiff bringing suit under § 1983 need not first exhaust available state judicial or administrative remedies (*Patsy v. Florida Board of Regents*, 1982). The Court, however, in *Farmer v. Brennan* (1994) did indicate that prisoners bypassing "adequate" internal prison procedures might be denied relief. The Court emphasized that "an inmate who needlessly bypasses such procedures may properly be compelled to pursue them."

In *Morgan v. Arizona Dept. of Corrections* (1997), the court addressed the issue of exhausting the prison system's grievance system prior to submitting a § 1983 action alleging an assault by other prisoners. The district court dismissed the action, finding that the prisoner failed to file an initial grievance under the corrections department's procedures, depriving the court of jurisdiction because he failed to exhaust his administrative remedies. According to the court, the PLRA has made exhaustion provisions mandatory rather than discretionary, and courts no longer have the discretion in the absence of exhaustion. The prisoner had requested a 30-day continuance to amend his complaint to prove that he had exhausted his administrative remedies.

Requiring exhaustion of administrative remedies presents a second potential problem. Maahs and del Carmen (1995) reported that in 1995 few states had a certified grievance system in place. This is primarily due to the slow and cumbersome certification process. Theoretically, this provision appears to assist in reducing the number of actions that can be filed by a prisoner, because it requires conflicts to first be confronted at the institutional level. Further examination, however, reveals that it may be unconstitutional, because the Supreme Court has traditionally held that such remedies need not first be exhausted. Also, if an institution does not have such a system in place, a lack of internal remedies may create more administrative problems than the Act was intended to resolve. In addition, this section limits the awards for attorney's fees and recovery of damages.

Luong v. Hatt (1997) is illustrative of a federal district court in Texas dismissing a prisoner civil action and denying the recovery of damages in conjunction with the PLRA. A prisoner brought an action against prison officials, alleging that they failed to protect him from an assault by other prisoners. The court dismissed the case, finding that the prisoner failed to demonstrate violations of his rights sufficient to support an order from the court requiring his transfer to another institution. The court also held that the prisoner could not recover damages in the absence of any indication that he suffered a "physical injury" within the meaning of the PLRA. According to the court, cuts, scratches, and minor bruises suffered by the prisoner did not constitute the requisite level of physical injury.

The United States Supreme Court has twice addressed the issue of whether it is constitutional to require prisoners to first exhaust administrative remedies before filing a lawsuit. In *Booth v. Churner* (2001), the Court held that Congress did indeed intend for prisoners to exhaust available remedies prior to filing a civil action. Before submitting his civil action, Booth only exhausted the first step of the institutional grievance system. The Court concluded that completion of every step is required by statute. It is not enough to file a grievance only at the institutional level; if further appeals are available, they must be completed prior to filing the action in federal court. Second, prisoners are not allowed to bypass the grievance system merely because they believe that doing so is an exercise in futility.

In a second case the Court reaffirmed its decision in *Booth*. In a unanimous decision, the Court ruled in *Porter v. Nussle* (2002) that prisoners in jails and prisons may not bring any action into federal court until they have exhausted administrative remedies available to them at the institutional level. Nussle filed a § 1983 lawsuit claiming that correctional officers used excessive force, that officers threw him up against a wall, pulled his hair, "kneed" him in the back, and struck him several times. He further claimed that the officers threatened to kill him if he reported the beating. The federal district court dismissed the case, relying on the exhaustion of administrative remedy requirement. He appealed and the appellate court reversed the lower court's decision, holding that exhausting administrative remedies did not apply to use-of-force allegations. The court made a distinction between conditions of confinement claims and use-of-force claims.

The United States Supreme Court granted certiorari and determined that Congress did not intend to divide prisoner petitions into subcategories for judicial review (i.e., civil actions and habeas corpus petitions). The Court concluded that Congress did not intend to exempt use-of-force cases from prison condition cases under the PLRA and that, therefore, prisoners could not skip the administrative remedy process at the institutional level. The Court held that the exhaustion of administrative remedies requirement was important so that correctional administrators could know of correctional officers' misconduct. Authorizing prisoners to bypass the internal grievance process excluded the possibility that administrators would take corrective actions when they might be warranted. The Court held that the PLRA's exhaustion requirement applied to all prisoner suits about prison life, whether they involved general circumstances or particular episodes, and whether they alleged excessive force or some other wrong.

Section 804 of the PLRA addresses the issue of filing fees. Generally, the filing fee for a civil action is approximately $150, and previously the fee had been waived for prisoners. The law now requires prisoners to pay the full filing fee, and it requires institutional officials to verify the funds that the prisoner may have at his or her disposal. Additionally, this section provides for the appointment of an attorney if any person is unable to afford one. Bona fide indigent prisoners will not be affected by this stipulation. The court will dismiss the action at any time if it determines that the poverty claim is untrue. Lower courts have begun to rule on this provision. In *Hampton v. Hobbs* (1997) and *Roller v. Gunn* (1997), both courts found the PLRA filing fee requirement to be rationally related to curtailing meritless prisoner litigation and that it did not violate the equal protection clause of the Fourteenth Amendment.

Section 809 provides for the revocation of earned good time or early-release credit of a federally incarcerated prisoner should that prisoner file a malicious or false civil action. It is, however, not definitive what characterizes a "malicious" civil action. Some guidance is given in this section because the PLRA has its own version of "three strikes and you're out." States that have legislated the three-strikes law incarcerate for life individuals who have three convictions of the same type of crime or violent crimes. The PLRA version provides that a prisoner who has had three previous lawsuits dismissed for failing to state a claim, or as frivolous or malicious, is banned from filing further lawsuits without paying the full filing fee in advance. The exception to this is if the prisoner is under "imminent danger or serious physical injury." Reaction by the courts to this provision appears to be split. In *Lyon v. Vande Krol* (1996), the court found the provision to be unconstitutional. In *Abdul-Wadood v. Nathan* (1996), however, the court upheld the provision.

Questions have frequently emerged as to whether prisoners must strictly adhere to the procedural rules of the PLRA prior to filing a civil lawsuit. In *Jones v. Bock* (2007), state prisoners brought separate § 1983 claims against correctional officials. The district courts dismissed the actions for failure to satisfy procedural rules, implementing the administrative exhaustion requirement of the PLRA. The appellate court affirmed the respective dismissals. The prisoners appealed to the United States Supreme Court and the Court granted certiorari, consolidating the actions. The Court reversed and remanded to lower courts. The Court held that a prisoner's failure to exhaust under the PLRA is an affirmative defense; a prisoner is not required to specially plead or demonstrate exhaustion in his complaint. The Court concluded that prisoners' § 1983 actions are not automatically rendered noncompliant with PLRA exhaustion requirements by the fact that not all defendants named in the legal actions had been named in the administrative grievance. The Court found that a prisoner's compliance with the PLRA exhaustion requirement as to some, but not all, claims, does not warrant dismissal of an entire action.

In *Shariff v. Coombe* (2009), state prisoners who were disabled brought legal actions claiming cruel and unusual conditions under the Eighth Amendment. The prisoners asserted that their safety in the prison was unprotected from other prisoners, that their mobility in wheelchairs was restricted to access to restrooms, that broken cement on ramps prohibited their wheelchairs from full mobility and several prisoners had received injuries from falling out of their wheelchairs. The prisoners asserted that food counters were higher than eye level and that reaching for food trays in the wheelchair was almost impossible, and several prisoners received burns on their bodies from hot beverages. The prisoners also filed claims under the ADA asserting that correctional officials were deliberately indifferent to their life necessities and posed an unreasonable risk of serious damage to their future health.

The district court rejected summary judgment to the defendants. The court held that prisoners were not required to exhaust institutional remedies under the Prison Litigation Reform Act (PLRA). The court ruled that prison officials provided evidence where accommodations had been to serve food to prisoners in wheelchairs with other alternatives. However, the court did find that the correctional officials failed to make reasonable accommodations for wheelchair-bound prisoners' access to restrooms, where prisoners soiled themselves regularly, and such failure denied prisoners minimal civilized measures of life's necessities and that there was an unreasonable risk of serious damage to their future health.

Searches and Liability

A fundamental tenet in operating correctional facilities is to keep contraband, including weapons and drugs, to a minimum, which can enhance the security and safety of prisoners and the officers that work there. Performing searches is at the core of this tenet. In many correctional facilities officers are required to conduct personal, cell, and facility searches on a regular basis. Strip and body cavity searches are also conducted. Prisoner searches have been the center of several lawsuits since the 1970s and the United States Supreme Court has addressed this issue in four cases.

Applying the intrusiveness/balancing test, the Court in *Bell v. Wolfish* (1979) approved a policy of strip searching all pretrial detainees in a federal detention facility. A strip search involves the nontouching and visual inspection of an undressed prisoner's body openings and fingers and toes by an officer of the same gender, normally having the prisoner "squat and cough," visually observing the prisoner's mouth (and lift the tongue), ears, and nose, having the prisoner run his hands through his hair and scalp, and having the prisoner lift his feet and genitals. The argument that allowing such a search policy would be abused by officers was outweighed by the need for increasing security within the facility. The Court noted that a prisoner in a detention facility had no reasonable expectation of privacy under the Fourth Amendment with respect to a prisoner's room or cell. A search warrant is not required prior to conducting the search and the decision in *Bell* allowed random searching of a detainee's cell.

In *Block v. Rutherford* (1984), the Court upheld its decision in *Bell* by holding that jail policies directing correction officers to conduct random cell and strip searches of prisoners returning to their cell after a visit were not unreasonable. The Court determined that the detainees had no right to observe the cell search. On the same day, the Court ruled in *Hudson v. Palmer* (1984) that a convicted prisoner does not have the right to an expectation of privacy in his or her prison cell, under the Fourth Amendment. During a cell search of the prisoner's cell contraband items were discovered, they were confiscated, and the prisoner was later found guilty of a disciplinary action. The prisoner claimed that his right to privacy was violated. The Court overturned the lower court's decision, holding that facility security overrides a prisoner's privacy right in a correctional setting. The Court held that unfettered access to prison cells by prison officials is imperative if contraband is to be ferreted out and sanitary conditions maintained. Finally, the Court held that searches that are conducted for harassment purposes and not supported by penological objectives are actionable.

Although the Court had opined on the constitutionality of conducting strip searches in *Bell*, many lower courts frequently ruled in favor of detainees filing legal actions challenging a strip search at time of admission in a jail. The issue raised many questions among the appellate courts on whether strip searches could be performed at time of jail admission, no matter how minor the offense, and without reasonable suspicion to believe a detainee was concealing contraband or weapons. In *Florence v. Board of Chosen Freeholders of the County of Burlington* (2012) the Court granted certiorari to address this issue.

Florence was arrested, charged with fleeing from officers, obstruction of justice, and use of a deadly weapon, plead guilty, and sentenced to pay a monthly fine. Over time, Florence fell behind in his payments and a bench warrant was issued for his arrest. He paid the outstanding balance a week later but the warrant remained active in the computer system. On a traffic stop, two years later, Florence was arrested by a New Jersey state trooper, and transported to the Burlington County Detention Center (jail). At the Burlington facility Florence was strip-searched, provided a shower with a delousing agent, and his body was examined for scars, marks, gang tattoos, and contraband in accordance with facility policy. He was then placed in a general population cell with another prisoner. Florence was transferred six days later to the Essex County Correctional Facility and was strip-searched upon admission. After the charges were dropped the next day, Florence was released from custody.

Florence filed a lawsuit claiming that his constitutional rights were violated based on the two unreasonable strip searches. The Appellate Court for the Third Circuit ruled that all persons admitted into the jail's general population could be strip-searched without reasonable suspicion irrespective of the nature of the lodging offense. Florence appealed and the United States Supreme Court agreed to review the issue of whether every detainee who will be admitted to the general population in a jail may be required to undergo a close visual inspection while undressed. Florence argued that detainees arrested for minor offenses should not be subjected to strip searches.

In a 5-to-4 decision, the Court began its analysis by recognizing its prior decisions in *Bell*, *Block*, and *Hudson*, and stated that the courts should pay deference to the decisions of corrections officials in their efforts to maintain order and security in jail facilities. The Court upheld the decision to authorize a blanket strip search policy and addressed several components for its decision underscoring a legitimate penological interest. First, the Court reasoned that operating a detention facility is a complex task and the courts should ordinarily defer to their expert judgment in such matters. Second, the Court ruled that correctional officers have significant interest in conducting a thorough search of detainees to reduce the risk of allowing contraband, weapons, and drugs into the facility. The Court noted that detainees commit over 10,000 assaults against correction officers annually and many more against other prisoners, so conducting searches can assist in increasing the security and internal order of the facility. Third, the Court noted that gangs exacerbate the problem by creating grave threats to security, initiating thefts, violence, committing assaults, and they approach other prisoners in packs to take contraband from them, placing the entire facility at risk of security. Fourth, the Court underscored the need to perform a strip search to check incoming prisoners for possible infections, wounds, injuries, and those who may need immediate medical attention.

Fifth, the Court reasoned that using the severity of the lodging charge is a poor predictor of who may be in possession of contraband. Persons confined for a misdemeanor can be just as violent as a felon. Further, those charged with a "minor" offense may make a quick decision to hide illegal substances to avoid getting into more trouble at the time of their arrest. Moreover, they may also be coerced into bringing contraband into the facility by another during transport to the jail. Exempting those arrested of a minor offense from a standard search policy places them at a greater risk and would result in more contraband being brought into the facility, thereby placing the entire facility at a security risk.

The Court noted that this was not an example of a case where detention officers intentionally humiliated a prisoner; it was not an example involving touching the prisoner, and not a case where the prisoner was isolated for a short period of time without ever being placed in a general population cell. Allowing a blanket policy for a strip search at time of admission, regardless of the arresting charge, the Court grants more deference to correctional officials and supports the need to operationalize the search policy. Correctional officials are encouraged to review their policy and revise it as warranted in accordance with the Court's decision and to train officers to perform all searches in a professional manner.

Liability and Parole Decisions

The most frequently used prison sentence is the indeterminate sentence, which stipulates a minimum and maximum number of years to be served. For example, an individual may receive a sentence of five to ten years for breaking and entering into a residence. In many states, the prisoner may be eligible for parole (early release) just prior to his five-year minimum or before the maximum term is served. The state parole board has jurisdiction and authority to decide when a prisoner is released on parole. With this decisionmaking authority, issues of liability often emerge for the parole board and subsequently for the supervising parole officer.

The United States Supreme Court has examined decisionmaking by a parole board. In *Martinez v. California* (1980), the Court held that the Parole Board of California was absolutely immune from liability in its decision to parole a prisoner who committed a homicide five months after release. Martinez sued the state of California after his daughter was murdered by a parolee who was a known sex offender. He brought a state claim and a § 1983 claim, asserting that the parolee deprived his daughter of life without due process. The lower courts found in favor of the defendants, and Martinez appealed the decision to the U.S. Supreme Court. The Court held that under these circumstances of the decision to parole, the death was too remote a consequence of the parole board's action to hold it responsible. The Court further stated that the decision to parole the inmate was an action by the state and that the action of the parolee five months later cannot be fairly characterized as state action. The Court upheld a state statute providing absolute immunity from suit for the parole board as valid.

In *Sellars v. Procunier* (1981), the Court denied review and remanded the case to a lower court. The Ninth Circuit Court of Appeals determined that parole board officials' decision in granting parole was similar to that of a judge, who is absolutely immune from liability. The court stated that parole board members enjoy absolute immunity from lawsuits by individuals denied parole insofar as the suit attacks the decision on their parole. In *Montero v. Travis* (1999), a former parolee brought a pro se § 1983 action against parole board officials, alleging that his parole was revoked in violation of his due process rights. The district court dismissed the case and the appeals court affirmed. The appeals court held that the parole board commissioner who presided over the parole revocation hearing was entitled to absolute immunity, notwithstanding the official's administrative function. The official was serving in a quasijudicial function when he revoked the parolee's parole. The court further held that the claim against a second parole board official was frivolous given the failure to allege facts describing the official's personal involvement in the alleged constitutional violations.

Likewise, the Tenth Circuit Court of Appeals found that the Utah Parole Board was entitled to absolute immunity in *Malek v. Haun* (1994). A parolee brought a § 1983 action against parole board members, alleging that he was denied the opportunity to appeal the parole board's decision to deny parole. The court determined that the parole board has complete discretion in making parole decisions once an offender is eligible, and is immune from civil liability.

Parole officers, however, have qualified immunity and may be liable for actions that violate a parolee's rights. In *Greer v. Shoop* (1998), the administrator of a decedent's estate brought a § 1983 action against state probation and parole officers based on their failure to warn the decedent that a parolee placed into the decedent's home, who had been the decedent's boyfriend, was infected with HIV. The district court entered summary judgment for the defendants, and the appeals court affirmed. The appeals court held that the defendants were entitled to qualified immunity because the law was not clearly established at the time of the incident. Likewise, in *Olds v. Hogg* (1991), a prisoner brought a § 1983 action against parole officers in Missouri, alleging that they had made false statements in a pre-parole hearing report. The federal district court found that the parole officer was entitled to qualified immunity from § 1983 damages for liability and granted summary judgment.

One of the primary issues that parole officers face is the task of performing searches of parolees and their property to ensure that they are abiding by the conditions of the parole. The court's views on probable cause and conducting a search are different for parolees than free citizens, as the parolee is still serving a sentence but under supervision in the community. The status of the prisoner is slightly altered and therefore application of the Fourth Amendment is slightly altered as well.

In *United States v. Tucker* (2002), a parolee convicted for possession of child pornography appealed his conviction, challenging a warrantless parole search of his residence. The district court held that the parole search was supported by reasonable suspicion and that seizure of the defendant's computer was justified under the plain view doctrine. The court noted that probable cause is not required for a parole search that is conducted under a valid parole agreement and that the defendant had agreed to allow searches of his residence, diminishing his expectation of privacy.

In *Williams v. Consovoy* (2006), a former state prisoner brought a § 1983 claim against members of the parole board, a psychologist who contracted with the state to provide mental health services, and others, alleging that his arrest for a parole violation and the subsequent decisions of the parole board violated his Fourth and Eighth Amendment rights. The lower court granted summary judgment and the appellate court affirmed and held: (1) the claim against the parole board members and the arresting officer was not cognizable under § 1983; and (2) the psychologist enjoyed absolute immunity. According to the court, regardless of the fact the federal habeas relief was no longer available, the parole revocation decision had not invalidated a revocation decision. The court held that the private psychologist who contracted with the state to perform the evaluation and presented his findings to the adjudicative parole board, which then relied on his report and expertise in reaching its ultimate decision to deny the prisoner parole, acted as an arm of the court and enjoyed absolute immunity from a civil lawsuit alleging the wrongful denial of parole.

A parolee brought a legal action against a parole officer in *Giddings v. Joseph* (2007). The parole officer directed a warrant officer to return a parolee to the mental health unit of the prison from a halfway house for attempted suicide because he had cut his wrists. The parolee claimed that the parole officer was deliberately indifferent to his mental health needs and should have been transported to the hospital rather than to the prison. The court granted summary judgment on behalf of the parole officer. The court ruled that the parole officer was entitled to qualified immunity from the Eighth Amendment claim that she was deliberately indifferent to the parolee's need for medical treatment for a self-inflicted cut on his arm, noting that the cut was not serious because the parolee did not experience significant blood loss or infection, and the officer was indifferent to the cut as she transported him to the prison for medical care.

In *Drogosh v. Metcalf* (2009) a parolee was arrested and brought a § 1983 lawsuit against a parole officer and the lodging facility, alleging false arrest and unlawful detention in violation of the Fourth Amendment. The district court granted summary judgment in favor of the defendants on all claims but one against the parole officer's unlawful detention. The parole officer appealed and the Sixth Circuit Court of Appeals affirmed the lower court's decision. The court ruled that the parolee's confinement in jail for 13 days without a probable cause hearing violated the Fourth Amendment. The court held that the parole officer shouldered the responsibility to ensure the arrestee receive a prompt probable cause hearing after the warrantless arrest for alleging a parole violation and denied qualified immunity for failing to comply with the requirement.

Summary

Prisoners have used § 1983 as the primary vehicle for filing actions against correctional officials that allege constitutional rights deprivations for more than 40 years. From the mid-1970s to the late 1990s, prisoner civil litigation flooded the court system and many subsequent decisions have significantly affected correctional operations. Correctional litigation is comprised of a wide array of topics, but this chapter has dealt with the standard most commonly applied to prisoner allegations.

A common standard applied to correctional issues is that of "deliberate indifference." The standard is applied to correctional issues in prisons in accordance with the Fourteenth, Fifth, and Eighth Amendments, and in jails under the Fourteenth and Fifth Amendments. Deliberate indifference means that officials have consciously chosen to disregard the rights of a prisoner. It is a high standard for the plaintiff to prove and is applied by the courts on a case-by-case basis. Primary issues include medical and mental health care, conditions of confinement, and failure to protect. The United States Supreme Court has also expanded the standard to apply to issues relevant to environmental hazards in confinement facilities and claims filed under the ADA. Because of its common applicability in correctional matters, correctional officials should be aware of their custodial responsibilities in light of this standard.

Liability issues also emerge when confining the mentally impaired. Detention facilities house a significant number of this population. Whether in prison or jail, supervising and medicating the mentally ill raises certain liability concerns that officers and correctional officials should address. Procedures and practices for involuntarily medicating these prisoners should be implemented and officers should receive periodic training in how to respond to this population.

Perhaps the most significant impact on prisoner litigation has been the establishment of the Prison Litigation Reform Act. The PLRA was passed by Congress and has been implemented in an effort to reduce the number of frivolous lawsuits filed by prisoners. The PLRA pinpoints prison condition litigation and since 1996 its restrictions have reduced the number of civil actions filed by prisoners. As a result, habeas corpus petitions have increased sharply. Prisoners who file "frivolous" claims may be subject to losing earned good time, and prisoners in many situations must first submit an institutional grievance in an effort to resolve a complaint prior to filing a civil claim. In most cases, filing fees must be paid by prisoners. The PLRA applies to state correctional institutions and jails alike. The United States Supreme Court has twice addressed Congress's intent to require prisoners to exhaust administrative remedies before filing a civil action. This factor alone has more than likely assisted in reducing the number of lawsuits that prisoners file. The Court does not distinguish between classifications of lawsuits in applying the requirement. Correctional agencies should continue to ensure that their internal remedy mechanisms are functional in an effort to resolve prisoner disputes at the institutional level.

References

Alexander, E. (1996). Inmate advocate raises questions about PLRA's constitutionality. *Correctional Law Reporter, 8*(19), 26.

Black's Law Dictionary (2004). (8th ed.). St. Paul, MN: West Publishing Co.

Bober, D., & Pinas, D. (2007). Prisoners' rights and deliberate indifference. *The Journal of American Academy of Psychiatry and the Law, 35,* 388–391.

Krantz, S. (1997). *The law of sentencing, corrections, and prisoners' rights* (5th ed.). St. Paul, MN: West Publishing.

Maahs, J. R., & del Carmen, R. V. (1995). Curtailing frivolous section 1983 inmate litigation: laws, practices, and proposals. *Federal Probation, 59,* 53–61.

Maruschak, L. (1997). HIV in prisons and jails, 1995: *Bureau of Justice statistics bulletin.* Washington, DC: U.S. Department of Justice.

Maruschak, L. (2010). *Medical problems of prisoners: Bureau of Justice statistics.* Washington, DC: U.S. Department of Justice.

Maruschak, L., & Beavers, R. (2009). *HIV in prison: 2007–2008: Bureau of Justice statistics bulletin.* Washington, DC: U.S. Department of Justice.

Palmer, J. W., & Palmer, S. E. (1999). *Constitutional rights of prisoners* (6th ed.). Cincinnati, OH: Anderson Publishing Co.

Plitt, E. A. (1997). *Police civil liability and the defense of citizen misconduct complaints manual.* Chicago, IL: Americans for Effective Law Enforcement, Inc.

Ross, D. L. (1997). Emerging trends in correctional civil liability cases: a content analysis of federal court decisions of title 42 United States code section 1983: 1970–1994. *Journal of Criminal Justice, 25,* 501–515.

Schlangeer, M. (2003). Inmate litigation. *Harvard Law Review, 6,* 1555–1706.

Silver, I. (2010). *Police civil liability.* New York, NY: Matthew Bender & Co.

Vaughn, M. (1996). Prison civil liability for inmate-against-inmate assault and breakdown/organizational theory. *Journal of Criminal Justice, 24,* 139–152.

Vogt, R. P. (2000). What is deliberate indifference? *CorrectCare Quarterly Newsletter, Fall,* 1–2.

Describe the liability factors and possible means of risk reduction associated with police pursuits. Discuss the Scott v. Harris case and include reference to applicable constitutional and case law

12

Section 1983 Actions in Law Enforcement

OVERVIEW

The essence of contemporary law enforcement has made the patrol officer a prime target for litigation. In a democratic society police represent the legitimate force of government to compel citizens, if necessary, to obey laws that the majority of citizens, at least theoretically, have participated in creating. Despite the legitimacy of police authority and power, there are many citizens in society who resist such authority. When the government, through law enforcement, is required to intervene in the lives of the citizenry, a conflict emerges between the protection of individually protected constitutional rights and the exercise of the rule of law. In a democracy, an informal contract exists whereby citizens have a duty to abide by the law. When that contract is breached, other citizens rely on the police to intervene and enforce the law.

Intervening and responding on behalf of society by enforcing the law is the point at which the police become vulnerable to civil liability. When police officers perform their primary functions, they must be accountable to the rule of law. Just as citizens must comply with the law, police must know the law, make prudent decisions when enforcing the law, and exercise their authority within the boundaries of the law. A vast majority of police officers perform their duties in accordance with their sworn oath of office. As in many professions, there are some officers who cross the line, violate their oath, and exercise their authority outside its legal limits. As previously described in this text, § 1983 was enacted so that citizens who believe their protected rights have been violated by police may redress such actions.

Enforcing the First and Fourth Amendments through police intervention can generate civil actions against the police. When a protester exercises his or her freedom of speech at a rally, police may have to intervene if the protester violates the law. The protester may be arrested through the use of force and charged with a crime. The protester may later file a civil lawsuit claiming that his or her right to freedom of speech was denied, that he or she was falsely arrested and imprisoned, and that the officers used excessive force when making the arrest. The officers may have acted within their legitimate authority, but must be able to defend their actions. This chapter will examine § 1983 actions that arise out of common functions that the police perform regularly. In reviewing these cases, officers should consider their state's statutes and their agency's policies and practices.

False Arrest

Police officers are authorized to enforce the law and to arrest law violators. Officers frequently are sued for false arrest and false imprisonment. "Arrest" is defined as taking a person into custody against his or her will for the purpose of criminal prosecution or interrogation (*Dunaway v. New York*, 1979). An arrest occurs only when there is a governmental termination of freedom of movement through means intentionally applied (*Brower v. County of Inyo*, 1989). There must be some form of restraint used by the police, because words alone are insufficient. As a Fourth Amendment issue, arrest is a type of seizure, because a person's liberty must be restricted by law enforcement officers, such that the person is not free to leave. Allegations of false arrest or false imprisonment are actionable under both state tort law and § 1983.

Arrest is a legal conclusion that is used to describe a complex series of events that have taken place (Walker & Hemmens, 2008). Depending upon the circumstances, there are at least three possible components of an arrest. First, an essential component is the intent of the arresting officer to take the person into custody. Without the requisite intent there is no arrest, even though a person may be temporarily detained. Stopping a speeding motorist and citing him or her for violating the posted speed limit is not an arrest. There is no intent on the part of the officer to take the person into custody.

Second, under criminal law, an officer making an arrest must have the authority to restrict the person's liberty. An officer acting within the "scope of his authority," as provided by law, may make a legal arrest, providing that the elements for the arrest exist. An example may be when an officer arrests under an invalid warrant or makes an arrest for a misdemeanor not committed in his or her presence, where such an arrest is not authorized by state law. Arrest authority is granted by state law and agency regulations.

Third, the person must come under the control and custody of the officer. This can be accomplished by two means. First, a person may voluntarily submit to the authority and control of the officer. Second, the officer may use physical force to take the person into custody. In *United States v. Mendenhall* (1980), the U.S. Supreme Court stated that a person is seized only when, by means of physical force or show of authority, his or her freedom of movement is restrained. Informing a person that he or she is under arrest shows the intent of the officer, but does not constitute an arrest. The required restraint of the individual accompanied by taking control of the person is necessary.

In order to validate the arrest, the officer must have probable cause. In *Draper v. United States* (1959), the Supreme Court defined probable cause as: "facts and circumstances within the arresting officers' knowledge and of which they had reasonably trustworthy information are sufficient in themselves to warrant a man of reasonable caution in the belief that an offense has been or is being committed." This is applied on a case-by-case basis. The officer may form probable cause through three means: (1) his or her knowledge of the facts and circumstances; (2) acquiring information through a third party or an informant; or (3) gaining information and corroboration. Pursuant to federal constitutional standards, probable cause is required in all arrests, whether the arrest is being made with or without a warrant.

Claims of warrantless arrests without probable cause constitute one of the most frequently litigated issues in § 1983 cases, as the arrest is unquestionably a "seizure" of a person under the Fourth Amendment (Silver, 2010; Walker & Hemmens, 2008). In a false arrest claim, the plaintiff asserts that the arresting officer or officers deprived him of his liberty without proper authority. The plaintiff will generally allege that the officer acted without probable cause.

Claims of false arrest may also emerge when an officer executing an arrest warrant arrests the wrong person or an individual not named in the warrant. The officer must demonstrate that the arrest was valid and that he or she was acting in accordance with probable cause. In *Brodnicki v. City of Omaha* (1996), probable cause existed when a nine-year-old girl described a suspect, identified his car license plate, and identified the plaintiff in a showup at his home. A few inconsistencies in matching the plaintiff to the initial description did not alter the determination. The showup was not impermissibly suggestive and probable cause existed prior to it.

Compare, however, *Washington v. Lambert* (1996), in which the court denied qualified immunity to officers. The court held that a forcible stop involving displaying weapons, cuffing, frisking, searching the car, and detention in a patrol car for up to 25 minutes was a functional arrest. This intrusive action was not warranted by any alleged resemblance to armed robbery suspects. The court determined that under ordinary circumstances, when police have only reasonable suspicion to make an investigatory stop, drawing weapons and using handcuffs and other restraints will violate the Fourth Amendment. The court further held that only factors such as uncooperativeness, information that the suspect is currently armed, suspicion of committing a violent crime, and specificity of information about the crime may permit intrusive action. In this case the factors were extremely vague and the suspects did not match the descriptions.

In *Iacobucci v. Boulter* (1999), the court denied qualified immunity for arresting an individual for videotaping a meeting in which the person was not disorderly. The nondisruptive conduct of the plaintiff in videotaping a public meeting was legal, despite the fact that the arresting officer repeatedly told him to cease recording. The court stated that a police officer is not a law unto himself; he cannot give an order that has no colorable basis and then arrest a person who defies it. Further, in *Spiller v. City of Texas City* (1997), arresting a person for uttering a profanity was invalid. An arrest made by a plainclothes officer for disorderly conduct for demanding that the officer move his vehicle away from a gas pump was not based on probable cause. The court determined that the word "damn" was not likely to incite an immediate breach of the peace under Texas law, and it was unreasonable to arrest an individual for merely using one profane word.

The court also denied qualified immunity to officers in *Beier v. City of Lewiston* (2004). Beier and his wife were separated and seeking a divorce. Beier's wife was granted a protective order by the court and the judge ordered him to stay 300 feet away from her residence and place of employment. The order prohibited him from visiting his two sons. Several days later, Beier attended church where he was a member and sat a few rows behind his wife and sons. Beier's wife called the police after he would not leave on the request of one of his sons. Beier's wife informed the responding officer that she had an order and that her husband was violating it, but she did not show it to the officer, nor did he inquire about its stipulations or ask to read it. The officer instructed Beier to leave, but he claimed that he was not violating the order and asked the officer to review it. A second officer responded and they arrested Beier for violating the order. A scuffle ensued as one of Beier's sons attempted to intervene. The officers were trained in how to assess, serve, and enforce protection orders and they admitted that they were supposed to review the contents of an order to determine whether a violation had occurred.

Beier was arrested for violating the order, resisting arrest, and malicious injury to property. The charges were later dismissed.

Beier filed a lawsuit for false arrest in violation of the Fourth Amendment. The lower court and the appellate court denied the officer's motion for qualified immunity. The appellate court concluded that the officers did not have probable cause to arrest Beier as they incorrectly relied upon his wife's statement that he was violating the order. Probable cause could not be established by relying on the wife's incorrect understanding of the order. The officers should have relied on the contents of the order, not their unsubstantiated understanding of the order's terms. The court reasoned that there were no exigent circumstances warranting the failure to determine the applicable terms of the order. The court determined that the officers should have asked dispatch for details of the order and failed to review the order themselves. Because the officers made no attempt to review the contents of the order, the arrest of Beier was unjustified.

In *Bryson v. City of Tacoma* (2008), the court concluded that officers arresting an individual who was suspected of passing a forged check were granted summary judgment. Bryson entered a Bank of America branch to cash a payroll check from his employer. The teller checked his account number and found a negative balance of $32.00 and informed him that the overcharge would have to be paid prior cashing the check. Bryson refused to go to another bank to cash it and insisted on cashing the check. The teller became suspicious and attempted to scan it through the telescanner, which proved unsuccessful. She also noted that the paper stock of the check was thinner than most payroll checks, which further heightened her suspicions about the validity of the check. The teller contacted her supervisor and he contacted the bank that issued the check. The bank faxed over information to the supervisor and the check was indeed a forgery. Police officers responded to the Bank of America to investigate the check fraud. Bryson was detained, handcuffed, and placed in the patrol car. Bank employees informed the officers of the situation and the officers attempted to contact Bryson's employer, who issued the check. The employer could not be reached and the officers also noted that the check stub number of the payroll check did not match the corresponding number of the presented check. Based on probable cause, the officers arrested Bryson on a charge of forgery. A later call to Bryson's employer revealed that the check was valid, having been issued from a different account. Bryson filed a suit claiming false arrest. The city filed a motion to dismiss and the court granted the motion.

Bryson argued that the officers did not have probable cause to arrest him. He contended that every reason for suspecting him of committing a crime was unsubstantiated. The court rejected the argument and held that Bryson would have to show that either the policy of arrests performed by the city were specifically detrimental to him or were deliberately put in place to harm him. He would also have to show that the city had a pattern of unlawful arrests. The court held that there was no evidence that the city had a practice in place whereby officers acted outside the scope of probable cause when making arrests and dismissed the case.

In *Thomas v. City of Peoria* (2009), an arrestee brought a § 1983 lawsuit against the city and a prosecutor seeking relief on behalf of a class of similarly situated individuals who had been arrested by the city for parking tickets. The arrestee had been arrested after an officer mistakenly identified him as an individual who had nine unpaid parking tickets and a warrant out for his arrest. The arrestee claimed that the city had an unconstitutional practice of arresting people for not paying their parking tickets. The appellate court upheld the district court's decision to grant summary judgment for the defendants. The court ruled that the fact that an otherwise reasonable arrest was not for an "arrestable" offense would not make it unconstitutional, that an arrestee for a "nonjailable" offense would not violate the Fourth Amendment, and the prosecutor was entitled to absolute immunity from damages for her action in filing a motion for an arrest warrant.

False Imprisonment

False imprisonment is the unlawful confining of a person, which deprives that person of his or her liberty. False imprisonment may occur because of false arrest or, more commonly, as the result of an illegal detention after a valid arrest (Silver, 2010). An excessive delay in producing an arrestee before a magistrate may give rise to a valid § 1983 action. For example, a person may be legitimately arrested in accordance with probable cause, but held in a detention facility uncharged for 15 days (false imprisonment). The United States Supreme Court held in *Baker v. McCollan* (1979) that a "mistaken identity" arrest and a short detention under a warrant failed to give rise to a § 1983 action. The warrant was valid and the arrest was reasonable at the time it occurred. The fact that the police failed for several days to even investigate the plaintiff's assertion of innocence did not violate any constitutional right.

Prolonged detention can give rise to a false imprisonment claim under § 1983. The United States Supreme Court determined in *County of Riverside v. McLaughlin* (1991) that delays of up to 48 hours, if not taken for improper purposes, may be actionable. In *Kyle v. Patterson* (1997), the court ruled that a 61-hour delay before presentation before a magistrate due to the prosecutor delaying about what charges to bring against the arrestee was unconstitutional. Compare, however, *Sanchez v. Swyden* (1998) and *Brennan v. Township of Northville* (1996), in which qualified immunity was granted despite delays in bringing the arrestees before a magistrate. In *Sanchez*, officers detained the plaintiff for 26 hours before taking him before the magistrate. In a mistaken identity arrest, officers possessed the actual suspect's photos, fingerprints, and tattoo information within two hours of the arrest. *Baker* was cited and more than negligence was required. In *Brennan*, the court, citing *McLaughlin*, found that the overnight detention of an arrestee for 22 hours for domestic violence without giving an opportunity to post bail was not actionable under § 1983. The court concluded that there was no constitutional violation, no harassment, nor was a magistrate available that evening.

In *Brady v. Dill* (1999), officers mistakenly arrested an individual on a valid warrant. He was arrested and placed in detention for 36 hours over a weekend. Officers attempted to contact the prosecutor and judge but were unsuccessful. After discovering their mistake, the officers failed to release the arrestee. The plaintiff filed a § 1983 action, claiming false imprisonment. The officers' failure to release was qualifiedly immunized, at least because they had actually attempted to secure the person's release. The court held that in egregious cases where officers failed to inform a prosecutor or judge, liability would most likely attach. Although prolonged detention occurred in this case, the court acknowledged that neither the judge nor the prosecutor was available and that the officers made a bona fide effort to contact them.

In *Sivard v. Pulaski County* (1992), qualified immunity was denied on a false imprisonment claim. A 17-day detention between a warrantless arrest, a hearing, and a continued post-hearing detention, due in part to a probable cause finding and also an out-of-state request to detain a warrant obtained one month after the arrest, was illegal. Even though the defendants were orally informed of the indictment within hours of the arrest, they failed to comply with the ordinary promptness requirements or the state of Indiana's Extradition Act by not bringing the arrestee before a magistrate who could have ordered further detention.

The court granted summary judgment to arresting officers in *Wilder v. Village of Amityville* (2003), when a protester was arrested for attempting to block the removal of a tree. When town officials attempted to remove a tree, Wilder and other protesters cited religious and environmental concerns and stood in front of the tree, blocking workers from cutting it down. Police officers responded and a sergeant instructed Wilder to leave numerous times. Wilder claimed that while she was playing the flute she became confused about what the sergeant wanted her to do. The sergeant moved her, handcuffed her, and charged her with obstructing a governmental function in the second degree. Wilder sued, claiming false arrest, excessive force, false imprisonment, malicious prosecution, and interference with her free speech rights.

The federal district court granted summary judgment to the sergeant. The court concluded that the sergeant had probable cause to arrest Wilder for obstructing governmental administration, and her other claims also failed. The law prohibited a person from intentionally preventing public servants from performing their official functions. It was undisputed that Wilder failed to move when ordered several times by the sergeant. Her excessive force claims failed because although her wrists may have been sore, they were uninjured, and this was not enough to be considered to be unlawful conduct in a lawful arrest situation. Her claims of expressing her right to free speech also failed as she could not prove that the village harbored any ill-will against her.

In *Estate of Cloanigner v. McDevin* (2009), a former detainee who had been seized by deputies for a psychological evaluation, brought a § 1983 lawsuit against deputies for asserting that his Fourth and Fourteenth Amendment rights had been violated. The detainee had called a hospital to report an adverse reaction to prescription medication and threated suicide, stating that he "had access to many weapons." The hospital called 911 and deputies were dispatched to the residence. The deputies knew that the detainee had made several suicidal threats in the past, had responded to the residence previously, and that firearms had been discovered at the home. Acting on "exigent circumstances," the deputies entered the home and took the detainee into custody so that a psychological evaluation could be performed.

The detainee filed a lawsuit and the appellate court found that the lower court's decision to award summary judgment to the deputies was proper. The court ruled that the deputies had probable cause to seize and detain the detainee for a psychological evaluation, and that exigent circumstances existed, supporting the warrantless seizure of the detainee.

Police Pursuits

A common task of many patrol officers is operating their police vehicle in a high-speed pursuit. Such pursuits may involve citizens attempting to elude police. The chase may involve misdemeanants or felons. It is not uncommon for the driver, passenger, or an innocent third party to be seriously injured or die, because many pursuits end in crashes. As a consequence, it is highly likely that a § 1983 lawsuit will be filed against the officers involved and the police agency.

Research studies on police pursuits are limited (Beckman, 1987; Gallagher, 1989; NIJ, 1998; Falcone et al., 1994). Alpert (1997), however, conducted a national study on the training of police officers and their agency policies on engaging in pursuits. He studied 436 agencies of 737 contacted. Of the respondents, 90 percent indicated that they had written policies on allowing and restricting officers to pursue fleeing motorists. Sixty percent require officers to be trained in pursuit driving in the police academy (14 hours) and provided an average of three hours of in-service training annually.

In an attempt to perform their legally sworn duties when engaged in a pursuit, law enforcement personnel frequently find themselves in a no-win situation. They are criticized for pursuing and for not pursuing an eluder. While police may be open to civil litigation, Kappeler et al. (1997) found that plaintiffs prevail in approximately 31 percent of the § 1983 claims filed against them. The lawsuit generally asserts that the officer, by initiating the pursuit, should be held liable for violating the constitutional rights of the injured party. The lawsuit may also claim that the officer was motivated by the intent to harm, failed to follow agency policy and training, and acted with indifference to the rights of the injured party. Frequently, supervisors will also be named in the civil litigation for failing to train, supervise, and direct officers in regard to engaging in such pursuits.

Several issues have emerged regarding the practice of police officers performing high-speed pursuits. One important issue surrounding police pursuits is that of whether pursuits and roadblocks constitute a "seizure" under the Fourth Amendment. The United States Supreme Court in *Brower v. County of Inyo* (1989) determined that roadblocks designed to stop an individual from fleeing from the police are "seizures" under the Fourth Amendment. The plaintiff asserted a viable claim that placing a large tractor-trailer across the highway as a "roadblock" behind a curve without illumination and the pursued driver being blinded by police car headlights as he approached constituted an "unreasonable seizure." Applying *Brower*, the court in *Frye v. Town of Akron* (1991) reviewed a high-speed police chase involving a motorcycle in which the passenger died. The accident was not a constitutional seizure in the absence of any evidence that the officer intended to seize the person by colliding with them to force them off the road. If there was any evidence that the officer acted so recklessly as to amount to a complete disregard for the safety of the passenger, a substantive due process claim may be stated. The court concluded that proof of the department not providing training to its officers concerning high-speed pursuits may, however, state a policy claim against the government entity. Compare, however, the court's decision in *Adams v. St. Lucie County Sheriff's Department* (1992). Several deputies from the St. Lucie County Sheriff's Department attempted to stop a motorist for committing a misdemeanor. The driver sped off and deputies engaged in a high-speed pursuit. During the chase, the deputies intentionally rammed the eluder's car, which later crashed, killing the passenger. The court denied qualified immunity for the deputies. The court determined that intentional ramming constituted an unreasonable seizure that would have been apparent to a reasonable officer.

BOX 12.1   *COUNTY OF SACRAMENTO V. LEWIS* (1998)

In *Lewis*, a deputy attempted to stop a motorcyclist (with a passenger) who had driven between two deputies' patrol vehicles at a high rate of speed. The pursuit, which exceeded 80 miles an hour, ended when the motorcycle overturned, and the deputy's vehicle skidded into the motorcycle. The driver of the motorcycle survived, but the passenger was killed. The driver of the motorcycle attempted to elude the deputies because he was restricted from operating the motorcycle. In operating their police vehicles at speeds of more than 80 miles per hour, the deputies violated their department's policy regarding proper pursuit speeds.

Lewis's family filed a § 1983 claim under the Fourteenth Amendment asserting the deprivation of Lewis's substantive due process right to life. The lower court granted summary judgment for the deputy, but the Ninth Circuit Court of Appeals reversed, holding that the appropriate standard in a police pursuit is deliberate indifference to a person's right to life. The Supreme Court granted certiorari to examine the issue of determining the appropriate standard in police pursuit cases. The Court rejected the standards of deliberate indifference and reckless disregard. The Court determined that in circumstances of a high-speed chase aimed at apprehending a suspected offender, where unforeseen circumstances demand an instant judgment by the officer who feels the pull of competing obligations, only a purpose to cause harm unrelated to the legitimate object of the arrest will satisfy the "shocks the conscience" test. Chases conducted with no intent to physically harm suspects or worsen their legal plight do not give rise to the substantive due process liability.

This is a significant case because the Court for the first time established that the "shocks the conscience" standard was the appropriate standard in police pursuit cases. While the decision involved the death of a passenger, its broad language appears to apply to all injuries, including injuries sustained by bystanders, regardless of whether the police vehicle or the pursued vehicle was involved in the accident. This is a high standard for the plaintiff to overcome, because the intent and motive of the officer to cause harm must be proved.

A second important issue concerning high-speed police pursuits addresses the appropriate standard of review the courts apply in such cases. Over the years, lower courts have applied different standards, such as deliberate indifference, shocking to the conscience, and objective reasonableness to police pursuits in determining whether liability should attach. These standards have caused confusion among the courts, police, and lawyers. The U.S. Supreme Court, in *County of Sacramento v. Lewis* (1998), agreed with the philosophy of many lower courts concerning pursuits by endorsing the "shocks the conscience" standard (Box 12.1). The Court concluded that a high-speed pursuit will violate substantive due process only where a purpose to cause harm unrelated to the legitimate object of the arrest "shocks the conscience."

After the *Lewis* decision, a few lower courts applied the standard with varying interpretations. In *Trigalet v. City of Tulsa* (2001), officers pursued a motorist who stole a minivan. There was no indication that the fleeing suspect had committed any violent felony or was known for violent behavior. The eluder drove through several stop signs, at speeds of more than 40 miles per hour, and later drove through a red light, where he struck another vehicle, killing the three occupants. The estates of the victims sued the city, claiming that it was liable for civil rights violations for its policies and practices governing high-speed chases. The department's policy stated that all pursuits were to be supervised and that officers were to terminate pursuits "when the hazards outweigh the benefits." The officers allegedly did not inform any supervisor of the pursuit. The city requested summary judgment, but the lower court refused their request and they appealed. The appellate court reversed, concluding that the officers' actions did not violate the plaintiffs' constitutional rights. Testimony revealed that the officers had received 24 hours of hands-on training regarding operating a vehicle and additional training on the philosophy of pursuits. The court stated that the officers would violate a bystander's substantive due process rights only when they acted with reckless indifference to the risk created and directed by their actions toward the bystander. Here, nothing indicated that the officers intended to harm the victims. Thus, the officers did not violate the victims' constitutional rights. The court further stated that because the officers did not violate the victims' constitutional rights, the city could not be held liable.

In *Puglese v. Cobb County, Georgia* (1998), the court found that it was reasonable to shoot a fleeing intoxicated felon to end his flight and because the driver had driven his vehicle at the officer. The court ruled that the shooting was a seizure under the Fourth Amendment in accordance with *Brower*, was reasonable under *Graham v. Connor* (1989), and did not shock the conscience, despite a collision and injury sustained by the driver. Similarly in *Scott v. Clay County* (2000), the court ruled that police shooting the tires of a fleeing vehicle did not rise to the "shocks the conscience" level. The Sixth Circuit Court of Appeals ruled that a chase lasting more than 20 minutes, reaching speeds ranging from 80 to 100 miles per hour, and officers shooting the tires out, with two bullets hitting the passenger in the car, was not shocking to the conscience. The driver of the car attempted to drive over an officer prior to the chase. The court stated that the driver led the officers on a high-speed chase and attempted to harm the officer, and thus the officer was justified in firing at the vehicle in order to seize it. The officer could not violate the passenger's rights because he did not know she was there.

The Third Circuit Court of Appeals affirmed summary judgment for officers involved in the pursuit of a stolen vehicle in *Davis v. Township of Hillside* (1999). Matching the description of a stolen vehicle, two patrol officers in separate patrol cars attempted to investigate the theft as the vehicle was stopped at a stop sign. As the officers approached the driver of the stolen vehicle, he pulled away. A pursuit reaching speeds of more than 70 miles per hour ensued. Officers activated their overhead lights but not their sirens. One patrol car bumped the rear of the eluder's car, causing the driver to hit his head on the steering wheel, rendering him unconscious. The car spun out of control, hitting a parked car, which struck a pedestrian standing on the sidewalk. The pedestrian (Davis) suffered severe injury and filed a civil action against the police. The lower court granted summary judgment and Davis appealed.

Davis argued that the officers' ramming of the eluder's vehicle amounted to deadly force and that such action was foreseeable where harm or injury that "shocks the conscience" was likely. The appellate court concluded that the officers were performing a lawful duty by attempting to investigate the stolen vehicle, and faced lawless behavior when the driver drove off. The officers' actions were taken out of necessity, not to cause injury. The court reasoned there was no evidence that their actions, if reckless or imprudent, were "tainted by an improper or malicious motive." Their actions did not shock the conscience and the court subsequently affirmed summary judgment.

Because of the stringent standard established in the *Lewis* case, many plaintiffs are seeking relief in state courts when a pursuit ends in a fatality. Claims are filed in accordance with wrongful death statutes. In *Nguyen v. City of Westminster* (2002), police observed a stolen van and attempted to stop it but the driver fled from them. The chase traveled through a high school parking lot, and through an adjacent athletic field. The van proceeded into a second parking lot, where numerous students were standing. The officer twice rammed the van but it continued toward the students. The van hit a pool of water, skidded, and crashed into a trash dumpster, striking and seriously injuring several students. The family sued for negligence and after a student died the family added a wrongful death claim. Under California law, the officer was immune from liability for the death and injury resulting from operating an emergency vehicle in a pursuit of a suspected criminal. The lawsuit therefore was directed at the city for adopting a faulty pursuit policy that contributed to the death of the student. The city's policy identified 11 factors for officers and supervisors to consider when engaging, continuing, or discontinuing a pursuit. Such factors included the seriousness of the offense, the safety of the public and officers, traffic concerns, location of pursuit, speed, time of day, radio communication, and road conditions, to mention a few. The policy also directed that the officer should use his or her discretion as the policy could not address every conceivable factor involved in a pursuit. Determining that the policy satisfied the law's requirement, the court granted summary judgment to the city and the family appealed.

The appellate court affirmed the lower court's decision. The court noted that the city followed the law when it designed its policy. The law was intended to encourage public agencies to adopt clear and specific standards that were intended to reduce the frequency of accidents but to leave the agency discretion as to when to conduct vehicle pursuits without threat of liability. The policy alone made the officer immune, regardless of whether he followed it. Because the policy complied with the law, the city was immune from liability.

Conversely, in *Ewing v. City of Detroit* (2002), the plaintiff prevailed in a pursuit case. Police engaged in a high-speed chase and the driver of the vehicle crashed into a third party. As a result of the collision an innocent motorist and her child were severely injured. The family filed suit in state court, claiming that the police were the proximate cause of the injuries. The court agreed and awarded the family $2.2 million.

Many suspects are willing to risk their lives as well as the lives of others (including the police) to avoid being apprehended. The ability to pursue a fleeing suspect is an essential aspect of effective law enforcement. The International Association of Chiefs of Police reports that police engage in about 250,000 pursuits annually, resulting in 500 deaths (Pape, 2006). The U.S. Supreme Court remarked in *Illinois v. Wardlow* (2000) that headlong flight is the consummate act of evasion: it is not indicative of wrongdoing but it certainly suggestive of such. This philosophy, however, falls short of providing guidance to the police when making a decision to pursue a fleeing motorist. In *Scott v. Harris* (2007), the United States Supreme Court had occasion to examine a police pursuit in order to determine proper police practices and to determine whether using stopping maneuvers is objectively reasonable (Box 12.2).

BOX 12.2   *SCOTT V. HARRIS* (2007)

Deputy Reynolds observed a car driven by Harris traveling at 73 miles per hour in a 55-mile-per-hour speed zone. Reynolds activated his overhead lights, which also activated the in-car video system. Harris accelerated away and Reynolds radioed for assistance and turned on his siren. Harris drove erratically, crossing the center line and almost striking other vehicles. Harris pulled into a parking lot and deputy Scott joined the pursuit. Harris drove through the parking lot and Scott followed him. Harris continued to drive recklessly, reaching speeds of 90 miles per hour. Scott radioed for permission to perform the Precision Intervention Technique (PIT) maneuver and his supervisor granted permission. Scott made contact with Harris's back bumper, causing Harris's car to leave the roadway and crash. Harris sustained injuries that left him a quadriplegic.

Harris filed a § 1983 action, claiming that the use of the PIT maneuver amounted to deadly force in violation of his Fourth Amendment constitutional rights. Harris argued that Scott violated the deadly force criteria established in *Tennessee v. Garner* (1985). The district court and the appellate court denied summary judgment, holding that ramming an eluding vehicle under the circumstances amounted to deadly force. Scott appealed and the United States Supreme Court granted certiorari. In an 8-to-1 decision the Court reversed the appellate court's decision and granted summary judgment for Scott (with Justice Stevens dissenting). The Court watched the video and found that it contradicted Harris's account and that his reckless driving posed a danger to the public, awarding qualified immunity.

The Court concluded that Scott's actions of bumping Harris's car were objectively reasonable under the Fourth Amendment. Harris posed a danger and an imminent risk to himself and to the community and Scott's seizure was objectively reasonable under the rapidly evolving circumstances. The Court determined that Harris's behavior created the need to terminate the chase and actions taken by Scott were justified in eliminating the risk under the circumstances.

The Court's decision in *Scott* established a guide for future pursuit cases for the police and civil liability (Hughes & Edwards, 2008; Ross, 2008). There are several issues which emerge from this decision. First, assisting the Court in making its ruling was the videotape. The majority agreed that from seeing the incident, the video clearly contradicted Harris's account. The Court's collective agreement determined that Harris's actions posed an imminent risk to the public and that Scott's actions were reasonable under the Constitution. The Court reasoned that a reasonable jury, therefore, after watching the video, would conclude that Scott's actions were reasonable. Thus, such determination warranted qualified immunity for Scott. The Court posted the video on its web site (http://www.supremecourtus.gov/opinions/video/scottv .harris.rmvb).

Viewing videotapes as part of the evidence relied upon by a court is not new. Numerous cases have been decided in the past by using a videotape to assist a court in rendering a decision. According to the Court, Harris's conduct was so reckless as depicted by the video that the case did not need to be presented to a jury. Such behavior overwhelmingly convinced the Court that the issue of qualified immunity need not be addressed. It is projected that more courts may view videotapes of incidents with more regularity than in the past based on this decision and qualified immunity granted to officers, as long as the conduct is supported by the Constitution. The Court held that such decisionmaking during the discovery stage does not negatively impact the stages articulated in its decision in *Saucier v. Katz* (2001). Prompted by the *Scott* decision, the court in *Lewis v. City of West Palm Beach* (2009; see Chapter 12) viewed a videotape of officers restraining a violent arrestee who later died after restraint. The court granted summary judgment to the officers, stating that the video confirmed the officer's need to use reasonable force by restraining the combative suspect.

Further, the Court examined whether Scott's use of force was justified by relying on its decision in *Graham v. Connor* (1989), rejecting the *Tennessee v. Garner* standard (1985). The Court held that the facts in Harris were vastly different and that *Garner* had no applicability. The Court held that the issue of deadly force was not at question, rather they addressed whether Scott's actions were objectively reasonable, holding that it was reasonable for an officer to stop a fleeing motorist who created a danger to the community by ramming his car from behind. According to the Court, not stopping a dangerous suspect posed a greater risk of harm to the community. Endorsing the objective reasonableness standard established in *Graham*, the Court focused on Scott's actions in relation to the risk of harm and danger posed by Harris's actions and distinguished a car chase from an unarmed foot pursuit, commenting that "pursuits are extremely more dangerous." Relying on the *Graham* standard, the Court has also apparently added new criteria independent of *Garner*, which included dangerousness of flight as part of the reasonableness standard. The dangerousness of flight component will be assessed on a case-by-case basis and cannot be mechanically measured. The police cannot mechanically calculate the degree of risk that a suspect will take or the degree of harm that a suspect will invoke to elude capture.

This decision obviously does not justify the use of lethal force on any fleeing suspect. It does provide a framework for assessing the potential for danger and the degree of danger the suspect posed by his conduct in flight from the police. It also provides for an analysis of the reasonableness of an officer's actions, which is to be viewed within the totality of circumstances facing the officer, the split-second decisionmaking that officers are forced to make, and how rapidly events can unfold, all factors emphasized in the *Graham* and *County of Sacramento v. Lewis* cases. The Court supports the position that the police may eliminate the risk of a fleeing suspect who is attempting to elude them by driving recklessly and places others in danger, even when it places the fleeing motorist at risk of serious injury.

The decision in *Scott* has been applied by the lower courts. In *Bingue v. Prunchak* (2008), police engaged in a pursuit covering one hour at speeds reaching 100 miles per hour. The pursuit involved a dozen police vehicles and a police helicopter. A responding officer sideswiped a vehicle that had stopped on the road to allow police vehicles to pass by. Both vehicles spun out of control and the motorist sustained injuries and filed a legal action against the police. The appellate court ruled that officers were entitled to qualified immunity because they acted reasonably and did not act with intent to harm anyone. The court further ruled that officers acted solely with the motivation to stop the fleeing suspect, who was endangering the community.

In *Beshers v. Harrison* (2007), Beshers was refused service at a package store after he attempted to steal beer from the store. A surveillance tape showed the truck that Beshers was driving and officer Harrison spotted it at a gas station. Beshers fled from Harrison and a pursuit began. Beshers swerved to avoid a roadblock set up by officers and he ran a red light at an intersection and struck another motorist's vehicle. Beshers operated his truck from 55 to 65 mph. Rather than stop, Beshers continued to flee from the officers and Harrison rammed his truck, causing it to flip over several times, killing him on impact. The appellate court awarded Harrison qualified immunity, holding that Besher's conduct was undeniably dangerous. The court held that the *Scott* decision compelled it to conclude that Harrison's use of force was objectively reasonable and did not violate the constitutional rights of Beshers.

High-speed pursuits are a high liability area in policing, despite the standard established in the *Lewis* and the *Scott* decisions. As discussed in Chapter 6, claims attacking administrators revolve around failure to train, failure to supervise, and failure to direct officers through established written policies and procedures. Police pursuits are a highly controversial topic with the public, the news media, and the courts. It is critical that administrators provide a written policy for their officers and that policy training, as well as behind-the-wheel training, be provided. Boxes 12.3 and 12.4 illustrate components that should be considered when deciding to engage in a pursuit and identify essential elements of a pursuit policy (Nerbonne, 1998; Michigan Municipal Risk Management Authority, 2007).

Administrators should also consider adopting a pursuit management continuum, which provides guidance in decisionmaking for officers (Ashley, 2006). This continuum is similar to that of a use-of-force continuum that has been used in law enforcement and corrections for many years. The pursuit continuum graphically illustrates various types of pursuit circumstances and aligns recommended pursuit tactics (control) for officers to consider based on the situation. The Ashley continuum can be divided into three suspect activities based on the severity of the hazards involved in the flight of the suspect and three levels of pursuit control

---

BOX 12.3   FACTORS IN DETERMINING WHETHER TO UNDERTAKE A POLICE PURSUIT

- Type of crime involved
- Type of location where pursuit occurred
- Time of day or night
- Likelihood of harm from not apprehending the suspect
- Availability of backup
- Weather and road conditions
- Condition of the police vehicle
- Safety of officer and citizens
- Traffic conditions
- Communication with supervisor
- Presence of passengers in fleeing vehicle
- Likelihood of apprehending the suspect
- Officer's knowledge of the area
- Whether suspect can be apprehended later
- Whether suspect has been positively identified

BOX 12.4   ESSENTIAL COMPONENTS OF A PURSUIT POLICY

- Department philosophy regarding pursuits
- Definition of high-speed pursuits
- Initiation of a pursuit
- Activation of emergency equipment
- Use of marked versus unmarked vehicles
- Pacing
- Notification of supervisor
- Bumping and ramming
- Safety of officer
- Pursuits in and out of jurisdiction
- Compliance with state and local laws
- Use of roadblocks
- Use of strips
- Number of police vehicles
- Types of crimes
- Speed limits
- Authority to terminate
- Radio communications
- Information on suspect when available
- Shooting from or at a moving vehicle
- Environmental factors (weather, roads, city, highway, residence, business, rural, etc.)
- Safety to citizens
- Defining supervisory role
- Description of alternatives that may be used
- Establishing the speed that police vehicles may travel
- Requiring reports and review process
- Tracking the number and nature of pursuits annually

---

tactics, including trailing techniques, blocking techniques, and contact techniques. The concept is to teach officers how to assess suspect activities and respond with reasonable and justifiable techniques based on the numerous variables involved in any pursuit. The continuum should be integrated with the pursuit policy, combined with classroom and scenario-based field training, to enhance the decisionmaking and motor skills of officers.

In *Sykes v. United States* (2011), the United States Supreme Court ruled on a sentencing case with implications for police pursuits. Sykes was arrested and found guilty of federal felony firearms charges. Sykes was found guilty and because he had three prior convictions for violent felonies, he received an enhanced sentence under federal sentencing guidelines. Sykes appealed the sentence enhancement arguing that one of the prior convictions was not a violent felony. The conviction related to fleeing from a law enforcement officer, and under Indiana law, it is considered a violent crime. The Court granted certiorari to decide whether fleeing from a law enforcement officer qualified as a crime of violence.

Under Indiana law, flight from law enforcement with a vehicle after being ordered to stop through words or emergency equipment constitutes a Class D felony. The Court explained that police activated their emergency equipment for a traffic stop, Sykes refused to stop and a chase ensued. Sykes drove on the wrong side of the road, drove through yards, and weaved back and forth through traffic, passed through a fence, and struck the rear of a house. Sykes fled on foot and was discovered by the aid of a canine. In his appeal, Sykes did not dispute that his fleeing was a felony, but argued such action was not a violent felony.

The Court defined what constituted a violent crime from federal statutes stating that it must be an offense that otherwise involves conduct that presents serious potential of risk of physical injury to another. The Court further asserted that when a perpetrator defies a law enforcement command by fleeing in a car, the determination to elude capture makes a lack of concern for the safety of property and persons of pedestrians and other drivers an inherent part of the offense. A criminal who takes flight creates a risk of this dimension, and takes action similar in degree to the danger involved in arson, which also entails intentional release of a destructive force dangerous to others. The attempt to elude capture is a direct challenge to an officer's authority and is a dangerous act that dares, and in a typical case requires, the officer to give chase. The felon's conduct gives the officer reason to believe that the defendant has something more serious than a traffic violation to hide.

Confrontation with police is the expected result of vehicle flight and it places property and persons at serious risk of injury. Risk of violence is inherent in vehicle flight. It is well known that when offenders use motor vehicles as their means of escape they create serious potential risks of physical injury to others. Fleeing from a police officer invites, even demands, pursuit, and as it continues, the risk of an accident accumulates. Based on these factors, the Court ruled that felony vehicle flight constitutes a violent felony under the federal Armed Career Criminals Act.

There are several implications from this decision. All officers and administrators should check to determine if their state has an eluding statute like Indiana. Second, it is important to observe how state courts will apply this decision to police pursuits. Third, this decision aligns with the Court's decision in *Tennessee v. Garner* (1985), which authorizes lethal force when the suspect threatens an officer with a weapon or there is probable cause to believe the suspect has committed a crime that involves the infliction or threatened infliction of serious bodily harm, lethal force may be used to prevent escape, when a verbal warning is provided, if feasible. As a result of this decision, the use of lethal force may be supported and justified by officers when engaged in a pursuit, based on incident variables. Third, the Court emphasized that fleeing from the police is a provocative and dangerous act that requires that an officer give chase, which supports police officers pursing fleeing felons. Finally, the Court's decision, which defines fleeing the police as a violent felony, supports an agency's pursuit policy directing officers to pursue such felons eluding apprehension. Pursuit policies should be revised as warranted in accordance with the Court's decision.

Failure to Protect

Section 1983 claims emerging from a failure to protect assert that the police officer's action or inaction caused harm to the plaintiff. To state a cause of action, the plaintiff must show that a police officer or municipality was aware of a particular danger or risk to which the plaintiff was exposed, and/or the injury occurred while the plaintiff was in the immediate control of the police. Common claims for failure to protect involve allegations of failure to intervene, failure to arrest a drunk driver, delay or failure in responding to a call, failure to protect a witness, leaving citizens in a place of danger, domestic violence situations, and failure to summon assistance. In a highly publicized case, the city of Milwaukee, Wisconsin, settled out of court for $850,000 for claims of failing to intervene and failing to protect a 14-year-old boy from Jeffrey Dahmer in *Estate of Sinthasomphone v. City of Milwaukee* (1995). Police were summoned to investigate a youth who was drugged, bleeding, and running naked in the neighborhood. After investigating, the officers came to believe that the incident involved a homosexual love matter between the youth and Dahmer (it was unknown to the officers at the time that he was a serial killer). The officers left the youth in Dahmer's custody in his apartment, where he was later murdered by Dahmer. The estate filed suit against the city, alleging that the officers violated the rights of the youth by not intervening.

An important case on liability under § 1983 for claims of failure to protect comes from a case that is unrelated to policing. The U.S. Supreme Court in *DeShaney v. Winnebago County Department of Social Services* (1989) held that there is no constitutional right to protection under the due process clause. This decision holds that, with some exceptions, the state and its officers are not liable under § 1983 for failure to protect persons from injury caused by private persons (Box 12.5).

This decision is important to public officials. Absent any duty to protect, it makes little difference whether inaction was intentional, malicious, reckless, or negligent, so long as the public officials in some substantial way do not actively participate in the infliction of harm (*Bryson v. City of Edmond*, 1990). The Court in *DeShaney* stated that one element under § 1983 was absent—the violation of a constitutional right. A § 1983 action cannot succeed when the harm comes from the hands of a third person. However, governmental entities that detain or incarcerate prisoners could be sued under § 1983 for failure to protect. Thus, officials working in detention centers and prisons must provide security to those in their custody.

In *Stemler v. City of Florence* (1997), the court denied qualified immunity to officers who physically forced a woman to accompany her intoxicated boyfriend in his truck and drive away, resulting in an accident and her subsequent death. She had been beaten by her boyfriend earlier. While custody was not required in this case, it was present. The court determined that constitutional arbitrariness was a predicate for liability. The court further ruled that police officers should know that they cannot force an incapacitated woman to drive away with an obviously drunk man who they believed had beaten her. This action of the police, the court stated, "is a chilling and unacceptable vision of the role of the police in our society."

In *Dodd v. Jones* (2010), an intoxicated driver struck a motorist who had been lying injured on the road after his own apparent alcohol-related accident. He sued two highway patrolmen who responded to his accident for failure to protect him from the intoxicated driver. A federal appeals court upheld summary judgment for the defendants, as the evidence did not show that they had taken the plaintiff into custody and held him against his will, triggering a duty to

BOX 12.5   *DESHANEY V. WINNEBAGO COUNTY DEPARTMENT OF SOCIAL SERVICES* (1989)

After a divorce, four-year-old Joshua DeShaney was placed into the custody of his father. Over a period of time, social workers received several complaints that Joshua was being abused by his father. The department of social services took limited measures to protect the boy, but did not remove him from his father's custody. Joshua was later beaten by his father and sustained permanent brain injuries that caused him to be mentally retarded. His father was prosecuted, found guilty of child abuse, and sentenced to prison. His mother filed a § 1983 action against the department of social services, claiming that it violated the child's Fourteenth Amendment right to due process by failing to protect him from his violent father. The district court held in favor of the county, and the appellate court affirmed.

The United States Supreme Court examined the issue of whether the state has a duty to protect individuals not in its custody from harm by a private person. The Court decided that the Fourteenth Amendment does not require a state to protect a person from harm by a private person who is not in its custody. While the Fourteenth Amendment does protect citizens from the actions and power of the state, it does not impose any requirement on the state to protect its citizens' life, liberty, and property from invasion of a private party. The Court concluded that a state's failure to protect an individual against private violence does not constitute a violation of the due process clause.

This decision is significant because the Court held for the first time that state and public officials are not liable to citizens for failing to protect them from harm incurred through the actions of a private person. While this case does not involve criminal justice personnel, it is important for those who have care and custody of prisoners and detainees. The Court reasoned that when the state takes a person into custody and detains that person against his or her will, the Constitution imposes a duty to provide some level of protection against harm for that person. This would apply to detention centers and correctional facilities. The state has some responsibility to provide for the safety of those in its custody. A breach of such a duty would subject the state and its officers to civil liability.

protect him. The officers did not move the motorist, awaiting the arrival of an ambulance, as they feared he had suffered a spinal injury, but they did attempt to stop the oncoming vehicle driven by the intoxicated driver, who ignored their directions.

In *Decoria v. County of Jefferson* (2009), a police officer allegedly arranged for a sex offender to stay at a home a few days before he raped a child there. The child's mother sued, claiming that the officer exposed the child to a danger she would not otherwise have faced, in violation of her substantive due process rights. At the time of the incident, the law was clearly established that an officer who acted with deliberate indifference to affirmatively placing a person in a danger that he or she otherwise would not have faced violates that person's constitutional rights. The appeals court ruled, however, that the question of whether the officer violated the child's rights when his actions were not aimed at the child, but at a third person (here the sex offender) who later harms the child had not previously been decided in the Ninth Circuit. The officer was therefore granted qualified immunity, as he did not violate clearly established law.

Domestic Violence

Responding to domestic violence situations can, in many jurisdictions, involve a considerable amount of time for the police. Generally, the police do not owe a constitutional duty to protect people from domestic violence. In light of *DeShaney*, it has been argued that there is a special duty to provide protection from domestic violence, including spouse abuse. Liability, however, will not normally attach against police officers in domestic violence incidents unless the officer or the department increases an individual's danger or interferes with other actions that may have been available (such as informing an abused spouse not to go to court because they would protect her [Plitt, 1997].

Congress passed the Violence Against Women Act in 1994. The Act provides for powerful criminal and civil enforcement tools for holding perpetrators accountable for committing such crimes as sexual assaults, stalking, domestic violence, and other violent crimes against women. In 2000 and 2005, Congress expanded and improved the legal tools of the Act to address additional violent crimes against women. The Office on Violence Against Women was subsequently created to implement the components of the legislation in an effort to improve the criminal justice response to domestic violence crimes.

Some of the national statistics on domestic violence include the following (Durose, 2005; Rennison, 2003):

- A significant number of police calls for service are related to domestic crimes
- It is the leading cause of injury to women in the United States
- The American Medical Association estimates that women's male partners assault two million American women annually
- Approximately 85% of the victims of domestic violence are women
- Approximately 1.3 million women and 835,000 men are physically assaulted by an intimate partner
- On average, more than three women are murdered by their husbands or boyfriends in the United States every day
- Intimate partner violence made up 20% of all the fatal violent crimes against women in 2001
- Nearly 25% of the women and 7.6% of the men were raped and/or physically assaulted by a current or former spouse, cohabitating partner or dating partner/acquaintance
- 49% of violent crimes committed against family members were committed against a spouse
- 89% of the spouse abuse victims were female and 86% of the dating partner victims were female
- About 35% of the emergency room calls were a result of domestic violence
- It is estimated that 503,485 women are stalked by an intimate partner annually in the United States and 76% of the female victims were stalked by the person who killed them;
- Family violence costs the nation from $5 to $10 billion annually in medical expenses, police and court costs, shelters and foster care, sick leave, absenteeism, and non-productivity.

Further, Truman (2011) reported in the annual National Criminal Victimization Survey (NCVS) that from 1993 to 2010, violent crime decreased by 70 percent and declined by 40 percent from 2001 to 2010. Truman reported that violent crime between intimates (spouse, boyfriend/girlfriend, former intimate, or acquaintance) declined slightly from 1993 to 2010. Female intimate victimization in violent crimes was four times higher than for men (22% v. 5%).

Orders of protection, often referred to as protective orders or restraining orders, are frequently used as a civil remedy to provide some level of protection for domestic violence victims seeking to end abuse by another (Hughes et al., 2007). Protective orders serve to eliminate or restrict unlawful contact with the victim and the assailant. They serve to provide a legal sanction to dissuade further abusive behaviors, which can include: stalking, no contact orders, establishing visitation procedures with minor children, court order counseling, etc.). The protective order provides the police with an enforcement tool that provides a level of legal protection to the victim. Protective orders also give an offender the ability to remain in the community to continue to work and provide financial assistance to victims as long as compliance with the order and the law are maintained (Buzawa & Buzawa, 2003).

The victim in domestic violence civil litigation generally asserts that procedural or substantive due process rights were violated. In a substantive due process claim, the victim-plaintiff seeks to force officers to provide battered women with protection whenever the state is aware of their situation. In a circumstance in which a state has provided, through legislation, protection to victims through a protective or restraint order, the plaintiff will seek to induce the police department to actually provide the protection. The argument may be that protection should be provided in accordance with state law rather than through the Constitution and the state is obligated to provide such protection.

Clearly domestic violence situations pose a significant problem for the police community. Out of these types of situations varying liability claims have emerged. While no individual has the right to demand or expect protection from all harm, when the police have knowledge and are "on notice" concerning a domestic violence situation, such as through a protective order, the potential for liability increases. It becomes paramount to respond to such calls for service when there is knowledge or the department has notice of such domestic problems. Gone are the days when these types of incidents could simply be dismissed.

In *Siddle v. City of Cambridge* (1991), a protection order created a protected interest on the part of a woman who was beaten and abused by her husband. The duty to enforce the law is, however, normally only owed to the public at large and not to any specific person. If complaints and enforcement regarding protective orders are treated differently from other types of complaints, an equal protection claim can be upheld. In *Siddle*, a woman had been abused and harassed by her husband and was granted a court-issued protection order. When her husband violated the order, she would summon the police. They responded every time she called. The prosecutor chose not to prosecute some of the violations of the protection order, which was not the fault of the police officers. The court granted qualified immunity to the police, because each time they responded, it was a reasonable response.

In *Sadrud-Din v. City of Chicago* (1995), liability attached against the department for failing to protect a wife from her husband, who had killed her. A female officer was married to a male officer and he had threatened to kill her on several occasions. She secured a protection order and also filed a complaint with the police department. Two officers had seen him point a gun at her. Over a period of time, several officers were summoned to her residence for this type of violent behavior. Two days before the husband shot and killed her, she called for help and two officers responded. She demanded that they arrest him but they failed to intervene and called their supervisor. The supervisor arrived and failed to intervene. Two days later, the husband killed his wife and himself. Her estate filed a § 1983 claim and the department argued that it had no duty to protect her. The court held that there was sufficient evidence to establish a special relationship, because they knew about the danger and played a part in placing her in a position of danger. There were more than six incidents in which no action was taken by supervisors or officers when the department had such knowledge.

Consider, however, *McKee v. City of Rockwell, Texas* (1989), in which the police were granted qualified immunity for not arresting the boyfriend in a domestic violence case. A woman was beaten by her live-in boyfriend and demanded that the police arrest him. While in the officer's presence, the boyfriend threatened to burn her belongings should she follow through on her complaint. The police decided not to arrest the boyfriend, because there was no evidence of an assault and he appeared to be calm and rational. The police decided to drive the woman to an undisclosed place, where later the boyfriend discovered and stabbed her. The court, citing *DeShaney*, found the case to be relevant to an equal protection claim, but ruled in favor of the officers, finding no constitutional requirement to arrest the boyfriend. The court further ruled that probable cause did not exist, given the lack of a noticeable injury and the fact that the woman was not trapped in the apartment. The court declined to consider a statement apparently made by the chief that officers do not like to make arrests for domestic violence, stating that this did not establish a policy of nonarrests. The court further found arrest statistics in domestic violence cases and other assault cases to be inconclusive in supporting the plaintiff's claim.

Citing *DeShaney*, the Sixth Circuit Court of Appeals in *Summar v. Bennett* (1998) affirmed the lower court's decision in favor of officers whom the plaintiff claimed had failed to provide protection. Summar was arrested for possession of marijuana and decided to offer his services as a confidential informant in exchange for an undercover officer's promise to inform the prosecutor of his cooperation and to assist in future drug investigations. The officer submitted the necessary paperwork and Summar became an informant for the officer. The officer asked that he assist in buying drugs and testifying against a drug dealer. Summar refused and the officer interpreted the failure as an abandonment of the earlier agreement. Several months later, the officer gave information to the prosecutor to prepare charges against a drug dealer and also gave the name of Summar as the confidential informant. The indictment stated that Summar had purchased drugs from the drug dealer. Several days after the indictment had been issued on the drug dealer, Summar was found shot to death. Summar's father filed a § 1983 action claiming the officer's actions exhibited a deliberate failure to protect the plaintiff's identity and personal safety, because it was foreseeable that harm would result should his identity become known.

The lower court dismissed the case and Summar's father appealed. The appellate court affirmed the lower court's ruling, holding that the officer did not have a special duty to protect

Summar. The court concluded that Summar voluntarily chose to act as a confidential informant and was not forced to do so by the officer. The court further added that Summar's voluntary decision to become a confidential informant, with all of the dangers it presented, not to mention his prior decision to fraternize with criminals in the first place, played a much greater role in his demise than did the officer's action in helping the prosecutor prepare the indictment.

The court in *Barber v. Guay* (1995) denied summary judgment to a deputy who arrested a mentally impaired individual for theft. The plaintiff was a veteran who had a psychological disability and was considered a "drunk." He was receiving psychological treatment at a Veterans' Administration hospital. The plaintiff claimed that the deputy illegally arrested him, used excessive force during the arrest, and failed to protect him due to his disability. The state dropped the theft charge. Despite the state's failure to prosecute, the court determined that the deputy did not make a false arrest. The court, however, ruled that the deputy was not justified in using force by improperly applying handcuffs on the plaintiff's wrist and knuckles, wrenching his shoulder, and throwing him headfirst into the patrol car. Such force, the court concluded, was excessive because the plaintiff did not resist arrest, did not attempt to flee, and did not pose a threat to the officers or others. In applying the force in such a manner, coupled with the plaintiff's disability, the court held that the deputy failed to protect him during arrest and custody.

In *Russell v. Steck* (1994), police were denied qualified immunity when they forced an inebriated person to drive home and injury resulted. An officer responded to a call regarding a drunk and disorderly person at a hotel. After being ordered by the officer to drive away, the guest later was injured in a car accident. The court held that *DeShaney* standards regarding a duty to protect applied and the officer created a danger, violating the person's Fourteenth Amendment due process rights. The court further concluded that a reasonable officer should have known that forcing a person to drive while intoxicated amounted to an unjustifiable intrusion on that person's interest in personal security.

A different theory of liability stemming from claims of failure to protect addresses property interests in enforcing restraining orders. Under the due process clause it was argued that a restraining order creates a property interest to the protected party, and failure to enforce the order by law enforcement officers deprives the party of due process of law. The United States Supreme Court addressed this argument in *Town of Castle Rock v. Gonzales* (2005; Box 12.6).

In arriving at its decision the Court reiterated its previous position that the Constitution does not require a duty of the government to protect a third party from harm and the ability of the states to enact legislation that recognizes such protection as a matter of state law if the state so chooses. The Court stated: "in light of today's decision and that in *DeShaney*, the benefit that a third party may receive from having someone else arrested for a crime generally does not trigger protection under the due process clause, neither in its procedural nor in its 'substantive' manifestations. This result reflects our continuing reluctance to treat the Fourth Amendment as 'a font of tort law.'" But it does not mean states are powerless to provide victims with personally enforceable remedies. Although the framers of the Fourteenth Amendment and the Civil Rights Act of 1871, 17 Statute 13 (the original source of § 1983) did not create a

---

BOX 12.6   *TOWN OF CASTLE ROCK V. GONZALES* (2005)

Jessica Gonzales obtained a restraining order against her estranged husband. The order was later modified and the husband was granted visitation rights on alternate weekends and the ability to visit the home to pick up the children. The husband picked up the children one evening and took them to an amusement park in Denver without prior arrangements with his wife. She called the police and sought their assistance in finding her children and enforcing the order when she became aware that her children were absent. The police informed her that there was nothing that they could do as the children were with their father but to call back later if the girls were not returned by 10:00 P.M. At 8:30 P.M., Mrs. Gonzales received a call from her husband who reported that he had the children and they were at the amusement park. She immediately called the police again, asking that an all-points bulletin be initiated for her husband, gave the police his description and a description of his vehicle, and asked that they make a check at the park. She was told by the police to wait until 10:00 P.M. to see if the girls returned. Mrs. Gonzales waited until 10:10 P.M. and called the police a third time and reported that the girls were still not home and the police told her to wait until midnight. At midnight she drove to her husband's apartment and did not find him home. She called the police and was told to stand by. After 40 minutes she filed a complaint at the police department and the police did not begin a search for her children. At 3:20 A.M. Mr. Gonzales showed up at the police department and began firing a rifle at the building. Officers returned fire and killed Mr. Gonzales. The officers searched the truck and found that Mr. Gonzales had killed his daughters.

   Mrs. Gonzales filed a lawsuit alleging that the inaction of police violated her procedural due process rights under the Fourteenth Amendment and that this violation led to the deaths of her children. The district court granted the town's motion to dismiss, but the Tenth Circuit Court of Appeals reversed, holding that Mrs. Gonzales had alleged a cognizable procedural due process claim because a Colorado statute established the state legislature's clear intent to require police to enforce restraining orders. The court also determined that Mrs. Gonzales had a protected property interest in the enforcement of the restraining order. The town appealed and the United States Supreme Court granted certiorari to examine the issue of property interests in enforcing restraining orders.

   The Court overturned the appellate court's decision, holding that the due process clause does not protect everything that might be described as a government "benefit." The Court reasoned that as Colorado law has not created a personal entitlement to enforcement of restraining orders, it does not appear that state law truly made such enforcement mandatory. The Colorado statute, the Court held, does not require an officer to arrest or to enforce a restraining order, but provides for allowances in discretion in enforcing a restraining order. The statute did not say anything about the right of a person to demand enforcement and arrest by the police. Even if the Court thought the statute mandated officer response, it is not clear that an individual is entitled to enforcement of the order constituting a "property interest." The Court held that Mrs. Gonzales failed to demonstrate that she was "entitled" to the protection of the police and due process property interests were not violated by the inactions of the police in her regard.

---

system by which police departments are generally held financially accountable for crimes that better policing might have prevented, the people of Colorado are free to craft such a system under state law.

   The application of this decision generally means that: (1) officers must be familiar with their state's statutes regarding the enforcement of restraining orders; (2) law enforcement generally has no constitutional duty to protect citizens from third-party harm; (3) a duty may be found if the police have "created" or "enhanced" the danger to an individual; and (4) a duty to protect may be more likely found in situations in which officers have an individual in custody against his or her will and the person is harmed. The following cases illustrate how lower federal courts have applied the *Gonzales* decision.

In *Tanner v. County of Lenawee* (2006), two deputies were dispatched to investigate a call regarding a suspicious person at a rural residence. The deputies were unaware that the "person" was the estranged husband who was looking for his wife at her sister's residence. He had attempted to gain entrance into the residence at 1:00 A.M. and found the doors secured and his wife called 911. The deputies approached the house and confronted the husband in the front yard. He displayed a handgun and the deputies took cover at their patrol car and he ran to the back of the house. While the deputies called for back-up, they heard five gunshots and then about one minute later heard six more gunshots. The deputies were instructed by their supervisor to secure the perimeter of the house as other deputies responded and wait until the emergency response team responded prior to entering the house, based on the gunfire.

Within several minutes, two children exited the house, followed by their mother. The deputies provided cover for them and took them to a waiting ambulance down the road from the residence. The deputies learned that the female who fled the house with her children had been shot twice and was the man's sister-in-law. She informed them that her brother-in-law had been drinking, shot his way into the house, shot her husband five times, shot her two times, shot his wife two times, and then shot himself. She was unsure who was dead or alive. Later, the emergency response team responded, entered the house, and found the wife and her estranged husband dead in the bedroom. The team also found the surviving female's husband, who been shot five times, still alive. He was flown by helicopter to a hospital and survived. He and his wife filed a federal civil rights lawsuit against the county, the two deputies, and the emergency response team. They claimed that the county failed to protect them from the assailant, and were denied their substantive due process rights based on the manner in which the situation was handled. They argued that the officers should have shot the assailant which would have prevented him from entering the house and that the deputies failed to enter the house once they heard gunfire. The appellant court affirmed summary judgment by the lower court determining that their constitutional rights had not been violated.

The appellate court disagreed with the arguments made by the plaintiffs. The court held that there was no proof that the deputies knew or should have known that person they confronted in the yard was the suspect. There was no evidence that the deputies knew that simply responding to the call and confronting the suspect would cause him to run to the back of the house, shoot his way in, and rampage through the house on a shooting spree, as opposed to shooting at the officers, or fleeing the area. The appellate court rejected the argument that the county's actions in setting up a perimeter around the house elevated the danger to the plaintiffs, or prevented emergency medical personnel from rescuing those inside. The court stated that there is no constitutional right to state-provided rescue services, so that there was no constitutional violation in preventing publicly employed medical personnel from entering the home. The court concluded that the deputies did not create or enhance the danger to the plaintiff.

In *Burella v. City of Philadelphia* (2007), the spouse of a police officer was shot and injured. He later turned the gun on himself and committed suicide. The surviving wife filed a civil lawsuit against the police department on a claim of a failure to protect her from her husband. She argued that her substantive procedural due process rights were violated on the basis that the police department failed to arrest her husband when she previously reported incidents of abuse after taking out protective orders against him. The lower court denied her claims and the appellate court affirmed. The appellate court held that a failure to act did not violate her rights or bring his assault on her within the realm of a "state-created danger" theory of liability. The court also rejected her claim of equal protection because there was no evidence from which a reasonable jury could find an unlawful custom or believe that a discriminatory motive was behind the failure to arrest the assailant. The court ruled that there was no constitutional duty to protect the plaintiff from abuse by her spouse.

In *Mata v. City of Kingsville, Texas* (2008), a victim of domestic violence from her husband (who was a police officer), claimed that her equal protection rights were violated. She alleged that officers unjustifiably stopped her on a number of occasions, that her husband stalked her in his patrol car, and that she was intentionally treated differently from other victims of domestic violence who were not married to police officers. The appellate court affirmed the lower court's denial of the claims, holding that the officers took steps to try to protect the wife, even over the objections of her husband and herself, including going to their home in response to a 911 call that was made and then rescinded, and filing various reports. The court concluded that any actual difference in treatment was the result of the wife's own requests, as she asked that only informal measures be taken to stop her husband's alleged violent actions.

In *Burke v. County of Alameda* (2009), a 14-year-old daughter ran away from the home of her mother and stepfather. Her mother and father were divorced. During an interview with an officer, she stated that her stepfather had struck her and also that he repeatedly grabbed her breasts. The officer, without contacting the father, and lacking a warrant, took the girl into protective custody. The father, mother, and stepfather sued, claiming that the officer violated their Fourteenth Amendment right to familial association. A federal appeals court upheld summary judgment for the officer because he had a reasonable basis to belief that the girl faced imminent danger of physical harm, and the officer was entitled to qualified immunity on claims arising from his failure to contact the father. The county, however, was not entitled to summary judgment on the father's claim that the failure to contact him violated his rights.

In *Smith v. Kansas* (2009), three officers went to the home of a man's brother, after the man's girlfriend told them that he had assaulted her and may have gone there. Two officers handcuffed the brother after he answered the door, while the third officer made a warrantless entry into the house to look for the suspect. A federal appeals court rejected the argument that the warrantless entry was justified by the possible presence inside the house of a domestic violence suspect with a child. No facts were asserted that would indicate that the suspect was a threat to his child or anyone else, and a belief that an unarmed domestic violence suspect may be present does not justify a protective sweep of the premises under these conditions. A jury could also find that the use of force against the brother was not objectively reasonable, since he did not resist and was given no time to comply with a request to step outside before he was forcibly removed and subsequently allegedly injured. The court rejected granting qualified immunity to the officers.

Searches

By nature of their law enforcement function, police officers search people, vehicles, residences, businesses, and other enclosed facilities. Police are authorized to conduct searches with a warrant. Warrantless searches incident to a valid arrest are limited to the person and the surrounding area (*Chimel v. California*, 1969). Searches are generally performed to discover contraband, fruits of a crime, instrumentalities of a crime, and evidence of a crime. The Fourth Amendment protects people from any governmental intrusion into a person's reasonable expectation of privacy and therefore police officers must abide by its requirements (*Katz v. United States*, 1967). The U.S. Supreme Court stated in *Johnson v. United States* (1948) that the point of the Fourth Amendment, which often is not grasped by zealous officers, is not that it denies law enforcement the support of the usual inferences that reasonable men draw from evidence. Its protection consists in requiring that those inferences be drawn by a neutral and detached magistrate instead of being judged by the officer engaged in investigating crime.

A search may be reasonable at its inception, but may become unreasonable in its execution (Silver, 2010). A search can be defined as any governmental intrusion into a person's reasonable and justifiable expectation of privacy. All searches must be based on probable cause. The key is the legal concept of "reasonableness." Many civil actions have been filed challenging the reasonableness of a search (Kappeler et al., 1997). In their study of more than 1,300 published § 1983 actions from 1978 to 1994, plaintiffs prevailed in 72 percent of the strip-search allegations. This category represented the largest winning percentage by the plaintiff, and the average award was $24,329. The Associated Press (2001) reported that the City of New York agreed to pay up to $50 million to settle a lawsuit on behalf of 50,000 people who were illegally strip-searched. The subjects of the searches, which were conducted by officers in the jail at Queens and Manhattan over the course of 10 months in 1996 and 1997, were often first-time offenders arrested for minor infractions such as loitering and disorderly conduct. The settlement will disburse awards that range from $250 to $22,500.

Police come into contact with many different people in a variety of situations. Stopping and detaining or frisking "suspicious" individuals during a street encounter has been controversial Fourth Amendment subject matter. The basic principle is that, even lacking probable cause, a police officer has the right to stop and detain a person whom he or she reasonably suspects has committed or is about to commit a crime (*Terry v. Ohio*, 1968). In *Terry* a police officer stopped a suspect on a city street after he observed the suspect and two other men "casing" a store. The officer stopped the suspect and conducted a pat-down search of the outside of his clothing for weapons without placing him under arrest. The officer removed a handgun from the suspect's coat pocket. The holding by the U.S. Supreme Court emphasized that police officers may detain a suspect and conduct a frisk only for the protection of the officer and are limited to patting down, rather than a full-scale search of the person. The officer must be able to reasonably articulate that the individual was armed and dangerous and have reasonable suspicion to stop and detain a person.

The Court expanded the stop-and-frisk to seizure of contraband detected through an officer's sense of touch during a protective pat-down search in *Minnesota v. Dickerson* (1993). Performing a *Terry* stop, an officer felt a lump in a suspect's coat. The search did not yield a weapon, but the officer felt a plastic bag that was later revealed to contain cocaine. The Court ruled that officers may seize contraband as long as they stay within the bounds of *Terry*. While the Court expanded the application of *Terry* to contraband, the Court found the seizure of cocaine in *Dickerson* to be unconstitutional, because the officer never thought the lump was a weapon and did not immediately recognize it as cocaine.

In *Painter v. Robertson* (1999), the court denied immunity to officers who ignored *Terry* requirements. Officers responded to a bar after the manager summoned them following a fight. When the manager would not consent to a search of the facility, the officers frisked him and found a handgun in his jacket. The officers knew the manager was a law-abiding person, carried a weapon, and had expelled several intoxicated and dangerous customers earlier in the evening. The court concluded that the officers failed to establish reasonable suspicion that the manager was armed and potentially dangerous. The court further ruled that the officers ignored the *Terry* requirements and denied them qualified immunity.

The court in *Gainor v. Douglas County, Georgia* (1998) found that officers made a *Terry* stop of an individual who was at the scene of a burglary. Officers responded to a burglary, detained an individual, then grabbed him because he became uncooperative. The court found that the officers' seizure of the individual was reasonable because it was initiated to question him. As he became uncooperative and attempted to leave, the officers grabbed him, which was reasonable and proportional under the circumstances, and placed him under arrest. The actions of the suspect, coupled with being at the scene with no visible means of transportation, established reasonable suspicion of criminal behavior. The court granted qualified immunity to the officers.

A warrantless search may be conducted incident to a lawful arrest, and probable cause is not needed. In *Osabutey v. Welch* (1988), the stop and search of a vehicle failed to yield any contraband. The court concluded that the automobile search and "search incident to arrest" exceptions applied and, based on an informant's tip, probable cause was present. In *Commonwealth v. Knoche* (1996), however, an officer's search of a passenger's purse for weapons was not justified as a search incident to arrest. The officer impounded a vehicle and offered the passenger a ride. He searched her purse for weapons prior to allowing her into the patrol car. The search was not an inventory search because the passenger was not arrested, and there was no probable cause or reasonable suspicion to perform the search. The court concluded that the officer should have obtained consent prior to searching the purse.

Searches incident to arrest are not always performed to discover contraband, but to ensure the safety of the officer, the arrestee, and others in the area. Where there is reasonable suspicion to believe that during a legal arrest an armed or dangerous person may be present, such as an accomplice, a "protective sweep" of the area is permissible. The rationale is that there may be other persons at the location who could pose a threat to the arresting officers or destroy evidence.

The United States Supreme Court held in *Maryland v. Buie* (1990) that conducting a limited protective sweep of an apartment was constitutional when based upon reasonable suspicion that other dangerous accomplices might be hiding in the apartment. The Court ruled that, as a precautionary matter, officers may search closets and other rooms immediately adjoining the place of arrest from which an assault may be launched. It is objectively reasonable to suspect without probable cause that an accomplice may be present and to perform a search of the area.

The lower courts have expanded upon this rationale. In *United States v. Biggs* (1995), the court upheld a protective sweep of the premises 20 to 75 feet away from the actual arrest location. The arrest of the suspect occurred inside a motel room and a search was conducted outside the motel. Officers had reasonable suspicion, based upon prior knowledge that others, who were armed, were present and they did not know if they were in the room or outside. Consider, however, *United States v. Blue* (1996). Federal agents had an arrest warrant for a suspect named Elton Ogarro. When drug enforcement agents entered the apartment, Ogarro was pushed through the door of another person's (Blue's) apartment. Officers began searching Blue's apartment and looked between his mattress and box spring. The court held that the search was unconstitutional. Although Blue was a potential danger to the agents, he was handcuffed and controlled by an agent larger than himself. According to the court, the bed, which was two feet away, was not accessible or within a "grab area." The court rejected the idea that the interior of the bed could have hidden a third person. In *United States v. Pixley* (1998), a protective sweep was considered unreasonable by the court. Officers arrested a suspect on the main floor of a home. A sweep of a second-floor bedroom, which involved searching under a mattress on a bed that would not conceal another person, was rejected by the court.

In *United States v. Gwinn* (2000), officers responded to a 911 call regarding a domestic violence situation. An officer was informed that Gwinn was inside a trailer threatening to kill his girlfriend. From behind his patrol car, the officer ordered Gwinn to exit the trailer. He complied, wearing only blue jeans. The officer applied handcuffs, performed a pat-down search, and placed him in the squad car. The officer entered the trailer to speak with the girlfriend, Diane Harrah, and a second officer entered the trailer and performed a protective sweep search. Harrah informed the first officer that Gwinn was drunk, had waved a handgun at her, and threatened to kill her. The officers searched for the handgun but instead found a shotgun under the couch. The officers seized the shotgun and retrieved Gwinn's boots and shirt. As the officer picked up the boots, he noticed they were heavy. Looking inside the boot, the officer observed a handgun, showed it to Harrah, and she confirmed that it was the weapon Gwinn had used to threaten her.

Gwinn filed a civil action for an illegal seizure during a warrantless search. The lower court agreed with respect to the shotgun, but refused with respect with the handgun, finding that the second search and seizure were proper based on the plain view doctrine. He appealed and the appellate court affirmed. The court held that the officer entering the trailer was proper because Gwinn was partially dressed and it was part of the officer's duty to care for an arrestee in his custody. There was no evidence that entering the trailer was pretexual. The intrusion was minor, temporary, and limited to the purpose of obtaining his boots and shirt.

Police are frequently confronted with searching for and seizing contraband or evidence of a crime from a home. The general requirement for performing a search or seizure within a home is to first obtain a warrant. Performing a warrantless search, however, is not always an unreasonable search that would give rise to a civil action, and the plaintiff bears the burden of proof. The United States Supreme Court in *Payton v. New York* (1980) held that, absent exigent circumstances, nonconsensual entry into a person's home is prohibited under the Fourth Amendment. There are a variety of rationales that constitute exigent circumstances. Some of the more common circumstances can involve a belief that a crime is being committed, hot pursuit of a suspect, protective sweeps, and searching for a criminal. Probable cause to believe that a crime is being committed is not per se an exigent circumstance. By these types of circumstances police are justified in entering a residence to effect an arrest, but their actions may be later scrutinized in a civil action. In *United States v. Timberlake* (1990), the court concluded that undercover officers who smelled PCP could not legitimately enter a location when there was no evidence that entry was initiated by fear of an explosion and there was no danger of evidence being destroyed.

In *United States v. Bates* (1996), the court held that an informant's tip regarding a weapon that was concealed in an apartment did not establish exigent circumstances to enter the premises and search for the weapon. Despite the door being barricaded and the potential for drugs being destroyed, the court reasoned that the presence of a weapon alone was insufficient to enter the apartment. There was no indication of violence and officers had not been threatened. Consider, however, the court's ruling regarding an entry into a home to search for an arrestee in *Valdez v. McPheters* (1999). Officers had an arrest warrant and reasonably believed that the suspect lived at his parents' residence. They also believed the suspect was in the home at the time the officers were there. Officers entered the home and arrested the suspect. The court upheld the entry because the officers possessed a valid arrest warrant and they "reasonably believed" the suspect lived at his parents' home, as evidenced by his lifestyle.

Likewise, in *Fletcher v. Town of Clinton* (1999), the court granted qualified immunity to officers who entered a home to enforce a domestic violence restraining order. Officers had previously received numerous calls for help from the female complainant and she would change her mind once the officers responded. Officers entered the home and, despite no evidence of violence, arrested the boyfriend, who had violated the restraining order and bail conditions. The complainant, who objected and interfered with the arrest, was also arrested and later filed a civil action against the police. The court granted qualified immunity to the officers for the warrantless entry due to exigent circumstances because the officers believed her safety was at risk.

Neither valid consent nor exigent circumstances allowed a warrantless entry into a home in *Howe v. State* (1996). The court concluded that a suspect merely stepping away from the doorway, without more information, was not clear and persuasive evidence that the person gave consent. Officers were at the home based on the belief that the suspect was growing marijuana, and had a generalized fear that he may have been destroying evidence by burning the marijuana, so they entered the home. The court held that even if there was probable cause to make the arrest, a warrantless search was not justified as being incident to arrest. Likewise, in *Guie v.*

Wright (1998), the court denied qualified immunity in the warrantless entry and arrest of a person identified by a police officer as a suspect in several armed robberies. Exigent circumstances were absent because several officers on the scene could have surrounded the house to prevent an escape.

The Sixth Circuit Court of Appeals affirmed summary judgment to officers when a woman consented to a warrantless search of her residence in *Saltsman v. Campbell* (1998). A department of social services worker was denied admittance into a house to check on the welfare of children inside as well as the alleged condition of the home. The worker returned to her office and her supervisor instructed her to return with a police officer. The next day the worker and an officer returned to the house and were met at the porch by the same woman. She informed them that her attorney had instructed her not to allow them entrance into the house and that they needed a search warrant. The officer informed her that he did not need a warrant, because he was with a social worker. The woman retreated inside and closed the door. After a few minutes she returned and on advice of her attorney consented to the search. During the search the social worker did not find any evidence to support the allegations and closed the case. The woman filed a § 1983 action claiming that her Fourth and Fourteenth Amendment rights had been violated. The lower court granted summary judgment to the officer and the appellate court affirmed.

The plaintiff claimed that the officer coerced her into allowing him into the house. The court concluded that the search was consensual and therefore was within the consent exception to the warrant requirement. She allowed the officer entrance into her residence on the advice of her attorney, and she was in constant contact with the officer the entire 20 minutes he was there. The plaintiff failed to show that the officer violated her constitutional rights.

The Third Circuit Court of Appeals determined that exigent circumstances existed when an officer heard "eerie silence" after loud crying in *United States v. Coleman* (2003). A woman who was noticeably upset, nervous, shaking, and talking fast, approached an officer and informed him that her sister was being beaten by her boyfriend (Coleman) a few blocks away. She also informed the officer that earlier she observed "a lot of blood" in the bedroom. The officer called for backup and two other officers responded. As the officers approached a common area of the apartment building, Coleman noticed them and ran back to the apartment and slammed the door shut. The officers could hear a female crying coming from inside the apartment and heard muffled voices, yelling and some kind of commotion. The officers began banging on the door repeatedly yelling "Police, open the door!" The noise continued for several more minutes, no one came to the door, and another officer arrived. Suddenly, the noise in the apartment ceased, which disturbed the officers, fearing for the woman's safety. The officers did not have a warrant to enter the apartment and after making a warning, an officer kicked in the door and the police entered. Inside the apartment the officers observed a woman sitting on a couch holding her young son. She had bruises on her neck and she was crying, shaking, afraid, talking fast, and hyperventilating. She told the officers that Coleman had held her against her will, had a shotgun, pointed it at her, and threatened to kill her. Coleman emerged from the bedroom. The girlfriend led the officers to the bedroom and showed them the shotgun under the bed. An officer retrieved the gun and also observed a plastic bag containing what appeared to be crack cocaine.

The police arrested Coleman and obtained a warrant to search the rest of the apartment for narcotics. The search yielded more cocaine and a scale. At trial, the court denied Coleman's motion to suppress the shotgun and drugs found in the apartment. The appellate court affirmed the lower court's verdict, stating that there were exigent circumstances justifying the officers' entrance into the apartment. The court ruled that exigent circumstances justify a warrantless entry where officers reasonably believe that someone is in danger, and that they must act to avert the danger. The sister's description of the apartment and the situation, hearing a commotion, crying, and yelling, followed by silence, and Coleman's reaction when the police entered the apartment, reasonably led the police to believe that a woman was in imminent danger.

In *United States v. Ray* (2007), officers were awarded summary judgment when they searched the residence of a person suspected of murdering four high school students. After a high school prom, four youths were shot to death in Huntington, West Virginia. A month later, a witness to the shootings informed investigators that he observed Ray commit the murders over a bad drug deal, and that he threw the weapon in the Ohio River. Based on this information and additional evidence, officers obtained a warrant to search Ray's residence for guns, ammunition, clothing, fibers, blood, hair, and other items connected to the crime. During the search investigators found a .40 caliber semi-automatic pistol and a 7.62-mm rifle and seized the weapons. Ray later filed suit claiming that the search warrant was insufficient to show probable cause, in violation of his rights.

The appellate court affirmed the lower court's decision to award summary judgment. The court ruled that the investigators' affidavit was based on probable cause. The court stated the totality of circumstances supported probable cause that Ray committed the homicides and included: (1) a corroborating statement by a witness; (2) the police department knew the type of car that Ray drove when leaving the scene; and (3) the vehicle matching the description was parked outside Ray's residence at the time investigators requested the search warrant. Further, the court held that additional items that the police knew about supported probable cause to grant the warrant. Ray attempted to argue that the investigators failed to make a direct link with the items on the warrant to the murders. The court stated that a direct link is not necessary to support an affidavit to search based on probable cause and as such, the search of Ray's residence was lawful.

In *United States v. Perkins* (2007), a county narcotics unit executed a search warrant at a small three-bedroom house. Officer Bartlett approached the front door with other officers, knocked on the door and announced, "Sheriff's office, search warrant," six times, and waited 30 seconds before entering. Officers could hear a commotion inside, breached the door, and forced their way into the residence. Inside officers confronted several people, including Perkins, whom they handcuffed. Officer Barlett asked if there were narcotics in the house and Perkins stated that there was marijuana and cocaine in the bedroom. The officers seized the narcotics and found a handgun near the bed where the narcotics were seized. Perkins was given her *Miranda* warnings and admitted that the gun was hers. She was later convicted and filed sued claiming that the officers violated her constitutional rights by failing to follow the "knock-and-announce" rule.

The court granted summary judgment to the officers, finding they satisfied the "knock-and-announce" rule. The court ruled that the officers waited 30 seconds prior to forcing entry and executing the warrant. The warrant was executed in the middle of the afternoon, they heard a commotion in the house, signaling the presence and activity of people, and the subject matter of the warrant (narcotics) had the potential of being easily destroyed. The court stated that, based on these factors, the officers met the components of the rule and concluded that the entry into the home was lawful.

In *Clark v. San Antonio* (2012), the Fifth Circuit Court of Appeals denied summary judgment to officers who entered a residence without first knocking and announcing. A confidential informant informed detective Arcuri that he had purchased methamphetamine from a person named "Randy" at his home. The informant further stated that "Randy" was allowing others to cook the meth at the home. Arcuri obtained a warrant from the magistrate to search the residence. Arcuri performed an investigation of the home and the owner prior to executing the warrant. Arcuri found that a Randy did not live there, that a woman paid the taxes on the house, that a car parked in the driveway was registered to Clark, and there was no history of criminal activity associated with the property. At the house, Arcuri noticed that someone was inside but was unable to determine who it was.

Arcuri sought approval to perform the search without knocking and announcing and the supervising sergeant granted the request. Arcuri led a team of seven plain clothes detectives and one uniformed officer to the house to execute the search around 9:40 P.M. The officer forced the door opened with a battering ram and the detectives entered the house. Clark was in the back of the house and two armed detectives approached her, ordered her to the ground, and handcuffed her. Another female (Bishop) was found in a bedroom and the detectives allowed her to dress and she was handcuffed. The two suspects were cooperative with the detectives and were questioned about the operation of a methamphetamine lab. They denied any involvement with illegal drugs. The detectives searched the home and did not find any evidence of drugs. A dog was brought to the home and it did not find any drugs. Detectives were on scene for about one hour and 45 minutes, released Clark and Bishop, left the scene, and did not pursue further investigation.

Clark and Bishop filed a § 1983 lawsuit claiming that their Fourth Amendment rights were violated when the detectives failed to knock and announce prior to entering the house to execute the search. The lower court granted summary disposition to the detectives and Clark appealed. The court reversed the lower court's decision and assessed the question as to whether exigent circumstances justified Arcuri's decision, which was approved by a supervisor, to enter Clark's house without knocking and announcing the team's identity and purpose. Arcuri argued that he decided not to knock and announce out of fear for his team due to an association of weapons at drug locations and that all potential drugs would be destroyed if he knocked on the door. The court held that in prior rulings, it is reasonable to wait 15 to 20 seconds after knocking and announcing on a search warrant for drugs, absent some exigent circumstance. Here, the court stated, the question is waiting a reasonable time after knocking and announcing and not announcing at all. The court reasoned that Arcuri failed to demonstrate exigent circumstance, which demonstrated that Clark would dispose of any drugs upon knocking and announcing and such entry prior to knocking or announcing was unjusti-fied. The court further ruled that Arcuri failed to show in his investigation that occupants of the home presented any threat of danger or safety to responding detectives. Specific facts and information and not generalizations about the concern for safety must be articulated to justify a no-knock entry. The court concluded that Arcuri failed to show reasonable suspicion based on particular facts as to the need to preserve evidence and officer safety, so exigent circum-stances did not justify the team's no-knock entry to Clark's home.

This decision is instructive. Officers seeking search warrants based on an informant's infor-mation are encouraged to ensure the veracity of the information provided. Officers are also reminded to articulate with specificity those facts that clearly demonstrate that a present dan-ger exists on location and may also pose a substantial risk that evidence will be destroyed if required to knock and announce.

Officers sometimes perform strip searches. Although an arrest may be valid, a strip search or body cavity search incident to an arrest may not be authorized. Every strip search and body cavity search must be justified by the circumstances of the arrest, or the search will be consid-ered unconstitutional. Civil liability may also attach.

Neither exigent circumstances nor probable cause existed in an arrest and strip search in *Flores v. City of Mount Vernon* (1999). A narcotics unit with a warrant searched a pub based on an informant's tip. The search failed to yield any narcotics within the pub. Three patrons and the bartender were arrested for drug possession even though there was no evidence that the bartender was involved in any criminal behavior. At the station house, the bartender was strip-searched, but not charged with a crime. The bartender filed a civil action and the court held that the officers lacked probable cause to arrest or strip-search the bartender. She was arrested without any evidence that she was harboring drugs, and no exigent circumstances supported the strip search.

While exigent circumstances did not play a part in *Nelson v. McMullen* (2000), the arrestee was strip-searched. An officer stopped a woman for speeding. Checking her license, he found an outstanding warrant for someone matching her name, date of birth, and general descrip-tion. The warrant indicated that the wanted person had a tattoo on her chest. The officer explained the warrant and instructed the woman to show him the tattoo. The woman refused to cooperate and go to the station house. The officer insisted on seeing the tattoo, and the woman exposed her breasts, revealing no tattoo. The woman filed a civil action, claiming an illegal search. The lower court granted summary judgment and she appealed. The appellate court affirmed the lower court's decision. The court agreed that a strip search is an extreme invasion of personal rights. The government, however, has a significant interest in pursuing lawful warrants and, in this case, confirming the woman's identity. While the officer did not have authority to conduct a roadside strip search, he did have reasonable suspicion to check her physical description. The court concluded that the officer did not ask for consent to search or command her to submit to a search. The plaintiff chose to pull her top down far enough to expose herself.

In *Doe v. Calumet City* (1993), the city decided to settle out of court a lawsuit involving strip searches of female arrestees. The case involved repeated strip searches of female traffic and misdemeanor arrestees by officers without the reasonable belief that they had weapons or contraband. The city had adopted a policy prohibiting such searches, but failed to supply it to the officers responsible for performing the searches. The city settled the suit for $6.1 million.

The United States Supreme Court addressed the issue of whether an officer could search a vehicle incident to arrest after the arrest was made outside the vehicle in *Thorton v. United States* (2004). Thorton was driving his vehicle next to an officer and slowed down so that he would not be directly across from him. The officer did not notice him until he slowed his vehicle. The officer allowed Thorton to pass him and ran a check on his plates and learned that the plates were for another car—*not* the one Thorton was driving. Thorton pulled over into a parking lot, parked his car, and left it. The officer pulled into the lot, confronted Thorton, asked him for his driver's license, and informed him that the plates did not match the car that he was driving. Thorton became nervous, sweating, licking his lips, and began to ramble. Fearing for his safety, the officer asked Thorton if he had any drugs on his person and he said no and allowed the officer to search him. During the pat-down search, the officer discovered several bags of marijuana and crack cocaine. After the search the officer secured Thorton in the patrol car and searched Thorton's vehicle and found a handgun under the front seat. Thorton was charged with possession of drugs and a handgun and asked that the court suppress the evidence based on an illegal search. Thorton argued that the officer could not search his vehicle because he initiated contact with him outside his vehicle. Thorton's motion was denied, he was convicted, and he appealed.

Ultimately the United States Supreme Court reviewed the case and affirmed the lower court's decision. The Court ruled that, after lawfully arresting a person, officers could search the arrestee and the area immediately surrounding him without first obtaining a warrant. The purpose of a search incident to an arrest is to secure any dangerous weapons and to prevent the concealment or destruction of evidence. If the arrestee was the recent occupant of a vehicle, the Court treated the passenger compartment as the area surrounding him, thereby making a search of the area a lawful search incident to an arrest. The Court reasoned that it did not make a difference that Thorton left his vehicle prior to the initiation of the police encounter. In its decision the Court did not distinguish whether the arrestee was outside or inside the vehicle, as the safety concerns for the officer are the same.

Special Response Teams

In response to incidents involving high-risk and extraordinary situations beyond patrol officers' normal duties, numerous police agencies and sheriffs' departments have developed special response teams (SRT). The purpose of these teams is to perform special tactical and weapons responses to situations that may involve hostage taking, barricaded individuals, high-risk drug seizure operations, executing warrants on known violent individuals, and other incidents requiring tactical procedures and weapons. These teams have been in operation since the late 1960s and, depending on the region of the country and the specific use of the team, the frequency of call-outs for the team can be quite high. Because of the high-profile nature of these teams, some of their operations have generated § 1983 claims. Plaintiffs may allege claims of excessive force, illegal arrest, illegal search or seizure, or delay in responding to a call-out. For example, civil litigation has been filed against several police departments based on the Columbine High School (Littleton, Colorado) shooting in 1999, in which two students killed 13 fellow students and later committed suicide. The family of one of the deceased victims sued the Jefferson County Sheriff's department for its alleged delay in the special response team's deployment to the incident (Denver Post, 2000).

The plaintiff in *Kirk v. Watkins* (1999) filed a § 1983 claim against a special response team when it executed a warrant for his arrest. An informant informed a drug task force unit that he had observed drugs, guns, and drug paraphernalia in Kirk's residence. The unit obtained a no-knock warrant to search the home, and the department's special response team was sent to execute it. Kirk was known to be violent, known to carry guns, and had a previous conviction for assault and battery with a deadly weapon. It was well known that if the police ever came to arrest him, he would use deadly force against them. The police approached the house and threw a flash-bang distraction device into the bedroom. The device landed on the bed and started a fire, which burned Kirk and his wife.

Kirk filed suit, claiming that the officers violated his constitutional rights. The lower court found in favor of Kirk and the officers appealed. The appellate court reversed and held that the officers were entitled to qualified immunity. The court concluded that the officers had reason to believe Kirk had loaded weapons, had threatened to kill officers if they attempted to arrest him, and had a history of violence. The purpose of the warrant was to arrest him and seize the drugs, which was a volatile combination. An officer could have reasonably believed that using a distraction device would lessen the possibility of injury in executing the warrant.

In *Boyd v. Benton County* (2004), the use of a flash-bang device by a response team to enter a residence was again criticized. A confidential informant informed police that three men that robbed a jewelry store two days earlier could be found at an apartment that he had frequented and where he had purchased drugs. The informant had been in the house and heard the men bragging about the heist. Officers watched the house and observed two of the men and they appeared to fit the description of the men who robbed the store. The two men left in their car and the police followed. A high-speed chase ensued and the officers arrested the two men. The third man was still in the apartment and the police radioed for the county SWAT unit to assist in securing the apartment. A briefing was conducted outlining the nature of entry, the number of people that may be in the apartment, the potential for high-powered weapons, and that the third man was potentially in the residence. As result of the briefing, the team supervisor decided that a "flash-bang device be used against the front wall of the apartment as it was believed that the risk of someone sleeping there was minimal. Without looking, a deputy on the team tossed in the flash-bang a few feet from the door and Boyd was burned on the arm when it ignited. Boyd sued the officers for using excessive force in violation of his Fourth Amendment rights when they threw in the flash-bang device. The lower court granted summary judgment for the officers and Boyd appealed.

The Ninth Circuit Court of Appeals affirmed the lower court's verdict, but commented that the officers used poor judgment. The court noted that the officers did not consider alternatives such as controlled evacuation of the premises. The officers' contention that an armed person might be situated in the loft of the apartment was insufficient to justify throwing the device, without either looking or sounding a warning first. The court noted that it cannot be reasonable to throw a device "blind" into a room with several innocent people nearby. Because there had been no case decided by the United States Supreme Court on what constitutes a Fourth Amendment violation when using a flash-bang, the court concluded that the officers were entitled to qualified immunity.

In *Tapia v. City of Greenwood* (1992), upon receiving information that a fugitive, who had an outstanding arrest warrant for murder, was in town to attend a funeral, the city's special response team was deployed. Information conveyed to the police was that Tapia's nephew was staying at her house. Upon arrival at Tapia's home, officers asked her to open the garage door and she left before the team entered the house. Tapia claimed she was ordered out of her house and forcibly pulled from the garage. The team searched the home but did not find the wanted nephew.

Tapia filed suit, claiming that the team conducted an illegal search and that the city failed to train its officers in regard to warrantless searches and failed to provide officers with policies with which to conduct searches. A jury awarded Tapia $200,000 and the city appealed. The appellate court reversed the judgment, stating that the search was not unconstitutional nor did there exist an unconstitutional policy directing the duties of the team in performing the search. The court further added that there was no evidence that the city failed to train the team about search warrants; therefore, the verdict could not stand.

Due to the volatile nature of the calls to which special response teams are deployed, civil actions have been filed citing that the actions, tactics, and weapons used to respond to such a situation violated the constitutional rights of the arrestee. Other claims have been filed that attack the tactical procedures the team used during a particular entry.

Tactical procedures used by a special response team were challenged in *Baldwin v. Seattle* (1989). Seattle police attempted to evict Baldwin for nonpayment of rent. When a police officer attempted to enter the residence to evict Baldwin, Baldwin killed the officer with a sword and barricaded himself in the apartment. The special response team responded, along with a hostage negotiation team. Baldwin refused to communicate for 17 hours, and the commander believed that further negotiating efforts would be pointless.

Commanders of the units decided that a tactical entry would be justified because Baldwin might be injured, officers having shot five rounds at him earlier. The plan called for tear gas to be launched into the apartment, followed by the use of a stun grenade, and then immediate entry. Unfortunately the response team experienced equipment failure and poor communications. When the apartment door was opened, Baldwin charged the officers and stabbed one officer in the knee with the sword. Baldwin was shot by an entry team member and then retreated into the bathroom. A stun grenade was thrown into the bathroom, and Baldwin stuck his sword out the open bathroom door. Baldwin exited the bathroom after the grenade exploded, and the officers (thinking he was going to charge them with the sword) shot him 21 times in the side and back.

Baldwin later died and his estate sued the city. The court ruled in favor of the estate and held that the decision to make a tactical entry was inappropriate and violated established procedure. The court further stated that a tactical response is a final option to be exercised only when the actions of the criminal subject cannot be allowed to continue without danger to any party (officer, hostage, or bystander). Examples of such actions requiring immediate intervention include the execution of hostages, gunshots directed at officers or bystanders, and attempts to escape from the area of containment.

In *Handle v. City of Little Rock* (1991), an entry team was summoned to remove people from trailers. A supervisor was on the scene and coordinated the team's response from outside the trailer. Handle was forcibly removed from the trailer, and as he was brought out by team members, he began screaming and cursing. He complained to the supervisor that the officers used excessive force against him. The supervisor did not see any readily observable injuries. Handle brought a civil action, claiming that the city and supervisors engaged in a custom and practice of using excessive force. The court granted summary judgment to the entry team and its supervisor. In support of his claim, Handle offered numerous citizen complaints that were filed against the team for using excessive force. The court rejected this theory because it was without merit. The court further held that Handle failed to show there was a custom requiring excessive force, police regulations fostering excessive force, or regulations that required officers to act unconstitutionally.

The deployment of a special response team was criticized in *Williams v. Richmond County, Georgia* (1992). Family members of a mentally impaired woman summoned police to assist in an involuntary commitment for treatment of the woman, who had refused transport to a mental health facility. A special response team was deployed after officers had spoken with the woman, and she threatened to shoot the officers and swung a butcher knife at one officer. The team responded, attempted to talk to her, and she again responded in the same manner. When she swung the knife at a team member, an officer shot her. They took custody of her and she was transported to the hospital. The family sued and the court determined that it was not an unreasonable use of force or seizure in light of the facts and circumstances of the situation. In *Salas v. Carpenter* (1992), neither the county nor the sheriff was liable for the death of a hostage taken at the courthouse. During a court proceeding, an individual took a hostage and made several demands. The special response team and hostage negotiation team later responded. After several hours, the sheriff ordered the removal of the teams and they were replaced with county personnel not trained in response team or negotiation procedures. The hostage was later killed and a civil action was filed. The court determined that the sheriff did not violate any of the hostage's constitutional rights, because there was no constitutional duty to have a special response team or trained hostage negotiators.

Allegations that a response team used excessive force measures emerged in *Federman v. County of Kern* (2003). Neighbors complained to the police about a man's odd behaviors at his home. Deputies from Kern County responded and after interaction with Federman, a sergeant determined that he needed to be taken into custody for an involuntary psychiatric evaluation. The sergeant did not advise Federman of this nor did he seek a warrant, but called the department's SWAT team. After four hours of surrounding the house and attempting to coax him out, the team lured him to a window and sprayed him with pepper spray. Simultaneously, five members of the team, armed with submachine guns and shotguns, kicked in the door and entered the house. Allegedly, Federman shot a rifle at the officers and they retreated. Team members fired three rounds of tear gas into the house, threw a flash-bang into the house, and reentered. Federman dropped his rifle, pulled a knife, and began walking toward the officers, in a final act of surrender, according to his family. The family stated that one officer fired four rounds of wooden less-lethal shots at Federman, but three other officers opened fire with standard munitions, striking him 18 times and killing him. The family sued the sheriff and the officers on claims of excessive force and a warrantless entry of the home. The district court denied summary judgment and the officers appealed.

The appellate court affirmed the lower court's decision and determined that the officers recklessly entered Federman's home with a SWAT team and violated his constitutional rights. The court held that officers aggressively entered the home without a warrant, to detain Federman for a psychiatric evaluation due to his "odd behavior," provoked him to resist, and turned a relatively minor situation into a fatal shooting. The court held that no reasonable officer could have believed that he was entitled to make such an entry. The family also showed that the officers used excessive force—Federman was not a suspect of any kind, and using lethal force against a person who was allegedly surrendering, was unreasonable.

SWAT team members and other officers were awarded partial summary judgment in *Estate of Bing v. City of Whitehall* (2006). Officers and eventually SWAT officers responded to a home where the occupant was shooting his weapon out of the house. Team members surrounded the home and attempted to persuade the man to exit the home unsuccessfully. Team members forcibly entered the house without a warrant by using pepper gas and a flash-bang grenade in an attempt to flush him out. Officers used a second flash-bang, which ignited the home, burning it to the ground. As the man exited the burning home, he pointed his weapon at the officers and they fired, killing him. The estate of the decedent filed a § 1983 lawsuit claiming that the use of the flash-bang device caused the house to burn and using lethal force were both excessive and unreasonable in violation of his constitutional rights. The appellate court affirmed that using the pepper gas and flash-bang device was reasonable, granting summary judgment. The court, however, denied summary judgment on the use of lethal force as there were disputes as to whether the man pointed his weapon at the officers and posed an immediate risk.

In *Long v. City and County of Honolulu* (2007) a SWAT team was activated to respond to a man shooting his rifle at motorists passing by his home and wounding two of them. Team members and a sniper took up positions around the home and observed the man with his rifle. The man observed the team and other officers near his house and began threatening them. Officers radioed that the man began shooting at them and yelling threats. The team sniper observed the man yelling and shooting at the officers, and shot and killed him. The family filed a lawsuit against the officers and the city, claiming excessive force in violation of the Fourth Amendment. The estate argued that the sniper should have waited until a light armored vehicle responded for safety reasons. The lower court granted summary judgment and the appellate court affirmed. The appellate court ruled that despite not waiting for the armored vehicle to respond, the man posed an immediate threat to the officers, and the sniper used objectively reasonable force in accordance with constitutional criteria.

In *Escobedo v. Bender* (2010), Escobedo called 911 and informed the dispatcher that he had been taking cocaine, was armed with a gun, and was going to shoot himself. He also reported to dispatch that he was seeing a psychologist and provided his phone number. He stated that he wanted to talk to someone, would not harm anyone else, but just wanted to talk about his addiction problem. Sergeant Taylor spoke with Escobedo over his cell phone for 25 minutes and decided to activate the Crisis Intervention Team (CIT) and the Emergency Response Team (ERT). On location the CIT negotiator spoke with Escobedo for a period of time over a phone and Escobedo informed him that he was thinking of killing himself and feared that the police would kill him. The negotiator also spoke to his psychologist on the phone but did not invite him to the location. The psychologist informed the negotiator that Escobedo did not have a history of using weapons or attempting suicide. Escobedo spoke with the negotiator and stated he was going to exit the house with his weapon but did not threaten to harm the police or the public.

The ERT commander believed that he heard Escobedo barricading the front door and became concerned for the safety of the community, as Escobedo possessed weapons, was threatening suicide, traffic on the street began to pick up, and believed that negotiations had stalled. The commander had suggested that the ERT use tear gas to force Escobedo to surrender and exit the residence but the negotiator advised to continue to attempt to talk him out. As the negotiator began speaking with Escobedo on the phone, ERT members, who had been on location for several hours, began preparing to launch tear gas into the residence. The ERT commander notified the negotiator to wind down the conversation with Escobedo. After about three minutes passed officers fired six rounds of tear gas into Escobedo's apartment over a period of about 10 minutes and the fumes were so strong that all communication attempts stopped by the negotiator. Four ERT officers were assigned to enter the apartment and waited for about 10 minutes before entering. ERT officers wore gas masks, two of them carried submachine guns, one officer carried a bean bag shotgun, and all carried Glock firearms.

The first officer breached the door and threw a canister of tear gas and waited for a response. After several seconds and no response, a second canister of tear gas was thrown into the apartment, and no response was noted by Escobedo. Officers threw a flash-bang grenade into the apartment, which produces a loud sound and a flash of bright light, momentarily stunning the person. The flash-bang exploded and created a fire and the officers quickly extinguished it. The officers determined that Escobedo was in the bedroom, yelled at him to surrender, but there was no response. The officers pushed on the bedroom door, which was blocked, and heard Escobedo yell that he had a gun pointed toward his head, and he was prepared to shoot himself. The officers threw a flash-bang grenade into the bedroom and then entered. The officers found Escobedo sitting in a closet with a gun pointed at his head and instructed him to drop the weapon. Escobedo quickly began to lower the weapon and two officers shot him fearing for their lives. Escobedo did not survive.

The estate of Escobedo filed a § 1983 lawsuit primarily claiming that the officers used excessive force in deploying excessive amounts of tear gas, flash-bang grenades, and using lethal force. The district court granted summary judgment to the ERT members who were on scene but did not actually participate in using force. The court, however, denied summary judgment to the officers who fired the tear gas into the apartment, the officers who deployed the two flash-bang grenades, and the two officers who used lethal force. The court also denied summary judgment on supervisory claims of failure to train.

Using the *Graham* standard, the appellate court affirmed the lower court's decision to deny summary judgment and found the use of the tear gas, flash-bang grenades, and ultimately the use of lethal force were excessive given Escobedo's threat level. The court held that when the ERT entered the apartment, Escobedo was not posing an immediate threat to the officers or to the public, the standoff was only three hours old, and the officers making the tactical decisions did not have all the relevant and critical information regarding the negotiations. Escobedo was not resisting arrest, fleeing from the police, or holding hostages. While Escobedo may have posed some level of threat or potential threat to the officers because he was armed and under the influence of drugs, taking the facts in the light most favorable to the Estate, he did not threaten to harm anyone but himself. Escobedo had not committed a crime, there were no efforts to arrest him for the commission of a crime, and there were no warrants for his arrest. The officers' own reason for the deployment of the force used was to seize Escobedo for a 24-hour mental health watch. According to the court, this scenario, coupled with the amount of tear gas utilized by the defendants, against the incapacitating level of tear gas necessary, the use of flash-bang devices within the tear-gas-filled room, and the throwing of the flash-bang device into a darkened room with no knowledge of the location of the individual inside that room was patently unreasonable.

Racial Profiling

The use of race solely as the bias for law enforcement decisionmaking has been a debatable tactic for many years. The debate has enlarged since the World Trade Center Towers were attacked on September 11, 2001. When it comes to using race as the criterion to screen, stop, question, or treat someone with a degree of suspicion in a proactive matter, it means that many perfectly innocent people will be forced to undergo scrutiny that others would not, based solely on their race. This is at odds with the constitutional principles of due process and equal protection.

Law enforcement officers must balance the interests of the individual against the interests of the government. Hickman (2005), reporting for the Bureau of Justice Statistics, defines "profiling" as racial profiling, or *stopping a person based solely on their perceived race or ethnicity instead of individualized suspicion.* Police agencies have been collecting traffic stop data for several years and Hickman reported that 29 of 49 state police patrol agencies in the United States have required their officers to report race and ethnicity for every traffic stop. Stopping motorists for traffic offenses based only on a demographic characteristic and without individualized suspicion is a violation of the U.S. Constitution and the constitutions of all states (Raterman, 2004). The question becomes "What is the proper response by law enforcement when using race and or other factors to stop, detain, and/or arrest someone in protecting citizens from threats to national security and or other types of criminals?"

The United States Supreme Court held in *Wayte v. United States* (1985) that the Constitution prohibits selective enforcement of the law based on race under the equal protection standards. The Court, however, ruled in *United States v. Drayton* (1999) that there is a diminished expectation of privacy in public transportation facilities (such as airports) and the conveyances that operate from them, and therefore individuals may be singled out for increased scrutiny. When other factors can be articulated combined with race it appears that surveillance and stopping, detaining, and arresting individuals may be justifiable. The Court's decision in *Whren v. United States* (1996) is instructive. Officers stopped Whren and others for traffic violations, even though departmental policies instructed undercover officers not to conduct traffic stops. The officers observed drugs in plain view, and the occupants of the vehicle were convicted on the basis of drugs discovered during the stop. On appeal, Whren claimed that the stop was a pretext to discover drugs and that such stops violated the Fourth Amendment's prohibition of unreasonable searches. The Court ruled that the officer's subjective motivation for making a traffic stop is irrelevant as long as there is probable cause to justify the traffic stop. The Court reasoned that the test is not whether the officer would have made the stop, but whether he "could have" made the traffic stop. In other words, if a person is committing or believed to be committing an offense, and the individual officer has sufficient reason to believe this is the case, a stop or detention will likely be upheld.

Lower courts have had occasion to examine cases alleging unconstitutional detentions based on factors less than probable cause. In *United States v. Moore* (2004), an appellate court upheld a lower court's decision not to suppress evidence acquired during a traffic stop. Detectives secluded themselves in an observation room at an Amtrak station to investigate drug couriers coming through the station who were using trains to distribute narcotics. The detectives spotted Moore, who saw them in the observation room, and expressed a "surprised" look on his face, and began to walk quickly away. The officers decided to stop and question him. By the time they reached the exit area, Moore had boarded a taxi and sped away. The detectives followed the taxi from a patrol car and an unmarked car. The officer in the patrol car stopped the taxi, and approached the driver, while the other detective approached the passenger side and asked Moore to answer a few questions. Unable to provide identification and giving inconsistent information about where he was going, which later proved to be false after a computer check, the officers asked Moore to step out of the taxi for a consent search. He complied and an officer felt a hard object in his jacket pocket. The officer reached in to retrieve the object and Moore fled. The detectives chased Moore into a hotel and found him hiding in a bathroom stall. The officers unwrapped the object and found 11 grams of crack.

The appellate court upheld the lower court's denial of Moore's suppression motion because Moore voluntarily consented to the search and the drugs were discovered pursuant to the search. The court held that as part of traffic stop, officers are permitted to question any passenger without triggering a Fourth Amendment violation. Further, the questioning of Moore and his responses to the questions did not violate his rights because Moore consented to the inquiries. The stop was not unconstitutional, as the taxi driver consented to the stop and questioning may occur as part of a lawful stop. Moreover, the search was not unlawful because Moore consented to the pat-down search of his outer clothing consistent with a *Terry* stop. The crack was admissible because Moore consented to the search.

In *United States v. West* (2004), agents of the Bureau of Alcohol, Tobacco, and Firearms (ATF) were finishing an investigation and from the vehicle in the parking lot of a sporting goods store, they observed a car parked in the lot. The occupants stared at the agents and became nervous and hesitant to leave their car. They finally exited their car and began walking toward the store, but continued to look back and forth at the agents several times. The agents became more suspicious and one called an employee inside the store. The two men purchased ammunition and as they approached their car, they nervously walked into each other as though they were unsure of their movements. Agents also noticed a small package in the waistband of the pants of one of the men.

The agents decided to approach the two men, identified themselves, and asked them what they were doing. West stated that they had purchased ammunition for a friend, and gave the agent his identification card when asked. The other man could not produce any identification. While one agent ran a background check, the other noticed that West began fidgeting with his car keys, which were in the ignition. The agent at the car discovered that West had a previous conviction for car theft and the agent conducting the background check learned that he also had prior arrests for drug violations, aggravated assault, and receiving stolen property. Moreover, he had an outstanding arrest warrant for violating probation. The agents arrested West and charged him with the felony probation violation of possession of ammunition. West asked the court to suppress the ammunition, claiming the agents' actions violated his Fourth Amendment rights. The court denied West's request and he appealed.

The appellate court affirmed, holding that momentarily detaining the two men was supported by reasonable suspicion that they were engaged in criminal activity and therefore the evidence was admissible. The court determined that under the Fourth Amendment, law enforcement officers are authorized to conduct a brief investigative stop if they could point to specific and articulable facts which, when taken collectively, a reasonable inference from the facts establishes reasonable suspicion to believe the suspects are engaged in criminal activity. The court stated that prior case decisions allow officers to investigate even legal behavior that supports reasonable suspicion, if based on the totality of circumstances, when actions lead to an inference of criminal activity. While nervousness in and of itself cannot support reasonable suspicion, the collective nature of the nervousness, the men tripping over each other, the clerk informing the agents that one man purchased ammunition, and noticing that West had a package in his waistband, all supported reasonable suspicion that the men were engaging in criminal activity. The court held that the agents did not violate West's constitutional rights.

In *United States v. McDonald* (2007), an officer responded to a call of an armed robbery and interviewed the victim. The victim reported that he had been robbed at gunpoint, that the perpetrator was a black male who left in a Mazda, and the victim provided a partial license plate number. The officer left to look for the vehicle and three blocks away he spotted a white Mazda with the license plate number matching the description. A black male, McDonald, was standing next to the vehicle and entered the car. The officer summoned back-up and they arrested McDonald. A search of the vehicle revealed cocaine, a handgun, and cash. McDonald filed a lawsuit claiming an unreasonable stop and racial profiling which violated his constitutional rights.

The lower court granted summary judgment and the appellate court affirmed. The court ruled that there was reasonable suspicion to conduct an investigatory stop and the officer received a description of the vehicle, with a license plate number, and a description of the perpetrator. The court held that looking for a black male who met the description of the perpetrator, who was black, failed to rise to a claim of racial profiling. The court held that the stop and arrest did not violate the constitutional standards for performing such a duty.

In *Ortega Melendres v. Arpaio* (2009), detainees of Hispanic decent brought an action against a county sheriff and deputies seeking relief from alleged practices of racial profiling, false arrest, and detention. The allegations filed by the detainees claimed that deputies profiled, targeted, and ultimately stopped and detained persons based on their race in violation of the Fourth and Fourteenth Amendments. The defendants filed a motion for summary disposition and the federal district court denied the motion. The court held that: (1) allegations were sufficient to state Fourth Amendments claims; (2) the allegations were sufficient to state equal protection claims; (3) the county was subject to municipality liability; and (4) the court refused to dismiss the county sheriff's office as non-jural entity.

The plaintiff was detained for four hours in a police holding cell without being apprised of any charges against him, and was then handed over to Immigration and Customs Enforcement officials. The court ruled that an allegation that deputies placed the Hispanic passenger of a speeding vehicle in full custodial arrest for violating United States Immigration laws, even after the passenger provided them with sufficient immigration documents, including a United States Visa containing a fingerprint and picture, a Department of Homeland Security permit was sufficient to state a claim for a Fourth Amendment violation for false arrest without probable cause. The court noted that an allegation that the deputies request for a Hispanic driver's Social Security card was not "standard procedure" for all routine traffic stops conducted by the county. Further, the court held that allegations that the county sheriff made a public comment that physical appearance alone was sufficient to question an individual about his or her immigration status, that the county's crime suppression sweeps had been allegedly targeted at area having a high concentration of Hispanics, and that the county had used volunteers with known animosity toward Hispanics and immigrants to assist in crime sweeps, were sufficient to allege discriminatory purpose, as required to state a § 1983 equal protection claim.

Summary

This chapter has examined seven areas in policing that can increase the liability potential for officers: false arrest, false imprisonment, pursuits, failure to protect, searches, racial profiling, and special response teams. These seven categories represent critical dimensions of police work and the potential for liability exposure. With the exceptions of failure to protect and police pursuits, each category is based on incidents controlled by court decisions emerging from the Fourth Amendment to the U.S. Constitution. Since 1950, the United States Supreme Court has decided more than 350 cases involving Fourth Amendment issues. When officers conduct searches and seizures, allegations of unreasonable conduct will emerge, providing an avenue of civil litigation.

Officers also engage in vehicle pursuits. Because pursuits are high-profile events, when a serious injury or death of a citizen results, they have spawned civil lawsuits under the

Fourteenth Amendment. The *Scott* decision underscores the objectively reasonable standard and the associated criteria that were previously established in *Graham*. Similar to other allegations of excessive force, officers will be judged based on the reasonableness of their actions and not what they might have considered in using force irrespective of the incident. Reasonableness of officers' actions in terminating a dangerous flight from capture in a high-speed pursuit will be assessed in accordance with balancing the government's interest in protecting the public from the risk of harm that a suspect poses by engaging in reckless and dangerous behaviors involved in pursuits. The rule that has been developed by the Court is that a police officer's attempt to terminate a dangerous high-speed car chase that threatens the lives of innocent bystanders does not violate the Fourth Amendment, even when it places the fleeing motorist at risk of serious injury or death.

The Court's decision in *Scott* is not a special license for police to use force irresponsibly or recklessly. To be granted summary judgment, the agency must demonstrate that officers acted reasonably and in accordance with the law. Administrators are encouraged to fully review the decision and provide training to their officers to reduce their liability exposure. Further, the Court's decision in *Sykes* defined that fleeing a police officer in a vehicle is considered a violent crime and administrators should revise their agency's policy as warranted and provide training to officers on how to implement the components of the case and agency policy.

Failure-to-protect allegations can also stem from violations of the Fourteenth Amendment. Failure-to-protect claims can cover a wide range of possible circumstances. The Supreme Court, in the *DeShaney* decision, however, made it more difficult for the plaintiff to prevail in failure-to-protect claims. The Court's decision in *Town of Castle Rock v. Gonzales* further restricts exposure to liability regarding protective orders. Collectively these two decisions will make it much more difficult for a plaintiff to prevail when alleging that the police failed to protect. Administrators, trainers, and officers should ensure that their policy reflects these two decisions and their state's statute regarding protective orders and their enforcement. Periodic training should be conducted to address this issue. In addition, allegations of racial profiling and bias have emerged as a concern in civil litigation. In light of national and local security concerns, policies, practices, and training that address this issue should direct officers in performing such duties within the framework of legal precedents.

The categories of litigation in this chapter represent areas of the law that are the most likely to change regularly. In light of the cases reviewed in this chapter, police administrators should keep abreast of the changes in the law and the potential for civil litigation. Administrators should keep their policies and procedures current with respect to each category and ensure that officers and supervisors in their department regularly review these policies and receive ongoing training. Training and direction provided for officers enforcing constitutional requirements of the Fourth Amendment may include: making arrests, conducting searches with or without a warrant, obtaining warrants, the scope of searches during short detentions, the scope of searches incident to a lawful arrest, proper methods for seizing items, proper intervention in domestic disputes, and engaging in pursuits of fleeing individuals.

Police officers also should be aware of their potential liability when performing these duties. Officers should be aware of the current status of the law and be familiar with their agency's policies and procedures. When practical, and as circumstances dictate, officers should obtain a warrant for arrests, searches, and seizures. Properly executing warrants is also important. Officers should be aware of circumstances that do not require a warrant. They should also adhere to the law, department policies, and training when performing these duties. Compliance with the law, acting reasonably and in accordance with probable cause, and properly using their authority will not totally protect officers from civil lawsuits. It will, however, be useful in defending a civil lawsuit from claims that the officer violated a citizen's constitutional rights and help to support the qualified immunity defense.

References

Alpert, G. P. (1997). *Police pursuits: policies and training*. Washington, DC: National Institute of Justice.

Ashley, S. (2006). Reducing pursuit liability. *The Law Enforcement Trainer, Jan/Feb*, 26–29.

Associated Press (2001, January 10). NY Settles Strip Search.

Beckman, E. (1987). Identifying issues in police pursuits: the first research findings. *The Police Chief, July*, 57–63.

Buzawa, E. S., & Buzawa, C. G. (2003). *Domestic violence: the criminal justice response* (3rd ed.). Thousand Oaks, CA: Sage Publications, Inc.

Denver Post (2000, September 10). U.S. Courts to Hear All Suits. A3.

Durose, M. R. (2005). *Family violence statistics: including statistics on strangers and acquaintances*. Washington, DC: Bureau of Justice Statistics, Department of Justice.

Falcone, D. N., Charles, M. T., & Wells, E. (1994). A study of pursuits in illinois. *The Police Chief, July*, 59–64.

Gallagher, G. P. (1989). Managing the risk of police pursuits. *Government Risk Management Reports, December*, 1–6.

Hickman, M. J. (2005). *Traffic stop data collection: policies of state police in 2004*. Washington, DC: Bureau of Justice Statistics.

Hughes, T., & Edwards, T. D. (2008). *Scott v. Harris*, police use of force, and high speed pursuits, born to run. *Law Enforcement Executive Forum, 8*, 95–106.

Hughes, T., Magers, J. S., & Fell, B. (2007). *Castle Rock v. Gonzales*: due process, police discretion, and mandatory enforcement of protective orders: the promised land? *Law Enforcement Executive Forum, 7*, 75–86.

Kappeler, V. E., Kappeler, S. F., & del Carmen, R. V. (1997). A content analysis of police civil liability cases: decisions of the federal district courts: 1978–1990. In V. E. Kappeler (Ed.), *Critical issues in police civil liability* (2nd ed.). Prospect Heights, IL: Waveland Press, Inc.

Michigan Municipal Risk Management Authority (2007). *Pursuit driving*. Livonia, MI: Author.

National Institute of Justice (1998). *Pursuit management task force*. Washington, DC: U.S. Department of Justice.

Nerbonne, T. (1998). *Policy development for emergency and pursuit driving: training manual*. Big Rapids, MI: Criminal Justice Institute, Ferris State University.

Pape, J. (2006, March 2). Local police satisfied with pursuit policies; agencies restrict chases, consider safety factors. *The Houston Chronicle*, 1.

Plitt, E. (1997). *Police civil liability and the defense of citizen misconduct*. Chicago, IL: Americans for Effective Law Enforcement.

Raterman, M. T. (2004). *Putting race in its proper place: profiling, law enforcement and post-9/11 America. A special report*. Boston, MA: Quinlan Publishing.

Rennison, C. M. (2003). *Intimate partner violence.* Washington, DC: Bureau of Justice Statistics, Department of Justice.

Ross, D. L. (2008). *Scott v. Harris*: seeing is believing. *Criminal Justice Review, 33,* 431–446.

Silver, I. (2010). *Police civil liability.* New York, NY: Matthew Bender & Co.

Truman, J. (2011, September). *Criminal victimization, 2010.* Washington, DC: National Criminal Victimization Survey. Bureau of Justice Statistics, Department of Justice.

Walker, J. T., & Hemmens, C. (2008). *Legal guide for police: constitutional issues* (8th ed.). Newark, NJ: LexisNexis/Matthew Bender.

13 ███

Liability and Wrongful Custodial Death

OVERVIEW

Police are increasingly taking custody of citizens who are intoxicated by alcohol or drugs, exhibit symptoms of a mental illness, and violently resist arrest, forcing officers to use higher levels of force, and nonlethal force equipment. A vexing problem has emerged from these confrontations, because annually a small number of arrestees die suddenly in police custody. The individual may be violent toward himself, others, or officers, requiring several officers to restrain him or her. In a majority of arrests, the person is physically controlled and restrained without being injured. In some cases, however, the arrestee was maximally restrained in a restrictive position, commonly referred to as being "hogtied" (hands and legs restrained, connected together, legs bent back toward the hips, and placed on his stomach). In a majority of cases the person has been controlled and restrained, and within minutes officers may notice that the once-combative person is unresponsive. Emergency procedures may be initiated and medical assistance summoned, and it is determined that the individual is dead, all within a few minutes or hours of the arrest.

Additionally, detention facility personnel confine a diverse population, who are often mentally impaired, intoxicated, depressed, hostile, or addicted. Members of this population periodically attempt or commit suicide while confined in a jail or police lockup. The estate of the deceased prisoner will generally file a civil action claiming that jail personnel were deliberately indifferent in protecting the prisoner from him or herself, indifferent to his mental or medical health needs, or were in some way negligent in performing their duties, which led to the prisoner's death. It is common for the estate to file a wrongful death claim against the agency administrators, the municipality or county, and the officers involved.

This chapter describes the civil liability issues commonly associated with wrongful custodial deaths, including deaths following restraint incidents and deaths due to prisoner suicides. Liability issues involving standards of care in state courts are examined, as well as the standards for use of force, restraints, medical care in accordance with actions based on claims of negligence, and § 1983. Sudden deaths in police custody after a use-of-force confrontation are emerging as a critical area in police civil litigation. While many of these lawsuits are settled out of court, cases that are decided by trial yield a number of important legal issues that are of concern to police officers and administrators. A custodial death normally results in a civil lawsuit by the estate. The plaintiffs attempt to demonstrate that the officers and the government entity should be held responsible for the wrongful death.

Wrongful Custodial Deaths

A lawsuit filed in a wrongful custodial death will allege that the agency as a whole was intentionally negligent, grossly negligent, or deliberately indifferent to the needs of the deceased. The lawsuit generally will assert that the department's custom, policy, and procedures (or lack thereof) were the "proximate cause" of the death. The plaintiff will attempt to show that the department ignores industry standards, historically ignores problems in the agency, and typically fails to correct constitutional deficiencies.

The claim may also assert that the department fails to keep abreast of changes in the profession, and that it takes a death or a lawsuit before the agency makes necessary changes. Allegations made against public officials in a sudden wrongful death suit generally include the following factors: that arresting officers used excessive force; that officers assaulted and battered the deceased; that the officers' use of restraints contributed to the decedent's death; that the officers were grossly negligent or deliberately indifferent to the medical and/or psychological needs of the deceased; that officers failed to assess or monitor the medical condition or provide medical assistance for the deceased; that officers failed to transport the deceased to the nearest hospital or summon medical assistance at the arrest scene; that the officers failed to follow department policy; that the decedent in a maximum restrained position was transported in a police vehicle that contributed to his death; that officers violated the decedent's constitutional rights; that officers acted outside the scope of their authority; and that officers conspired to injure or cause the death of the deceased.

The claim may also assert that administrative personnel failed to provide officers with policies that would direct them in responding to "special needs" arrestees (intoxicated or mentally impaired), failed to provide officers with training in how to properly respond and use control techniques with "special needs" arrestees, failed to provide officers with appropriate equipment to perform their duties, failed to supervise their officers, failed to train supervisors, negligently entrusted equipment to their officers without training or competency evaluation, condoned excessive force measures with arrestees, failed to articulate directives in how to transport "special needs" arrestees, failed to develop a protocol for responding to violent arrestees' medical/psychological needs, failed to conduct an internal investigation, or failed to conduct an independent investigation of the death, conspired to cause the death of the deceased, or covered up the death with an inadequate internal investigation. Each case will have numerous variables for the plaintiff to attack, although in any lawsuit not all initial allegations will withstand judicial scrutiny. The agency should, however, be prepared to defend each claim.

Negligence Components

The common law and statutes generally provide that police officers may take custody of the apparently mentally ill or those who appear to be dangerous (Silver, 2010). Negligence claims against police officers for wrongful deaths of arrestees are based on state tort law. Negligence tort definitions differ from state to state and are generally differentiated from other torts, as they include inadvertent behavior that results in injury or damage (Barrineau, 1994). In some states, slight negligence will suffice, while other states require gross negligence, which involves a reckless disregard of the consequences. When an arrestee dies in police custody, a presumption of negligence may arise if the arresting officers failed to follow department policies regarding force measures, use of restraints, medical concerns, and transporting procedures.

Wrongful death torts, usually established by law and found in all states, arise whenever a death occurs as a result of an officer's unjustified action (del Carmen, 1991). These lawsuits are based in state statutes and are brought by the estate of the deceased (Kappeler, 1997). Frequently, wrongful death claims emerge from a deadly force incident; however, deaths in custody after a physical force altercation and custodial suicides have become the subject of more wrongful death litigation. The possibility of a wrongful death lawsuit arises any time a death is caused by criminal justice personnel. However, no liability attaches unless the death was unjustified. Further, the claim must be based on a recognized tort theory. Compensatory and punitive damages can be awarded.

The standard applied in negligence torts is whether the officer's act or failure to act created an unreasonable risk to another. When police officers exercise custodial control over a person they have a duty to provide reasonable care (*Thomas v. Williams*, 1962; *Wagar v. Hasenkrug*, 1980; *Abraham v. Maes*, 1983). Custody applies to police arresting or transporting, and to detention officers confining prisoners and the mentally impaired. This means that the police have a legal duty to take reasonable precautions to ensure the health and safety of persons in their custody, render medical assistance as warranted, and treat arrestees humanely. Establishing negligence is difficult. To prove a negligence claim, four components must be established: legal duty, breach of duty, proximate causation, and actual injury.

A legal duty requires an officer either to act or refrain from acting in particular situations. The duty may arise from laws, customs, judicial decisions, or agency regulations (Kappeler et al., 1991). Second, once a duty has been proven by the plaintiff, it must be demonstrated that the officer breached the duty by failing to act in accordance with the legal responsibility. Courts recognize that the police are only liable to specific individuals and not the general public (*Harris v. District of Columbia*, 1991). Some special knowledge or circumstances must exist that sets the individual citizen apart from the general public and shows a relationship between that citizen and the police (Kappeler, 1997). Next, if the plaintiff can show that the officer owed a duty and breached that duty, it must be established that the officer was the proximate cause of the harm or the damage (Barrineau, 1994). A close causal link between the officer's negligent conduct and the consequent harm to the arrestee must be proven. This may be determined by asking, "But for the officer's conduct, would the plaintiff have sustained the injury, damage, or death?"

These components provide the structure in which a state tort claim for negligence in a wrongful custodial death will be examined. Proximate cause is defined differently by many courts. It may be enough to show that the officer's act or omission rose to a level that caused injury to or death of the arrestee. Other courts, however, may rely on a higher standard of recklessness, wanton conduct, or gross negligence before negligence will be attached. For example, in *Tindall v. Multnomah County* (1977), there was no negligence when an officer took an intoxicated individual to jail rather than a treatment facility after being notified by hospital personnel that they would not take drunks. The officer did not inform detention personnel that the arrestee had fallen and had a bump on his head. There was no violation of a state statute, because the statute applied only when the arrestee was incapacitated or in immediate danger, and if a treatment facility was available. A cause for liability was upheld in *Brinkman v. City of Indianapolis* (1967), however, when an officer took a severely sick man to jail rather than a hospital, provided no medical assistance, and notified his relatives that they could not post bond until the morning.

Special Duty of Care

Courts have also established that an officer may owe a special duty when he or she has reason to believe that the arrestee presents a danger to himself. When it is evident that a particular arrestee has a diminished ability or cannot exercise the same level of care as an ordinary person due to mental illness or intoxication, police must ensure that reasonable measures are taken in order to care for the person in their custody (*Thomas v. Williams*, 1962; *Shuff v. Zurich*, 1965).

The concept of special duty is based on two factors: (1) the officer's knowledge of the arrestee's mental state, and (2) the extent to which the condition renders the arrestee unable to exercise ordinary care. If it is foreseeable (i.e., a reasonable anticipation that the injury or damage is likely a result of an act or omission) that a circumstance shows that an arrestee's condition creates a hazard, a general duty of care is required of police that becomes a special duty of care that may lead to liability if the duty is breached. If an officer possesses sufficient knowledge of an arrestee's mental state or intoxicated condition and the arrestee is rendered helpless, a special duty may exist.

A special duty of care creates increased responsibilities and may include cases of unexpected custodial deaths. In *Fruge v. City of New Orleans* (1993), the estate brought a wrongful death claim for a diabetic arrestee who gave the appearance of intoxication. The arrestee was placed in an isolation cell, where he later was observed to be foaming at the mouth. He was transported to the hospital and died two hours later. The attending doctor stated that he had a moderately enlarged liver, which can cause sudden death. The court found that officers were negligent in their decision to incarcerate, because they owed a duty to a prisoner to protect him from harm and preserve his safety. The court concluded that the city failed in its responsibility by not ascertaining his medical condition and transporting him to a hospital. The arrestee's apparent intoxication triggered the need for a higher degree of care by the police.

In *Del Tufo v. Township of Old Bridge* (1996), the estate of an arrestee who died from a cocaine overdose while in police custody brought a wrongful death action for negligence. The estate claimed that officers failed to provide the arrestee with emergency medical assistance upon arrest. Officers responded to a traffic accident and found the driver sitting at the wheel with the motor running. Officers attempted to subdue and restrain him, but he struggled violently with them. Other officers responded and the driver was restrained with his hands behind his back and placed in the back seat of the patrol car. In the patrol car he began kicking the windows, and during transport the officer observed him to be shaking violently. At police headquarters the arrestee collapsed outside the car. The officer removed the handcuffs, began CPR, and radioed for medical assistance. The individual died an hour later at the hospital from cardiac failure due to ingesting 1.5 to 3.5 grams of cocaine.

The court acknowledged that the police have a duty to provide emergency medical assistance to those in their custody. The court rejected, however, the idea that drug abusers fall into the same category as the elderly and the mentally ill, because they have the responsibility to advise the police that they have consumed drugs—self-inflicted harm equates to self-care responsibility. The plaintiff failed to prove that the officers were the proximate cause of the death of the arrestee by a delay of medical care, and comparative fault was used as the defense for the officers: "a policy of individual responsibility for voluntary behavior."

The estate in *Brown v. Lee* (1994) brought a wrongful death claim when a prisoner died in the police lockup from an overdose of methylenedioxy-methamphetamine (also called Ecstasy). The plaintiff asserted that the sheriff had a duty to obtain medical treatment for him. The lawsuit alleged negligent failure to provide medical care and negligence in monitoring arrestees in the lockup. The prisoner was arrested on charges of disturbing the peace, because he was walking in the middle of traffic, sweating, and grimacing. The arresting officer detected the odor of alcohol and during transport asked him if he had used the drug Ecstasy. He denied any drug use, although he acted "hyper" and was sweating. During booking, the arrestee said he was fine. Medical attention was offered, but he refused and was placed in a cell.

During the night, a trustee noticed that the prisoner was experiencing breathing difficulties and shaking, and called for the officers. Responding officers found the arrestee dead. An autopsy revealed that he died from a drug overdose. The court acknowledged that officers owe a duty to provide care for arrestees and that a higher degree of care is owed to an intoxicated person who cannot care for himself. Because the arrestee denied being under the influence and rejected medical care when it was offered, and because the drug condition is often not fatal, the court dismissed the claim, stating that it is "unreasonable to impose a duty on the sheriff to provide medical treatment to every intoxicated arrestee."

These cases illustrate that courts determine whether a special duty exists on a case-by-case basis. The courts expect the police to provide a level of care and caution when taking custody of arrestees who exhibit signs of intoxication and mental illness. Legal duties are obligations recognized by the courts that require police officers to act or refrain from acting in a given situation (Kappeler, 1997). While a plaintiff may be able to prove that the officer owed a duty and breached that duty, he or she must next prove that the officer was the proximate cause of the injury or death. This is not a simple endeavor, because there are considerable differences among the courts' interpretations of "proximate cause." In these unexpected death cases, one method of determining this is to ask: "But for the officer's action, would the arrestee have died?" Careful consideration must be given to the decedent's medical and psychological history and his or her condition during the hours prior to arrest and during the arrest to determine the actual cause of death. In some incidents, the officer's action or inaction may be a significant factor and rise to a level of culpability that results in liability. The courts will determine the degree of knowledge the police had at the time or obtained relative to the arrestee's condition.

While a definitive test for foreseeability does not exist, the courts will rely on the facts of the particular case and on precedent when analyzing the case. Figure 13.1, as adapted from Kappeler, Vaughn, and del Carmen (1991), illustrates how the courts determine liability based on negligence factors, special duty, and knowledge or foreseeable factors concerning

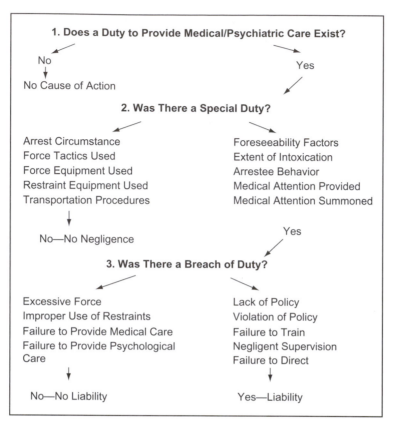

FIGURE 13.1 Liability Decision-making Model in Police Custodial Deaths. *Source: Adapted from Kappeler, V., M. Vaughn & R.V. del Carmen (1991). "Death in Detention: An Analysis of Police Liability for Negligent Failure to Prevent Suicide."* Journal of Criminal Justice *19:381–393.*

sudden/wrongful deaths in custody. Many courts will evaluate the case based on the totality of circumstances. Other courts, however, will consider the knowledge the officers had about the arrestee who exhibited symptoms associated with other sudden deaths and whether the death was foreseeable. The interaction between judicial decisionmaking and factual circumstances that indicate a breach of duty ultimately determines liability for negligent failure to prevent a wrongful death (del Carmen & Kappeler, 1991).

Wrongful Custodial Death Claims Under § 1983

Wrongful death actions are recognized in all states; therefore, such laws may be used in a § 1983 action. Section 1983 authorizes the application of any state remedial law that is consistent with the purposes of § 1983 to any situation for which federal civil rights laws do not provide an appropriate remedy (Silver, 2010). Wrongful death claims may be filed under § 1983 when the death has resulted from excessive force, failure to attend to medical needs, or any other

Table 13.1   Sudden Deaths in Police Custody Liability Issues Matrix

	Arrestee		
Issue	**Applicable Amendment**	**Precedent**	**Standard of Review**
Use of Force and Restraints	Fourth	Graham v. Connor (1989) Tennessee v. Garner (1985)	Objective Reasonableness
Medical/Psychological (§ 1983)	Fourteenth	Revere v. Mass. General Hospital	Deliberate Indifference
Policy/Custom	Fourteenth	Monell v. Dept. of Social Services (1978)	Deliberate Indifference Proximate Cause
Training	Fourteenth	City of Canton v. Harris (1989)	Deliberate Indifference
	Pretrial Detainees		
Use of Force and Restraints	Fifth and Fourteenth	Johnson v. Glick (1973) Bell v. Wolfish (1979) Rochin v. California (1952)	Shocks the Conscience Due Process Clause
Medical/Psychological	Eighth and Fourteenth	Estelle v. Gamble (1976) Revere v. Mass. General Hospital (1983)	Deliberate Indifference
Failure to Protect	Eighth and Fourteenth	DeShaney v. Winnebago (1989) Farmer v. Brennan (1994)	Deliberate Indifference Special Relationship
Policy/Custom	Fourteenth	Monell v. Dept. of Social Services (1978)	Deliberate Indifference Proximate Cause
Training	Fourteenth	City of Canton v. Harris (1989)	Deliberate Indifference

constitutional violation, and the conduct of the defendants was the proximate cause of the death under intentional tort principles (*Wright v. Collins*, 1985).

Unexpected custodial death cases filed under § 1983 are evaluated within the purview of the Fourth and Fourteenth Amendments, based on the standards of "deliberate indifference," "objective reasonableness," and "conduct shocking to the conscience." Table 13.1 presents a matrix that summarizes various liability issues, court decisions, and applicable standards of review when analyzing the factors involved in sudden deaths in police custody. Liability concerns regarding citizens who are arrested, restrained, and suddenly die shortly after arrest are analyzed according to the Fourth Amendment standard of objectively reasonable force, and primarily involve issues of excessive force/restraints, failure to train, failure to render medical/psychological care, and policy and customs issues that are alleged to have violated the decedents' constitutional rights. As an arrestee's status changes to that of a pretrial detainee, the standard of reviewing claims of excessive force relies on the "conduct shocking to the conscience" standard under the Fourteenth Amendment. Medical, psychological, and failure to protect concerns are generally examined under the Eighth Amendment deliberate indifference standard. Arrestee behaviors that are consistent with the inability to care for themselves, such as the intoxicated or mentally ill, pose a particular dilemma for responding officers. The following § 1983 case analysis of wrongful deaths in police custody reveals how the courts determine liability.

Excessive Force Claims

A significant number of sudden death restraint incidents involve the violent behavior of an arrestee, requiring police to use higher levels of physical control measures and nonlethal force equipment or implements. As a result, the primary claims filed against the responding officers are allegations of excessive force that occurred during arrest, at the station, or in a detention cell.

In *Estate of Phillips v. City of Milwaukee* (1996), officers used force to subdue a large schizophrenic man with ballpoint pens in each hand. After a lengthy struggle, he was subdued, handcuffed behind his back, and placed in leg restraints. He was on his stomach for one minute and suddenly stopped breathing. Cardiopulmonary resuscitation was initiated and emergency medical personnel responded, but they were unable to revive him. The arrestee died a day later, and the medical examiner determined that the restraint contributed to his death. The estate filed a § 1983 lawsuit for use of excessive force, denial of medical care, and failure to train. The court held that the officers did not use excessive force in controlling the arrestee. Police actions were analyzed based on the totality of circumstances and the resistive behaviors they encountered. Deliberate indifference to the medical needs of the deceased was not established and officers were shielded from liability under qualified immunity. Moreover, the court noted that "police officers facing unpredictable and oftentimes dangerous situations must be free to perform their duties utilizing their training, experience, and judgment with confidence that courts will not scrutinize their discretionary decisions with microscopic detail."

In *East v. City of Chicago* (1989), however, the court held that officers used excessive force when East died of a drug overdose in their custody. During a drug raid, East swallowed a packet of cocaine. Approximately four hours later, in the interrogation room at the station, he experienced hallucinations, began yelling, and attempted to hide under a table. Several officers removed him from under the table, kicked him in the head and between his legs, and hit him with a nightstick in an attempt to handcuff him. East told the officers that he had ingested cocaine, but they ignored him and responded "You're just afraid to go to jail." He was placed in a cell with another prisoner, who later informed police that East needed medical attention. At an unknown time, paramedics were summoned, responded, and transported East to the hospital, where he later died.

The court cited the *Graham v. Connor* (1989) decision, but acknowledged that the arrestee was in custody at the station when force was applied. They ruled that in post-arrest situations, when dealing with a pretrial detainee, the Fourteenth Amendment "shocks the conscience" standard applies. The officers were found liable for beating the arrestee, deliberate indifference to his medical needs under *Estelle v. Gamble* (1976), and the city was also liable for failing to train officers in the appropriate use of force.

In cases of sudden death after force is used, two questions are commonly asked: "Was the officer's force excessive?" and "Did the amount of force used contribute to the detainee's death?" Answering these questions is not easy. Excessive force claims stemming from arrests must be examined under the Fourth Amendment's "reasonableness" standard based on the Supreme Court's decision in *Graham*. The "reasonableness" inquiry in an excessive force claim is an objective inquiry. While there is no precise definition for the test of reasonableness, applying the standard requires careful attention to the facts and circumstances confronting the police, without regard to their underlying intent or motivation. Each case must be evaluated from the perspective of a reasonable officer on the scene, based on the severity of the crime, the resistance level of the arrestee, the threat posed by the arrestee, and whether the circumstances were rapidly evolving.

The courts recognize that use-of-force incidents can be tense and officers often must respond quickly, with the understanding that there are numerous variables to consider. Using the objective reasonableness standard, the court will determine whether excessive force was used by officers by evaluating the totality of the circumstances, including the unpredictability, danger, and violent behavior manifested by the arrestee, and whether the force or control tactics used were reasonable or proportional in light of the behavior encountered. Objectively reasonable and lawful force is force used at the moment it is needed and in response to the arrestee's behavior, regardless of the outcome. The *East* case, however, provides an example of excessive force, because officers kicked the arrestee in the head and between the legs, and then continued to beat him with an impact weapon. After establishing control, officers failed to provide timely medical assistance. In light of the circumstances, these tactics were considered excessive and disproportional. Failure to follow up with necessary medical care amounted to deliberate indifference.

Use of Restraint Claims

[handwritten: Describe use of force factors that may emerge from wrongful restraint deaths.]

Associated with excessive force allegations is a second level of claims that often asserts that the police maximally restrained the deceased, which purportedly contributed to his death. The assertion is frequently made that the deceased died as a result of "positional, postural, restraint, compressional, or mechanical asphyxia," because he was placed in the hogtied position. The claim may also assert that the individual died from asphyxia due to the weight of the officers on his body for an extended period during control and restraint. These allegations may be further supported by results of an autopsy or independent autopsy conducted by the estate claiming that the method of restraint contributed to asphyxia, which caused death. Moreover, this assertion will attempt to prove excessive force by using restraints without considering the obvious medical needs of the arrestee.

A federal court found the City of Chicago liable for contributing to the death of an arrestee who was under the influence of cocaine and phencyclidine in *Animashaun v. O'Donnell* (1994). While restrained and lying face-down on the ground, the arrestee began experiencing breathing difficulties. He was transported to the hospital in a maximally restrained position, where he was pronounced dead. His estate filed a § 1983 action, claiming that he had died from positional asphyxia due to the nature of restraint methods used by the police. The city contended that it was unaware of the relationship between restraining an arrestee in this manner and the occurrence of positional asphyxia. The plaintiff attached a memorandum of a similar death in 1988 regarding this problem, and the city deliberately ignored it. The court held that the city was on notice that its officers were responding to recurring situations yet chose to ignore it and this omission rose to a level of deliberate indifference in training their officers. Likewise, in *Johnson v. City of Cincinnati* (1999), policy and training issues that arose from *Monell v. Department of*

Social Services of New York (1978) were not dismissed. The court denied summary judgment because the city knew that taking custody of highly agitated people was a recurring problem, and it was aware of the potential risks of placing a person showing signs of delirium in a prone restraint that could result in sudden death.

Similarly, in *Cruz v. City of Laramie, Wyoming* (2001), the Tenth Circuit found that hogtying individuals with diminished capacity was excessive force and denied summary judgment for the city of Laramie. Cruz was found by officers to be naked and running wildly. Believing he was on some type of drug, officers summoned an ambulance; verbal calming attempts were unsuccessful. He fought with the officers, who restrained him with handcuffs, and due to his kicking, a nylon strap was placed on his ankles and connected to the handcuffs. Cruz calmed down, but officers noticed his face had blanched and removed the restraints. Although emergency medical personnel initiated CPR, Cruz died at the hospital. An autopsy revealed a large amount of cocaine in his system. His family filed a civil action claiming he died of restraint asphyxia, which was supported by one medical expert, while another medical expert claimed his death was solely from cocaine abuse.

A dispute emerged over whether Cruz was hogtied or hobbled. The lower court determined that had the officers separated Cruz's ankles further from his restrained hands, by two feet or more, Cruz would have been hobbled. The court reasoned that the hogtied restraint technique does not per se constitute a constitutional right violation; rather, officers may not apply the technique when an individual's diminished capacity is apparent. Such diminished capacity may result from intoxication, the influence of controlled substances, a discernible mental condition, or any other condition apparent to officers. The appellate court ruled that the officers knew Cruz was under the influence and using the hogtie restraint amounted to excessive force. Liability attached against the city for failing to train officers in the use of hobble restraints.

In *Price v. County of San Diego* (1998), an arrestee who had a history of methamphetamine use fought violently with police, was restrained in a hogtied position, stopped breathing, and died two days later in the hospital. A § 1983 claim for violation of constitutional rights, wrongful death, and excessive force was filed, along with state negligence claims. One medical examiner argued in court that restraint asphyxia contributed to the decedent's death, while another medical examiner testified that the hogtied position did not dangerously affect oxygen levels, nor contributed to the arrestee's death based on new medical research concerning restraint asphyxia (Chan et al., 1997). Based on the medical research, the judge ruled that hogtying in and of itself did not cause the arrestee's death, that the deputies did not use excessive force, and acknowledged that the consequences of abusing drugs led to a heart attack that, more than anything else, killed him. The case was dismissed. In a companion case, *Guseman v. Martinez* (1998), a federal district court in Kansas found that the police officers' method of restraint did not rise to the level of deliberate indifference, despite the arrestee dying in custody, and granted the city's motion for summary judgment.

Likewise, in *Young v. Mt. Ranier* (2001), the court awarded summary judgment to the defendant officers despite Young's dying in restraints. Police officers responded to a call that Young was exhibiting bizarre behaviors and was extremely agitated, and upon initial response found him lying on the ground. The officers attempted to take him into custody, but he struggled with them. The officers used pepper spray and restrained him with handcuffs and leg restraints. He was transported to the hospital, where he died. An autopsy revealed that Young had PCP in his system and the cause of death was listed as sudden cardiac arrhythmia. Young's parents claimed the officers were deliberately indifferent to his medical needs. The Fourth Circuit determined that the officers did not violate Young's rights, as he struggled and the officers were unaware that he had consumed PCP.

The *Graham* standard of using force is also applied to the reasonable use of restraints in controlling a combative arrestee. Liability attaches only if excessive force is used on an individual that proximately causes injury, in this case death. The use of restraints must be reasonably related to the behavior and safety of the individual, the need to control him or her, and the safety concerns of the responding officers. It is standard practice to handcuff an arrestee after a use-of-force altercation. In combative arrest scenarios (as illustrated by these cases), officers generally need to further restrain the person, as he or she frequently will kick and continue the violent behavior. In response to the citizen's behavior, police officers are authorized to graduate their response to the demands of any particular situation. It is reasonable to handcuff and restrain an individual's legs (*Maynard v. Hopwood*, 1997).

A federal district court found, however, that a restraint procedure known as the "total appendage restraint procedure" (TARP) amounted to excessive force and contributed to the death of an arrestee. In *Nelson v. County of Los Angeles* (2003), Nelson stood in the middle of street and began firing a loaded gun in the air and at passing motorists. Police were summoned and deputies from the Los Angeles County Sheriff's Department responded. Nelson was handcuffed and placed in the back seat of the patrol car and began thrashing around. The deputies removed him and placed him the "total appendage restraint procedure" (TARP). When the deputies secured him they noticed that he was unconscious. They rolled him over and observed that he was not breathing. Rescue personnel were summoned but could not revive him. The arrest and restraint process was videotaped from a deputy's car camera. An autopsy was performed and the pathologist reported that he died of positional asphyxia. The family filed a lawsuit alleging that the officers used excessive force and restraints that contributed to the wrongful death of their son. At trial the pathologist testified that the officers used the TARP procedure, which "hogtied" Nelson, compromising his breathing, and thus killing him. Nelson had an underlying heart condition and had cocaine in his system, but the pathologist did not believe these factors contributed to his death. Finding for the estate of Nelson, the jury awarded $2 million in compensatory damages. The court reduced the amount to $1.3 million as Nelson was 35 percent at fault.

The county appealed and the court affirmed the lower court's decision but found the award was excessive and ordered the amount reduced. The court determined that there was enough evidence to show that Nelson died due to the TARP procedure and positional asphyxia. The court found that Nelson's heart condition and cocaine use did not contribute to his death.

In *Hill v. Carroll County* (2009) deputies arrested a woman who responded to handcuffing by attacking one of them, forcing him to the ground, seizing his flashlight, and pummeling him about the head and shoulders. When she continued to resist efforts to place her in the deputies' vehicle, they placed her in four-point restraints, linking leg restraints to handcuffs with an additional set of handcuffs. She allegedly rode face down in the back of the car on the way to the jail, became quiet, and may have stopped breathing. At the jail, she was unresponsive and without a pulse, and attempts to revive her failed. An autopsy diagnosed fatal hypothermia with the exact cause of death uncertain. The woman was obese and hypertensive but neither drugs nor excessive amounts of alcohol were in her system. A federal appeals court rejected the argument that the deputies used excessive force to subdue the woman, and stated that it assumed the cause of death was positional asphyxia. The court found that the plaintiff failed to show that the use of the restraints was unnecessary, excessively disproportional to the resistance they faced, or objectively unreasonable in terms of its perils to the arrestee, who exhibited none of the additional contributing or associated factors that cast doubt on the propriety of such restraints in some cases, such as evidence of drug abuse or drug-induced psychosis. The appeals court also rejected a claim that the deputies acted with deliberate indifference, failing to adequately monitor the arrestee on the way to the jail.

In *Lewis v. City of West Palm Beach, Florida* (2009), the court granted summary judgment to officers who restrained a combative arrestee who died in custody. Officer Shaw encountered Lewis, who was disoriented, stumbling in the middle of the street and attempting to flag down passing vehicles. Shaw attempted to assist Lewis, who acted as if he was under the influence of narcotics. Lewis began to struggle against Shaw's efforts of control. Shaw maneuvered Lewis to the ground on his stomach and began handcuffing him. Officer Root responded, placed his knee on Lewis's upper back and neck and the handcuffs were secured. Other officers arrived and restrained Lewis's legs with a leg restraint. Lewis continued to struggle, breathe heavily, and fought against the officers. The officers attempted to place Shaw in a seated position, but he continued to kick and refused to sit up. Officers connected the leg restraints to the handcuffs and placed Lewis in a "hogtied" position. Within seconds officers observed that Lewis became unconscious and they removed the restraints and initiated resuscitation procedures. Emergency medical personnel responded and but were unsuccessful in reviving Lewis and he was pronounced dead. The medical examiner determined that the cause of death was sudden respiratory arrest following physical struggle against restraints and cocaine-induced excited delirium.

Lewis's family filed a § 1983 action claiming that the officers used excessive force by placing weight on his back during the restraint procedure and hogtied him, which asphyxiated him, causing his death. The family argued that the use of the hogtie procedure was unnecessary and that such procedure violated Lewis's constitutional rights. The family also sued the city, alleging that it failed to train the officers in the proper use of restraints with violent arrestees. The district court granted summary judgment for the officers and held that the officers' use of force should not be second-guessed and that their use of restraints was not unconstitutional. The appellate court affirmed. The court reasoned that the use of control techniques and the use of restraints were objectively reasonable under the tense and evolving circumstances.

The court held that the city was not liable and did provide regular training for the officers in the use of restraints. The training program was adequate to prepare the officers to respond to violent arrestees, was not deliberately indifferent, and did not violate Lewis's constitutional rights. According to the court, an officer placing knees on the back of a combative suspect in order to restrain him is not a violation of the Constitution.

Officers were granted summary judgment in *Galvin v. City of San Antonio* (2008), which involved the death of an arrestee during a violent use-of-force altercation. The decedent made numerous 911 phone calls and would then hang up. The officers encountered the man in the street while he was running and screaming, "Help me, help me!" as he ran away from them with an object in his hands. The officers attempted to physically control him and he resisted. They applied one burst of pepper spray and one application of the Taser. He continued to resist. After a struggle, the officers were able to control and handcuff him with his hands behind his back. The man became unresponsive and suddenly died. His family filed a lawsuit, claiming that he died of positional asphyxia, alleging that one of the officers sat on his back. The defendants filed for summary judgment and the court granted it. Relying on the *Graham* standard, the court held that the officers' use of force was objectively reasonable based on the circumstances and the demonstrated dangerous behaviors exhibited by the arrestee.

Compare, however, the court's ruling in *Arce v. Blackwell* (2008). Officers confronted a violent arrestee who displayed behaviors consistent with "excited delirium." They placed him prone on the ground to restrain him. During the restraint process he began yelling that he could not breathe and suddenly died. A lawsuit was filed, claiming excessive force. The court denied a motion for summary judgment, ruling that the officers were on notice that keeping a person prone and restrained who was in a state of excited delirium could die due to compressional asphyxia by placing pressure on his back. The court noted that the weight of the officers on the person's back contributed to the claim of excessive force in violation of his constitutional rights.

The use of restraints may be considered unreasonable force if they were used inappropriately to the need, officers were not trained in their proper use, or officers failed to follow the department's restraint policy. There must be proof that a particular violation of a federal right was a "highly predictable" consequence of the failure to equip police officers with specific tools to handle recurring situations. The question that emerges from these restraint deaths is whether asphyxia deaths are highly foreseeable or a predictable consequence of restraining persons prone in the hogtied position. The *Graham* standard of objectively reasonable force will be applied in restraint cases. The *Price* case is illustrative of this, as the court, relying on scientific evidence regarding "hogtying," found the restraint procedure in and of itself not to be excessive force and that it did not cause asphyxia. The court found that drugs caused the individual's death and not the restraint procedure. In analyzing these cases, courts will review the totality of circumstances, cause of death, extent of the person's medical or psychiatric condition, restraints authorized and methods used, other alternatives available, officer's perception of safety, and the resistive behaviors requiring further immobilization of the person. As evidenced in these cases, the courts are split in their opinions as to whether the hogtied procedure should be considered excessive force. This type of restraint litigation is still emerging and changes in court interpretations may be forthcoming.

Referring to the *Price* case (1998), the court's holding can be considered a pivotal decision in cases asserting a death due to positional asphyxia and sudden in-custody deaths. The court ruled that hogtying in and of itself is not considered excessive force. Medical research has determined that the prone restraint of a violent arrestee is not associated with a sudden

Table 13.2   Trends in Published Section 1983
Sudden Deaths in Custody Litigation

Year and Number		1985–1998 (95)			1999–2006 (120)	
		Police Prevailed	Plaintiff Prevailed		Police Prevailed	Plaintiff Prevailed
Factors	(#)	%	%	(#)	%	%
Drugs	(55)	57	33	(70)	59	41
Pos. Asphyx. & Restraints	(40)	58	42	(50)	60	40
Mentally Ill	(33)	58	45	(41)	59	41
Mentally Ill & Drugs	(25)	60	40	(38)	59	41
Physical Control	(95)	59	31	(120)	62	37
Pepper Spray	(49)	55	45	(39)	59	41
Baton	(30)	58	42	(9)	59	41
Combination	(95)	55	45	(120)	57	43
Fail to Train	(79)	80	20	(120)	68	32

custodial death, but rather it is the drugs, mental impairment, and medical history/condition of the arrestee that contributes to the death (Chan et al., 2004; DiMaio & DiMaio, 2006; Karch, 2006, Michalewicz et al., 2007; Ross, 2010; Wetli, 2006). Yet, despite the medical research, cases are still litigated and the courts appear to be closely divided on this issue, as Table 13.2 illustrates.

Table 13.2 shows the longitudinal time-series dispositions of the 215 § 1983 cases decided from 1985 to 2006 (Ross, 2007). Cases categorized from 1985 to 1998 were decided prior to the *Price* decision and cases categorized from 1999 to 2006 are post-*Price*. Research revealed that of the 95 case decisions published prior to the *Price* decision, 55 involved drug-related incidents and 40 involved positional asphyxia incidents. The outcome of these two factors shows that the police prevailed in 57 percent of the drug-related deaths and they prevailed in 58 percent of the positional asphyxia/restraint deaths. When a mentally impaired person was the decedent, the police prevailed in 58 percent of the cases and when the litigation involved a mentally impaired individual who was under the influence of a chemical substance, the police prevailed in 60 percent of the decisions. The remaining factors in Table 13.2 during this period illustrate what type of force was used in controlling the decedent beyond restraints, and will not add up to 95, as varying combinations of force were used to control the person. Physical control measures (including restraints) were used in all of the incidents, while pepper spray was used in 49 of the incidents and batons (impact weapons) were used in 30. Combinations of force measures were used in every incident. Police prevailed in about 57 percent of the claims. The police prevailed in 80 percent of the claims, citing a failure to train by command person-nel, although such an allegation was asserted in only 79 cases.

Post-*Price* decisions (1999 to 2006, 120 published cases) show similar results to previous years. Litigation in which illicit drugs caused the death continues to set the trend in these wrongful death claims. Cases involving the mentally impaired increased slightly, as did incidents with the mentally ill under the influence of a chemical substance. Incidents in which the police used an impact weapon declined considerably and incidents involving the application of pepper spray declined slightly. The change in the police prevailing in these published cases was negligible. The combinations of the types of force used when police prevailed increased only slightly. Failure to train claims were affected the most, as they declined to a prevailing ratio of two to one and were asserted in every lawsuit.

Several important elements are revealed in Table 13.2. Overall the police prevail in about 58 percent of the litigated cases, which has remained stable for the 21-year period. This shows that despite all of the medical research conducted during the past 10 years, indicating that the heath conditions and drug abuse of the suspect are more likely to cause the sudden in-custody death, defending and prevailing in these claims remains problematic for the police. The number of published cases involving the abuse of chemical substances, the mentally impaired, and the mentally impaired who abuse chemical substances increased slightly, and cases in which the police prevailed remained relatively unchanged. The police use of pepper spray declined slightly while the use of impact weapons has decreased considerably. These factors have perhaps been most affected by the increase of the police using Tasers on violent suspects. Since the late 1990s more than 5,400 police agencies (Hougland et al., 2005) have implemented the use of Tasers, thereby decreasing the use of other force equipment. While sudden in-custody deaths have occurred after the use of a Taser, case law research did not yield any published litigated § 1983 court decisions alleging that the death was caused by the Taser.

Deliberate Indifference to Obvious Medical or Psychological Needs

Beyond the claims of excessive force and improper use of restraints, allegations for failure to recognize behaviors and medical symptoms commonly associated with sudden custodial deaths will be filed. The duty to protect a detainee from harm and to provide reasonable medical care is based partially on the notion that the government is responsible for these individuals because it has deprived them of the ability to look after themselves (Silver, 2010).

The duty begins at arrest and continues through the process of detention. The police, however, are not considered absolute insurers of the health and safety of those in their custody. The assertion may be made that officers were deliberately indifferent to the medical or psychological needs of the arrestee. This legal claim may be framed within the context of the Fourteenth Amendment in accordance with the U.S. Supreme Court's decision in *City of Revere v. Massachusetts General Hospital* (1983). This case concluded that municipalities have a constitutional duty to obtain necessary medical care for detainees in their custody. Failing to obtain such care may rise to the level of deliberate indifference.

In *Harris v. District of Columbia* (1991), the estate brought a wrongful death claim under the Fourteenth Amendment, alleging that officers were deliberately indifferent to the decedent's medical needs and misused restraints. Harris was "freaking out" on PCP. He was handcuffed, with legs restrained, locked in a police van, and later transported to a hospital. Medical care was delayed at first due to filling out forms (per hospital policy), and then it was delayed because the forms were incorrectly completed, according to the attending emergency room physician. Harris was pronounced dead two hours and 20 minutes after the arrest, due to a drug overdose. The court held that the police had not entered into a special relationship when they restrained him and locked him in the van, in that he had not been formally committed, either by conviction, involuntary commitment, or arrest. Thus there was no duty to obtain medical assistance. Officers were entitled to qualified immunity because they acted reasonably in light of the circumstances. The court also noted that the officers had not entered into a special relationship requiring a duty to provide medical care, because Harris demonstrated a lack of care for himself when he ingested the PCP. The court's reasoning compared the police officers' duty of custody with that of ambulance drivers, stating that "they are not subject to a constitutional obligation every time they pick up a patient."

In *Cottrell v. Caldwell* (1996), police officers responded to a 911 call and arrested a man with a history of mental illness who had stopped taking his medication. The family wanted the officers to transport him to the hospital. After a 20-minute struggle to control the individual, he was subdued, restrained with handcuffs and leg restraints, and placed face-down on the floor of the car. He was transported to the station and during transport died of "positional asphyxiation." Using the deliberate indifference standard, the court ruled that in "custody mistreatment claims," gross negligence is not part of the standard of review. The standard is deliberate indifference to a "substantial risk of serious harm." The plaintiff must show a deprivation that is "objectively, sufficiently serious," meaning that the officers' actions resulted in the denial of the minimal civilized measure of "life's necessities." The court found no evidence that the officers knew of, and consciously disregarded, the risk that the arrestee would suffocate, and the plaintiff failed to show a violation of due process. The police did not act with deliberate indifference to the medical and due process rights of the arrestee, nor did they use excessive force in restraining him.

In *Simpson v. Hines* (1990), the estate brought a § 1983 action against 10 officers for alleged excessive force and lack of medical care under the Fourth and Fourteenth Amendments, as well as state claims. The chief of police was sued on grounds of failure to supervise. After an arrest and confrontation, officers were attempting to search an individual at the station. The arrestee was in a drug-induced state, became violent, and refused to be searched. A struggle ensued, and one officer placed him in a "neck hold," while other officers grabbed his arms and legs and forced him to the floor in order to handcuff him. A large officer sat on his chest. After control was established, the arrestee was rolled on his side, handcuffed with his hands behind his back, and his legs were restrained. Once restrained, the arrestee became silent, and was left in his cell to recover. During the night he was checked twice, and the officers noted that he did not move from that position. Approximately five hours later, an officer noticed a pool of blood near his head. Rigor mortis had apparently occurred. The medical examiner reported that the arrestee died as a result of asphyxia due to trauma to the neck during the struggle to subdue him. On the medical claim the court held that the officers were deliberately indifferent to the medical needs of the deceased by leaving him unconscious in the cell. The court stated that the officers owe a duty of reasonable care to pretrial detainees under the Fourteenth Amendment.

The applicable standard with regard to medical care issues is deliberate indifference pursuant to *Estelle v. Gamble* (1976). The plaintiff must establish actual omissions that are sufficiently harmful to evidence deliberate indifference to serious medical needs. To hold officers liable, it must be shown that they intentionally denied or delayed access to treatment or interfered with treatment. The Court in *Estelle* held that an inadvertent failure to provide adequate medical care does not rise to the level of a constitutional violation.

In *Hoyer v. City of Southfield and County of Oakland* (2003), five officers responded to contain a mentally impaired man, partially clothed, who was running in traffic. Officers attempted to make verbal contact with him, but he ignored them. An officer attempted to control him and he violently fought with responding officers. One officer struck him with a baton three times, while another officer sprayed him with pepper spray, another officer applied a brachial stun to the side of his neck and several knee strikes to the outside of this thigh in an effort to control him. All of these attempts were unsuccessful, but the officers eventually were able to place him on the ground, control, and handcuff him. Hoyer was transported to the jail and three officers received treatment at the hospital for injuries sustained. Within 20 minutes, Hoyer became violent in his jail cell and began banging his head on the wall, shouting, and attempting to destroy the toilet. Paramedics were summoned and an extraction team forcibly removed him from the cell. During transport in the ambulance he became unresponsive and later died at the hospital. The family filed a lawsuit claiming excessive force and deliberate indifference to Hoyer's medical condition. The family claimed that the officers should have transported him directly to the hospital rather than the jail. The pathologist who performed the autopsy reported that Hoyer died due to acute cocaine intoxication, with about 4 grams of cocaine in his system, and agitated delirium. The court granted summary judgment to both of the defendants. The defendants were not found to be deliberately indifferent to Hoyer's medical condition nor used excessive force in subduing him.

In *Mann v. Taser, Inc.* (2009), the estate of an arrestee brought a § 1983 claim against arresting deputies, the sheriff, and Taser International alleging that the use of the Taser by the deputies caused her death. At the arrest, the arrestee violently and aggressively resisted arrest by the deputies, would not comply with officers' instructions to comply, and demonstrated behaviors that she was a danger to herself and others in the community. The plaintiff's counsel argued that one deputy was aware of the decedent's prior methamphetamine history and argued that the Taser application contributed to her death.

The Appellate Court for the Eleventh Circuit affirmed the lower court's decision for summary judgment on behalf of the Sheriff's department finding that the decedent posed a significant risk of danger to herself, requiring control. The court found that the deputies' use of the Taser was reasonable and was not the cause of her death. The court noted that even though the decedent showed signs of "excited delirium," a decision to transport her to the jail rather to a hospital failed to demonstrate deliberate indifference to her medical condition. The court found that the deputies summoned emergency medical services personnel on scene to treat the decedent after the application of the Taser and they did not recommend transport to the hospital reasonable. Further, the court noted that the plaintiff's medical expert could not opine with medical certainty that the Taser application caused the decedent's death in light of consumption of methamphetamine and the history of consumption.

In *Galvin v. San Antonio* (2010), officers acted in an objectively reasonable manner in their gradual escalation of the use of force against a yelling, cocaine-intoxicated man who they encountered while responding to a 911 call indicating that shots had been fired. The suspect ran from the officers, threw something at them, and charged at one officer. He exhibited great strength and the officers used increased force as he continued to resist efforts to subdue him, beginning with verbal warnings, and subsequently using pepper spray, hand-and-arm manipulation techniques, and finally a Taser, following which the man continued to struggle, but the officers were at last able to handcuff him behind his back while he was facedown. The man died following the struggle, but the court noted that the officers had used no force at all until he attacked one of them, and that they reacted to a "rapidly evolving, volatile situation" with "measured and ascending responses."

The courts do not hold police officers to the same level of care as a physician, although officers have a responsibility to determine the medical or psychological well-being of a person in their custody. The plaintiff may attempt, however, to prove that officers failed to provide medical needs under the ruling in *DeShaney v. Winnebago County Department of Social Services* (1989). In this case, the United States Supreme Court recognized that a special relationship can exist between the state and a person, giving rise to a constitutional duty on the state to assume some responsibility for the person's medical needs, only "when the State takes a person into its custody and holds him against his will." Police officers are under no constitutional obligation to protect or provide medical services to the general public, even if they know of a particular person's need and regardless of whether that obligation is imposed by state tort law, unless the government has entered into a "certain special relationship" with the person. There are three primary components that must be considered in determining whether a "special relationship" may exist for medical purposes, which include that the police: (1) created the danger to which the plaintiffs were exposed; (2) had knowledge of the impending danger; and (3) had custody of the plaintiff. Thus, liability for police officers may attach when the need for medical care of an arrestee in their custody was created after a use-of-force situation (e.g., baton strikes, physical control techniques, during restraint, etc.) and the person sustained an injury, and officers knew that the person needed medical assistance through verbal inquiry or assessment or requests made by the individual. As illustrated in the *Harris* case, medical care liability in sudden custodial deaths may not attach, because in a significant number of incidents the police take custody and restrain an individual after they have already consumed drugs or alcohol. With this in mind, police officers should take reasonable precautions to assess and monitor the condition of the arrestee, and summon medical care as warranted after a violent use-of-force restraint confrontation.

Failure to Train

Section 1983 claims of failure to train focus on the U.S. Supreme Court case of *City of Canton v. Harris* (1989). The plaintiff must show that the custom or policy of the department was to ignore officer training and that this was the moving force behind a constitutional violation. In custodial death cases, the plaintiff must show that the alleged lack of training with regard to the use of force and restraints and the alleged lack of medical or psychiatric care for "special needs" prisoners is closely related and actually have caused the officers' deliberate indifference to the serious medical needs of the arrestee.

A frequent claim in unexpected death actions is allegations that police supervisors failed to train officers. As indicated in Table 13.2, it is common for plaintiffs to file allegations that police supervisors failed to train officers. In 32 percent of the post-*Price* decisions, the courts have found command personnel liable for failure to train. The assertion is that officers have not been properly instructed or trained by the supervisor or agency and thus lack the skills, knowledge, or competency required in a range of items, such as: use of appropriate force measures, including the use of restraints and other equipment; recognizing the hazards of drug-induced violent behavior; deficiency in training to obvious medical or psychiatric behaviors; recognizing the risks of hogtying; and a lack of training in policies and procedures for responding to "special needs" prisoners (those intoxicated or mentally impaired).

In *Elmes v. Hart* (1994), a § 1983 claim and state tort claims were filed by an estate when an arrestee who was high on LSD and marijuana died in police custody. Officers responded to a disturbance at a party where they observed an individual choking a female guest. Due to an intense struggle, several officers were needed to subdue the violent male. Handcuffs and leg restraints were secured on the kicking arrestee, and he was hogtied with flexcuffs and leg restraints. The medical examiner was summoned to the scene and found the arrestee hogtied and learned that he had stopped breathing after several minutes of being hogtied. An ambulance was summoned, but there was no attempt to resuscitate, because there was no CPR mask available, and officers were fearful of contracting AIDS. They had felt for a pulse and, finding none, thought CPR would be futile. Death was caused by "mechanical asphyxiation." The court ruled that the officers did not "intentionally kill the arrestee." An excessive force claim was made against the officers in which the court found that the officers used excessive force in arresting the deceased. The city, however, was not found to be deliberately indifferent for failing to train its officers.

In *Swans v. City of Lansing* (1998), the jury found in favor of the estate of an arrestee who died in a detention cell. Upon being admitted into the detention center, Swans kicked the booking sergeant in the head and fought with officers. He was restrained with handcuffs but the officers were unable to secure him in a restraint chair. He was forcibly moved to a cell where he continued to violently fight with the officers. In the cell, five officers and a lieutenant attempted to further restrain him with a Kick-Stop restraint strap, like they had used in numerous other situations with violent detainees. The strap broke and the officers restrained Swans with additional handcuffs and leg irons connected to his ankles. The officers left Swans on his side/stomach, monitored him by closed circuit television, and returned to the cell within 10 minutes. The officers found Swans lying in urine and unresponsive. They moved him to the hallway, removed the restraints, initiated CPR, and summoned medical personnel. Medical personnel found him pulseless, continued life-saving efforts, and transported him to the hospital where he was pronounced dead. An autopsy revealed that he died from cardiac dysrhythmia caused by postural asphyxia during custodial restraint. The jury determined that officers used excessive force, misused the restraints, and that administrative personnel had failed to train, supervise, and direct officers in how to properly respond to and restraint mentally impaired detainees. The jury awarded $10 million to Swans' estate.

The court in *Pliakos v. City of Manchester, New Hampshire* (2003) held that physically controlling a combative subject who twice kicked and beat off a police dog, fought with several officers, fought through a two-second burst of pepper spray, was not unreasonable nor excessive force. After Pliakos was restrained he remained on his stomach for approximately three minutes, became unresponsive, and later died. Pliakos suffered from bipolar affective disorder, an enlarged heart, and was under the influence of cocaine during the confrontation. Pliakos' estate claimed that the chief failed to train officers in properly restraining agitated persons and monitoring them while in restraints. The court reasoned that in light of the circumstances the officers did not violate their training and it was not unreasonable to keep Pliakos restrained on his stomach for his and the officers' safety.

In *Sanders-Burns v. Plano* (2010), an officer responding to a call about an altercation allegedly handcuffed a participant and left him on his stomach facedown against the floor while questioning others present, resulting in the man dying from positional asphyxia. A federal appeals court found that there was no evidence showing that the death resulted from inadequate training policies of the city that employed the officer.

Conversely, the court found in *Watkins v. New Castle County* (2005) that the department was deliberately indifferent to the training needs of its officers regarding factors pertinent to positional asphyxia. Officers responded to a domestic call to remove a man from the residence. A person at the scene informed the officers that he had a long history of cocaine abuse. The officers met the man and noticed that he had a dazed look on his face, spoke incoherently, and complained of feeling sick. The man engaged in a struggle with him and then he tensed up. The officers struck him in the face several times, struck him on the wrist with a collapsible baton, sprayed pepper spray in his eyes. He fell to the floor and an officer dropped his weight on his back to handcuff him. The officers held him down on his chest and secured his wrists and ankles together. Within several minutes he became unresponsive and died. The court denied summary judgment and found that the evidence revealed that the department failed to adequately train its officers in the risks of cocaine-induced delirium and the potential serious health consequences of restraining persons with their hands and ankles bound together.

Claims of excessive force and failing to train officers in the proper use of the restraint chair have been filed due to the deaths of several detainees in detention facilities. In *Jones v. Devaney* (2004) and *Bishop v. Corsentino* (2004), prisoners became combative, requiring officers to further restrain them in the restraint chair due to their continued self-injurious behaviors. The prisoners were placed in the chair, monitored, and later became unresponsive. Life-saving efforts were initiated and both prisoners died due to unspecified medical conditions. In both cases the courts granted summary judgment, as it was shown that the officers were guided in the proper use of the chair by agency policy. Training in the policy and the mechanics of using the chair was provided by the agency and the policy also provided for officer monitoring and intervals of medical personnel assessment. In both cases the procedures and officer training was followed, and the courts determined that the use of the chair failed to amount to excessive force in restraining the violent prisoners.

Section 1983 claims of this nature will focus on the U.S. Supreme Court case of *City of Canton v. Harris* (1989). The Court established that the inadequacy of police training may serve as a basis for § 1983 liability only when the failure to train amounts to deliberate indifference to the rights of persons with whom the police come into contact. The plaintiff must show that the custom or policy of the department was to ignore officer training and that this was the moving force behind a constitutional violation. In custodial death cases, the plaintiff must show that the alleged lack of training with regard to the use of force and restraints and the alleged lack of medical or psychiatric care for "special needs" prisoners is closely related and actually caused the officers' deliberate indifference to the serious medical needs of the arrestee.

The courts appear to be split on the issues of failure to train officers regarding restraint and use-of-force procedures, and recognizing symptomologies of medical and psychological care for these arrestees. For example, in *Swans v. City of Lansing* (1998), *Johnson v. Cincinnati* (1999), *Cruz v. City of Laramie, Wyoming* (2001), and *Watkins v. New Castle County* (2005), the courts denied summary judgment on claims of failure to train. The courts noted that administrators were deliberately indifferent to the training needs of their officers when they contact and intervene with the mentally ill and/or those who are experiencing a drug-induced psychosis. In the *Cruz* case, the court specifically held that there must be more than 14 inches separating the restraints between the ankles and wrists when restraining a violent arrestee who appears to be under the influence of drugs. Moreover, the *Swans* case is illustrative of how a jury may view restraining a mentally impaired person who suddenly dies in police custody. Further, in *Weigel v. Broad* (2008), the Tenth Circuit Court of Appeals found a constitutional violation when troopers failed to follow their subject control training by placing weight on the back of a prone arrestee who died of asphyxiation during restraint.

Conversely, in the decisions of *Sims v. Greenville* (2000), *Bozeman v. Orum* (2002), *Hoyer v. City of Southfield* (2003), *Pliakos v. City of Manchester, New Hampshire* (2003), *Bishop v. Corsentino* (2004), and *Jones v. Devaney* (2004), the courts held that officers used proper force and followed their policies and training, granting summary judgment. These cases are instructive as the officers had received training in responding to the mentally impaired, training on substance abuse, and training in use-of-force techniques, multiple officer response, and restraint training. As evidenced in these case examples, the courts are more likely to grant summary judgment to the responding officers and agencies when they can justify the appropriate level of force, based on the circumstances facing them, and when the officers have been provided with proper training, and were guided by policy.

Claims Against Detention Personnel

The claims most frequently filed against detention officers are allegations of excessive force, positional asphyxia, and failure to provide medical care, like their police counterparts. The jury returned a "no cause" for action verdict in *Love v. Bolinger* (1998). During a hearing to determine the competency to stand trial of a bipolar individual, the detainee became agitated and rushed the judge's bench. Five officers struggled with the detainee and sprayed him twice with pepper spray. Once he was finally subdued, his hands were secured in front with two sets of handcuffs. He was escorted from the courtroom, down one floor, to a padded cell in the detention center. The detainee continued to struggle during the escort and fought with officers, kicking them once they placed him in the cell. While officers were removing the handcuffs, one officer noticed he had stopped breathing, and began CPR, while another officer summoned medical personnel. Within several minutes paramedics responded and continued life-saving efforts. A pulse was restored but it stopped during transport to the hospital, where he was pronounced dead. The estate filed a § 1983 action, claiming that he died of asphyxiation from a choke hold and the officers placing their weight on him in the cell. Two other pathologists reviewed the autopsy and each determined that he died of an enlarged heart. Over five days the jury listened to the officers' and expert witness testimony. They found in favor of the officers, finding they did not use excessive force, nor did they cause the death of the detainee.

Detention facilities have experienced sudden custodial deaths of detainees who have consumed a quantity of drugs prior to admission. In *Smith v. Wilson County* (2000), Smith died of acute cocaine intoxication in the detention center and his family filed a § 1983 action against the facility for failing to provide medical care at time of arrest and while confined. Smith resisted arrest for failing to stop at a stop sign. Officers noticed he was chewing something and he attempted to remove it. Smith stated he swallowed a marijuana cigarette, and then said it was rock cocaine, and then said it was marijuana. The arresting officer asked if he wanted medical attention, Smith refused, and he was transported to the police department for processing. At the station, Smith informed the lieutenant that he had not swallowed cocaine. The lieutenant instructed the officer to take Smith to the magistrate. The magistrate set Smith's bond and Smith did not complain about needing medical care nor did he appear to be under the influence of drugs. He was booked into the detention center, being unable to post bond. Smith was placed in a holding cell and shortly became agitated and began yelling. Officers moved him to an isolation cell and Smith stated that the "rock of cocaine he swallowed is killing me." Smith then stated he only swallowed a marijuana cigarette. Officers did not summon medical personnel, as Smith did not appear to need medical treatment.

During a standard security check three hours later, Smith was found unconscious in his cell. Medical personnel were summoned and life-saving efforts were initiated but proved unsuccessful and Smith was pronounced dead at the hospital, approximately five hours after he was arrested. The autopsy revealed that Smith had not suffered any "acute external injuries." The pathologist determined the cause of death to be from cocaine intoxication, which caused an idiosyncratic reaction of the heart due to Smith's heart being enlarged from extensive cocaine abuse.

The family filed a legal action claiming the arresting officers used excessive force in taking Smith to the ground and were deliberately indifferent in failing to provide medical care in violation of his Fourth and Fourteenth Amendment rights. The court awarded summary judgment to the arresting officers. The family also filed claims against the detention facility officers and the sheriff for wrongful death, officers failing to recognize and respond to a medical emergency, and failing to train, supervise, and direct officers in the care of intoxicated prisoners, under the Fourteenth Amendment. The court also granted summary judgment to the detention personnel, finding no evidence that the officers or the sheriff were deliberately indifferent to Smith's medical needs.

In *Sims v. Greenville County* (2000), a detainee was being moved from a holding area to a holding cell in order to serve a meal. The detainee resisted the detention officers, and four officers took him to the floor. One officer applied a choke hold on the fighting detainee. The detainee was maximally restrained with handcuffs and leg restraints and placed in the holding cell. The detainee became unresponsive and attempts at medical intervention were unsuccessful. He later died and the pathologist determined that the cause of death was positional asphyxia. A legal action claiming that the officers used excessive force and inappropriately used a "multiple officer takedown" technique was filed on behalf of the detainee. Claims against the sheriff alleged that he failed to train officers and instituted an unconstitutional policy of using a multi-officer takedown maneuver. The appellate court affirmed summary judgment by the lower court, determining that Sims failed to present evidence that the defendants used excessive force. Sims failed to show that the sheriff maintained unconstitutional policies that would subject detainees to excessive force measures.

In *Bozeman v. Orum* (2002), the estate of a deceased detainee brought a § 1983 claim against the sheriff and several officers, alleging the force used caused his death, thereby violating his Fourteenth Amendment right against the use of excessive force. The detainee had become violent in the jail and the officers had threatened to "kick his ass" if he did not cease. He continued and the officers apparently punched or slapped the detainee and he subsequently died as a result of the officers' actions. The court granted summary judgment to the officers and sheriff, noting that some level of force was necessary to restore order where the detainee was going through a mental breakdown in his cell. The court noted that the sheriff had provided adequate training in the proper use of force, including training on positional asphyxia, and was not liable for failing to train or supervise the officers.

In *Loggins v. Carroll County, MS* (2009), a woman died after being placed in four-point restraints and put into a vehicle facedown for transport to jail. Upholding summary judgment for the defendant deputies and county in a federal civil rights lawsuit, the court, assuming the facts in the light most favorable to the plaintiffs, assumed that the decedent died from positional asphyxia. The plaintiffs, however, failed to show that the use of the restraints was unnecessary, or excessively disproportionate to the resistance the deputies faced from the prisoner, so that no reasonable jury could have found that the deputies used excessive force to subdue her. The plaintiffs also failed to sufficiently prove a claim for alleged inadequate monitoring of the prisoner during transport.

The incidence of a sudden death in custody after a period of restraint is a rare event. Although rare, the risk of death may occur during any arrest situation and may occur during the use of any less-lethal force control measure. Burch (2011) reported that from 2003 to 2009, there were 4,813 arrest-related deaths reported to the Bureau of Justice Statistics, which are underreported. These deaths were the result of the individual attempting to elude control and arrest. Excluding homicides and deaths from suicide during an arrest, deaths as a result from intoxication, accidents, natural causes, and undetermined causes resulted in 1,314 deaths. During the same period 98 million arrests were made (Burch, 2011). Therefore, the likelihood of a sudden in-custody death is estimated at less than a one-percent chance from occurrence and statically negligible.

While the courts appear to be split regarding the science of what causes a sudden in-custody death after a period of restraint, which can impact summary judgment dispositions, research studies on human subjects reveal that the physiological condition of the arrestee is statistically more responsible for the sudden death and not the control measures or less-lethal force equipment used by the police or detention officers. This finding rests on several levels. First, since the use of the Taser has increased, a controversy has emerged suggesting that it is responsible for causing the sudden custodial deaths of many arrestees. Laub (2011) reported for the National Institute of Justice that after a three-year study by a panel of 30 physicians, academics, and law enforcement officials, the use of the Taser is substantially safe when used according to manufacturer's instructions. The panel reviewed 175 peer reviewed journal articles and reviewed 300 death incidents that occurred after the use of the Taser.

The panel concluded that the Taser did not cause or contribute to the death in a significant number of deaths and reported that the risk of death after using the Taser is 0.025 percent. The panel concluded that the risk of death from using a Taser is less than other force measures available to the police. The panel reported that there is no conclusive medical evidence within the state of current research that indicates a high risk of serious injury or death from the direct or indirect cardiovascular or metabolic effects of short-term conducted energy device (CED) exposure in healthy, normal, nonstressed, nonintoxicated persons. Current medical research in humans and animals suggests that a single exposure of less than 15 seconds from the Taser is not a stress of a magnitude that separates it from the other stress-inducing components of restraint. Finally, the panel concluded that deaths after exposure to a Taser application were more likely related to other factors underscoring the decedent's physiological and psychological condition rather than the Taser. The panel suggested that multiple applications or prolonged applications should be used with caution.

Second, it has been argued that the prone restraint of a violent person contributes to a sudden death through a condition commonly referred to as positional asphyxia. Ross studied all the published human subject studies performed on restraint asphyxia (2010). Ross reported that 10 studies were published that used human subjects to measure the effects of prone positioning after restraint. Of the studies examined three were excluded that did not require subjects to raise their heart rate prior to the restraint experiment and who failed to adhere to statistical sound research methods. Of the remaining experimental studies, two combined the use of pepper spray prior to restraining the respondents to measure the effects of the spray during a period of restraint. None of the studies found a statistical significant measure that would support the notion that restraining a person in a prone position, or hogtying or hobbling the person, with or without being exposed to pepper spray, posed a risk factor for asphyxia.

The findings of the Ross analysis were also confirmed by Hall et al. (2012). Hall and her research team studied 1,255 arrest incidents in which arrestees were restrained over three years in a city of a population of 1.1 million residents. Individuals arrested fought with the police and may have been exposed to a Taser application, pepper spray, or other less-lethal force measure in order to control the person. Arrestees experienced behaviors consistent with alcohol intoxication, mental distress, drug intoxication, or a combination of intoxication and mental distress.

All arrestees were handcuffed. Some of the arrestees were restrained prone, kneeling, or standing. Some of the arrestees were controlled by straps secured around their ankles but none were restrained by using the hogtied method. Only one person died during the study and the decedent was not placed in a prone position, but died from cardiopulmonary collapse unrelated to the restraint process. The researchers concluded that the risk of sudden death following the police use of force and restraint is low (0.08%, with a confidence interval of 95%) and that prone positioning for restraint is not associated with a sudden death in their cohort. The researchers also recommend monitoring all individuals restrained regardless of the position for signs of medical distress.

Third, a panel of emergency room physicians studied 18 peer reviewed journal articles that were published on the medical condition referred to as Excited Delirium Syndrome (EXDS), to determine whether it is a disease and what role it may play in a sudden in-custody death (Vilke et al., 2011). Excited delirium is a physiological condition exhibited by psychological features. It may be caused by the illicit use of substances and or psychiatric illness (Hughes, 2011). The subject often exhibits hyperaggression, bizarre behavior, extreme agitation and violence, combativeness, unusual strength, a high tolerance to pain, and is often partially nude or nude at the time of police intervention. A majority of excited delirium subjects die after a violent struggle with police who are attempting to control the person. The person suddenly dies as a result of a combination of physiological and psychological factors intersecting with the abuse of illicit drugs producing abnormalities in the brain, and hyperthermia, all impacting the cardiovascular system.

The panel concluded that the condition of EXDS is a real medical condition with uncertain, likely multiple, etiologies. The risk of death is likely increased with physiologic stress during the restraint process where the person violently fights against control measures. The researchers recommend that control measures be used that will shorten the time span of the struggle and safely achieve physical control.

The scientific studies performed to date suggest that physiological and psychological factors of the person are statistically more likely to contribute to the sudden death in custody than from control measures and less-lethal force equipment used by police or detention officers. There is no risk-free control use of force technique or piece of equipment and caution must be used by officers when applying them in a use-of-force encounter. Adhering to agency use-of-force policies, training, and appropriate application of restraint and force equipment can place the officer and management in the best possible position to defend against a claim of a sudden wrongful death in custody.

In *Deshotels v. Marshall* (2011), the court acknowledged that the decedent died from excited delirium and not from the application of the Taser. A woman witnessed a man breaking into her garage and confronted him. The man fled and the woman's husband chased him down, tackling him in front of an apartment complex. The husband informed a passerby that the man had broken into his house and asked her to call 911. When officers arrived, the husband was standing near the man. Police approached the man and he took off running. One officer quickly caught the man and attempted to handcuff him but he resisted. Other officers came to assist and one warned the man that if he did not comply he would be Tased. The man refused and an officer conducted a five second drive-stun Tase to the man. After he still would not comply, the officer did the same thing once more. Finally, the officers handcuffed him but when they attempted to lift him off the ground, the officers noticed the man was limp. The officers removed the handcuffs, laid him on his back, and called an ambulance. The man later died at a hospital, and the reported cause of death was excited delirium. The court noted that the officers were responding to a burglary in progress, "a crime normally and reasonably expected to involve a weapon." Further the court noted the man initially fled, remained combative when caught, and refused to show officers his hands. Because of these circumstances, the court found the officers did not use excessive force and awarded summary judgment.

Suicides in Detention

Given the diversity of the prisoner population in confinement facilities and their medical and psychological backgrounds, a death while incarcerated should not be unexpected, although a rare occurrence (Kelly & Linthicum, 2006; Raba, 1998; Rold, 1998). Some prisoners of this population periodically attempt or commit suicide while confined in a jail or police lockup, or in prison. Researchers have estimated that a prisoner suicide in jail was from five to 16 times more likely than in the free society population (Hayes, 1983, 1989; Winfree, 1985). Ross (2001) reported that from 1978 to 1998, suicides accounted for 31 percent of the in-custody deaths in jails and police lockups, which accounted for about 134 suicide deaths on average annually.

Noonan and Carson (2011) reported that from 2000 to 2009 custodial deaths in jails declined about 13 percent and the following causes of death include suicide, 29%; illness, 54%; drug/alcohol intoxication, 6%; accident, 2%; homicide, 2%; and unknown causes, 7%. During the same time period, Noonan and Carson report the causes of deaths in state prisons include illness, 89%; suicide, 6%; homicide, 1.5%; drug/alcohol intoxication, 1.5%; accident, 1%; and unknown causes, 1%.

A suicide by a prisoner or pretrial detainee poses a serious problem for detention and prison personnel. Civil litigation in this topic area has increased since the 1970s, and millions of dollars have been awarded as a result of attempted or actual suicides. The prevailing trend for plaintiffs, however, declined during the 1990s and through 2005. These civil actions normally assert that the confining agency and its officers failed to take the proper measures to prevent such an incident.

A wrongful death claim resulting from a prisoner suicide may be brought under § 1983 or as described earlier under state tort law. In accordance with § 1983, the plaintiff's claim will invariably allege that the defendant was deliberately indifferent to the deceased by failing to properly screen the prisoner upon reception into a detention facility; failing to recognize signs of symptoms of suicide; failing to train detention personnel; failing to protect the prisoner from himself by providing a safe environment; failing to properly search the prisoner and seize items that might be used to commit suicide; a deficiency in the design and structure of the confining facility; failing to "watch" the suicidal prisoner on a continuous basis; and failing to provide mental health services (Cohen, 1992).

A typical complaint will allege multiple theories of liability. In *Frey v. City of Herculaneum* (1995), for example, an intoxicated arrestee hanged himself in his cell with bed sheets. The estate claimed that the defendants were deliberately indifferent to the medical needs of Frey insofar as they knew or should have known that he was a suicide risk; knew or should have known he was in immediate need of medical attention; inadequately monitored the jail cells; failed to take precautions to remove dangerous items from the arrestee's cell; and knew or should have known that the jail was defective and dangerous.

Suicide and Deliberate Indifference

In Chapter 9, the deliberate indifference standard was described and applied to correctional issues. Recall that deliberate indifference originated in *Estelle v. Gamble* (1976), which involved prisoner medical care issues. In *Bell v. Wolfish* (1989), the U.S. Supreme Court held that pretrial detainees at the very least possess the same rights as convicted prisoners. While the Court has never specifically recognized a prisoner's right to protection from self-harm, the principles and analysis of *Bell* and *Estelle* have been applied to prisoner suicide cases.

Consider, however, the *Farmer v. Brennan* (1994) decision, in which the Court held that in order for liability to attach in a civil rights action against correctional personnel, deliberate indifference to a prisoner's safety and health must be based on a showing that they were subjectively aware of the risk. Correctional officials are not absolute guarantors of the safety of prisoners, but cannot ignore obvious risks or dangers to prisoners in their custody. The official must be aware of the facts from which the inference could be drawn that a serious risk of harm exists. Although Farmer is not a suicide case per se, it is instructive in that it is a deliberate indifference case involving issues of "knew or should have known" and should strengthen the ability to defend suicide cases involving issues of knowledge. *Deliberate indifference* describes a state of mind that is more blameworthy than negligence and requires more than an ordinary lack of due care, but can be satisfied with less than acts or omissions with knowledge that harm will result. In *Hare v. City of Corinth* (1996), the Fifth Circuit applied *Farmer* standards to a pretrial detainee suicide claim. The court ruled that the duty not to be deliberately indifferent was minimally established. A check on the prisoner who had threatened suicide while in withdrawal from drugs consumed prior to arrest was made by an officer, although he failed to remove a blanket from the cell. The officer's belief that the detainee was too weak to tear it was objectively reasonable.

To prevail in a § 1983 suit for violation of rights under the Fourteenth or Eighth Amendments, the plaintiff must establish that the defendant displayed deliberate indifference to a "strong likelihood" of suicide rather than a mere possibility. The plaintiff must prove that officials were deliberately indifferent to the prisoner's serious needs. Deliberate indifference is more than making a mistake. In suicide cases, deliberate indifference means: (1) officials knew or should have known that the prisoner was a suicide risk and steps were not taken to prevent it; and/or (2) the officers and agency were deliberately indifferent to the prisoner's serious medical or mental health needs (Plitt, 1997). Accordingly, when an official fails to act in the face of an obvious risk of which he or she *should have been* aware, the official has not inflicted punishment in violation of the Eighth Amendment.

In *Popham v. City of Talladega* (1990), the court applied the "strong likelihood" test of deliberate indifference in the suicide of an intoxicated pretrial detainee. The estate brought a § 1983 action against city and jail officials, claiming that their son had the right to be protected from committing suicide while confined, that officials failed to properly monitor him, and that officers were not properly trained to recognize indicators of suicide. Popham was placed in a holding cell, and his belt, shoes, socks, and the contents of his pockets were removed. His cell was monitored by closed-circuit television, and he was periodically monitored physically. The last physical check was at 11:00 P.M. At 5:00 A.M., he was discovered hanging from his cell bars by his jeans.

The appeals court affirmed the lower court decisions that jail personnel were not deliberately indifferent because they were unaware of any suicidal tendencies. The court held that suicides in custody are analogous to the failure to provide medical care, and deliberate indifference is the proper standard of review in such cases, regardless of the status of the prisoner. The deliberate indifference standard as applied to suicide cases requires a strong likelihood, rather than a mere possibility, that self-inflicted harm will occur. Personnel followed standard procedures and a failure to train officers in screening for suicidal tendencies did not provide a basis for imposing liability. Further, in *Bell v. Stinger* (1991), the court ruled that although an intoxicated detainee threatened to kill himself and officers failed to respond or to remove his belt during a search, this did not rise to the level of deliberate indifference, because there was no "strong likelihood" of a suicide attempt.

In *Sanders v. Howze* (1999), the Eleventh Circuit Court of Appeals followed the same line of reasoning as *Popham*. After the lower court denied summary judgment, the appellate court reversed the decision and held that the jail officials were entitled to qualified immunity in the suicide of the detainee. Several weeks after his confinement, the detainee removed the razor from a disposable razor and cut his wrists. He was transported to the local hospital, per jail policy, and was later transferred to a state hospital, where he remained for several months. He returned to the jail and was placed in the general population, where within two days he used a pencil to reopen his earlier wound. He was again transported to the hospital and treated. He was transferred to the state hospital a second time and later released back to the jail and placed in an observation cell. The county petitioned the court for a psychiatric evaluation, but before the request was granted the detainee hanged himself with a bed sheet. The court ruled that jail officials were not deliberately indifferent to the needs of the detainee and followed established policy in responding to him.

Suicide Risk Factors

The question of whether a detainee's past or current behaviors are indicative of a suicidal "profile" often arises. This question posed is asserted by the plaintiff in many legal actions regarding custodial suicide. The claim is that the decedent "fit" the profile and officers failed to recognize it, and therefore should be held liable. In an attempt to establish a foundation for such an argument, the plaintiff will cite studies suggesting that the decedent characterized the "typical" in-custody suicide.

The use of a profile is highly controversial, and the research on suicide points toward patterns and risk factors that correctional personnel should observe. It is important to recognize that a definitive profile of potential custodial suicide on which all researchers agree does not exist (Plitt, 1997). With any research there are methodological problems that can skew the data.

Table 13.3   Prisoner Suicide Awareness Factors

- Nature of arrest/transporting from transporting officer
- Prisoner's mental state/mental health history
- Prisoner expresses feelings of hopelessness
- Prisoner expresses he is thinking about killing himself
- Prisoner's history of suicide attempts
- Prisoner's intoxicated state
- Prisoner shows signs of depression
- Prisoner shows concern about a loss: a job, family, position in community, etc.
- Prisoner's behavior is anxious, afraid, angry, strange
- Prior arrests and convictions
- Prisoner's medical/medication history
- Prisoner charged with a "shocking" crime

A significant problem in suicide research is that studies all examine the suicide without fully comparing the victim to other confined prisoners (Kennedy & Homant, 1988). In other words, why did other detainees in the same facility not commit suicide? Does one "profile" fit all prisoners and all locations? These types of questions are ignored in many studies. Rather than claiming that a prisoner fit a profile and committed a jail suicide, it would be more precise to state that a suicide happened to occur while a detainee was confined in a jail. Thus, a "typical suicide" does not exist in the confinement setting. What should be addressed are factors that may alert correctional personnel to potential risks of a detainee suicide and what constitutes awareness of suicide (see Table 13.3).

While such factors are not inclusive of every possible factor and may not apply to every detainee, they may be useful in training correctional personnel about the behavior of all detainees in housing assignments, and in potential medical care of the detainee. Understanding the behavior of all detainees in a detention or correctional setting can assist officers in being more proactive in reception procedures, removing items from a cell or from the detainee that could be used to commit suicide, utilization of cells and housing assignments, monitoring procedures, and services provided to prisoners. The mere fact that a detainee fits a "suicide profile," independent of other factors, does not support liability against correctional personnel that the prisoner was likely to commit suicide.

In *Zwalesky v. Manistee County* (1990), a detainee hanged himself 90 minutes after being placed in a detoxification cell at the jail. He had been arrested for spouse abuse, was intoxicated, and threatened to kill his relatives, the transporting officer, and himself. The court granted summary judgment to jail officials, because there was no showing that the jail officials violated any clearly established right possessed by the detainee.

Further, the court concluded that the right actually being asserted is the right of a detainee to be screened for suicidal tendencies and to have appropriate preventive measures taken. The general right to medical care, the court ruled, is not sufficient to establish a clear constitutional right to be screened for psychological problems.

In *Estate of Frank v. City of Beaver Dam* (1996), the estate of a detainee who committed suicide while confined in jail brought a § 1983 action against a detention officer. The court dismissed the case, holding that the officer was entitled to qualified immunity because he was not deliberately indifferent to the rights of the detainee. The court noted that although one officer was informed that the detainee had exhibited severe mood swings during transport to the jail, the detainee did not make any threats, cause any disturbances, stagger, slur his speech, or do anything bizarre that would have caused the officer to believe he was suicidal. The court determined that the detainee's quiet behavior as he walked to the cell and unresponsiveness to questions asked by the officer did not suggest that he was an imminent danger to himself. The court also noted that once the detainee was placed in his cell he later ate breakfast and engaged in a telephone conversation.

The district court in *Vinson v. Clarke County, Alabama* (1998) granted summary judgment to the defendant sheriff and detention officers in a detainee suicide. The estate brought a § 1983 claim against the sheriff and officers, asserting that the intoxicated detainee, with a blood-alcohol content of .205, clearly fit a suicidal profile in that he committed suicide within 30 minutes of confinement. The court determined that the county was not deliberately indifferent to the risks of suicide. The court further held that the risk of suicide among intoxicated detainees was not so obvious that the county's failure to remedy conditions of confinement that gave detainees the opportunity to commit suicide could be seen as showing deliberate indifference.

The Eighth Circuit Court of Appeals affirmed a lower court's decision to grant summary judgment for jail officials after a detainee committed suicide in *Liebe v. Norton* (1998). The court found that detention officers were not deliberately indifferent to the detainee's health and safety, because they classified him as a suicide risk, took precautionary measures by placing him in a holding cell, removed his shoes and belt, and periodically checked on him. The intake officer classified the detainee as a "suicide risk" because he admitted to previously attempting suicide and was taking clonazepam and Valium. Officers checked on the detainee at intervals ranging from 7 to 21 minutes, but did not turn on the audio system in the holding cell. The detainee used his long-sleeved shirt to hang himself from an electrical conduit in the cell. The parents asserted that the officers failed to supervise their son, and that the county failed to test officers on their policy manual regarding custodial suicides. The court found that the county was not deliberately indifferent to the training of officers, because the policy manual outlined their duties step-by-step.

The issue of suicide risk was examined in *Payne for Hicks v. Churchill* (1998) by the Seventh Circuit Court of Appeals. The parents brought a wrongful death action against city jail officials following the suicide of their son. The appellate court affirmed the lower court's dismissal on the suicide issue, but remanded the case on the excessive force claim. According to the court, the detainee's intoxication, his tattoo that questioned life, and his angry cursing did not indicate an obvious, substantial risk of suicide. The court found that failing to monitor the arrestee or recognize the risk of suicide was, at most, negligence. The man was admitted to a holding cell at 1:00 A.M. and died of suffocation after hanging himself with a blanket prior to 4:00 A.M.

Some courts, examining custodial suicides, have focused on the decedent's own responsibility in committing suicide rather on the alleged omissions of the officers. For example, in *Soles v. Ingham County* (2004), the court determined that the detainee was the direct cause of his death and not the actions or omissions of the detention officers or social worker. Frayer, the decedent, was placed in an observation cell for making comments about taking his life. After several days he promised a social worker that he would not kill himself and the social worker instructed officers to return him to the general population. During the afternoon prior to Frayer's suicide, a correctional officer noticed that he was acting strangely but did not transfer him back to the observation cell. Later that night Frayer committed suicide. His estate filed a legal action claiming that the social worker and the detention officer's actions amounted to deliberate indifference to Frayer's mental health needs. The court granted summary judgment to the defendants. The court concluded that Frayer's suicide was not the result of the defendants' actions or nonfeasance, but was a direct cause of his own actions. The court ruled that Frayer committed suicide while he was alone in his cell by hanging himself with a bed sheet, which was a result of his own volitional self-destructive action.

The Sixth Circuit Court of Appeals applied the deliberate indifference standard from the *Farmer* decision in *Bradley v. City of Ferndale* (2005) and also focused on the actions of the decedent. Bradley was admitted to the City of Ferndale's lock up facility and placed in a cell pending transport to the Oakland County jail on an outstanding warrant. Admitting officers could smell alcohol on Bradley and heard him state that an officer should give him a gun so that he could kill himself. Booking officers followed the standard booking process, and removed his belt, shoes, wallet, and jacket, but he was allowed to retain his shirt and pants. He was also given a blanket. Bradley was the only detainee in the lockup. At the time Bradley was admitted, Ferndale officers were handling a barricaded gunman situation, which left one officer, one supervisor, and a dispatcher at the stationhouse. At some point after placing Bradley in his cell, an officer observed him sleeping on his bunk with the blanket. The officers returned to monitoring the barricaded gunman situation. About 36 minutes after Bradley was placed in his cell, an officer made another cell check, and discovered Bradley unconscious, with the blanket tied around his neck. Officers immediately initiated CPR and summoned emergency medical personnel, but revival efforts were unsuccessful. Bradley's estate filed a § 1983 lawsuit claiming that the officers and city were deliberately indifferent to Bradley's known suicidal tendencies in violation of the Fourteenth Amendment.

The district court granted the defendant's motion for summary judgment and the plaintiff appealed. The appellate court affirmed the lower court's verdict. The court found that there was no evidence that the officers acted with deliberate indifference to the needs of Bradley. The court noted that the officers followed the proper booking procedures and departmental monitoring practices of making cell checks every 15 minutes. In fact, the court noted that the officers set a timer to remind themselves to make the checks. The court reasoned that removing the blanket from Bradley may have prevented his suicide but that did not equate to deliberate indifference and the policy of the department allowed numerous alternatives for officers to consider, but did not prohibit the removal of blankets. The court concluded that Bradley's own actions were the direct cause of his death and that the officers' actions did not manifest a conscious disregard for his welfare. Moreover, the court found no evidence that the city failed to train its officers in the risks and hazards of suicide prevention.

Failure to Train

As described earlier, claims of failure to train will frequently emerge in a wrongful death lawsuit. The same claim is commonly asserted in litigation arising from a suicide. The plaintiff will cite *Canton v. Harris* (1989), alleging that the agency was deliberately indifferent by failing to train officers in recognition of suicide indicators, policy issues, monitoring procedures, how to obtain medical or mental health care, and resuscitation procedures. As discussed below, the training standard of deliberate indifference is a high hurdle for the plaintiff to overcome.

In *Vine v. County of Ingham* (1995), a § 1983 claim was filed alleging deliberate indifference in training officers to recognize signs of drug or alcohol intoxication. In response to a disorderly conduct complaint, a deputy took into custody a male who complained of pain from ingesting methyl alcohol. Transport to a hospital was refused when the arrestee complained of stomach pain. The deputy transported the arrestee to the city lockup and transfer of custody was established. Vine was placed in the city lockup without medical examination, although he appeared intoxicated. During booking, he became belligerent and, due to prior suicide attempts, was placed in handcuffs in a maximum-security observation cell. During a security check later in the day, Vine was observed to have mucus or vomit coming from his mouth or nose. He had been in the cell for approximately two hours without medical attention, because officers thought he was sleeping. He was later transported to the hospital in a comatose condition and died shortly thereafter. The court ruled in favor of the officers, stating that there was no evidence of deliberate indifference to the medical needs of the arrestee, nor to the training of officers, because they had been trained in accordance with state minimum standards.

In *Pyka v. Village of Orland Park* (1995), the court granted summary judgment to city jail personnel in a case regarding the suicide of an 18-year-old detainee. The estate brought a § 1983 action claiming, among other things, that officials failed to properly train officers about the risks of prisoner suicides. The court held that officials were not liable for the suicide on the theory of failure to train officers on suicide awareness, absent any evidence that the municipality had a large suicide problem that it was ignoring or that statutes or regulations required officers to perform CPR on the detainee after he was discovered hanging in his cell.

In *Mathis v. Fairman* (1997), the Seventh Circuit Court of Appeals affirmed summary judgment granted by the lower court in a suicide that occurred in the Cook County Jail. The court found that jail personnel did not exhibit deliberate indifference toward the detainee. The court noted that after hearing that the detainee was fearful that someone might kill him, an officer placed the detainee in a holding cell and requested that a mental health professional speak with him. A psychologist concluded that the detainee did not pose a threat to himself, and officers placed him in the general population. The mother of the detainee alleged that jail officials failed to train officers about prisoner suicides and that they failed to adequately staff the facility. The court held that while it was the officer's first day on the job, he reported the strange behaviors of the detainee to a supervisor. These actions failed to rise to a level of deliberate indifference, despite only having completed a five-day orientation course. The court ruled that although officers may not have been trained in suicide prevention, the jail maintained a psychiatric unit for that purpose.

Compare, however, *Owens v. City of Philadelphia* (1998), in which the federal district court denied summary judgment to the defendants, ruling that the training program was deliberately indifferent to detainees' needs. According to the court, the detainee's statement to an officer that he felt "schizy" and that he was "going to hurt myself" raised questions of fact on issues of knowledge and deliberate indifference. The court held that it was not necessary to show that an officer believed harm would actually befall the detainee; rather, the plaintiff need only show that the official acted or failed to act despite his knowledge of substantial risk of serious harm. The officer summoned a psychiatrist knowing that she intended to issue a pass for the detainee to go to the mental health unit, but failed to note in the logbook the detainee's statement about harming himself. There was nothing in the record that indicated the pass was ever issued. The court further found that the officials' alleged conduct as policymakers with respect to inadequate training to prevent suicide by pretrial detainees was actionable under § 1983.

In examining claims for failure to train officers regarding issues of suicide awareness, a majority of courts are rejecting plaintiffs' claims if the defendants can show evidence of training or policies that direct officers in responding to detainees who exhibit a strong likelihood of suicide. For example, in *Harvey v. County of Ward* (2005), *Howard v. City of Atmore* (2004), and *Gray v. Tunica, Mississippi* (2003) the courts granted summary judgment, finding that the administrators had addressed issues surrounding suicides, including booking procedures, contacting health care personnel, initiating and monitoring detainees, and suicidal symptomologies, through training sessions and policies and procedures. In *Wever v. Lincoln County* (2004), however, the sheriff was denied qualified immunity on claims that he was deliberately indifferent to the training needs of detention officers and the risk of suicides in the jail. The jail incurred two suicides in a short period when officers gave blankets to detainees who were confined in isolation cells.

In *Forgan v. Howard County, Texas* (2007), a detainee committed suicide by hanging himself with his trousers. During the booking process the detainee stated that he was under a physician's care and had been prescribed numerous medications for mental illness, including depression. He indicated that he was not thinking about suicide at the time. Based on this information, the booking and classification officer classified the detainee as a "risk" for suicide and a 15-minute monitoring procedure was initiated. An hour later the detainee was discovered hanging in his cell and the family filed a § 1983 lawsuit claiming that the sheriff, the county, and the officers were deliberately indifferent for failing to protect the detainee, failing to follow monitoring procedures, and failing to adequately train officers in suicide prevention. The court granted summary judgment and the appellate court affirmed. The court disagreed with the plaintiff, ruling that the sheriff did have proper policies in place and that officers were trained in the proper responses to suicidal prisoners. The court further held that evidence of a single incident will fail to support a finding of inadequate training as a matter of custom or policy, for the purpose of establishing liability under § 1983.

Trends in Suicide Litigation

In order to assess trends in suicide litigation, Ross (2010) performed a 27-year longitudinal study of published § 1983 court decisions. Case collection yielded 2,079 published § 1983

Table 13.4   Prevailing Suicide Litigation Trends by Pre-/Post-*Farmer* and Correctional Entity

	Pre-*Farmer*: 1980 to 1993		Post-*Farmer*: 1994 to 2007	
Agency	CO (%)	Prisoner (%)	CO (%)	Prisoner (%)
Jail	682 (75)	225 (25)	550 (84)	101 (15)
Lock up	115 (55)	95 (45)	95 (75)	31 (25)
Prison	75 (68)	35 (32)	64 (85)	11 (15)
Total	871 (77)	356 (32)	709 (83)	143 (17)

cases. Using multiple legal data sources assisted in ensuring that all published § 1983 decisions from 1980 to 2007 were identified for analysis. Section 1983 suicide litigation was selected due to its more frequent occurrence and application.

Analysis of the published § 1983 cases involved three confinement entities: (1) county jails, (2) city lockups, and (3) prisons. From 1980 to 2007, the average daily population in jails, lockups, and prisons was approximately 2.1 million prisoners (Sabol & Minton, 2008). In 2006 there were 3,061 county jails, 1,975 police lockups, and all 50 states operated prison facilities (Hickman & Reeves, 2006). City lockups are confinement facilities that generally hold detainees from 20 to 72 hours; jails are operated by the county and confine pretrial detainees and sentenced individuals from 24 hours to two years in some jurisdictions; and prisons confine sentenced prisoners for more than one year. Comparisons of the trends were made among these three confinement facilities.

Table 13.4 illustrates prevailing party trends and shows that prisoners have a low probability of winning a claim associated with a custodial suicide. "Prevailing party" means that a jury found in favor of correctional personnel, or that the court found sufficient evidence to warrant a jury's judgment in the case, or that the court awarded summary judgment without the case progressing to trial. Jails comprised 75 percent of the litigation while lockups accounted for 16 percent, and prisons accounted for nine percent. Prior to the *Farmer* decision, prisoners prevailed in 32 percent of the cases. In the pre-*Farmer* period, custodial personnel in lockups and prisons collectively prevailed in 61 percent of the litigation, 14 percent below the prevailing rates of jails. Overall, prevailing percentages in jails were the highest of the three agencies but experienced the lowest percentage increase, nine percent.

Correctional personnel prevailed by a three-to-one ratio over the study period, 76 percent to 24 percent. Since the *Farmer* decision, correctional personnel prevailed in 83 percent of the litigation, or about a four-to-one ratio. Comparing the two periods, police lock ups were less likely to prevail than prisons and jails, but made the largest gain in prevailing patterns, netting a 20 percent increase since the *Farmer* decision. Further, since *Farmer*, prisoners in state prison prevailing rates were cut in more than half of the published decisions (32% to 15%). By the end of the study period, the total prisoner prevailing rate decreased by almost half, from 32 percent to 17 percent.

These litigation trends show the impact of the *Farmer* decision on custodial suicide litigation, as prisoner plaintiffs' prevailing percentages have been cut almost in half. This is due to a stricter, narrower definition, and a heightened standard of deliberate indifference that embraces a subjective definition to that of criminal recklessness (Scarfile, 2006). This requires a plaintiff to show that correctional officials knew and ignored an excessive risk to a prisoner's safety. In conjunction with this strict definition, some courts have added further definitional language and include that the prisoner must show a "strong likelihood rather a mere possibility" that the suicide is impending. As the research reveals, the *Farmer* decision has brought more stability in the law concerning custodial suicides. A successful plaintiff must show evidence that a correctional official had an actual subjective knowledge of a serious risk of harm to the health of a prisoner and disregarded the risk.

The research found that more than 90 percent of the lawsuits filed by a plaintiff included at least four claims against the confining agency. Typically these lawsuits include claims of: failure to protect and monitor the prisoner; failure to provide medical and mental health services; failure to train officers and provide them with policies; and failure to properly admit and classify the prisoner. The following cases illustrate these trends.

In *Branton v. City of Moss Point* (2007), the estate of the decedent who hung himself in the city jail filed a § 1983 claim under the Fourteenth and Eighth Amendments, asserting claims of failure to train, failure to adopt a policy for safe custodial care of suicidal prisoners, and failure to provide medical care for suicidal prisoners. The decedent was housed in the jail on a charge of drunk driving and was combative during the booking process. During booking the detainee was asked if he was suicidal or if he ever attempted suicide previously and he responded "no" to the booking officer. He was housed in a protective cell and provided a sheet and blanket. A cell check made by an officer two hours later found the detainee hanging with the bed sheet around his neck and he did not survive despite medical intervention efforts. The defendants moved for summary judgment and the court denied the motion. The court determined that the officers were deliberately indifferent to the medical needs of a combative and intoxicated detainee and that the city's training of its officers was deficient, which increased the risk of personal harm to the detainee.

A female detainee attempted suicide by hanging, which left her severely brain-damaged. Her family filed a § 1983 lawsuit in *Mombourquette ex rel. Mombourquette v. Amundson* (2007). She alleged that the sheriff, detention officers, and nurses of the jail violated her constitutional rights by: failing to protect her from harming herself, maintaining deficient policies, failing to provide health care and safety for prisoners, and failing to train and supervise officers. The defendants filed for summary judgment and the court denied it, agreeing with the plaintiff's claims. Evidence was submitted that showed a jail lieutenant intentionally and deliberately disregarded the risk of protecting the detainee as he removed another female from her cell to engage in sexual misconduct with her at the same time the detainee was attempting suicide. The court found that the sheriff's dismissive attitude toward the complaint exhibited deliberate indifference toward the detainee's health care and safety and in general to all prisoners. The court also found that the jail nurse and officers were deliberately indifferent to the detainee's medical care. The court determined that there was evidence to show an affirmative link between the sheriff's failure to properly train and supervise personnel and the failure to prevent the detainee's suicide, which supported a claim of deliberate indifference.

In *Cooper v. County of Washtenaw* (2007), a detainee had demonstrated violence at the time of the arrest and during initial booking at the jail. At his arraignment the court decided to place him on suicide watch until his sentencing. Upon his return back to the jail, detention officers placed him on a 15-minute suicide watch and placed him in an observation cell. On the day of his sentencing, two officers transported the detainee to the court but the releasing jailers did not inform the transporting officers that he was a suicide watch. The transporting officers had the detainee changed into street clothes from a tearaway gown in the observation cell prior to transport to court. During the transport to court and while in court the detainee was calm. After sentencing the prisoner was placed in a holding cell while paperwork was completed. The prisoner used his shirt and hung himself. The prisoner's estate filed a lawsuit against all of the officers, claiming deliberate indifference. The lower court granted summary judgment and the appellate court affirmed but reversed regarding one of the officers.

The appellate court held that the standard for deliberate indifference is whether the official knows of and disregards an excessive risk to inmate health and safety. Detention officers and one transporting officer were granted summary judgment. One officer, however, who was responsible for watching the prisoner in the court's holding cell, was denied summary judgment. The court concluded that the officer should have been aware of the prisoner's risk of suicide. The court stated that the officer went to the observation cell to pick up the prisoner, saw that he was under a suicide watch, had a tearaway gown on, and had him change into street clothes prior to the transport. The court ruled these factors supported the requisite knowledge that the prisoner was at an excessive risk of suicide, underscoring the claim of deliberate indifference.

In *Conn v. City of Reno* (2010), officers transporting a woman to a jail for civil protective custody witnessed her attempting to choke herself by wrapping a seatbelt around her neck, screaming that they should kill her or she would take her own life. They failed to either take her to a hospital or report the incident to jail personnel. She was released and then detained again. During the second detention, which was less than 48 hours after the suicide threat, she hung herself in her cell. The court rejected summary judgment and found that the officers acted with deliberate indifference to the decedent's serious medical needs so that they were not entitled to qualified immunity. The city was also liable for failing to adequately train the officers on suicide prevention and reporting, but claims relating to alleged failure to discipline the individual officers were rejected.

In *Minix v. Canareccii* (2010), a mental health patient at a state hospital was on leave from the hospital to attend a family funeral, and was arrested for theft and battery after getting separated from his mother. During booking at the jail, officers noticed that he had laceration scars on his neck and wrist, and he admitted having attempted suicide during the previous month. The detention officer arranged for him to continue receiving medication he was taking to inhibit suicidal thoughts. He was placed on suicide watch for a time, but taken off it after he allegedly denied having suicidal thoughts. He was again placed on suicide watch after refusing his medication, and after a blade was found missing from his razor. When he was later again taken off suicide watch, he used a bed sheet to hang himself from the bars on his cell window. The decedent's estate filed a § 1983 lawsuit claiming deliberate indifference to his mental health needs. The court granted summary judgment for defendant jail officials, as the evidence presented was insufficient to meet the standard of deliberate indifference to the risk of suicide.

Summary

Two emerging areas of liability that have increased allegations of wrongful deaths have been described. Sudden deaths in police custody are a rare occurrence after a use-of-force confrontation, but the liability potential for a wrongful death can be critical. Law enforcement officers and administrators have many responsibilities for individuals in their custody. The police are not absolute guarantors of health, but they do owe a duty of care to arrestees in their custody who otherwise cannot care for themselves.

Based on case analysis, police agencies can insulate their officers and themselves from liability by taking a proactive stance in considering the following policy and training recommendations. Because these arrest situations allege excessive force, administrators are encouraged to first review and revise their use-of-force policy to ensure that officers are directed in using "objectively reasonable" force in accordance with the *Graham* holding. It should direct officers in the proper escalation and de-escalation in a variety of physical force techniques and equipment based on the arrestee's behavior. Included in the force policy should be a section devoted to the use of authorized restraints. This section should direct officers in using department-issued restraint devices that specify how to further restrain combative and "special needs" detainees. Because in a significant number of these incidents more than three officers respond, officers should receive training in "multiple officer response" or "team-takedown response." Such training can assist officers in using physical control techniques and force equipment more efficiently when faced with a violent encounter (Ross & Chan, 2006; Ross, 2010; Hall, McHale, Kader, Stewart, MacCarthy, & Fick, 2012).

A second area of concern is transportation. Preliminary questions that need to be addressed are: Under what circumstances will police transport a maximally restrained person? How many officers should be involved? What type of vehicle will be used? If police do not transport, who will? These issues need to be examined and addressed pursuant to policy prior to the need arising. Procedures that direct officers in responding to the mentally or chemically impaired (special needs detainees) should be revised or developed. This policy should be structured within state standards for dealing with detainees who require medical or psychiatric treatment or hospitalization. The policy should direct officers in how to respond to this population, when to summon backup or a supervisor, when to summon medical or psychological assistance, and to what facility they should be transported. Taking proper precautions with at-risk detainees begins with policies that direct officers in justifiable decisions when encountering such individuals.

In compliance with the *Canton* decision, administrators are also encouraged to provide officers with regular training relevant to the policies identified. In many jurisdictions, police frequently encounter "special needs" individuals. As shown in the case examples, regular training should be provided in assisting officers in responding to "special needs" individuals, in recognizing behaviors and symptoms associated with in-custody deaths, such as the mentally ill and intoxicated. Officers should routinely receive realistic training that addresses skill competency and use-of-force decisionmaking in all authorized physical control tactics and restraint equipment (Ross & Jones, 1996; Ross, 2011). Further training should be regularly provided to officers in how to assess the medical/psychiatric condition of detainees, monitoring needs of detainees in restraints, and when to summon medical assistance for detainees involved in a violent force confrontation. Administrators are encouraged to require officers to maintain certification in first aid and CPR in order to help them recognize and respond to medical emergencies. Finally, periodic training that addresses the critical issues to be contained in an incident report should be provided.

If an agency experiences an in-custody death or suicide, the administrator should immediately contact his or her risk manager and legal counsel, and ensure that a thorough internal investigation is conducted. Using an independent agency to conduct the investigation should be considered. Moreover, the administrator is encouraged to immediately initiate an ongoing file by compiling all relevant policies, officer incident reports, training files of personnel involved, autopsy report, attending physician reports, emergency medical personnel reports, investigation reports, statements of all witnesses, photos and video of the incident scene, retrieving/saving all taped radio communications throughout the incident, in order to develop a timeline of the incident.

Liability concerns regarding custodial suicides were also discussed. The standard of review in these cases is whether there was a strong likelihood that the detainee or prisoner would commit suicide and whether officials were deliberately indifferent to a substantially known risk of harm. It is common for the plaintiff to allege that the decedent fit a suicide profile and that officers failed to recognize such symptoms.

While a "typical" suicide profile is nonexistent, the review of cases illustrates that detention agencies are likely to prevail in this type of litigation when proactive measures have been instituted and followed by agency personnel. It is important to underscore that maintaining a detention or correctional facility requires an understanding of prisoner behavior. Guidelines that direct officers in the performance of their duties in order to provide an orderly and safe operation should be developed. Not all custodial suicides can be prevented, but many can be averted through proper planning and careful adherence to a system of fundamental correctional strategies. This system should include a twofold approach: policy development and training. When developing a suicide awareness policy, administrators are encouraged to consider the following components: intake screening/assessment procedures for all prisoners, proper classification/ housing of prisoners, levels of supervision and monitoring protocols, documentation of security checks, communication between detention officers and health care workers, when to summon health care professionals, detailed reporting, investigation of a suicide, and debriefing of facility personnel (Ross, 2010). Administrators should ensure that all directives comply with state minimum standards and court decisions for confining prisoners.

Moreover, all personnel having contact with prisoners should be trained in policies that direct decisions in responding to and supervising prisoners. Training should involve recognizing and understanding human behavior and common prisoner behavior, particularly toward understanding behavior of the mentally impaired and the chemically addicted.

References

Barrineau, H. E., III (1994). *Civil liability in criminal justice* (2nd ed.). Cincinnati, OH: Anderson Publishing Co.

Burch, A. (2011). *Arrest related deaths: statistical tables.* Washington, DC: Bureau of Justice Statistics, Department of Justice. 1–43.

Chan, T., Vilke, G., Neuman, T., & Clausen, J. (1997). Restraint position asphyxia. *Annals of Emergency Medicine, 30,* 578–586.

Chan, T., Neuman, T., Clausen, J., Eisele, J., & Vilke, G. (2004). Weight force during prone restraint and respiratory function. *The American Journal of Forensic Medicine and Pathology, 25,* 185–289.

Cohen, F. (1992). Liability for custodial suicide: the information base requirements. *Jail Suicide Update, 4,* 1–9.

del Carmen, R. V. (1991). *Civil liabilities in American policing: a text for law enforcement personnel.* Englewood Cliffs, NJ: Brady.

del Carmen, R. V., & Kappeler, V. (1991). Municipal and police agencies as defendants: liability for official policy and custom. *American Journal of Police, 10,* 1–17.

DiMaio, T. G., & DiMaio, J. M. (2006). *Excited delirium syndrome: cause of death and prevention.* Boca Raton, FL: CRC Press.

Hall, C. A., McHale, A., Kader, A. S., Stewart, L. C., MacCarthy, C. S., & Fick., G. H. (2012). Incidence and outcome of prone positioning following police use of force in a prospective, consecutive cohort of subjects. *Journal of Forensic and Legal Medicine, 10,* 1–7.

Hayes, L. M. (1983). And darkness closes in . . . a national study of jail suicides. *Criminal Justice and Behavior, 10,* 461–484.

Hayes, L. M. (1989). National study of jail suicides: seven years later. *Psychiatric Quarterly, 60,* 7–29.

Hougland, S., Mesloh, C., & Henych, M. (2005). Use of force, civil litigation, and the taser: one agency's experience. *FBI Law Enforcement Bulletin, March,* 24–30.

Hughes, E. (2011). *A special panel review of excited delirium: special report.* Washington, DC: Weapons and Protective Systems, and Technologies Center, National Institute of Justice.

Kappeler, V. (1997). *Critical issues in police civil liability* (2nd ed.). Prospect Heights, IL: Waveland Press, Inc.

Kappeler, V., Vaughn, M., & del Carmen, R. V. (1991). Death in detention: an analysis of police liability for negligent failure to prevent suicide. *Journal of Criminal Justice, 19,* 381–393.

Karch, S. B. (2006). *A brief history of cocaine* (2nd ed.). Boca Raton, FL: CRC Press.

Kelley, M. F., & Linthicum, G. (2006). Mortality in jails and prisons. In M. Pursis (Ed.), *Clinical practice in correctional medicine* (2nd ed.). Chicago, IL: Mosby Publisher.

Kennedy, D. B., & Homant, R. J. (1988). Predicting custodial suicides: problems with the use of profiles. *Justice Quarterly, 5,* 441–456.

Laub, J. (2011, May). *Study of deaths after electro muscular disruption.* Washington, DC: National Institute of Justice, U.S. Department of Justice. 1–74.

Michalewicz, B. A., Chan, T. C., Vilke, G. M., Levy, S. S., Neuman, T. S., & Kolkhurst, F. W. (2007). Ventilatory and metabolic demands during aggressive physical restraint in health adults. *Journal of Forensic Science, 52,* 171–175.

Noonan, M. E., & Carson, E. A. (2011, December). *Prison and jail deaths in custody: 2000–2009, statistical tables.* Washington, DC: Bureau of Justice Statistics, Department of Justice. 1–34.

Plitt, E. A. (1997). *Police civil liability and the defense of citizen misconduct.* Chicago, IL: Americans for Effective Law Enforcement.

Raba, J. (1998). Mortality in prisons and jails. In M. Pulsi (Ed.), *Clinical practice in correctional medicine.* St. Louis, MO: Mosby, Inc.

Rold, W. J. (1998). Legal considerations in the delivery of health care services in prisons and jails. In M. Pulsi (Ed.), *Clinical practice in correctional medicine*. St. Louis, MO: Mosby, Inc.

Ross, D. L. (2001). Assessing in-custody deaths in jails. *American Jails, November/December*, 13–25.

Ross, D. L. (2007). An analysis of civil liability and sudden in custody deaths in policing. *Law Enforcement Executive Forum, 7*, 7–30.

Ross, D. L. (2010). The use of force, science, liability, and restraint asphyxia. *Journal of Law Enforcement Executive Forum, 10*(1), 35–56.

Ross, D. L. (2010, March/April). Liability trends of custodial suicides. *American Jails*, 37–47.

Ross, D. L. (2011, December). Liability for failure to train and police use of force. *Special Edition Monograph of the Journal of Law Enforcement Forum*, 59–79.

Ross, D. L., & Chan, T. C. (2006). *Sudden deaths in custody*. Totowa, NJ: Humana Press.

Ross, D. L., & Jones., M. (1996). Frequency of training in less-than-lethal force tactics and weapons: results of a two-state study. *Journal of Contemporary Criminal Justice, 12*, 250–263.

Scarfile, S. L. (2006). Issues in the third circuit: deliberate indifference or not: that is the question in the third circuit jail suicide case of *Woloszyn v. Lawrence County*. *Villanova Law Review, 51*, 1133–1154.

Silver, I. (2010). *Police civil liability*. New York, NY: Matthew Bender & Co.

Vilke, G., DeBard, M. L., Chan, T. C., Ho, J. D., Dawues, D. M., Hall, C., et al. (2011). Excited Delirium (EXDS): defining based on a review of the literature. *The Journal of Emergency Medicine, 4*, 1–9.

Winfree, L. T. (1985). Rethinking American jail death rates: a comparison of national mortality and jail mortality: 1978, 1983. *Policies Studies Review, 7*, 641–659.

14

Conclusions: Shifting
Directions in Civil Litigation

OVERVIEW

With the decisions by the United States Supreme Court in *Monroe v. Pape* (1961) and *Monell v. Department of Social Services* (1978), § 1983 was resuscitated and expanded. These two decisions have had a profound impact on liability in criminal justice. Since these decisions, numerous cases have been filed alleging that police and correctional personnel misused their authority, which has underscored varying types of liability claims over 40 years. Regardless of position or rank, criminal justice practitioners remain vulnerable to civil litigation and, based on past trends of § 1983 lawsuits, nothing indicates that its use will decline in the future. What appears to be occurring in the civil litigation landscape are shifts in the use of § 1983 and civil lawsuits against public officials.

The law, civil liability, and American jurisprudence are dynamic. As societal conditions change, so do our laws. These changes manifest shifts in legal thinking, establishment of legal standards, and application of these standards to activities of personnel in the criminal justice system. This text has illustrated emerging areas that place criminal justice personnel today in a more vulnerable position of civil liability than in the 1960s. In this chapter, several apparent shifts in civil litigation in criminal justice agencies are addressed in order for practitioners to consider the best possible ways to avert future legal claims.

Cases

The United States Supreme Court's decisions in *Monroe* and *Monell* have assisted in paving the way for line officers and administrators to be held liable under § 1983. Although § 1983 was enacted in 1871, it lay dormant for many years until a shift in the judicial scrutiny of official misconduct changed the interpretation and application of the statute. Civil liability in criminal justice is still evolving, particularly in areas of supervisory and administrative issues. If the past can predict the future, more shifts and expansions in areas already litigated should be expected, as well as new decisions in emerging areas.

Court decisions have established new or significantly expanded legal standards of review in civil liability. Three examples are worth noting. First, in less than 20 years, a shift in case precedents has been noted in the type of immunity granted to public officials. Today, criminal justice personnel possess qualified immunity. Qualified immunity is considered an affirmative defense when allegations are made (*Harlow v. Fitzgerald*, 1982).

Second, a common standard the U.S. Supreme Court has established to review numerous criminal justice topics is that of "deliberate indifference." This standard is applied to police and correctional activities. Since it was first applied in *Estelle v. Gamble* (1976), the Court has expanded its use to include such correctional issues as: conditions of confinement (*Wilson v. Seiter*, 1991), failure to protect (*Farmer v. Brennan*, 1994), and environmental tobacco smoke (*Helling v. McKinney*, 1993). It has also incorporated the standard to the Americans with Disabilities Act with application to prisoners (*Pennsylvania Dep't of Corrections v. Yeskey*, 1998).

In policing and corrections, the Court has shifted the standard by further expanding it to include administrative liability. The Court in *City of Canton v. Harris* (1989) held that a government entity may be held liable for failing to train its employees. This shift has spawned numerous lawsuits and is the foremost claim asserted against administrators today. The standard has also been applied to hiring practices of administrators (*Board of County Commissioners of Bryan County v. Brown*, 1997). Clearly, the standard of deliberate indifference, through the Court's expansion to correctional and police activities, provides a major example of the shift in judicial thinking of applying case precedents. The standard has been applied to Eighth, Fourth, and Fourteenth Amendment issues, making it one of the most common standards in which the courts review actions of criminal justice personnel.

Third, from 1985 to 1992, the Court shifted in its legal thinking in excessive force litigation. From 1973 to 1985, *Johnson v. Glick* (1973) was the precedent-setting case regarding the use of force, although not a Supreme Court decision. The standard of review was applied to issues pertaining to police and correctional officer use of force. The standard used by the courts to examine use-of-force issues at that time was the "shocks the conscience" test. In 1985 the U.S. Supreme Court significantly shifted the use-of-force analysis by separating lethal force decisions by police officers in *Tennessee v. Garner* (1985) and lethal force used in corrections during riots in *Whitley v. Albers* (1986). These two cases marked the first time the Court addressed use-of-force issues and also made a distinction between using lethal force in police situations and using lethal force in corrections.

In *Graham v. Connor* (1989), the Supreme Court made a further shift in assessing force issues by holding that all police use of force is to be considered a Fourth Amendment seizure. The Court established specific standards by which use-of-force cases are examined. The Court further established the "objective reasonableness" standard for analyzing all police use of force. Three years later, another shift in use-of-force cases in corrections took place in the Court's decision in *Hudson v. McMillian* (1992). The Court ruled that serious injury to a prisoner is not to be considered when correctional officers use force. The case established a new standard of review when considering claims of excessive force that may violate the cruel and unusual punishment clause of the Eight Amendment when the force is used maliciously and sadistically for the purpose of causing harm.

These four cases again illustrate a shift in the Court's thinking about civil liability in criminal justice in the use-of-force area. In a short period (1985 to 1992), the Court shifted its former rationale about use-of-force issues and established two decisions with guidelines that specify the legal requirements of using force in corrections and in policing. Two of the cases deal with force used under the Fourth Amendment and two deal with force used under the Eighth Amendment. The Court has clearly bifurcated the use of force by criminal justice personnel. As a result, numerous claims have been filed by citizens or prisoners asserting that their constitutional rights have been violated through the use of excessive force by officers.

Seeking qualified immunity in civil actions is an important component for defendants when asking a court to consider granting summary judgment. The United States Supreme Court's decision in *Brosseau v. Haugen* (2004) further clarified the application of qualified immunity. The Court underscored the two-part test established in their decision in *Saucier v. Katz* (2001) by noting that qualified immunity operates "to protect officers from liability." If an officer had fair notice that his or her conduct is unlawful and is clearly established through case law decisions, that conduct must be viewed within the context of the law and the facts and circumstances that faced the officer at the time of the conduct. If the law is not clearly established at the time of the officer's conduct, the officer should not be subject to liability. Thus, qualified immunity would be granted to the defendant officer or agency. The Court noted that while *Garner* and *Graham* provide standards of review when assessing claims of excessive force, the standard is general and may apply to varying circumstances. According to the Court, the shooting in the *Brosseau* case did not "clearly" underscore the established law of shooting a "fleeing suspect in a vehicle" that would preclude granting qualified immunity. The Court held that the shooting is far from the obvious one where *Graham* and *Garner* alone offer a basis for such a decision. Because the plaintiff could only show a "handful" of cases relevant to the shooting, the Court held that the cases by no means "clearly established" that Brosseau's conduct violated the Fourth Amendment rights of Haugen. Qualified immunity applies to the discretionary functions of the officers and is available on an individual basis. It is an affirmative defense made by an officer through his or her counsel. As these cases show, the courts will make their decisions on a case-by-case basis. The key to qualified immunity includes being proactive prior to performing the duties of a police or correctional officer.

While the Supreme Court provided more clarification regarding granting qualified immunity, it also made clear that an officer will be held liable when he or she knowingly violates the law. The Court's decision in *Groh v. Ramirez* (2004) firmly reminds officers to follow the law while performing their sworn duties. When asserting a claim of qualified immunity, the officer must show that he or she was following the established law at the time of the incident. This suggests that officers actually must be knowledgeable of state law and constitutional law. Officers must show that their actions were reasonable under the circumstances and that a reasonably trained officer would know that the conduct was constitutional or unconstitutional, depending on the situation. These factors should be addressed in agency policy and procedures, as demonstrated in the *Groh* decision. Officers need to train on a regular basis and be evaluated on their performance to ensure that they are complying with policy and that their conduct conforms to constitutional mandates. When performing their sworn duties, officers should clearly and completely document their actions and rationale for actions taken. Adhering to these elements will assist in being granted qualified immunity with more success.

The Court's ruling in *Pearson v. Callahan* (2009) provides clarification and a slight shift in considering the process and procedures involved in determining qualified immunity. In its decision the Court maintained that the two-step procedure outlined in *Saucier v. Katz* (2001) should not be regarded as an inflexible requirement. The Court explained that it, as well as lower courts, have experienced the shortcomings associated with the procedures, such as a lack of judicial resources and litigating parties' expenditures of costs and additional resources during the discovery phase due to delays. Further application of the *Saucier* rule also made it difficult for affected parties to obtain appellate review of constitutional decisions having a serious prospective effect on their operations. The Court stated that *stare decisis* did not prohibit them from determining whether the Saucier decision should be re-evaluated or modified. Revisiting precedent is appropriate when a departure would not disturb a prior holding. After all, the Court held, the precedent was judge-made and adopted to improve court operations, not a statute promulgated by Congress. Thus, the Court still recognizes that the procedure in *Saucier* is frequently beneficial; but it should, however, no longer be considered as mandatory in all cases.

In *Messerschmidt v. Millender* (2012), the Court further clarified what factors are necessary in securing a search warrant and how qualified immunity is applied in civil litigation. The Court found that it was reasonable when an officer, seeking a search warrant, relied on his experience, supporting the request with articulable rationale with detailed facts, and having the petition reviewed by supervisors and a prosecutor as proper conduct underscored in the law. Such conduct entitled the officer to qualified immunity. The case should be read in its entirety in order to review the salient principles of law and to appropriately apply them.

The Court's decision in *Town of Castle Rock v. Gonzales* (2005) underscores its previous position that the constitution does not require a duty of the government to protect a third party from harm and the ability of the states to enact legislation that recognizes such protection as a matter of state law. The Court stated: "in light of today's decision and that in *DeShaney*, the benefit that a third party may receive from having someone else arrested for a crime generally does not trigger protection under the Due Process Clause, neither in its procedural nor in its 'substantive' manifestations. This result reflects our continuing reluctance to treat the Fourth Amendment as 'a font of tort law.'" Because this decision provides further deference to law enforcement responses regarding protective orders, it may be overlooked by the police and administrators. Rather, the decision should serve as a reminder to law enforcement to ensure that a system is in place that directs officers in the proper response in enforcing protection orders. Thus, the application of this decision generally means that: (1) officers must be familiar with their state's statutes regarding the enforcement of restraining orders; (2) law enforcement generally has no constitutional duty to protect citizens from third-party harm; (3) a duty may be found if the police have "created" or "enhanced" the danger to an individual, and (4) a duty to protect may be more likely found in situations in which officers have an individual in custody against his or her will and the person is harmed. Review of the law, procedural practices, and revisions of policies is recommended in light of this decision.

The Court's ruling in *Scott v. Harris* (2007) provides another example of a shift in assessing liability emerging from police pursuits. In making its decision the Court was aided by the video of the incident, which clearly showed that Harris's reckless driving and eluding the officer created an imminent risk of harm to the community and the officer. With such danger created, the Court adopted the position that such a review of police actions in pursuits is best framed within the objective reasonableness standard in accordance with the Fourth Amendment. The Court found that Scott's use of the Precision Intervention Maneuver (PIT) was reasonable under the totality of circumstances.

This decision by the Court is a marked shift from prior decisions regarding police pursuits, as the justices applied the *Graham* standard to the facts in *Scott*. The Court reasoned that because Harris posed a danger to the community, balancing the need for Scott to stop Harris's reckless actions justified the use of the PIT maneuver. For the Court, all that mattered was whether Scott's actions were reasonable. The Court ruled that a police officer's attempt to terminate a dangerous high-speed chase that threatens the lives of innocent bystanders does not violate the Fourth Amendment, even when it places the fleeing motorist at risk of serious injury or death. The Court focused on the dangerousness-of-flight component created by Harris in assessing Scott's response in determining that it was objectively reasonable and they were not prepared to reward reckless behavior without impunity.

The *Scott* decision underscores the objectively reasonable standard. The rule applied by the court in police pursuit incidents examines the risk of dangerousness of flight posed by the eluding suspect and whether the officer's actions were reasonable irrespective of the incident. In reviewing the reasonableness of the officer's actions, courts will balance the government's interest in protecting the public from the risk of harm posed by the suspect. This decision is in deference to law enforcement officials but does not provide a special license to make decisions recklessly about determining the types of techniques to apply in terminating a high-speed pursuit. Policies and procedures in response to suspect flight and officers' response in pursuits through appropriate techniques should be addressed in the policy followed by training.

The Court's decision in *Sykes v. United States* (2011) provides further clarification on its evolving concern of the dangerousness of police pursuits. The decision defines a suspect fleeing in a vehicle from police as a violent crime. This decision enlarges police pursuits, underscoring the dangerous task officers confront when involved in high speed pursuit. Agency policy revisions should be made in accordance with the decision and officers should receive ongoing training in this high-profile, dangerous, and risky responsibility.

These shifts in Supreme Court decisions underscore the fact that the law is constantly changing and legal standards are continually expanded and revised. The shifts also illustrate the need for practitioners to keep abreast of changes in the law in order to perform their responsibilities in compliance with legal standards.

Administrative Issues

Officers as Plaintiffs

One of the most notable shifts in civil liability during the 1990s was the increase in the number of officers who filed civil actions against their own departments (MacMannus, 1997). Administrators have perhaps become accustomed to citizens and prisoners filing legal actions against the department, but now must be aware of the emerging area of officers bringing suit against the department for a variety of reasons. The most common area of litigation involves employee-initiated lawsuits alleging sexual harassment (Vaughn et al., 2001; Ross, 2000; Worrall & Gutierrez, 1999). Vaughn, Cooper, and del Carmen (2001) reported that Texas chiefs revealed that 12 percent of the civil litigation in 1998 through 2000 was filed by their own employees and that employees prevailed in 41 percent of the cases. Actions were filed for sexual harassment/sex discrimination, disciplinary actions, employment discrimination (hiring, promotion, and discharge), overtime/compensation/pay issues, First Amendment issues (speech/political rights/religion), race discrimination/reverse discrimination, disability discrimination, and employee search/privacy/Fourth Amendment issues. From 2000 to 2008, trends in officer-initiated lawsuits have been focused on sexual harassment allegations, due process claims stemming from wrongful discharges, claims surrounding the ADA, and First Amendment issues.

The Texas chiefs' study revealed that many of the employee-initiated lawsuits were settled out of court, and average awards were higher than citizens' awards settled out of court. Ross reported that not only do employee-initiated lawsuits emerge from sexual harassment claims, as well as other areas cited, but officers commonly file civil lawsuits against administrators for failing to train in various dimensions of the job and failure to train to competency levels in using job-related equipment.

An increase in officers as plaintiffs should direct administrators in seeking better practices and methods for managing personnel. Previous research (Scogin & Brodsky, 1991) reveals, and Texas chiefs agree in their survey, that treating people fairly is a significant approach to reducing lawsuits. Other methods include better screening of applicants, better supervision, more and better training, early identification of problem officers, following agency policies, and holding officers accountable (Vaughn et al., 2001).

In a series of United States Supreme Court decisions, the Court addressed administrative liability issues, which were presented in Chapters 6, 7, and 9. Administrators are encouraged to fully review *City of Ontario, CA v. Quon* (2010), *Connick v. Thompson* (2011), *Los Angeles Co. v. Humphries* (2010), *Ashcroft v. Iqbal* (2009), and *Straub v. Proctor Hospital* (2011). These decisions generally provide deference to administrators in the areas of supervision, training, and policy and procedures. They further provide an analysis of management practices and guide administrators in shoring up management practices in order to more effectively supervise subordinate personnel and enhance agency operations. In addressing the managerial components expressed in these decisions, the Court's rulings assist in insulating administrators from liability when they enact, implement, and enforce policies that direct the officers within legal boundaries.

Department of Justice Investigations

With the passage of the Crime Bill in 1994, §§ 14141–14142 of Title 42, United States Code, the Department of Justice (DOJ) was authorized to investigate patterns or practices of misconduct in local police departments and requires the collection of statistics on "police abuse." The statute grants authority to the DOJ to file a civil action on behalf of citizens to obtain declaratory or equitable relief.

Arguably, Section 14141 is one of most significant measures that affects police reform, management practices, and accountability. The DOJ has conducted 22 investigations since 1996, resulting in seven consent decrees and six memorandums of agreement. One case was dropped by the DOJ. Investigations are ongoing in eight agencies (2006). This marks a significant shift in federal oversight of local, state, and county police agencies.

Passage of this legislation has ushered policing into a new era in which the federal government can dictate sweeping changes in the policies and practices of a law enforcement agency. This provision has significantly affected law enforcement operations. In many cases, a revamping of the entire system of police practices has occurred. Mandated changes in reporting, recording, and tracking all aspects of officer and citizen interactions are required in the consent decrees. Revisions in officer performance evaluations and the department's disciplinary system have in most cases been overhauled as well. Start-up and maintenance costs required of a department in order to comply with the stipulations of the consent decree are enormous.

While police accountability is a legitimate concern, it remains debatable whether § 14141 has been successful in achieving police reform or will bring reform to law enforcement. Since 1999, Department of Justice investigations in accordance with the statute continue to assess patterns and practices of alleged constitutional violations in many police agencies. Investigations are more likely to end in a settlement agreement. Moreover, the DOJ is performing investigations of alleged criminal conduct of criminal justice personnel in accordance with § 242 with more regularity. Since 1997, this statute has been used with more regularity and since 2003 the number of investigations has slightly increased. Conviction rates are high and the disposition of these convictions result in a significant number of prison sentences.

Rather than speculate about the utility of the statute, based on the past trends of its implementation, police administrators should focus on instilling proactive measures that can minimize the likelihood that the federal government will initiate such an investigation in their department. This provision has opened an additional door of liability concern for administrators and officers alike. Police administrators are encouraged to read the stipulations contained within these consent decrees to learn valuable lessons of how to avoid such investigations (see the Justice Department's Web site: www.doj.gov.). Further, administrators are encouraged to regularly assess the policies and practices in the department with respect to hiring practices, training practices, citizen complaint policies, use-of-force training, tracking of use-of-force incidents and traffic stops, practices involving searches and seizures, responding to calls for service, remediation of problem officers, supervising officers, internal affairs investigations, and disciplinary procedures. This will show the community that the department is seeking to increase the organizational effectiveness of the department and is taking proactive measures to avert claims of tolerating a culture of abusing the constitutional rights of citizens. To that end, administrators are encouraged to consider the risk management suggestions identified below and incorporate them into their management system as warranted.

Adopting Risk Management Strategies

Despite the upward trends in civil liability against criminal justice personnel since the 1960s and recognizing that filing of lawsuits will not be declining anytime soon, studies reveal that public officials win more frequently, and that trend is continuing to shift to higher percentages over time (Ross, 1997, 2000; Vaughn et al., 2001). In response to the ongoing potential of civil litigation, many police agencies have adopted proactive measures to reduce the number of lawsuits and place themselves in a better position to defend a civil action. This is directly related to an administrator's management philosophy. This does not entirely imply that liability is solely and directly linked to the management or leadership style of an administrator, but there are facets that link the administrator to liability by his or her practices and policies.

For example, a noteworthy shift by many police agencies since the 1980s is the adoption of some version of "Community-Oriented Policing" (COP). Adopting COP has forced a change in management approaches and policies, and has expanded officer participation in organizational goal setting and decisionmaking at the street level. Tremendous strides have been made in reducing crime rates in many jurisdictions in the United States. As a result, COP has been touted as a major innovation in policing and highly recommended by many criminal justice scholars.

Implementing COP strategies should result in the decline of civil liability over time. Studies that specifically examine the relationship of COP and civil liability are limited. Worrall and Marien (1998), however, hypothesize that due to COP's philosophy of expanding the officer's street-level decisionmaking and advocating more creative risk-taking in solving problems, the risk of civil liability is likely to increase. They theorize that the more risk-taking officers engage in, the greater the chances of civil liability exposure. In theory, COP embraces internal and external changes in managing the police organization and providing police services to the community. Many COP programs are implemented to modernize the agency, change departmental behavior and operations, and change policies and practices, while delegating to officers more input and decision making authority. Community-oriented policing fully recommends developing partnerships in the community intended to improve police-citizen relationships. If these ideals are incorporated with proper guidelines such as effective supervisory practices; training officers in COP; and implementing, monitoring, and evaluating such practices; liability should be reduced. This should be a fertile ground for future scholarly research and practitioner assessment.

Community-oriented policing is not necessarily a panacea for civil liability in the departments that implement it. A shift in management approaches through COP may create one net outcome in the reduction of civil lawsuits. While studies in this area are limited, the literature recommends that administrators apply risk management strategies to varying management styles that can assist in reducing the number of civil lawsuits (Gallagher, 1990; Collins, 1993; Alpert & Smith, 1994; Katz, 1995; Parsons, 1997; Ross & Bodapoti, 2006; Ryan, 2008).

Regardless of whether the criminal justice agency is police or correctional in nature, adopting a system of risk management within a management philosophy can reduce exposure to civil liability and is a proactive management strategy to avoid liability. Risk management identifies problem areas within an organization and addresses the situation through risk control strategies. In light of the ongoing nature of civil litigation and varying shifts in liability, administrators should consider developing risk management approaches as a method for reducing their exposure to liability. A job assessment that reviews the frequency of critical job tasks by examining calls for service, citizen complaints, incident reports, and past litigation and case decisions is an important step in initiating a risk management program. Once a job assessment is performed, job descriptions, as well as policies and procedures, can be revised.

A critical component of implementing a risk management program is to ensure that all policies are current. Policy formulation and effective supervisory implementation can provide a viable strategy in controlling police civil liability (McCormick, 1996; Ryan, 2008). Policies can serve as guides for officer actions in the field, and when properly enforced by supervisors, assist in keeping officers accountable for proper conduct. While policies cannot be written for every conceivable encounter an officer might face, they should provide a range of options for officers to consider when responding to a variety of situations. Implementing proactive risk management strategies assists in reducing the magnitude of the inverse relationship that exists in criminal justice agencies; that is, when an agency increases the professionalism of the agency, it serves to lower or reduce the opportunities for liability. Criminal justice practitioners should work on instituting best practices in order to place themselves in the best position to successfully defend a civil lawsuit.

Risk Management and Officer Training

Since the *City of Canton v. Harris* (1989) decision, police and correctional administrators have frequently been cited for failing to train their employees. This is the most frequently cited area when a citizen or prisoner files a claim against administrators, followed by failure to supervise and failure to direct officers (Ross, 2000; Archbold et al., 2006). Kappeler, Kappeler, and del Carmen (1996) reported that from 1978 to 1994, claims of failure to train were won by administrators in only 45 percent of the cases. Ross revealed that from 1989 to 1999, a marked shift took place in favor of administrators in 10 commonly litigated areas in policing. During the 10-year review, administrators prevailed in 64 percent of the claims. While this indicates a significant shift in the winning margin, employees began to file more lawsuits against their departments.

As the trend to prevail in claims increases, criminal justice administrators must remain committed to providing ongoing training for their officers and supervisors. Chapter 7 indicated the 10 most litigated areas in policing and areas in which correctional training should be addressed. These 10 areas identify key topics for training and represent a practical starting point in which regular training should be addressed. Other training topics should include legal issues of arrests, searches, and civil liability of employees, and the constitutional limits of using force. Topics for correctional training should also include prisoner management in housing units, use of force and the use of restraints, verbal skills, report writing, legal and liability aspects of the job, searches and security measures, medical care issues, suicide awareness, classification, critical incident response, supervising special needs populations, and sexual harassment.

An ongoing commitment should also be made to training supervisors. A primary shift in much of the § 1983 litigation since the *Monell* decision is to name the supervisor along with the officer in the lawsuit. There are eight theories of potential supervisory liability, and commonly a plaintiff will assert that supervisory personnel should be held liable for a combination of these theories, such as failure to train, failure to supervise, and failure to discipline. Administrative and supervisory training is therefore critical to organizational operations and reducing civil liability.

Supervisory training is very important for limiting liability. As noted in this chapter and as described throughout the text, new decisions made by the Court create shifts in legal directions establishing the need for ongoing training in civil liability for officers and supervisors.

Supervisors should be trained in proper policy implementation and enforcement, expectations of the job and job descriptions, personnel evaluations, sexual harassment/sex discrimination, hiring and firing practices, officer coaching and counseling, and the agency's progressive disciplinary process.

Training is an administrative function that can enhance employee skills, proficiencies, and decisionmaking. Training is a fundamental component of risk management. It can improve overall organizational effectiveness and is a viable approach to reducing the risk of civil liability.

Liability Shifts in Corrections

Prison Litigation Reform Act

Most notable in correctional § 1983 litigation is the passage of the Prison Litigation Reform Act of 1996 (PLRA) and its impact on prisoner litigation. This act was passed by Congress to reduce the number of frivolous lawsuits filed by prisoners. Since its implementation, a shift in § 1983 prisoner filings has occurred. The number of annual prisoner filings has been reduced by approximately 50 percent since 1996, which indicates that the goal of Congress in passing the legislation has been accomplished. The United States Supreme Court has also determined that it is constitutional to require prisoners to exhaust remedial measures at the institutional level prior to filing a civil lawsuit in its decisions in *Booth v. Churner* (2001) and *Porter v. Nussle* (2002). Both decisions underscore the requirement and trends show that prisoner litigation has been considerably reduced as a result.

A by-product of the PLRA is the increase in prisoners filing habeas corpus petitions regarding sentencing issues and conditions of confinement. For approximately 20 years (1976 to 1997), habeas corpus petitions were rarely used by prisoners due to the increased use of § 1983. Since the PLRA was enacted, the use of writs of habeas corpus has been growing steadily. This shift shows that since 1996 habeas corpus petitions have increased by about 60 percent.

Another trend in corrections is the use of consent decrees as a result of prisoner civil litigation. For more than 30 years, many prisons and local jails have consented out of court to stop or start certain practices. Overcrowding has been a prominent issue that has prompted numerous consent decrees. Most state prison systems and numerous detention facilities have been forced to expand their bed space by building new facilities. This has come at a huge price to taxpayers. The consent decree does not result in a loss when compensatory damages are awarded; rather, the cost is from building new facilities and staffing them with the proper number of personnel. Operating the contemporary correctional facility is a large-budget item despite the fact that monetary damages may be awarded in prisoner litigation.

The PLRA assists in not only reducing the filing of frivolous prisoner lawsuits, but also terminates existing court-ordered consent decrees, unless there are continuing constitutional violations. The PLRA only provides for consent decrees when a court finds "harm" occurring within a facility and may order such a decree to correct such harm. While the PLRA has affected the use of consent decrees, the Civil Rights of Institutionalized Persons Act (CRIPA) allows the DOJ to investigate constitutional deprivations of those confined in varying types of institutions. This should be of concern to correctional officials as prisons, jails, and youthful offender facilities make up about 60 percent of the institutions that have been investigated and/or placed under a consent decree. Enforcement trends of CRIPA show that the DOJ is investigating allegations of abuse of prisoners when it has been shown that there have been a number of repeated blatant constitutional violations. Even so, CRIPA provides another methodology for plaintiff prisoners to bring allegations of constitutional violations against the agency and administrators must be prepared to defend against such claims.

Recognizing that prisoner litigation is comprised of a sizeable amount of civil actions annually, the Court took occasion to reassess the PLRA's requirement for prisoners to exhaust institutional remedies prior to filing a legal action. In *Jones v. Bock* (2007), the Court reiterated its prior holding in *Porter* that there is no question that exhaustion of institutional remedies is mandatory under the PLRA prior to filing a lawsuit. However, the Court held that the lower courts that were requiring a prisoner to demonstrate in their complaint that all institutional remedies had indeed been exhausted need not be cited within a legal complaint. The Court clarified that when a court is presented with a lawsuit with both exhausted and unexhausted claims, the court can allow the exhausted claims to proceed rather than dismissing the entire suit. The Court also ruled that the PLRA did not require a prisoner to name each defendant in his administrative grievance in order to name the defendant in his subsequent lawsuit.

The Court's decision creates a slight shift from prior rulings in accordance with the PLRA, although the core requirement of exhaustion of administrative remedies remains intact. Protocol implications emerge on two levels that correctional officials should recognize. First, the Court's decision strikes down additional court rules that previously exceeded their legitimate authority in managing their court dockets. Second, officials should note that prisoner litigation may proceed more slowly in the system now than in the past, as additional requirements that were once tacked on by the lower courts are lifted. Officials should also note that prisoners are not required to name each defendant in an institutional grievance in order to name a defendant in a subsequent legal action.

In *Florence v. Board of Chosen Freeholders of the County of Burlington* (2012), the Court determined in a 5-to-4 decision that strip-searching all persons at the time of booking in preparation for being housed in the general population, regardless of the charge, was constitutional. While the Court addressed concerns regarding searches at the time of confinement in three prior decisions, the decision in *Florence* marks the first time the Court squarely addressed the issue of strip searches at the time of admission, regardless of the charged offense. The question had been at issue in the lower courts for many years, and their decisions added to the unsettled nature of the topic. This decision is a major shift and change in the way jails and prisons across the country may conduct searches at the time of booking. The Court's decision is in deference to correctional employees, which is clearly underscored by its concern to increase officer safety and institutional security. Based on the decision, commensurate policy changes are recommended followed with training for agency officers in order to fully implement the case decision.

With their holding in *Wilkins v. Gaddy* (2010) the Court did not depart from its decision in *Hudson v. McMillian* (1992) but reaffirmed it. The Court took occasion to clarify the appropriate standard for reviewing a prisoner's claim of excessive force in accordance with the Eighth Amendment. According to the Court, the Fourth Circuit Court of Appeals had deviated from the *Hudson* holding by requiring a prisoner to demonstrate that he or she sustained "a degree" of injury in order to prevail in an excessive force allegation. The Court reiterated as it did in *Hudson*, the shift in the core judicial inquiry is not the "extent of injury" sustained by a prisoner through the use of force, but whether the force used was applied maliciously and sadistically to cause harm. This legal standard, in accordance with the Eighth Amendment, applies when assessing a use of force claim brought by a convicted prisoner.

Sexual Harassment and Sexual Misconduct

An emerging trend in civil litigation in state prisons and detention facilities is claims of sexual harassment. Male supervisors and correctional officers alike are vulnerable to allegations of sexual harassment by female officers, and during the 1990s more allegations were filed and successfully litigated than in previous years. The shift in this litigation brought before lower federal courts prompted the United States Supreme Court to decide three cases that address this issue. While these cases are not criminal justice–related, they apply to all employees and administrative personnel. A system that does not tolerate such behavior, that includes policies and procedures, training, proper investigation, and appropriate discipline, must be in place. Criminal justice administrators should work to ensure that such violations do not occur and respond appropriately should allegations surface.

The Supreme Court has specifically addressed sexual harassment and constructive discharge issues in its decision in *Pennsylvania State Police v. Suders* (2005). This is the first time the Court has addressed an allegation of constructive discharge as it relates to claims of sexual harassment in a criminal justice agency. This reveals that the subject matter of sexual harassment continues to be of prime importance in the workforce, despite the advances in case law, policy changes, and implementation of the law and policy. Further, claims of sexual harassment show the primary area where an officer becomes plaintiff and files legal actions against his or her own department. This case also shows a shift in the theory of sexual harassment claims. With this ruling, it is highly predictable that more claims of constructive discharge will be integrated into allegations of sexual harassment, particularly when the plaintiff has terminated his or her employment due to an alleged hostile environment. Administrators are encouraged to review their current policies and practices as they relate to this important decision.

Sexual misconduct, mostly by male correctional officers with female prisoners, has emerged as a civil liability issue during the past 10 years. A study prompted by Congress and conducted by the General Accounting Office (GAO, 1999) in three state prison systems identified numerous reports and claims of sexual misconduct with female prisoners. Further, two additional state prison systems settled out of court regarding allegations against male officers by female prisoners. More lawsuits can be expected, and administrators and officers should work toward eliminating such behavior.

Officer Performance

Despite the growing trend in filing lawsuits and shifts in civil litigation in criminal justice, officers generally win more often than they lose when named in a civil lawsuit. Lawsuits commonly filed against officers include false arrest and imprisonment, excessive use of force, improper searches and seizures, failure to protect, delay or denial of medical care, and vehicle pursuits. When an officer loses in a civil lawsuit, compensatory and punitive damages may be assessed. This shift in awarding punitive damages by the courts remains intact since the United States Court decision in *Smith v. Wade* (1983). This is important as punitive damages are assessed in particularly egregious situations and for blameworthy conduct outside the scope of the officer's authority. As such, strict compliance with the law is required.

Criminal justice practitioners should regularly review agency policies and procedures and seek out supervisors when questions arise. Officers should keep abreast of changes in the law. Frequent changes are noted with Fourth Amendment issues and routinely include making arrests with or without a warrant, searches and seizures, and false arrest or imprisonment. Changes and shifts in the law frequently occur in corrections with Eighth Amendment issues. Keeping current with legal requirements, performing duties within their mandates, and making sound decisions in compliance with agency policy can reduce the occurrence of civil lawsuits. To assert a successful defense of qualified immunity, officers must demonstrate that they acted within the constraints of the law, their experience, and training.

Officers should also maintain competency in job duties that require physical skills (Siddle, 1997) and operating equipment. A common theme in civil liability involves lawsuits claiming that an officer used excessive force and improperly used his or her baton or handcuffs or sprays. Officers should strive to maintain proficiency and competence in all authorized equipment and control techniques. Whether the officer used reasonable force will be determined on the facts of the case, the officer's perception in using force, and the resistive behaviors of the individual. In use-of-force encounters, officers may have to use varying types of equipment and physical skills. Maintaining proficiency in empty-hand control techniques and other equipment can help to prevent civil lawsuits.

Further research of liability trends of published cases and other sources indicates that claims of police use of excessive force and wrongful deaths rank in the top five most frequent litigated topics (Ross & Bodapoti, 2006; Archbold et al., 2007). Within these categories, two sub-components of case law that are worthy of consideration have emerged. First, the use of varying less-lethal equipment in policing and corrections has shifted the trends in litigation. Since the late 1990s more agencies have been using Tasers and are applying them with more frequency (Farber, 2007; Houghland et al., 2005; Smith et al., 2007). Accompanying the frequent use of the Taser is the corresponding trend of litigation regarding the alleged excessive application. To date, a plaintiff rarely prevails in such claims (Smith et al., 2007).

Further, since the 1990s, correction officials have been using the restraint chair for violent prisoners in jails and prisons with more frequency. Like other applications of equipment, civil lawsuits have been filed by plaintiffs alleging the excessive use of force.

Applications of these two types of force equipment require that officers justify their appropriate use. A review of the extant case law in these areas reveals that corresponding policy, training, and proper field application be implemented. Policy and training should stress under what circumstances the equipment is to be used, that it be used within the manufacturer's specifications, the duration of its use, the type of suspect resistance for its application, how the equipment affects the body, monitoring the person through the use of the equipment, and the potential need for summoning medical personnel to assess the suspect after the use of the equipment.

Second, research of the liability trends of sudden in-custody deaths after a violent confrontation with a suspect reveals that defendant officers and criminal justice agencies prevail by only a slight margin. While the occurrence of a sudden death after violent confrontation is statistically rare, given the number of arrests made by the police where any force is used, such a death will generate a multimillion-dollar lawsuit. A review of the emerging trends of published case decisions over 30 years on the subject reveals that policy and training should address: the use of empty-hand control techniques for controlling violent suspects; less-lethal force equipment use; use of restraints when subduing a violent subject; monitoring the medical condition of the suspect after control; summoning medical personnel as needed; and implementing appropriate transportation strategies. Maintenance of these recommendations by officers and supervisors in these two emerging liability categories can place the criminal justice agency in the best position to defend against a potential civil lawsuit.

Moreover, the decision in *Brian v. McPherson* (2010), where an officer applied a Taser during arrest, notes a full review by criminal justice agency officers and administrators. Although not a Supreme Court decision, and the *Graham v. Connor* (1989) standard remains applicable, the court defines that the use of a Taser is an "intermediate"-level use of force. The decision provides instructive guidance and a slight shift on how the courts will examine allegations of excessive force when using a Taser.

Summary

Shifts in civil litigation require all employees in criminal justice agencies to continually seek methods for complying with court mandates and strategies for reducing the risk of lawsuits. Innovations in management philosophies, technology, risk management approaches, and decisionmaking are all necessary to ensure that civil liability issues are addressed within each agency. The days of adopting a "head in the sand" approach toward civil litigation are outdated, lead to stagnant organizations, and heighten the risk of civil litigation. Administrators and officers must work together to accomplish the mission of the organization while remaining cognizant of legal changes that affect agency operations. In this way, according to Kappeler (1997), "criminal justice executives and officers must begin to monitor shifting judicial philosophies of law enforcement and the responsibility to society while being mindful that today's actions directly affect the future of liability law and their colleagues within the system."

References

Alpert, G. P., & Smith, W. C. (1994). Beyond city limits and into the woods: a brief look at the policy impact of *City of Canton v. Harris* and *Woods v. Ostander. American Journal of Police, 10*, 19–40.

Archbold, C. A., Lytle, D., Manis, J., & Bergeron, L. (2007). Police civil liability incidents that result in litigation: an examination of the causes and costs. *Law Enforcement Executive Forum, 7*, 61–73.

Archbold, C. A., Lytle, D., Weatherall, C., Romero, A., & Baumann, C. (2006). Lawsuits involving the police: a content analysis of newspaper accounts. *Policing: An International Journal of Police Strategies and Management, 29*, 625–642.

Collins, S. C. (1993). Managing liability for municipal law enforcement agencies. *Practicing Law Institute: Litigation and Administrative Practice Course Handbook Series, 490*, 497–508.

Farber, B. J. (2007). Civil liability for use of Tasers, stunguns, and other electronic control devices: Part I. *AELE Monthly Law Journal, 3*, 101–109.

Gallagher, C. P. (1990). Risk management for police administrators. *The Police Chief, 57*, 18–29.

General Accounting Office (1999). Women in prison: sexual misconduct by correctional staff: *Report number GGD-99-104*. Washington, DC: General Accounting Office.

Hougland, C., Mesloh, C., & Henych, M. (2005). Use of force, civil litigation, and the Taser: one agency's experience. *FBI Law Enforcement Bulletin, March*, 24–30.

Kappeler, V. E. (1997). *Critical issues in police civil liability* (2nd ed.). Prospect Heights, IL: Waveland Press, Inc.

Katz, D. M. (1995). County pools seek to form $20 M captive. *National Underwriter, 102*, 11–12.

MacMannus, S. A. (1997). Litigation cost, budget impacts, and cost containment strategies: evidence from California cities. *Police Budgeting and Finance, 17*, 28–47.

McCormick, R. J. (1996). Police perceptions and the norming of institutional corruption. *Police and Society, 6*, 239–256.

Parsons, R. L. (1997). Risk management strategies in policing: *Police administrator's training manual*. Big Rapids, MI: Criminal Justice Institute, Ferris State University.

Ross, D. L. (2000). Emerging trends in police failure to train liability. *Policing: An International Journal of Police Strategies and Management*, 169–193.

Ross, D. L., & Bodapoti, M. (2006). An analysis of the claims, losses, and litigation of law enforcement agencies in Michigan. *Policing: An International Journal of Police Strategies and Management, 29*, 38–57.

Ryan, J. (2008). Managing law enforcement liability risk. *PATC E-Newsletter, Public Agency Training Council*

Scogin, F., & Brodsky, S. L. (1991). Fear of litigation among law enforcement officers. *American Journal of Police, 10*, 41–45.

Siddle, B. K. (1997). *Sharpening the warriors' edge*. Millstadt, IL: PPCT Publications.

Smith, M. R., Petrocelli, M., & Scheer, C. (2007). Excessive force, civil liability, and the Taser in the nation's courts: implications for law enforcement policy and practice. *Policing: An International Journal of Police Strategies and Management, 30*, 398–422.

Vaughn, M. S., Cooper, T. W., & del Carmen, R. V. (2001). Assessing legal liabilities in law enforcement: police chiefs' views. *Crime & Delinquency, 47*, 3–27.

Worrall, J. L., & Gutierrez, R. S. (1999). Professional notes—potential consequences of community-oriented policing for civil liability: is there a dark side to employee empowerment? *Review of Public Personnel Administration, 19*, 61–70.

Worrall, J. L., & Marien, O. (1998). Emerging liability issues in the implementation and adoption of community oriented policing. *Policing: An International Journal of Police Strategies and Management, 21*, 121–136.

Table of Cases

Cases Cited in Chapter 1
Overview of Civil Liability

Cooper v. Pate, 382 F.2d 518 (7th Cir. 1964)
Kesler v. King, 29 F. Supp. 2d 356 (S.D. Tex. 1998)

Cases Cited in Chapter 2
Foundations for Liability

Herman v. County of York, 482 F. Supp. 2d 554 (M.D. Pa. 2007)
O'Guinn v. Lovelock Correctional Center, 502 F.3d 1056 (9th Cir. 2007)
Seremeth v. Board of County Commissioners Frederick County, No. 10-1711 (4th Cir. 2012)
Waller v. City of Danville, 212 F. Supp. 2d 162 (4th Cir. 2007)

Cases Cited in Chapter 3
Civil Liability Under State and Federal Tort Law

Ayers v. O'Brien, 13 NY3d 456 (N.Y. 2009)
Abraham v. Maes, 436 So. 2d 1099 (La. Dist. Ct. App. 1983)
Allen v. City of New York, 480 F. Supp. 2d 689 (S.D.N.Y 2007)
Alfrey v. United States, 276 F. 3d 557 (9th Cir. 2002)
Azure v. City of Billings, 596 P.2d 460 (Mont. 1979)
Baker v. Chaplin, 517 N.W.2d 911 (Minn. 1994)
Becker v. Porter County, WL 500562 (N.D. Ind. 2009)
Bivens v. Six Unknown Federal Narcotics Agents, 403 U.S. 388 (1971)
Bodan v. DeMartin, No. BCo25408 (L.A. Superior Court, 1994)
Boyer v. State, 322 Md. 558, 594 A.2d 121 (1991)
Brown v. Bryan County, Oklahoma, 1410 F.3d 1410 (5th Cir. 1995)
Butterfield v. Forrester, 103 Eng. Rep. 926 (1809)
Byrd v. New York Transit Authority, 568 N.YS.2d 628 (A.D. 1991)
Calogrides v. City of Mobile, 475 So. 2d 560 (Ala. 1985)
Carlin v. Blanchard, 537 So. 2d 303 (La. Dist. Ct. App. 1988)
Carlson v. Green, 446 U.S. 14 (1980)
Carroll v. City of Quincy, 441 F. Supp. 2d 215 (D. Mass. 2006)

Cases Cited in Chapter 4

Civil Liability and Federal Law: Section 1983 Litigation

Alliance to End Repression v. City of Chicago, 561 F. Supp. 537 (N.D. Ill. 1982)

Alyeska Pipeline Service Co. v. Wilderness Society, 421 U.S. 240 (1975)

Benton v. Maryland, 395 U.S. 784 (1969)

Brandon v. Holt, 469 U.S. 464 (1985)

Brawner v. Irvin, 169 F. 694 (C.D. Ga. 1909)

Bynum v. District of Columbia, 412 F. Supp. 2d 73 (D.D.C. 2006)

Cabral v. U.S. Department of Justice, 587 F. 3d 13 (1st Cir. 2009)

Carey v. Pipus, 435 U.S. 247 (1978)

Chapman v. Houston Welfare Rights Organization, 441 U.S. 600 (1979)

Chester v. Beard, 657 F. Supp. 2d 534 (M.D. Pa. 2009)

Daniels v. Williams, 474 U.S. 327 (1986)

Drumgold v. Callahan, 806 F. Supp. 2d 405 (D. Mass. 2011)

Errico v. Township of Howell, 50120 Lexis (D.N.J. 2008)

Franklin v. Aycock, 795 F.2d 1253 (6th Cir. 1986)

Gideon v. Wainwright, 372 U.S. 335 (1962)

Graham v. Richardson, 403 U.S. 365 (1975)

Hensley v. Eckerhart, 461 U.S. 424 (1983)

Hughes v. Rowe, 449 U.S. 5 (1980)

Hutchings v. Corum, 501 F. Supp. 1276 (W.D. Mo. 1980)

Jackson v. Austin, 241 F. Supp. 2d 1313 (D. Kan. 2003)

Kentucky v. Graham, 473 U.S. 159 (1985)

King v. Marci, 993 F.2d 975 (2d Cir. 1993)

Knopp v. Johnson, 712 F. Supp. 571 (W.D. Mich. 1989)

Lewis v. Casey, 518 U.S. 343 (1996)

Limone v. United States, 597 F. Supp. 3d. 79 (1st Cir. 2009)

Los Angeles v. Lyons, 461 U.S. 95 (1983)

Maher v. Gagne, 448 U.S. 122 (1980)

Maine v. Thiboutot, 448 U.S. 1 (1980)

Monell v. Department of Social Services, 436 U.S. 658 (1978)

Monroe v. Pape, 365 U.S. 167 (1961)

Ousley v. Town of Lincoln, 313 F. Supp. 2d 78 (D.R.I. 2004)

Powers v. Lightner, 820 F.2d 818 (7th Cir. 1987)

Screws v. United States, 325 U.S. 91 (1945)

Sick v. Manzanares, 270 F. Supp. 2d 1265 (D. Kan. 2003)

Smith v. Wade, 461 U.S. 30 (1983)

Spell v. McDaniel, 824 F.2d 1380 (4th Cir. 1987)

Robinson v. California, 370 U.S. 660 (1962)

United States v. Classic, 313 U.S. 299 (1941)

West v. Atkins, 108 U.S. 2250 (1988)
Will v. Michigan Department of State Police, 491 U.S. 58 (1989)
Wilson v. Garcia, 471 U.S. 261 (1985)
Wolf v. Colorado, 338 U.S. 25 (1949)
Woodard v. Correctional Medical Services of Illinois, 368 F. 3d 197 (7th Cir. 2004)

Cases Cited in Chapter 5
Defenses to Civil Litigation and Risk Management

Aczel v. Labonia, No. 03-7414 (2d Cir. 2004)
Anderson v. Creighton, 483 U.S. 635 (1987)
Apostol v. Landau, 957 F.2d 339 (7th Cir. 1992)
Bradley v. Fisher, 80 U.S. 335 (1872)
Brisco v. Lahue, 460 U.S. 325 (1983)
Brosseau v. Haugen, 543 U.S. 194 (2004)
Chew v. Gates, 744 F. Supp. 952 (C.D. Cal. 1990)
City of Ontario, CA v. Quon, 560 U.S. ___ (2010)
Cleavinger v. Saxner, 474 U.S. 193 (1985)
Conner v. Alston, 701 F. Supp. 376 (E.D.N.Y. 1988)
Ex parte Young, 209 U.S. 123 (1908)
Forrester v. White, 484 U.S. 219 (1998)
Gomez v. Toledo, 446 U.S. 635 (1980)
Gooden v. Howard County, Maryland, 954 F.2d 960 (4th Cir. 1992)
Groh v. Ramirez, 540 U.S. 551 (2004)
Hans v. Louisiana, 134 U.S. 1 (1890)
Harlow v. Fitzgerald, 457 U.S. 800 (1982)
Jacobs v. Dujmovic, 752 F. Supp. 1516 (D. Colo. 1990)
Los Angeles Co. v. Humphries, 131 U.S. 447 (2010)
Malley v. Briggs, 475 U.S. 335 (1986)
Monell v. Department of Social Services, 436 U.S. 658 (1978)
Pearson et al. v. Callahan, 555 U.S. 751 (2009)
Pierson v. Ray, 386 U.S. 547 (1967)
Procunier v. Navarette, 434 U.S. 555 (1978)
Saucier v. Katz et al., 533 U.S. 194 (2001)
Schwab v. Wood, 767 F. Supp. 574 (D. Del. 1991)
Scheuer v. Rhodes, 416 U.S. 232 (1974)
Supreme Court of Virginia v. Consumers Union, 446 U.S. 719 (1980)
Tarantino v. Baker, 825 F.2d 772 (4th Cir. 1987)
United States v. Clarke, 33 U.S. (8 Pet.) 436 (1834)
United States v. Cancelmo, 64 F.3d 804 (2d Cir. (1995)

Cases Cited in Chapter 6
Administrative and Supervisory Liability

Atchison v. Monroe Municipal Fire and Police Civil Service Board, WL 1677744 (La. Court of Appeals, 2011).

Ashcroft v. Iqbal, 566 U.S. 662 (2009)

Atchinson v. D.C., 73 F.3d 418 (D.C. Cir. 1996)

Bastia v. Rodriguez, 702 F.2d 393 (2d Cir. 1983)

Beck v. City of Pittsburgh, 89 F.3d 966 (3d Cir. 1996)

Bell v. City of Miami, 733 F. Supp. 1475 (N.D. Fla. 1990)

Benavides v. County of Wilson, 955 F.2d 968 (5th Cir. 1992)

Bivens v. Six Unknown Fed. Narcotics Agents, 403 U.S. 388 (1971)

Board of County Commissioners of Bryan County v. Brown, 520 U.S. 397 (1997)

Brown v. Benton, 425 F. Supp. 28 (W.D. Okla. 1978)

Campbell v. City of New York, 2004 U.S. Dist. Lexis 7656 (S.D.N.Y.) [unpublished opinion]

Castagna v. City of Seal Beach, 2005 Lexis 7775 (Div. 3, 4th Cal. App.) [unpublished opinion]

City of Canton, Ohio v. Harris, 489 U.S. 378 (1989)

City of Oklahoma City v. Tuttle, 471 U.S. 808 (1985)

City of Ontario, California v. Quon, 560 U.S. ___ (2010)

City of St. Louis v. Praprotnik, 485 U.S. 112 (1988)

Cox v. District of Columbia, 821 F. Supp. 1 (D.D.C. 1993)

Day v. Civil Service Commission of Borough of Carlisle, 948 A.2d 900 (Pa. Commw. 2008)

Diaz v. Martinez, 112 F.3d 1 (1st Cir. 1997)

Duckworth v. Whiesnant, 97 F.3d 1393 (11th Cir. 1996)

Estate of Brutsche v. City of Federal Way, Lexis 11653 (W.D. Wash. 2007)

Estate of Larsen v. Muir, Lexis 8316 (10th Cir. 2006)

Estelle v. Gamble, 429 U.S. 97 (1976)

Estep v. Dent, 914 F. Supp. 1462 (W.D. Ky. 1996)

Farmer v. Brennan, 114 S. Ct. 1970 (1994)

Ford v. Brier, 383 F. Supp. 505 (E.D. Wis. 1974)

Flynn v. Sandahl, 58 F.3d 283 (7th Cir. 1995)

Gaines v. Choctaw County Commissioners, 242 F. Supp. 2d 1153 (S.D. Ala. 2003)

Garris v. Rowland, 678 F.2d 1264 (5th Cir. 1982)

Giroux v. Sherman, 807 F. Supp. 1182 (E.D. Pa. 1992)

Grancid Camilo-Robles v. Diaz-Pagan, No. 97-2260061 (1st Cir. App. Ct. 1998)

Grandstaff v. City of Borger, 767 F.2d 161 (5th Cir. 1985)

Graham v. District of Columbia, 795 F. Supp. 24 (D.D.C. 1992)

Gutierrez-Rodriguez v. Cartagena, 882 F.2d 553 (1st Cir. 1989)

Hardeman v. Kerr County, Tex., WL 2264113 (5th Cir. 2007)

Haynes v. Marshall, 887 F.2d 700 (6th Cir. 1989)

Hirschfeld v. New Mexico Corrections Department, 916 F.2d 572 (10th Cir. 1990)

Cases Cited in Chapter 7

Liability for Failure to Train

Cases Cited in Chapter 8
Operating Criminal Justice Agencies Under a Consent Decree

Brady v. Maryland, 373 U.S. 83 (1963)
City of Canton v. Harris, 489 U.S. 378 (1989)
Groh v. Ramirez, 540 U.S. 551 (2004)
Hazelwood School District v. United States, 433 U.S. 299 (1977)
International Brotherhood of Teamsters v. United States, 431 U.S. 324 (1977)
Mason County v. Davis, 927 F. 2d 1473 (9th Cir. 1991)
Mapp v. Ohio, 367 U.S. 643 (1961)
Monroe v. Pape, 365 U.S. 167 (1961)
Monell v. Department of Social Services of New York, 436 U.S. 658 (1978)
Printz v. United States, 512 U.S. 898 (1997)
Terry v. Ohio, 392 U.S. 1 (1968)
United States v. City of Columbus, No. CIV A. 2: 99CV1097 (S.D. Ohio 2000)
United States v. Terrell County, Ga., 457 F. Supp. 2d 1359 (M.D. Ga. 2006)

Cases Cited in Chapter 9
Personal Issues and Liability

AFGE Council 33 v. Barr, 794 F. Supp. 1466 (N.D. Cal. 1992)
Almond v. Westchester County Dept. of Corrections, 425 F. Supp. 2d 394 (S.D.N.Y. 2006)
Anderson v. City of Los Angeles, WL 1137335 (Cal. App. 2d Dist. 2011)
Anthony v. County of Sacramento Sheriff's Department, 845 F. Supp. 1396 (E.D. Cal. 1994)
Barth v. The Village of Mokena, 2004 U.S. Dist. Lexis 8316 (E.D. Ill.)
Board of Regents v. Roth, 408 U.S. 564 (1974)
Boxer X v. Harris, 437 F.3d 1107 (11th Cir. 2006)
Brockmeyer v. Dun & Bradstreet, 335 N.W.2d 834 (Wis. 1983)
Briggs v. Waters, 484 F. Supp. 2d 466 (E.D. Va. 2007)
Brown v. City of Detroit, 715 F. Supp. 832 (E.D. Mich.1989)
Burlington Industries, Inc. v. Ellerth, 524 U.S. 742 (1998)
Chaos v. Ballista, 630 F. Supp. 2d (D. Mass. 2009)
Christensen v. Harris, 529 U.S. 576 (2000)
City of San Diego v. Roe, 543 U.S. 77 (2004)
Clark v. New York City Housing Unit Authority, 562 N.Y.S. 2d 637 (A.D. 1990)
Cleveland Board of Education v. Loudermill, 470 U.S. 532 (1985)
Davoll v. Webb, 194 F.3d 1116 (10th Cir. 1999)
Diaz v. City of El Central, DO43517 (4th Div. 3 Cal. App. 2005) [unpublished opinion]
Erickson v. Wisconsin Department of Corrections, WL 3290202 (7th Cir. 2006)
Evans v. Leelanau County Sheriff's Department, No. CL 94-78765- NM (1994)

Spades v. City of Walnut Ridge, 186 F.3d 897 (8th Cir. 1999)

Speed v. Ohio Dept. of Rehabilitation and Correction, 646 N.E.2d 273 (S.D. Ohio 1994)

Spicer v. Commonwealth of Virginia Department of Corrections, 66 F.3d 705 (4th Cir. 1995)

Stachowski v. Town of Cicero, 425 F.3d 1075 (7th Cir. 2005)

Staub v. Proctor Hospital, 131 U.S. __ (2011)

Stroud v. Shelby County Civil Service Commission, 2006 Tenn. App. Lexis 89

Summers v. The City of Dothan, AL No. 10-15361(11th Cir. 2011) [unpublished]

Sutton v. United Airlines Inc., 974 U.S. 1943 (1999)

Thomas v. Galveston County, 953 F. Supp. 504 (S.D. Tex. 1997)

Van v. Miami-Dade County, 509 F. Supp. 2d 1295 (S.D. Fla. 2007)

Vaughn v. City of Puyallup, WL 110516 (2008)

Ware v. Jackson County, Missouri, 150 F.3d 873 (8th Cir. 1998)

Williams v. Philadelphia Housing Authority, 380 F.3d 751 (3d Cir. 2004)

Williamson v. City of Houston, Texas, 148 F.3d 462 (5th Cir. 1998)

Women Prisoners v. D.C., 877 F. Supp. 634 (D.D.C. 1994)

Wright v. Rolette County, 417 F.3d 879 (8th Cir. 2005)

Cases Cited in Chapter 10

Use of Force in Law Enforcement and Corrections

Austin v. Hopper, 15 F. Supp. 2d 1210 (M.D. Ala. 1998)

Beaver v. City of Federal Way, 507 F. Supp. 2d 1137 (W.D. Wash. 2007)

Birdine v. Gray, 375 F. Supp. 2d 874 (D. Neb. 2005)

Bond v. Queen, 71 F.3d 1151 (1st Cir. 1999)

Bordanaro v. McLeod, 871 F.2d 1151 (1st Cir. 1989)

Brazier v. Cherry, 293 F.2d 401 (5th Cir. 1961)

Brockington v. Boykins, 637 F. 3d 503 (4th Cir. 2011)

Brothers v. Klevenhagen, 28 F.3d 345 (5th Cir. 1994)

Bryan v. McPherson, 630 F. 3d 805 (9th Cir. 2010)

Buckley v. Haddock, [unpublished] USCA, No. 06-00053CV-5 RS-MD (11th Cir. 2008)

Calamia v. City of New York, 879 F.2d 1025 (2d Cir. 1989)

Campbell v. Sikes, 169 F.3d 1353 (11th Cir. 1999)

Carter v. City of Wyoming, Lexis 24988 (W.D. Mich. 2007)

Carver v. Bullock, 168 F.3d 481 (4th Cir. 1999)

Casaburro v. Giuliani, 986 F. Supp. 176 (S.D.N.Y. 1997)

Chapman v. Martinez, [unpublished] No. 8:05CV-133 (E.D. Neb. 2008)

Chimel v. California, 395 U.S. 752 (1969)

Colston v. Barnhart, 130 F.3d 96 (5th Cir. 1997)

Cotton v. Busic, 793 F. Supp. 191 (S.D. Ind. 1992)

Cruz v. Escondido, 126 F.3d 1214 (10th Cir. 1997)

Danley v. Allyn, 485 F. Supp. 2d 1260 (N.D. Ala. 2007)

Cases Cited in Chapter 11
Section 1983 and Correctional Liability Issues

Cases Cited in Chapter 12

Section 1983 Actions in Law Enforcement

Cases Cited in Chapter 13
Liability and Wrongful Custodial Death

Abraham v. Maes, 436 So. 2d 1099 (La. Dist. Ct. App. 1983)

Animashaun v. O'Donnell, 1994 U.S. Dist. Lexis 17339 (N.D. Ill.)

Arce v. Blackwell, [unpublished] No. 06-17302 (9th Cir. 2008)

Bell v. Stinger, 937 F.2d 1340 (8th Cir. 1991)

Bell v. Wolfish, 441 U.S. 520 (1979)

Bishop v. Corsentino, 371 F. 3d 1203 (10th Cir. 2004)

Bozeman v. Orum, 199 F. Supp. 2d 1216 (M.D. Ala. 2002)

Bradley v. City of Ferndale, 148 Fed. Appx. 499 (6th Cir. 2005)

Branton v. City of Moss Point, 503 F. Supp. 2d 908 (S.D. Miss. 2007)

Brinkman v. City of Indianapolis, 231 N.E.2d 169 (Ind. Ct. App. 1967)

Brown v. Lee, 639 So. 2d 897 (La. Dist. Ct. App. 1994)

City of Canton v. Harris, 489 U.S. 378 (1989)

City of Revere v. Massachusetts General Hospital, 463 U.S. 239 (1983)

Conn v. City of Reno, No. 07-15572, (9th Cir. 2010)

Cooper v. County of Washtenaw, unpublished No. 06-1013 (6th Cir. 2007)

Cottrell v. Caldwell, 85 F.3d 1480 (11th Cir. 1996)

Cruz v. City of Laramie, Wyoming, 239 F.3d 1183 (10th Cir. 2001)

Del Tufo v. Township of Old Bridge, 685 A.2d 1267 (N.J. 1996)

DeShaney v. Winnebago County Department of Social Services, 489 U.S. 189 (1989)

Deshotels v. Marshall, No. 11-301-10, (5th Cir. 2011)

East v. City of Chicago, 719 F. Supp. 683 (N.D. Ill. 1989)

Elmes v. Hart, 1994 Tenn. App. Lexis 278 (Tenn. Ct. App. 1994)

Estate of Fank v. City of Beaver Dam, 921 F. Supp. 590 (E.D. Wis. 1996)

Estate of Phillips v. City of Milwaukee, 928 F. Supp. 817 (E.D. Wis. 1996)

Estelle v. Gamble, 429 U.S. 97 (1976)

Farmer v. Brennan, 511 U.S. 285 (1994)

Forgan v. Howard County, Tex. 494 F.3d 518 (5th Cir. 2007)

Frey v. City of Herculaneum, 44 F.3d 667 (8th Cir. 1995)

Fruge v. City of New Orleans, 613 So. 2d 811 (La. Dist. Ct. App. 1993)

Galvan v. City of San Antonio, No. 8-51235 (5th Cir. 2010) [unpublished]

Galvin v. City of Antonio, Lexis 106894 (W.D. Tex. 2008)

Graham v. Connor, 490 U.S. 386 (1989)

Gray v. Tunica County, Mississippi, 279 F. Supp. 2d 789 (N.D. 2003)

Guseman v. Martinez, 1 F. Supp. 2d 1240 (D. Kan. 1998).

Hare v. City of Corinth, 74 F.3d 633 (5th Cir. 1996)

Harris v. District of Columbia, 932 F.2d 10 (D.C. Cir. 1991)

Harvey v. County of Ward, 352 F. Supp. 1003 (D.N.D. 2005)

Hill v. Carroll County, 587 F.3d 230 (5th Cir. 2009)

Howard v. City of Atmore, 887 So. 2d 201 (N.D. Ala. 2003)

Cases Cited in Chapter 14
Conclusions: Shifting Directions in Civil Litigation

Subject Index

Index of Cases